Dr. L. Calisti
30 Orchard Cir.
Westwood, Ma. 02090
617-326-7973

John Krefeldt
Engr. Design
Tufts
Medford MA
02155

ORGANIZATION STRATEGY
A Marketing Approach

ORGANIZATION STRATEGY
A Marketing Approach

E. RAYMOND COREY
Professor of Business Administration

STEVEN H. STAR
Assistant Professor of Business Administration

DIVISION OF RESEARCH
GRADUATE SCHOOL OF BUSINESS ADMINISTRATION
HARVARD UNIVERSITY
Boston · 1971

© COPYRIGHT 1971 BY THE PRESIDENT AND FELLOWS OF HARVARD COLLEGE
Second printing 1975

Library of Congress Catalog Card No. 79–132151
ISBN 0–87584–088–4

Faculty research at the Harvard Business School is undertaken with the expectation of publication. In such publication the authors responsible for the research project are also responsible for statements of fact, opinions, and conclusions expressed. Neither the Harvard Business School, its Faculty as a whole, nor the President and Fellows of Harvard College reach conclusions or make recommendations as results of Faculty research.

Printed in the United States of America

FOREWORD

This book is evidence of the Harvard Business School's continuing commitment to research in marketing. Professors Corey and Star focus upon the crucial relationship between corporate organization and the marketplace. The market environment is one of the greatest single influences shaping organization structure in modern corporations. Businesses organize to pursue market strategies. As markets grow and develop, as customer needs evolve, and as competitive imperatives intensify, organization structure adapts to the changing environment. Thus strategy shapes organization. Similarly, the way a business is organized influences its choices of strategies and goals. Hence organization shapes strategy. The organization design process is best understood as a dynamic process.

Organization design should also be understood as an optimizing process involving trade-offs. The price of specializing organizational units by product, or market segment or task, for example, may be a loss in the flexibility of the resources of the business. Also, the larger and more cost-efficient a business is, the less it may be able to focus on the needs of individual customer groups. Organization strategy is a critical element of total corporate strategy. It is a matter of managerial art.

Professors Corey and Star identify and describe the underlying logic of modern corporate organization at the division (or "business") level and of basic organizational processes such as planning, operating, and expanding the business through new product development. This perspective differs from previous studies which have taken a corporate level view. Their research cuts across a range of industries so that the fundamentals of organization patterns may be seen apart from industry setting. They focus on thirteen large businesses, all leaders in their industries, but they have confirmed their intensive case observations by surveying in lesser depth the experiences of over 500 other large companies.

A few of the research questions posed and answered in this study should suffice to establish its interest for all businessmen: What should be the considerations which come to bear on determining how large the business unit should be, how broad its product lines, and the range of markets it serves? What design principles should guide the planning of the program-resource structure? How should program managers and resource managers work together in developing plans, implementing programs, and generating growth? What determines the balance of power between programs and resources in the shaping of overall business strategy?

The financial support for this research project came from the allocation of funds from gifts to the School by The Associates of the Harvard Business School and from two Graduate Research and Study Grants made to the School by The General Electric Foundation. For such support we are most appreciative.

Soldiers Field
Boston, Massachusetts
October 1970

LAWRENCE E. FOURAKER
Dean

PREFACE

Possibly no other subject claims as much of the time and attention of top corporate managers as problems of organization structure and processes. Such problems are difficult to diagnose and to treat skillfully, involving as they do both the strategic and the human dimensions of the business. Moreover, there are few guidelines which businessmen may use in dealing with structural design. There has been much useful writing on the human aspects of organization; much less has been written that is helpful to managers on the subject of formal organization structure. Corporate managements tend to work in isolation one from another in dealing with organization problems. Events and environmental pressures tend to influence them in similar directions, but there is little interchange of ideas and experiences.

The study is an effort to provide a conceptual scheme which will be useful to top corporate managers and to teachers and students of business in dealing with organization problems at the division (or the "business") level. The scheme is the distillation of experiences in thirteen large businesses, confirmed to the extent possible by a survey of more than 500 other large businesses.

The authors' interest in this area began with the development of a series of problem cases at Du Pont's Textile Fibers Department. One case, written as a background note, described the Department's organization and how it had been changed twice in a three-year period. Our students showed a much greater interest in the note than in the problem cases. As one studied Du Pont's organizational changes, the relationship between strategy and organization was clearly demonstrated. One could begin to understand, as well, the roles and interrelationships of product managers, market managers, and resource managers in complex organizations.

Then, the arduous task of gathering and analyzing other case histories was undertaken. It was successfully completed because of the close cooperation the authors received from managers in the companies described in this book. Their willingness to share with us their experiences in coping with problems of organization structure was the *sine qua non*. We are grateful to them, indeed.

The study is designed to be used in different ways. The conceptual scheme is laid out in the six chapters for those readers who want an overview of the subject. Then, for those who may have an interest in studying particular companies, the thirteen cases are included. Following each case is a commentary which deals with the unique aspects of that situation and draws out, as well, such generalizations as could contribute to the overall scheme.

We are grateful to three Faculty members who reviewed the manuscript and gave us excellent suggestions: Professor Alfred D. Chandler, Jr. (business historian, author of *Strategy and Structure,* and a member of the Faculty of Johns Hopkins University), Dean Lawrence E. Fouraker (Director of Research at the Harvard Business School at the time this study was written, and now Dean), and Associate Professor Ralph G. M. Sultan (in the Marketing Area at the Harvard

Business School). We wish also to express our thanks to Associate Professor James P. Baughman, Associate Director of the Division of Research, who skillfully steered this study through to completion when Dean Fouraker assumed the leadership of this School. He was most ably assisted by Miss Ruth Norton, Editor and Executive Secretary of the Division of Research, who painstakingly reviewed the manuscript and took it into print.

We are grateful to Mrs. Ellen Schadegg and Miss Bonnie Green. They worked hard and long in typing notes, cases, and manuscript from the beginning through a series of revisions.

Our deepest gratitude is to our wives, Charlotte Worrall Corey and Brenda Schwalb Star. They provided the constant encouragement and help that saw us through to the completion of this study.

Finally, it must be said that the ideas and opinions expressed in this study are ours alone. Managers in the businesses we studied gave us the facts as they saw them. But we must take the responsibility for the interpretation of those facts and their use to develop and illustrate our conceptual scheme.

E. RAYMOND COREY
STEVEN H. STAR

Boston, Massachusetts
September 1970

TABLE OF CONTENTS

1. INTRODUCTORY COMMENTS 1
   The Matter of Terminology . . . The Distinction Between Programs and Businesses . . . Emerging Themes . . . The Plan of Study
2. DEFINING THE PRODUCT/MARKET SCOPE OF THE BUSINESS . . . 7
   Defining Integrated Business Units . . . Resource Size and Efficiency: *Economies of Scale; Resource Organization and Specialization; Resource Integrity; Summary* . . . Market Scope: *A Qualifying Note; Market Decentralization; The Business as a Framework for Planning and Measuring Performance; Summary* . . . The Need for Program Managements
3. PROGRAM STRUCTURES 17
   Unilateral and Bilateral Program Structures . . . Simple and Complex Program Management Units . . . Program-Attached Resources . . . Market Segmentation and Program Organization . . . Segmentation Schemes and Phases of Growth . . . Summary . . . Significance of Program Organization Design
4. RESOURCE STRUCTURES 27
   The Role of Resource Management . . . The Delineation of Resource Structures . . . Program-Specialized Resource Units . . . The Positioning of Specialized Resource Units . . . Field Sales Organization: *Sales Management Functions; Field Sales Specialization; Specialization of Individual Sales Representatives* . . . Summary
5. PROGRAM-RESOURCE RELATIONSHIPS: PLANNING, OPERATING, AND GROWING THE BUSINESS 37
   Planning: *Annual Planning Processes; The Program-Resource Balance in Strategic Planning; Summary* . . . Program-Resource Coordination Functions: *Coordination Through Product Management; Interface Managers in Resource Departments; Independent Scheduling Functions; Summary* . . . New Product Development . . . The Dynamics of Interaction
6. SURVEY RESULTS AND SUGGESTIONS FOR FURTHER RESEARCH . . . 52
   Results of the Questionnaire Survey . . . Toward Further Research: *The Concept of Scale Economies in Organization; The Concept of Power in Program-Resource Relationships; The Utilization of External and Internal Resources; Organizing for Multinational Business Operations; Resource Structures*

CASES AND COMMENTARIES

LOCKHEED AIRCRAFT COMPANY: LOCKHEED-GEORGIA COMPANY . . . 61
   Development of Gelac's Organizational Structure . . . Gelac Matrix Organization . . . The Programs . . . The Corporate Steering Committee . . . The Branches

COMMENTARY ON LOCKHEED-GEORGIA COMPANY 102
   Factors Leading to a Matrix Structure . . . Role and Authority of Program Directors . . . Role and Authority of Branch Heads . . . Projectizing Resources . . . Resource Allocation . . . Organizing for Commercial and Military Markets . . . Summary

INTERNATIONAL BUSINESS MACHINES CORPORATION: DATA PROCESSING
DIVISION 108
    Development of the IBM Corporate Structure . . . Data Processing Division: Organizational Development . . . Data Processing Division: Organization in 1966 . . . Applications Development in the Data Processing Division . . . Setting Quotas . . . Sales Support . . . The GEM Region

COMMENTARY ON IBM DATA PROCESSING DIVISION 146
    Structuring a Business . . . The Evolving Structure of the Resource Functions . . . The Emergence of Industry Programs . . . The Product Programs Organization . . . The Field Sales Organization . . . Future Organizational Developments . . . Summary

MOBIL OIL CORPORATION: NORTH AMERICAN DIVISION 156
    Historical Background . . . Case Organization . . . The Marketing Department in 1967 . . . The Commercial Marketing Department . . . The Resale Marketing Department . . . A Field Marketing Division . . . Headquarters Staff Departments . . . Marketing's Role in Planning and Forecasting . . . Product Supply . . . Product Planning and Development

COMMENTARY ON MOBIL NORTH AMERICAN DIVISION 179
    Definiton of the Business . . . Defining Marketing Programs . . . The Planning System and Product Allocation . . . Summary

E. I. DU PONT DE NEMOURS AND COMPANY: TEXTILE FIBERS
DEPARTMENT 187
    Organization of the Textile Fibers Department in 1951 . . . Consolidation of the Five Fiber Divisions . . . Further Organizational Changes . . . Controlling the Operations of the Sales Divisions

COMMENTARY ON DU PONT TEXTILE FIBERS DEPARTMENT . . . 197
    Strategy and Organization . . . Understanding the Organizational Structure

GENERAL FOODS CORPORATION: POST DIVISION 201
    Development of the Post Marketing Organization . . . Marketing Organization as of August 1966 . . . The Marketing Plan . . . Sales Planning . . . Relations with Advertising Agencies . . . Marketing-Manufacturing Relationships . . . Product Development

COMMENTARY ON GENERAL FOODS POST DIVISION 225
    Program and Resource Structures . . . Planning: Form and Process . . . Program-Resource Relationships . . . The Product Development Process . . . Summary

GENERAL ELECTRIC COMPANY: HOUSEWARES DIVISION 231
    The Old Product Department Organization . . . Proposed Reorganization . . . The New Organization after September 1964 . . . The General Electric Marketing and Distribution Operation . . . The Product Design and Production Operation . . . Universal Manufacturing Company . . . General Electric Distribution Company

COMMENTARY ON GENERAL ELECTRIC HOUSEWARES DIVISION . . 254
    The Case for Consolidation . . . Structuring the New Business . . . Organization of Field Sales . . . Product Development Processes . . . Summary

FORD MOTOR COMPANY: NORTH AMERICAN AUTOMOTIVE OPERATIONS . 261
    Evolution of the Ford Organization, 1957–1967 . . . Case Organization . . . The Development of North American Automotive Operations . . . North American Automotive Operations in Early 1967 . . . The Ford Division . . . Trucks . . . The Ford Dealer Organization . . . The

Autolite-Ford Parts Division . . . North American Automotive Operations in Late 1967 . . . Organizational Changes in Other Ford Operations

COMMENTARY ON FORD NORTH AMERICAN AUTOMOTIVE OPERATIONS . . 289
E Pluribus Unum . . . The New Product Development Group — Concept and Structure . . . Program-Resource Structure in the Sales Group . . . Strategy and Organization . . . An Evolving Structure . . . Ford of Europe and Ford Tractor as "Businesses"

SEARS, ROEBUCK AND CO. 296
Organization . . . Recent Developments . . . Merchandising . . . Four Buying Departments . . . The Field . . . Planning, Logistics, and Product Development

COMMENTARY ON SEARS, ROEBUCK AND CO. 326
An Interpretation of History . . . Understanding Sears Today . . . A Concept of the Sears Organization . . . Resource Allocation Procedures . . . The Buying Departments . . . The Roles of Parent and Field in Formulating Marketing Strategy . . . Product Development Strategy and the Implications for Organization . . . An Overview — and the Future

MONSANTO COMPANY: ORGANIC CHEMICALS DIVISION 336
Organization in 1967 . . . The Plasticizer Product Group . . . Division Reorganization

COMMENTARY ON MONSANTO ORGANIC CHEMICALS DIVISION . . . 354
Program-Resource Structure . . . Planning . . . Product Development Processes . . . Division Reorganization . . . Summary

MONSANTO COMPANY: AGRICULTURAL DIVISION 358
Organizational Structure . . . International Sales . . . Product Development . . . Pricing . . . Scheduling . . . Planning and Budgeting

COMMENTARY ON MONSANTO AGRICULTURAL DIVISION 367
Agricultural Division Organization

MONSANTO COMPANY: INTERNATIONAL DIVISION 370
The Overseas Division . . . Monsanto Europe . . . Emerging Problems . . . Appraisal and Restructuring . . . The Evolving Organization — Structure and Interfaces . . . A Revised Charter for the International Division

COMMENTARY ON MONSANTO INTERNATIONAL DIVISION 385
A Structure for World-Wide Strategies

CHAS. PFIZER & CO., INC.: PFIZER INTERNATIONAL 390
Product Lines . . . Geographical Location of Pfizer International Activities . . . Historical Development of Pfizer International Organization . . . Organization in Early 1965 . . . 1965 Organizational Changes . . . The Future

COMMENTARY ON PFIZER INTERNATIONAL 409
By Way of Prediction

FORD MOTOR COMPANY: TRACTOR DIVISION 412
Organization . . . Product Development . . . Manufacturing . . . Equipment Operations . . . Sales and Marketing . . . Tractor and Implement Operations — U.S. . . . Ford Tractor Operations — Europe . . . Overseas Tractor Operations

COMMENTARY ON FOOD TRACTOR DIVISION 432
Basic Organization . . . Organization of the Marketing Function . . . The Future

INDEX TO COMPANIES AND COMMENTARIES 435

CHAPTER 1

Introductory Concepts

Organization design begins with the market. Businesses are structured to carry out strategies in the markets they serve. It follows that as market conditions evolve, as strategies are reshaped, and as customer groups change in character, organization structure must change accordingly.

Since World War II rapid organizational change has characterized large and growing companies more than ever before. Growth *per se* is one reason. The organizational framework for handling a $50 million business will be obsolete long before the business reaches the $500 million point. Another is the fast changing character of served markets. A third is the rapid technological development of new products. Still another is the wide ranging diversification of companies into new products and new markets, and a spreading out of operations to embrace national and world markets. The framework for a business with a single product line, a single customer group, a single geographic market is quickly outgrown when the business broadens its product and market scope. Finally, one must note the profound effects on corporate organization of intense competition, a factor forcing structural change in order to survive and grow.

Even within the past decade, experimentation in organizational design in large companies has led to important innovations in ways of structuring a business to deal with the management problems brought on by growth and by market and product proliferation. In particular *program structures* have emerged as a device for helping business managements to plan and carry out multiple strategies in widely ranging markets. Thus, within a business it is becoming increasingly common to find product or program management units each having the responsibility for developing a marketing strategy for a line of products or for a particular set of the company's customers. Allegheny-Ludlum Steel Corporation, for example, has product managers for stainless steel sheets, stainless steel castings, carbon steels, and silicon and electrical steels, among others. International Business Machines has industry program managers for such markets as airlines, utilities, distribution, and government.

Although program management structures are highly formalized in many large corporations, no one arrangement can be described as common. Schemes vary among companies with regard to how program management is positioned organizationally and how it functions. Nevertheless, much has been learned and the experimentation carried out in innovative companies provides useful guidance for industry in general.

The Matter of Terminology

The intricacies of modern corporate organization are such that the traditional "line" and "staff" dichotomy is of little value in understanding organizational design. The terms are used more to infer degrees of authority than to describe roles and functions. The line, by implication, commands and directs; the staff provides supporting services to the line. Line and staff are used, not infrequently, to imply status in a managerial hierarchy, with line managers perceived as having higher status than their staff counterparts. Dealing as it does, then, with status and authority inferences, the line-staff classification misses the great subtleties of formal organization structure.

And yet no common terminology has developed to replace it. One of the great difficulties of comparing organizations from one enterprise to another is that each has developed its own, often unique, nomenclature. Similar functions in different organizations will often have different names or titles. What is needed, then, is to look past the titles to understand tasks and to base comparisons on functional descriptions of these tasks.

For purposes of this study it will be useful to provide a common terminology for organizations in a wide range of businesses and industries from consumer goods to defense, from retailing to industrial.

We begin with a definition of the market. A *market* may be perceived broadly as a need which generates potentially effective demand. A market must have identifiable customers with purchasing power to buy products and/or services which satisfy this need. Within a market there are *segments,* consisting of groups of customers who have homogeneous patterns of purchasing behavior and product use.

The transportation market, for example, may be segmented by rail, automobile, ship, and air transportation. It may be further segmented by personal, business, and military use. In the air/business segment, a classification scheme might differentiate between public transportation and private aircraft. The segmentation scheme may be, and often is, drawn more finely for purposes of planning and implementing marketing strategies and for organizing business operations.

Segmentation schemes are a matter of art, not science, and schematic variations are infinite. Because organizations are designed to serve markets, the definition of market segments becomes the critically important beginning point for designing organizational structures.

A *program* is a total strategic plan for serving a particular market segment. It provides for product design, pricing, channels of distribution, advertising, promotion, and field selling; for product supply and customer service. In the longer run, it also includes the development of new products and services which the business is to supply to the market.

Business *resources* are the physical facilities, manpower, technical skills, and capital utilized in carrying out programs. What might be termed the *basic resources* would include the physical facilities, personnel, and working capital employed in procurement, manufacturing, research, engineering, field sales, wholesale and retail distribution systems, and customer service. *Promotional resources* would include personnel in advertising departments and agencies, in departments for developing and producing promotional materials, and personnel and facilities for customer education. It will be noted that some of these resources are *internal* while others are *external* to the business. Although this distinction is meaningful for purposes of organizational design, it should be recognized that many resources external to the corporate entity are essential parts of the system for planning and implementing market strategy.

In addition, the business will include *information services* for the gathering and analysis of data used for planning, control, and appraisal purposes: budgets and measures, marketing research and economic research data.

The large corporation will include, as well, *resource support services* which focus on the establishment of policies and standard practices for their respective resource units throughout the enterprise and on programs for developing resource manpower and facilities. At the corporate level in General Electric, for example, are such organizational units as Manufacturing Services, Engineering Services, and Marketing and Public Information Services. These are groups of professionals who aid in the development of personnel and of management practices in their counterpart units in more than a hundred GE business departments.

Finally, there is a range of organizational resources that provide *corporate support and development services,* directed not at specific programs and resources but at the development of the corporation as a whole and at the conduct of its relations with environmental groups. One might list these services among others: corporate financial; legal; public relations; stockholder relations; personnel; organization planning; long-range planning. These units deal with outside interests, assist top management in formulating plans and policies, develop financial resources, and plan structural changes in the organization. These types of activities are often located at corporate headquarters and sometimes at operating levels, as well, as extensions of counterpart headquarters units.

What might be called a "division" or "product department" in many companies is called a *business* in this study. It has an integrated set of resources with which to plan and implement one or more programs. A business includes the personnel, physical facilities, and technical skills for designing, making and/or buying, promoting and selling certain products or services. These products or services may be related by a common technology (e.g., electronics, optics), a common materials base (e.g., petroleum, lumber), common production processes (e.g., chemical distillation, metal fabrication), common distribution facilities (e.g., retail department stores), and/or common managerial knowledge and skills (e.g., real estate development, consulting services).

Within the business, there are, in addition to programs and resources, certain *coordination* functions which will be identified and described in this study. They coordinate programs and basic resource activities and are instrumental in allocating resources to programs and in matching the level and timing of resource efforts to program needs. A business organized by both resources and programs which are integrated by means of coordination functions is said to have a *matrix organization*.

Finally, the *enterprise* is defined as a multibusiness structure administered by a headquarters management.

The *enterprise*, then, may be divided into several relatively self-contained *businesses* each with the requisite *resources* for planning and carrying out *programs* serving *market segments*. Resources may be *internal and external* and may be further classified for purposes of this study as *basic, promo-*

Exhibit 1. Matrix Organization (Schematic Diagram)

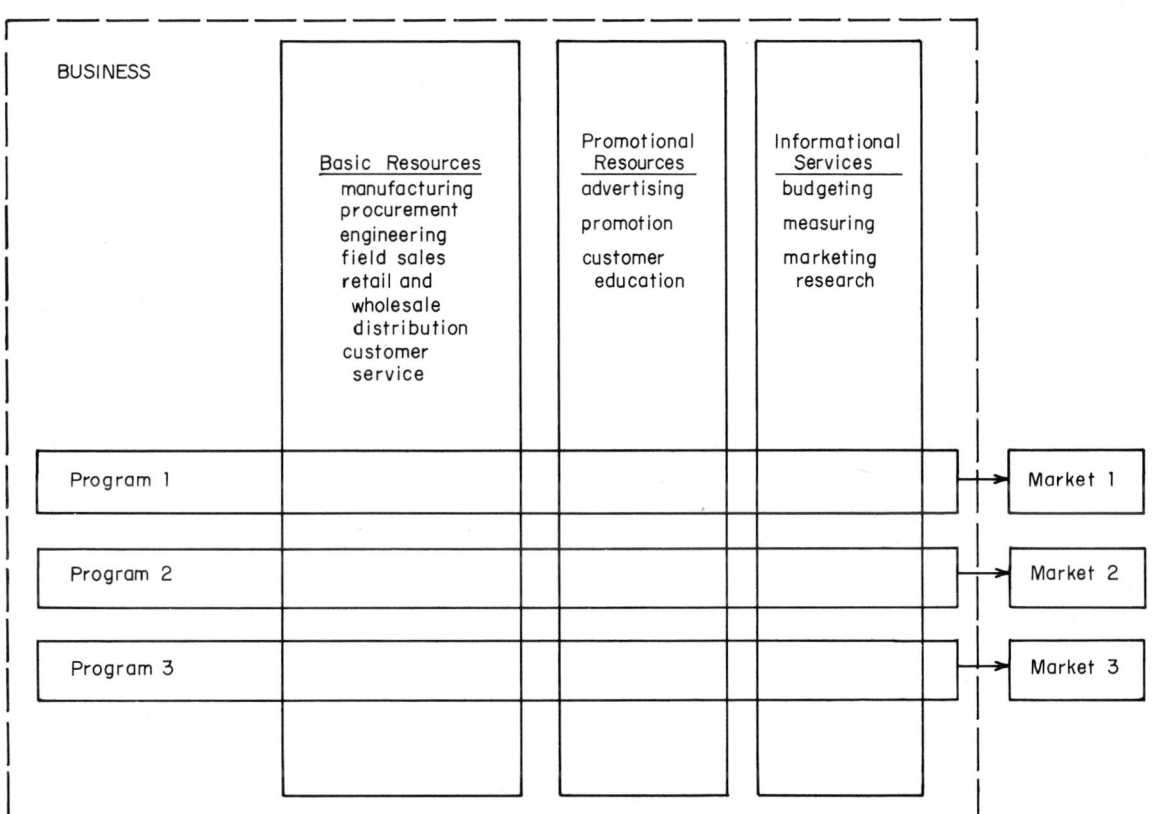

Exhibit 2. Schematic Concept of the Enterprise

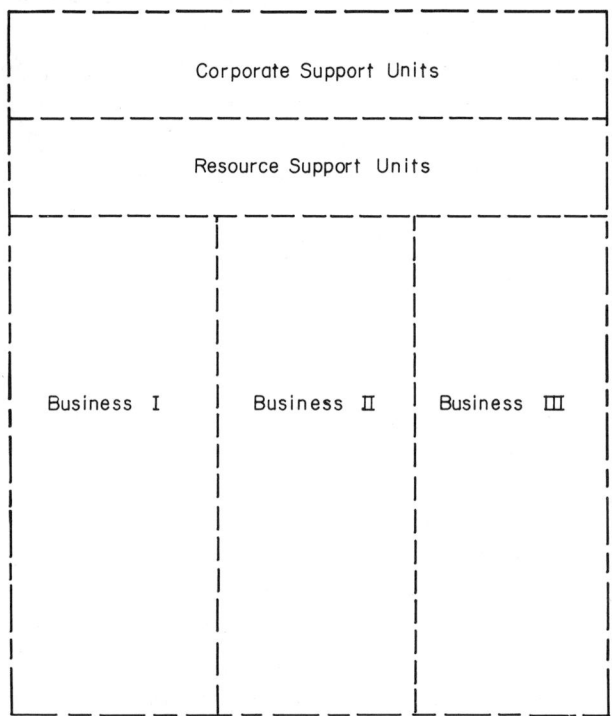

tional, information, resource support, and *corporate support. Coordination* functions are needed to integrate resource activities by programs. A business that is organized both by programs and by resources has a *matrix organization.* (Exhibits 1 and 2.)

The Distinction Between Programs and Businesses

In practice the "program"-"business" distinction does not fall out as neatly as this classification scheme would suggest. There is a range of organizational forms in which programs have their own resources in varying degrees instead of being dependent on the common resources of the business.

At one end is the multiprogram business, in which the program management units have no resources of their own and share instead those of the business unit. The program management group may consist of one or a few people who are concerned with developing strategy and with guiding and coordinating the efforts of the several resource units of the business in carrying out that strategy. A modification is the structure in which certain of the programs have some of their own resources. A program management unit might, for example, have its own specialized sales force or technical service group but be dependent on the manufacturing, engineering, and other resources of the core business. Moving further along the scale, a so-called product department may be self-sufficient except for a single basic resource. For example, the department may have its own manufacturing, engineering, and information resources but share with other sister departments the services of a "pooled" sales force. A product department may, in fact, mount several programs. At this point, it would be appropriate to recognize the product department itself as constituting a "business."

Finally, at the other end of the scale we might have a fully self-contained one-program "business." At this point we have come full circle. Thus, the distinction between a "program" and a "business" is a matter of degree. And, in fact, programs may become businesses as more and more of the resources which serve the program become autonomous to it, and as the program unit becomes self-sufficient.

Emerging Themes

A central idea in this study is that in successful companies, organization structure responds to market environment. The business, for example, seeks naturally to achieve a size where it can realize full-scale economies in such functions as manufacturing, distribution, and research. What this size may be will depend significantly (although not exclusively) on the market environment — its diversity, servicing requirements, and the technical complexities in the use of the product by customers.

The business seeks as well to be large enough to achieve *market integrity*. Often market programs impinge one on the other at the market level. They may have common customers, or they may be competitive in nature. The business will tend to be defined in a way that interrelated marketing programs are drawn together organizationally under a single management so that these programs may be coordinated.

The business will seek, on the other hand, not

to be so large that its management is no longer responsive to customer needs, market opportunities, and competitive behavior.

Within the business, the program structure reflects the scheme by which the management segments its markets for strategic purposes. Segmentation schemes, for example, may be based on the way customers buy, on the way in which they use the product, or on the countries or regions in which customers are located. A perceptive definition, for organizational purposes, of the markets the business serves is critical to its success.

The business which is of sufficient size to achieve scale economies and which is also structured to serve a number of market segments needs effective coordination between programs and resources for strategy planning and implementation. Resource output has to be allocated according to some priority system. Resource efforts need to be integrated by programs. Successful companies have developed effective coordination processes by which plans are made, adjusted as changing market conditions dictate, and carried out.

Another major theme that emerges from case evidence is that organization is a matter of balance. There is a balance to be achieved in the extent to which organizational units are specialized or generalized. The structure may provide, for example, for specialization of the field sales force by product or by type of customer. It may call for engineering and research units which are specialized by technical discipline or by marketing program. There are trade-offs to be made in these decisions, and the market advantages of specialization must be weighed against the greater flexibility and lower costs of not specializing.

There is a balance, too, that must be struck between the program and resource dimensions of the business in planning strategy. These two dimensions of the organization tend to pull the business in different directions. Resource managers are likely to favor paths of business growth which will utilize and develop existing technical skills, plant capacities, and distribution systems. Program managers tend to influence strategy in the direction of pursuing market opportunities which may require new and different resources.

Each in its own way, the companies we have studied seek continually to build balanced and coordinated organizations designed to meet needs and opportunities in diverse markets. Because these markets are themselves undergoing continuous change, the pursuit of effective organization design, relevant for carrying out today's programs and planning for tomorrow's, never ends.

The Plan of Study

This is an exploratory study. It is based on thirteen case studies drawn from ten large companies in as many different industries. Each case study describes the organization and organizational changes in one business in a multibusiness enterprise. In some instances, the business accounts for a very large part, if not the bulk, of the total revenues of the enterprise: Sears' Domestic Retailing Operations; Ford's North American Automotive Operations; Mobil's North American Division; IBM's Data Processing Division. In other cases, the business is one of a number and while it is among the largest in its industry, it does not dominate the enterprise: Lockheed-Georgia; Du Pont's Textile Fibers Department; General Foods' Post Division; General Electric's Housewares Division; Monsanto's Organic Chemicals Division; Monsanto's Agricultural Division; Monsanto's International Division; Ford's Tractor Division; Pfizer International. Except for the IBM case, these studies do not provide data on organization structure at the corporate headquarters level.

Each of the ten large companies is a recognized leader in its field. They are innovators in organizational design. Their leadership positions establish a presumption that their organizational structures have successfully adapted to the market environments they serve.

These large companies were selected for study not only because they have led in organizational experimentation but also because in large organizations one can see the structures more finely articulated. Because of their size, they can afford a degree of organizational specialization that the smaller companies cannot. Also, large companies often serve a wider range of markets with broader product lines and need relatively sophisticated structures to conduct a multiplicity of programs.

The study was designed purposely to cut across different industries: in this instance, data processing, petroleum, aerospace, chemicals, small electrical appliances, packaged foods, automotive, retailing, pharmaceuticals, synthetic fibers, and industrial and farm equipment. In this study, we identified organizational patterns apart from industry setting.

In addition to making in-depth studies of thirteen businesses in ten large companies, we surveyed through a mail questionnaire more than 500 other large companies. The purpose of the survey was to test hypotheses that developed from the analysis of case data. The organizational patterns which were identified in the case studies were, in fact, confirmed in the much broader survey sample.

Chapter 2, which follows, describes the considerations which are important to the management of the enterprise in delineating business units, in defining the product and market scope of each business, and in giving it a complement of resources. Chapter 3 considers the program structure — how program management units are defined in market and/or product terms, the different types of program management structures and their functions.

Chapter 4 then looks at the resource organization of the business, how it is designed and how basic resources are organized to serve the programs. Chapter 5 deals with the processes through which resources and programs relate to each other in the planning of overall business strategy by programs, in day-to-day operations to carry out strategy, and in "growing" the business, i.e., new product development. In this chapter we identify and describe three types of program-resource coordination functions.

Chapter 6 reports the results of the statistical survey to establish that organizational patterns which may be seen in the case studies are, in fact, widespread.

The thirteen case studies follow, each with an analytical commentary. The analysis compares each business to the common patterns and seeks to explain variations primarily in terms of the history of the organization, its traditions, and its strategy. The objective is not merely to explain variations but to understand, as well, why the organization has evolved as it has. Finally, many of the commentaries have pressed forward to the point of predicting further organizational evolution. Broadly speaking, modern enterprises seem to follow a somewhat predictable pattern of structural change.

The cases were prepared through the generous cooperation of managerial personnel in the subject companies. We have sought to record the facts as top managers in these companies have reported them to the authors. The chapters and the case commentaries, however, are the work of the authors alone and are not the interpretations and predictions of company personnel. That should be made abundantly clear at the outset. The analysis of the material is intended to develop a conceptual framework which goes beyond each individual case and may be usefully applied to corporations in general.

CHAPTER 2

Defining the Product/Market Scope of the Business

According to Chandler's history[1] of the organization of American business enterprises, the structural form of corporations has evolved markedly over the past hundred years. In the 1870s nearly all businesses were unifunctional; that is, they were engaged either in manufacturing, or wholesaling, or retailing. By the end of the 19th century the large enterprises which had emerged in many industries were multifunctional structures shaped to pursue a single business. These companies produced or purchased materials and supplies, manufactured, and sold directly to wholesalers and/or retailers. Then, by the end of World War I, large enterprises such as E. I. du Pont de Nemours and Company, which were engaged in diverse businesses, devised a multidivisional form of organization with a number of operating departments and a headquarters management directing the affairs of the overall enterprise.

Du Pont serves as a useful example of how organizational structure evolved as the scope of the enterprise broadened.[2] Before 1902 the Du Pont company operated several plants for making explosives while the Du Pont family also held controlling interests in other large powder companies. One of these was the Repauno Chemical Company formed in 1880 by Lammot du Pont to manufacture a new type of explosive: dynamite. With a few exceptions these plants sold their output through agents who marketed the products of many companies. In 1902 the Du Pont interests were consolidated into a new corporation, E. I. du Pont de Nemours Powder Company. A nationwide sales organization was formed, the nucleus of which was the sales department in Repauno Chemical. Engineering, traffic, and purchasing departments were established and a development department was put in place in this new structure to work on product and process improvement. With further elaboration but no major revamping, this organization served the company until 1921.

In 1910 Du Pont acquired the Fabrikoid Company, a leading manufacturer of artificial leather. In the same year plans were laid for making pyroxylin (celluloid) products in sheet, rod, tube, and photographic film forms. In 1917 the Du Pont management moved to expand the artificial leather and pyroxylin ventures and to add dyestuffs, paints, and varnishes to the product line. While these products had in common the fact that their manufacture was closely related to that of nitrocellulose (used in making explosives), they went to different markets and in some instances used new types of materials.

The diversity of markets greatly increased decision making and administrative burdens on Du Pont's management. The coordination of purchasing, manufacturing, marketing, and product development for each of the new lines became exceedingly difficult.

In the postwar recession of 1920–1921 each of Du Pont's new lines suffered large losses, underscoring the inadequacies of the existing organiza-

---

[1] Alfred D. Chandler, Jr. *Strategy and Structure* (The M.I.T. Press, Cambridge, 1962), pp. 24–25.
[2] *Ibid.*, pp. 52–113.

tion when it came to handling so many diverse ventures.

In September 1921 the company was reorganized. Five product or Industrial Departments were created as well as eight "staff" or Auxiliary Departments and a Treasurer's Department.

The head of each Industrial Department had full authority and responsibility for the operation of his business subject only to the authority of an Executive Committee. He had in his organization such functions as purchasing, manufacturing, sales, engineering, research, control, and traffic, which he needed to carry out a total business strategy. His performance would be appraised in terms of the return he produced on the investment placed at his disposal.

Responsibility for overall corporate policy determination, for the appraisal of the performance of the Industrial Departments, for coordination and overall administration was vested in the Du Pont Executive Committee. This committee had no authority or responsibility for operating decisions and its individual members could only advise, not direct, managers in the Industrial Departments. The work of the Auxiliary Departments was in areas which were not directly related to the operation of one or another of the Industrial Departments. Among these were Legal, Purchasing (for major purchases), Development (for business expansion and new ventures), Engineering (for major construction), Chemical (for research and consultation), Advertising, Traffic (for traffic activities not carried out within the five departments), and Services (such as medical, welfare, real estate, safety, fire protection, and inspection).

The crisis of 1921 had called for imaginative organization planning and for a bold restructuring. The multidivisional arrangement has since provided the framework for phenomenal growth in sales volume, in the number of ventures undertaken, and in profits.[3] Moreover, it has set an example for corporate managements to observe and in many instances to follow.

In modern corporations, the "businesses" by which the total enterprise is delineated are continually being redefined and realigned. A new business may have its early development as the offshoot of some existing business. When its size permits it to be established as a unit which is self-sufficient in resources, it may be cut loose to pursue independently its unique business objectives. By the same token, some "businesses" may not achieve a size sufficient to support an integrated set of resources and may be merged into other related businesses. Or as "businesses" develop, they may become increasingly related to other "businesses" at the market level and may eventually be consolidated with them for strategic as well as cost-economy reasons.

The segmentation of the enterprise into a series of "businesses" has been called "decentralization." On the surface, it has seemed that large corporations swing periodically from extensive decentralization to recentralization and back again. Certainly there are many examples in large corporations of excessive decentralizing, which occurs when there are attempts to establish units as "businesses" when they are not sufficiently large or strategically independent of other businesses to be viable. But lying behind these apparent swings of the pendulum are often the more fundamental realignments that take place because of business growth, evolving strategies, and changes in the market environment.

Defining Integrated Business Units

A business is defined in terms of the product lines it manufactures (and/or procures) and sells, the resources it contains, and the markets it serves. Generally, a business is built around a cluster of product lines related in technology, market, and/or production processes, and large enough in total sales volume to support an integrated set of basic resources: engineering, procurement, manufacturing, financial, and sales.

What are the factors which are taken into account in modern corporations in segmenting the enterprise into a series of businesses, and in continually revising this structure? In delineating the business structure, corporate managers strike a

---

[3] As of 1968, there were twelve Industrial Departments accounting for sales of $3.5 billion (Du Pont *Annual Report*, 1968).

balance among factors which pull in opposite directions when it comes to the size and to product/market scope.

On the one hand, the business must be large enough so that it can afford to maintain certain critical resources and to operate them on an efficient scale. Second, the business should further embrace programs which are related at the market level to facilitate the coordination of market strategies that might otherwise be in conflict. Third, the scope of the business — its resources, products, and markets — must be such as to establish a realistic framework for forecasting, strategic planning, and goal setting. That is, product/market scope must be significant so that the broad trends which affect the business can be appraised and dealt with strategically within the bounds of the business. It follows, as well, that the business should be so defined that its performance may be usefully measured. Whether the performance of a business may be usefully measured depends on the extent to which its operating managers control key strategic decision making as well as the resource activities through which strategy is implemented. All of these factors encourage the structuring of business units which are broad in scope.

On the other hand, the market scope of the business must not be so broad that it is inflexible and does not respond quickly to customer needs, to the tactics of competition, and to its unique market opportunities. Nor should it be so large as to become ponderous in its internal communications and control. Such factors tend to encourage a narrower scope of the business unit.

Each of these factors will be examined in the discussion that follows.

Resource Size and Efficiency

In a profit-making business the efficient utilization of resources is of critical importance if the business is to be successful in the market place. The scope of the business unit will tend, then, to be large enough so that its key resource departments can operate efficiently.

The efficiency of the resources which make up the business depends on several factors. The first is size and economies of scale. Up to some point, the larger a resource unit the more efficient it may be. In addition, large resource units may be able to afford a higher degree of specialization within the resource organization than smaller units. Finally, resource efficiency is dependent on the unit's being "whole" or complete and self-contained. A resource is obviously less efficient when certain essential functions are missing. It has difficulty as well in functioning when the resource is broken up organizationally and cannot be centrally managed.

Economies of Scale

It has long been recognized that as a resource unit increases in size, up to some optimum point, the cost per unit of output declines while the quality of the output may increase. The point of optimum efficiency will depend often on technical factors. It may be that unless a resource unit is of a certain minimum size and the volume of its output is also at some threshold level the unit is relatively inefficient.

Scale Economies in Manufacturing: Manufacturing provides many illustrations of this phenomenon. In chemical manufacturing processes, for example, it will usually be uneconomical to construct a plant of less than some minimum size and, up to a point, the larger the plant the lower the unit cost of output. The Monsanto Organic Chemicals case notes that:

In 1967 the largest plasticizer[4] plants enjoyed significant manufacturing scale economies over plants of lesser size. It was believed that even larger plants would soon be built in which unit manufacturing costs would be even lower than the costs in any existing plant. Industry production capacity tended to be added periodically and in large chunks.

In some other types of manufacturing processes, capacity may be added easily in small increments and even a relatively small operation may be as efficient as a much larger one. This may be charac-

---

[4] Plasticizers are high boiling liquids or solids used to improve the processing of plastic resins and to impart flexibility and softness to the finished plastic material.

teristic, for example, of job-shop machine tool operations.

Scale economies in manufacturing, of course, go well beyond plant operations. They apply, as well, to the purchasing of materials and parts and to inventory costs.

A compelling consideration, for example, leading to the consolidation of Ford's domestic automotive businesses into a single business, North American Automotive Operations, was the economies that could be realized by designing, making, and stocking common parts for all lines: Ford, Lincoln, and Mercury.

Scale Economies in Research and Engineering: Optimum size is probably more easily determined for manufacturing resources than for such other resources as research and engineering. Nevertheless, scale economies are highly relevant here, too, although difficult to measure.

In technical industries a research unit, to be viable and productive, may need to be staffed with a range of scientific talents and may require substantial investments in laboratories and pilot plants. Investments in research and development may have to be made over long stretches of time before commercially exploitable results are forthcoming.

Scale Economies in Marketing: In the marketing area, scale economies apply to at least three types of resources: promotion, the field sales organization, and the distribution system.

With regard to promotion, companies which market nation-wide, and which are therefore able to justify national advertising, may benefit from scale economies not available to smaller, regional marketers. Television advertising rates, for example, favor national network users.

Advertising scale economies vary by type of product. Some products such as soap, cigarettes, toothpaste, packaged foods, and portable household appliances may be highly advertising elastic; that is, increased advertising expenditures will tend, up to a point, to produce increased sales and profits. In these industries, the magnitude (or "critical mass") of advertising required to be an efficient and profitable competitor is so great that a few large producers account for a major share of the market.

The formation, in 1959, of the Mobil North American Division, combining U.S. and Canadian operations, had significant promotional advantages.

In the retail motorist market a unified approach for branding, advertising, service station design, and consumer credit was possible. With the increasing mobility of the U.S. and Canadian population, a single overall gasoline marketing strategy for these markets was indeed desirable. Economies could be realized, moreover, through the use of national television network and magazines. A single distribution system including retail stations, wholesalers, and distributors was possible.

There are also marketing scale economies in selling. At the field sales level, a certain minimum sales volume is required to support a geographically dispersed field sales organization, to elicit the support of a distributor organization, and, where needed, to support a product service function. How large a field sales and service resource needs to be to be efficient will be affected greatly by the degree of dispersion or concentration of customers, their individual purchasing potential, and the technical requirements of selling to them.

The scale economies for field sales resources and promotion would be one thing for the Du Pont Textile Fibers Department, dealing with large buyers in geographically concentrated markets. The marketing scale economies would be quite different for Procter & Gamble, selling Crest toothpaste through tens of thousands of retail outlets in markets that are widely dispersed geographically. The sales volume needed to support an economically efficient marketing effort (promotion and the field sales system) could be far greater for the latter.

Constraints on Scale Economies: In some instances, businesses are constrained from reaching a level of maximum resource efficiency because of arbitrary restrictions. One such constraint may be our laws prohibiting monopoly. Another constraint concerns trade barriers.

For example, Ford's markets for automobiles were restricted in some Latin American countries by laws which allowed only locally manufactured automobiles and trucks to be sold. The purpose of such legislation was to create a national automobile industry. In some of these countries, Ford built assembly and manufacturing facilities to stay in the market, but only a very limited line was offered in order to minimize unit manufacturing, engineering, and servicing costs.

Trade restrictions which force businesses to operate within national boundaries may prevent them from achieving optimum scale economies. Operating at relatively high cost (and price) levels, such businesses may survive only because all competitors are similarly constrained.

When the constraints are eased, however, it may become necessary to increase the scale of the business to remain competitive.

For example, Ford of Europe was formed through a merger of the operations of the British and German companies largely because of the significant tariff reductions that accompanied the development of the European Economic Community. In addition there was the possibility that further significant tariff reductions would follow if EEC and EFTA (European Free Trade Area) merged. With all of Western Europe as its market, Ford of Europe had the potential for scale economies well beyond that of the individual British and German companies.

The essential point is that business units tend to increase in size as long as there are economies to be realized by increasing the scale of operation of some critical resource: manufacturing, or research, or engineering, or promotion, or the field sales system. The level of operation of the other resources will, of course, be expanded commensurately although scale economies may not necessarily be operative in the case of these other resources.

Resource Organization and Specialization

In at least two cases in this study, the scaling up of resource units permitted increased functional specialization and made possible a form of organization that was not practical on a smaller scale.

In the case of the General Electric Housewares Division, the Division was established by merging three GE product departments, all making and selling small portable appliances. As a part of this reorganization, nine housewares manufacturing plants were consolidated into a single Product Design and Production Operation. A major perceived advantage of this consolidation was the possibility of specializing plants by product lines, while centralizing purchasing for items common to all plants. Important cost savings would result.

At Ford Motor Company the formation of a single Product Development Group in 1967 for all car and truck lines was the culminating step in the formation of a single domestic business, North American Automotive Operations. Until then, separate product development functions had been maintained for Ford cars and trucks and for Lincoln-Mercury. At corporate headquarters, there was, in addition, an advanced product planning function concerned with longer run vehicle design. The Ford case study indicates that the old arrangements had not facilitated the coordination of annual model changes with longer run advanced design planning. Nor did the old system provide for effective working relationships between the Ford and Lincoln-Mercury Product Planning and Engineering Offices on the one hand and the engineering design functions in the manufacturing divisions.

In the new Product Development Group, product planning was organized by car lines (Ford, Lincoln-Mercury, and Advanced Car Product Planning). The engineering function was organized at one end by type of vehicle (light cars — Mustang, Falcon, Fairlane, Montego, Cougar — and "custom" cars —Ford, Mercury, Lincoln, Thunderbird) for translating product planning concepts into performance specifications, and at the other end by car systems (body, chassis, power train, and electrical).

The new Product Development Group was therefore structured to have effective working relationships with the vehicle divisions on the one hand and with Manufacturing (which was organized by vehicle subsystems) on the other. It provided for a degree of specialization, functionally and technically, hitherto impossible. Its formation was a major step toward achieving parts commonality across vehicle lines.

Resource Integrity

In the development of business units, compelling pressures are at work on management to "flesh out" the business — to make it whole — in terms of needed resources and to achieve a working integration of resource activities. Sometimes in designing the organizational structure of the business, important functions are missing. Under these circumstances, management will tend to fill in the resources that the business lacks, simply in response to its competitive environment.

Sometimes a "natural" resource unit may, in fact, be split among two or more businesses in the corporate structure or part of it may be internal and part external. The initial response on the part of the managements of the several businesses may often be to establish a coordinating mechanism to avoid conflicts, to resolve questions of work priority, and to integrate resource operations with other functional activities. Frequently, however, coordinating devices fail to meet the need and resource integrity — or "wholeness" — often has to be established by consolidating the several businesses involved or by creating fully self-contained resource units for each of the businesses.

For example, before 1959 Mobil operated in the United States through three companies, each with producing, manufacturing and marketing activities: Magnolia Petroleum Company in the Southwest, General Petroleum Company in the West, and the Socony Mobil Oil Company in the eastern two-thirds of the United States. The presidents of Magnolia and General Petroleum reported to the president of Socony Mobil. The directors of the production, manufacturing, and marketing functions in Socony Mobil exercised line authority over their own functions and in addition held staff responsibility for coordinating their functions in other parts of the country. Under each of these three "functional" directors, a coordination committee established general policies. The committees had limited influence, and Magnolia and General Petroleum had been relatively free of outside functional direction. As a result, there was a marked lack of coordination among the three companies, particularly in marketing and product supply activities. There was, for example, a large volume of transfers of petroleum products among the three operating companies, and the lack of adequate coordination of product flows resulted in significant inefficiencies in supply and distribution.

In 1959 the Mobil Oil Company (later renamed the North American Division) was established which included all operations in the United States and Canada. Socony Mobil became the parent company and no longer engaged in operations. A major advantage of the reorganization was that it placed in a single functionally organized operating company (Mobil Oil) direct control of all crude oil supply, refining, and transportation in the United States and Canada.

Mobil's experience demonstrated that the enterprise, when delineated into autonomous, regionally restricted businesses, was unable to cope with sudden shifts in supply and demand and, in fact, was not able to supply its markets efficiently under stable market conditions. Coordination of product flows through headquarters committees was not effective. Instead the business had to be defined in large units covering large geographic areas, such as the United States and Canada, in order to have self-contained functional resources and to make it possible for a single operating management to integrate these resources effectively.

Summary

Strong pressures may often be at work to increase the size of business units in order to achieve increased efficiencies. Larger resource departments may be able to realize economies of scale. At higher levels of operations it may be possible to achieve the "critical mass" needed to support large and low-cost plants, a full range of specialized competence in engineering, research, and product development, and a certain threshold level of advertising and distribution. The consolidation of like businesses may provide cost saving opportunities in the management of inventories and in all basic resource functions such as purchasing, engineering, manufacturing, and promotion.

There is, as well, the consideration of efficiency of organizational design at work. It is often possible to structure large resource units in ways that will enhance their productivity and their effectiveness in coordinating with other organizational units.

The size at which a business will achieve maximum scale economies will vary widely indeed. Because the examples on which the above conclusions were based were all drawn from large companies, the importance of designing large-sized business units would tend to be stressed. Many small companies, however, operate at efficient levels and significant growth would not necessarily produce unit manufacturing cost reductions or increased marketing efficiencies. Again, optimum size in a manufacturing operation is a function of the nature of the production process and the logistical system needed to supply markets. In marketing, optimum size is a function of the size and geographic scope of the served market, the relative concentration of customers, their information and service needs, and the nature of the distribution systems (wholesale and retail) needed to reach them.

Market Scope

Just as resource efficiency considerations may tend to weigh on the side of forming larger rather than smaller business units, market factors may also press in the same direction. There is a strong tendency on the part of corporate managements to consolidate business units when these units are perceived as serving markets with common characteristics. These may be markets in different geographic areas, or they may be markets for products that are related in use. Important benefits may be realized by serving through one business, rather than several, those customers whose operations are geographically dispersed or who buy a number of products from the enterprise. The industrial customer, in particular, develops continuing and multidimensional relationships with his suppliers. The supplier-customer involvement may include technical development, product service, delivery, allocation in periods of short supply, negotiation on price and other conditions of sale. These aspects of the customer relationship cannot be carried on independently by several business units and in different geographic territories without generating conflict and incongruities.

Part of the pressure to merge geographically decentralized businesses comes through growth and the tendency for each to expand territorially and to come in conflict. Part of the pressure arises, too, from the desire to maintain a consistent posture with large customers whose operations sprawl across the territories without "due regard" for the way their suppliers are organized to serve them.

Until 1964, for example, Monsanto operated abroad essentially through a large number of overseas subsidiaries and agents who handled exports from Monsanto's domestic divisions. As the number of subsidiaries had increased during the 1950s and early 1960s[5] and as sales volume grew, certain basic problems emerged. Some member companies began competing with each other and with Monsanto's domestic divisions in third-country markets. In the case of polystyrene, Monsanto manufactured this plastic in the United States and eight other countries. Monsan-

to's agents (in third countries) were free to buy from any of these sources, and in a few cases would whipsaw one against the other on price. Monsanto encountered difficulties, too, in dealing with large international customers. Both Monsanto's domestic Organic Chemicals Division and its large British subsidiary, Monsanto Chemicals Ltd., for example, sold rubber chemicals to the large rubber companies, most of which operated tire factories all over the world. These sales efforts, as well as product development programs for rubber chemicals, were uncoordinated and often in conflict.

Another difficulty, according to Overseas Division executives, was that the development of markets abroad was impeded because the domestic divisions tended to give first priority to domestic customers in periods of short supply and to be interested in export trade primarily when supplies were ample.

In 1964 the domestic divisions were given profit responsibility for their respective product lines worldwide. They were to plan and execute world-wide strategies. A new International Division would "administer" overseas activities and would contribute foreign market expertise in formulating investment plans and market strategies. Agency agreements in many European countries were terminated. Many investments abroad were consolidated into seven "member companies." The domestic divisions moved then to develop world-wide strategies.

Out of conflicts at the market level had come the framework for developing unified strategies and dealing with world-wide customers.

The consolidation of businesses which serve different geographic areas with essentially the same product lines, or the same markets with different products, may offer opportunities for segmenting these markets in some new and more useful way. There may be the possibility for "putting it all together and slicing it another way" for strategic and organizational purposes. The larger market scope provides the basis for a broader range of strategic options.

For example, the Du Pont Textile Fibers Department grew originally as five separate, fully integrated businesses — rayon, acetate, nylon, "Orlon," and "Dacron." Many weavers and other industrial users were potential customers for more than one of these fibers. At the same time each fiber had widely different uses requiring different application technologies.

Customers objected to being solicited by five Du

---

[5] Monsanto made its first foreign investment in a Welsh company in 1920. Between 1920 and 1950, it made a number of other investments abroad including investments in Monsanto Chemicals Ltd. (England), Monsanto Canada Ltd., Monsanto Chemicals (Australia) Ltd., and Mitsubishi Monsanto Chemicals Company (Japan). In 1967 these were the four largest overseas member companies in volume of sales. Between 1950 and 1965 Monsanto made 43 new foreign investments.

Pont salesmen each promoting a different type of synthetic fiber and each competing with the others. Users of synthetic fibers wanted sales representatives from Du Pont who understood their product lines and production processes and who could serve as a source of useful technical ideas.

By consolidating these five businesses into one synthetic fibers business the Du Pont management created an organization that could deal much more effectively with customers in different market segments. The Textile Fibers Department established a single multifiber field sales force. It set up market program units for four broad market segments, men's wear, women's wear, home furnishings, and industrial products. Each of these market segments had a potential demand for all five fibers.

In establishing one fibers business, Du Pont resolved the problem of conflict at the customer level. More importantly, it developed a segmentation scheme by type of end-product rather than by type of fiber, which provided a more useful framework for planning and implementing marketing strategy.

A Qualifying Note

While there are important strategic advantages in defining business units in such a way as to embrace in each business those programs that are related at the market level, it is not always practical to do so. It may be that to embrace all market-related programs in a single business unit would be to create business units so large and so diverse in the manufacturing and engineering functions as to be unmanageable. Then the problem of coordinating market-related programs must be solved in other ways. At General Electric the product departments make and sell tens of thousands of products many of which go to the same customers and/or utilize common distributor systems. To provide a degree of market coordination and to gain field distribution economies, General Electric uses "pooled sales operation." The Power Generation Sales Division, for example, sells the products of 8 product departments, while the Power Transmission and Distribution Sales Division represents approximately 40 product departments. The Industrial Sales Division, which markets primarily to end-users and original equipment manufacturers, performs selling functions for more than 45 product departments. Agency and Distributor Sales Operation, similarly, represents about 35 departments to General Electric distributors.[6] By the same token, any one product department may draw on several of these field sales resources.

Market Decentralization

Consolidations of businesses related at the market level are motivated largely by the desire to establish *market integrity*. Merging like businesses is a way of eliminating inconsistencies and conflict in dealing with customers. It often leads as well to scale economies in resource operations and to the development of a position of greater market power.

However, market *de*centralization is also a common phenomenon. Market integrity may be better established by *breaking up* a business which serves so many diverse markets that its management cannot respond adequately to customer needs. The business's competitive position may deteriorate as it is outmaneuvered on price, falls behind on service, and fails to be innovative in product development.

In December 1967 Monsanto's large and profitable Organic Chemicals Division was reorganized into six businesses: Food and Fine Chemicals, Rubber Chemicals, Petroleum Additives, Paper Chemicals, Functional Fluids, and Plasticizers and General Chemicals. Until then, Organic Chemicals had been operated as a single business.

The following paragraphs are excerpts from an internal memorandum describing the new organization and its rationale:

Up to now the Organic Division has been organized as though it were one business—organic chemicals. The line departments have been in the traditional functional pattern of Manufacturing, Marketing Research, Development, and the various administrative functions. As the size of the division increased, product directors were introduced to assist the General Manager on a staff basis to coordinate the functional groups with respect to an emerging number of different customer groups or "businesses."

The Division has been quite successful in continuing its total growth as well as growth in its several businesses. In addition, new and different businesses have been developed within the Division charter.

---

[6] These data are given as of early 1970.

With greater size it has been increasingly burdensome to maintain the past high standards of customer service and quick response to the many different business interests. The general management burden has been further aggravated by the stepped-up rate of developing new products and obsoleting old products and the related changes in manufacturing processes in each of the several businesses. With this situation in mind, the Division conducted an intensive study of its functions, markets, and system of operation with particular emphasis on its methods of planning and executing the wide variety of programs called for.

As a result of its study, *the Division has concluded that it is no longer just an organic chemical business; instead, it is a number of separate businesses who happen to employ organic chemicals, for the most part, to meet the requirements of distinctly different markets. Furthermore, by orienting itself to market requirements, a much wider vista for future growth opens up. Under this concept, for example, future products may not necessarily be limited to chemicals. In turn, this may lead to better earnings on investment than is possible in the capital-intensive general chemical manufacturing.* [Italics added]

A clear market focus, then, is essential if the business is to meet customer needs and competitive challenges. The Organic Chemicals memorandum says one thing more: singularity of focus is important if the business is to pursue growth opportunities in its markets that may take it beyond its immediate competence. Growth opportunities may call for new technical skills and new production resources. This kind of growth might well have been constrained in an Organic Chemicals business serving many different markets because the difficulties of managing the business would greatly increase if resources were diversified to pursue wide-ranging market opportunities.

In a sense we have come full cycle. The move to break up Organic Chemicals into six businesses in 1967 is similar to the 1921 reorganization at Du Pont where the company decentralized its business to form five fully integrated business departments. Du Pont was perhaps the first business to make this move. By 1967 decentralized business structures had become a common organizational form, understood and well accepted. Perhaps that is why the Monsanto Organic Chemicals reorganization seemed to be a relatively casual move while it took a sharp recession to precipitate the restructuring at Du Pont.

The Business as a Framework for Planning and Measuring Performance

Forecasting, planning, setting objectives, and measuring performance are important modern techniques in the conduct of business. If a top corporate management is to pursue some set of long-term goals and is to allocate resources accordingly, it must, indeed, plan and appraise in terms of the individual businesses that make up the enterprise. It follows that the business structure should provide a suitable framework for planning and measuring. The market scope of the business is an important consideration; planning must necessarily be in terms of some distinct market or significant market segment. The degree of control the manager of the business has is also relevant; he should have reasonable control over key strategic decisions and the critical resources needed to implement the business strategy.

Between 1956 and 1964, when Ford's North American Automotive Operations was formed, Ford's domestic organization was moving step by step from a business structure decentralized by car lines (Ford, Lincoln, Mercury, Continental, and Edsel) to a single car and truck business. In discussing Ford's organization during the early 1960s, one Ford executive commented (in 1967):

> Our organization was sort of a half-way house. On the one hand, the Ford and Lincoln-Mercury Divisions had far less autonomy than they had had in the late 1950s. On the other hand, the Company tended to treat them as if they were still autonomous, as profit centers with control of their own destinies.
>
> To some extent, the vehicle divisions never had been really autonomous. In this business, there are several really big decisions each year: the product program including styling, the marketing budget, and the capital budget. These decisions could never have been delegated to the divisional General Managers. They are simply too important!
>
> Transfer prices have also been a problem. It was extremely difficult to establish meaningful transfer prices for parts and assemblies "purchased" by the vehicle divisions from the manufacturing di-

visions, since reliable "market" prices for many of these items could not be obtained.

I am not suggesting that these problems were new in the early 1960s. They were not. But as the product divisions became less and less integrated, the basic weaknesses of our organizational structure became more and more apparent.

For two reasons, therefore, the Ford business structure, when decentralized by car lines, provided an inadequate framework for performance appraisals of management. First, decision making on some of the critical elements affecting division performance did not rest with division managements. Second, transfer prices had to be negotiated between the manufacturing divisions and the vehicle divisions, all of which had profit responsibility. When market prices do not exist to provide a realistic benchmark, transfer prices become difficult to establish and are determined largely by negotiation. What is being negotiated fundamentally is the split of corporate profits among organizational units. Division profits, under these circumstances, may become more a measure of negotiating skill than of overall business performance.

Summary

Market scope is a significant dimension of the business, and strong pressures exist to define the business in such a way that it has *market integrity*. Pressures exist to consolidate like businesses that are delineated by geographical area or businesses that market products going to common customers and related in use. Marketing (advertising, promotion, field selling) scale economies may be realized. The larger business unit can take a consistent posture with customers who buy several products or who may deal with the company at widely dispersed locations. Market scope, moreover, describes the span of opportunity. In theory the broader the span the more choice the business management has in committing resources to market and/or product development opportunities. On the other hand, the business which embraces a number of diverse markets tends to become less responsive to the needs of customers in each market and is constrained in pursuing market growth opportunities.

Finally, in defining a business in terms of its product and market scope and the resources it contains, the ability to plan and measure business performance is a relevant factor. If the business does not have market integrity, it does not usually provide a good framework for forecasting, planning, and setting objectives. If the manager of the business does not have authority to make key strategic decisions and to control the critical resources by which strategy is implemented, his performance and that of the business cannot be usefully appraised.

The Need for Program Managements

In defining the product, market, and resource scope of the business, corporate managements work to achieve a delicate balance. Decentralization (as at Du Pont in 1921 and at Monsanto Organic Chemicals in 1967) is intended to produce *manageable* business units, responsive to customer needs, competitive behavior, and new market opportunities. Consolidation of related business (as at Mobil, Ford, Monsanto International, General Electric Housewares, and Du Pont Textile Fibers) may be needed to achieve market integrity, resource integrity, and scale economies in such resource functions as manufacturing, marketing, research, and engineering.

What seems clear, however, is that at their optimum levels of operations, business units generally are serving several market segments with relatively broad lines of products and pursuing simultaneously a range of product/market strategies. The need exists for structuring the business so that its management can develop and execute widely different strategies without losing sharpness of focus in each of its markets. Organizations must be structured to plan multiple market strategies and to coordinate the activities of large resource units in serving different markets simultaneously. In the next chapter, we consider in some depth the factors which lead business managements to build program organization structures and how these structures are designed.

CHAPTER 3

Program Structures

A *program,* by definition, is a total strategic plan for serving a particular market segment. A *program management* unit has responsibility for developing such a strategy and guiding resource effort in its execution. The *program structure* in a business provides for a series of organizational units, which together plan and monitor the business's several market strategies. As defined in the first chapter, a business organized by both resource units and program units is called a *matrix organization*.

The program structure provides the framework for planning and tailoring overall business strategy to individual market segments. It is the vehicle, as well, for allocating resource capacity to individual market programs and for coordinating resource effort by program.

An example of a well-developed program structure and a useful description of the role of program management may be found in the case on the General Foods' Post Division.

The Post Division had three product/market management units: Cereals, Pet Foods, and Beverages and Miscellaneous Products. Each of the three was headed by a product group manager who supervised the work of several product managers. In the case of cereals, for example, there were product managers for nutritional cereals, children's (presweetened) cereals, family cereals, and miscellaneous (e.g., bran) cereals. Through long experience Post Division management recognized that its competition was different for each of these categories; that customer buying behavior differed for each — some categories responded more to advertising, others to in-store display, and others to price promotions. Yet in advertising, pricing, special promotions, and distribution the marketing strategies for cereals had to be tightly coordinated.

Each Product Manager prepared an annual marketing plan for each brand to which he was assigned. These marketing plans included quarterly sales volume objectives, a general marketing strategy, analyses of competitive activity, and specific plans for advertising, promotion, packaging, pricing, product changes, and marketing research. The marketing plan had to be approved ultimately by the General Manager of the Post Division, after a series of reviews and recommendations by lower level marketing management.

When a marketing plan had been approved, the Product Manager was responsible for its implementation. He worked closely with one or more advertising agencies and the various Post departments. He presented his marketing strategy to an advertising agency, for example, and asked it to prepare advertising copy and media plans. He then reviewed this material carefully, and decided whether to recommend its approval by higher management. If his recommendation was approved, he then worked with the agency to execute the plan. In general, the Product Managers worked with Post staff departments in virtually the same way as they did with outside advertising agencies. They had no direct authority, but were expected to make sure that the various elements of a brand's marketing plan were implemented effectively. According to the Advertising and Merchandising Manager, "Persuasion in the best interests of the business with strong emphasis on data, judgment, and logic (was) the Product Manager's best tool."

This is one example. As one moves into a study of organizational design, however, it becomes apparent that there are several different types of program management structures, and that the choice among them is determined largely by product and market characteristics. Many program management organizations are, of course, like the Post Division in the respect that they have *product/*

market managers, managers whose scopes of responsibility are defined in product terms. This is called a *unilateral* structure. By contrast, a *bilateral* structure has both *product* and *market* managers. In the Du Pont's Textile Fibers Department, for example, there are product managers for acetate, nylon, "Orlon," and "Dacron." There are also market managers for the men's wear, women's wear, home furnishings, and industrial markets into which synthetic fibers go.

Another point of difference: some program structures are organized in pyramidal form in the respect that they provide for major program groups and *subprogram* units for each. Both General Foods Post Division and Du Pont Textile Fibers were so designed. Under the Men's Wear manager at Du Pont Textile Fibers, for example, were subprogram units for Boys' Wear, Furnishings and Sportswear, Tailored Outerwear, and Utility Clothing. This may be termed a *complex* structure. A *simple* structure would be one in which there are no such subgroupings.

Finally it is interesting to observe how program structures differ significantly in the extent to which the program units have their own special resources — a small sales force or a product service group, for example. Some program units have no such resources; others may be equipped almost to the point of being self-sufficient businesses.

The discussion which follows examines these variations and the circumstances under which one or another organizational form is appropriate. Then at the end of the chapter we will look at different types of market segmentation schemes by which business managements delineate program structures. What considerations, it will be useful to ask, bear on the choice of one of these over the others? Of all the critical judgments that must be made in designing the organizational structure of a business, none is so important as this one: how will the business segment its markets for strategic planning purposes?

Unilateral and Bilateral Program Structures

Generally, the bilateral scheme which provides for both product and market management units is appropriate when the markets for a product are quite diverse and when end-use technology varies markedly from one type of customer to another. The unilateral arrangement which has only product/market management units is usually found under the opposite circumstances; that is, where the customer groups are not greatly different one from another in the way they buy and use a product, as in the case of General Foods' Post Division.

As noted above two businesses included in this study, Du Pont's Textile Fibers Department and International Business Machines, both developed bilateral program structures.

In IBM's Data Processing (marketing) Division, the Industry Program Department included 16 market program management units delineated on terms of customer industries. These were Aerospace, Manufacturing, Process, Distribution, Printing and Publishing, Consultants and Service Bureaus, Insurance, Communications, Utilities, Finance, Medical, Federal Governments, State and Local Governments, Education, Airlines, and Transportation (Rail; Motor).

Industry Program managements prepared sales forecasts and marketing strategy plans for their respective market segments. They prepared and conducted educational programs for both IBM salesmen and customers. They worked with the field branches to develop effective sales strategies and to enlist the full support of field sales representatives, systems engineers, and field engineers in their assigned markets. Each Industry Program unit also developed Type II computer programs ("software"). These programs were designed for specific application (such as retail inventory control, industrial process control, and airlines reservations scheduling). Finally, Industry Program managements were active in initiating requests for new and improved equipment for their respective markets.

There were *also* Product Marketing Managers in the Data Processing Division, one for System/360, another for Special Systems, and a third for New Business. Under each one there were two to four Product Managers for such categories as Large Systems, Intermediate Systems, Small Systems, Programming Systems, and Data Acquisition and Control Systems.

Product Administrators were responsible for the continuing development of the product line. They received ideas for product line additions and equipment improvement from industry program managements, from field personnel, and from the constant monitoring of competitive offerings. They worked with personnel in the Systems Development Division to estimate the market potential of proposed new products and to achieve the development of products that would fill customer needs and be profitable for IBM. Product Administrators prepared instructional materials, conducted product information seminars, and worked with field personnel on problems of selling and servicing equipment. Finally, they worked with Systems Manufacturing on production and delivery schedules.

This is an instance where there is significant diversity among market segments, especially in terms of end-use applications. "Software" was relatively unique for each of the 16 segments which IBM's management identified for organization and planning purposes. As noted, bilateral program structures are often found in businesses which face such market diversity.

The same condition (significant market diversity) obtained in the case of synthetic fibers.

Synthetic fibers markets range broadly from nylon for tires, for example, to nylon for women's hosiery. Across this wide range, application technology and the manufacturing processes in which synthetic fibers were used as a material varied greatly. Thus, when the five synthetic fibers businesses were consolidated into one in Du Pont's Textile Fibers Department, the organization plan called for both Merchandising (market) Managers and Sales Programs (product) Managers.

The Merchandising Managers forecast synthetic fiber consumption in their markets and made market strategy plans. They also developed specific plans to help Du Pont's direct customers move their products through trade channels. They promoted the use of Du Pont fibers both through advertising and through promotional work with their respective channels of trade.

The Sales Programs Managers were oriented to products. Each Sales Programs Manager was charged with looking after the "health" of his particular fiber: rayon, acetate, nylon, "Orlon," and "Dacron." He worked with the Merchandising Managers to assure that the plans they were making would provide for the full exploitation of the market potential for his fiber. His other areas of interest included scheduling production, allocating available supplies, and planning new plant capacity. Each Sales Programs Manager took an active part in the development of new fiber grades and new fabrics. He solicited ideas from field personnel and estimated the potential sales volume for a proposed new fiber and the price it might bring. New ideas were discussed with representatives from Research and Manufacturing. If the response was favorable, the Sales Programs Manager reviewed the idea with interested Merchandising Managers and requested their help in promoting the new grade of fiber in the specific applications for which it had been developed.

At IBM and Du Pont, market program managers focused on strategy development and implementation in the market. Product managers were concerned with developing new product variations and moving them into the on-going marketing stream. They were concerned as well with the efficient utilization of the businesses' product development and manufacturing resources. At Du Pont in particular, the Sales Programs Managers' work, broadly speaking, was concerned with seeing that the plants served Du Pont's several markets, and that this capacity was maintained and used efficiently as well. It had to do, further, with working to channel plant output into the most promising and profitable markets.

A bilateral structure was appropriate at IBM and Du Pont. Planning and strategy formulation were usefully approached from a market viewpoint, but management attention had to be focused, as well, on individual products. Both the synthetic fiber and computer industries were in phases of rapid technological development. It was essential for Du Pont and IBM to lead product developments in their respective industries and at the same time to maximize the return to be derived from investments in plants and laboratories.

Simple and Complex Program Management Units

Program management units may have subprogram structures for the development and implementation of substrategies. These are *complex* program organizations. They are useful when there are strong strategic ties among what might otherwise be relatively independent programs. For example, subprograms may be related with regard to such aspects of strategy as pricing, advertising, technical product development, and relations with key customers.

It is worth noting that in the Du Pont Textile Fibers organization both the broad program and subprogram groupings were laid out in terms of end-use markets. At the Post Division the structure was delineated at both levels by product.

The subprogram organization may also be laid out usefully in terms of *markets* in instances where the basic program organization is delineated by *products*. Interestingly, program management units may also be organized at the subprogram level by a *geographic* breakdown where marketing strategy needs to be tailored to differences among geographic markets.

Monsanto's Organic Chemicals Division provides a useful instance of a complex program management organization where there were subprogram structures delineated both by market and geographically. This Division's business was large (in excess of $250 million a year) and diversified, and its products[1] went into a wide range of markets. About three-fourths of the Division's business came from a limited number of large buyers, each of whom accounted for purchases of more than $500,000 a year. These large customers often bought a number of different Monsanto products and purchased both in the United States and abroad. Because of its range of products, the Division's management had to formulate and implement marketing plans for each of 60 product lines. Marketing programs had to be tightly coordinated, especially as they applied to major customers.

The initiative for strategy development resided primarily with seven Market/Product Group Managers. It was at this level that product strategies were formulated. Under each there were subprogram managers responsible for planning product strategy by end-use market. In the case of the plasticizer line, one of the seven product groups, marketing plans were formulated for such plasticizer applications as vinyl plastic flooring, wire and cable insulation, plastic film and sheeting, and plastisols. The individual *market* strategies were the building blocks for a total *product* strategy. It was important that the program structure be laid out initially along product lines before being subdivided by markets. Pricing strategy had to cut across markets. Product supply had to be allocated to markets according to relative profitability and growth potential.

In 1964 Monsanto's domestic divisions were each given responsibility for developing world-wide strategies for their products, and for implementing them through the International Division. Then the Market/Product Group Managers in Organic Chemicals added a *geographic* dimension to their organizations. The scheme that was worked out provided for an Organic Director of Sales in each of four areas: Europe, Canada, Latin America, and Asia-Pacific. These men would report administratively to the area managers and would have a dotted line reporting relationship to the Organic Chemicals Director of Marketing in the United States.

Reporting to each of the four Sales Directors would be counterparts for each of the Market/Product Managers in the United States. These overseas Marketing Managers would work with the U.S. Market/Product Managers to develop strategies by areas. Marketing Managers would provide information on their markets as inputs for world-wide strategy formulation. Once plans were made, they worked in their respective areas to see that they were implemented. They were the geographic "outreach" for program management teams at Organic Chemicals headquarters in the United States.

Thus, on the one hand product programs were broken down by markets and on the other by geography. Such an arrangement provided for the coordination of subprogram strategies across multinational accounts, for tailoring strategy by geographic area, and for developing individual programs for end-use markets and yet preserving a consistency in product pricing and promotion.

Even within a market as homogeneous, relatively speaking, as the United States, it may be useful to provide, in the program structure, for tailoring market strategy by geographic area.

At Sears, for example, the buying departments in the Merchandise Department procure the merchandise that is sold through Sears stores and catalogs. The items the buying departments stipulate as "basic-basic" must be carried by all stores with over 32,500 square feet of selling space. "Basic-basic" merchandise accounts for 46% of Sears dollar sales at retail. The greater part of dollar sales are represented by the selections of "division managers" in the retail store

---

[1] The Organic Chemicals Division, for example, made a line of chemicals for the rubber industry, and another for the paper industry. Its products also included food ingredients, fine chemicals for pharmaceuticals, petroleum additives, plasticizers and resins, and functional fluids.

system. Similarly promotional and advertising materials are selected at the field level from those prepared in the Headquarters Merchandise Department.

This is a form of tailoring a total strategy to consumer wants and needs in different geographic markets.

Program-Attached Resources

In its most basic form, a program management unit has no resources of its own; it utilizes the common resources of the business for carrying out its strategy. Often, however, program units do, in fact, have certain resources which are identified as being part of it. Under what circumstances, it may be asked, do we find that program management units have resource complements and when do they share with other programs the common resources of the business?

Program management units tend to develop their own program-attached resources when it is economically justifiable; that is, when the program can utilize fully the capacity of a resource unit of efficient size, and when the function is unique to the program. Programs also develop their own resources, external or internal, when the common resources of the business do not have a particular capability which the program needs or when the common resource is not organized to serve the program well.

When it is impractical for program management units to have their own specialized resources, they may have the capability to aid in the development, for their purposes, of the resources on which they rely. It may be, for example, that a program management unit has personnel for training field sales representatives in product applications. Program management units also often house technical service groups to assist field representatives and work with customers.

For example, the North American Division of Mobil Oil Corporation had program management units in its Marketing Department for a wide range of markets. Many of these had program-attached resources. The Marine and Aviation Departments, for example, had their own direct sales forces. The selling task in each case was technically specialized. It called for a detailed knowledge of the industry and of individual customers. While market potential was large, there were a relatively small number of large buyers in each case and they were easily reached with a small selling organization.

Mobil's Industrial Department, which dealt with industrial lubricants, did not have its own sales force. The market ranged from small job shops to large manufacturing plants and was widely dispersed. It did, however, have resources for training new industrial products salesmen in the field sales organization. It provided engineering services, specialized by user industry, to assist in resolving field sales problems. In addition, the Industrial Department had a seven-man unit which worked with manufacturers of industrial machinery to arrange for the recommendation of Mobil lubricants in operating manuals. It prepared and published the widely recognized Industrial Engine Builders Book.

The Tires, Batteries, and Accessories Department of Mobil Oil had its own resources for procuring tires, batteries, and accessories to be sold through Mobil's network of gasoline stations. These were nonpetroleum products and Mobil did not manufacture them.

Other instances of resources attached directly to individual programs are found at the IBM Corporation:

In particular, each Industry Marketing Program Manager had his own technically skilled personnel for developing Type II "software" programs. Since data processing applications varied greatly from one customer group to another, it was logical that each industry program unit have its own "software" development resources. On the other hand, "hardware" product development was not unique for each user industry and that was the responsibility of the Systems Development Division.

At least one IBM program, the Airlines Industry, also had its own field sales and systems engineering personnel and did not draw on the regional organization. Because airlines reservation systems were highly specialized, because there were relatively few potential customers, and because each such customer was a potentially large user of IBM equipment, it was useful and economical to have program-attached resources for sales and systems engineering. Moreover, such an arrangement would facilitate the coordination of systems development, sales, installation, and servicing effort by individual customer. The concentration and coordination of effort that would be achieved strengthened IBM competitively in this important market.

The Government, Education, and Medical (GEM) group of programs shared a field sales organization and, like Airlines, did not utilize the resources of the regional selling organization. But unlike Airlines, there were a large number of large and small potential customers in these three market categories. In the case of GEM, however, the reasons for having specialized field sales resources were twofold. First, customer buying behavior in these markets was different from that which characterized industrial purchasing behavior. It would be advantageous to have field salesmen who understood institutional customers and could develop experience in dealing with them. Second, the GEM Region could be well structured geographically to deal especially with federal government agencies. Hence, the GEM Region had been delineated geographically to take account of customer locations. For example, the GEM Midwest Region had been drawn so the responsibility for NASA Space Flight Centers could be assigned to one district within the region. These considerations were important because buying decision-making influences were frequently dispersed geographically within the customer organization.

Another type of IBM resource activity, designing industry-oriented training programs, was found attached directly to the industry program management units. These programs were conducted by the Data Processing Division's Education Department for personnel in the district selling organizations. In addition, as the case indicates, industry managers and their staff sometimes held seminars at headquarters or in the district or branch offices.

At IBM, therefore, certain resources were specialized by industry program and attached to the program organization. In all such cases, resource effort was specialized by industry: the development of Type II programs, selling and systems engineering for Airlines and GEM, and designing and conducting industry-oriented training programs. In all cases, specialization was economically justifiable. In one instance, Airlines, specialization by application was needed; in another, GEM, special expertise in customer purchasing patterns was required.

Market Segmentation and Program Organization

The discussion has presumed, thus far, that program management organizations will be delineated along the lines of some optimal segmentation scheme. We shall now consider how the markets a business serves should be segmented for organizational purposes.

The markets a business serves may be defined in terms of *products, end-use applications, buyer behavior patterns,* and *geographic area.* The program structure may be delineated along any one or any combination of these dimensions. The most useful way of delineating the structure will depend on which dimension of marketing strategy is the most critical.

For example, in structuring the Industry Program organization, it should be noted that IBM segmented the computer market for the most part in terms of *application* (or "software") *technology.* Computer applications in the "airlines" market were markedly different from those in "distribution" and different again from data processing applications in "insurance" and "utilities." In addition, customer buying behavior tended to be relatively homogeneous within each segment.

The identification of "Federal Government," however, as a market segment for organizational purposes was predicated on *customer buying behavior* as opposed to *application technology.* "Federal Government" is a tremendously large customer group with a very wide range of applications. Many, if not most, of these applications — such as payroll accounting, process control, and logistics — were like those in the manufacturing, distribution, or insurance market segments. But the buying behavior of "Federal Government" is different from that of other market segments, and centralized buying decision making and the use of competitive bidding procedures are key characteristics.

While decision making in government agencies is centralized, it is also complex. In any one procurement, there are likely to be a number of decision-making influences at different locations (both geographically and organizationally) which need to be identified and to be addressed each in terms of its particular interests in the procurement. At the same time the widespread use of competitive bidding procedures in the government leads to the use of somewhat different marketing strategies (with price as the major factor) than is the case in commercial markets.

In view of these considerations, marketing to the federal government is a field of its own; expertise in government marketing requires in-depth knowledge of government organization structure and procedures, and a working knowledge of the people who participate in one way or another in procurement decisions. Furthermore, unless this knowledge is continually updated, such expertise may quickly become obsolete because government organization and procedures change frequently and personnel turnover may be rapid. All these factors vary from one federal government organization to another and lead to a program structure broken down by government agency.

"State and Local Government," "Education," and "Medical" were combined with "Federal Government" at IBM in 1965. The single program known as the "GEM Region" emerged. These four market segments were perceived as being related and also somewhat similar in buying characteristics. In many instances medical and educational data processing expenditures are financed by state, local, and federal agencies and personnel in these agencies become involved in purchasing decision making. In addition, procurement in these markets is often (but not always) by competitive bid and the buying decision-making process is complex.

In consumer goods markets, useful segmentation schemes may hinge on subtle differences in buyer behavior. The management of General Foods' Post Division made such distinctions, for example, in segmenting the breakfast cereal market (into nutritional cereals, children's cereals, family cereals, and other cereals) and apportioning it for strategic purposes among four product managers.

Sears' management recognized important differences between consumer buying behavior at retail stores compared with catalog sales. Consumers tend to buy more of certain types of items (such as children's clothing) through catalogs and more of other merchandise (such as large household appliances) through retail stores. Each takes a different type of promotional effort and different pricing strategies. Sears has developed separate marketing programs in each broad product category for each of these channels — retail store and catalog.

Because market structure is continually evolving, segmentation schemes may become obsolete for organization and strategy purposes and may need to be recast.

When Alfred Sloan originally conceived the General Motors structure, it was based on segmenting the market by price brackets. As Sloan described it:

"It seemed to me that the intelligent approach would be to have a car at every price position, just the same as a general conducting a campaign wants to have an army at every point where he is likely to be attacked." [2]

Hence, in the original scheme, Cadillac was the General Motors offering in the highest price category and Chevrolet in the lowest. Oakland, Buick, and Oldsmobile were at intermediate points and the Pontiac was brought out in 1925 to fill the price bracket between Chevrolet and Oldsmobile.[3]

As the automobile market in this country has developed and as car product lines have proliferated across price categories, it is doubtful that the original scheme is still a useful way of segmenting the market according to buyer behavior. Other segmentation approaches are probably more useful for marketing program purposes (e.g., "small or light cars," "sports cars," "family cars-utility," "family cars-prestige," "recreation vehicles," "light trucks," "heavy trucks," "fleet vehicles," and "leasing").

We have considered three ways of segmenting markets for organizational purposes: by product, by end-use technology, and by buyer behavior, for both industrial and consumer markets. The ultimate choice should favor that scheme which matches the most critical dimension of marketing strategy, whether it be product knowledge, knowledge of customer buying behavior, or expertise in product end-use applications.

A fourth dimension along which markets may be segmented is the *geographic* one. Local or regional market environments may be differentiated greatly by buyer behavior, governmental regulations, and competitive conditions. How to tailor marketing programs to these environmental circumstances may be the most critical consideration in developing strategies. Under these circumstances, program management is likely to be decentralized geographically.

For example, in Pfizer International, program management responsibilities rested on the Area Managers and the Country Managers. With sales of $223 million in 1964, Pfizer International operated plants in 27 countries and marketed in more than 100 countries. Its product lines included pharmaceuticals (antibiotics

---

[2] Chandler *Strategy and Structure,* p. 143.
[3] *Ibid.*

and other ethical prescription drugs), agriculture and veterinary products (such as animal feed supplements and vaccines, and pesticides), chemicals (fine chemicals, bulk pharmaceuticals, petrochemicals and plastics), and consumer products (cosmetics and toiletries).

Ten geographic Area Managers reported directly to the President of Pfizer International and exercised line supervision over Country Managers. According to a company position description, it was "the responsibility of each Area Manager to plan, develop, and carry out Pfizer International's business in the assigned foreign area in keeping with company policies and goals. This involves, for the area assigned, the managerial planning and integration of products imported from established plants located elsewhere; . . . and direction of manufacture (where applicable) and marketing of products." He was to prepare annual and long-range product plans for his area.

Country Managers had profit responsibility. In most cases a single Country Manager managed all Pfizer activities in his country. In some of the larger, well-developed countries of Europe there were separate Country Managers for pharmaceutical and agricultural products and for consumer lines. A Chemicals Manager covered the United Kingdom and the countries in the European Economic Community.

Except for the fact that New York headquarters exercised control over the to-the-market prices of certain products, especially prices of widely used pharmaceuticals, Area and Country Managers had considerable autonomy in planning and managing the Pfizer International business in their respective geographic areas. This was appropriate because each area, and some countries within areas, provided unique market and regulatory environments. In the case of pharmaceuticals and agricultural and veterinary products (Pfizer International's most important lines), national laws affected formulations, dosages, labeling, distribution, and often price. Trade restrictions affected the flow of bulk pharmaceuticals and chemicals and packaged products, and might in effect require the establishment of manufacturing plants to supply local markets. Competition, too, varied significantly from area to area. These were the factors to which marketing strategy had to respond.

Segmentation Schemes and Phases of Growth

Segmentation schemes that are useful at one time and under one set of conditions may become obsolete as these conditions change. Different stages of product development and market growth may call for different segmentation schemes. Different stages of economic growth in areas of the world and even within a country call for different schemes.

In general, it might be hypothesized that geographic segmentation systems will tend to give way to product segmentation. Geography tends to become a decreasingly significant factor for strategic planning as markets in different regions and countries become more homogeneous and as product use patterns in different areas become similar.

Product segmentation schemes, especially those established during the initial stages of market development, will tend to be replaced by application and buyer behavior schemes for organizing and strategy planning. This is because in the early stages of product development, knowledge of the product and how it is used is most essential to commercial success. In the later stages, product knowledge becomes less critical in marketing strategy as customers become educated in its uses. In stages of product maturity (when there is little significant technical development of the product), competitive strength may hinge on developing expertise in diverse end-use applications, in dealing effectively with customer groups which exhibit heterogeneous patterns of purchasing behavior — and in organizing accordingly. It may be useful to recall the following examples:

In the structuring of Monsanto's international operations, the company moved by steps from geographically decentralized businesses to world-wide product departments. Conflicts among Monsanto subsidiaries operating in different countries and inability to work effectively with large customers, themselves operating in many countries, had created pressures to move from geographic organization structure to a product/market one.

Pfizer International was moving in the same direction. In 1965 the Pfizer International management established new Vice Presidents for Development in New York for the company's major product lines: pharmaceuticals, agricultural chemicals, industrial chemicals, and consumer products. These men were to assist the company's president in the determination of strategies for these lines.

Du Pont Textile Fibers moved from defining its

markets solely in product terms (rayon, acetate, nylon, "Orlon," and "Dacron") to organizing in terms of end-use markets (men's wear, women's wear, home furnishings, and industrial). In the early stages of product development, what significant markets might exist could not be clearly foreseen. As markets emerged, the critical dimension of strategy became end-use applications, knowing the customers' businesses, and how synthetic fibers could be used in the products they made.

Finally, organizational structuring based on end-use application and buyer behavior segmentation schemes tends to emerge simply as the business grows. Or, stated differently, large size may be a prerequisite for using a program structure delineated by end-use application and/or buyer behavior. When a company serves a number of diverse markets, such an organization structure requires large numbers of skilled managers and technicians to man it. These organizational "overheads" may be supported only by a large business base.

It is interesting to note that IBM adopted a program structure with 16 industry market program management units (and a large number of product management units, as well) about 1958. In that year IBM sales were $1,418 million.

Summary

A program structure provides a framework for breaking down the tasks of planning and implementing strategy in a business by individual market segments. It is, as well, a scheme by which resource capacity may be allocated to markets and resource effort may be coordinated.

Program structures may be *unilateral* (providing for unified market/product managers) or *bilateral* (with separate *market* and *product* managers). Unilateral program structures tend to develop in businesses which serve relatively homogeneous markets, such as the markets for packaged foods and for military aircraft. Bilateral program structures logically emerge in businesses where diverse markets are served by a technically related line of products and where market strategy as well as application technology varies considerably from one market to another (e.g., synthetic fibers and computers). In such cases *market* program managers are concerned with the development and implementation of market strategies, while *product* program managers play a major role in new product development, in market introductions, and often in coordinating production schedules with market program needs. The *product* manager will frequently have primary responsibility for the balancing of *market* program needs against the need for preserving the "health" of manufacturing and research investments in his products. He will thus be concerned with maximizing the long-run return on the total investment in the product program.

Individual program management units may have subprogram structures for the development and implementation of substrategies, along product end-use and/or geographic lines. In this study, these have been termed *complex* program organizations. They are useful where there are strong strategic ties among what might otherwise be relatively independent programs. In particular, a geographical substructure provides a framework for tailoring an overall strategy to regional market conditions and yet allowing for tight coordination among these subprograms. Coordination may be essential on pricing, advertising, technical product development, and relations with key customers.

Program management units often have certain resources attached to them directly. In this situation, the function performed is generally unique to the program; it cannot be suitably performed by a shared resource department, and a program-attached resource is therefore justifiable. Programs often have their own capabilities for developing (training) and assisting (through supplying technical service and promotional materials) the common resources upon which they depend, both external and internal.

Market segmentation schemes for strategic planning and organization purposes may be promulgated along any of four lines. Markets may be segmented in *product* terms; that is, the market is defined as all customers, existing and potential, for a specific product. Markets may be segmented in terms of user or application *technology* (as at the Du Pont Textile Fibers Department and to a large extent at IBM). They may be segmented in accordance with buying behavior characteristics (a good example is IBM's Government, Education, and Medical — GEM — industry program categories). Finally, they may be segmented geographically (as at Pfizer International) in recognition of a situation where important distinctions exist in market conditions from one geographic area to another. The choice among these four market segmentation schemes will depend on what kind of expertise (knowledge of product, application, buyer behavior, or geographic market conditions and the ability to deal with that dimension) is most critical to marketing success.

A market segmentation scheme which may be appropriate at one stage of market and product development may become obsolete at some later stage. Geographic schemes tend to give way to product schemes as (1) distinctions among regional markets (regarding product use and buyer behavior) tend to diminish, and (2) as conflicts develop in regional markets among geographically organized units. Product schemes, particularly those established in the early phases of market development, may yield to end-use application and buyer-behavior schemes. Knowledge of the product *per se* tends to become a less important dimension of marketing expertise; tailoring selling strategies to the ways buyers use the product and to their buying behavior patterns becomes more important.

Significance of Program Organization Design

The considerations, suggested in this chapter, which bear on program structure pose a series of choices for business managements. They are critical choices. How a management perceives its markets, how it organizes to serve these markets and to formulate strategies is fundamental to the success of the business. The organizational *framework* for planning strategy is an important determinant of the *substance* of strategy. The organizational framework presumes a certain delineation of the markets a business serves. If the definition of these market segments is not perceptive and sensitive to the market environment, the strategies the organization produces will be defective.

Organizational design is not a matter of statistical determination; it is a work of managerial art. The structural framework laid down must reflect the stage of product and market development and the nature of the market environments.

CHAPTER 4

Resource Structures

As a program structure begins to emerge and grow in a business, the resource organization tends to be restructured in order to meet the needs of the programs. New resource units may appear. Some resource units may be consolidated to achieve integration of effort. Others may be split up because fundamental differences in types of work done in the same resource department create difficulties in organization, operations, and personnel development. Very often program-specialized units will be established *within* resource departments (i.e., resource units which serve the specific needs of individual programs while not being attached to them organizationally). Other resource units will continue to apply effort to the broad range of programs.

The discussion that follows focuses on resources and on how they are structured to meet program needs. We are concerned here with such basic resources as procurement, manufacturing, product engineering (development), field (or customer) engineering, and sales.

The discussion begins with a statement on the role of resource management. It offers some ideas that bear on the overall structuring of the resource organization of the business. The chapter then looks at the development of program-specialized units within the several resource departments. Under what circumstances should resource units be specialized by individual programs? When is it useful to have program-*specialized* units in the *resource* departments as opposed to program-*attached* resource units in the *program* organization?

Finally, the chapter considers in depth the matter of field sales organization: the respective roles of regional and district managements, and the organization of field sales activity by type of customer or by product. Evidence from our case studies provides very useful ideas in this area. Moreover, field sales organization is an especially critical aspect in this study of market-oriented organization strategy.

The Role of Resource Management

The responsibility of the resource manager is to deploy the internal technical skills, personnel, physical plant, facilities, and inventories that he controls to the maximum interest of the business. He is similarly responsible for maintaining the strength of the external resources on which the business depends. He takes responsibility, as well, for the growth and development of these internal and external resources so as to meet long-run program and business objectives.

Resource managers have responsibility for allocating to the programs the assets they control. In effect, they deploy company resources to a portfolio of programs. In the program planning stages, a resource manager assesses the demands which the programs collectively will impose, and will determine whether, in fact, the load is manageable. Program plans may then be adjusted to the capacities of the respective resources and the resources, as well, may be scaled up or down. As program strategies are carried out and as plans are adjusted in response to market demand and competitive behavior, resource managers adjust the allocation of effort accordingly.

Because plants, laboratories, and offices are often decentralized geographically and because resources in part consist of highly visible personnel and physical facilities, resource managers often assume certain responsibilities for company-community relations. Plant managers, district sales managers, and laboratory managers commonly serve as interfaces between the company and local civic groups, labor organizations, and local and state and national governments. This function is relevant to resource management in that it is concerned with maintaining a favorable local environment for resource activities in addition to discharging the social responsibilities of the enterprise.

The role of the resource manager, then, is to allocate resource effort to programs, to develop the assets he manages, to meet long-run program objectives, and to maintain a favorable external environment for resource activities.

In meeting these responsibilities, resource managers have an interest in assuring that the programs actually utilize the resources which are available, since resource growth and development can take place only if there is "program through-put."

This concern was particularly relevant in the case of Monsanto's International Division. According to the Division Charter, it was to serve primarily as a set of resources for implementing abroad the world-wide strategies formulated by the headquarters' divisions. In addition, it provided inputs for strategy formulation. A 1967 policy statement charged International with the responsibility for safeguarding investments in member companies abroad. In practice, International would be concerned that operating division product strategies were such that the viability of member companies abroad would not be jeopardized and that the profitability of individual investments overseas would be watched carefully.

One International Division manager noted that "what's best for the product strategy is not always best for Monsanto in each country. Part of ID's responsibility is to see that the country organizations remain strong as product strategies are developed and implemented."

The Delineation of Resources Structures

Proper organization of resources is no less critical to the success of a business than the organization of program management. Resource and program structures bear important relationships to each other. Understandably, as program structures emerge, organizational changes must take place on the resources side of the business as well. Some resource departments are split so that certain functions can be organized independently of one another. Some resources develop specialized units to work on particular programs. Often the resource units establish special activities which have the function of serving as interfaces between the resource and the several programs.

A particularly interesting aspect of the evolution of the IBM organization is the way in which the resource units in the data processing business were redefined as this business grew and its product line changed.

IBM's data processing business was established as a separate entity in November 1956. At that time, the business had four divisions: the General Products Division, the Data Systems Division, the Data Processing Division, and the Advanced Systems Development Division.

Two of these four divisions had both product development and manufacturing responsibilities: the General Products Division for small systems and the Data Systems Division for large systems. The Data Processing Division handled both domestic sales and the servicing of computers in use (customer engineering). Advanced Systems Development Division was to identify new market opportunities and work on advanced designs.

The distinction between large and small systems gave way with the development of Systems/360, a single product line covering the full range of applications. Then the product development and manufacturing functions were separated. A Systems Development Division handled product development and a new Systems Manufacturing Division was responsible for production. In addition, the sales and customer engineering functions were segregated with the Data Processing Division handling the first and a new Field Engineering Division the second. By 1965, then, product development, systems manufacturing, sales, and customer engineering were all organized as separate functions.

We can postulate that three factors may have led to the separation of the four functions organizationally. First, differences in time cycle: the case tells us that the Data Processing Division was heavily oriented toward day-to-day sales activities and therefore field engineering tended to receive inadequate management attention. The two functions needed to be organized separately to strengthen customer engineering as an element of marketing strategy.

The systems development function and manufacturing, too, could be differentiated in terms of time horizons. Clearly, systems development operated with longer time cycles than manufacturing, which was focused on meeting near-term production deadlines.

Second, the way in which the function should be structured is another factor. As the selling function developed, it became organized both in the field and at headquarters by market or customer industry group. In contrast, field engineering was best organized along product lines. Product specialization rather than specialization by user industry was the more critical dimension along which to organize field engineering.

Third, providing a proper organizational framework for personnel development is a relevant consideration. The split between sales and field engineering was recognized, for example, as benefiting the professional growth of IBM field engineers. Probably the same consideration would apply in the case of systems development and manufacturing. The former function would call for more scientifically trained personnel. Their career paths and professional development would go along different lines from most manufacturing personnel.

There were several important factors which led IBM's management, then, to the segregation of product development and manufacturing, and the splitting of sales and field engineering. The reasons that were suggested had to do with differences among these functions as to the time horizons in the work they did, the development and advancement of personnel in each function, and the way in which these functions should be organized internally.

There is at least one other consideration which affects the question of whether a resource function should be integrated with or independent of another resource function. It relates to the values, perspective, and points of view that are brought to bear on resource activities and resource management decision making.

In the reorganization of the Du Pont Textile Fibers Department, a Textile and Industrial Products Research unit (TIPR) was transferred from the Research Division to the Sales Division. While TIPR was a research unit, its work was with customers on the use of Du Pont fibers. Located in the Research Division, TIPR management might find it difficult to assess the relative commercial importance of solving customer problems and to set work priorities accordingly. Located in a research setting, TIPR might tend, then, to establish priorities in terms of technical interest rather than market potential. By transferring this unit to the Sales Division, Du Pont's management had placed TIPR in a different "value setting" and had facilitated TIPR's working relationships with customers and with field sales personnel.

The IBM and Du Pont Textile Fibers cases contribute, then, to an understanding of the overall design of the resources organization. They suggest that delineation is based significantly on such factors as (1) the time horizons of resource work, (2) the way the work should be organized, (3) the setting for personnel development, and (4) the appropriate perspective and values that should influence resource decision making.

Program-Specialized Resource Units

In the preceding chapter, we considered the matter of *program-attached* resource units. We noted that an individual program management unit might have its own field sales force, or technical service facility, or product training group, for example. An alternative organizational scheme is to have *program-specialized* units in the resource departments, which are directly identified with individual programs.

The basic consideration, as we noted in the preceding chapter, appears to be the economic utilization of resources. If resources are divisible by programs and, so divided, can function efficiently, specialization is indicated. Often, however, that is not the case. The heavy press facility for making forgings at Lockheed-Georgia, for example, has far more capacity than any one program requires, and its use must be shared by all programs.

A second determining factor in the specialization of resource units by program is the uniqueness of the skill or knowledge which each program requires. A primary reason for specializing field sales personnel by type of customer, for example, is that product application problems vary widely from one user industry to another. In the research area, the technical skills and knowledge needed may vary greatly from one product line to another.

Finally, the relative scarcity of a particular resource is a consideration. Scarce resources must be shared.

Positioned in a resource department, program-specialized personnel usually have "two bosses." They receive "business direction" from program management and "administrative direction" from resource management. Administrative direction might include responsibility for training and professional development, performance reviews, salary recommendations, supervising the development and execution of a work program, and coordinating program activity internally and externally with outside resources and customers. Strategy direction and guidance, however, might be initiated by program management. Such guidance might come in the form of direct instruction or as program plans which the resources utilize in planning resource activities.

What are the factors to be considered in decisions to organize certain resource functions by program?

The Lockheed-Georgia case speaks of how the "branches" (resource departments) were "projectized" (specialized by programs) at various organizational levels for the C-5A, the C-141, the C-130, and the JetStar. In the Engineering Branch there were three departments working on design engineering for the C-130, C-141, and C-5A respectively. There were, in addition, six functional departments, responsible respectively for structural engineering, subsystems engineering, advanced design engineering, development test engineering, research, and engineering administration. These functional departments differed in the degree to which they were projectized. At some organizational level, usually, there were teams assigned to specific programs. Some functions, however, such as advanced structures design, were not projectized at any level and worked on each of the programs as need arose. The level at which "projectization" took place generally depended on the specific tasks to be performed and the level of effort required for the various programs at particular points in time. In commenting on his organization the Chief Engineer pointed out that it was necessary to retain maximum flexibility within functionally specialized departments and, at the same time, provide the Program Managers with readily identifiable (and thus controllable) resources.

In the Manufacturing Branch, the departments were not projectized except for assembly. Most manufacturing functions did not lend themselves to projectization, and it was most efficient for the various programs to share the same resources.

Within Manufacturing, a Director of Materiel was responsible for procurement, subcontracting, and material handling. A typical aircraft contained 40,000 to 50,000 separate procurement items. Moreover, the percentage of subcontracted subassemblies (by weight) ranged up to 60% in the case of the C-141. The Procurement Division purchased stock items and was not organized on a program specialized basis. The Subcontracts Division, however, working with vendors of major subassemblies, was projectized with separate departments working on each of the major programs. Subassemblies were unique to each aircraft; a high degree of coordination was needed on matters of engineering design, quality control, and delivery scheduling between vendors and internal program specialized personnel.

A separate Quality Assurance Branch established quality control policies, tested all incoming materials, assemblies, and subassemblies at various stages of manufacture, and subjected each aircraft to a rigorous inspection (including flight test) before delivery. The inspection function was organized on a combined functional and project basis with certain divisions responsible for fabrication and tool inspection, and materiel inspection, and others for the JetStar, C-141, C-130, and C-5A. The last four divisions were responsible for monitoring final assembly, while the first two divisions monitored earlier stages of the production process for all aircraft.

As a matter of organization strategy, the timing of resource specialization in all branches was a critical factor. Usually, new programs were initiated in the "general" or "unprojectized" resource units until the level of effort became so large as to call for specialized resources. Branch Heads had far more flexibility in deploying unprojectized units as needs arose and would not then commit them to specific programs until it was clear that the program would in fact materialize and would call for a significant level of effort.

The pattern was therefore one of projectizing at a fairly high organizational level each function that was unique to the program: design engineering, subcontracting for subassemblies, assembly, and final inspection. Other resources had to be used across programs because an efficient unit of these resources had more capacity than could be utilized fully by any one program: advanced structural engineering, procurement (of stock items), fabrication, and tool inspection. In Manufacturing an efficient, indivisible unit might be a large machine tool; in Engineering it might be a team of specialists in a technical discipline; in Procurement the optimum size of an efficient unit might be a function of the volume level of procurement necessary to command the lowest prices from suppliers. Consequently, the desirability of projectizing a particular resource depended both on the size of an efficient unit of that resource and on the size of the program.

The Positioning of Specialized Resource Units

Chapter 3 considered the circumstances under which we find certain resources as part of the program management organization, and in the first part of this chapter we looked at the matter of establishing program-specialized units in the resource departments. Given the desirability of specializing resource units by program, the question is raised as to what considerations determine whether program-specialized units should remain in the resource departments or be attached directly to programs.

The positioning of specialized resource units — either as part of the program organization or as part of the resource department — will depend, initially, on where its direction should come from. It may be that the unit requires a type of guidance and control that is discipline-oriented, and it should therefore be in a basic resource setting and have technical supervision. It may be that professional growth and development of personnel is better fostered in a resource department as opposed to a program management environment. Finally, it may be desirable for the management of the business to preserve some flexibility in the assignment of personnel and facilities to programs. It is apparently easier to reallocate resources that are not directly attached to programs. An *absence of concern* about these three considerations suggests that specialized resources might well be program-attached to provide a direct link with program management.

Field Sales Organization

The implementation of program strategy at the market level is heavily dependent on the effectiveness of the field sales organization. The ties between market program management and the field sales resource tend to be particularly strong. The need for close program-sales integration is evidenced by the fact that in all but the Lockheed-Georgia case, program management units and the field sales organization were both part of a Marketing Department.

Two aspects of field sales organization are important for purposes of this study: (1) the role of sales management at different levels, and (2) the specialization of sales representatives in the field by product or customer group.

Sales Management Functions

A field sales organization of any significant size has management levels which may range from region to district to branch. Because of the inherent nature of field sales work, these management units are always geographically dispersed. What functions do these different levels typically perform? Generally, these intermediate levels between headquarters management and the individual field sales representative provide *reporting links* and work on the development of the sales organization as a critical resource.

At IBM there were three regions, 20 districts, and 225 branches as of 1966. Line selling and systems engineering work were done in the branches. District managers served as reporting and performance review points for the branch managers. Approximately 10 to 12 branch managers reported to each district manager, making it possible for the latter to maintain a close surveillance of branch operations and to advise, counsel, and appraise his branch managers. This direct working relationship was an important link to Data Processing Division headquarters and served as well to maintain morale for branch managers at widely dispersed locations.

The district and regional offices also served as levels

for developing and consolidating detailed sales and financial plans and budgets. In the other direction, they translated overall quotas and sales objectives into goals for field branches.

A major concern of the districts and regions was personnel: recruiting, training, promoting, appraisal, and compensation. In this respect, the regional and district offices shared Data Processing Division headquarters responsibilities for developing resource competence in the field selling function.

Regional and district offices also served as the locus for certain specialized resource functions. In particular, there were education centers in each district for training IBM and customer personnel. While the needs of a single branch would not justify maintaining a complete educational unit for each one, the amount of training required for the several branches in a district could easily support a complement of skilled teaching personnel and physical facilities at the district level.

Regional and district offices provided, in addition, an "outreach" for DPD headquarters market operations and product programs managers. Their representatives, located at regional and district offices, disseminated industry market programs and product programs to the field and served as conduits for market information inputs to headquarters program planning activities. Systems engineering managers in the districts similarly served as two-way conduits, disseminating information to systems engineers in the fields sales organization, working on manpower planning and career development, and passing back information to the Systems Engineering Department at DPD headquarters.

Finally, district and regional managers participated directly in the selling function. They provided "high level" contacts with key customers, worked on critical competitive situations, and brought the resources of the field organization to bear on strategically important accounts.

Thus, region and district offices (1) provide a reporting relationship for the branches, (2) are conduits for planning and setting sales objectives, (3) contribute importantly to resource development through sales recruiting, training, and promoting activities, (4) serve often as the locus for specialized resource units such as educational facilities, (5) provide program dissemination and field information points for programs developed at headquarters, and (6) contribute directly to sales work.

In companies such as Sears, Mobil, and Ford, which have extensive retail distribution systems, the field sales organization also has an important function to perform in the development and maintenance of retail outlets and distributor organizations. This will often involve real estate acquisition, retail store construction, and personnel training. It will require the dissemination of promotional programs and the administration of control and reporting systems. It will encompass, as well, the development and administration of standards for retail store performance. In the case of Mobil and Ford this is an *external* resource development function; for Sears it is *internal*.

Field Sales Specialization

A field sales force, responsible for selling a broad line of products, may elect to have all salesmen sell all products to all classes of customers. It may alternatively have branches which are specialized by product or by customer group (e.g., IBM). It may, as a third possibility, not specialize the branches but specialize individual field salesmen within branch offices (e.g., Du Pont Textile Fibers).

The considerations which bear on the question of program specialization in sales organizations are fundamentally the same as in other functional resources. Resource divisibility and flexibility are important, and generally a field sales organization is regarded as a highly divisible resource, easily specialized if other considerations favor doing so. These other considerations are often economic in nature. The advantages in terms of improved service to the customer and potentially higher sales volume of specializing salesmen are weighed against the increased costs of covering a geographic area. For example, the costs of having ten sales representatives, each selling a different product line, travel over the same territory would be greater than having each man sell all product lines in one-tenth of the territory. But the uniqueness of sales knowledge and skills required to sell different product lines or to deal effectively with different customer groups may be critical. When the several marketing programs which a business conducts vary considerably one from another in these respects, the need to have program-specialized sales personnel are likely to outweigh cost-of-coverage considerations.

IBM began to specialize its field sales branches by user industry in the late 1950s. The need for specialization arose because computer applications varied greatly among such customer groups as the airlines, retailing establishments, and hospitals. "Software" programs tailored to applications in each user industry were being developed, and at headquarters the Data Processing Division marketing organization began to prepare industry marketing programs. In addition, sales had increased to $1.2 billion in 1957 and to $2.2 billion in 1961. The sales volume base and the market potential were considered by IBM's management to be sufficiently great to support specialization by user industry both at headquarters and in the field.

Specialized branches each responsible for a particular customer group were established first in the major cities. In New England, IBM's District 1 began to specialize in 1964. Prior to that time each branch office in the district covered the gamut of customers located in its assigned territory, although individual salesmen were specialized in some instances by user industry.

By early 1966 the District had ten branches which varied considerably in the degree to which they were specialized. A Finance branch, for example, was responsible for sales to banks and other financial businesses throughout the entire District. An insurance group handled sales to insurance companies in Metropolitan Boston, Rhode Island, New Hampshire, and Maine, while a Hartford branch was responsible for insurance accounts in that area and in western Massachusetts and Vermont as well as utilities in western Massachusetts. The Cambridge branch was given all university and hospital accounts in greater Boston. In general, the branches in the eastern part of the District (Boston, Massachusetts; Providence, Rhode Island; Concord, New Hampshire; Portland, Maine; Montpelier, Vermont; and Worcester, Massachusetts) were the most specialized, and the branches in the western area of the District (Hartford, Connecticut; Springfield, Massachusetts; New Haven, Connecticut) were the least specialized.

What are the circumstances under which industry specialization at the branch level can be justified? The reorganization of IBM's District 1 (the New England states) provides some useful clues. The District manager listed six criteria: (1) the geographic concentration of accounts in an industry group; (2) IBM's market penetration in that industry; (3) the travel costs of covering a geographic area using industry-specialized salesmen. (The first three considerations are interdependent in the respect that they relate the costs of supporting an industry-specialized field sales force to the volume of business available in the industry in a geographic area); (4) the uniqueness of applications in an industry and the special selling skills required to work with customers on those applications; (5) the extent to which competitors offered applications-specialized talent to a particular industry (these factors concern the relative competitive advantages of specializing); and (6) the amount of specialized talent available in a district that could be brought to bear on a given industry market. (The last is a matter of the effective utilization of scarce resources.)

To develop and maintain applications-specialized selling resources for 15 industry groups in 20 districts requires a large sales volume base. Because of its size IBM had a clear advantage over smaller competitors whose sales could not support this amount of specialized talent. As stated earlier, competitors might, then, tend to specialize in certain industries rather than attempt to compete with IBM "across-the-board."

Industry specialization at the field sales level has one disadvantage. It reduces the flexibility the company has in moving sales personnel to different assignments. This is an inherent problem in the specialization of any resource. In the Lockheed-Georgia case, for example, the head of the Engineering Branch speaks of the need to commit specialized resource units to programs but yet to maintain reserves of uncommitted personnel to give him flexibility in meeting urgent short-term needs.

Specialization of Individual Sales Representatives

The problem of whether or not to specialize *individual* field salesmen is not fundamentally different from the question of whether to specialize at the branch level. The basic consideration, again, is an economic one. It depends on the sales pattern relative to the costs of coverage. If the geographic concentration of customers, sales per account, and total sales volume are all high, specialization may be a practical alternative. Then, other considerations become relevant. Is specialization desirable because the nature of the selling task is different for different classes of customers or for different products in the line? Or, it may be that the range of products is so great that it would be difficult for each salesman to master all the facts he should know to sell the entire line effectively. It may be that the products are used for such a wide range of customer applications that individual representatives cannot be knowledgeable about the use of the product in all these market segments.

At General Electric when the three departments all making and selling household portable appliances (Portable Appliances, Home Care and Comfort Products, and Clocks and Personal Care Products) were merged into a single business in 1964, the three sales forces were consolidated into one. These sales forces were selling GE appliances to approximately 900 distributors, of which 180 carried all three lines, 370 carried the portable appliances and clock lines, and 350 carried only the clock line.

In the organization of the new Housewares business, the Division management attempted initially to have each salesman selling to wholesale distributors carry all product lines but ultimately reverted to specialization by product within the district sales organizations. In the meantime, however, General Electric Distribution (a company-owned distributor of Housewares Division products), calling on retail dealers, continued to follow the "full basket" approach; that is, that each salesman sell all Housewares Division products to his retail accounts. Why was it logical to specialize salesmen calling on wholesale distributors but not those who served retail store accounts?

According to Housewares Division executives, there were several reasons why the "full basket" concept had not worked for the sales force calling on wholesale distributors. While some distributors had complained that they had to deal with too many salesmen under the old organization, there were more complaints about inadequate sales assistance under the new organization.

In particular, many distributors had explained that since their own salesmen carried the "full basket" (they could not afford product specialization), HD salesmen should have detailed knowledge of individual products and product features. One of the main functions of the HD sales force, these distributors believed, was to train distributor sales personnel. If HD salesmen were not more specialized than distributor salesmen, there was relatively little they could offer in the way of assistance and training.

Equally important, the salesmen themselves did not like the new organization. As one salesman explained: "The basket was simply too full. It is impossible for one man to master such a wide range of products; you just don't sell clocks the way you do irons. There was too much; I could rarely get a distributor to give me enough time to go through my entire book."

Moreover, HD had franchised different distributors for its various product lines. Clock distributors were generally smaller and more numerous than portable appliance distributors, for example. As a result, HD sales representatives had to deal with a greater variety of distributors, and they complained that they had to work much harder to achieve a given level of sales.

The return to product specialization in the field sales force gave regional managers a certain flexibility in making assignments to salesmen. In the New England territory, for example, the regional manager then assigned two men exclusively to portable appliances, because the training of distributor sales personnel on product features and promotional tools was especially important to the success of this product line. Clocks, personal care products, and the Handy Hannah[1] line were grouped and assigned to other salesmen, since these lines were sold through small distributors, including drug wholesalers, the great majority of whom did not carry the Housewares Division's other product lines. Then, there were some salesmen who carried heaters, electric blankets, and fans since these items had offsetting seasonal sales patterns.

By contrast, General Electric Distribution (GED) which sold to retail stores *did* operate under the "full basket" concept, with each salesman selling the complete line. According to the GED general manager, selling to retailers required intensive coverage of a relatively small geographic territory. If a salesman handled only certain product lines, his territory would have to be enlarged to maintain his sales performance. In addition, most independent distributors were relatively small and carried literally thousands of different items. Retailers had become accustomed to working with such distributors, who could not afford to specialize. Moreover, a major task in selling to retail stores apparently was to achieve good display and in-store promotion of the full line of products.

The factors which favored specialization by product line in the Housewares Division sales force had to do primarily with perceived differences in the selling task among the several product lines. The Boston regional

---

[1] The Handy Hannah line of portable appliances was marketed originally by the Universal Manufacturing Company. In March 1965 General Electric acquired this company, and its product lines were then distributed through the Housewares Division.

manager, given the freedom to specialize his sales force or not as he saw fit, elected to specialize. His criteria in making sales assignments had to do first with *differences in the selling task* (two men were assigned exclusively to portable appliances, because the training of distributor sales personnel was particularly important here; clocks and personal care products were grouped because they required contacts with many small distributors, including drug wholesalers, who did not carry the other Housewares Division lines). Second, he was concerned with the economical use of his sales personnel.

Apparently the cost of territory coverage did not seem to be an important consideration in organizing the HD salesmen. Based on his own experience, the Boston regional manager made the intuitive judgment that the higher sales and profits that came through product specialization more than offset the increased travel costs incurred by several salesmen covering the same geographic area, sometimes calling on the same accounts. Relative to the size of orders salesmen received from distributors, on the average, travel costs did not seem important.

To the General Electric Distribution manager, however, cost of territory coverage was the key consideration. His salesmen called on a great many small retail accounts and the average order received was significantly smaller than in the case of distributors. Moreover, the selling task for GED representatives was not perceived to be very different from one type of retailer to another, or from one product line to another. Apparently sales training for retail store clerks was either not practical or not as important as instructing distributor salesmen in product features. Nor were retailers accustomed to being called on by several sales representatives from one supplier, each specialized in a particular product line. Hence, the case for sales specialization at the GED level was not at all compelling and travel cost considerations weighed strongly in favor of having each sales representative cover all accounts in a small geographic area.

If it can be established that costs of territorial coverage are not such that the specialization of salesmen is ruled out, it offers important advantages. Sales effort can be tailored to the needs of different classes of accounts. Field sales personnel can develop a mastery of the products assigned to them. District managers have flexibility in balancing work loads to achieve thorough coverage of their respective territories. They can match the particular selling talents of individual salesmen to the needs and "personalities" of individual customers.[2]

Summary

The primary function of the resource manager is to deploy the technical skills, personnel, and physical assets he controls, and to use these resources in meeting the immediate strategic objectives of the several programs. He is responsible, too, for developing resources to meet long-run programs and overall business objectives. Resource managers also assume certain responsibilities for company-community relations to maintain a favorable external environment for resource activities.

In delineating the overall resource structure of the business, it is useful to differentiate resource functions in terms of (1) time horizons of the work, (2) the way they should be organized, (3) the type of personnel required and their development and advancement needs, and (4) the values and perspective that are necessary for effective effort. Such functions as manufacturing, product development, customer service, procurement, and field sales will differ along these dimensions and are usefully established as separate resources.

To serve program needs, units within each of the business's resources may be specialized by program. The basic consideration is the economic utilization of resources. If certain resources are divisible by program and if, so divided, they can function efficiently, specialization is indicated. In particular, the specialization of resources by program is useful if programs call for unique skills. Whether specialized resource units should be part of the program organization or remain in the resource department will depend, in the first instance, on what kind of direction a resource unit needs. It may require supervision of a technical

---

[2] The New England district sales manager of a large multi-product company once commented to a Marketing class at the Harvard Business School: "Among my salesmen I have 'cherry-pickers,' 'wheelers and dealers,' 'negotiators,' and 'introverts,' and I have customers to match them all!"

nature, for example, and might then be better positioned in the resource department. In addition, professional development of its personnel may be better fostered in a resource department environment. Finally, a resource department "home" may be indicated to give resource managers greater flexibility in the reallocation of resources to programs.

We considered two aspects of one particular key resource, the field sales organization: field sales management and the matter of specializing field sales resources by product or type of customer.

The functions of field sales management at regional and district offices are (1) to provide a reporting relationship for branch offices, (2) to serve as conduits for planning and setting sales objectives, (3) to contribute to resource development through personnel recruiting, training, and advancement activities, (4) to serve as program dissemination and field information points for headquarters program managements, (5) to contribute to sales work, and (6) to provide a base for specialized resource units such as training facilities. In companies such as Sears, Mobil, and Ford a key function of field sales management is to develop and maintain extensive retail sales systems and distributor organizations.

Whether or not to specialize field sales branches and individual sales representatives is primarily determined by cost considerations. The price of specializing may be increased costs of territory coverage. If the cost increment is relatively small because customers are concentrated geographically, and if sales per account and potential sales volume are high, specialization has important advantages. Field sales strategy can be tailored to the specific needs of particular customer groups. Sales personnel can develop expertise in their assigned products and/or in the product application problems of their assigned customer groups. District managers gain flexibility in deploying field sales personnel so as to balance work loads and take advantage of salesmen's particular talents in covering their territories.

CHAPTER 5

Program-Resource Relationships: Planning, Operating, and Growing the Business

The two preceding chapters have described program structures and resource structures in business units. It remains now to consider the ways in which program planning and resource effort are integrated to plan, operate, and "grow" the business.

This chapter describes, first, the short-range (annual) planning processes and discusses, as well, the program and resource influences that are at work in longer run strategy formulation.

Annual planning provides an *a priori* apportionment of resources to programs to meet stated strategies. As the business moves into the period for which it has planned, resource efforts need to be coordinated by program and adjusted in response to program revisions. The discussion considers, then, the program-resource coordinating functions in implementing program plans. In the companies that have been studied we can identify and describe specialized organizational units that perform coordination functions.

The chapter concludes with a discussion of organizational functions and processes for new product/market development: in other words, growing the business. Generating new products and developing new markets is often a specialized function in dynamic and growing companies.

Planning

The allocation of resources to programs is often determined initially in the preparation of annual plans, which we designate *short-term planning*. Short-term planning is a process for developing a series of program strategies and rationing limited resources among these programs. In the longer run, resources are not fixed; a major objective in *long-range planning* is to provide for resource development as well as the formulation of program strategies. In long-run planning, both program strategies and business resources are variables. In short-run planning, programs are tailored to the available resources.

In the discussion that follows annual planning processes are described. Then, consideration is given to the influences emanating from program management, on the one hand, and from resource management, on the other, in shaping long-range business strategy. In the planning process there seems to be a "balance of power" between these two dimensions of the matrix organization that is significant in the shaping of strategic objectives.

Annual Planning Processes

The annual planning procedures described in our case studies vary widely from one company to the next. Something of a common pattern, however, emerges. In the initial stages of a one-year plan broad growth and profit objectives, based often on trends and forecasts of economic factors, are prepared for the total enterprise at headquarters levels. These provide parameters within which detailed planning may take place.

In a second stage, individual program sales and profit forecasts are prepared and aggregated to determine how closely the sum of program forecasts comes to meeting overall business or enterprise goals. If the business is organized both by product and by market (i.e., a bilateral structure), forecasts may be prepared for products and also for markets. These two independent forecasts are then brought into line by an examination of forecasting assumptions.

In a third stage, individual program plans are elaborated with the help of resource managers. The sum of resource effort demanded is appraised in light of resource supply or capacity. Further adjustments may then be made in program needs and objectives (and, if possible, in resource capacity) to bring program requirements and resource limits into line and to establish priorities.

The sequence of steps may vary somewhat but the process of bringing forecasts by market and by product into line, of adjusting program needs to resource capacity, and of matching the sum of program goals with overall business goals is typical. It is a recycling process. Effective planning systems seem to be characterized by an immense amount of interchange between top management and operating management, among program, product, and resource managers, and between headquarters and field, before plans are formalized.

When program plans become formal, after being approved at top management levels, they are then typically translated into a series of detailed objectives for the several resource units. Production schedules are developed, targets are established for field sales, research programs are planned, and advertising budgets are prepared — all with specific time dimensions.

Here, for example, is a description of annual planning at the Post Division of General Foods:

The product managers prepared their marketing plans one section at a time. Sales forecasts, spending needs, and profit estimates were based on historical data, competitive trends, and judgment. When a product manager had made his first rough cut at these figures, and received concurrence from his product group manager, he submitted his estimates to the Advertising and Merchandising Manager for review. The Advertising and Merchandising Manager attempted to gauge the validity of the relationships on which the forecasts were based and at the same time to determine how well, in the aggregate, the various marketing plans fitted with the division sales and profit objectives.

On the basis of his analysis and discussions with the Post Marketing Manager, the Advertising and Merchandising Manager frequently suggested changes in these preliminary forecasts. This generally occurred in late October. The product managers then prepared new forecasts which they submitted upward for approval. Again, the Advertising and Merchandising Manager reviewed them, but now in terms of a firmer divisional volume plan on which other departments based their planning and forecasts. Volumes were modified as more current consumer data became available.

During this same period (October to December) the product managers wrote the other sections of their marketing plans. In doing so, they worked with the Post Promotion, Art Services, Sales Planning, and Marketing Research Departments, and outside advertising agencies. The product manager generally presented a brand's marketing strategy to its advertising agency, for example, and asked the agency to prepare copy and media strategies. He reviewed these in detail, working with the agency to achieve modifications he considered appropriate. He then showed the strategies to his product group manager, who might also suggest changes. When the strategies were approved, the agency began to prepare copy and media schedules. Again, the product group manager reviewed these materials informally during preparation.

Similarly, the product manager presented his general objectives and strategies to the Promotion and Marketing Research Departments and asked them to prepare detailed plans. He worked with members of these departments in much the same way as he worked with account executives at the advertising agencies — reviewing alternative plans, suggesting changes, and consulting with his product group manager.

In most cases the Advertising and Merchandising Manager reviewed the various sections of a brand's marketing plan informally, before it was formally presented to him for approval in December. When it was presented to him there were "few surprises," although he might request minor modifications.

When the Advertising and Merchandising Manager had approved the brands' marketing plans, they were brought together into a divisional plan. The Advertising and Merchandising Manager worked closely with the National Sales Manager, the Marketing Manager, and the General Manager to establish the final divisional plan. This plan was submitted to the corporate management of General Foods in late February or early March.

After a brand's marketing plan had been "published," it was necessary to communicate elements of its content to the various departments responsible for implementing it. Although this was done in a variety of ways, the formal procedure was through the "plans letter."

A typical plans letter described what had to be done, and by whom, to achieve a given objective. In many cases this information was summarized in the form of a time schedule. Plans letters were written by the product managers and signed by the Advertising and Merchandising Manager or the Marketing Manager. The product plans letter was an action document authorizing the commitment of resources.

In most cases the product manager also communicated with the various departments on an informal basis, telling them when a plans letter would come out and what it would contain.

The importance of establishing top management guidelines in the planning process as a way of controlling the level of commitment of business resources is illustrated in this description of planning at Sears:

For planning purposes, Sears divided the year into two six-month periods. Several months before the beginning of a new period, the headquarters Economic and Marketing Research Department prepared economic and business forecasts which it submitted to corporate management. Using these data, corporate management developed a forecast of company sales for the next six-month period. The forecast was stated in the form of a percentage change over the same period during the previous year; for example, "Sales in existing facilities should increase 3.5%; total sales (including new stores) should increase 5%."

This forecast was sent with a covering letter to the buying departments and territories. While both were required to develop their own forecasts, it was expected that these forecasts would not deviate markedly from the company forecast. In practice, any major deviation from the company forecast had to be supported with strong reasons, and management was reluctant to approve forecasts above the company forecast.

Management's reluctance to approve forecasts higher than the company forecast was due primarily to its strong concern with inventory control. The "sales and inventory budget" prepared by each store and the store's forecast were, in fact, tied closely together. The forecast sales for a given division, for example, when divided by the appropriate inventory turnover for that division, gave the average inventory level for the division during the period in question. Thus, the greater the territory forecasts, which were composites of group, zone, and store forecasts, the higher the level of inventory the stores were authorized to carry.

The Program-Resource Balance in Strategic Planning

Since programs and resources may be perceived as the two dimensions of a matrix organization, it is understandable that the shaping of total business strategy will be influenced by each. It is also understandable that program and resource managements will approach business strategy formulation from somewhat different points of view.

Program managers typically want to respond to customer needs as they see them. Resource managers tend to favor business strategies that preserve and develop resource strength. These orientations may come into natural conflict. The choice of opportunities, which is basic to strategy, may move in one direction or another depending on the relative strength of the programs and the resources. And sometimes, when the business has a high long-term investment in a resource, external or internal, long-term strategy may be *resource constrained*. That is, strategy may be shaped to preserve the resource investment.

At Ford Motor Company, a major concern in planning program strategy was preserving and building the strength of the dealer organization, a resource that the company had spent more than 60 years developing. Programs that might possibly have utilized other channels of distribution were put through the Ford dealer system. Commercial fleet sales of cars and trucks to large and small accounts were handled, for example, through dealers. The Ford case notes, however, that "a considerable number of major fleet accounts wished to have a single contact within the Ford Division, or required a level of expertise frequently not available at the dealer level. To provide the required expertise at the local level, Fleet Merchandising Managers . . . were appointed in each district. These specialists, who were highly knowledgeable concerning the kind of economic analysis necessary to sell to major fleet accounts, helped the dealers to sell to fleet accounts by assisting them to plan their sales strategies and by calling on the accounts."

Conceivably, Ford might have handled the commercial fleet program on a direct basis were it not for a concern for dealer profitability and the strength of the system.

What determines the balance of power between programs and resources in the shaping of overall business strategy? In strategy councils, the relative strength of programs is likely to depend, in part, on how long the program structure has been in place. A program management structure is often introduced as a "staff" function which is to serve the "line" resource structure. By implication, program management is to play a secondary role in strategy councils. As times goes on, however, the program structure becomes established and gains informal authority through the planning and implementation of program strategies and through the setting of objectives by which resource effort must be guided and measured. Time seems to run in favor of program management, and program managers play an increasingly important role in formulating business strategy.

Programs seem to gain strength, as well, to the extent that they have their own program-attached resources or have program-specialized units in the resource departments to which they can directly relate. At IBM the industry program units had both types of resource units, and seemed to exercise considerable influence in shaping IBM strategy.

A smaller number of large programs may speak with a stronger voice in strategic planning than a large number of small programs. Lockheed-Georgia's four Program Directors wielded considerable influence. Each managed a program that was critically important to the business. Three of the four had the implicit power of a large and important customer (the U.S. Government) behind him. All four were at the Vice Presidential level, while the resource managers were Branch Heads.

Summary

To recapitulate, annual planning is the process by which strategy is set and fixed resources are allocated to programs in the short run. The planning process may be guided initially by a set of overall business objectives based on broad forecasts of the economic and business environment. At the program level, managers work within these guidelines to forecast by product and by market. Then, through program and goal adjustments, overall business objectives are brought into line with the sum of program forecasts and goals. Program needs are adjusted to resource capacity and the short-range strategy is gradually articulated. When formally approved, program strategies then become translated into specific schedules and plans for the resource units.

The balance of strength between the program and the resource structure influences the shaping of overall business strategy. There is a natural tendency for program managers to be acutely responsive to market needs. Resource managers tend to influence strategy in such a way as to preserve and nurture resource strength. That is, resource management will wish to see the business move in a direction that will fully utilize its existing resources and provide opportunities for resource development. We have used the term *resource constrained* to refer to strategies that are strongly influenced by such considerations.

Clearly, the interests of long-run market programs and of resources must be balanced if the business is to make profitable use of its current portfolio of assets and talents while changing to meet the shifting needs in the markets it serves. A narrow and prolonged commitment to existing resources may limit growth and work to competitive disadvantage.

Given a balance of power between programs and resources in overall business strategy formulation, what determines their relative strengths? The maturity of the program structure is one factor. Another is the extent to which programs are self-sufficient through having program-attached resource units or through having a direct relation with program-specialized units in the resource departments. A third consideration is whether there are a limited number of large programs in a business or a larger number of small ones. Under the former condition the program management structure seems to gain strength in business strategy councils.

Annual planning is a "first approximation" in resource allocation. As the business moves into the period for which managers have planned, there is constant interaction between programs and resources in program implementation. Programs are continually adjusted to respond to market changes and to reflect changes in resource output. This requires coordination. Program-resource coordination under operating conditions is therefore the next important topic to consider.

Program-Resource Coordination Functions

A business, as we have seen, will often pursue multiple strategies in a range of markets and implement these strategies through a set of common resources. A critical function in strategy implementation is therefore the day-to-day interpretation of program needs to the resources (both internal and external), the allocation of resource effort to programs in accordance with some set of priorities, and the coordination of resource effort by programs.

It is possible to identify three different types of coordinating functions in the case studies: product management, interface management, and resource scheduling.

Product managers in the program structure often have major responsibility for coordinating manufacturing schedules to meet market demands. They also exercise authority in the area between the product development function and marketing programs, guiding product development in response to market demands and competitive activity. This product development function is considered in more detail in the final section of this chapter.

Interface managers in resource departments also guide the allocation of resource effort to programs. They screen program demands and set priorities on the allocation of resource effort, presumably balancing the needs of customers, on the one hand, with the efficiency of resource utilization, on the other.

The third type of coordinating function is *resource scheduling* as performed by units independent of both the program and the resource structures. Businesses in which independent units are established to play a coordination role seem to be those in which day-to-day resource coordination by program is highly complex. Independent scheduling units seem also to be especially useful in businesses where there are acute problems in allocating limited (in the short run) product supply to a number of markets. In these cases the way in which product output is allocated to markets may have a significant impact on business profitability.

All three types of coordination functions work toward meshing program needs with available resources. The nature of the business seems to be the prime determinant of which of these approaches to program-resource coordination — or which combination of approaches — will be used. This is the next subject to consider.

Coordination Through Product Management

In bilateral program structures, in particular, product managers move between manufacturing and market programs, on the one hand, and product development and market programs, on the other, to serve the "balanced best interests" of both programs and resources. One of their fundamental concerns is to maximize the short-run return on investment in production facilities. They also work to maintain a cost-competitive product line and to preserve and increase the utility of the manufacturing resources for the products they manage. These objectives are partly accomplished by helping to set production priorities that will result in low-cost operations. They are also accomplished by assuring that plants and development laboratories, in fact, serve customer needs. There are trade-offs between maintaining efficient production and satisfying (sometimes) erratic customer demand. Product managers frequently make these judgments.

The Du Pont Textile Fibers Department case describes the role of the Sales Programs (product) Manager in a bilateral structure:

In general, each Sales Programs Manager was charged with looking after the "health" of his particular fiber and for serving as a clearing house for all information on it. Specifically, he worked with groups in the sales, research, and manufacturing organizations on scheduling production, allocating available supplies, planning new plant capacity, developing new products and new applications, and promoting the use of his fiber in the market.

In planning production schedules, each Sales Programs Manager met with production personnel about the middle of each month to work on schedules for the month following the month immediately ahead. In the case of fibers that might be in short supply, the Programs Manager and plant personnel for that fiber established "grants" or "reserves" for each sales region.

Another function of each Sales Programs Manager was to aid in planning new plant capacity for his fiber. He had the task of developing the long-range sales estimates on which plant investment decisions would be made. In doing so, he drew on the knowledge and judgments of Sales personnel and Merchandising Managers.

As new plant capacity was added, the Sales Programs Manager had the responsibility for determining the end-product markets in which efforts would be made to place the additional fiber output. These decisions were made in a way that would "build a sound market base" for the particular fiber. Sales Programs Managers were particularly interested, therefore, in building diverse end-product markets for their fibers and in avoiding excessive dependency on any one end-product application.

In determining the distribution of additional supplies of a fiber, the Sales Programs Manager relied heavily on the recommendations of both Merchandising Managers and Regional Sales Managers.

In addition to meeting with representatives from Manufacturing in connection with production schedules and plant expansion, each Sales Programs Manager had continuing contact with plant personnel on other matters. The size and pattern of inventories, for example, were determined by Sales Programs Managers and plant personnel with the Programs Managers taking major responsibility for such decisions. Problems having to do with the production of new fiber types were also handled by Programs Managers working with both plant and research personnel. As one means of maintaining close touch among men representing these three functions in the Textile Fibers Department, a Coordination Committee had been established for each fiber. This committee included the Sales Programs Manager, representatives from the plant making the fiber, and from those research groups concerned with the technical development of the fiber and its uses. This committee met weekly.

Interface Managers in Resource Departments

The product manager in the bilateral program structure described in Du Pont's Textile Fibers Department case is equally concerned with market and program needs, and resource strength. By comparison, the market/product manager in a unilateral structure usually seems more single-minded in representing market needs, and he negotiates with *interface managers* in resource departments to supply those needs.

At Monsanto's Organic Chemicals Division, for example, the Technical Production Managers in the Manufacturing Department functioned as interface managers:

The Technical Production Manager was the link between the plant and Marketing. Product Directors, Product Managers, and field salesmen could not deal directly with the plant on matters involving major or minor changes in product specifications and deliveries. Requests for such changes went through the Technical Production Manager, and he decided whether a proposed change would be advantageous based on cost, profit, and customer considerations. He was described by the Director of Manufacturing as "an umbrella over the plant to keep the plant from having its energies drained off on things we really shouldn't do."

In a unilateral matrix organization, it is important that interface functions exist in the resource departments and that they work effectively. In the absence of such a function, resource effort may be fragmented as resource personnel at all levels are "hit" with the demands of program managers. Work priorities may then be determined more by personal relationships and persuasion than by an objective appraisal of the relative needs of the several programs.

At General Foods' Post Division where market/product managers worked with the several resources to plan and implement strategies, interface arrangements varied greatly from one resource to another. In the case of field sales, the function was carried out by the Sales Development Manager who reported to the National Sales Manager. In the planning stage, the Sales Development Manager represented the sales force in meetings with individual product managers, in order to assure that the sales support called for in the marketing plans was in fact feasible, that the product management objectives were compatible with sales objectives and that no sales conflicts existed between one set of plans and another. Each product marketing plan called for various kinds of sales force support — introducing new products, selling a trade deal, modifying in-store shelving arrangements. As part of its work,

Sales Development then translated individual product marketing plans into an integrated set of objectives and sales plans for each district.

Post Division Marketing Research worked with product managers to prepare plans for carrying out market studies. Marketing Research, in effect, performed an interface function between product programs and outside market research organizations.

The lack of strong interface functions in the case of two resources, one internal and one external, created some difficulties.

The Operations Manager (in charge of manufacturing) noted that there was a tendency for product managers to make unreasonable and time-consuming demands on plant personnel. In addition, he indicated that the product managers did not fully assess the implications of their promotional plans for the Operations Department. If a special label promotion, for example, was to begin at a time when the plant still had old-label inventory, the plant had to hold the old-label inventory until the promotion was over. For lack of an effective interface function, difficulties in relationships between plant personnel and product managers tended to be moved toward top management levels for resolution.

In the case, too, of product management relations with the Post Division's five advertising agencies (an external resource) an interface function seemed to be needed. Advertising agency personnel believed that agency creativity was stifled because copy recommendations had to be screened through successive layers of Post marketing management personnel before final approval. At each level agency recommendations could be rejected or sent back for modification. According to the agency, such a procedure tended to favor "acceptable copy" at the expense of "creative breakthroughs." Had there been an Advertising Department which functioned in a manner similar to the Marketing Research Department, it might have been able to provide an interface between the agencies and the product programs so as to create a climate for creative work.

A single interface point representing a resource can coordinate program activities with regard to that resource, can communicate program needs to resource managers, and can suggest modifications in program demands to fit resource capabilities. A single interface point may also aid the resource in setting its own work priorities and in scheduling its own activities.

To perform well, the interface manager needs a good working knowledge of the operations of the resource he represents. He needs to understand its capabilities and its limitations. He needs, as well, to have a good sense of the market pressures at work on market/product managers and of the need to respond if the business is to remain healthy.

Independent Scheduling Functions

In addition to product management and interface management, there is a third type of coordinating activity: the independent scheduling function. In three instances in our case studies, formal scheduling functions had been established which were independently positioned in the organization of the business. They were located neither in the program structure nor in the resource structure. In two instances — Mobil's North American Division and Monsanto's Agricultural Division — they were needed to match demand to product supply in a wide range of markets almost on a daily basis. In the third case, Lockheed-Georgia, a Master Scheduling Branch worked to coordinate and schedule activities by project in the basic resource departments. The purpose of the Master Scheduling Branch was to maximize the utilization of division resources (and to minimize cost) while meeting Lockheed-Georgia's contractual commitments.

In all three instances the scheduling and resource coordination task was particularly complex. An independent scheduling function is a vehicle for making trade-offs at operating levels among programs and between cost and customer considerations. Through this organizational unit, such matters could be handled at operating levels instead of moving up the management chain for resolution.

Fundamentally, the task of the scheduling function in the three cases was *to satisfy given levels of demand in the several markets the business served at the maximum profit without sacrificing long-run market position.* For example, at Mobil's North American Division (NAD), the Supply, Distribution, and Traffic Department had responsibility for matching refinery output with market demand. One executive explained SD&T's function as follows:

The North American Division operates 9 [geographically dispersed] refineries. . . . It markets several thousand products in 43 states. In theory, any given refinery could supply any market area with any product (up to capacity) at some cost. But making money in this business depends upon careful calculations. These calculations are the responsibility of SD&T.

Refineries are half the equation. A given refinery can produce various mixes of products. But costs depend on the mix. The cost/mix relationship in turn depends on the grade and type of crude oil being run and varies from one refinery to another.

Marketing is the other half of the equation. To some extent, Marketing can vary the mix of products which it sells and the geographic areas in which it sells them. At any given time there is some combination of discretionary sales, crude inputs, refinery schedules, and transportation methods which will maximize profits for Mobil. We're never perfect, but it is SD&T's job to get us as close to that optimum as possible.

SD&T's function is difficult to describe because it's hard to know where to break into the circle. I suppose it starts with Marketing's forecasts: what quantities of what products it expects to sell in which areas. SD&T then asks, in effect, how can we supply (i.e., make and transport) this demand most economically? And does it pay to supply this demand? Might Mobil make more money by selling some other product mix to some other group of customers?

I know it sounds awfully complex, but we've been in this business for quite a while, and have a pretty good idea of how it ought to go. And we've split up the job; no one piece is all that difficult.

Given the constraints on supply — relatively fixed refinery capacity in the short run, limited flexibility in product mix — and the shifting demands of markets, the system by which Mobil allocates output to markets and balances an immensely complex supply-demand situation is critical to its growth and profitability.

The annual profit plan was the initial step in the process. It was used by the Supply, Distribution, and Traffic Department to plan refinery runs and shipment schedules. It was also the basis for setting volume and profit goals, by market, for the program management units and the field sales divisions.

With the annual plan under way, SD&T used current detailed information on refinery capacities and short-run market forecasts to revise the supply schedule every two months. Within that schedule, changes were made on a day-to-day basis to respond to short-term shifts in market demand and to variations from planned manufacturing schedules.

If Mobil could sell all that it produced — and no more — in markets that could be economically served from its refinery locations, the planning and scheduling process might have ended there. However, SD&T's work went beyond scheduling North American Division refineries and included outside purchases, "swaps," and sales. It was in this way that NAD ultimately equated its supply with demand by product, by market, and by geographic area.

A central concept running through this phase of SD&T's activities was that certain market segments took priority over others. The needs of these priority market segments would be satisfied first. The retail gasoline market clearly would have high priority. Mobil has immense investments in service station facilities; thousands of dealers depend on Mobil supplies. Any short-term failure to satisfy demand could have a far-reaching impact on the health of the retail distribution system and on market share.

Some other markets were "discretionary." Discretionary sales might be made in large quantities on a bid basis. If Mobil had refinery capacity available and there was no more profitable alternative, the output could be sold at prices that would cover costs and yield a small profit. These customers typically bought on a "spot" basis and NAD's management had no commitment to serve them as a continuing source of supply.

Thus, SD&T made optimizing decisions at the margin. It directed Mobil's refinery capacity toward its most profitable utilization, recognizing at the same time NAD's commitment to serve as a reliable source of supply for certain channels of distribution and certain classes of customers. It met these commitments by buying outside when and where this was necessary. It would also move excess output as profitably as possible to market segments which traditionally purchased on a price basis.

At Monsanto's Agricultural Division the Planning and Operations group performed a comparable function. This group determined what products the plants would manufacture and allocated plant output to different markets.

The Agricultural Division manufactured plant foods (fertilizers), blasting agents, animal feed additives, and pesticides. Some of the Division's products could be classified as commodities and others as proprietary items.

The various plant foods and blasting agents were closely related, since all used the same basic material. In simple terms, ammonia could be sold as ammonia (as either a raw material or a fertilizer), or it could be upgraded to form nitric acid or ammonium nitrate. Ammonium nitrate, in turn could be sold as a fertilizer, or it could be combined with fuel oil to form a blasting agent. The feed additives and pesticides were each relatively independent with regard to manufacturing processes.

From a manufacturing point of view it was also useful to differentiate between commodity products and proprietaries. In general, it was necessary to produce commodities at full capacity on a year-round basis if costs were to be kept low enough to realize a profit. Price levels for proprietaries, on the other hand, were high enough to allow considerable flexibility in manufacturing scheduling. As one executive explained: "On commodities we have to sell all that we can make. On proprietaries, we have to make all that we can sell."

The Divisions's distribution mix varied markedly from product to product. Commodity fertilizers and insecticides were sold to resellers or upgraders, because the Division was not able to distribute its full product through other channels. The distribution of pesticides varied, depending upon the geographic area in which they were used (the Division had retail outlets in some areas, but not in others). Feed additives were sold to resellers and large feed mills. Blasting agents were sold direct to mines and quarries, although the basic material (ammonium nitrate) was also sold to resellers.

While the Division's pattern of distribution was moving closer to the consumer on several fronts, the most notable development was the establishment of Monsanto Agricultural Centers (MACs). These outlets sold fertilizers, pesticides, and a variety of agricultural services. By early 1967 the Division operated approximately 150 MACs, located primarily in the corn belt of the Middle West. In commenting on the MACs, one executive explained: "The farmers have been taught that 'fertilizer is fertilizer,' to be bought wherever he can get the best deal. We are trying to change this, to differentiate our products on the basis of service and availability."

Scheduling was the responsibility of the Planning and Operations group in the Administration Department. The manager of the group explained his function as follows:

We are the traffic cops. We determine which products we *should* make, who *should* get the product, and how to get it there. While the actual decisions are made by the product managers, we tell them what their decisions *ought* to be — from a strictly economic point of view.

Our function could be in the Marketing Department or in the Manufacturing Department. It is better where it is, because of our neutrality. A marketing man has one objective — to sell. Some are more profit-conscious than others, but this is not necessarily a good thing. If he worries too much about profits, a marketing man may be too cautious.

We have one, and only one, concern: Where can we make the most money? We are doing our job right when most people are dissatisfied with what we are doing.

On plant foods the product managers develop sales plans on a day-to-day basis. We look at the sales requirements and the plant capacities, and compute a nitrogen balance. If there is not enough product to go around, the product group must decide which product it wants to make. But we tell them which product mix will make Monsanto the most money.

Similar decisions must be made with regard to customers. Some customers (because of location and quantities taken) are simply more profitable than others. We run the numbers and make a ranking, but it's up to the product group to decide. Some customers will still be around next year; others will not.

An awful lot of planning goes into this process. During the off-season, we and the product managers work out detailed plans as to who will get what under which circumstances. But we look at the weather when we get up each morning. It's just that kind of business.

We have a computer model which we use in our basic planning and to evaluate our performance after the fact. During the peak season, the computer is not much use. You can't get data into the computer fast enough.

But our people are good — and experienced. If

one of our plants is going to fall behind schedule today, we know it almost as quickly as the plant manager does. We can then shift schedules — to make sure that the customer who needs it first gets it first.

The MACs have a man assigned here who tells my men which MACs to ship to. He also buys products for the MACs from outside sources. We generally give the MACs service, but we will let their inventories run down if it's in the Company's best interest.

Monsanto's Agricultural Division works in a product/market environment which has strikingly similar characteristics to that of Mobil's North American Division. It is interesting indeed that it came up with the same organizational response: an independent and powerful scheduling function. Each of these two businesses experiences unpredictable shifts in demand in a wide range of markets. In each case raw material inputs and manufacturing outputs vary in ways that cannot be foreseen. The scheduling function responds to these variations in a fashion which optimizes short-run profits and long-run market position. Inevitably, this function has to take into account relative customer priorities and company commitments to supply certain markets. It is important under these circumstances that the scheduling function be independent of both the selling and the manufacturing functions if it is to serve as a balance wheel between marketing and manufacturing cost considerations.

At Lockheed-Georgia the reasons for having an independent scheduling function (the Master Scheduling Branch) were somewhat different in degree. To a large extent Lockheed-Georgia's work was developmental and called for close integration of engineering, manufacturing, procurement, quality control, and marketing effort. Trade-offs had to be made among existing contracts. The Division was continually involved in bidding on new contracts and, when successful, in building up its resources to handle new contractual commitments. The scheduling task was most complex and critical. The scheduling function was therefore highly specialized and independent of both the program and the resource organizations.

Lockheed-Georgia's programs (the C-5A, C-141, C-130, JetStar, and Aerospace) were in various phases of research, engineering design, and production. Other programs were in the early design and proposal stages.

The Master Scheduling Branch was responsible for three major functions: (1) master scheduling, (2) program coordination, and (3) program evaluation. Seven department managers reported to the Director of Master Scheduling. The Program Evaluation Department was responsible for preparing reports on program status. The Master Scheduling Department was responsible for establishing and maintaining an up-to-date master schedule which took into account all of Lockheed-Georgia's contractual requirements. Five Program Coordination Departments (C-130, JetStar, C-141, C-5A, and Aerospace) were responsible for assuring that each branch had scheduled its activities in such a way that individual program schedules would be achieved.

It was frequently necessary to make trade-offs among individual programs. A decision to shift some C-130 production out of the plant to make room for the C-5A, for example, might minimize expense for the Division as a whole, but increase expense somewhat for the C-130 program. Consequently, it was often necesary to negotiate with several program and/or branch managers simultaneously. According to the Director of Master Scheduling, this procedure made it possible to resolve interprogram conflicts without submitting them to the Lockheed-Georgia President.

The Program Coordination Managers worked closely with their Program Directors, briefing them regularly on program status. According to the Director of Master Scheduling, the Program Coordination Managers really reported to the Program Directors. It was important that they were located in the Master Scheduling Branch, however, since a change in the schedule of one program was likely to affect the overall master schedule.

Summary

The coordination of program plans with resource effort, and the allocation of resources, is provided for in organization structures in several ways. *Product managers* in a bilateral program structure move between market program managements and managers in manufacturing to serve the balanced best interests of both the programs and resources.

Interface managers representing individual resources (both external and internal), and often located in resource departments, are found where there is a unilateral program structure. Interface managers screen and translate program demands on resources and attempt to satisfy program needs while preserving resource efficiency.

Scheduling managers, positioned independently of program and resource structures in the business organization, are found in businesses where scheduling and coordination problems are especially complex. They work to match demand in a wide range of markets with limited resources and product supply at a maximum profit.

All three types of coordinating functions have essentially the same objectives: to assure that the entire business is market-oriented, to maximize the profitability of a given level of demand, to preserve and increase the market utility of investments in plants, laboratories, advertising, and field sales organizations. The coordinating function performs a trade-off role, balancing program (market) interests and manufacturing and engineering (cost) considerations. It relieves top management from having to arbitrate day-to-day choices between market and cost considerations and between one program and another.

A high degree of objectivity is essential for coordination managers. They can be particularly effective if they possess a working knowledge of the resources to which they relate; if they understand resource capacities; if they know how to make the most of the skills of resource personnel. Coordination managers must have a sense, as well, of market needs and opportunities, of customer demands, and of competitive pressures. In particular, they should "know their way around the business."

New Product Development

Organizational arrangements for "growing" the business are usually specialized. New product development, as an activity, is commonly set apart from those for planning and implementing ongoing programs. But just as the coordination functions described above play a key role in adjusting strategy and carrying out programs on a day-to-day basis, new product development depends significantly on a coordination function. The coordinating function in this case seems often to assume the role of initiating projects and of meshing marketing, technical, manufacturing, and cost considerations in the selection of opportunities. In addition, it sets product development tasks for the basic resources.

In businesses where there are bilateral program structures, product managers again fill the initiating-coordinating role on product development. The Product Managers at IBM and the Sales Programs Managers at Du Pont had major development responsibilities. In other cases organizational units independent of the program structure function in this capacity (e.g., Commercial Development in Monsanto's Organic Chemicals Division, the Car Product Planning Activity in Ford's Product Development Group, and Product Planning in General Electric's Housewares Division).

The need for an independent product development coordination function arises because the time horizons in product development are significantly longer than in selling and manufacturing. In addition, the required managerial perspective is different from that which characterizes the research environment, on the one hand, and the market environment, on the other. Thus, for example, the Director of Commercial Development at Monsanto's Organic Chemicals believed strongly that his function should be separate from Research and from Marketing. He noted:

Commercial Development is the "patient money" department. Normally, we work on a project for three or more years. In Marketing, every Product Manager has a lot of products to worry about and focuses on short-range budgets. If CD were part of Marketing, the longer range development projects would have to take second place. Moreover, Marketing tends naturally to think that if the customers want it, it should be done — and that is not always the case.

Commercial Development needs also to be separate from Research. It works best as an independent market place voice able to take issue with Research. Research people develop something and then want to take it out to the market, and Commercial Development has to be free to contribute a commercial judgment on projects.

The importance of having balanced appraisals of new product ideas is an important consideration in the organizational positioning of the product development function. Again:

At Ford, Car Product Planning Offices and Car Product Engineering Offices had been located in the Ford and Lincoln-Mercury Divisions of the company's Sales Group until late 1967. At that time these units were transferred to the newly formed Product Development Group. A major advantage of establishing a separate Product Development Group was that it would be in a position to give balanced consideration to market appeal, plant investment commitments, and manufacturing costs. Presumably the Car Product Planning function in a vehicle division setting had been especially responsive to market considerations, as opposed to cost and investment factors.

In the cases mentioned above the product development units did not themselves do the actual technical research and engineering work of developing new products. Research departments and engineering groups did that. The product development unit exercised initiative in generating a flow of new product ideas. These might come from program managers and resource personnel in the business. They might come out of studies of competitive developments, or from a scanning of the technical/scientific horizon.

Product development therefore moves ideas through a screening process and makes judgments of potential market demand, technical feasibility, required capital investments, and cost factors. Ideas which survive the screening process move into technical research. In this stage, the product development coordination unit may seek to achieve resource commitment to the effort and to provide for formal reviews at critical points. In the technical research stages, the product development unit will also work to bring market influences to bear on the technical effort so that the end-result will meet customer needs at competitive prices.

As the technical work nears completion, product development may then participate in the initial commercialization work. This may take the form of preparing product information materials and salesmen's product training programs (as at IBM). It may even involve making the initial sales to customers (as at Monsanto Organic Chemicals).

There are important advantages to carrying out the initial commercialization effort through a specialized product development function. The task at this stage is highly educational. Quick feedback is needed as customers begin to test the product. Close coordination is needed among research, manufacturing, and marketing personnel, on one side, and customers, on the other, to deal with application problems. The market development effort may therefore be most effective if responsibility is highly centralized. To move new products too quickly into regular sales channels may be to sacrifice quick feedback of, and response to, market reactions at a time when they are most needed.

The most detailed descriptions of product development processes are contained in the cases we wrote at IBM and Monsanto Organic Chemicals. In both businesses a rapid rate of new product development was an important element of strategy. At IBM, for example:

Within the IBM Product Programs Department individual product administrators were assigned to specific products.

The first step was the generation of a requirement. This could come about in a variety of ways, such as product requests from Market Operations or the field sales force, Product Programs Department analyses of competitive developments, or a strategic decision by IBM management to enter a new market or field. In general, the product administrator prepared a formal statement of the product requirement, in terms of product features, programming support, and applications, and worked with Systems Development Division (SDD) to develop formal product specifications.

After the initial specifications had been prepared, SDD visited a number of IBM customers to gauge their reactions to the proposed product. In particular, these "case studies" attempted to ascertain which applications the new equipment would be used for, and how much demand there was for alternative combinations of product features and application capabilities. The product administrator generally worked closely with SDD on these case studies. Following their completion he and his counterpart in SDD generally modified their original requirements and specifications.

After the case studies had been completed, SDD prepared two types of forecasts. The first forecast assumed that the new product would have certain features, would be delivered at a certain date, would be used in certain applications, and would have one of three different prices. Given these assumptions, a volume forecast was prepared for each price level.

The forecasters then obtained manufacturing cost estimates at each of the three volume levels. Assuming these manufacturing costs, the second forecast estimated product profitability at each of the three price/volume combinations. Frequently, the product administrator negotiated with SDD during the preparation of these forecasts, varying some of the assumptions in order to arrive at acceptable volume and profit forecasts.

SDD's case studies and initial forecasts were then submitted informally to the industry managers and regional staffs at a series of meetings. At this point the product administrator generally prepared detailed analyses of the market potential for the proposed product and compared its cost/performance characteristic with that of competitive products.

The market operations managers and regional staffs then "reacted" to the proposed product. In some cases their reactions might be directed at product features, e.g., "the proposed product needs faster printing or more programming support if it is to be competitive." In other cases, they criticized the forecasts themselves, e.g., "We cannot sell as many units as you say we can, unless you improve the product in the following ways. . . ."

On the basis of these reactions, the product administrator negotiated changes in specifications and forecasts with SDD. At the same time, competitive or technological developments might also suggest modifications in the original plan. At any rate, a new set of specifications and forecasts was prepared for DPD (Data Processing Division)[1] reaction. In general, DPD then requested further changes, and further negotiations took place. On a typical product, this cycle might be repeated three or four times during an 18-month period.

As the proposed announcement date approached, the product administrator began to coordinate the preparation of support materials, such as teaching manuals, product brochures, demonstration films, and news releases. According to one product administrator, this was a difficult job, since preparation had to begin before the final decision to introduce the product had been reached. Consequently, he had to get the various staff departments to prepare the materials for which they were responsible, without absolute assurance that they would actually be used. Since the final decision to introduce a product was often reached only several weeks before the announcement date, and all materials had to be distributed to the branches by the announcement date, it was necessary to complete all writing, artwork, plates, and plans while the final decision was still pending.

The final decision depended on DPD's willingness to concur with SDD's specifications and forecasts. As noted above, formal concurrence was based on a complex set of continuing negotiations and discussions between SDD and DPD. When DPD finally did concur with SDD's plans, it became responsible for selling and installing the forecast quantity of the proposed equipment.

At Monsanto's Organic Chemicals Division, product development was structured as follows:

Although it was at one time a part of the Research Department, Commercial Development (CD) in Organic Chemicals was split out in 1957 to become a separate functional department reporting to the General Manager. It was charged with the responsibility for defining new market opportunities, proposing research and development projects, monitoring these projects at every stage, and then introducing new products to the market in the initial stages of commercial development. Initially, CD prepared a Pre-Research Appraisal (PRA) which identified a market need, specified the kind of product required and the market potential (estimates of market potential were developed jointly by CD and Marketing) for such a product at given price levels. It indicated the technological skills needed to develop and support the product, the nature of existing competition, and the advantages Monsanto might have against the competition. The PRA was then sent to the Research Department with a request for technical appraisal of the proposed product. A technical appraisal included an assessment of the "state of the art," technical disciplines required beyond the Research Department's existing capabilities, facilities, manpower and time needed, and the probability of success.

If the proposal survived the technical appraisal stage, it was submitted formally along with the PRA to a Product Director for approval. With his approval both CD and Research became committed to undertaking the project.

During the research stages, Project Analysis (PA) reports were issued jointly by CD and Research to keep the top management informed on the status of the project. The PA reports covered both research and commercial progress.

As research neared completion, CD worked on the preparation of a business strategy, identifying

---

[1] The Data Processing Division had responsibility for the marketing functions for IBM's Data Processing Group.

key customers, targeting a market position for the new product, indicating price levels, and preparing plans for any new capital investment that would be needed.

At a point in time — if Research had succeeded — the new product was transferred from Research to Commercial Development. At this point, Research prepared a report detailing the performance of the new product against the "ideal" and against competitive offerings, and estimated full-scale production costs. CD at this juncture either accepted or rejected the new product and, if the former, issued a Project Analysis report detailing a Commercial Development program.

CD then began initial market introduction of the product. Promotional devices such as technical bulletins and visual aids and an advertising program were prepared, prices were set with the cognizant Product Director, calls were made on customers, and feedback on customer reactions and their experiences in using the product was obtained and analyzed. On the basis of these results, commercial development was extended to obtain broad customer acceptance, and forecasts were made of sales and of plant capacity needed to satisfy demand. As the commercialization effort progressed, CD began working closely with Marketing, first to work out a detailed strategy plan based on early market feedback and then to set a time for transferring the new product to Marketing.

At the time of transfer, a Transfer to Sales report describing the total commercialization effort and its results was prepared jointly by CD and Marketing in the form of a total product strategy for the new product, including a detailed Sales Plan showing how the new product would be integrated into the full product line and promoted.

Summary

In technically dynamic companies, product development initiative and coordination responsibility tends to reside in specialized organizational units. In businesses with bilateral program structures, product managers often take on this function. In other instances, separate "Commercial Development" or "Product Planning" departments move among the several resource departments and the market to generate and screen new product ideas. Product development groups which are set apart from the market programs and resource structures may be better able to provide for a balanced consideration of market, technical, cost, and investment factors in making new product decisions. These groups may be actively involved in the early stages of market development. At this stage, quick response to initial market reactions is critical. At this stage, too, promotional effort may often have a high educational content. Thus, the nature of the task calls for a specialized, highly focused commercialization effort which product development groups can supply.

To grow the business is to disrupt it. The "management of disruption" is often the responsibility of product managers, product development, or product planning organizational units. The long-run success of the business may hinge on their effectiveness.

The Dynamics of Interaction

Taken together the three parts of this chapter deal with the dynamics of interaction among programs and resources in the growing business. We have identified and described critically important organizational components, the interfaces, which serve as focal points for the relationships between programs and resources.

We have described the key processes by which resource effort is allocated to programs: annual planning, day-to-day scheduling procedures, and the processes for developing new products. The skill with which these processes are designed and the qualifications of the people who manage them — the program, resource, and interface managers — are of vital importance in the effective conduct of the going business.

Finally the chapter has developed the idea that a balance of power exists between programs and resources in the strategy councils of the business and suggests factors which weigh in that balance. The relative weight which program and resource managers bring to bear in strategic planning is most significant. If the resource management functions dominate, the direction of business growth may be constrained by an emphasis on fully utilizing and developing existing resources although market opportunities may lead in other, more profitable directions. If program management dominates, long-run strategic effort may be more dispersed, less restricted by a sense of need for using and preserving existing plants and financial, manufacturing, engineering, and research skills.

The extremes are usually undesirable. The business manager's task is an optimizing one: to make the most of the existing resources in the short run, while pursuing new and promising market opportunities which may call for new kinds of skills and resources.

Chandler has developed the theme that structure follows strategy, that when strategy changes, the organizational structure adjusts to accommodate to new directions. It must be recognized, as well, that the direction of strategy is certainly a function, in part, of the kind of organization which produces it and the balance of power within the structure. Today's organization is an important influence molding tomorrow's strategy which in turn shapes tomorrow's organization. Organizational design, the way in which planning processes are structured, the relative dominance of one organizational dimension over another — these are the factors which determine how the business will respond to its market opportunities, and therefore they will strongly influence the direction of its growth.

CHAPTER 6

Survey Results and Suggestions for Further Research

This chapter summarizes the major findings of a questionnaire survey which was conducted as part of this research project. When most of the case studies and commentaries had been completed, the authors concluded that there were a number of generalizations which seemed to cut across the individual companies and industries which had been studied. The most significant of these generalizations were:

(1) At operating levels, business organizations often consist of program units and resource units.
(2) The more diversified a business's products or markets, the more likely it is to have a program structure.
(3) The type of program structure (product, market, or both) which a business has is a function of the type(s) of diversity with which it is faced.
(4) Businesses which have program structures tend to be more active in new product development than businesses which do not have program structures.

The questionnaire survey was intended to assess the applicability of these generalizations to a much larger sample of companies than it had been feasible to study in detail. A questionnaire was prepared, pretested, and mailed to the presidents of the 1,000 largest U.S. manufacturing companies in August 1968; a follow-up questionnaire was sent to the nonresponding companies in the sample one month later. Five hundred and seventeen usable replies were received by November 1, 1968.[1]

[1] The design, methodology, and findings of this survey are described fully in Steven H. Star, "Organizing for Diversity: The Use of Program Organizations in Large U.S. Manufactur-

Results of the Questionnaire Survey

The findings of this survey lend considerable support to the organizational patterns we observed in the sample of firms described in the cases and in the preceding chapters. Seventy-seven percent of the businesses in the sample reported that they had some form of program structure. While businesses in certain industries (e.g., chemicals) tended to have program management units more frequently than businesses in other industries (e.g., transportation equipment), at least 50% of the businesses in each industry classification studied [2] reported that they used program managers. Similarly, even though businesses with more than $50 million annual sales were more likely to have program structures than smaller businesses, a majority of the smaller businesses also reported that they used program managers.

There was a striking relationship between the amount of product and/or market diversity faced by a business and its use of program managers. In all industry and size classifications, the more diversified a business's products and/or markets, the more likely it was to have a program structure.

Of the 397 businesses which reported that they had program management units, 163 (41%) had product-market program managers; 39 (10%) had market program managers; and 195 (49%) had both product program managers and market managers. As we had hypothesized, our survey data suggest that the type of program structure used by

ing Companies" (1969), an unpublished doctoral dissertation which may be consulted at Baker Library, Harvard Graduate School of Business Administration.

[2] SIC 2-digit industry classifications 19–39.

a business tends to be a function of the type of diversity with which it is faced. Businesses which sell diverse products to a relatively homogeneous market typically use product-market program managers; businesses which sell a relatively homogeneous product line to diverse markets typically have market program managers; and businesses which market diverse products to diverse markets are likely to have both product program managers and market program managers. This latter tendency is especially pronounced among larger businesses which presumably can most easily afford highly elaborated program structures.

According to the survey data, the responsibilities of product program managers and market program managers tend to be quite different, especially in businesses which have both types of program managers. As may be seen in the accompanying table, the frequency with which product and market program managers are assigned selected responsibilities varies significantly, and the responsibilities of each tend to fall into distinct clusters.

centage of the product program managers also have responsibility for coordinating the activities of the field sales, manufacturing, design engineering, and research resources as they apply to individual products.

A similar clustering of responsibilities may be seen in the case of the market program managers. In this case, marketing planning, promotion, and field sales are the most frequently assigned responsibilities. Marketing planning would seem to represent the critical element in the market program manager's job; his primary task is to plan for individual markets. The two elements of marketing strategy which lend themselves most to "tailoring" for individual markets (field sales and sales promotion) are present almost as frequently, apparently because they are critical to the success of a market-tailored marketing plan.

In the next cluster, we find advertising, product planning, and pricing. All three of these elements are critical to a successful marketing program, but there is generally less opportunity to make inde-

Areas of Responsibility for Product and Market Program Managers

Product Program Managers (n = 358)	*Market Program Managers* (n = 234)
Marketing Planning (82.1%)	Marketing Planning (76.9%)
Product Planning (81.8%)	Promotion (68.4%)
	Field Sales (67.5%)
Promotion (67.6%)	Product Planning (54.7%)
Pricing (65.6%)	Advertising (53.4%)
Advertising (62.0%)	Pricing (52.1%)
Field Sales (52.0%)	Research (27.4%)
Manufacturing (50.8%)	Marketing (26.4%)
Research (46.6%)	Design Engineering (24.4%)
Design Engineering (45.3%)	

These clusters suggest that the responsibilities of product and market program managers differ to a considerable degree. Product program managers are almost always responsible for marketing planning and product planning, the two activities most closely related to providing specialized attention to individual products. A significant number of the product program managers are also responsible for promotion, pricing, and advertising, the three processes which lend themselves most to differentiation among products. Finally, a smaller per-

pendent decisions in these areas for a single market segment.

Finally, market program managers are least frequently responsible for working with those resources which are furthest removed from the market, and are generally not specialized on a market basis. Manufacturing, research, and design engineering would all seem to fall into this category. While these resource activities are in the bottom cluster for both types of program managers, product program managers have responsibilities in these areas almost twice as frequently as market program managers.

On the basis of the case data, program organizations seem to be particularly useful when developing and introducing new products. In the survey, a rough approximation of "success" in this area was obtained by asking each respondent what percentage of current sales was accounted for by products developed since 1963. When the responses to this question were compared with other variables, a number of interesting relationships were found. Most significantly, businesses with program organizations seem to have been considerably more successful in developing and introducing new products than businesses without program organizations. For example, 36.9% of the 358 businesses which had product program managers reported that more than 20% of 1967 sales were accounted for by new products, while only 19.8% of the businesses without product program managers made this claim.[3]

Certain types of program organizations seem to be more closely related to success in developing and introducing new products than others. In general, businesses whose program managers had considerable authority and responsibilities cutting across several areas (e.g., sales, advertising, engineering, logistics) were more successful in developing and introducing new products than businesses whose program managers had more limited authority or responsibilities.

It should also be noted that the relationship between having a program organization and success in new product development is limited to those businesses which have either product-market program managers or *both* product and market program managers. Businesses which have *only* market program managers do not seem to be any more successful in developing and introducing new products than businesses which do not have program organizations.

* * * * *

Organizational structure is a highly complex subject, dependent to a considerable degree on the unique circumstances faced by individual firms. Nevertheless, certain patterns emerge; and some of these patterns may be studied through survey research. The findings reported in this chapter corroborate our analysis of individual case studies in two important respects:

(1) They suggest that the type of organizational structures with which we are concerned are characteristic of a large number of companies, in a wide range of industries.
(2) They support certain key relationships observed in the case data (e.g., between market and product diversity and program organizations; between program organizations and success in new product development).

The survey thus provides a supportive framework within which to view our analyses of individual case situations. Its findings increase our confidence in conclusions drawn from a limited number of case studies.

Toward Further Research

This study has identified and described broad concepts in the organization of large corporations. In particular, it has been concerned with the ways in which integrated businesses within an enterprise are structured to serve a wide range of markets.

From the outset, we have viewed this study as being exploratory in nature. One of our major objectives has been to identify areas where further research is needed. Several areas of research which show particular promise of producing significant results are reviewed below.

The Concept of Scale Economies in Organization

A major determinant of the size and product and market scope of the business unit is the optimum efficient scale of key resources. Businesses tend to become larger when they are able to achieve economies of scale. Competition forces the business to seek minimum unit costs, and unit

---

[3] This finding does not necessarily imply that successful new product activities are a function of having a product program structure in place. Extensive new product activities may themselves create pressures which encourage the development of a program form of organization.

costs, up to some point, tend to decline as volume increases.

Statistical studies of the "production function" in economics are an attempt to quantify such scale economies. Manufacturing engineers, for example, seem to be able to provide accurate estimates of scale economies in the manufacturing process. We still know very little about scale economies in nonmanufacturing processes, however. What are the relevant parameters for field sales, advertising and promotion, and research and development, for example?

It is likely that scale economies in these processes will take the form of a step function, where a certain threshold (a "critical mass") must be attained before a business can successfully carry out a particular type of activity. To compete successfully in the mass market for branded packaged goods, for example, a business generally needs an extensive field sales organization and high levels of advertising and promotion.

In other fields (e.g., computers), only large companies are able to support a high degree of specialization across a wide range of user industries. While smaller competitors are able to specialize in a limited number of user industries or applications, they are unable to compete "across-the-board" with their larger competitors.

To some extent, it should be possible to quantify scale economies and threshold levels ("critical mass") in nonmanufacturing processes. These concepts have close analogies in microeconomic theory, which uses them to explain the structure of individual industries. If we are able to quantify these concepts, we may be able to use them to explain the organizational structures of individual businesses.

The Concept of Power in Program-Resource Relationships

In Chapter 5 we suggested that the "balance of power" between program management units and resource management units is significant in determining the strategic course a business will follow. Program management units tend naturally to be highly responsive to the needs of their markets, while resource management units are understandably concerned with the preservation and development of the resources for which they are responsible. When these objectives are in conflict, as they often are (especially in the short run), that dimension of the business with the greatest "power" is likely to prevail in management councils.

As noted in Chapter 5, several factors seem to be most influential in determining the balance of power between programs and resources. On the basis of case data, we hypothesized that program management units tend to have considerable power: (1) when they have been in existence for a relatively long time; (2) when they have program-attached resource units, or there are program-specialized units in the resource departments; and/or (3) when there are a relatively small number of large programs.

These three factors are consistent with case data and seem intuitively reasonable. Nevertheless, it would be useful to test these hypotheses against a larger sample of businesses. We were unable to do so in our questionnaire survey because we could not devise a suitable technique for measuring "power." Other disciplines (perhaps political science) may have techniques which could be usefully employed in this area.

The Utilization of External and Internal Resources

Businesses are continually confronted with the question of whether to establish a particular resource internally, or whether to purchase the output of such a resource from an outside supplier. In procurement management, questions of this type are known as "make or buy" decisions. In engineering, there is frequently a question of whether to augment a firm's engineering manpower or use contract engineers during periods of heavy engineering workload. In marketing, typical questions of this type include: (1) whether to use independent channels of distribution or develop a wholesaling or retailing organization; (2) whether to use an outside advertising agency or prepare advertising copy internally; and (3) whether to use outside marketing research firms or develop internal marketing research capability.

These questions are all related in that they are

concerned with the relative advantages of developing and maintaining internal resources versus employing external resources. Some of the factors which influence such decisions are fairly obvious. Critical mass and scale economies may dictate the choice of an external resource when an individual business (because of its limited size) cannot come close to meeting the costs of an outside supplier. Another consideration is the extent to which it is important to control and direct resource activities (e.g., the control which Sears' management has over retail selling through its retail store system). Generally, but not always, internal resources are more controllable. Or a firm may require a degree of flexibility which it can only obtain through using an external resource (e.g., an aerospace firm which uses contract engineers when preparing a proposal for a government contract).

Another area which needs further research is the question of how to work most effectively with external resources. The management of General Foods' Post Division, for example, was concerned about how to structure its product managers' relationships with its advertising agencies to develop imaginative advertising programs.

These considerations suggest the following research questions:

(1) What factors should be taken into account when choosing between external and internal resources to perform a particular task?
(2) How may these factors be quantified?
(3) How can program managements work effectively with external resources?

Organizing for Multinational Business Operations

This study contains three cases dealing with the organization of multinational businesses: Monsanto International Division; Pfizer International; and Ford Tractor Division. In each case there is a need to maintain a balance between an organizational emphasis on individual products or groups of customers, on the one hand, and on different geographic areas (generally, countries), on the other hand. The organization of a multinational business differs from that of a domestic business in one major respect: the geographic (or political) dimension requires more organizational emphasis in multinational business than it does in domestic business. Thus, Monsanto has an International Division responsible for maintaining the strength of its country organizations, even though worldwide profit and program development responsibility resides in its product divisions. Pfizer International has area and country organizations, which are subdivided into program units corresponding to "staff" program management units at headquarters. And Ford Tractor, which operates its product development and manufacturing operations as world-wide resource organizations, has chosen to organize its marketing operation on a geographic basis, even though it sells diverse products to several distinct customer groups.

The geographic dimensions of a multinational business have a particularly significant impact on the basic marketing functions (selling, advertising, and promotion). In a multinational business, marketing strategy (and program management structures) thus tend to be three-dimensional (product, customer group, country). This is the case, for example, in Monsanto's Organic Chemicals Division.

Meshing these three dimensions (product, customer group, country) in planning and implementing multiple marketing strategies is difficult. It leads to complex organizational structures. Much more research is needed on how to design multinational business structures, and how to devise effective working relationships within them.

Resource Structures

Most businesses group their major resources in traditional functional departments such as Engineering, Manufacturing, and Marketing. As noted in Chapter 4, such functional departments may be divided into subfunctions (e.g., marketing research, advertising, field sales); program specialized units (e.g., banks, utilities, airlines); or combinations of these at different levels of programs and resources. Moreover, certain resource units may be removed from a functional department and located in a program organization (e.g., "Airlines" field sales at IBM).

Traditional resource groupings have been taken for granted in business (and in business education). Other organizational schemes might usefully be explored. Research is needed on the organization of resources within a business. It is quite likely that the grouping of such resources into the traditional functional departments may not always be appropriate.

CASES AND COMMENTARIES

Lockheed Aircraft Corporation: Lockheed-Georgia Company	61
International Business Machines Corporation: Data Processing Division	108
Mobil Oil Corporation: North American Division	156
E. I. du Pont de Nemours and Company: Textile Fibers Department	187
General Foods Corporation: Post Division	201
General Electric Company: Housewares Division	231
Ford Motor Company: North American Automotive Operations	261
Sears, Roebuck and Co.	296
Monsanto Company: Organic Chemicals Division	336
Monsanto Company: Agricultural Division	358
Monsanto Company: International Division	370
Chas. Pfizer & Co., Inc.: Pfizer International	390
Ford Motor Company: Tractor Division	412

Lockheed Aircraft Corporation: Lockheed-Georgia Company

The Lockheed-Georgia Company (Gelac), with headquarters in Marietta, Georgia, was one of nine operating divisions of the Lockheed Aircraft Corporation.[1] Gelac's primary business was the development and manufacture of fixed wing aircraft, particularly in the military air cargo field. In 1965 Gelac employed more than 20,000 persons and had sales in excess of $500 million.

When Lockheed took over Air Force Plant No. 6, it sent a nucleus of managers and technicians from California to Georgia. Since there were relatively few skilled factory workers in the Marietta area at this time it was necessary to undertake a massive training program. By early 1952 Gelac employed 10,600 persons, and had completed the first phase of its B-29 contract.

Table 1. Major Operating Units of Lockheed Aircraft Corporation: 1965

Division	Principal Products	Location
Lockheed-Georgia Company	Military & commercial transport aircraft	Marietta, Georgia
Lockheed-California Company	Military aircraft	Burbank, California
	Supersonic aircraft (SST)	
Lockheed Missiles and Space Company	Polaris missiles	Sunnyvale, California
	Agena satellite-boosters	
	Military & civilian space programs	
	Space, missile, oceanographic & information research	
Lockheed Propulsion Company	Large rocket motors	Redland, California
Lockheed Electronics Company	Military, industrial & aerospace electronic devices	Plainfield, New Jersey
Lockheed Shipbuilding & Construction Company	Shipbuilding & heavy construction	Seattle, Washington
Lockheed Aircraft Service Co.	Aircraft modification and maintenance	Ontario, California
Lockheed Air Terminal	Airport operation	Burbank, California
Lockheed Aircraft International	Licensing, Joint Ventures	Los Angeles, California

Gelac began operations in 1951, when the Lockheed Aircraft Corporation was awarded a contract to operate Air Force Plant No. 6 in Marietta, Georgia.[2] At the same time, Lockheed was awarded contracts to modify B-29 bombers and produce B-47s at the Marietta facility.

[1] The Lockheed Aircraft Corporation was a diversified manufacturer of military and commercial aircraft, ballistic missiles, space systems, electronic devices, ships and other products (See Table 1). Sales in 1965 were $1.8 billion, up from $1.6 billion the preceding year. Earnings in 1965 (including a $2 million special credit) were $54 million.

[2] Air Force Plant No. 6 was the largest aircraft plant under one roof in the United States; its main factory building alone contained more than 75 acres of floor space.

Before the B-29 modification contract was 50% completed, Lockheed began to build the B-47 six-jet bomber. Designed by Boeing, the B-47 was the most sophisticated bomber of its era. The B-47 was in such heavy demand during the Korean conflict that the U.S. Air Force found it necessary to expand its production base by adding two other contractors. The first Lockheed-made B-47 flew in December 1952. By 1956, when the program ended, Gelac had built 396 B-47s.

In 1952 Lockheed was awarded a contract to build the C-130, a propjet airlifter designed by Lockheed-California. Lockheed's management decided to manufacture the C-130 in Marietta, and work began there in 1953. As the B-47 program neared completion, Gelac concentrated its full attention on the C-130 program. The first production C-130 was flown in April 1955. By 1966 Gelac had built almost 1,000 C-130s, and production was expected to continue into the 1970s.

During the mid-1950s Lockheed-California designed a highly advanced twin-jet military utility (passenger/cargo) transport known as the JetStar. In 1957 the program was transferred to Gelac, where the JetStar was further developed to compete with an aircraft developed by the McDonnell Aircraft Company to satisfy a request by the Department of Defense. The JetStar was converted to a four-engine configuration and won a competition with McDonnell's entry. The military had planned to order at least 300 JetStars but, in fact, ordered only 16.

Development of the JetStar as an executive jet had paralleled its development as a military aircraft. When expected military orders did not materialize, Gelac decided to market the JetStar as an executive jet. It became necessary to write off losses of more than $60 million and shut down the JetStar production line for 14 months in 1963–1964. By mid-1966, however, more than 90 JetStars had been sold.

In 1961 Gelac won its first contract for an aircraft completely designed in Marietta. The C-141 StarLifter was a 158-ton fanjet cargo-troop carrier, intended for use by the Military Airlift Command. Flight tested in December 1963, the C-141 began squadron service in April 1965. The 100th C-141 was delivered in April 1966.

In late 1965 Gelac was selected to develop and manufacture the C-5A, under a contract valued at approximately $1.4 billion. This contract followed a period of intense competition with the Boeing and Douglas aircraft companies, and firmly established Gelac as the dominant company in the growing military aircargo field. The C-5A, which was to enter production in 1967, was an extraordinary aircraft by any standard. Over 80 yards long, the C-5A would be able to carry 250,000 lbs. of payload 3,700 miles at speeds in excess of 500 miles/hour.[3] According to Gelac executives, it would be able to land on a semi-prepared 4,000 foot runway (as compared with over 7,000 feet for a typical commercial jet), and could carry 844 passengers in a commercial passenger version. *Air Force and Space Digest* of December 1965 estimated an eventual market of up to 1,200 C-5As, with a value of $17 billion.[4]

By 1966 Gelac had thus become a major developer and manufacturer of aircraft. In the 15 years that Lockheed had operated the Marietta facility, Gelac had modified B-29s, built and modified B-47s, production designed and built the C-130 and the JetStar, completely designed and built the C-141, and won the largest single contract in aviation history, the C-5A. In 1966 Gelac was manufacturing the C-130, the JetStar, and the C-141, and was preparing to manufacture the C-5A. In addition, it was actively developing new aircraft (including VTOL[5] Hummingbird), and was engaged in such other fields as nuclear research and materials handling.

By this time Gelac had built or acquired a number of facilities to expand the capacity of its operations. These included an industrial products facility 15 miles from the main plant, a nuclear laboratory 40 miles away, a complete machine shop 90 miles away, and three subassembly feeder plants in neighboring states. When several additional facilities needed for the C-5A contract were completed, Lockheed's total investment in Gelac facilities would be approximately equal to that of the government.

Development of Gelac's Organizational Structure

Prior to 1960 Gelac operated through a basically functional organizational structure headed by a divisional General Manager. With the aid of one and later two Assistant General Managers, he supervised the work of several Branch Heads, responsible for functional departments such as Engineering, Manufacturing, and Marketing.

In 1960, when it became apparent that the JetStar program was not progressing as planned, one of the two Assistant General Managers was given responsibility for all aspects of the program. While functional personnel working on the JetStar continued to report to their Branch Heads, the Assistant General Manager now had general management responsibility for the JetStar.

Gelac's basically functional organization (now modified somewhat in the case of the JetStar) continued until early 1961, when Gelac submitted its proposal for the C-141 contract. By this time "program management" had become an accepted concept in the Air Force, and the C-141 program was assigned to an Air Force System Program Office (SPO) within the Air Force Systems Command. The SPO was

---

[3] Or 100,000 lbs. of payload 6,300 miles.
[4] Vol. 48, p. 36.

[5] Vertical takeoff and landing.

headed by a colonel whose sole responsibility was the successful completion of the C-141 program.

In its C-141 proposal, Gelac proposed to designate an Assistant General Manager (vice presidential level) as Program Director for the C-141 program. The Assistant General Manager, as Program Director, would work directly with C-141 personnel in the functional branches, although these personnel would continue to report to their respective Branch Heads. He would be fully responsible for the successful completion of the C-141 program, working on a continuing basis with the SPO Director. He would thus be the Gelac counterpart of the SPO Director. This organization was activated in February 1961, several months prior to the award of the contract.

In August 1961 the General Manager's title was changed to President, and the Assistant General Managers became Vice Presidents. In late 1961 the Gelac management organization thus consisted of a President, a Vice President in charge of JetStar and C-130, a Vice President in charge of the C-141 program, and a number of Branch Heads.

It soon became apparent that the C-130 program, having to share a Program Director with the JetStar program, would be at a disadvantage in obtaining branch resources. Consequently, in early 1962, a third Vice President, in charge of the C-130 program, was appointed.

During this period the branches themselves were projectized [6] to differing degrees. As a Program Director/Vice President reviewed the organization chart of a branch, he would eventually encounter one or more men who worked full time on his program. In some cases, a function would be projectized at the highest level, with a manager (reporting to the Branch Head) devoting his full attention to a given program. In other cases, a function was projectized one or more levels below the department manager.

A Program Director/Vice President for the C-5A was appointed prior to the submission of Gelac's final proposal for the contract. Since the C-141 award, the Air Force had increased its emphasis on program management to the extent that it now insisted that major programs be headed by high-level Program Directors. Moreover, it was increasingly clear that the Air Force wanted contractors to projectize at the highest level practicable. Therefore, C-5A managers would, in almost all cases, report directly to the Branch Heads, and were given responsibilities coinciding with responsibilities assigned to individual managers in the C-5A SPO.

Gelac Matrix Organization

In June 1966 Mr. W. A. Pulver was President of the Lockheed-Georgia Company. Acording to a company document, he was "accountable to his assigned Corporate Group Vice President for the profitable operation, growth, and perpetuation of his company. "Although Mr. Pulver occasionally became involved in particular problems and opportunities, he tried, to the greatest extent practicable, to leave operations to his Program Vice Presidents and Branch Heads. According to several Gelac executives Mr. Pulver managed his company by concentrating his attention on planning, product policy, organization, executive development, and corporate, government, and community relations.

Ten executives reported to Mr. Pulver (see Exhibit 1). Four of these executives were Vice Presidents, responsible for specific programs. Five Branch Heads, responsible for functional departments (Engineering, Marketing, Manufacturing, Quality Assurance, and Logistic Support) also reported to Mr. Pulver, as did the Director of Administration, who was responsible for the Finance, Master Scheduling, Legal, Public Relations, Industrial Relations, and Management Services Branches. While all of these executives reported directly to Mr. Pulver, it was clearly understood that the Vice Presidents and Administrative Director were at a higher organizational level than the Branch Heads. In theory, the Vice Presidents carried with them the President's authority as it applied to their programs.

Under Gelac's matrix organizational structure, all company resources were under the control of the Branch Heads. Only a secretary (and possibly an assistant or two) reported to each Vice President. All other personnel, whether working on several programs concurrently or permanently assigned to a single program, reported through the branch organizations to the Branch Heads. The Branch Head and his department managers were responsible for evaluating the performance of all personnel in their branches, and recommending raises and promotions when appropriate. Similarly, any facilities assigned to a branch were allocated to the various programs by the Branch Head and his subordinates.

Since a Vice President was at a higher organiza-

---

[6] "Projectization" refers to the establishment of a separate management structure with control over the resources that remained within a branch but were assigned to a given program.

tional level than the Branch Heads, he could when appropriate "instruct" a Branch Head to assign facilities or personnel to his program. As long as his instructions did not create conflicts with other programs, or branch plans and budgets, such an instruction created no problems. If, however, two or more programs wished to use the same facilities or personnel at the same time, it was necessary for the Branch Head to make a trade-off. He generally did so through negotiations with the Vice Presidents concerned, although occasionally such conflicts had to be resolved by the Gelac President.

In practice, conflicts of this sort were rare. Most decisions concerning the allocation of resources were made below the Branch Head's level. The Manager of Design Engineering for a given program might, for example, wish to increase the size of his department (if allowed by the budget) or obtain an engineer with particular competence in a specific area. He would then meet with his counterparts in other programs and determine what resources they were willing to make available to him. In most cases, managers at this level worked closely together and readily understood each other's objectives.

Moreover, most decisions concerning specific programs were made below the Branch Head level. Each Vice President chaired a Program Directorate or program team,[7] composed of "projectized" managers in each of the branches. The Program Directorates and teams met regularly, reviewing progress to date and making plans for the future. At these meetings a "projectized" department manager brought up any problems he faced and received his instructions. If his assignments did not require him to use resources outside of his existing department (this was usually the case), there was no need for him to consult with branch management. In most cases, however, "projectized" managers kept their branch managements informed and frequently asked higher level branch personnel for advice on specific problems.

In commenting on Gelac's organizational structure, several executives pointed out that it violated some of the early precepts of organizational theory. A "projectized" manager in a branch really had two bosses, whose desires might often be in conflict. Similarly, the Branch Heads worked for all four Vice Presidents, each of whom was concerned primarily with only his own program. Nevertheless, these same executives were strongly convinced that matrix organization, despite the theoretical problems, worked extremely well in practice. To a large extent, they attributed the organization's success to the people within it. Gelac executives, they pointed out, had worked together for a long time and were acutely sensitive to each other's problems. Many conflicts which, in theory, could only be resolved by the divisional President were easily resolved through face-to-face discussions at lower levels of the organization.

The Programs

This section will describe each of the four major programs and the resources available to each of the Program Directors.

C-130

Lockheed-California won the contract for the basic design and prototype construction of the C-130 in 1952. The C-130 was a medium-sized jetprop transport capable of carrying military payloads or 35,000 lbs. up to 1,600 nautical miles. Since Lockheed-California was heavily engaged in commercial propjet Electra production at this time, responsibility for production design and manufacture of the C-130 was assigned to Lockheed-Georgia. The first C-130 was delivered to the Tactical Air Command (TAC) in 1956; by 1959, 231 C-130s had been built, including 12 for the Australian government.

By 1958 initial and follow-up orders were nearing completion, and it seemed that the C-130 program would soon have to be phased out. Gelac developed the C-130B, however, which had larger engines and increased range. As a result, Gelac was able to sell additional C-130s, to foreign governments as well as to the Department of Defense.

Between 1959 and 1966 Gelac developed several advanced versions of the C-130, intended to extend the life cycle of the aircraft. Among these were C-130 tankers, weather reconnaissance aircraft, search and rescue aircraft, and versions with considerably increased range and payload capabilities. As a result of these and similar product improvements, Gelac management expected to have delivered or booked more than 1,000 C-130s by the end of 1966.

---

[7] The Program Directorate and program teams operated similarly, but the former designation was used only for the C-5A program. The term "Program Directorate" originated in the C-5A management proposal and was intended to suggest a more formal organization than that existing on other programs.

During 1965 and 1966 Gelac began to market the C-130 aggressively to the commercial market. The commercial version of the C-130 was identified as the L-100. A commercial certificate was obtained in September 1965 (at a cost of $1.5 million), and efforts were made to sell the L-100 to commercial carriers in the United States and abroad. By September 1966, several had been sold to Zambia for use during the Rhodesian crisis, to Alaska Airlines, and to Delta Airlines for use of its U.S. cargo routes. The Delta purchase was considered particularly significant, since it represented the first purchase of a specialized cargo aircraft by a U.S. commercial air carrier.

C-130 Organization

The C-130 Program Director in 1966 was Vice President T. F. Morrow, who had been assigned to the C-130 in 1964. The C-130 had been under a Vice President since early 1962, when it had been decided to give the C-130 organizational status equal to that of C-141.

Mr. Morrow's organization consisted of a secretary and personnel assigned to him in the various functional branches. In the Engineering Branch, a C-130 Engineering Program Manager reported to the Branch Head, the Chief Engineer, and supervised an Engineering Project Organization of 150 persons. Other engineering functions, such as structural engineering, were projectized for the C-130 at lower levels, if at all. In the Manufacturing Branch, a C-130 Assembly and Modification Manager reported to the Production Manager who reported to the Branch Head, the Director of Manufacturing Operations. Other C-130 manufacturing activities, such as parts fabrication, were unprojectized.

In the Marketing Branch a C-130 Sales Department Manager reported to the Director of Government Sales who reported to the Branch Head, the Director of Marketing. In addition, the Commercial and Export Sales Department, whose manager reported to the Director of Marketing, was actively engaged in C-130 sales.

In the other branches (Finance, Logistic Support, Master Scheduling, Quality Assurance, etc.) one or more departments worked full time on the C-130. In some cases, C-130 managers reported to the Branch Heads; in others they reported to other functional managers, who in turn reported to the Branch Heads.

According to Mr. Morrow, the C-130 organization was for the most part well suited to his current needs. After ten years engineering and manufacturing had become fairly routine, although they were complicated somewhat by the many versions of the C-130. In manufacturing, for example, it was often necessary to build several different versions on the same assembly line during the same month.

In marketing, however, Mr. Morrow would have preferred a separate department responsible for all C-130 sales, rather than a C-130 Military Sales Department and an unprojectized Commercial and Export Sales Department. According to Mr. Morrow, the major objective in mid-1966 was to sell additional C-130s, and thus keep the production line running. While he recognized the primary need for customer orientation, he believed that product knowledge — in depth — was an important prerequisite in selling a proved aircraft such as the C-130.

JetStar

The JetStar was initially designed and prototyped by Lockheed-California in 1957 in response to an Air Force requirement for a utility jet. The procurement called for several aircraft companies to build off-the-shelf aircraft, to be competitively flight tested. Since the California company was heavily engaged in Electra production at this time, final development and manufacture were assigned to Gelac. Capable of flying 17 passengers at 570 mph in its military version (known as the C-140), the four-engine swept wing JetStar represented a significant break-through in aircraft design and won the Air Force competition in 1959.

Preliminary Air Force planning led Lockheed to expect that the military would order 300 to 400 JetStars. Gelac began production in 1959, only to learn in 1961 that the new Secretary of Defense (Mr. Robert McNamara) did not believe that the Air Force needed an aircraft such as the JetStar. The Air Force finally agreed to purchase only 16 JetStars.

At the start of 1962 Gelac had completed over 30 JetStars (management had authorized 45 production aircraft). Most of these, but not all, had been sold to U.S. corporations. In the absence of a sizable military order and in view of the slow commercial market acceptance of this class of aircraft, Gelac temporarily ceased JetStar production in February 1962. By January 1963 the business airplane market appeared promising enough for JetStar production to recommence. The result of this sequence of events was a production interruption of 11 months.

Under a program of tight budget and schedule control, stepped-up marketing activity, and increased commercial customer responsiveness, the renewed JetStar program met its management objectives. By mid-1966, Gelac had sold more than 90 JetStars, of which 80 had been delivered. According to a Gelac brochure, "JetStars [were] in use around the world, flying five chiefs of state and other high government officials, as well as the executives of more than 50 of the country's top corporations." In 1966 the JetStar production rate was approximately two a month.

JetStar Organization

The JetStar Program Director was Vice President R. I. Mitchell.[8] Like the other Program Directors, Mr. Mitchell worked with personnel assigned to the functional branches. In the Marketing Branch, JetStar sales department managers responsible for military and commercial sales reported through Directors of Government Sales and Commercial Sales to the Director of Marketing. In the Manufacturing Branch, a JetStar Production Manager reported to the General Assembly Manager who reported to the Director of Manufacturing Operations. In the Engineering Branch, the JetStar Project Division reported to the Chief Advanced Design Engineer who reported to the Chief Engineer.

According to the JetStar Commercial Sales Manager, the JetStar program differed significantly from other Gelac programs. Although minor modifications in the JetStar were occasionally made, it was primarily a case of selling an off-the-shelf product. Moreover, the market for the JetStar consisted primarily of large U.S. corporations, a market toward which no other Gelac program was directed.

In selling the JetStar it was first necessary to identify likely prospects. Since JetStar was the "Cadillac of corporate jets" in both performance and price, sources such as *Fortune's* annual listing of the 500 largest U.S. industrial corporations were useful in locating potential buyers. JetStar promotional materials were sent to all likely prospects at least annually, and the sales force attempted to call on key prospects on a regular basis.

In most cases, a company likely to purchase the JetStar already had at least one executive aircraft.

---

[8] In addition to his responsibility as Program Director for the JetStar, Mr. Mitchell had reporting to him the Lockheed-Georgia Nuclear Laboratory located in Dawsonville, Georgia. This organization was established in the late 1950s to perform radiation testing services for the development of an all-nuclear aircraft. Additionally, Mr. Mitchell's duties included program direction of Gelac's VTOL aircraft projects and the activities of the Research Laboratories.

JetStar salesmen called on the chief pilots of such companies, stressing the operational advantages of JetStar over competing corporate jets. According to the JetStar Commercial Sales Manager, it was virtually impossible to sell a corporate jet without the enthusiastic support of the customer's chief pilot.

Nevertheless, the decision to buy a JetStar was generally made by top corporate management. It was often difficult, however, for a salesman to obtain an appointment with a corporate president or board chairman. A variety of means was used to get around this difficulty. Most important was the use of demonstration flights. As one salesman explained: "I recently accompanied the President of the XYZ company on a flight to the West Coast. Normally, I couldn't get five minutes of this man's time. On the flight, I got to talk JetStar for more than two hours."

High-level Lockheed executives also approached potential customers. Mr. Mitchell, for example, often called on key prospects with whom his salesmen would have been unable to get an appointment. Similarly the President and the Chairman of the Board of the Lockheed Aircraft Corporation were instrumental in making a considerable number of JetStar sales.

In selling the JetStar, Gelac salesmen stressed logistic support. As part of its marketing effort, Gelac stocked spare parts for the JetStar in several field warehouses, promising delivery within 24 hours. (The military stocked its own spares for all aircraft, including JetStar.) In the Logistic Support Branch, a JetStar Support Department reported to the Manager of Customer Services. This department was responsible for spare parts, service, and training of customer personnel.

In commenting on the Gelac organization, Mr. Mitchell said:

I am perfectly satisfied that the JetStar, despite its relatively small contribution to sales and profits, is getting more than its share of emphasis and resources. When you have as many programs as we have, there has to be some squeeze and push. Manufacturing can't keep everybody happy all of the time, and it may be difficult to get five engineers when the C-5A program is looking for fifty.

What we need is more commercial emphasis across branch lines. Few other airframe companies are as capable of dealing with the Air Force and Department of Defense as we are. This is not just a question of marketing; it involves engineering, manufacturing, quality control, etc. We must build a similar capability in the commercial field.

Perhaps we need a Vice President to take charge of

all commercial programs in order to fully develop and market commercial counterparts of our military products. Such a Vice President would be responsible for building an organization totally responsive to the commercial market.

C-141

In 1961 and 1962 Gelac was awarded contracts to build 132 C-141s. The first aircraft completely designed by Gelac, the C-141 was a four-jet cargo-troop carrier capable of carrying 94,000 lbs. of cargo or 145 men at speeds up to 550 mph.

The first C-141 was delivered to MAC on April 23, 1965. On April 22, 1966, Gelac delivered the 100th C-141. In the course of its first year of operations, numerous tributes were paid to the aircraft's performance and to Gelac's success in making deliveries on schedule and within cost. In mid-1966 the C-141 was playing a crucial role in the Vietnam conflict, almost doubling MAC airlift capabilities to Southeast Asia.

By June 1966 Gelac had delivered 120 C-141s, of which about 108 were operational. The original contract had been increased to 284 aircraft, which would allow production to continue through February 1968. Nevertheless, Gelac executives were concerned about the future of the C-141 program. Attempts were being made to find corollary missions for the C-141 as had been done with the C-130, but it seemed likely that the C-5A would soon replace the C-141 as a strategic airlifter. As Gelac executives pointed out, the C-5A was itself an extension of the C-141 since the C-141 and the C-5A had approximately the same missions. This made it difficult to extend the life of the C-141 program beyond 1968.

C 141 Organization

In mid-1966 the C-141 Program Director was Vice President A. E. Flock. As noted above, the C-141 had been the first Gelac program to have a Vice President as official Program Director. Prior to the award of the contract, C-141 development and marketing had been carried out by projectized departments within the functional divisions of the branches. During the early phases of the program, these departments had been small groups of people at relatively low organizational levels. As efforts on the C-141 program mounted, these departments grew in size and were given greater status in the branch organizations. By 1962 C-141 program managers reported to the heads of most of the major branches.

The C-141 Program Director was responsible for all phases of the C-141 program. In mid-1966 he was primarily concerned with manufacturing (164 aircraft were still to be built under present contracts) and marketing, although several major engineering projects were also underway in an effort to develop corollary missions for the C-141.

Mr. Flock worked closely with his program managers in the various functional branches. A C-141 program team[9] met weekly to discuss progress to date and significant problems. The Master Scheduling Department prepared a weekly report on program status, which Mr. Flock used as the agenda for his program team meetings.

In commenting on his program organization, Mr. Flock pointed out that he considered personnel working on C-141 in the branches as "my people." In general, he worked directly with these personnel, rather than the Branch Heads, although it was occasionally necessary to go to a Branch Head when a particular problem arose. According to Mr. Flock, the Gelac organization worked well — giving him what he needed to accomplish his job, while, at the same time, providing branch personnel with the direction and guidance necessary for the successful completion of their tasks.

The C-141 Engineering Program Manager said that Gelac's organization had made it relatively easy to transfer large numbers of people from the C-141 program to the C-5A program. He had in certain cases objected to the transfer of particular men, but problems in this area had been worked out between him and the C-5A Engineering Program Manager. Because the timing of the C-5A engineering build-up coincided perfectly with the reduction of engineering efforts on the C-141, it had been possible to fill virtually all key positions in the C-5A program with existing personnel.

The C-141 Sales Department Manager officially reported to the Director of Government Sales, who reported to the Director of Marketing. He pointed out, however, that he really reported functionally to Mr. Flock, with whom he worked very closely.

The C-141 Sales Department consisted of five men in addition to the manager. One was a sales trainee, who worked primarily on sales planning. The other four were sales representatives. One was responsible for sales efforts in the Washington area. A second

---

[9] Exhibit 2 shows the C-141 program team personnel as they were positioned organizationally within the functional branches.

was assigned full time to MAC. The other two men worked full time on developing corollary missions for the C-141, in an effort to extend production beyond February 1968. In this last function, it was necessary to work with a long chain of command, establishing requirements at the user level and then selling them to the systems analysts at the Department of Defense.

Among the corollary missions being considered for the C-141 in mid-1966 were the following:

(1) Airborne Warning and Control Systems (AWACS)
(2) C-141 Tanker
(3) C-141 Bomber
(4) C-141 Navigational Trainer

Personnel in each of the branches were assigned to the proposed corollary missions, to establish feasibility, determine costs, draw preliminary designs, etc. Often these personnel were located in a C-141 program department. In the case of AWACS, however, a program organization was beginning to take form.

AWACS was to be an airborne warning and control system, able to locate enemy aircraft or missiles and direct defensive weapons to their targets. In July 1965 Gelac and two other manufacturers were awarded six-month study contracts. At stake was whether the Lockheed C-141, the Boeing 707, or the Douglas DC8 would be the "platform" to which AWACS would be fitted. In late 1966 two of the three manufacturers would be selected to carry out a one-year study contract.

Shortly before the Requests for Proposal on the AWACS six-month study contract were issued, in July 1965, the C-141 Sales Manager, who had been following the AWACS program closely, was appointed AWACS Program Manager. At first he continued to report to the Director of Government Sales, but he was transferred to the C-141 Program Director later in 1965.

The original AWACS study contract resulted in the Gelac expenditure of $1.1 million, of which $250,000 was funded by the government. When the AWACS Program Manager needed funds, he went to the C-141 Program Director, who, in turn, submitted the request to the Gelac Research and Development Committee.[10] If the request was granted, the Program Manager had to convince the Branch Heads to assign resources to the AWACS program. As he explained:

"It's one thing to get the money and another to get the men. When I was first put in charge of the AWACS program, my biggest problem was staffing the program at a level commensurate with requirements to accomplish the task."

In mid-1966 small groups worked on AWACS in each of the functional branches. In most cases, these groups received their direction from project leaders, who reported to department managers located several levels below the Branch Head. Although the Program Manager exercised no direct administrative authority over the project leaders, they took their task assignments from the Program Manager and directed their groups accordingly, with technical guidance and assistance from branch management. After completion of the study phase and entry into formal CDP [11] competition in late 1967, the project would probably become a formal organization vested with both technical and administrative authority.[12]

C-5A

On September 30, 1965, Gelac was selected by the Air Force to develop and build the C-5A jet transport. The initial airframe contract, which called for Gelac to develop the C-5A and deliver 58 aircraft, was valued at approximately $1.4 billion. Under the terms of the contract, the Department of Defense had an option to purchase 57 additional aircraft for approximately $600 million.

Air Force and Space Digest described the operating characteristics of the C-5A as follows:

Wide recognition has been given to the C-5A's unprecedented cargo-carrying capacity — 100,000 pounds of payload for 6,300 miles (San Francisco–Tokyo or Honolulu–Saigon) or 250,000 pounds of cargo for 3,700 miles (New York–Paris). This is about three times the work capacity of the Lockheed C-141, the smaller brother of the C-5A, which is now entering service. The C-141 itself is a prodigious worker. One C-141 StarLifter is the equivalent of seven piston-driven C-124 aircraft over long hauls such as the transpacific routes. And a fleet of 132 C-141s, which will be available in the next few years, will more than double the present U.S. military airlift capacity to Southeast Asia.

---

[10] The Research and Development Committee consisted of the President, four Vice Presidents, Administrative Director, and several major Branch Heads. It was responsible for allocating Gelac's R&D budget (established by corporate management) to unfunded research and development projects.

[11] Contract Definition phase.

[12] The difference between formal and informal authority was not clear. It was related to formal salary and performance reviews and the formal authority to spend money, but there were few observable differences in the way project leaders (informal) and program managers (formal) operated. In either case, the manager directed a group of persons who viewed themselves as assigned to the program in question.

The C-5A has an important added virtue that no other transport can claim. It can carry virtually any of the Army's heavy equipment, including the fifty-ton Main Battle Tank. Another key feature is the aircraft's relatively low operating cost. According to DOD estimates, the C-5A will cost about fifty percent more to operate than the C-141. But it will do three times the work so that the direct operating costs in cents per ton-mile should be about half of the C-141's. Since the C-141 is expected to carry cargo under optimum conditions at four to five cents per ton-mile, the C-5A apparently has a real chance of getting this figure down to two cents.

The truly revolutionary implications of such economics are obvious, but also difficult to comprehend completely. Essentially the C-5A will allow the US to place formidable land forces on any trouble spot in the world within twenty-four hours. These Army units will not be "token" light infantry forces of the type that are now rushed in by air in emergencies. The C-5A will move heavy mechanized infantry and armored divisions, complete with tanks, trucks, artillery, and combat supplies.

A force buildup that would take more than a month with current sea and airlift will be achievable in a week with a fleet of 100 C-5As. A comparative example is provided by Operation Big Lift in 1963, which required 204 transport planes to airlift 15,000 unequipped troops to Europe in sixty-three hours. Once at their destination the men picked up tanks, trucks, ammunition, and other supplies which had been pre-positioned. Less than 100 C-5As could move the same number of troops plus their tanks, equipment, and supplies the same distance within 24 hours.[13]

The C-5A award followed a period of intense competition between Lockheed, Douglas, and Boeing. In early 1962 Boeing attempted to convince the Air Force of the need for an aircraft like the C-5A. Gelac, heavily involved in accomplishing the C-141 contract (barely one year old), and convinced that the C-5 requirement was well downstream, took little action. By 1963, however, it had become clear that the Air Force wanted a C-5A type aircraft, and Gelac began to compete in earnest. According to Gelac executives, the C-5A would be the follow-on to the C-141 as a strategic air transport. It was thus vital to the continued success of the company.

When Gelac first committed resources to the C-5A (1963), it established small marketing and engineering teams. Each team consisted of one or two people drawn from the C-141 program. At this early stage, the teams had no formal identity and were located several levels below branch management.

[13] *Air Force and Space Digest,* Vol. 48 (December 1965), p. 33.

In May 1964 the Air Force requested proposals for C-5 conceptual studies. In order to prepare its proposal, Gelac increased the size of its marketing and engineering teams to several hundred persons. These teams were headed by members of the original C-5A team, who now devoted much of their time to coordinating the efforts of all the various branches as preparation for the big competition took shape.

Gelac was one of three contractors awarded study contracts in June 1964. At this time a larger and more formally organized study team, consisting of personnel from engineering, manufacturing, marketing, operations analysis, and finance, was established. The entire study team was put under the general direction of Mr. T. R. May, who was also the C-130 Program Director at that time. The marketing and engineering leaders from the original team were given responsibility for coordinating the program; they reported directly to Mr. May.

The study contract was completed in September 1964. The Air Force requested proposals for the Contract Definition phase in December 1964. Gelac, Boeing, and Douglas all submitted proposals and all three were awarded contracts to perform the Contract Definition phase. The end result of this phase was firm proposals from each company to develop and manufacture the C-5. On the basis of these proposals, the C-5A contract would be awarded.

At this point, Vice President T. R. May was appointed Program Director/C-5A and Mr. T. F. Morrow became C-130 Program Manager. During the next six months the C-5A team grew to 2,000 people, working full time on the C-5A proposal. During this period, the original members of the team served as group leaders, reporting to both their branch managements and the Program Director. The original marketing and engineering leaders continued to coordinate the total effort, reporting to the Program Director.

In commenting on Gelac's success in the C-5A competition, the Deputy Director of Marketing (who had been C-5A Marketing Manager) stressed the importance of strategy. Gelac's strategy on the C-5A had been to give the customer what he wanted, i.e., to meet *all* requirements but not to exceed them where additional costs were involved. This strategy depended heavily upon defining "the customer" as being both the Office of the Secretary of Defense and the Air Force, with strong implications for the importance of cost and cost-effectiveness, as well as aircraft performance meeting all requirements. An alternative strategy could have been one of deliberately exceeding military requirements, accepting the attendant increase in total program costs.

Timing was also an important aspect of proposal strategy. It was essential to begin early in order not to fall behind competitors, but there were considerable risks in reaching a peak too soon. If the peak came too early, it was possible to become "locked-in" to design concepts that were not in accord with the customer's latest thinking.

In the case of C-5A, Gelac had brought its proposal efforts to a peak later than its major competitor. According to Gelac executives, this decision was based on marketing information suggesting that the formal request for final proposals would be received at a later date than had been at first expected. This proved correct, and Gelac was better able to respond to last minute changes in requirements than its competitors.

In early 1964, for example, Gelac's C-5A team consisted of about 90 persons, whereas Boeing had already assigned more than 1,000 persons to the project. In late 1964, just prior to the Request for Proposal for the Contract Definition phase, Gelac closed the gap rapidly, transferring large numbers of engineers from the C-141 program. According to the executive who had been engineering team leader at the time: "Our timing was just right. Marketing predicted the date of the RFP perfectly. But I was very worried for a while. I never thought we would have enough time and resources."

After the contract award the C-5A team was formally designated a program. In six of the eleven branches, C-5A Assistant Program Managers were appointed, reporting to both branch and program management. In virtually all classes, the C-5A Assistant Program Managers had been members of the C-5A team prior to the rapid build-up in late 1964.

C-5A Program Organization

A Deputy Program Manager and eleven Assistant Program Managers[14] reported to Vice President T. R. May.[15] Nine of the Assistant Program Managers were also members of functional branches, and two (the Configuration Manager and the Data Manager) were not assigned to the branches. Exhibit 3 is an organization chart of the C-5A Program Directorate. Exhibit 4 shows the same executives in their functional branch positions.

In the C-5A proposal, Gelac described its C-5A program organization as follows:

A bilateral [matrix] type of organization was selected for C-5A because it combines the most desirable qualities of a complete project organization and a fully functional organization. This organizational approach provides strong, centralized program management, avoids costly duplication of facilities and personnel; promotes the interchange of technical and administrative knowledge between programs, organizations, and people; affords flexibility in applying company resources to meet individual program requirements; and ensures prompt and effective support to individual programs.

The Lockheed-Georgia Company's basic organizational structure is depicted in Figure v. [This is the structure shown in Exhibit 1.] It is a bilateral or matrix organization with functional branch heads responsible for engineering, manufacturing, finance, and other major functions. Additionally, vice presidents are responsible as program managers for integrated program management and direction, drawing upon the resources of the functional branches as necessary to accomplish program objectives.

Lockheed has established the organization shown in Figure vi[16] to direct the C-5A program. The Vice President and Program Manager, T. R. May, is assigned full responsibility for the C-5A program. Mr. May's authority stems directly from the company president who has designated him to speak for the company and provide program direction on all C-5A activities. The relationship of the Lockheed C-5A program directorate and the basic functional organization is depicted in Figure vii. The major C-5A project units established exclusively for the C-5A program are identified with their appropriate C-5A assistant program managers along the vertical axis and with their parent functional branches along the horizontal axis. This [matrix] organization plan for the C-5A offers the following advantages over other plans evaluated during Phase IB:

- Provides top management visibility for the C-5A program and establishes short, clear lines of communication within the company.
- Places responsibility for directing the program squarely with the senior management personnel comprising the C-5A program directorate to the

---

[14] The C-5A Assistant Program Managers were organizationally equivalent to the functional program managers for the other programs. According to Gelac executives, the new title was intended to emphasize the close working relationship between the C-5A Program Director and his key representative in each of the functional branches.

[15] In addition to his C-5A management responsibilities, Mr. May had reporting to him directly the manager of Lockheed Industrial Products, located in a separate facility in Atlanta, Georgia. This organization produced aircraft ground support and nonaircraft products. Its function was not directly tied to any aircraft program.

[16] Figures vi through viii, on pages 71–73, show organizations and assignments as of September 1965, when the final proposal was submitted. Information as of September and October 1966 is provided in Exhibits 1 through 14.

Figure vi. C-5A Program Directorate Organization, September 1965

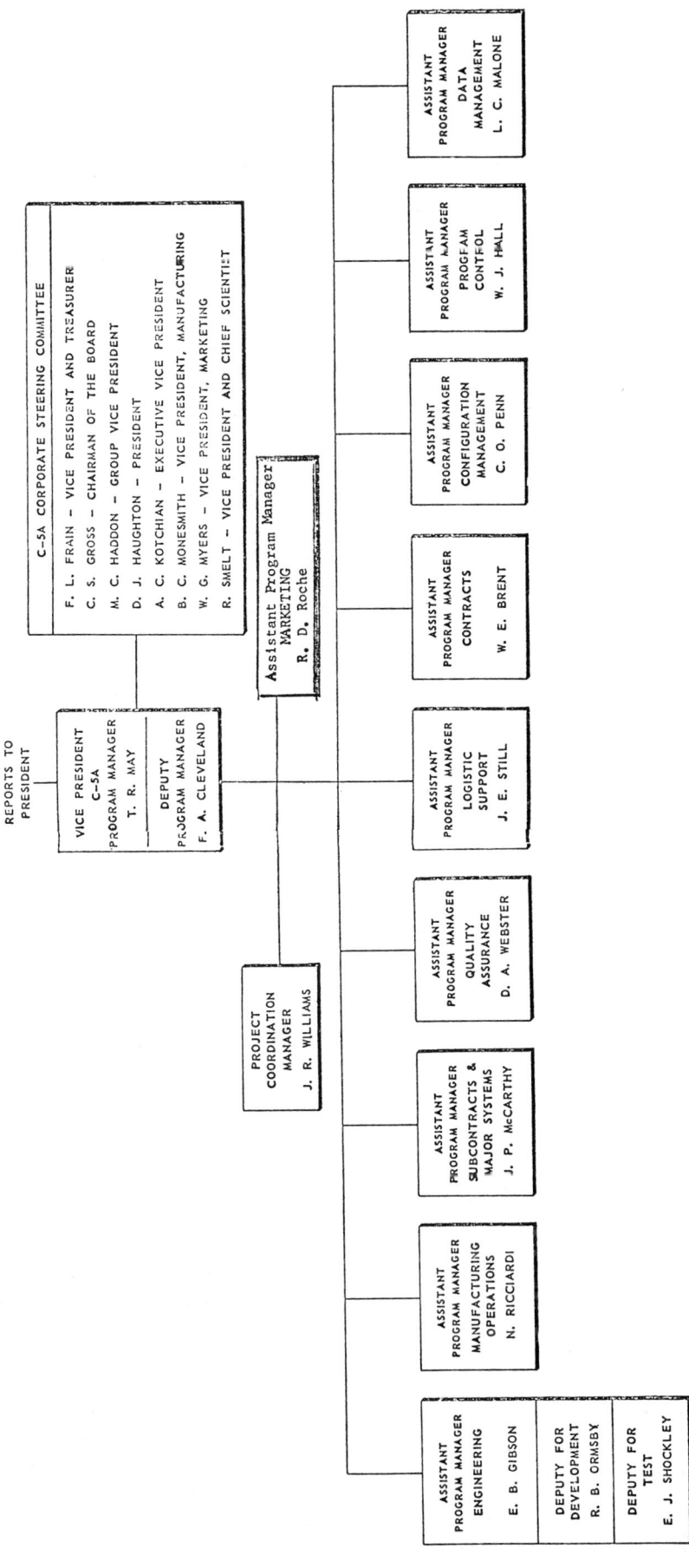

Figure vii. C-5A Program Organization Plan: Project/Functional Matrix, September 1965

Figure viii. C-5A Management Team, September 1965

C-5A SYSTEM PROGRAM OFFICE	AIR FORCE PLANT REPRESENTATIVE	LOCKHEED C-5A PROGRAM DIRECTORATE
System Program Director COL. W. E. RANKIN	PROGRAM MANAGEMENT	T. R. MAY Vice President and Program Manager
Assistant Program Director M. C. CHASE		F. A. CLEVELAND Deputy Program Manager
Deputy Director Engineering B. V. LOWRY	ENGINEERING	E. B. GIBSON Assistant Program Manager Engineering
Chief Configuration Management Division	CONFIGURATION MANAGEMENT	C. O. PENN Assistant Program Manager Configuration Management
Chief Program Control Division LT. COL. J. LOUDERMILK	PROGRAM CONTROL	W. J. HALL Assistant Program Manager Program Control
Deputy Director Procurement & Production G. E. OSTER	PROCUREMENT	J. P. McCARTHY Assistant Program Manager Subcontracts & Major Systems
Deputy Director Test and Deployment	TEST	E. J. SHOCKLEY Deputy for Test

SYSTEMS ENGINEERING DIRECTOR C. B. HARGIS, JR.

exclusion of all other duties and responsibilities, thereby focusing attention on C-5A performance, cost, and schedule requirements.
- Applies to the C-5A program the cumulative knowledge and experience of the senior management in the functional organizations in overall program planning and problem solving which require the broadest base of management judgment.
- Promotes the interchange of technical and administrative knowledge between programs, organizations, and people.
- Ensures prompt and effective support and services to the C-5A program.

The C-5A Lockheed organization depicted in Figure vi is parallel in many respects to the System Program Office organization in the Air Force. A direct counterpart Lockheed position is established for every major position within the System Program Office. This relationship, shown in Figure viii, provides important management interfaces with key Air Force systems management personnel and implements the Air Force-Industry team concept described in the 375 series of Air Force systems management documents.

In commenting on his program organization Mr. May stressed the importance of the Program Directorate.

These men [the Assistant Program Managers] are the ones who really run this Program. They know their functions, and what has to be accomplished in their Branches. Until recently we met as a Directorate every day, after lunch. Now we meet three times a week. These meetings are invaluable for keeping me informed, for coordinating the work of the various Branches. We have set up a Program Control Center, a special conference room where we maintain up-to-date data on program status and hold our meetings.

I believe strongly in delegation. I tell my Assistant Program Managers that the way to get ahead is to make decisions one level above their positions. At the same time, I do not believe that a manager should manage by exception, and deal only with problems as they come up. I want to be informed of both problems and opportunities, to be able to give positive direction to the Program as a whole.

L-500

The Air Force's C-5A competition required that the contractors explore possible commercial applications of the aircraft. Upon winning the C-5A contract in September 1965, Gelac increased its activity in developing a commercial derivative. To head this effort, the Director of Government Sales in the Marketing Branch, Mr. W. D. Perreault, was promoted to C-5A Commercial Program Manager. In its commercial versions, the C-5A was to be known as the L-500. Mr. Perreault reported to the C-5A Program Manager, Mr. T. R. May.

According to Mr. Perreault, a large market was developing for commercial cargo aircraft and the C-5A type showed considerable market potential. The management of Gelac had decided to participate in this commercial market, but had not yet determined whether a C-5A derivative was the best approach. Past experience suggested that the airlines were reluctant to accept a military aircraft derivative even though major changes requiring a very large investment were made. The airlines, for example, had no interest in the C-5A's ability to carry outsize cargoes or to land on short, semiprepared runways. These characteristics, which were highly important to the military, added weight and cost to the aircraft without providing commercial advantages, since the airlines carried relatively small, low-density cargo and had access to long runways at their regular airports. The impact of these characteristics on the aircraft's payload, and consequently on its lifetime earnings, seemed to be unacceptable to the airlines.

Despite these considerations, Mr. Perreault believed that the L-500 could find a significant market among the world's airlines, particularly in cargo service. He felt that the most serious problem facing Gelac was its lack of commercial orientation. As he explained:

Gelac is in good shape with regard to doing business with the military services. We are well established in the military cargo business and our people are, in effect, a part of the military team and have ready access to people in all commands and at all levels. We are on top of this business and we feel that the military recognizes our capabilities.

Unfortunately, Gelac is in a weak position in the commercial field. While Lockheed Aircraft Corporation has had some very successful commercial programs in the past, Gelac is known as a manufacturer of military aircraft. This puts us at a disadvantage when competing with our commercially oriented competitors. Fortunately, the recent sale of commercial C-130 aircraft to several airlines — Delta, Alaska, Zambian Air Cargoes — is making a favorable impression.

Mr. Perreault went on to explain the status of the L-500 program organization in 1966:

As you know, we have now projectized the L-500. To date, this means that I have been appointed Program Manager, given a budget, and assigned the responsibility to determine our best approach in developing a commercial derivative of the C-5A. Like other project managers at Gelac, I have no personnel, but instead work with people in the various branches to pursue all phases of our L-500 effort. These people range from individuals to small teams with their own managers within the various functional departments and branches.

My biggest job has been to get my program staffed. Ideally, I would like to have these people assigned full time to the L-500 program rather than to use a transient staff of the same size. This would considerably reduce the flexibility of the individual Branch Heads in responding to a wide variety of division needs. For instance, the Chief Engineer would be very reluctant to detach specific members of his various departments and thus impact his ability to respond to other critical program needs.

There is a definite advantage within the branches to be able to move their specialists from one assignment to another as requirements develop in all phases of the overall Gelac operations. When the Air Force expresses an interest in a new bomber, tanker, or command and control aircraft, the Engineering Branch feels it must be able to respond with senior people without needless coordination to get these engineers freed up from activities which have been developed along projectized lines, such as the L-500. Yet each time people are diverted from the L-500 program, it disrupts our progress toward developing this vital commercial capability.

The Corporate Steering Committee

According to Gelac executives, Lockheed's Corporate Steering Committee played an important role in guiding the company's activities on major programs. The Corporate Steering Committee consisted of ten to twelve corporate officers, including the Chairman of the Board, the President, and the functional Vice Presidents. It visited each of Lockheed's nine operating units at least every two months, generally for two days.

During these two-day periods, each Gelac program was examined in considerable detail. The Program Managers and their staffs made semiformal presentations (often lasting several hours), supported with slides and quantitative data. A typical presentation (on the C-5A) included 60 detailed slides and charts. A partial listing of these slides will be found in Exhibit 5.

In discussing their meetings with the Corporate Steering Committee, Gelac executives stressed the fact that these were working sessions, rather than formal "after-the-fact" reviews. Corporate executives asked detailed questions, and made specific suggestions for action. "Action decisions" were listed in the minutes of the meeting and became, in effect, instructions to the executive concerned.

The Branches

This section of the case will describe Gelac's major branch organizations. An effort has been made to reduce the length of the text by including organization charts, Exhibits 6 through 14,

Engineering

In September 1966 the Engineering Branch consisted of approximately 7,000 engineers; 5,000 of these engineers were Gelac employees and 2,000 were contract engineers hired as part of the C-5A engineering build-up. Some of the contract engineers were located in Gelac facilities in Marietta; others were located in remote offices in the United States and Great Britain.

The Engineering Branch had grown considerably since the establishment of Gelac in 1951. At first, Gelac's mission had required primarily liaison engineering, the translation of other people's designs for production in Marietta. As the company's mission changed with the addition of the C-130, JetStar, and C-141, additional functions were added, until by early 1960 Gelac had acquired a full range of engineering functions. The C-5A program, with its heavy demands for engineering manpower, had required a massive recruiting effort and the use of contract engineers (a common practice in the aerospace industry).

The Engineering Branch consisted of two types of departments: (1) three Engineering Program Departments, each headed by an Engineering Program Manager,[17] and (2) six functional departments, responsible respectively for structural engineering, subsystems engineering, advanced design engineering, development test engineering, research, and engineering administration (see Exhibit 6).

The three Engineering Program Departments, which were responsible respectively for the C-130, C-141, and C-5A, were primarily concerned with design engineering. Besides supervising design engineering for their programs, the Engineering Program Managers were members of a Program Directorate or program team, and had overall schedule and budget responsibilities for the engineering aspects of their programs.

The functional departments differed in the degree to which they were projectized. In general, there were at least several levels of functionally specialized divisions below the department manager. At some point, however, the subdivisions were generally broken down into groups or teams assigned to specific programs.

---

[17] In the case of the C-5A, an Assistant Program Manager.

The level at which projectization took place was generally a function of the specific tasks to be performed and the level of effort for the various programs at particular points in time.

In mid-1966, for example, the Structural Engineering Department was heavily involved in work on the C-5A program. As Exhibit 7 shows, the Structural Engineering Department was divided into four functional divisions. Each division, in turn, was divided into a "general" department and a C-5A department. The "general" departments were further divided into program groups or functional groups. The functional groups, in turn, were almost always divided into smaller groups working on particular programs.[18]

New programs, such as the L-500, were generally staffed with personnel in the "general" departments until such time as the level of effort required formal program organization. Similarly, the JetStar Engineering Program Manager now reported to the Chief Advanced Design Engineer (rather than the Chief Engineer) since effort on this program was no longer at a high level.

The Chief Engineer monitored the work carried out in his branch through weekly program status reports. These reports, prepared for the Program Managers, allowed the Chief Engineer to determine how well his branch was doing on each of the programs assigned to it. In addition, the Chief Engineer continually monitored the assignment of branch resources to each of the programs, to ensure, for example, that each program was receiving its proper share of various categories of engineering manpower.

In commenting on his organization, the Chief Engineer pointed out that it was necessary to retain maximum flexibility within functionally specialized departments and, at the same time, to provide the Program Managers with readily identifiable (and thus controllable) resources on a continuing basis. Moreover, it was necessary to plan for the future, to ensure that the branch would have the skills and manpower required by changing technologies and aircraft requirements.

Manufacturing

Reporting to the Director of Manufacturing Operations were two Assistant Directors (responsible respectively for the C-141 and the C-5A) and nine functional Division Managers (see Exhibit 8). All resources of the branch were under the control of the functional Division Managers.

For the most part, the divisions were not projectized, except at very low levels. According to the Director of Manufacturing, most manufacturing functions did not lend themselves to projectization, since it was most efficient for the various programs to share the same resources. For example, heavy machine tools could only be utilized fully if shared by several programs.

The Assembly Division was an exception to this pattern. It was divided into JetStar, C-130, and C-141 Assembly Divisions. In this case, high-level projectization was practicable, since each program had its own assembly line. The C-5A program, because of its size, had its own Assembly Division, the manager of which reported to the Director of Manufacturing.

The two Assistant Directors were responsible for overseeing manufacturing operations for the programs to which they were assigned. While reporting to the Director of Manufacturing, they worked closely with their Program Vice Presidents and were members of a Program Directorate or program team.[19] In addition, each Assistant Director was assigned general responsibilities by the Director of Manufacturing. The C-141 Assistant Director, for example, had general responsibility for most production shop operations.

The Director of Manufacturing was frequently faced with conflicts among the major programs. If one program was 4% behind schedule and another 11%, for example, the Vice President of the latter program was likely to demand an explanation. Similarly, when it became necessary to assign work to outside subcontractors, the Program Vice President concerned was likely to resist strongly.

According to the Director of Manufacturing, conflicts of this sort could usually be worked out but required detailed supporting information and a great deal of patience. As he explained, "It may be true that a dog can serve only one master, but most of us — fortunately — are more intelligent than a dog."

Materiel

Within the Manufacturing Branch, the Director of Materiel was responsible for procurement, subcontracting, and materiel handling. The importance of

---

[18] Some highly specialized functions were not projectized at all. The Advanced Structures Department, for example, consisted of 50 engineers who did work for each of the programs as the need arose.

[19] The Assistant Directors obtained the concurrence of the Director of Manufacturing before committing the branch to do something at a meeting of their Program Directorate or team. Such concurrence was necessary, one Assistant Director explained, because the branch often had to agree to carry out a task before it had found a way to do so.

this function may be seen in the fact that a typical aircraft contained 40,000 to 50,000 separate procurement items. Moreover, the percentage of subcontracted subassemblies (by weight) ranged up to 60% in the case of the C-141.

Three Assistant Directors and four division managers reported to the Director of Materiel (see Exhibit 9). The three Assistant Directors worked on general assignments and had coordinating responsibility for the C-5A program, the C-130 and JetStar programs, and the C-141 program respectively. The four divisions were functionally oriented, responsible respectively for Materiel Requirements and Operations, Materiel Procurement, Materiel Handling, and Subcontracts. The C-5A program had its own subcontracting and procurement departments, which reported to the Assistant Director responsible for the C-5A program.

The Materiel Requirements and Operations Division worked closely with personnel in the Engineering, Manufacturing, and Master Scheduling Branches to establish requirements and lead times for outside purchases. The Procurement Division purchased items on an off-the-shelf basis. The Subcontracts Division worked with vendors of major subassemblies. In general, purchases in the former category were made on a competitive fixed-price basis while the latter category required complex subcontracts, often with incentive provisions.

The Subcontracts Division was projectized, with separate departments working on each of the major Gelac programs. According to the Director of Materiel, projectization was not desirable in other procurement activities, since the programs were often able to achieve volume discounts through combined purchase from a common supplier.

Quality Assurance

The Quality Assurance Branch was responsible for the overall quality of Gelac products. The Quality Assurance Branch established quality control policies, tested all incoming materials, tested assemblies and subassemblies at various stages in the manufacturing process, and subjected each aircraft to a rigorous inspection (including flight test) before delivery to a customer. According to Gelac executives, quality assurance was extremely important in the aircraft industry, accounting for as much as 8.5% of manufacturing expenses.

Quality Assurance was at branch level, rather than, for example, part of the Manufacturing Branch. Gelac executives agreed that an independent branch was desirable, since Quality Assurance, in effect, performed an audit function with regard to the work of the other branches.

The Quality Assurance Branch was organized on a functional basis, with directors in charge of flying operations, inspection, and quality engineering respectively (see Exhibit 10). The inspection function was organized on a combined functional and project basis, with divisions responsible for fabrication and tool inspection, materiel inspection, JetStar inspection, C-141 inspection, C-130 inspection, and C-5A inspection. The last four divisions were responsible for monitoring final assembly operations; the first two divisions monitored earlier stages of the production process. This breakdown of functional and project responsibilities corresponded closely to the organization of the Manufacturing Branch.

The Director of Inspection pointed out that the branch had both auditing and marketing responsibilities. On the one hand, it represented the customer, assuring that the aircraft he received were of the highest possible quality. On the other hand, it was the branch's mission to sell Gelac quality to the customer, to convince him that Gelac's quality assurance procedures ensured that his aircraft were free of significant defects. As a result of this dual function, the Quality Assurance Branch served as an important interface between the company and the customer.

Master Scheduling

The Master Scheduling Branch was responsible for three major functions: (1) master scheduling, (2) program coordination, and (3) program evaluation. Seven department managers reported to the Director of Master Scheduling (see Exhibit 11). The Program Evaluation Department was responsible for preparing reports on program status. The Master Scheduling Department was responsible for establishing and maintaining an up-to-date master schedule, which took into account all of Gelac's contractual requirements. Five Program Coordination Departments (C-130, JetStar, C-141, C-5A, and Aerospace, i.e., miscellaneous) were responsible for assuring that each branch had scheduled its activities in such a way that individual program schedules would be achieved.

The Program Evaluation Department prepared a number of standard reports for Gelac and Air Force managements. Among these were daily program status reports, weekly graphical program status reports, and monthly "briefings" for the Air Force. Copies of these reports were also submitted to corporate management.

The Master Scheduling Department sought to schedule work in such a way as to maximize utilization of division resources (and minimize cost) while at the same time fulfilling all contractual obligations. In doing so, it was frequently necessary to make trade-offs between individual programs. A decision to shift some C-130 production out of the plant to make room for the C-5A, for example, might minimize expense for the division as a whole but increase expense somewhat for the C-130 program. Consequently, it was often necessary to negotiate with several program and/or branch managers simultaneously. According to the Director of Master Scheduling, this procedure made it possible to resolve inter-program conflicts without submitting them to the Gelac President.[20]

The Program Coordination Managers worked closely with their Program Directors, briefing them regularly on program status. According to the Director of Master Scheduling, the Program Coordination Managers really reported to the Program Directors. It was important that they were located in the Master Scheduling Branch, however, since a change in the schedule of one program was likely to affect the overall master schedule.

Each Program Coordination Manager wrote a report on the "health" of his program weekly. This report was sent to all Gelac Program and Branch Managers, the Gelac President, and top corporate executives. Under company policy, no Gelac executive other than the Program Coordination Manager was to see this report prior to its publication. According to Gelac executives, this policy was intended to ensure that significant problems and difficulties were brought to top management's attention promptly.

A considerable portion of the branch's work was carried out through interbranch committees. Most important of these were the First Aircraft Master Scheduling Committees (FAMSCOs)[21] and the Configuration Change Boards (CCBs).[22] These committees were responsible for coordinating the plans of the various branches, ensuring, for example, that the schedule of engineering design releases was in accord with the planning schedule of the Manufacturing Branch. On a major program, as many as five FAMSCOs might work simultaneously, specializing in various parts of the aircraft under consideration.

The Program Coordination Managers (or their deputies) served as chairmen of these committees. According to the Director of Master Scheduling, the chairman was responsible for recognizing major impasses between functions, and calling meetings of successively higher level personnel until the conflict was resolved. In general, the working level FAMSCOs were able to resolve routine conflicts, and policy issues were resolved by the Program Directorate or team, and occasionally the Branch Heads.

Logistic Support

The Logistic Support Branch was responsible for providing spare parts, service, and maintenance training to Gelac customers. Prior to November 1965, Logistic Support had been a major organization within the Marketing Branch. It was established as a separate branch at that time, however, as a result of the Air Force's increased emphasis on logistics management.

Three executives reported to the Director of Logistic Support (see Exhibit 12): (1) the Director of Supply and Service, (2) the Director of C-5A Logistic Support, and (3) the Manager of Support Operations. The Director of Supply and Service and the Director of C-5A Logistic Support performed essentially the same functions, except that the former was responsible for three programs (C-130, JetStar, C-141) and the latter only one.

The Logistic Support Branch was operated as a profit center. Each year the Director of Logistic Support prepared a revenue forecast which served as his sales target for the year. The branch sold spare parts packages, ground handling equipment, training aids, and maintenance training programs to both military and commercial customers. In addition, the branch assigned technical representatives to most major military installations (where Gelac aircraft were based) and to commercial customers to provide maintenance assistance, gather performance data, and conduct on-the-job training of customer personnel.

---

[20] It had recently been decided, for example, to remove JetStar manufacturing activities from the main plant to a separate building. This move would make room for the C-5A program and, at the same time, protect the JetStar program from encroachment by the larger programs.

[21] The FAMSCOs were made up of part-time representatives of each of the functional branches. Particular emphasis was placed on scheduling the first aircraft since the schedule established for this aircraft would largely determine future manufacturing schedules. Moreover, certain important interfunctional relationships (e.g., release of basic engineering drawings to manufacturing) were primarily related to the manufacture of the first aircraft.

[22] The CCBs consisted, for the most part, of the same personnel as the FAMSCOs. The CCBs were primarily concerned with the effect of changes in specifications and manu-

facturing processes on the master schedule. If the wing configuration was changed, for example, engineering drawings had to be released and orders had to be placed on vendors in much the same way as for the first aircraft.

According to the Director of Logistic Support, there were significant differences between military and commercial customers. The military generally purchased a year's supply of spare parts for each new aircraft, afterwards buying spare parts on a competitive basis. Commercial carriers generally purchased spares from OEM (Original Equipment Manufacturers) suppliers. JetStar owners (generally, major corporations) purchased spares from Gelac as the need arose, demanding rapid delivery. Similarly, military and commercial customers had different requirements in the areas of maintenance training and training aids.

Finance

The Finance Branch was divided into three major divisions: (1) Program Pricing and Control, (2) C-5A Program Control, and (3) Accounting and Financial Services (see Exhibit 13). The Program Pricing and Control Division was divided into departments responsible for the C-130, C-141, JetStar, and spares. Each of these departments performed functions similar to those performed by the C-5A Program Control Division. The four Program Control Managers served their Program Directors in the same way as a controller would serve a divisional general manager. They prepared regular and special reports, worked with engineering and manufacturing to develop price recommendations, and monitored program expenditures to make sure they were within budget.

According to the Director of Finance, the Program Controllers were far more marketing-oriented than was usually the case in large companies. This was particularly true in the pricing area. He noted that:

> In order to make money in this business it is necessary to propose a price low enough to get the contract, and yet assure that the contract terms can be met at a profit. This is extremely difficult on most programs, since we have to commit ourselves to a price before we have developed the product. For this reason, our people must have in-depth knowledge of product features, market conditions, and development and manufacturing processes.

Marketing

The Marketing Branch was responsible for gathering information on future requirements, selling Gelac's approach to these requirements, selling the product, and "keeping the customer sold" after a contract had been awarded. In addition, it had the broad mission of advising Gelac management concerning market conditions, competitive developments, relevant technologies, and broad strategies and tactics in pursuit of new business. According to the Director of Marketing, the branch's primary responsibility was to ensure that the company remained customer-oriented.

In the military market, these missions required continuing contacts at various levels of the Department of Defense. Although using commands customarily generated requirements, actual decisions were generally made at the DOD level. After a contract had been signed, it was necessary to satisfy the DOD, SPO, and using command, while, at the same time, developing corollary missions to extend the life cycle of the product.

Contacts with the various levels of the customer's organization were maintained in two ways. The Lockheed Aircraft Corporation operated 21 Corporate Field Offices in major cities and the headquarters of major commands. These field offices were shared by all Lockheed divisions, but individual salesmen in the larger offices specialized in particular products. In most cases these specialized salesmen were former employees of the division whose products they sold. According to Gelac executives, the Corporate Field Offices made it possible for the divisions to be represented in locations where they would have been unable to justify full-time salesmen. In addition, the offices took responsibility for a wide range of administrative matters that would have been difficult to handle from Marietta.

The bulk of the selling effort was carried out by Gelac salesmen. Although sales assignments varied considerably (see below), at the lowest level individual salesmen were generally responsible for selling a particular aircraft to a particular customer. These salesmen called on their customers regularly, exchanging information on operational requirements and Gelac's approaches in them. In many cases appointments were arranged by the resident Corporate Field Office representative, who accompanied the Gelac salesman on his calls.

The Marketing Branch was organized in six major divisions, three of which were involved in direct sales (see Exhibit 14). The other three divisions were responsible respectively for marketing services (bid and proposal preparation, sales promotion, customer relations, general administration), contract administration, and marketing planning (marketing research, economic analysis, long-range planning).

The three direct sales divisions were responsible respectively for government sales, commercial sales, and export sales. The Government Sales Division was divided into six product sales departments — C-5A, C-130, C-141, C-140 (the military version of JetStar), VTOL, and Development Sales — and one department responsible for sales to a particular customer. The Export Sales Division sold all Gelac products in the export market, and the Commercial Sales Division sold all Gelac products to commercial customers.

Before August 1966 there had been a separate JetStar Sales Division divided into Military and Commercial Sales Departments. According to Marketing Branch executives, the JetStar Sales Division had been separate at this point in time in order to give increased sales emphasis to this program. In the same period commercial and export sales had been combined in one division.

In August, however, the old Commercial and Export Sales Division was split into two divisions. The establishment of a separate Commercial Sales Division, responsible for all commercial sales, would give increased emphasis and visibility to the important commercial market, according to the Director of Marketing. Furthermore, the JetStar Sales Division was eliminated. In the future JetStar military sales would be handled by the Government Sales Division, JetStar commercial sales by the Commercial Sales Division, and JetStar export sales by the Export Sales Division.

In commenting on his branch organization, the Director of Marketing pointed out that the sales requirements for each aircraft and customer were different. For this reason, it was not desirable to projectize direct sales completely, with a separate sales department for each aircraft. Instead, it seemed best to establish broad customer groupings (Government Sales, Commercial Sales, Export Sales), and leave it to each Division Sales Manager to assign his men in such a way as to cover the complete market and the complete product line.

The Director explained that the success of this organization depended on the willingness of individual salesmen to communicate with one another. It was essential, for example, that individuals selling the same product or dealing with the same customer keep in close contact with each other — whether or not they were in the same sales division. In general, working level contacts of this sort were maintained without difficulty.

* * * * *

Gelac's marketing efforts had, over the years, been directed primarily toward the military aircraft market. Although Gelac anticipated significant growth in the commercial air cargo market, that market had not developed very rapidly. By 1966 Gelac Marketing was clearly faced with the need for a major sales effort in the commercial field. With the L-100 (C-130), L-200 (C-141), and L-500 (C-5A), the company's product line included a full range of all-cargo aircraft. Significant problems were still to be overcome (Would the airlines, for example, be willing to commit themselves to nonconvertible all-cargo aircraft?), but Gelac executives were increasingly optimistic concerning the potential of the air-cargo market. Several executives expressed the hope that commercial sales would eventually represent 50% of Gelac revenue.

Increased emphasis on commercial sales, however, would raise significant questions concerning Gelac's organization. One executive stated the problem as follows:

Our decision to enter the commercial market with large cargo aircraft was preceded by considerable analysis of many critical problem areas. The first problem concerned the size of the market, and Gelac's ability to meet the market's needs. On the basis of considerable market research, we are convinced that the long-awaited air cargo expansion is here . . . now. Our prediction of requirements clearly indicates a sizable market, and there is no question that Lockheed "Freight-Shaped" aircraft — the L-100, L-200, and L-500 — and the facilities and know-how available all add up to having a full measure of capability.

A second important problem was that of clearly recognizing the difference between the military market and the commercial market, and taking steps to change our organization, management, and operations to accommodate the dual market. The differences we refer to are significant. They start right with the engineering design optimization choices and go through the whole system . . . specifications, production, quality assurance, sales, financing, logistic support. There are some who think these differences are so critical that a company cannot successfully serve both the military and the commercial markets. They cite the Boeing and Douglas corner on the commercial market as evidence. We don't agree at all. As a matter of fact, we are convinced that *combined* design, production, and support offer advantages to both . . . advantages we can reflect in our schedules, prices, and quality. The learning curves are heavily complementary. But we recognize that it will work well only if we keep our "customer-oriented" policy in mind, and make sure our system does indeed serve two masters.

This leads to a third problem. What organizational structure will not only permit but indeed will enhance this strategy? We think it imperative that each of our dominant functional Branches contain a large "commercial" division, within which commercial projects are established. It may well be that these commercial functional divisions should report to a new Vice President of Commercial Programs. He would then have both the direct functional and project authority. You'll recognize this as another form of our flexible matrix organization, with which we have worked so successfully on our concurrent military programs. This would give our commercial programs top management visibility, all of the resources and experience of the top management in the functional branches, and not only permit but promote technical interchange. And even more important, the matrix organization concept is specifically designed to provide a customer-oriented management and team. We fill customer requirements . . . not sell products. And there's a world of difference.

Exhibit 1. Organization Chart of General Management, June 1966

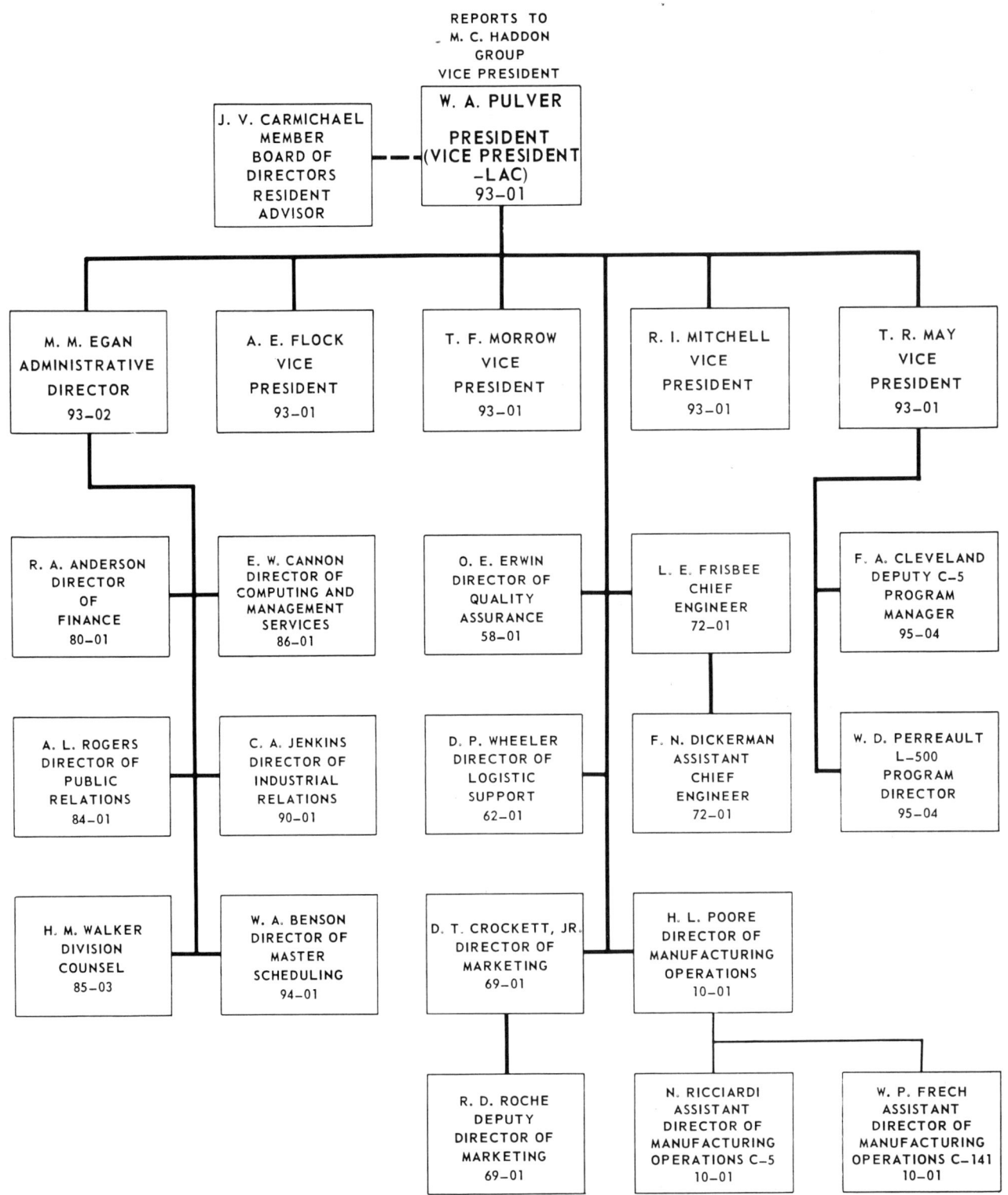

Lockheed-Georgia Company 83

Exhibit 2. C-141 Organization Chart, September 1966
Chart No. 1

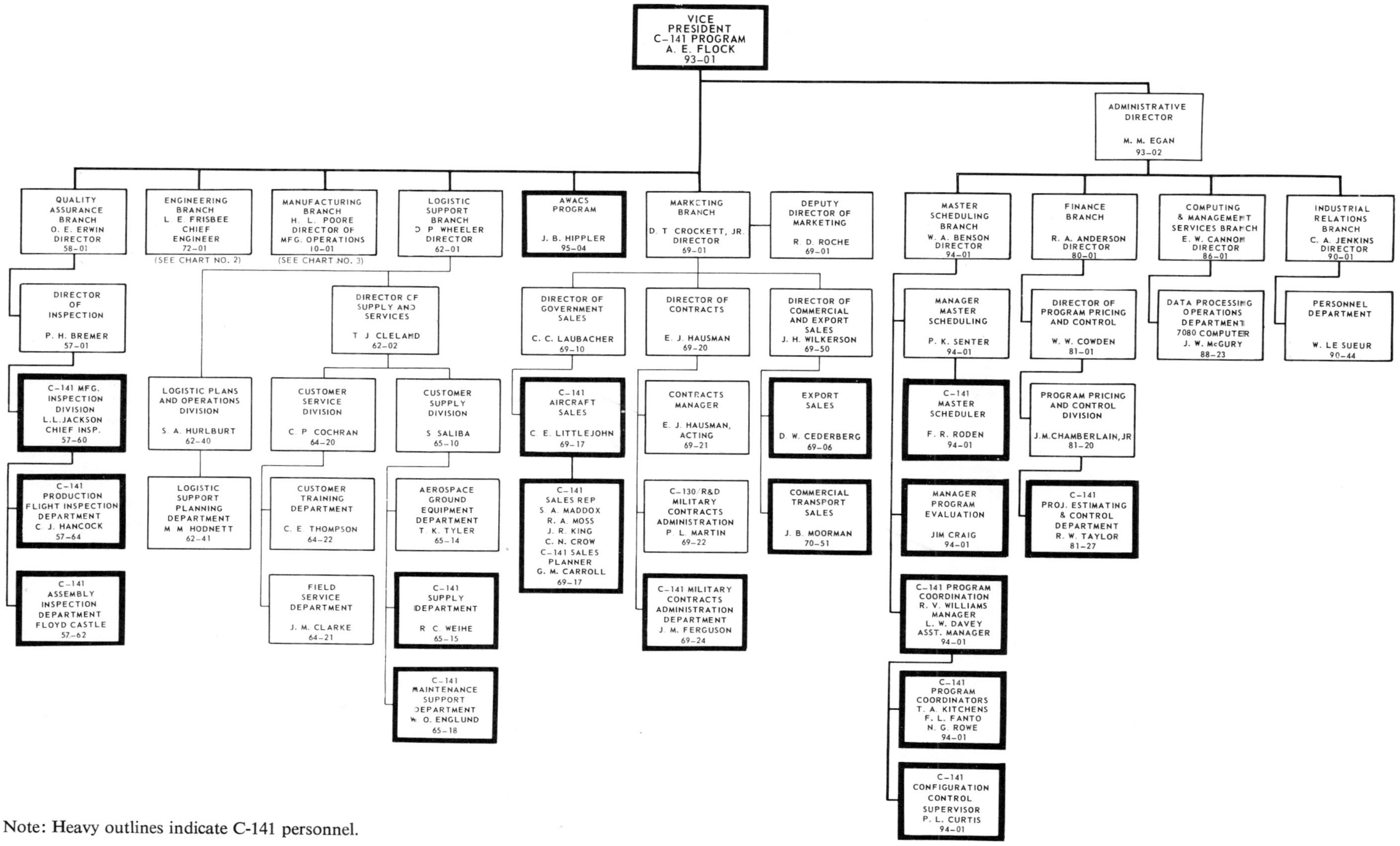

Note: Heavy outlines indicate C-141 personnel.

84 Cases and Commentaries

Exhibit 2 (continued). Chart No. 2

REPORTS TO VICE PRESIDENT C-141 PROGRAM

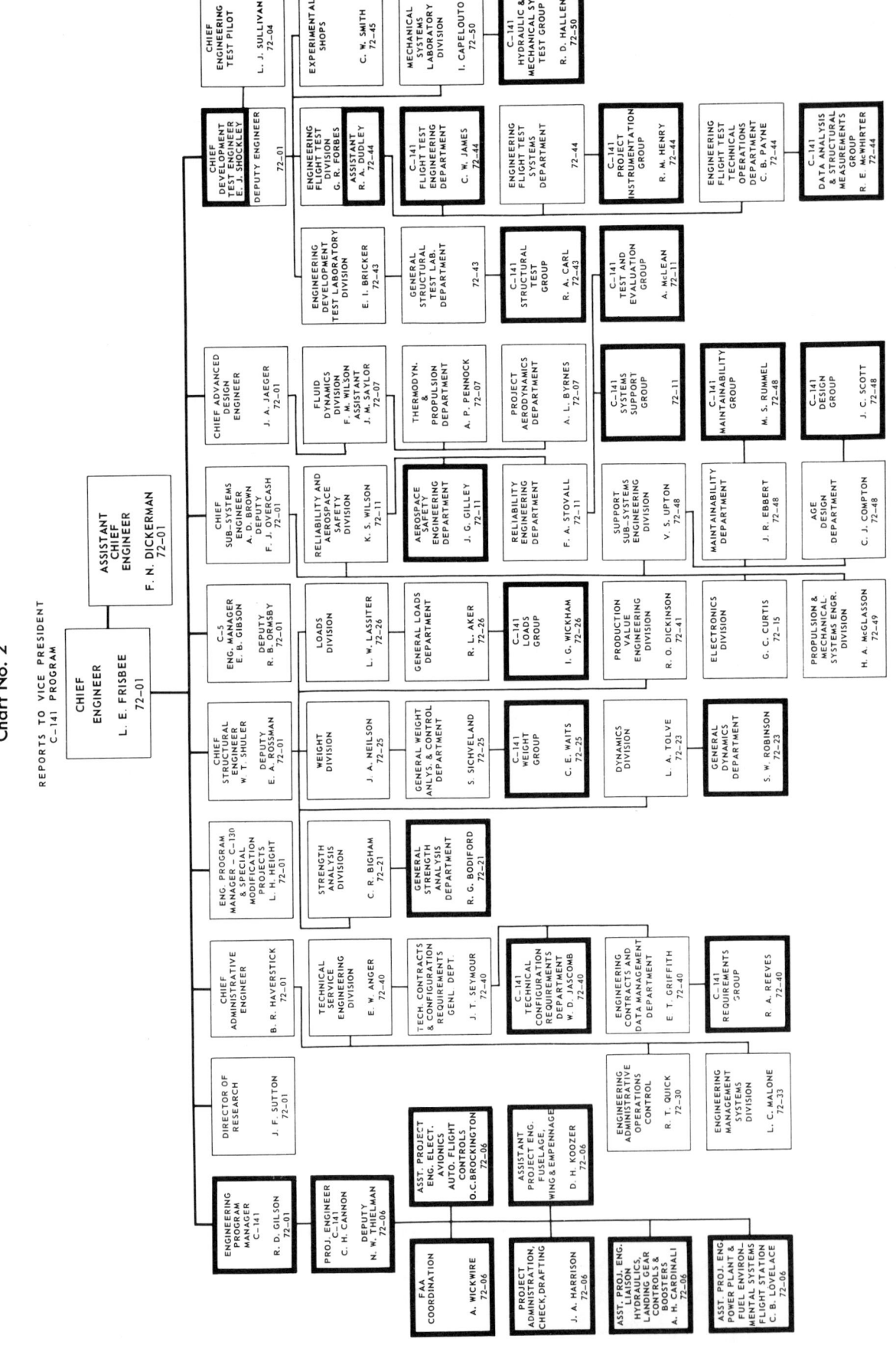

Exhibit 2 (continued).
Chart No. 3

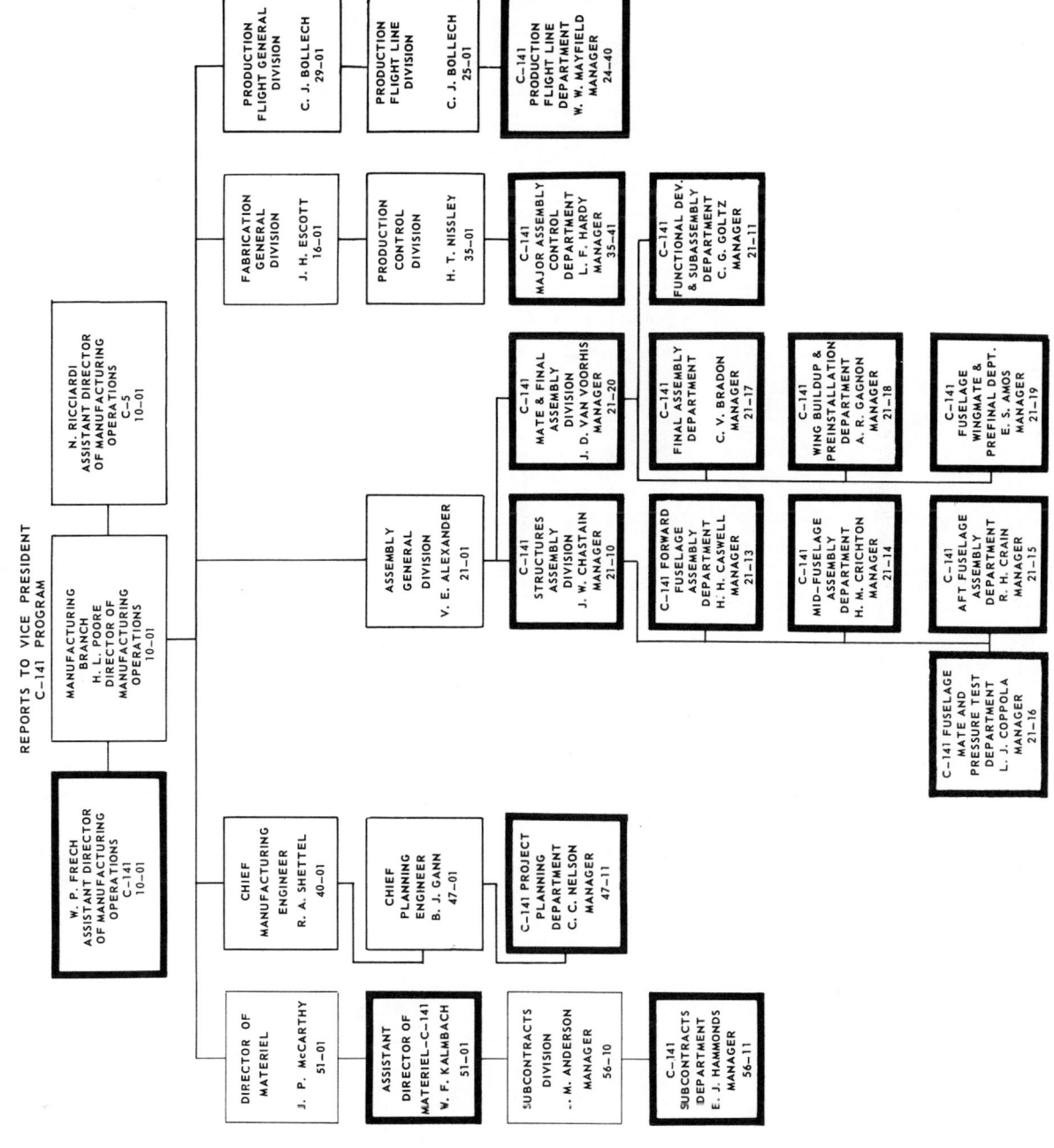

86 *Cases and Commentaries*

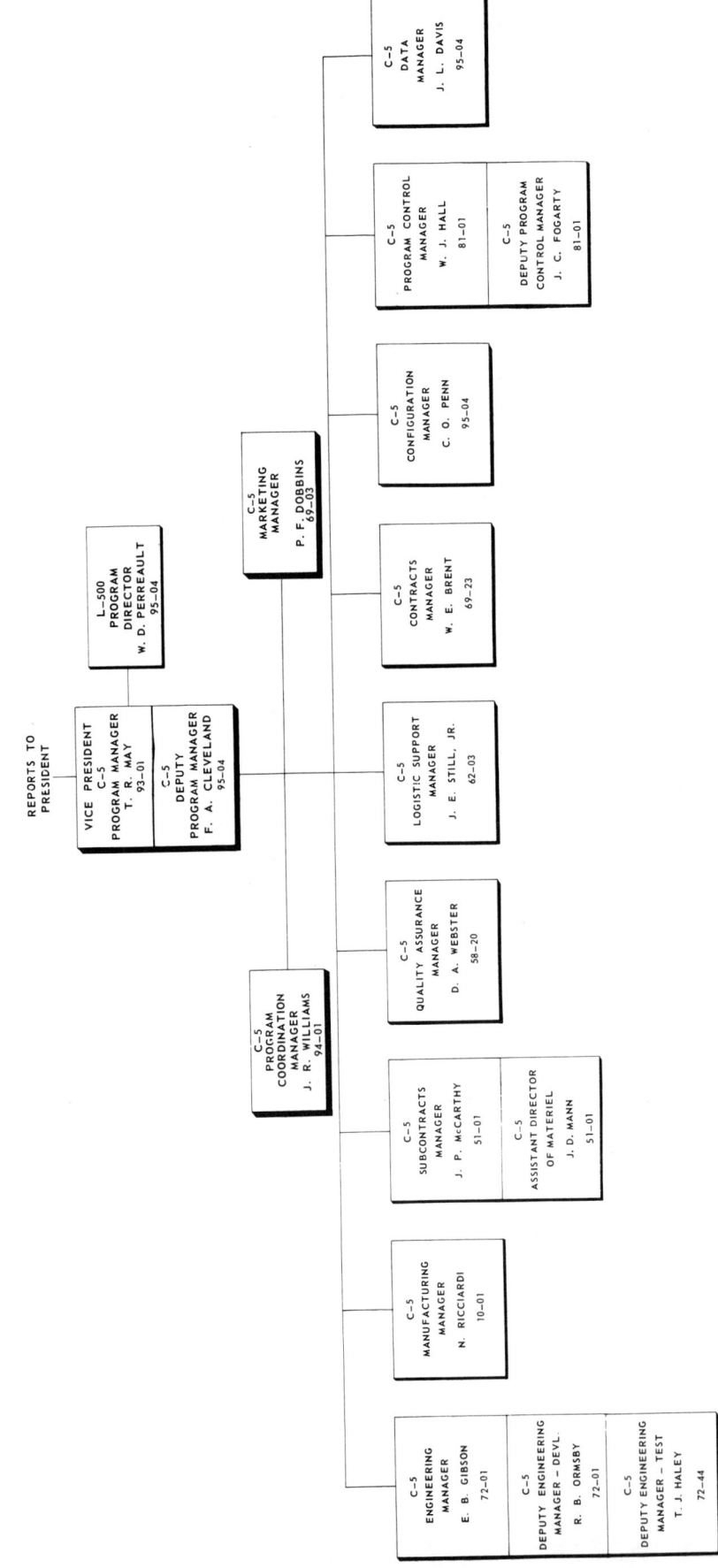

Exhibit 3. Organization Chart of C-5A Program Directorate, September 1966
Chart No. 1

Lockheed-Georgia Company 87

Exhibit 4. C-5A Program Organization (in Functional Branches), September 1966
Chart No. 2

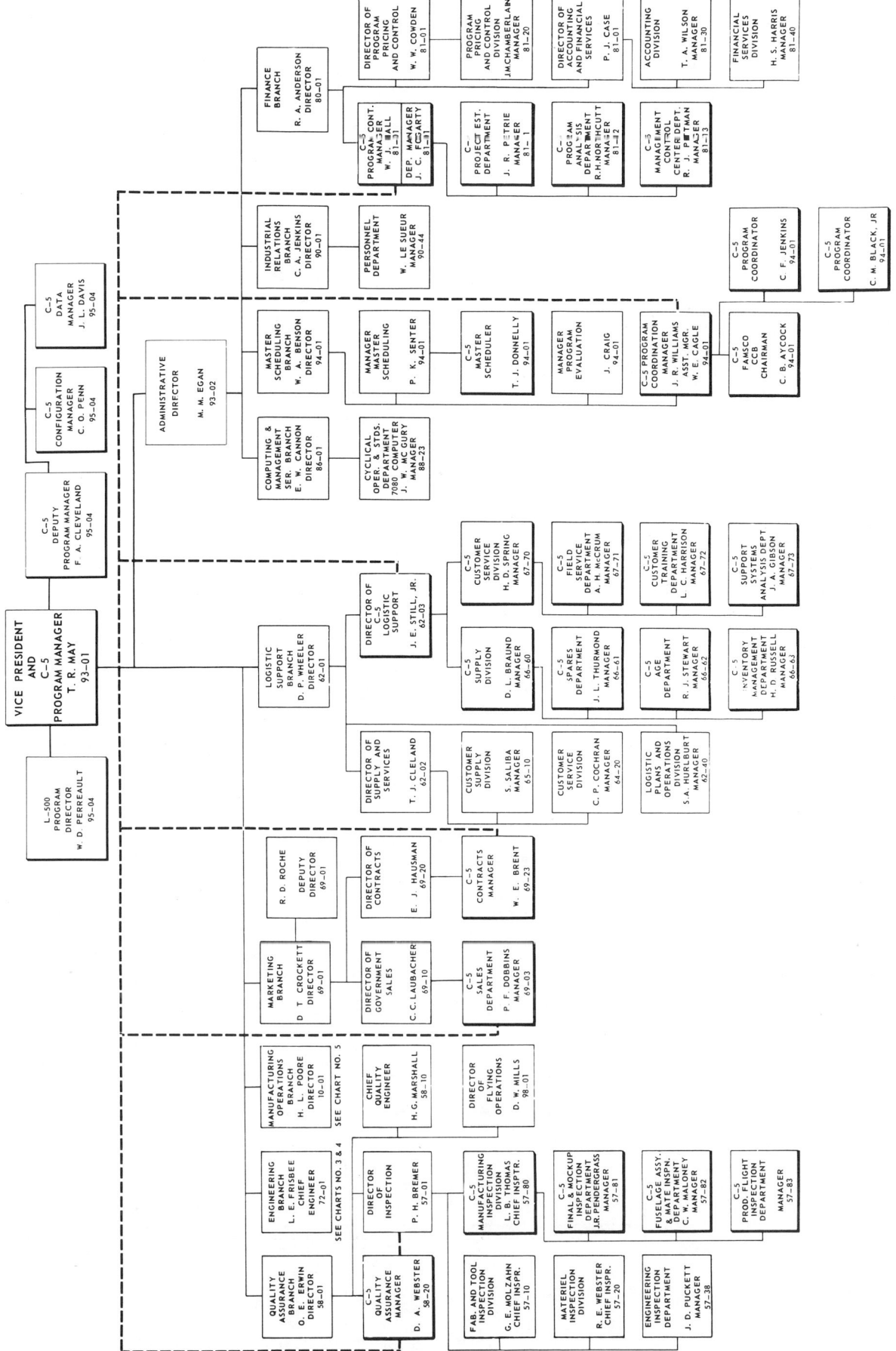

88 Cases and Commentaries

Exhibit 4 (continued).
Chart No. 3

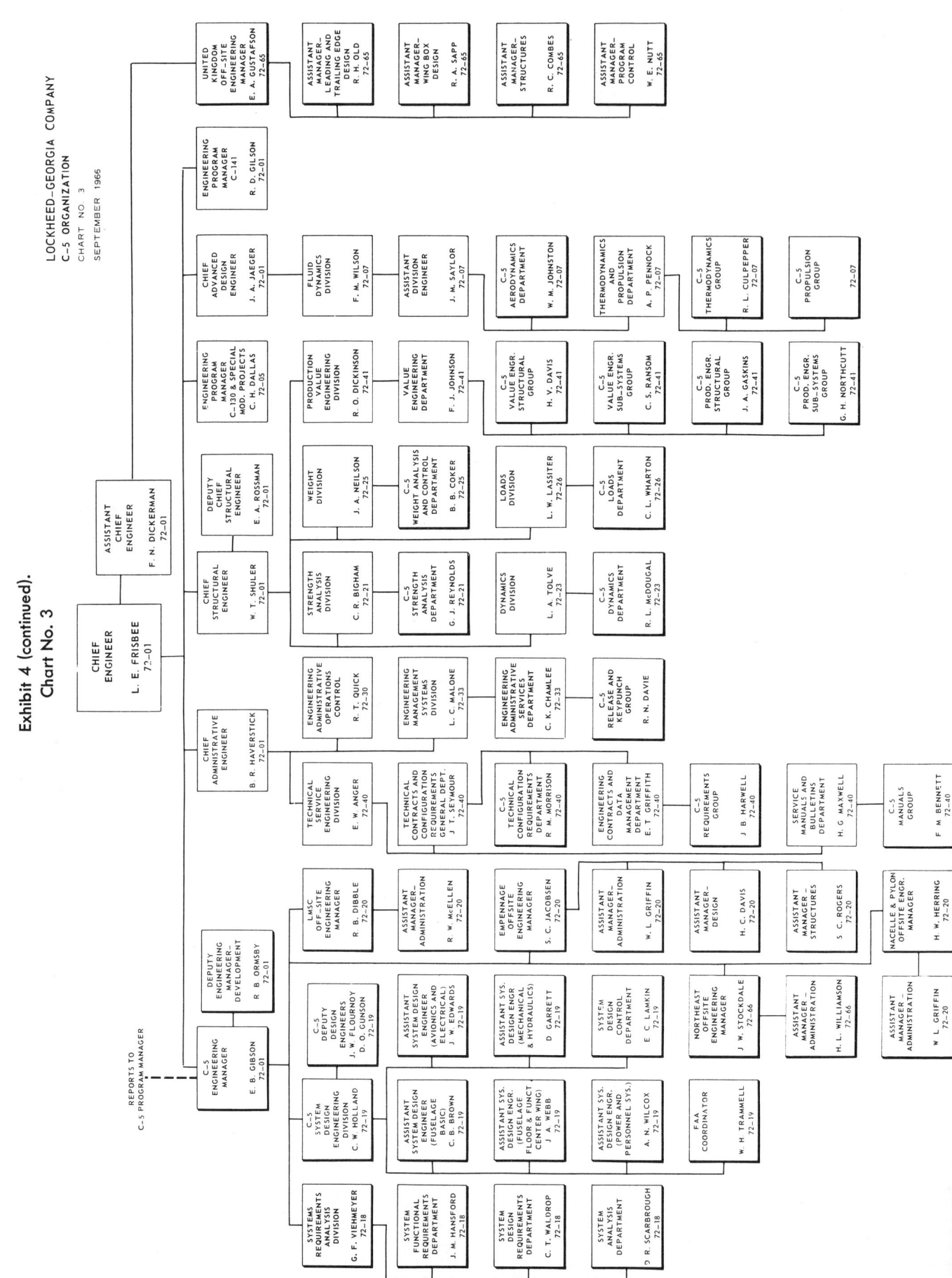

Exhibit 4 (continued).
Chart No. 4

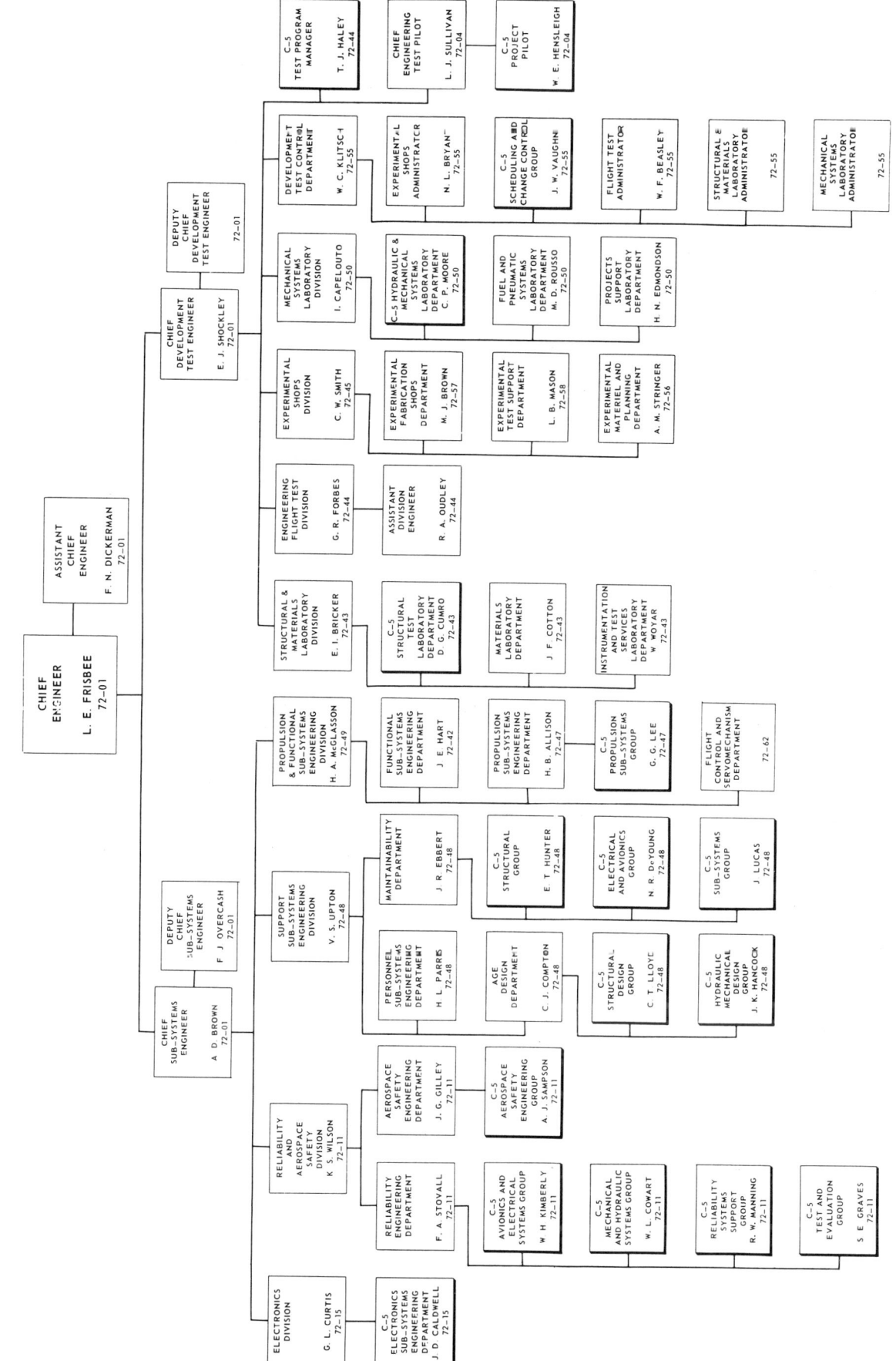

90 Cases and Commentaries

Exhibit 4 (continued).
Chart No. 5

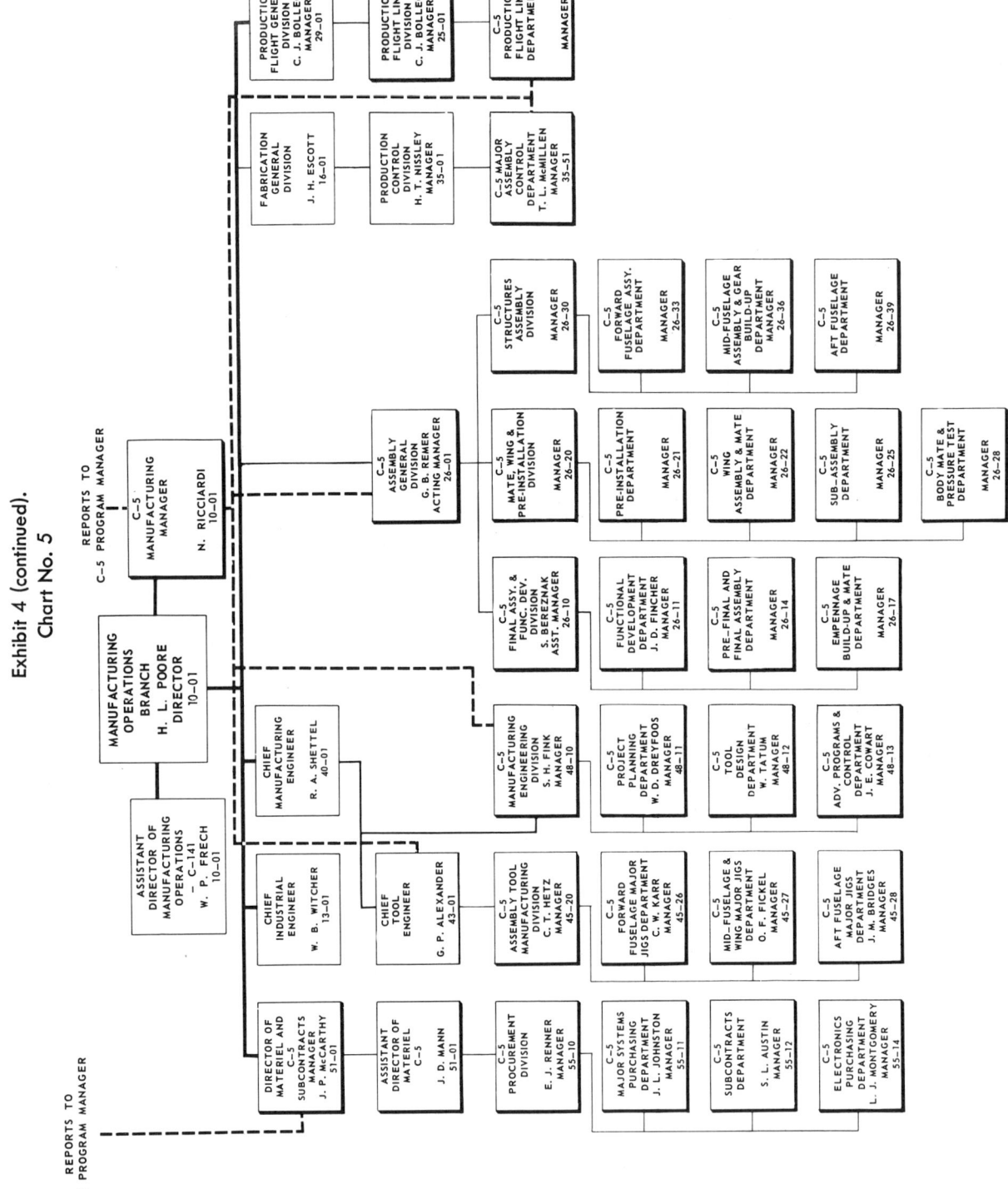

Exhibit 5. List of Slides Used in a Typical C-5A Presentation to the Corporate Steering Committee

Marketing

Program Change Proposal Funding
C-5 Program Schedule: Two Months Ago . . . Today
Engine CDP Schedule
AF Design Requirements Review
Alternative Submittal Strategies
PDP Proposal Preparation Plan and Schedule
Systems Management Plan and Implications
AF-SPO Organization & Gelac Counterpart Plan
Competitors Organization Plans
Gelac Organization Alternatives
Integrated Logistic Support Requirement/Plan
Past and Projected Formal Customer Brrifings
3rd and 4th Quarter Detailed Contact Plan
Sales Activity Review and Plan
AF/DOD Source Selection Procedures
Competitors Aircraft Descriptions and Sales Activities

Engineering

Recommended Design/Payload Analysis with G.E. Engine
Recommended Design/Payload Analysis with P&W Engine
Relative Total System Cost as a Function of Design Cruise Mach Number
Relative Cost of Speed on a Fixed Thrust Basis
Increased Floor Area and Payload Capabilities
Ten-Year Operational Costs for C-5 Fleet
C-5 FAA Certification Status and Plan
C-5 FAA Airport Performance
Configuration of Commercial C-5
High Density Passenger Version
Summary — Direct Operating Costs of Commercial C-5
Advanced Airborne Command Post Configuration
Resized C-5 — G.E. Powered Design
Resized C-5 — P&W Powered Design
Comparison: Aspect Ratio 9 and 7.75 Wings
G.E. Engine Inlet Review
C-5 Landing Gear Flotation
System Engineering Management Plan . . . Control Center
Project Organization Planning
Engineering Control/Costs

Manufacturing

Fuselage Paint Analysis
Relocation of Factory Assembly Area
Proposed Empennage Gantry
Manufacturing Analysis Chart for Aircraft Sections
Master Models: Requirements and Analysis
Tool Engineering Specifications
Flow Charts — Major Airplane Sections
Material Flow Description
Potential C-5 Subcontractors
C-5 Major Subcontracts
C-5 Major Components and Systems
Subcontract Bidding Concepts
Subcontract Bid Evaluation
Competitor Subcontract Activity

Finance

PERT Cost Plan and Model
C-5 Work and Breakdown Structure
Flexible Sharing Ratio Proposal Plan
AF Single Package Procurement Plan
Pricing Status and Schedule

Public Relations

C-5 Public Relations Plan and Schedule
Trade Publication Coverage
Security Restrictions

Exhibit 6. Organization Chart of Engineering Branch, September 1966
Chart No. 1A

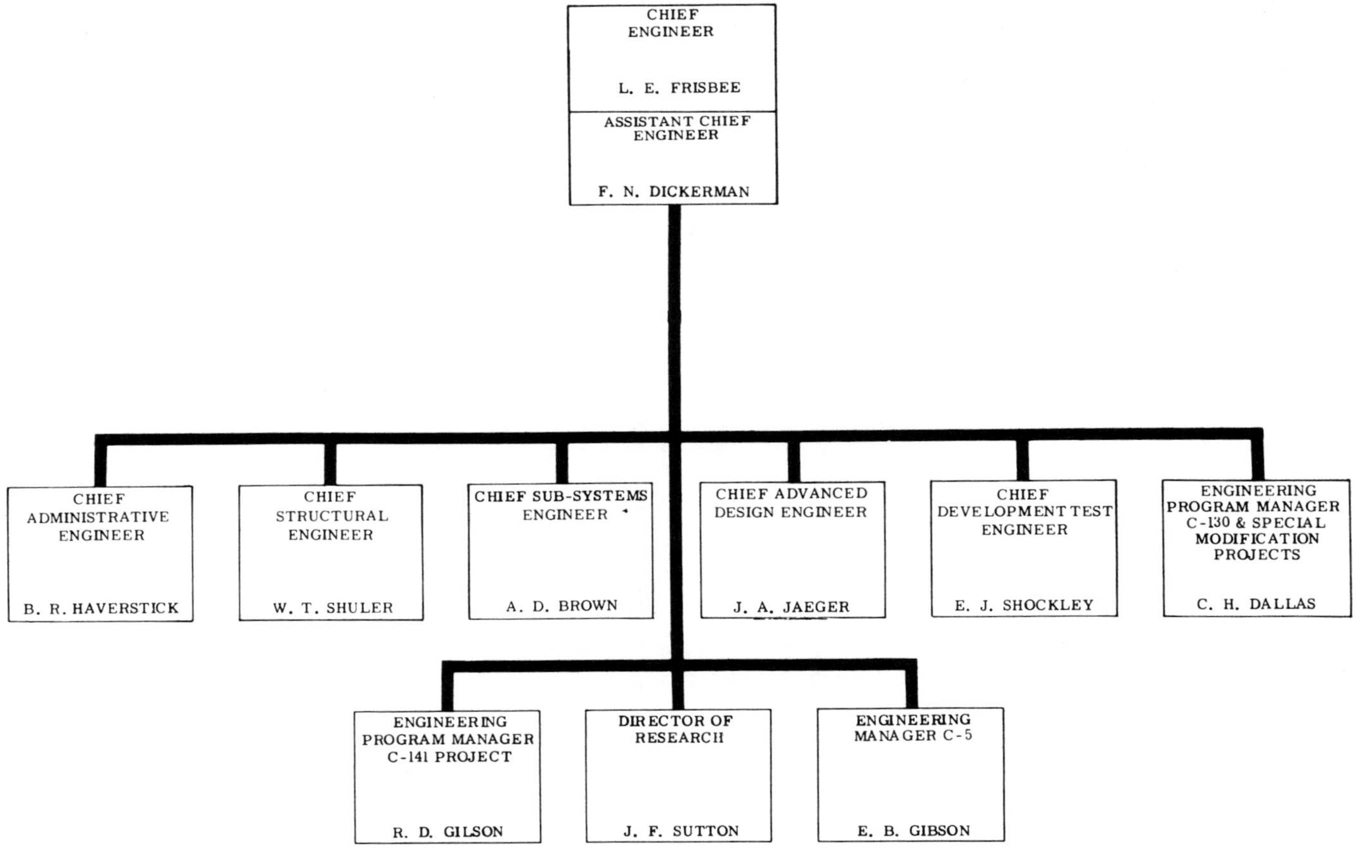

- **CHIEF ENGINEER** — L. E. FRISBEE
- **ASSISTANT CHIEF ENGINEER** — F. N. DICKERMAN
  - **CHIEF ADMINISTRATIVE ENGINEER** — B. R. HAVERSTICK
  - **CHIEF STRUCTURAL ENGINEER** — W. T. SHULER
  - **CHIEF SUB-SYSTEMS ENGINEER** — A. D. BROWN
    - **DIRECTOR OF RESEARCH** — J. F. SUTTON
    - **ENGINEERING PROGRAM MANAGER C-141 PROJECT** — R. D. GILSON
  - **CHIEF ADVANCED DESIGN ENGINEER** — J. A. JAEGER
    - **ENGINEERING MANAGER C-5** — E. B. GIBSON
  - **CHIEF DEVELOPMENT TEST ENGINEER** — E. J. SHOCKLEY
  - **ENGINEERING PROGRAM MANAGER C-130 & SPECIAL MODIFICATION PROJECTS** — C. H. DALLAS

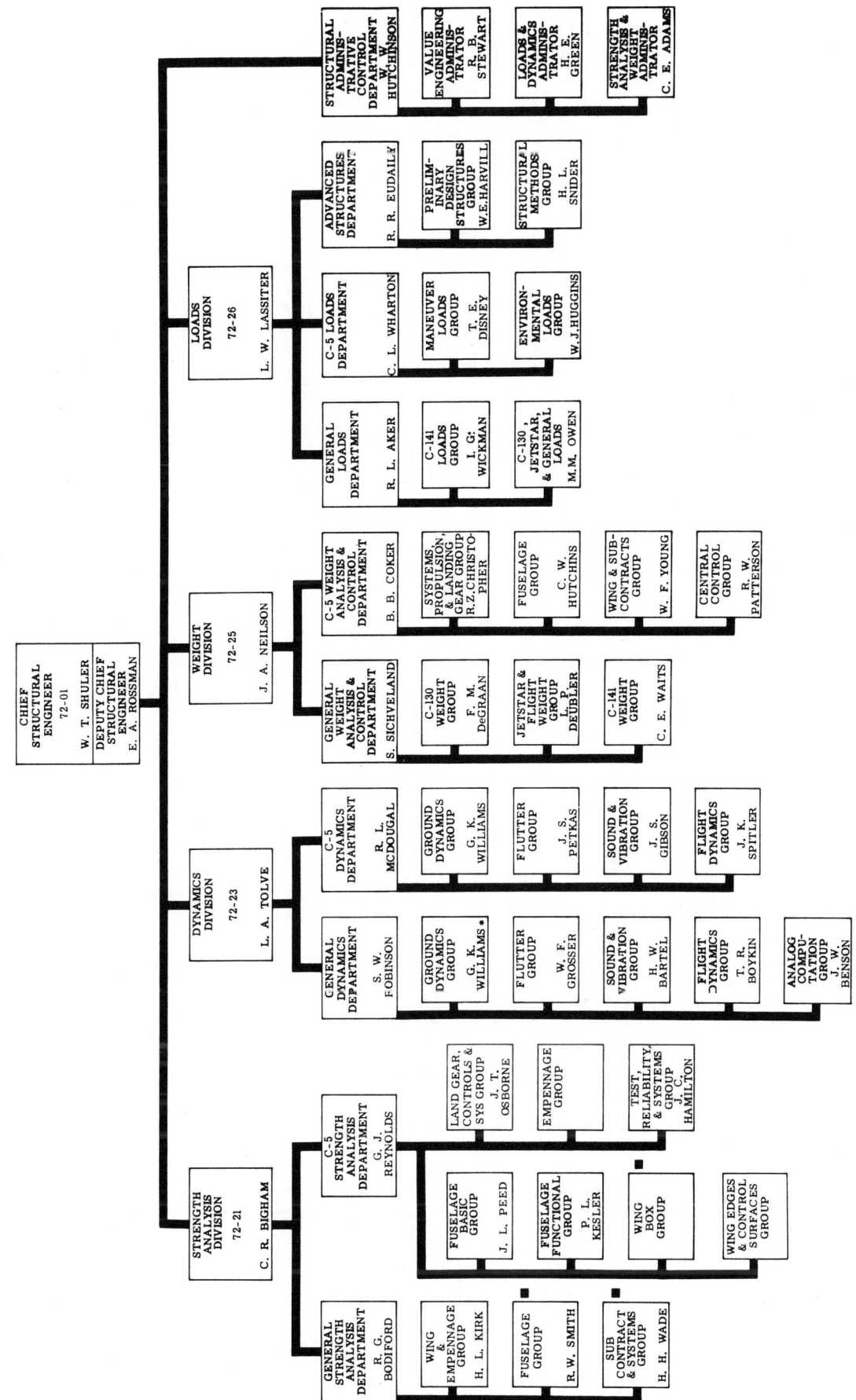

Exhibit 7. Organization Chart of Structural Engineering Branch, September 1966
Chart No. 3A

94 *Cases and Commentaries*

Exhibit 8. Organization Chart of Manufacturing Branch, September 1966

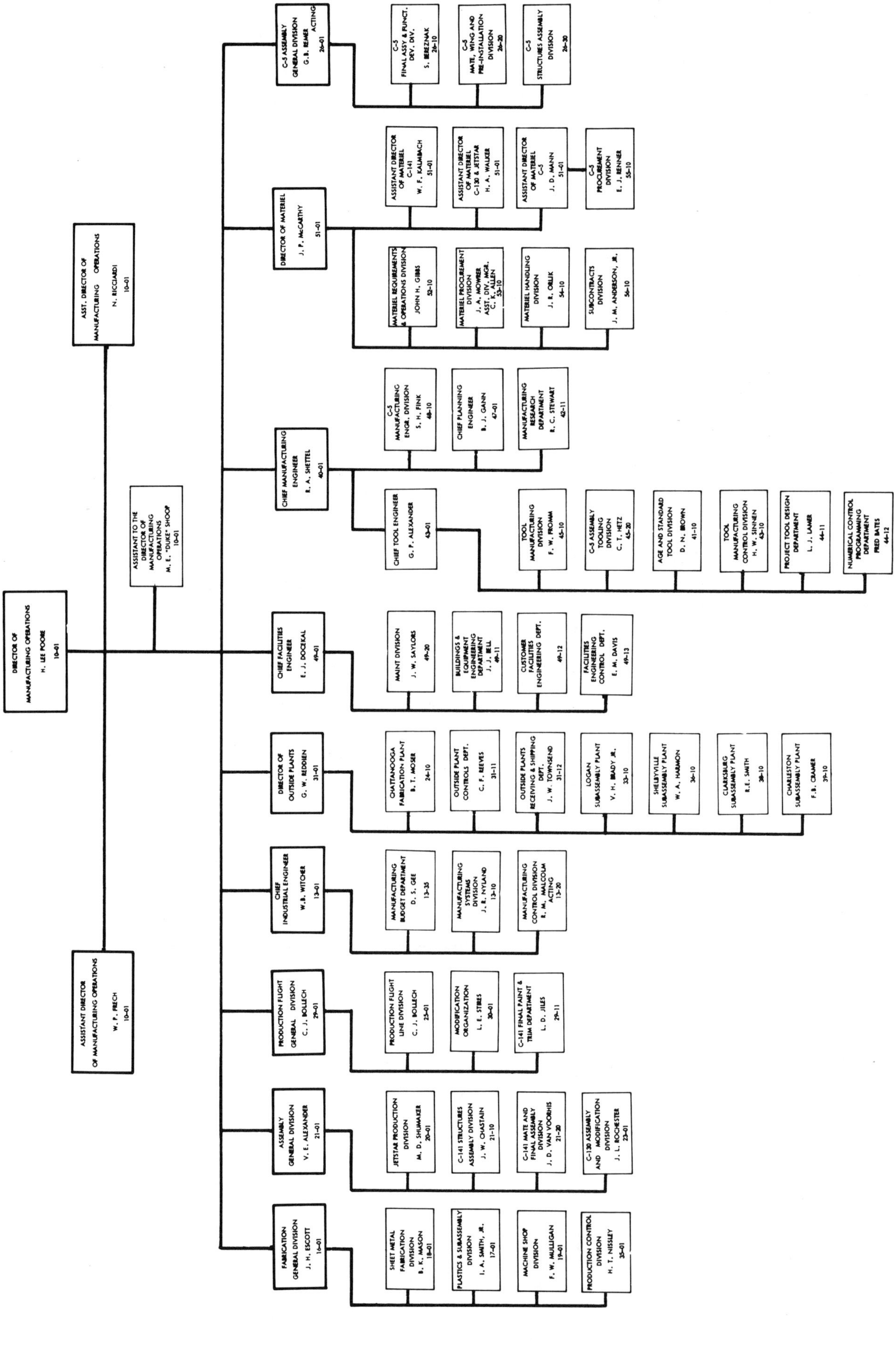

Exhibit 9. Organization Chart of Materiel Section, Manufacturing Branch, September 1966

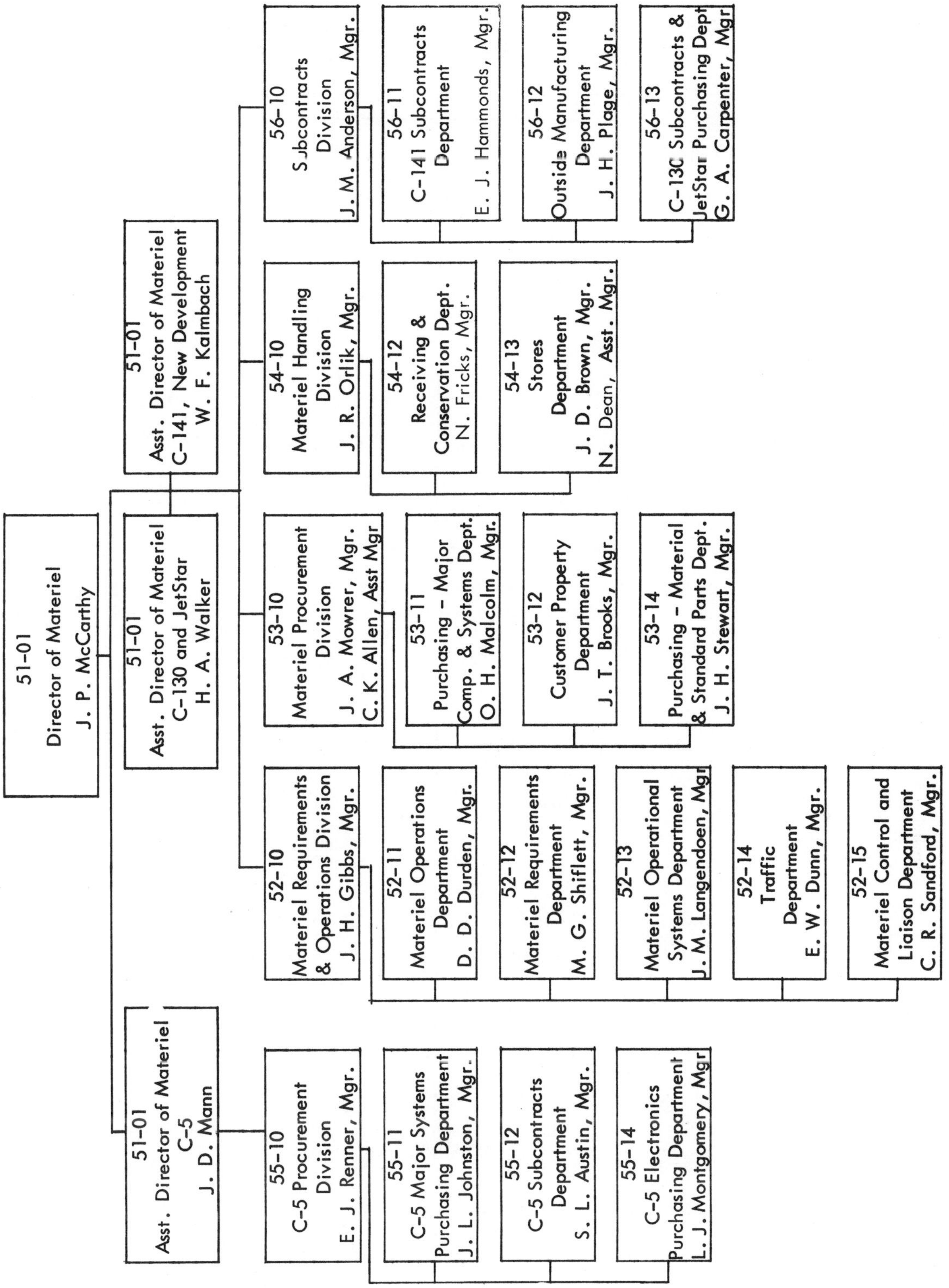

Lockheed-Georgia Company 95

96 *Cases and Commentaries*

Exhibit 10. Organization Chart of Quality Assurance Branch, October 1966
Chart No. 1

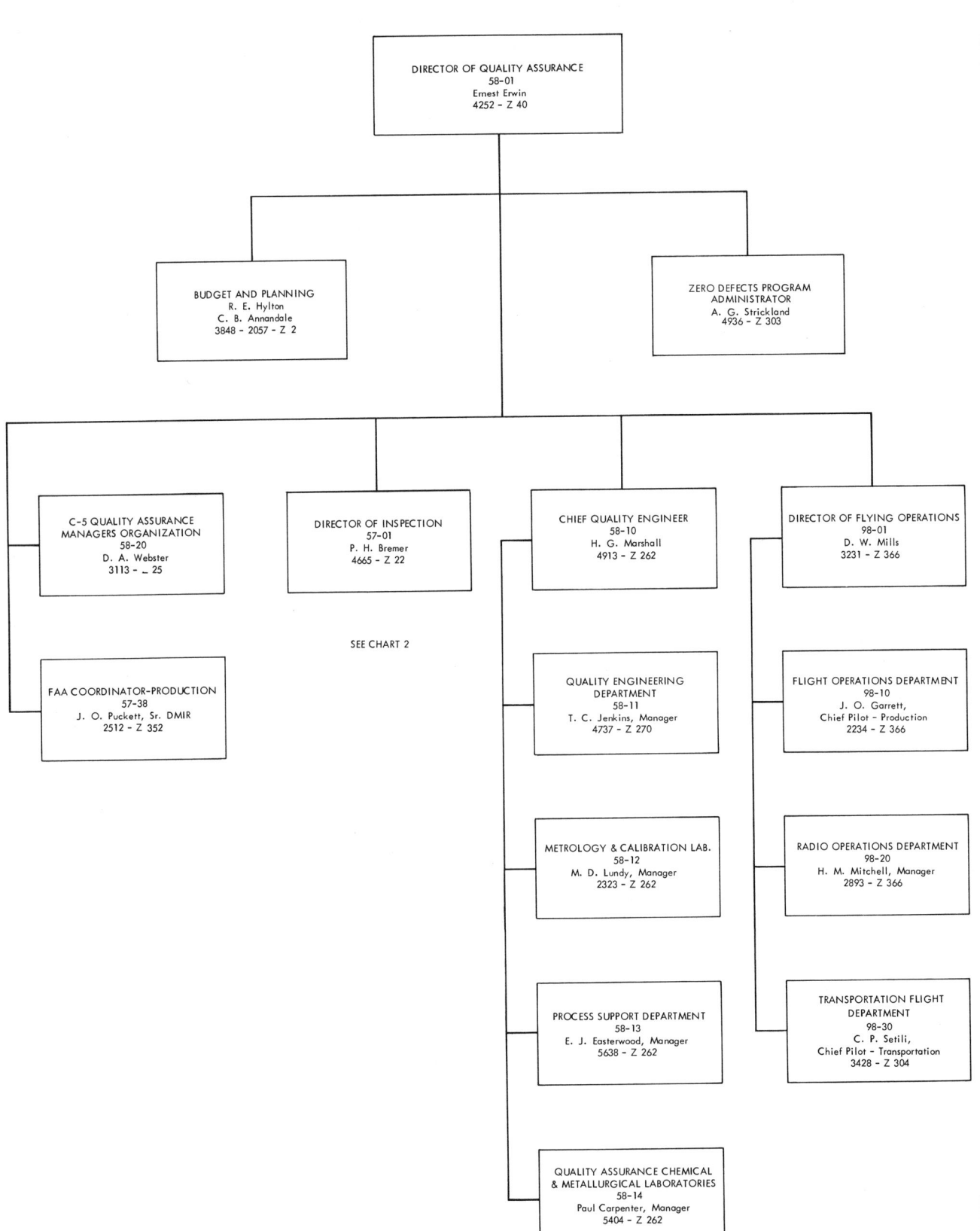

Exhibit 10 (continued).
Chart No. 2

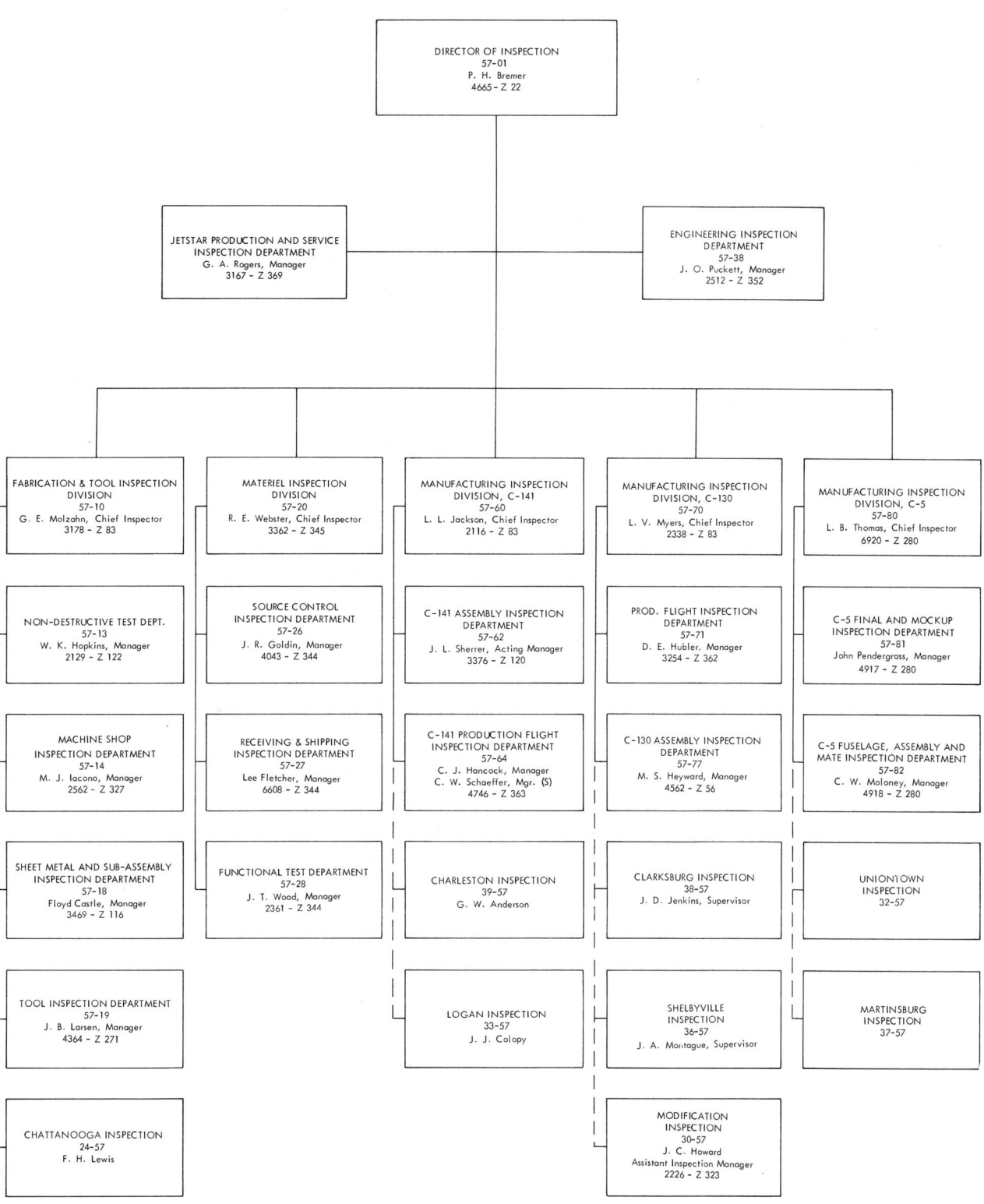

98 *Cases and Commentaries*

Exhibit 11. Organization Chart of Master Scheduling Branch, August 1966

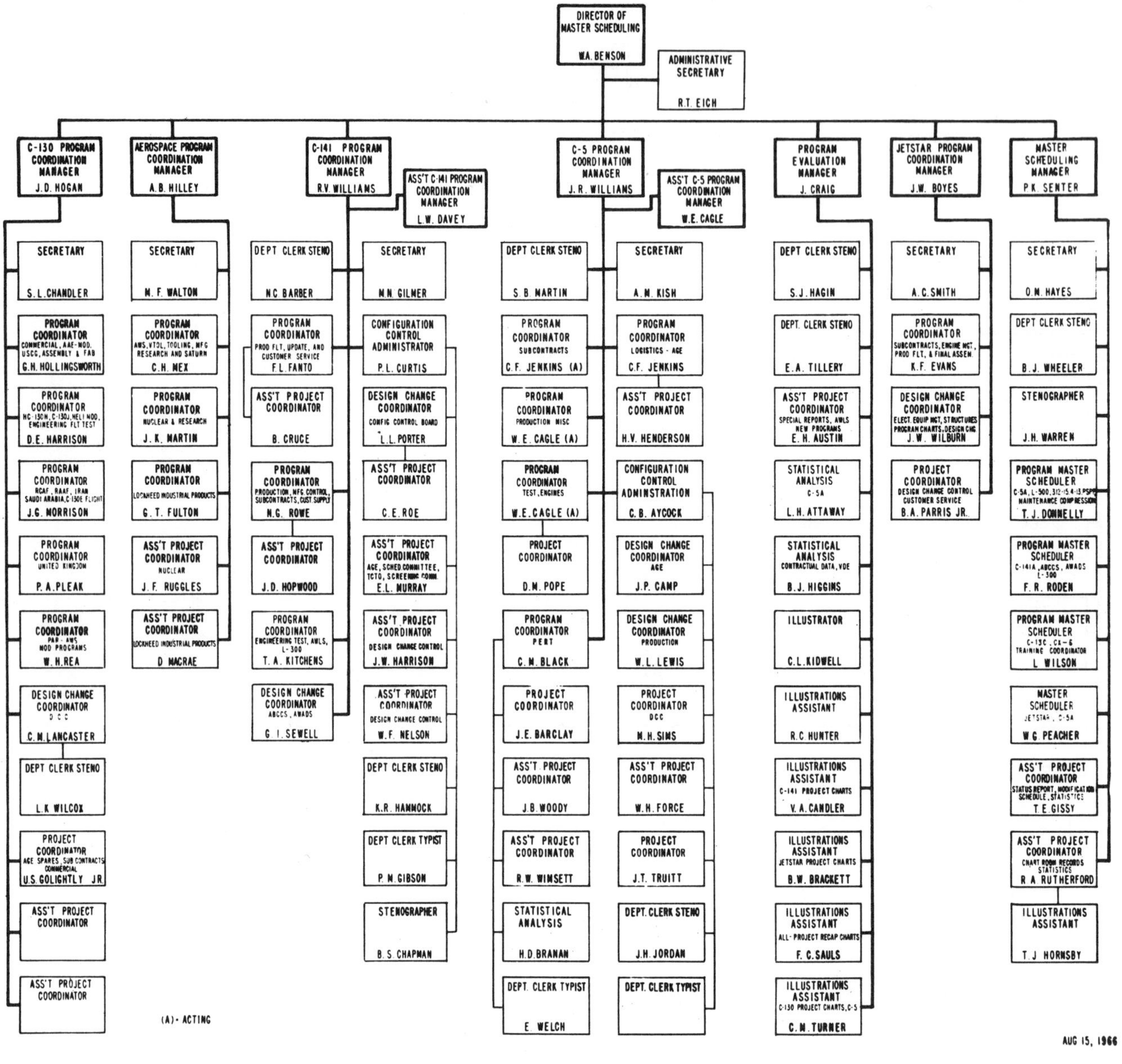

Exhibit 12. Organization Chart of Logistic Support Branch, October 1966

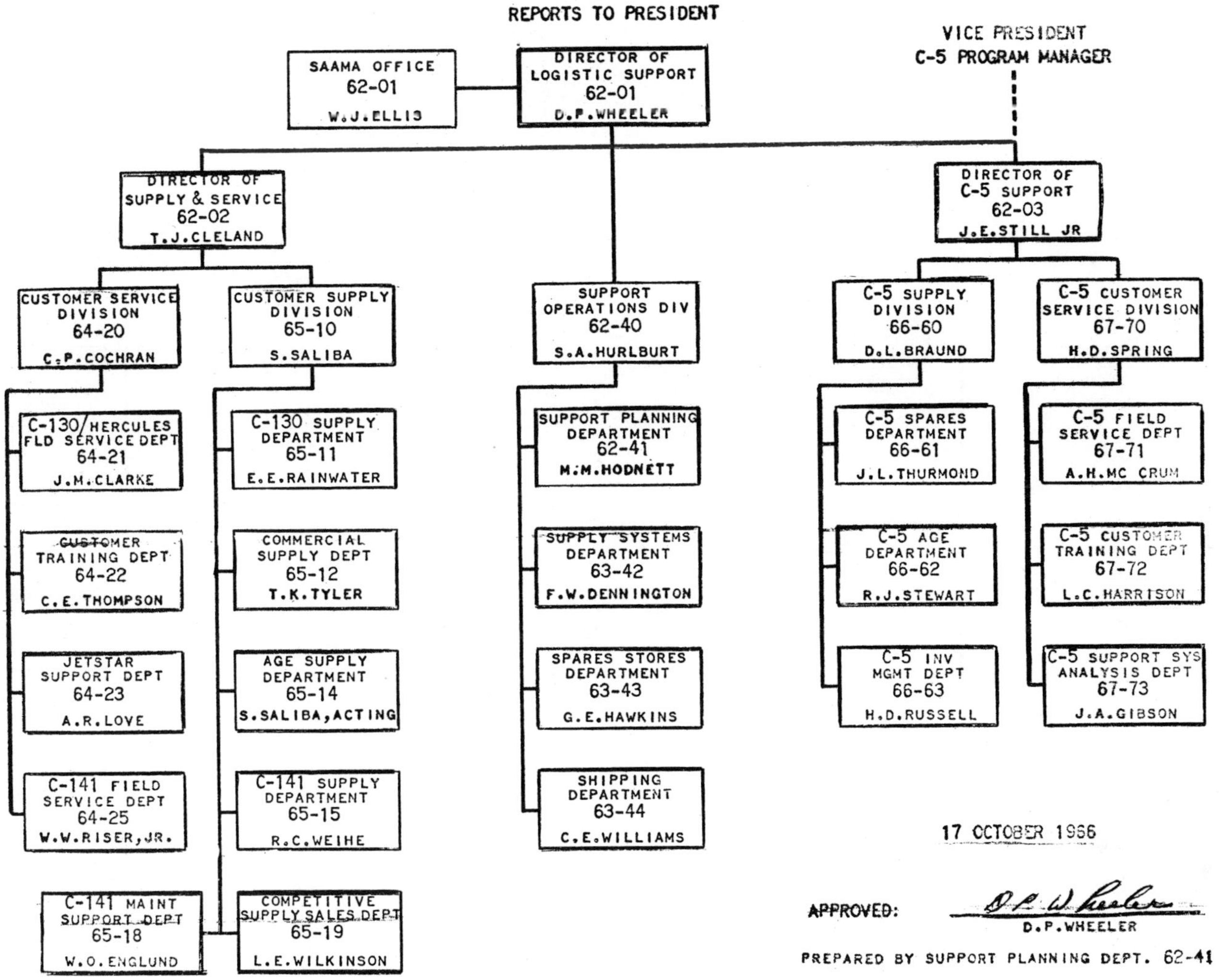

REPORTS TO PRESIDENT

- SAAMA OFFICE 62-01 — W.J. ELLIS
- DIRECTOR OF LOGISTIC SUPPORT 62-01 — D.P. WHEELER
- VICE PRESIDENT C-5 PROGRAM MANAGER

DIRECTOR OF SUPPLY & SERVICE 62-02 — T.J. CLELAND

- CUSTOMER SERVICE DIVISION 64-20 — C.P. COCHRAN
  - C-130/HERCULES FLD SERVICE DEPT 64-21 — J.M. CLARKE
  - CUSTOMER TRAINING DEPT 64-22 — C.E. THOMPSON
  - JETSTAR SUPPORT DEPT 64-23 — A.R. LOVE
  - C-141 FIELD SERVICE DEPT 64-25 — W.W. RISER, JR.
  - C-141 MAINT SUPPORT DEPT 65-18 — W.O. ENGLUND
- CUSTOMER SUPPLY DIVISION 65-10 — S. SALIBA
  - C-130 SUPPLY DEPARTMENT 65-11 — E.E. RAINWATER
  - COMMERCIAL SUPPLY DEPT 65-12 — T.K. TYLER
  - AGE SUPPLY DEPARTMENT 65-14 — S. SALIBA, ACTING
  - C-141 SUPPLY DEPARTMENT 65-15 — R.C. WEIHE
  - COMPETITIVE SUPPLY SALES DEPT 65-19 — L.E. WILKINSON

SUPPORT OPERATIONS DIV 62-40 — S.A. HURLBURT

- SUPPORT PLANNING DEPARTMENT 62-41 — M.M. HODNETT
- SUPPLY SYSTEMS DEPARTMENT 63-42 — F.W. DENNINGTON
- SPARES STORES DEPARTMENT 63-43 — G.E. HAWKINS
- SHIPPING DEPARTMENT 63-44 — C.E. WILLIAMS

DIRECTOR OF C-5 SUPPORT 62-03 — J.E. STILL JR

- C-5 SUPPLY DIVISION 66-60 — D.L. BRAUND
  - C-5 SPARES DEPARTMENT 66-61 — J.L. THURMOND
  - C-5 AGE DEPARTMENT 66-62 — R.J. STEWART
  - C-5 INV MGMT DEPT 66-63 — H.D. RUSSELL
- C-5 CUSTOMER SERVICE DIVISION 67-70 — H.D. SPRING
  - C-5 FIELD SERVICE DEPT 67-71 — A.H. MC CRUM
  - C-5 CUSTOMER TRAINING DEPT 67-72 — L.C. HARRISON
  - C-5 SUPPORT SYS ANALYSIS DEPT 67-73 — J.A. GIBSON

17 OCTOBER 1966

APPROVED: D.P. WHEELER

PREPARED BY SUPPORT PLANNING DEPT. 62-41

100 Cases and Commentaries

Exhibit 13. Organization Chart of Finance Branch, October 1966

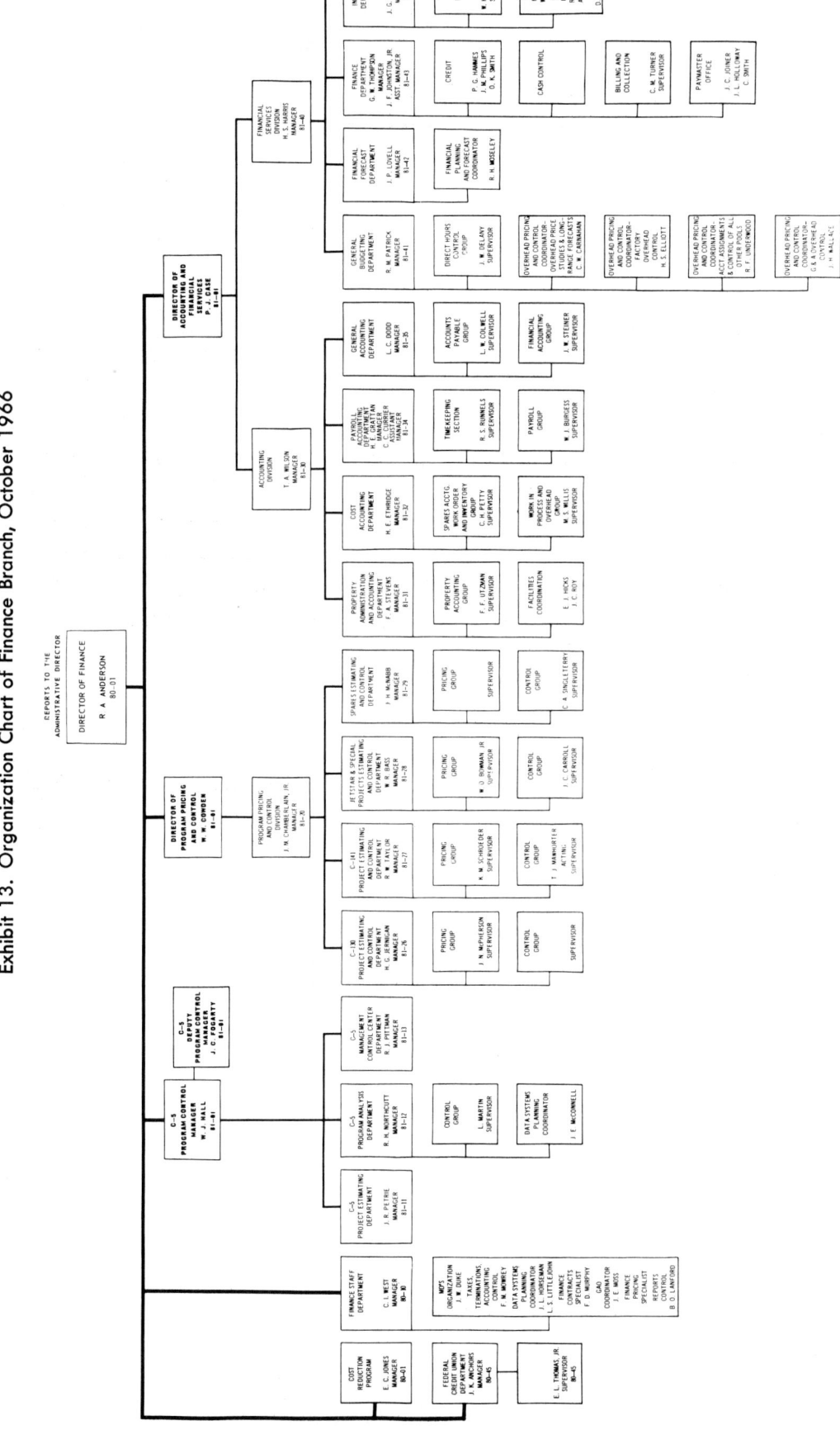

Exhibit 14. Organization Chart of Marketing Branch, August 1966

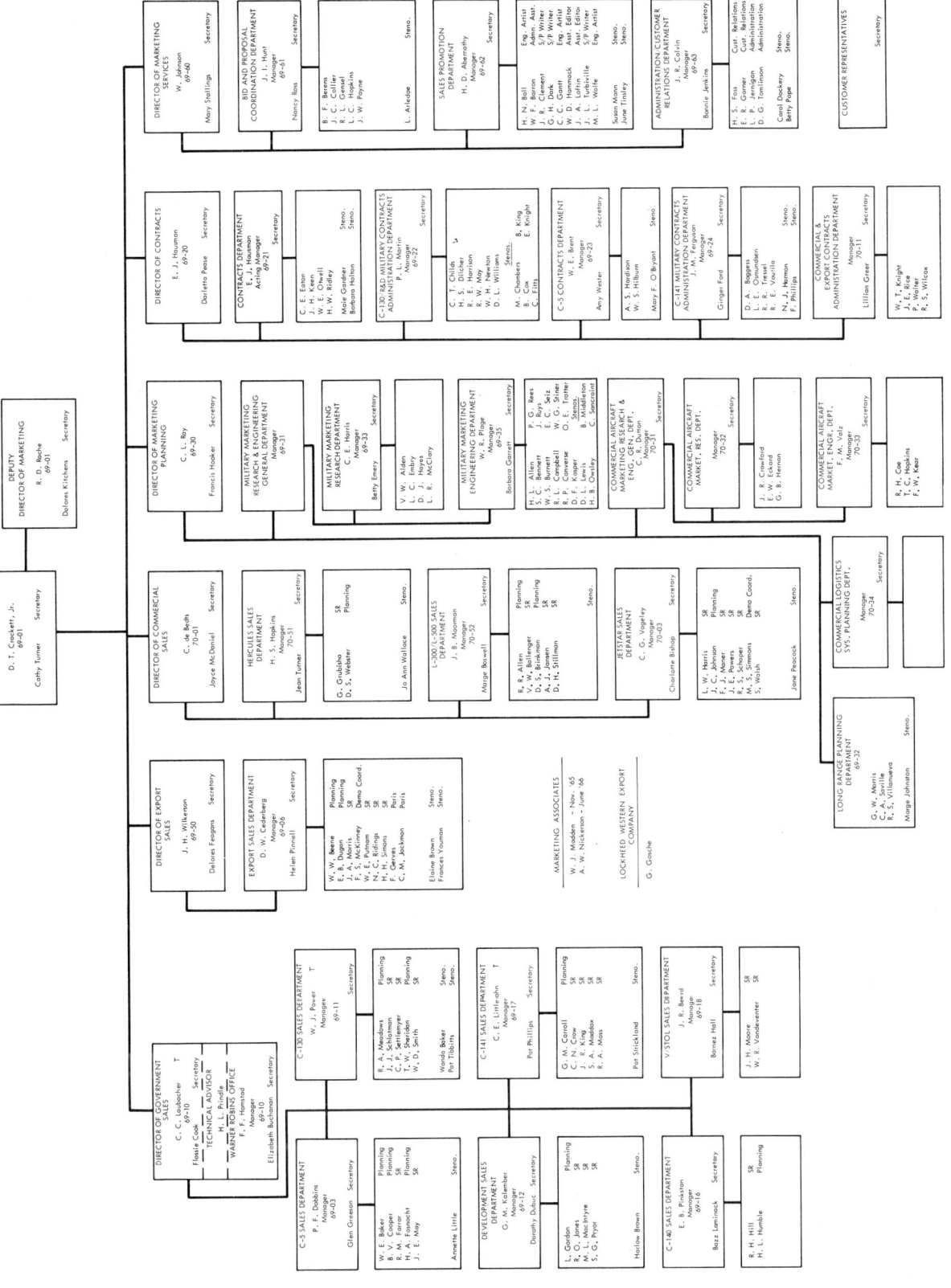

Lockheed-Georgia Company 101

COMMENTARY

Lockheed-Georgia is a business that grew and developed around a facility, Air Force Plant No. 6, which Lockheed Aircraft Corporation contracted to operate in 1951. For almost ten years this plant was essentially used as a production facility for modifying B-29 bombers and building B-47s and C-130s. The B-47 was designed by Boeing and the C-130 by Lockheed-California. In the mid-1950s Gelac was also assigned the Lockheed-California designed JetStar, and this aircraft was further developed by the Georgia division.

With the C-141, however, Gelac became a fully integrated business, self-sufficient in engineering, production, and marketing. As Gelac became an integrated business around 1960, it began to develop a program structure. In the Lockheed-Georgia case history, one can see the emergence of a program structure and can easily trace the influences at work moving Gelac in this direction.

The case then provides some insights on the respective roles of Branch Heads and Program Directors, their degree of authority, and the way they work together. There is, in addition, a useful description of how the resources are allocated to the several programs, and the circumstances under which resource units are "projectized" — assigned exclusively to individual programs.

One organizational problem apparently has troubled the Gelac management — the question of how to organize if the company is to be equally effective in both military and commercial markets. Strongly oriented toward defense production, the company has played a far less important role in the markets for commercial aircraft. Two large competitors, Boeing and Douglas, have been the major suppliers of aircraft to the commercial airlines. Gelac's management foresees the development of large commercial air cargo markets and is concerned about how best to organize in order to compete for a major share of these growing markets.

Factors Leading to a Matrix Structure

A program management unit was first established at Gelac in 1960 for the JetStar. The program was not progressing well. By placing responsibility for the program in the hands of one executive a sharper focus on problems could be achieved. In addition, the JetStar program became more visible to top management. One program director would serve as the source of information on JetStar progress and as a point of control.

A year later, the second program unit was established when Gelac submitted its proposal for the C-141 contract. In this instance the organizational arrangement was made to meet the needs and wishes of the Air Force customer. The Air Force, itself, had just adopted a program management concept. The C-141 program had been assigned to an Air Force Systems Program Office (SPO). It would significantly enhance Gelac's chances for winning the competition to propose establishing a C-141 program management unit in Gelac to work directly with the C-141 SPO team.

In 1962 a C-130 program director was appointed. With the establishment of separate program directors for some programs, it became apparent that other contracts would be at a disadvantage in the competition for resources.

In the case of the C-5A, a program director was formally appointed to head the contract definition phase of the work in the competition with Boeing and Douglas. Again, Gelac stipulated in its proposal to the Air Force customer that if it won the competition, the C-5A contract would be carried out under the direction of a Program Director who, like the JetStar, C-130, and C-141 Program Directors, would be a Vice President. The Program team would be organized to match the C-5A SPO team that had been established. The customer was assured, then, that the C-5A effort would be structured to facilitate close working relationships between the Air Force and Gelac. The customer knew, too, that by virtue of his reporting status, the C-5A Program Director would have sufficient authority within Gelac to "get things done."

There were three reasons, then, for setting up a program structure at Gelac: (1) to focus management attention on a program in trouble (JetStar); (2) to meet the needs of the customer and facilitate working relationships with him (C-141, C-5A); and (3) to avoid placing another program at a disadvantage in competing for resource effort (C-130).

Theoretically, the alternatives to establishing a matrix organization were, on the one hand, to establish each program as a self-contained business unit, with its own resources; and, on the other, to simply attempt to operate the business without a program overlay. What did Gelac gain by adopting a program structure?

The advantages as Gelac's management perceived them were:

1. Efficient utilization of resources: A program structure avoids the costly duplication of skills and physical facilities for each program and facilitates the sharing of scarce resources among the several contracts. It preserves resource integrity, allowing the business to be organized by resource units, each on a large enough scale to operate efficiently.
2. Resource flexibility: As the demands of some programs decline and as needs of others increase, resources could be shifted among programs.
3. Interchange of technical and administrative knowledge: A matrix organization facilitated professional interchange so that useful tools, techniques, and technical knowledge developed for one program could be applied to others.
4. Top management control: Overall division performance could be measured in terms of major programs, giving Gelac's top management the information on which action could be taken to meet Gelac's contractual commitments profitably for the company. In addition, the assignment of responsibility to Program Directors for program performance and to Branch Heads for resource efficiency established a high level check-and-balance system.
5. Customer relations: Program Directorates paralleled Air Force Systems Program Offices, facilitating working relationships with the customer's organization. This is an especially important consideration in a development contract, because the work is necessarily shaped as it progresses by knowledge of customer requirements, on the one hand, and technical feasibility, on the other.

Role and Authority of Program Directors

It is useful to note that the Program Directors did not directly control the resources working on their respective contracts. Only a secretary and perhaps an assistant reported to each Program Director, the case study indicates. Instead, he chaired a program team made up of the managers in each of the branches who were assigned directly to his program. The Program Director was responsible for making plans, monitoring progress, and taking action through members of the program team to resolve problems.

Program Directors had high organizational status, a fact that undoubtedly reflects the customer's insistence that program heads be at a high level and able to speak and act for top management. Program Directors were Vice Presidents, having the authority of the President as it applied to their respective programs. Branch Heads were Directors, lower in organizational status. In theory the Program Directors could instruct the Branch Heads. In practice, the Program Directors worked through their teams. In cases of interprogram conflicts for branch resources, the Branch Head, in effect, negotiated with the Program Directors concerned to make trade-offs.

Although the Program Directors did not have line authority, they were, in fact, responsible for directing the program, according to the statement in the C-5A proposal. Their ability to carry out this responsibility stemmed from the influence they exercised as Vice Presidents. It also derived in large part through their working relationships with "projectized" personnel in the branches. A "projectized" manager recognized a dual reporting relationship and worked at serving his Program Director as well as his Branch Head. It is significant that the C-141 Program Director referred to personnel in the branches who were working on his project as "my people."

Role and Authority of Branch Heads

The Branch Heads controlled the resources: engineering, manufacturing, quality assurance, procurement. They allocated resources to programs. Their authority in this area is evidenced by the comment of the AWACS Program Manager who had to convince Branch Heads to assign resources to his program: "It's one thing to get the money and another to get the men."

Branch Heads recognized, however, that they worked for the several programs and sensed a split responsibility. As the Director of Manufacturing said: "It may be true that a dog can serve only one master, but most of us, fortunately, are more intelligent than a dog." The Branch Heads clearly functioned as balance wheels, shifting resources to meet, within the limits of their capabilities, the needs of the programs and at the same time attempting to utilize their resources efficiently.

The Branch Heads were directly responsible for development, performance evaluation, compensation, and advancement of personnel in their branches. They were also concerned with the longer-run growth of the facilities, technical skills, and manpower of their branches to serve the business.

In all of this, one might well ask what role was left for the President. He is described as not involving himself directly in operations; he was concerned, instead, with planning, product policy, organization, executive development, and relations with Gelac's customers, suppliers, and the community in which it operated.

Projectizing Resources

In the branch organizations certain resource units were allocated directly to individual programs, others worked on several or all programs. It is interesting to note the considerations that seemed to bear on decisions to "projectize" resource units or to leave them "unprojectized." In the manufacturing branch, heavy machine tool centers had to serve all programs if they were to be utilized fully. On the other hand, it was logical to projectize assembly operations in the manufacturing branch since there were assembly lines for each aircraft, the JetStar, C-130, and C-141.

In Materiel, a Procurement Division purchased standard items and was unprojectized, but the Subcontracts Division was responsible for procuring major subassemblies and had separate departments for JetStar, C-130, and C-141. C-5A had its own procurement and subcontracting departments under an assistant director reporting to the Director of Materiel.

By having a single procurement operation for off-the-shelf items, Gelac's purchasing power with vendors was enhanced. On the other hand, by projectizing subassembly procurement, Gelac personnel could work effectively with subcontractors on the technical and engineering problems of subassemblies uniquely designed for specific aircraft. Moreover, contractual relationships with these vendors tended to be complex.

In Engineering, resource units were projectized at various levels. The larger the program, the higher the level of projectization was, because the level of effort called for correspondingly large resource commitments. Even so, some highly specialized units, such as the advanced structures department, were not projectized and worked on all programs as needed.

A major consideration, then, was the economic use of resources. If the capacity of an economically efficient unit was greater than could be fully utilized by a single program, it was not projectized. This would be true of a heavy press, for example, or a 50-man technical engineering unit such as the Advanced Structures Department.

Program-unique functions, such as subassembly procurement and production assembly operations, were projectized. Program-common functions, such as standard parts procurement, were not projectized. And in the latter case, the function had more bargaining power vis-à-vis outside vendors through the consolidation of purchasing of "off-the-shelf" items for all projects.

In structuring the sales function in the marketing branch, Gelac's management was torn between organizing primarily by customer group (government, commercial, and export) and organizing by product. Before mid-1966, there had been a separate JetStar Sales Division but after that point JetStar sales were subsumed under the three customer categories.

Major differences in purchasing behavior, in spare parts service requirements, and in product specifications on the part of government, commercial, and export customers would argue strongly for a basic specialization by customer group. Two considerations might lead alternatively to a product specialization, at least in part. One would be the need to give adequate attention to a relatively small program (JetStar). The second would be the desires of Program Directors to have projectized sales organizations for their respective aircraft. Thus the C-130 Program Director favored a single C-130 sales unit for all customers, arguing that it was important for sales representatives to have detailed product knowledge. By implication, product-specialized sales representatives could be more effective than ones having in-depth customer knowledge. The argument had to do only with commercial and export sales where the selling function was unprojectized and not with government sales, which were divided into product sales departments.

As a matter of organization strategy, one might note that the timing of resource specialization was a critical factor. Usually, new programs were initiated in the "general" or unprojectized resource units until the level of effort became so large as to call for a formal program structure. Branch Heads had far more flexibility in deploying unprojectized units as needs arose and would not then commit them to specific programs until it was clear that the program would in fact materialize and would call for a significant level of effort.

In the case of the C-5A, the timing of the build-up of the program team was credited with being an important factor in Lockheed's success in winning the bid. Had the build-up come too soon, management believed, Gelac might have developed design concepts prematurely and become committed to them before customer thinking had fully taken shape.

Resource Allocation

A major problem area in the operation of a matrix organization is the allocation of branch resources to programs. In this case the problem is all the more critical because the work was far from routinized and called for close coordination of the work of the several branches. The scheduling of resource effort for each program is both complicated and critical.

At the highest levels, program budgets serve to indicate the relative amount of effort each branch is to expend on each program. At operating levels, resource effort is allocated in the short run through formalized scheduling procedures. In the Master Scheduling Branch, one department was responsible for maintaining an overall schedule of work on all projects. There was also a program coordination department for each project; these were concerned with scheduling in the branches to meet target dates. The Master Scheduling Branch had to balance a concern for the efficient utilization of Gelac resources with the need to meet the company's various contractual commitments. Personnel in Master Scheduling, then, often negotiated trade-offs with program coordination managers in the utilization of branch resources. Interprogram conflicts that could not be resolved at this level were noted in weekly reports by program coordination managers to all Program Directors, Branch Managers, and other top corporate executives. This procedure served to assure that top management attention was quickly drawn to important schedule and cost deficiencies. The case indicates, however, that few interprogram conflicts had to be passed up to this management level for resolution.

Thus, because the allocation of resource effort was very complicated and because interbranch coordination by programs was critical, scheduling was established as a separate function. This function included units, on the one hand, responsible for the efficient utilization of Gelac resources, and, on the other, units concerned with the successful completion of each program. Working in physical proximity, managers of these units were constantly involved in making trade-offs. Interprogram conflicts for the use of resources were settled usually at this level and direct confrontations among Program Directors and Branch Heads were avoided.

Organizing for Commercial and Military Markets

At three points in the case Gelac executives indicated a concern that the company was not organized to deal as effectively with commercial markets as with military. One Program Director suggested that Gelac might well have a Vice President for all commercial programs, responsible for developing and selling commercial counterparts of military products. Another executive spoke of having a large "commercial" division in each of the "dominant" branches and possibly having the commercial divisions report to a Vice President, Commercial Programs.

Such a move would recognize that commercial aircraft are designed and engineered differently from military aircraft and that customer purchasing procedures, motivations, and decision-making processes are similarly quite different. It is difficult for one organization to be equally responsive to the needs of two such different types of customers. It will tend, therefore, to become oriented more toward one group than the other. This orientation is likely to go beyond the sales function and to extend to engineering, manufacturing, procurement, and logistics as well, since tight coordination among these branches is needed in aircraft development, production, and servicing.

One might speculate that establishing a new business unit, comparable to Gelac itself, for commercial contracts would provide an even better framework for competing in commercial markets. Such an arrangement would provide a single market focus throughout the business from the top management on down. But a significant base of commercial business would be needed to support such an arrangement, and until that materialized, work on commercial contracts would necessarily have to share the resources being utilized predominantly by government contracts. In the meantime, having large commercial units in the branches and a Commercial Vice President would give top management visibility and organizational thrust to the effort to build commercial sales.

Summary

The Gelac case suggests a range of pressures leading toward the development of a program overlay: one contract needed close top management attention because it was in difficulty; another needed to be organized as a program to provide close integration with the cognizant Air Force Systems Program Office; another needed a program management to assure that it received the resources it needed in competition with the other programs.

As the Lockheed-Georgia management perceived it, the matrix structure helped to assure resource flexibility, a focus for management control, resource integrity and efficiency, and close working relations with the military customer.

Program Directors did not directly control the resources working on their respective projects. But they had authority commensurate with their responsibility both because of their status as Vice Presidents and because they worked with "projectized" personnel in the branches, assigned directly to their programs.

Branch Heads balanced the needs of the several programs in allocating resources to each. They were responsible, in the short run, for the efficient utilization of the resources they managed. In the long run, they were charged with developing resource strength and capability to meet the needs of the business.

In the branches, resource units were "projectized" when (1) a resource unit, large enough to be complete and efficient, could be fully utilized by a single program and (2) the resource function was unique for that program.

The allocation of resource effort to programs was complicated by the need to integrate closely the work of the several branches by programs and by the frequent changes in the needs of individual programs as technical design, schedule, and cost parameters were shifted. This function was handled on a day-to-day basis by the Master Scheduling Branch. Master Scheduling, working through representatives of both the branches and the programs, was involved in making the trade-offs that kept Gelac's contractual commitments in balance. Interprogram conflicts that could not be resolved at this level could then be isolated for top management attention.

The need for having a separate scheduling function, located outside of the engineering, manufacturing, logistics, and marketing branches, is to be explained by the fact that Gelac's work was largely developmental, requiring an unusual degree of coordination of functional effort.

International Business Machines Corporation: Data Processing Division

The International Business Machines Corporation (IBM) is the world's largest manufacturer of data processing systems and related products. Sales for 1966 of $4.2 billion placed IBM ninth in *Fortune*'s annual listing of the 500 largest U.S. corporations. Sales had increased sharply over 1965 volume of $3.6 billion, and profits after taxes had grown from $477 million in 1965 to $526 million in 1966. (For a ten-year financial summary, see Exhibit 1.)

The story of IBM's growth is one of the most exciting chapters in the history of American industrial enterprise. Before World War II, IBM was the acknowledged leader in the punched card tabulating field, but sales had reached only $53 million in 1939. During the war IBM began to develop concepts that would eventually lead to the data processing revolution of the 1950s, but company management believed that the sales potential of the computer was severely limited. In the late 1940s, when the true potential of the computer was finally realized, IBM found itself significantly behind several major competitors.

The 1950s were a decade of intense competition. IBM came up from behind, and according to trade sources,[1] obtained an estimated 80% market share by the end of the decade. In achieving its dominant position IBM stressed commercial rather than scientific applications, with emphasis on medium-sized business computers such as the highly successful 1400 series, which was introduced in 1959.

The early 1960s were marked by a resurgence of competition, as several major manufacturers either concentrated their resources on market segments IBM had not emphasized (e.g., small scientific computers) or attempted to meet IBM head on in the general business computer field. At the same time, significant changes were taking place in computer technology. The following changes seem most significant for our present purposes:

[1] See *Forbes*, July 1, 1962, p. 28.

(1) Cost/performance ratios improved considerably during the late 1950s and early 1960s. Each "generation" of computers was much faster than its predecessors, and had significantly more data storage capability. Nevertheless, to the extent direct comparisons are possible, each new generation sold or rented for a lower price than its predecessor.

(2) As computer technology advanced, an ever-increasing number of applications were developed. Where computers had previously been used primarily for solving mathematical problems and carrying out fairly routine accounting procedures, they were now also used for such diverse applications as on-line process control, typesetting, and logistics management. Moreover, it was generally agreed that the range of application possibilities would continue to increase markedly through the 1960s and 1970s.

(3) To an increasing extent, machine independent programming languages were becoming an essential ingredient in computer marketing. These languages were user-oriented rather than machine-oriented, and were thus easier to work with than the older machine language had been. During the 1950s it had been necessary to have highly skilled programming competence at virtually all data processing installations. After the development and refinement of machine independent programming languages such as COBOL and FORTRAN, the customer generally expected to require a lower level of programming competence. Moreover, COBOL or FORTRAN, once learned, could be used to program a number of different types of computers.

(4) Type II programs were also growing in importance. These programs, which were generally developed by the computer manufacturer, could be used by the customer with relatively few modifications. Typical Type II programs were used for linear programming, PERT, typesetting, and certain accounting applications.

(5) Program compatibility became increasingly important as customers came to realize that the cost of writing new programs for a new computer installation could often be as large as the cost of the equip-

ment itself. IBM's System/360, which was introduced in 1964, was designed in such a way that a customer could shift from one model to another (as his requirements changed) without major reprogramming. Moreover, in many cases it was possible to replace previous generation computers (e.g., the 1401) without major reprogramming.

(6) Tele-processing (i.e., direct communication between computers, or between a central computer and outlying terminals) had become a reality by the early 1960s. Consequently, it was increasingly important that the various types of data processing equipment purchased by a customer be completely compatible with each other.

Developments such as those listed above had significant implications for IBM's strategy and organization. The present case focuses primarily on IBM's marketing organization, the Data Processing Division (DPD). It first traces the historical development of the IBM corporate structure and the organization of the Data Processing Division. It continues with a description of the organization of the Data Processing Division in early 1966 and then focuses on the processes through which line and staff personnel worked together to develop new products and applications and to increase sales.

Development of the IBM Corporate Structure

1954 Structure

Prior to 1954 IBM was organized on a functional basis. Five line departments (Manufacturing, Finance, Service, Sales, and Engineering) and eight staff departments (Product Planning and Market Analysis, Electronic Data Processing Machinery Development, Counsel, Budgets, Personnel, Defense Contracts, Economic Research, and *Think* magazine) reported directly to IBM President Thomas J. Watson, Jr. Exhibit 2 shows the corporate organization chart as of May 1954.

During this period, IBM had three major product lines: (1) electric typewriters, (2) electric accounting machines, and (3) time equipment. In general, each department carried out its function for all three product lines, except that all international activities were handled by a separate subsidiary, the IBM World Trade Corporation.

The field sales and service organization was divided into 14 districts, which supervised the activities of 187 branches. The district managers reported to both the Sales Department and the Service Department, and were responsible for selling and servicing the entire IBM product line.

1954–1956

In November 1954 two executive vice presidents were appointed. One was responsible for data processing manufacturing and accounting, and for corporate finance, personnel, and legal matters. The other was responsible for data processing product development, planning, service, sales, and education, and for corporate research, education, and recruiting. The appointment of the two executive vice presidents was intended to lighten the president's work load, speed up decision making, and improve top management's ability to arrive at proper corporate decisions in complex matters.

During 1955 and 1956 IBM retained its basically functional structure but split out divisions responsible for military products, electric typewriters, supplies, and the Service Bureau Corporation.[2] The functional department managers now concentrated their efforts on the growing data processing business and the time equipment business, reporting to President Watson through the two executive vice presidents. Exhibit 3 shows the Corporate Organization Chart as of June 1956.

Weaknesses of the 1954 Organization

An internal memorandum, drawn up in 1956, cited six major weaknesses of the IBM organization:

(1) The size and complexity of the business placed a very heavy load on the president and the two executive vice presidents. Management of the company was concentrated in the hands of these three men.
(2) Division of responsibility for data processing between the two executive vice presidents created the necessity for constant consultation between the two and for adjudication of interfunctional issues by the president. More issues were forced to the top for decision than should have been, and more divided responsibility existed than was reasonable in a business as large as IBM.
(3) Decision making was slowed to the point where operations were being impeded.
(4) Controls and measurement of performance were inadequate.
(5) Forward planning was notably lacking.
(6) The staff concept was not adequately recognized or developed.

---

[2] The Service Bureau Corporation operated facilities that processed customers' data in accordance with a published schedule of fees.

In early 1956 Mr. Watson decided to retain a management consulting firm to study the IBM organizational structure. At the same time, he appointed two executives to work with the consultants and implement whatever organizational changes were decided upon.

The Williamsburg Conference

The consulting firm presented its report in July 1956. During the next several months IBM's top management devoted almost full time to analyzing the report and making plans for implementation. By November a new plan of organization had been agreed upon; in its major ingredients, it followed the consultant's recommendations. On November 28 the new organization was announced to more than 100 members of IBM's management at a conference held in Williamsburg, Virginia.

The new organization, shown in Exhibit 4, established four operating groups: (1) a single division (given group status) responsible for all domestic data processing activities; (2) the IBM World Trade Corporation (also given group status); (3) a group containing the Electric Typewriter Division and the Supplies Division; and (4) a group containing the Military Products Division, the Service Bureau Corporation, the Time Equipment Division, and the Special Engineering Products Division.[3] A separate corporate staff group was responsible for all corporate staff functions except organization, executive development, and budgets, which were established as corporate departments reporting directly to the president. The two executive vice presidents became the heads of the Data Processing Division and the Corporate Staff group respectively. They joined the three other group executives and President Watson on the corporate management committee, which reviewed key operating proposals and developed policies and plans for the corporation as a whole.

According to IBM executives, the new organization accomplished several major objectives: (1) it completely separated executive responsibility for line and staff functions, which had been shared by the two executive vice presidents; (2) it divided operations into manageable segments and consolidated the previously divided data processing business; (3) it integrated domestic and international activities more closely; and (4) it provided a basic structure suitable for growth.

---

[3] The Special Engineering Products Division designed and built custom designed hardware on a special-order basis.

1959 Reorganization

The Williamsburg organization continued essentially unchanged until May 1959. By that time the data processing business had grown so significantly that it was no longer considered a manageable segment of the company's business. In essence, the manager of the Data Processing Division was confronted with problems similar to those which had led to the 1956 reorganization. For example, Data Processing Division sales in 1959 were greater than total corporate sales in 1955.

The 1959 reorganization divided the Data Processing Division into four divisions: (1) the General Products Division, which was to develop and manufacture small data processing systems and unit record equipment; (2) the Data Systems Division, which was to develop and manufacture large data processing systems; (3) the Advanced Systems Development Division, which was to identify new market opportunities and develop specifications for advanced data processing systems; and (4) the Data Processing Division, which was responsible for all domestic data processing sales and customer service.

Under the new organization (see Exhibit 5), the data processing development and manufacturing divisions and the data processing marketing division reported to different group executives. Decisions concerning the data processing business as a whole were made by the Corporate Management Committee.[4]

1965 Reorganization

In early 1965 the three data processing product divisions (the Components Division,[5] the General Products Division, and the Data Systems Division) were reorganized on a functional basis. Whereas the three divisions had previously been responsible for both development and manufacture of their product lines (components, small systems, and large systems respectively), the new organization assigned all three product categories to two new divisions. One division, the Systems Development Division, was responsible for all data processing development activities (except for certain types of projects which were assigned to the Advanced Systems Development Division or the Federal Systems Division). The other new division,

---

[4] The composition of the Corporate Management Committee changed several times between 1959 and 1965. In general, it consisted of the chairman, the president, and the group executives.

[5] The Components Division was established in 1962 to manufacture some of the components used in IBM products and thus lessen dependence on outside suppliers.

the Systems Manufacturing Division, was responsible for all data processing manufacturing activities. Both new divisions reported to the same group executive. The Data Processing Division and the Field Engineering Division[6] reported to a different group executive, who, in turn, reported to a different senior vice president.[7] (See Exhibit 6, the Corporate Organization Chart in 1965.)

IBM executives cited several reasons for the 1965 reorganization. System/360, which encompassed a single product line for both small and large users, had made the old distinction between the product missions of the General Products Division and the Data Systems Division obsolete. In the past there had been some overlapping and competition between the two divisions, which, in general, was considered a good thing. The General Products Division, for example, had developed small systems, in terms of price, with large system performance capabilities. Now, with an integrated product line, such competition did not seem advantageous, especially since top management wished to be able to control development expenses more closely than it had in the past.

1966 Reorganization

In April 1966 the IBM president became chairman of the executive committee of the Board of Directors. One senior vice president was promoted to president; the other to vice chairman of the board. Mr. Thomas Watson, Jr., remained chairman of the board and chief executive officer.

The four senior executives formed the corporate office. As members of the corporate office they focused on long-term trends, developments in corporate policy, and other matters of a general management nature. The president and the vice chairman of the board had "contact responsibility" [8] for assigned groups, but they were not directly responsible for the operating performance of an individual organizational unit.

Group assignments were also changed at this time, generally in the direction of wider scope. Certain group executives performed many of the integrative functions previously performed at the senior vice president or corporate level. In particular, the components, systems development, systems manufacturing, data processing (marketing), and field engineering divisions were now placed under a single group executive, who was expected to coordinate their plans and activities, and present integrated plans for the entire data processing complex to corporate management.

IBM executives explained that the new organization made it possible for the corporate office to plan for the company as a whole, reviewing plans that had already been brought together for each major business. In the past, top management had performed the integrative function itself, assuring, for example, that the plans of the data processing development, manufacturing, field engineering, and marketing divisions fitted together. Now, top management would receive already integrated plans and could evaluate them in terms of the goals and objectives they had set for the corporation as a whole. (See Exhibit 7, the Corporate Organization Chart of 1966.)

Data Processing Division: Organizational Development

1959 Organization

The 1959 corporate reorganization limited the responsibilities of the Data Processing Division (DPD) to marketing and customer service, whereas previously they had also included development and manufacturing. In forming his new organization (Exhibit 8) the DPD General Manager kept three "line" re-

---

[6] The Field Engineering Division, which was responsible for equipment maintenance, was established in late 1964. Prior to this time, field engineering had been part of the Data Processing Division. According to IBM executives, there were three major reasons for the field engineering split-off:

(1) As a result of the rapid growth of the data processing business, the Data Processing Division had grown considerably in size. The split-off made it possible to reduce the size of DPD to manageable proportions, without materially altering its basic marketing mission.
(2) Because the Data Processing Division was so heavily oriented toward day-to-day sales activities, field engineering tended to receive inadequate management attention. In particular, this was believed to affect the professional growth and career opportunities available to IBM field engineers.
(3) In general, it seemed best to organize DPD around customer groups, or types of applications. In contrast, field engineering was most efficient when organized along product lines, with product specialization within specific geographic areas.

[7] Two senior vice presidents had been appointed in 1964. Their appointment was intended to lighten top management's work load and make additional time available for long-range planning, field visits, and external demands.

[8] The member of the corporate office with contact responsibility for a group served as the communications channel between the group executive and the corporate office.

gions and four "staff" headquarters departments as they had been established in 1956.

The three regions were responsible for sales and service in the East, Midwest, and West. The Regional Managers had direct responsibility for the revenue and expense results of their regions. Seventeen geographic districts, each headed by a district manager, were divided among the three regions. One hundred and ninety branch offices, each headed by a branch manager, reported to the 17 district managers.

Each branch was responsible for sales and service in a given geographic territory. Although branch organizations varied somewhat, in general there were sales representatives,[9] systems engineers,[10] and customer engineers[11] reporting to the branch manager. In addition, each branch had an administrative organization which was responsible for branch accounting, office services, and the processing of orders and invoices.

At division headquarters the controller, director of marketing administration, director of marketing programs, and manager of customer engineering reported to the DPD General Manager. The controller was responsible for division accounting and related administrative functions. The director of marketing administration was responsible for sales policies, personnel, planning, and internal communications. The director of marketing programs was responsible for sales planning, advertising, promotion, education, and new product introductions, including DPD's relations with the three data processing product divisions. The manager of customer engineering (i.e., field engineering) established general policies in his field, and worked with customer engineering managers in the regions and branches.

Industry Specialization

In the late 1950s IBM had begun to specialize major segments of its data processing sales effort along in-

---

[9] Sales representatives were responsible for "account control," which meant that they had complete responsibility for all relations between IBM and the accounts assigned to them. In general, a sales representative was thoroughly familiar with the problems faced by his accounts and guided them through the entire data processing cycle (familiarization, systems design, ordering, employee training, programming, installation, debugging, service, and upgrading).

[10] Systems engineers were highly trained specialists who worked with the sales representatives on designing systems, choosing equipment configurations, preparing programs, and installation.

[11] Customer engineers were responsible for equipment maintenance and certain aspects of installation.

dustry lines. DPD had divided all its data processing accounts into key customer industries (e.g., manufacturing, finance), and forecast sales on this basis. At the same time, the DPD headquarters marketing organization began to prepare industry marketing programs, tailored to the requirements of specific industries.

In conjunction with the new emphasis at DPD headquarters, members of the field sales force had begun to specialize in specific industries. These sales representatives attended industry schools, where they studied the management information problems of a given industry. After such instruction, a salesman was generally assigned accounts in the industry in which he had specialized.

By 1960 it was apparent that industry specialization had been a sound strategy, and DPD began to extend the concept further. In several major cities, specialized branches responsible for several industries were established. Where previously a multibranch city might have had a "down-town" branch, a "north-side" branch, and a "south-side" branch, it might now have a branch specialized in manufacturing and distribution; a branch specialized in insurance and banking; and a third branch responsible for serving the remaining accounts on a city-wide basis.

Headquarters Organization: 1962–1964

In 1962 the DPD president[12] appointed two vice presidents. The Vice President-Headquarters operations was responsible for marketing, systems design, field engineering, finance, and administration. The Vice President-Field Operations, to whom the three Vice Presidents and Regional Managers now reported, was responsible for the line field organization. According to DPD executives, this organizational move was intended to lighten the DPD president's work load, and reduce the number of departments and regional managers reporting to him.

In 1963 a Vice President-Marketing was appointed, to be responsible for the marketing functions previously assigned to the Vice President-Headquarters Operations. In particular, the Vice President-Marketing was responsible for product marketing (facilitating the availability and exploitation of a fully competitive product line) and industry marketing (assuring that each of the 15 industries into which DPD had divided its market received adequate marketing attention.) According to DPD executives, these two functions had

---

[12] The title of the General Manager of DPD had been changed to President after 1959.

grown so much in importance that top management believed that they should be separated from the other headquarters functions.

In 1964 the Vice President-Management Controls[13] became president of DPD and the position of Vice President-Field Operations was eliminated. Consequently, six vice presidents (Management Controls, Marketing, and four[14] regional vice presidents) now reported to the DPD president. This organization is shown in Exhibit 9.

The Federal Region

In 1963 responsibility for marketing standard data processing products to the federal government was transferred to the Data Processing Division from the Federal Systems Division, which also developed, manufactured, and sold special systems and military products to the federal government. The reasons for this shift, which were complex, are described in some detail on page 130. In essence, IBM was confronted with changed conditions in the federal market in the early 1960s and decided that standard data processing equipment sales should be separated from IBM's defense-oriented business.

When DPD assumed responsibility for federal marketing it established a Federal Region, with headquarters in Washington. The Federal Region had a large Washington organization, but no branches outside the Washington area. Sales to government organizations headquartered outside of Washington were made by branches in the geographic regions, with staff marketing support from the Federal Region. In early 1965, however, 16 branches with predominantly federal accounts were transferred from the geographic regions to the Federal Region.

The Market Operations Department

In early 1964 the scope of the Industry Programs Department, which reported to the Vice President-Marketing, was considerably expanded. Prior to 1964, two types of personnel had been involved in DPD industry marketing. On the one hand, 15 industry managers in the headquarters industry programs department prepared marketing programs and forecast sales for their industries. On the other hand, each regional vice president had a staff of industry marketing specialists, who disseminated industry marketing programs to the field sales force.

In early 1964 the 200 industry marketing specialists in the regions were put under the control of the industry managers at headquarters in White Plains. They continued to be located physically in the regional headquarters but their activities were now directed by the industry managers.

In March 1965 the manager of industry programs, who previously had reported to the Vice President-Marketing, was promoted to the new position of Vice President-Market Operations, reporting to the DPD president. According to the DPD president, the job of Vice President-Marketing had become too big for one man to handle effectively. Now the Vice President-Marketing would concentrate on product marketing, seeking to insure the availability of a fully competitive product line. The Vice President-Market Operations would be responsible for planning and coordinating DPD's industry-oriented marketing strategy. (See Exhibit 10, Organization Chart of Data Processing Division, March 1965.)

The National Airlines Sales Organization

In January 1965 responsibility for sale and installation of airlines reservations systems was transferred from the geographic regions to the airlines industry manager at headquarters. IBM had recently installed the SABRE reservation system at American Airlines, and now wished to make similar sales to other airlines. Because of the highly specialized nature of airlines reservations systems, and the small number of potential customers, DPD management believed that a separate sales organization, with headquarters in White Plains and branch offices in several major markets, would be more effective than the geographically oriented field sales organization in reaching this market.

The GEM Region

In November 1965 the scope of the Federal Region was increased through the addition of state and local governments, educational institutions, and medical accounts to its previous mission. At the same time, the name of the region was changed to the GEM (Government, Education, Medical) Region, and the region was assigned an additional 17 branch offices.[15] The industry managers responsible for state and local government, education, and medicine were transferred from the Market Operations Department to the GEM

---

[13] The title of Vice President-Headquarters Operations was changed to Vice President-Management Controls in early 1964.

[14] Including the new Federal Region vice president (see below).

[15] In January 1966 GEM was assigned two additional branches.

Region. Like the Federal Region, the GEM Region would have line responsibility for sales made to accounts served by its branch offices and staff responsibility for sales made by branches in the geographic regions.

In announcing the establishment of GEM, the DPD president made the following statement:

> Last February we established 16 new branch offices in the Federal Region. This move was designed to meet changing customer requirements and to improve our service to customers in this region. I want to congratulate everyone involved for making that move a success.
>
> Now — since "nothing succeeds like success" — we are extending the scope of the activities of the Federal Region to include State and Local Government, Education, and Medical industry marketing. Our studies and analyses have shown that the interests and data processing needs of customers and prospects in these fields are closely related to those of the Federal Government. By making them part of the new Government-Education-Medical Region we improve our ability to meet customer needs. We also help everyone concerned function more effectively in this interrelated marketing area.
>
> The integration of these related marketing areas within the GEM Region increases the power of industry specialization as a sales and service tool. Those of you who are already specializing in an industry will find yourselves working with specialists in related fields, pooling your talents in finding answers to customer problems. Basically, customers are interested in results. By providing service in response to specific customer requirements, you will enhance your position with that customer.
>
> The GEM Region improves our marketing position. In so doing, it provides for those of you in the region improved opportunities for personal achievement. I am confident you will take full advantage of these opportunities and that your combined capabilities will successfully implement the change we are announcing today.

Data Processing Division: Organization in 1966

The rest of this case focuses on the processes through which product and industry marketing personnel worked with the geographically oriented field organization. Line authority passed directly from the DPD president to the regions, districts, branches, and ultimately individual salesmen, but IBM also encouraged the active participation of staff personnel in its overall marketing effort. According to the DPD president, the influence of the product and industry marketing personnel at headquarters was felt at all levels of the DPD organization, and was a highly important element in the operation of the division.

Headquarters Organization: The Marketing Department

The headquarters Marketing Department was organized in five departments: Product Programs, Systems Engineering, Marketing Education, Communications (i.e., advertising, promotion, press relations, and internal communications), and Product Scheduling.[16]

The Product Programs Department was a major part of the Marketing Department. It was responsible for interfacing with the Systems Development and Systems Manufacturing Divisions,[17] and assuring that DPD's product requirements were satisfied. It established priorities for product requests from the field organization, and had to concur with the plans for a new product before the product could be announced.

The Product Programs Department was organized along product lines. Reporting to the Director of Product Programs were three product marketing managers (System/360; Special Systems; and New Business) and four managers responsible for various staff and service departments. Reporting to each product marketing manager were several product managers, each of whom was responsible for a smaller category of products (e.g., small systems; intermediate systems; large systems). Finally, reporting to each product manager were several product administrators, each of whom was responsible for one or more specific products.[18]

The Systems Engineering Department was responsible for disseminating information to systems engineers in the field sales organization. In addition, it was concerned with manpower planning and career development in the systems engineering function.

The Marketing Education Department had line responsibility for basic product training and advanced sales schools conducted at IBM manufacturing locations. It also supervised the activities of the district education centers, on a staff basis, and was responsible for the preparation of the overall DPD education plans and budgets.

The Communications Department was responsible for the DPD advertising, sales promotion materials and press relations, business shows, audio-visual materials, internal communications, and sales conventions.

---

[16] See Exhibit 11, Organization Chart of the Marketing Department.

[17] These divisions reported to the same Vice President and Group Executive as did the president of DPD. See Exhibit 7.

[18] See Exhibit 12, Organization Chart of the Product Programs Department.

The Product Scheduling Department was responsible for recommending changes in delivery and manufacturing schedules established by the product divisions. Product scheduling was a very important function, since there was generally a backlog of orders for most products, and IBM was committed to sequential delivery under a consent decree.

Headquarters Organization:
The Market Operations Department

The Vice President-Market Operations was responsible for industry marketing. DPD divided its market into 16 major industrial classifications,[19] and attempted to market to each industry on an individual basis. Sales forecasts for each industry were prepared annually, and industry managers were assigned quotas. In order to meet their quotas, industry managers were active in a number of areas ranging from designing marketing programs to coordinating specialized sales schools. In 1966 industry managers were also taking a major role in the development of new products and programs required by their industries.

The Market Operations Department was divided into five major departments: Manufacturing and Distribution Industries, Transportation Marketing, Service Industries, Scientific Development, and Cross-Industry Operations (see Exhibit 13, Organization Chart of Market Operations Department). The Cross-Industry Operations Department was responsible for non-scientific applications that cut across several industries, and provided administrative services for the Market Operations Department. The Scientific Development Department was responsible for scientific applications (e.g., PERT, linear programming) which cut across several industries. The three industry departments were divided into 12 industry groups, each headed by an Industry Manager. Each Industry Manager had a headquarters staff, which varied with the size and nature of his industry. In addition, industry representatives and their staffs were located in regional offices, but reported to the industry managers (for example, see Exhibit 14, Organization Chart of Manufacturing and Distribution Industries Department[20]).

---

[19] Aerospace, Manufacturing, Process, Distribution, Printing and Publishing, Consultants and Service Bureaus, Insurance, Communications, Utilities, Finance, Medical, Federal Governments, State and Local Governments, Education, Transportation, and Airlines.

[20] There were four other industries in DPD (Federal, State and Local Government, Education, and Medical), which were organized similarly but reported separately to the GEM Regional Manager.

Field Organization: The Branches

The branch was the basic unit of DPD's field organization. In 1965 there were 225 DPD Branches. Each branch was headed by a branch manager who was responsible for achieving his branch sales quota. The branch manager reported to a district manager, who also had quota responsibility.

The branches differed considerably in organization and assignment. In the larger markets, branches generally were specialized according to industry. In Chicago, for example, there were separate branches for finance, insurance, distribution, public services, and manufacturing, as well as several branches handling unspecialized accounts on a geographic basis. In the smaller markets, branches generally were responsible for all accounts in a given geographic area. Even in these branches, however, salesmen were industry-specialized to the degree practicable.

The Evanston Manufacturing Branch: The Evanston branch was responsible for all manufacturing accounts in the greater Chicago area. Prior to early 1965 it had also been responsible for several railroad accounts, but they had been assigned to another branch early in the year.

The Evanston branch management team consisted of a branch manager, two marketing managers, two systems engineering managers, and an administration manager, all of whom reported to the branch manager. Twelve salesmen reported to each marketing manager, while 14 systems engineers reported to each systems engineering manager. The administration manager supervised a staff of 57 persons through several administration operations managers.

Each marketing manager was responsible for accounts throughout the branch's territory. There was no effort to specialize the marketing managers' responsibility by type of manufacturing account (e.g., large v. small) or geography. Instead, the branch manager assigned individual salesmen to the marketing managers on the basis of experience level and need for supervision. In general, the branch manager attempted to balance the workload between the two marketing managers, assigning each approximately the same number of experienced and inexperienced salesmen, accounts, and revenue.

The Rockford Branch: The Rockford branch was unspecialized and was responsible for all accounts in the Rockford, Illinois, area. Its management team, headed up by a branch manager, consisted of a marketing manager, a systems engineering manager, and an administration manager.

The marketing effort was carried out by nine salesmen (supervised by the marketing manager) and nineteen systems engineers (supervised by the systems engineering manager). Six salesmen spent more than 80% of their time on manufacturing accounts, and three salesmen spent all of their time on new accounts. Two of the six salesmen who specialized in manufacturing were also specialized in finance and insurance.

The Boston Commercial Branch: The Boston Commercial Branch was responsible for finance, insurance, and services (public utilities, telephone, and transportation). Its responsibility for finance covered all of District 1 (New England), but its responsibility for insurance was limited to New Hampshire, Maine, and Eastern Massachusetts. In the services industry, the branch's responsibility varied from one type of service to another. It covered public utilities in New Hampshire, Maine, and Eastern Massachusetts; telephone companies in the area serviced by the New England Telephone and Telegraph Company (headquarters in Boston); and transportation in the immediate Boston area. Airlines, it should be noted, were covered by a separate airlines branch (see below).

The Boston commercial branch management team consisted of a branch manager, three marketing managers, and three systems engineering managers. There was no administration manager, since an area administration department, which reported to the District 1 administration manager, provided administrative services to all branches in the Boston area.

Each of the industries covered by the Boston commercial branch was assigned to one marketing manager and one systems engineering manager, who worked together in marketing to accounts in their industry. Ten salesmen and twenty-one systems engineers were assigned to finance, eight salesmen and sixteen systems engineers to insurance, and six salesmen and thirteen systems engineers to services. Several of the salesmen and systems engineers assigned to finance were located in Hartford but reported to the Boston finance marketing manager.

Field Organization: The Districts

In 1966 there were 20 DPD districts. The largest district (Chicago) consisted of 15 branches, while the smallest (Metropolitan New York Finance and Insurance) contained only 4 branches.

In most cases, the headquarters of a district was located in a major city and had responsibility for a number of branches dispersed throughout the surrounding territory. There were, however, several exceptions to this pattern. Branches in the New York metropolitan area were divided among three districts, each of which specialized in several industries. In the Southwest, several branches located within the geographic boundaries at District 17 were assigned to District 20, since District 20 had a heavy concentration of accounts in the aerospace industry in which these branches were specialized.

A district management team typically consisted of a district manager, an assistant to the district manager, a district systems engineering manager, a district education manager, and a district administration manager. The district manager was responsible for the entire district and generally worked closely with his branch managers, reviewing their results on a weekly or monthly basis, and visiting the branches fairly frequently. In addition, he generally took an active part in hiring and promoting personnel in his district and called on key customers when a major installation was being considered or a significant problem arose.

The assistant to the district manager was primarily concerned with planning and evaluating sales programs and performance. The district systems engineering manager had a staff relationship with branch systems engineering managers. The district education manager was in charge of the District Education Center (see below), and was responsible for all formal training activities in the district. The district administration manager supervised any *Metropolitan Area Administration managers* located in his district and worked with the branch administration managers in those branches where the administration manager reported to the branch manager.

District 1: District 1 was responsible for the sale and installation of IBM data processing systems in the New England states. In early 1966 District 1 *was the largest district in terms of business volume in the Eastern Region.* The district consisted of a district headquarters organization, a district education center, and ten branch offices.

Prior to January 1964 District 1 had been almost completely unspecialized. Individual salesmen were already specialized in particular industries, but each branch office covered a wide range of industries located in its geographic territory. Between January and June 1964 district management prepared a plan for specialization of the branches along industry lines. According to the district manager, there were several reasons for making a change at this time. First, and clearly most important, the District 1 growth rate had fallen well behind the national average, and a major restructuring seemed to be in order. Second, district management believed that it was not getting adequate leverage from its specialized sales force. Although individual salesmen were specialized in key industries, the number of salesmen specialized in a particular industry in an individual branch was generally too small to warrant adequate support at the branch level. Finally, regional and divisional management had asked District 1 to consider reorganization along industry lines.

After considerable analysis, district management concluded that specialized branches were desirable. Since District 1's territory was not large geographically and most of its accounts were concentrated in two major metropolitan areas (Boston and Hartford), it would be possible to assign almost all the salesmen specialized in a particular industry to one, or at most two, branches, which would cover the entire district.

The implementation of the decision to specialize the branches was complicated by a number of factors. While it might have been desirable to specialize all industries and branches at one time, the various industries and branches differed significantly in the degree to which they could be specialized immediately. In commenting on these differences, the district manager listed six factors which he considered in determining the appropriate degree of specialization for a given industry.

(1) Center of gravity. Is most of the industry's business concentrated in one or two metropolitan areas, or is it widely dispersed throughout the district?
(2) How much application specialization does this industry require? Some industries (e.g., finance) were characterized by highly unique applications, whereas others (e.g., manufacturing and distribution) had a great many applications in common.
(3) Talent available. The district had highly specialized personnel in some industries, but not in others.
(4) Degree of competition. IBM faced stronger competition in some industries than in others. All other things being equal, the specialization of the highly competitive industries was probably more important than the specialization of the less competitive industries.
(5) Degree of penetration. Data processing was more firmly established in some industries than in others. In most cases, the specialization of high penetration industries was probably more important than the specialization of low penetration industries.
(6) Cost of coverage. Some industries would be more expensive to cover from a single branch than others. Differences in this area depended primarily on the travel expense necessary to sell and install the equipment and applications appropriate to a given industry.

Acceptance of the district plan by regional and DPD management was followed by the announcement on June 27, 1964, of Phase I of the district reorganization. For the most part, Phase I was limited to the four branch offices in the Boston metropolitan area (Boston, Salem, Natick, and Cambridge).

The Boston branch was reorganized into three groups. The Finance group was responsible for sales to banks and related businesses throughout the entire district. The Insurance group was responsible for sales to insurance companies in all of Metropolitan Boston and Western Massachusetts. The Service group, which was primarily concerned with utilities, transportation, and state and local government, was responsible for all of Metropolitan Boston.

At the same time, the Cambridge branch became responsible for all universities and hospitals in greater Boston, and for the federal government in greater Boston, and the Providence area. The Salem branch became responsible for manufacturing and some general accounts, while the Natick branch took over responsibility for distribution and some general accounts. Both Salem and Natick now covered accounts in the entire greater Boston area.

In commenting on these moves, district management pointed out that the assignment of district-wide responsibility for finance to the Boston branch was the most radical move made at this time, especially since banking accounts were widely dispersed throughout the district. Two reasons for this move were cited: (1) IBM was not doing well in this industry in New England, and (2) there were highly qualified personnel, specialized in finance, in Boston and several of the outlying branches.

During 1965 several additional organizational moves were made. In January the Boston branch extended its coverage of the insurance industry to Rhode Island, New Hampshire, and Maine, and the Hartford branch took over responsibility for insurance in Western Massachusetts and Vermont and utilities in Western Massachusetts. In February all federal accounts were transferred to the newly established Federal Region. In April the Salem and Natick branches were closed, and their accounts were assigned to a new manufacturing and distribution branch in Waltham, on the outskirts of greater Boston. In July District 2's New Haven and Bridgeport, Connecticut, branches were assigned to District 1 as part of a reorganization in the New York metropolitan area. In November most of District 1's government, education, and medical accounts, and the Cambridge branch, were assigned to the new GEM region.

In early 1966 the District thus consisted of ten branches, which varied considerably in the degree to which they were specialized. In general, the branches in the eastern part of the District (Boston Commercial; Boston Manufacturing and Distribution; Providence; Concord, N.H.; Portland, Maine; Montpelier, Vt.; and Worcester, Mass.) were the most specialized, and the branches in the western area of the District (Hartford, Springfield, and New Haven) were the least specialized. District management had now concentrated its attention on the western area, however, and expected to carry out a major reorganization in the near future.

Field Organization: The Regions

The four regional vice presidents, who reported directly to the president of DPD, were responsible for DPD's field operations. Three regional vice presidents were assigned geographic territories (East, Midwestern, and West). The fourth was in charge of the GEM Region. The three geographic regions differed somewhat in organization. Differences were minor, however, and the Midwestern Region was like the others in all essential respects.

The Midwestern Region: The Vice President of the Midwestern Region reported to the DPD president, but also worked closely with the vice presidents of marketing and market operations, and was in frequent contact with the other regional vice presidents. He was responsible for seven districts (Cleveland, Cincinnati, Detroit, Chicago, Minneapolis, Kansas City, and New Orleans) in a territory including all or part of 22 states.

Three staff managers also reported to the Vice President of the Midwestern Region. The manager of staff services supervised the regional counsel and personnel planning. The manager of finance and administration was in charge of control, financial planning and analysis, data processing services, equipment and order control, and branch office administration. The manager of marketing services supervised the managers of systems engineering, product programs, promotional services, marketing planning, new business marketing, education, and scientific marketing.[21]

Representatives of the Market Operations Department were also located at regional headquarters. These industry specialists had reported to the regional marketing services managers until January 1964, but now reported to the industry managers in White Plains.

[21] See Exhibit 15, Organization Chart of the Midwestern Region.

Although they limited their activities to the Midwestern region, they were considered part of the divisional staff rather than members of the regional organization.

Experiments in Field Sales Organization

In early 1966 DPD was experimenting with several new approaches in its field sales organization.

Account Teams: A limited number of major accounts were assigned to account marketing managers. An account marketing manager was assigned to a single large account and reported directly to his branch manager. He supervised an account team of a minimum of eight sales representatives and systems engineers. The account team was assigned a single quota, and all members of the team were on an incentive compensation plan. Only those systems engineers assigned to account teams were eligible for incentive bonuses.

New Business Branches: In January 1966 seven branches located in major metropolitan markets were designated new business branches. These branches specialized in small accounts with limited data processing requirements. As an account assigned to a new business branch grew in size, it would be transferred to a branch specialized in its industry.

Field Systems Centers: In early 1966 sixteen Field Systems Centers were established to provide systems engineering support to the branches in their districts. According to IBM executives, there were many new applications that required highly sophisticated systems engineering skills in which the branches were not yet completely self-sufficient. When a branch was confronted with an application of this sort, it could request help from the Field Systems Center in its district. Field Systems Center personnel would provide high-level skills necessary for specific applications and, at the same time, train branch systems engineering personnel in the new applications.

Product Development

Product development was the formal responsibility of the Systems Development Division,[22] which carried out the actual development work. The Data Processing Division provided SDD with market information and made specific requests for new products. In general, the Product Programs Department, which reported to

[22] The place of the Systems Development Division (SDD) in the DPD organization is shown in Exhibit 7.

the DPD Vice President-Marketing, was responsible for working with SDD.[23] Requests for new products submitted to SDD by the Product Programs Department were generally accompanied by market data and other supporting documents. SDD was free to undertake, or not undertake, any project provided that its decision could be justified on economic or strategic grounds. It was necessary for DPD to concur in SDD's sales forecast for a new product before the product could be announced. When DPD agreed with an SDD forecast, it promised, in effect, to sell the forecast quantity of the proposed product, provided that the product was delivered on schedule at the proposed price.

The Product Programs Department used three major sources of information in determining which products to request from SDD. These were requests from the field sales organization and from the Market Operations Department, and information generated by analyses of competitive activities.

Each region submitted a Marketing Requirement Report to the Product Programs Department every month. These reports summarized new product requests originated by the branches and transmitted through the districts. When a number of requests for a similar item were received, or a particular request seemed unusually promising, the Product Programs Department conducted a market survey to gauge overall demand for the proposed product.

In addition, the Product Programs Department sent representatives to the branches to obtain product requirements directly. These product specialists met with branch managers and their personnel, and also accompanied salesmen on customer calls. Besides collecting requests for the new products, the product specialists conducted surveys intended to ascertain the demand for new products already proposed.

The industry managers in the Market Operations Department also submitted requests for new products to the Product Programs Department. In general, these requests were limited to input-output equipment with applications in only one or two industries. According to the Director of the Product Programs Department, the Market Operations industry managers generally operated under the assumption that Product Programs would generate requests for general product features (e.g., central processing units), while they would request specific features that could help them sell to their industries.

Once a month, the DPD president held a "state of the union" meeting, which was attended by representatives of the Product Programs Department and the Market Operations Department. During the morning session the performance of each industry currently below its plan was reviewed. In some cases, unsatisfactory performance was attributed to deficiencies in the product line. During the afternoon session representatives of the Product Programs Department dealt with these shortcomings, either by explaining what was being done to correct a deficiency, or by agreeing to take action. In some cases, the Product Programs Department took the position that a proposed addition to the product line should not be made, either because the forecast demand for the new item was not adequate or because the deficiency would be remedied by a longer term development program. In other cases, the Product Programs Department suggested that a more detailed study of the product requirement be made.

Prior to the meeting the Product Programs Department received copies of the reports prepared by Market Operations personnel on the several industries. In the opinion of a number of executives, this formal procedure, which was intended to provide adequate time for preparation of replies, was not really necessary since the industry managers and the Product Programs Department were in close day-to-day contact. The state of the union meetings mainly filled the function of bringing unresolved problems to the attention of top management.

The Product Programs Department also tracked competitive developments on an ethically gathered basis. This activity ranged from the use of clipping services to careful analysis of reports from the branches concerning the reasons for every lost sale. Most major manufacturers of data processing equipment exchanged copies of all publicly available new product announcements, promotional brochures, etc. According to the Director of Product Programs, analysis of competitive developments rarely turned up anything new but frequently changed the priority assigned to a product feature already under consideration.

The Product Administrator: Within the Product Programs Department individual product administrators were assigned to specific products. The activities of a given product administrator depended on his product assignment and the stage of development his product was in. The following paragraphs describe the activities of a "typical" product administrator, as

---

[23] A similar department in the World Trade Corporation also submitted requests for new products to SDD.

he brought his product from the early conceptual stage to market introduction.

The first step was the generation of a requirement. This could come about in a variety of ways, such as product requests from Market Operations or the field sales force, Product Programs Department analyses of competitive developments, or a strategic decision by IBM management to enter a new market or field. In general, the product administrator prepared a formal statement of the product requirement, in terms of product features, programming support, and applications, and worked with the Systems Development Division to develop formal product specifications.

After the initial specifications had been prepared, SDD visited a number of IBM customers to gauge their reactions to the proposed product. In particular, these "case studies" attempted to ascertain which applications the new equipment would be used for, and how much demand there was for alternative combinations of product features and application capabilities. The product administrator generally worked closely with SDD on these case studies. After their completion he and his counterpart in SDD generally modified their original requirements and specifications.

Next, SDD prepared two types of forecasts. The first forecast assumed that the new product would have certain features, would be delivered at a certain date, would be used in certain applications, and would have one of three different prices. Given these assumptions, a volume forecast was prepared for each price level and manufacturing costs were estimated at each of the three volume levels. Assuming these manufacturing costs, the second forecast estimated product profitability at each of the three price/volume combinations. Frequently, the product administrator negotiated with SDD during the preparation of these forecasts, varying some of the assumptions in order to arrive at acceptable volume and profit forecasts.

SDD's case studies and initial forecasts were then submitted informally to the industry managers and regional staffs of DPD at a series of meetings. At this point the product administrator generally prepared detailed analyses of the market potential for the proposed product and compared its cost/performance with that of competitive products.

The market operations managers and regional staffs then "reacted" to the proposed product. In some cases their reactions might be directed at product features, e.g., "the proposed product needs faster printing or more programming support if it is to be competitive." In other cases, they criticized the forecasts themselves, e.g., "We cannot sell as many units as you say we can, unless you improve the product in the following ways. . . ."

On the basis of these reactions, the product administrator negotiated changes in specifications and forecasts with SDD. At the same time, competitive or technological developments might also suggest modifications in the original plan. At any rate, a new set of specifications and forecasts was prepared for DPD reaction. In general, DPD then requested further changes, and further negotiations took place. On a typical product, this cycle might be repeated three or four times during an 18-month period.

As the proposed announcement date approached, the product administrator began to coordinate the preparation of support materials, such as teaching manuals, product brochures, demonstration films, and news releases. According to one product administrator, this was a difficult job, since preparation had to begin before the final decision to introduce the product had been reached. Consequently, he had to get the various staff departments to prepare the materials for which they were responsible, without absolute assurance that they would actually be used. Since the final decision to introduce a product was often reached only several weeks before the announcement date, and all materials had to be distributed to the branches by the announcement date, it was necessary to complete all writing, artwork, plates, and plans while the final decision was still pending.

The final decision depended on DPD's willingness to agree with SDD's specifications and forecasts. As noted above, formal concurrence was based on a complex set of continuing negotiations and discussions between SDD and DPD. When DPD finally did concur, it became responsible for selling and installing the forecast quantity of the proposed equipment.

Applications Development in the Data Processing Division

In 1966 the largest single item in the Market Operations Department's budget was "Industry Development." An expenditure on industry development generally resulted in a Type II Program. A Type II Program[24] was an integrated set of computer instruc-

---

[24] A Type I Program was related to machine usage rather than customer applications. Type I Programs were developed by the Systems Development Division.

tions that could be used by a large number of accounts to carry out common applications. Typical Type II Programs were used for shop floor scheduling, utility billing, airlines reservations, and retail inventory management.

Prior to 1964 Type II Program development was carried out by individual DPD branch offices and a group in the Advanced Systems Development Division (ASDD) (see Exhibit 7). As IBM's activities in this area grew in importance, management decided to improve coordination and control by consolidating all Type II Program development in a single division. In 1964 this mission was assigned to DPD, and the applications development group in ASDD was transferred to DPD.

Within DPD responsibility for Type II program development was given to the Market Operations Industry managers, who established industry development groups to work on applications within their industries. At the same time a set of formal standards and procedures, similar to those used in product development, was established.

In early 1966 more than 150 Type II programs were being developed by DPD. Among the most significant of these programs were IMPACT (Inventory Management Program and Control Technique) and a real-time airlines reservations program. These programs are described in the following paragraphs.

IMPACT

In 1964 the Distribution Industry Manager established a 26-man group to develop a program for retail inventory management. The Advanced Systems Development Division had been working on a similar project, which was transferred to DPD at this time.

The ASDD-developed program was tested with a customer in early 1965 and modified in several respects as a result. It was then "generalized" and tested with five other customers, and again modified and tested. Finally, in January 1966 retail IMPACT was announced as an important adjunct to the System/360 marketing program.

Typically, a salesman specialized in the distribution industry would give a seminar on IMPACT for the top managers of his key retailing accounts. He would then collect sample data on inventory levels and stock outs, and use IMPACT to establish optimal inventory levels for the sample items. He would present his findings to management as evidence of how System/360, with IMPACT, could increase the retailer's profits.

According to the Distribution Industry Manager, IMPACT by May 1966 had already proved to be an effective marketing tool. Although the retail industry had historically been slow to adopt modern inventory management techniques, retail management was currently undergoing a "scientific management" revolution. As a result, it was receptive to new ideas, especially when, as in the case of IMPACT, dramatic increases in profits could be demonstrated.

Airlines Reservations System

The Airlines Industry group was primarily concerned with marketing advanced reservations systems to major airlines. IBM had made an agreement with American Airlines in 1959 for the joint development of the SABRE airlines reservation system. SABRE, which was fully operational in 1964, made it possible for reservations personnel to determine immediately the availability of space on any American flight and confirm reservations in a matter of seconds. The system, which represented a significant advance in real time tele-processing technology, consisted of more than 2,000 separate terminals and a central processor capable of handling over 2,000 messages per minute.

By the time American's SABRE had gone "on-the-air," IBM had sold similar systems to two other major airlines. Since IBM had a major lead over its competitors in this field, it decided to develop and market a relatively standardized airlines reservations system, which, unlike its predecessors, could use System/360.

Because of the specialized development task involved, and the magnitude of the job, an Airlines Industry development group was established in DPD. This group was expected to spend about 150 man years developing a general purpose reservations program. Forming the core of this group, which consisted of 255 persons in late 1965, were about 100 persons who had worked on SABRE in the Advanced Systems Development Division.

During the planning stages it was apparent that an extraordinary amount of detailed systems knowledge would be required to sell the airlines reservations system. Because of the advanced nature of the system, almost all of IBM's talent in this area was concentrated in the systems development effort. Some of this talent could have been sent out to existing branches, on either a temporary or a permanent basis, but even then the branches would have lacked the capability necessary to install the systems. For these reasons, it was decided to establish a separate airlines sales organization, which would report to the industry manager and work closely with the development group.[25]

In commenting on his organization, the Airlines Industry Manager pointed out that there were only 25 major airlines in the United States, which made it possible to cover the entire market with relatively few branches. Nevertheless, he had experienced several problems of remote management. Because the airlines branches were so highly specialized, each consisted of only a few people who confined their efforts to one or two airlines. This raised problems in the areas of manpower scheduling (systems engineer work loads, in particular, tended to vary widely) and group identity. As a result, the Airlines Industry Manager closed several of his smaller offices in early 1966, transferring their accounts to larger airlines branches.

Setting Quotas

Each year the DPD president received two divisional quotas from IBM corporate management. The first quota, Net Sales Record Increase (NSRI), set the target for additional data processing equipment to be sold during the year. The second quota, Net Installed Record Increase (NIRI), set the target for equipment actually to be installed during the year.

The president divided the quotas among the four regions. Like the president, each regional vice president was responsible for meeting his quotas and was evaluated according to his success in doing so. The regional vice presidents divided their quotas among the district managers in their regions. The district managers, in turn, divided their quotas among their branch managers, who made the final assignment of quotas to individual salesmen, whose compensation was closely tied to their success in meeting quotas.[26]

Product and Marketing functions received quotas equal to the total DPD quota. The two groups broke their quotas down by product or industry, and assigned quota responsibility to individual product or industry managers. These managers were not compensated according to their quota achievement and were not eligible for membership in the Hundred Percent Club. Nevertheless, achievement of quota was a highly important element in the evaluation of their performance.

Although product and industry quotas helped line management set geographic quotas, line managers below the regional vice presidents were not responsible for industry or product quotas.[27] DPD management believed that the branches should be primarily concerned with meeting the needs of their customers and should not try to sell specific pieces of equipment. For this reason, branch managers were not informed of product quotas, except, on occasion, when marked deviation from quota suggested that a particular set of applications was not receiving adequate attention.

The Division Quota

The Planning Department, which reported to the Vice President-Management Controls, was responsible for coordinating the preparation of DPD's five-year long-range plans and two-year operating plans. Since the first year of a two-year operating plan represented the current year's budget, the Planning Department was also responsible for coordinating its plans with the division's annual quota and budget.

While two-year operating plans were far more detailed than the five-year plans, the processes through which they were developed were similar. In each case it was necessary to obtain forecasts of installations of IBM equipment from each of the 16 industry groups, collate them with the forecasts of the product divisions (through the Product Programs Department), and combine them in a revenue forecast. At the same time, expense forecasts were made by the field organization and functional staffs, and collated with the plans of the 16 industry groups. Finally, the revenue and expense forecasts were brought together in a two-year or five-year plan and presented to corporate management.

Industry quota distributions to regions and districts were prepared simultaneously by the industry managers and the Planning Department. The industry managers prepared their allocations on the basis of

---

[25] Airlines branches, which reported to the Airlines Industry Manager, were established in Chicago, New York, Atlanta, and Los Angeles. In addition, sales representatives were based in Tulsa, Kansas City, San Francisco, Seattle, and Miami.

[26] Under a typical DPD compensation program, a salesman who made quota exactly would receive compensation made up of 50% of base salary and 50% of incentive pay. A salesman who achieved none of his quota received only the base salary, and a salesman who reached 50% of his quota received total compensation equal to 75% of what he would have received had he achieved 100% of quota. Above 100% of quota, however, incentive compensation increased at a considerably accelerated rate; i.e., a salesman who achieved 110% of quota received compensation equal to more than 110% of what he would have received had he achieved only 100% of quota.

[27] Beginning in 1966 District Managers were to be responsible for industry quotas assigned to them by their Regional Vice Presidents.

detailed account and applications knowledge, while the Planning Department used a mathematical model. Generally, the two sets of allocations were close together, and differences were resolved by investigating the reasons for them. In some cases, the industry manager might have failed to consider a relevant factor which was included in the mathematical model. In other cases, the industry manager might have included relevant information not available to the mathematical model. According to the manager of the Planning Department, the two sets of allocations in effect served as checks on each other, and thus resulted in a better allocation than could have been obtained by either method independently.

When DPD received its annual quota, the target approved by corporate management was generally somewhat higher than that forecast by the Planning Department. When this occurred, the additional revenue quota was not allocated to the industries on an arbitrary or pro rata basis. Instead, the Planning Department went back over each of the industry forecasts to determine which industries had the highest probability of achieving additional quota.

Product Quotas

The Product Programs Department was assigned the divisional quota. It broke this quota down by product type, in accordance with its product forecasts. The manager of the Product Programs Department then assigned quotas to his product managers. The product manager quota was a "memorandum quota," which meant that it was intended to serve as a guide, rather than a target for which he would be held strictly accountable. The product manager was expected to provide adequate sales support for his product and to monitor the sales of his product closely.

If sales of a particular product were considerably below forecast, the product manager generally initiated a study to find out why. In one case, for example, a new product was both less expensive and more efficient than the IBM equipment it was intended to replace. Nevertheless, sales of the new product were well below forecast. The product manager then arranged for a computer analysis of users of the old equipment who had not ordered the new equipment. After locating "prime targets" for the new equipment in this way, the product manager sent a list of prime targets to each region. These lists were broken down by district and branch, which made it easier for the regional vice presidents to work with individual branch managers.

In commenting on activities of this kind, one product manager pointed out that such tactics, although effective, could only be used selectively. Line managers were not responsible for meeting product quotas, and were only interested in product quotas in those instances where such information helped them meet their geographic quotas. Failure to meet a product quota might suggest that more attention should be given to particular customers or applications, but it might also mean that the sales force was meeting customer needs more effectively with another type of equipment.

Industry Quotas

The Market Operations Department was also assigned the divisional quota. This quota was distributed to the 16 industry managers, following an analysis by the Planning Department of sales forecasts prepared by each industry. These forecasts were based on sales trends, analysis of competitive activity, and estimates of sales to major accounts.

The Market Operations Department industry managers then divided their quotas among the industry representatives located in the regions. The regional industry representatives were expected to motivate the line organization to achieve their industry quotas. They did so in a variety of ways, ranging from holding industry seminars to working directly with specialized branches and salesmen. In addition, they tried to encourage the district managers to assign realistically high quotas to specialized branches, as well as to geographic branches with salesmen specialized in their industries.

In commenting on the industry quota, one regional industry representative said that he would prefer to see industry representatives evaluated on some basis other than sales. He pointed out that the industry manager, whether located in White Plains or the field, had no real control over actual sales. It was possible, for example, that an industry representative was doing an excellent job, but was not getting enough support from the sales force.

Field and District Quotas

In distributing his regional quota to his districts, one regional vice president used three approaches:

(1) IBM had compiled extensive data regarding the average sales potential of each sales representative. The regional vice president was thus able to obtain one set of quota figures from the manpower planning table of the districts.
(2) The regional industry specialists prepared guide lines of the amount of sales they expected to achieve in each district. By combining the industry guidelines

for each district, the regional manager obtained a second set of quota figures.

(3) The regional vice president's staff projected sales trends for each district. By applying these trends to the present year's regional quota, a third set of district quotas was established.

The regional vice president's staff then prepared an analysis of the accuracy of each of the three methods, had it been used during the previous year. While quotas were never in fact assigned on the basis of just one method, this analysis gave the regional vice president a "feel" for the amount of weight he should assign to each of the three approaches.

The regional vice president then went over all these data and established final quotas on the basis of his own judgment. In general, the three approaches suggested roughly similar quotas, and he more or less took the average. When he had determined district quotas, the regional vice president held a meeting at which all his district managers were present. At this meeting he gave each district manager an envelope containing quota and budget for the year. According to the regional vice president there was rarely any discussion or negotiation concerning district quotas.

Branch Quotas

District 11: After receiving his quota from the regional vice president, the manager of District 11 (Chicago) divided it among his 14 branch offices. Although most of his branches were specialized to some degree, the district manager made little use of the industry quota guidelines prepared by the industry managers in the Market Operations Department. Instead, he distributed the district quota on the basis of the historical sales trends of the individual branches and his knowledge of key accounts. At the district level, he pointed out, a district manager was able to know his branches well enough to have a good "feel" for what they could do.

In 1965 the district manager had not received industry quota guidelines until one week after he had set the branch quotas. He had been pleased to find that his distribution had not differed significantly from that suggested by the industry managers. He had protested to the Market Operations Department, however, when he learned that prior to the formal quota announcement several of the regional industry representatives had told their specialized branches what their quotas would be.

The district manager was also disturbed by a "rumor" that branch quotas would soon be set by the regions rather than the district managers. He explained that the rumored change was probably intended to give the industry managers greater influence over individual branch quotas. While he agreed that closer coordination between industry and branch quotas might be desirable, he believed that the district managers should retain responsibility for setting branch quotas. If the district managers lost the power to set quotas, he argued, their relationships with their branch managers would be seriously undermined.

District 1: The manager of District 1 (New England) used a different method to establish branch quotas. Prior to receiving his district quota from the region, he asked each branch manager what his quota for the next year should be. The branch managers then submitted written quota "requests," broken down by individual accounts and sales territories.

When the district manager received his district quota, he compared it with the "requests" submitted by his branch managers. For 1966 he found that the two totals were within 1% of each other.

In making his final assignments of branch quotas, the district manager did not necessarily give each branch exactly what it had requested. Instead, he and his assistant went over each branch's request in detail and made adjustments where they seemed to be called for. According to the district manager, District 1 had acquired an exceptionally able group of branch managers during the past several years, and it was rarely necessary to deviate markedly from the branch quota requests in assigning the final branch quotas.

Setting Salesmen's Quotas: Branch managers used a variety of methods in distributing their branch quota to individual salesmen. In some cases, the branch manager divided his quota among his marketing managers, who subdivided their quotas among the salesmen reporting to them. In other cases, the marketing managers worked with the branch manager in assigning the quota to individual salesmen.

The branch and marketing managers had detailed knowledge concerning the sales potential of each account and the capabilities of individual salesmen. Through a variety of means, branch management estimated the potential of each account and the percentage of the branch's total potential that account represented. Since each account was the responsibility of an individual salesman, the salesman's quota generally reflected the share of total branch sales potential his accounts represented. Most branch managers adjusted quotas derived in this way to reflect the experience of individual salesmen, however.

It was common practice for branch managers to

assign 105% of the quota that the branch received from the district. Approximately 80% of IBM salesmen generally made or exceeded quota, but most branch managers wished to have the additional insurance of overassigned quotas. Moreover, the surplus, or "house quota," gave the branch manager flexibility in assigning accounts to new sales representatives. If an experienced sales representative was promoted, for example, the branch manager might want to assign his account to a relatively inexperienced salesman. Although the sales potential of the accounts was unchanged, the inexperienced salesman could not realistically be expected to do as well as the experienced salesman would have done. The "house quota" allowed the branch manager to assign fewer quota points to each account after such a personnel change than he had in his original distribution.

Using Quotas to Set Priorities

As noted above, DPD used two types of quotas: Net Sales Record Increase (NSRI) and Net Installed Record Increase (NIRI).[28] The total quota of a region, district, branch or salesman consisted of the sum of an NSRI quota and an NIRI quota. In some cases, the mix might be 70% NSRI and 30% NIRI; in other cases it might be 60% NIRI and 40% NSRI.

By varying the quota mix, management at each level of the DPD organization was able to vary the amount of emphasis the next level placed on (1) *selling*[29] *new equipment* or (2) installing equipment already on order. If management wished to emphasize new equipment sales, for example, it might set the quota mix at 60% NSRI and 40% NIRI. Conversely, if management wished to emphasize equipment installation (and thus current revenue) it might change the mix to 60% NIRI and 40% NSRI.

Sales Support

Selling, installing, and servicing a data processing system required a complex set of relationships between the customer and IBM personnel. In most cases, it was necessary to make a careful analysis of customer requirements, recommend changes in the customer's operating systems, determine alternative configurations of hardware and programming support, and provide aid and counsel to the customer during his transition to new equipment.

In order to coordinate this complex set of activities and prevent confusion on the part of the customer, IBM utilized the principle of account control. According to this principle, every present or potential user of data processing equipment was assigned to an individual salesman, who was responsible for the customer's complete satisfaction. While the customer would normally have contact with systems engineers, product and industry specialists, and customer engineers, the salesman who had account control was expected to serve as the focal point in meeting the customer's needs.

Because of the complex nature of data processing marketing, the salesmen and systems engineers working on a given account often needed to bring IBM resources outside of their direct control to bear on specific problems. In some cases, help was found in other divisions. More often, however, these resources were located in the line organization — at the branches, districts, and regions. In other cases, it was necessary to enlist the help of personnel or resources located at DPD headquarters in White Plains. This section of the case will describe some of the staff services available to DPD salesmen, and the way in which they were utilized. In addition, it will describe some of the methods used by industry and product marketing in seeking to help and encourage the field sales organization to achieve product and industry quotas.

Education

According to one IBM executive, education was the most important element in IBM's marketing mix. When IBM first entered the data processing field, relatively few potential customers had even the most rudimentary knowledge of what a computer was, how it worked, or what it could do. During this period the IBM mission was largely an educational one. Managers and sales representatives had to be taught how to sell an entirely new type of product; customers had to learn an entirely new set of concepts; and customer employees had to learn new jobs.

Although awareness and knowledge of data processing had become much more widespread by the mid-1960s, the situation had not changed fundamentally. New generations of computers, more sophisticated applications, and increasingly widespread use of data processing kept IBM active in the educational field. New accounts still had to be educated from the very

---

[28] Actually, there were several additional special quotas (e.g., out-of-territory sales; on-schedule quota points) which also were part of the total quotas. In this case, however, only NSRI and NIRI are considered.

[29] "Selling" in this instance means either outright sales to customers or lease arrangements.

beginning, although now they were likely to begin with more advanced equipment and applications. Old accounts, while sometimes possessing relatively sophisticated internal capability, still had to be instructed in the use of new equipment for new applications. IBM personnel worked hard to keep abreast of new developments in the field, whether in hardware, software, programming, or applications.

As a result, IBM was engaged in a great many educational activities. An adequate description of these activities would fill several volumes. Consequently, the present case will confine itself to a broad outline of several educational activities that seem particularly relevant to an understanding of the relationships between the field organization and product and industry marketing.

The District Education Center: IBM's educational activities were carried out in a variety of facilities, ranging from corporate education centers to branch office conference rooms. Most formal instruction took place at district education centers, however. Each district education center was directed by a district education manager, who reported to the district manager. Generally, a district education center was responsible for both customer and IBM employee education.

The Boston District Education Center was located in a modern building in the heart of the business district. In 1966, 50,000 student days were devoted to its various educational activities. For planning purposes, it broke its activities down into five categories. These categories, and the approximate amount of time to be spent on each in 1966, are listed below:

(1) Basic Sales and Systems Engineering Education (for both new salesmen and Systems Engineers)   14%
(2) Customer Programming Instruction   63%
(3) Customer Executive Seminars   8%
(4) Updating of IBM Personnel   10%
(5) Customer Unit Record Equipment Instruction   5%

Basic Education for Salesmen: When a new salesman was hired by IBM, he was assigned to a training program. Depending on the trainee's qualifications (e.g., technical vs. nontechnical college education) and the industry to which he was assigned, the basic training program varied from 42 weeks to 92 weeks. In all cases, however, the training program consisted of several formal schools (lasting from three to nine weeks) and extensive field experience. After the training program the new salesman was assigned to a territory and was responsible for meeting a quota.

A nontechnical college graduate whose first territory would be in the smaller business field (generally, small commercial applications) received the following basic training:

Basic Data Processing Course	7–9 weeks
Field Sales Experience	15–20 weeks
Application School	3 weeks
Field Sales Experience	12–16 weeks
Sales School	2 weeks
Assigned to a New Business Territory	

The training program for a technical college graduate who was to be assigned a geographic or industry (but not new business) territory was approximately as follows:

Computer Systems Training (CST)[30]	10 weeks
Field Sales Experience	26–52 weeks
Basic Systems Training	4 weeks
Field Sales Experience	8 weeks
Application School	3 weeks
Field Sales Experience	8 weeks
Territory	2 weeks

Regardless of the training program to which he was assigned, a new salesman was assigned to a branch office where he received all his field sales experience. During his training program, the district education manager was responsible for his progress. Most of his formal course work was taken at the district education center, and the district education manager, fully aware of the short-range and long-range goals of the Product Programs Department and Market Operations, monitored his on-the-job field sales training to insure that he was exposed to a variety of sales situations.

Industry Education for Salesmen: By 1965 the majority of DPD salesmen were specialized in a particular industry. In general, these salesmen received formal industry training at IBM education centers or at colleges and universities. Such training covered the nature of an industry, its problems, and its method of operations. After such training a salesman was expected to work with his customers as a fellow expert in their businesses.

The industry oriented training programs, while administered by the DPD Marketing Education Department, were generally designed by members of the

---

[30] Compared with the emphasis on unit record, Model 20, and small accounts in the Basic Data Processing Course, which the nontechnical graduate took, CST stressed computer systems throughout and the problems that larger customers faced.

Market Operations Department. In addition, industry managers and their staffs held seminars covering sales to their respective industries as the need arose. These seminars were sometimes held in White Plains but were more likely to be held at a district or branch office. Specialized branches generally had their own industry training programs and frequently requested instructors from the Market Operations Department. Unspecialized branches generally were informed when an industry representative would be holding classes in their areas, and they were free to send their sales representatives to the classes.

Industry managers believed that seminars of this sort were extremely effective in helping them to achieve their industry sales quotas. In most industries, the major potential was in new applications in existing accounts, rather than in new accounts. Since each additional application was generally more sophisticated than the application preceding it, new business was largely dependent on increased sales and systems engineering sophistication. As one industry manager pointed out, "If we are to make our quota next year, we have to motivate our salesmen to seek out and then sell applications which have just recently became possible. While a systems engineer can design the system for the application, he will never have a chance to do so unless the salesman is able to determine that the potential is there."

Product Education: The Product Programs Department shared responsibility for product education with the Education Department. When a new product was announced, the Product Programs Department helped to coordinate the preparation of educational materials and made certain that the sales representatives and systems engineers received adequate instruction in the new product, its applications, and its relationships with other parts of the IBM line.

Formal product instruction was carried out at the district education centers, but some personnel attended classes at the national training center and factory locations. Formal product education rarely took place at the branches, although special classes were held on some occasions. Representatives of the Product Programs Department might, for example, visit a branch in order to demonstrate the applicability of a new product to an industry assigned to the branch.

During late 1965, following the successful 1964 introduction of System/360, some interesting problems developed for branch managers. All sales and systems engineering personnel had received training in the new System/360 equipment, but the newer salesmen and systems engineers had relatively little experience with the older types of equipment. Since most accounts were still using the older equipment, and would continue to do so for some time, it was necessary for sales representatives to seek new applications for the old equipment as well as sell new equipment. Because the more experienced personnel were best qualified to work with the old equipment, but were at roughly the same level of competence as the new personnel with regard to System/360, there was some tendency to have the older personnel concentrate on new applications for older equipment and newer personnel concentrate on System/360. Doing so would soon make the older personnel obsolete, however, and branch managers were forced to train new personnel on the old machines as well, even though such training would be of use for only a relatively short period of time. Moreover, except for the very basic training new personnel received upon joining IBM, branch managers had to rely largely on their own resources in training their new personnel to work with old machines. However, programmed instruction courses and problem-sets helped make up for the lack of formal classes on unit record and 1400 series equipment.

Customer Education: IBM activities in the area of customer education ranged from management seminars for company presidents to on-the-job training for key punch operators.

Management seminars were generally held at the invitation of the branch office or industry managers in Market Operations. The Market Operations industry representative responsible for an area notified the branches of the date of the seminar and the subject to be discussed. Individual salesmen then invited appropriate customers to attend, often accompanying them to the seminars. Customers paid their own expenses, but the branches were expected to pay for the participation of branch personnel.

According to one industry manager, these seminars were extremely effective in selling new applications to IBM customers. Salesmen generally were enthusiastic about the seminars and did all that they could to encourage their customers to attend. In some cases, however, industry representatives had to "sell" a seminar to the sales force and, through them, to the customers. In other cases, limited industry resources made it impossible to hold as many seminars in a given area as the sales force requested.

Moreover, industry seminars often created budget problems for the branch manager. An industry marketing program might call for heavy participation by the branches in a seminar program at a time when branch budgets were already under pressure. If the branch manager allowed his salesmen to participate, he ran the risk of exceeding his budget for the year. If he did not allow his salesmen to participate, industry representatives might complain that he was not cooperating with their marketing programs.

Other customer programs were also used by branches, such as courses on concepts for middle and executive management. These courses helped customers to understand not only the products but also their own role in managing computer operations to make them more effective management tools.

Industry Marketing Programs

Each year the Market Operations Department prepared a series of marketing programs. Each program generally dealt with a particular industry or an application within an industry. A typical marketing program would describe the application and its most likely users, suggest the amount of sales and systems engineering effort that should be expended, schedule educational programs for IBM and customer personnel, and distribute a wide range of sales support materials. In some cases, sales support materials were quite sophisticated. A simulation program which allowed a potential user to observe a demonstration using his own data might, for example, be included in the marketing program.

In most industries, specific marketing programs were the responsibility of the regional industry representatives. Generally, an industry representative designed one or more marketing programs for the entire country. Such programs usually focused on opportunities existing in his region and were the outgrowth of his approach to them. In some cases, however, industry managers assigned responsibility for a marketing program to an industry representative on the basis of a national need, rather than on promising work that had been done in his region.

While industry marketing had no formal control over the implementation of its marketing programs, it generally received excellent cooperation from the line organization. In New York City, for example, specialized district and branch marketing personnel often met with industry managers to review industry marketing programs while they were still undergoing preparation. According to one industry manager, such cooperation was not surprising, since the marketing plans provided the resources needed by the line organization in order to achieve its quota. In some cases, of course, individual programs met sales force resistance. Some industry representatives complained when this occurred, but it was widely believed that most problems in this regard arose from inadequacies in the marketing plans.

Nevertheless, several industry representatives complained that it was often difficult to get branch managers to take their salesmen out of the territories to attend meetings concerned with specific marketing programs. The industry representatives wished to use these meetings to disseminate information *and* increase salesmen's interest in particular applications, whereas the branch managers were more interested in receiving industry assistance after a specific sales opportunity was located. According to one industry representative, the resources of the industry marketing organization were geared to continuing marketing programs, which required broad participation rather than individual sales efforts. He and his staff were more than willing to work with the branches on specific marketing opportunities, even to the extent of accompanying salesmen on sales calls, but he did not have enough resources to do so on a regular basis. The purpose of industry marketing programs, he pointed out, was to make the specialized knowledge of the industry organization available to the branches on a continuing basis.

Industry Role in Resource Allocation

Industry marketing took an active role in the staffing of the line marketing organization. While line management was formally responsible for the selection and allocation of personnel, the trend toward industry specialization had greatly increased industry marketing's influence in this area. If a district manager needed several industry specialized salesmen for one of his branches, for example, he would generally turn to the appropriate industry manager for help in locating them. Similarly, industry managers had a vital interest in the selection of branch and marketing managers for branches specialized in their respective industries. When a vacancy in one of these positions occurred, the industry manager generally submitted a list of qualified candidates to the district manager, who chose among them. If the district manager was unwilling to accept any of the proposed candidates, he generally asked Market Operations management for additional names.

Industry management was also concerned with the level of resources assigned to its specialized branches. One industry manager, for example, had visited his largest branch, and concluded that its "headcount" should be increased substantially. According to his analysis, IBM's position in his industry would deteriorate considerably unless more personnel were assigned to this branch.

The industry manager presented his request to the district manager, who told him that he agreed that the branch should have more "headcount" but that he did not have the manpower available. The industry manager then went to the regional vice president, and together they worked out a program for providing resources from elsewhere in the region and company. Eventually, the regional vice president assigned 32 additional men to the branch.

This shift in personnel led to problems. When the 1966 branch quotas were announced, the industry manager found that the branch in question had received a considerably larger quota than that suggested by the industry guidelines. The district had raised the branch's quota in accordance with the increase in its personnel. The industry manager believed that his suggested branch quota had taken the personnel increase into account and that the higher quota would have a bad effect on branch morale. He pointed out that the new personnel would not be really effective for at least a year.

Line Management's Role in Sales Support

The sales force also received support from line management. Although regional, district, and branch managers spent most of their time managing the resources assigned to them, they also participated in specific sales efforts. This section of the case will describe several ways in which line management worked with the sales force, but is not intended to be all-inclusive.

The Midwestern Regional Vice President's "Hot Five": The Midwestern regional vice president required each of his district managers to submit to him a list of his five most critical sales situations each week. These lists, which were known as the "hot five," were prepared by district managers from similar reports submitted to them by their branches. The reports received by the regional vice president described the critical sales situations in terms of equipment, competition, probability of success, and probable decision date.

When the regional vice president received the "hot five" lists, he held a meeting with the key members of his marketing staff. At these meetings, he and his staff went over each critical situation in some detail, and asked what they, as regional management, could do to improve IBM's chance of winning.

In commenting on the "hot five," the regional vice president pointed out that this procedure made it possible for him to bring the region's key resources to bear on critical situations. He realized that the system only worked if the branches did in fact report their critical situations to their district managers, and admitted that there were often significant pressures for them not to do so. Nevertheless, he believed that almost all branches did report their critical situations candidly, particularly since they could be held accountable later for not doing so. Each branch was required to report every lost sale and explain why it had been lost, and the regional manager's staff collated these reports with the "hot five."

District Management: District managers generally limited their direct involvement in making sales to strategy meetings with their branch managers. At these meetings, the branch manager outlined his key sales prospects and his strategy for making the sales. The branch manager's sales strategy included sales and systems engineering assignments, use of marketing programs materials or resources, and choice of equipment and programming package. The district manager generally reviewed the branch manager's strategy in some detail, and made suggestions concerning the timing of resource allocation and the use of marketing aids.

On many occasions, however, the district managers took direct part in the sales effort. When appropriate, a district manager would accompany a sales representative on a visit to a customer.

The Branch Manager: Branch managers were very much involved in almost all major sales efforts. They worked closely with their salesmen in setting and reviewing strategy and visited almost all potential customers.

Branch managers also used customer visits to gather information that could help them give assistance to their salesmen. Virtually all branch managers had sales experience, and in the case of specialized branches that experience was generally in the industry in which the branch specialized. Having more experience than most salesmen, the branch manager was frequently able to spot application possibilities that the salesmen otherwise would have missed. As the manager of a specialized manufacturing branch explained: "I usually drive over to the customer's plant with the salesman assigned to the account. On the way over we talk about the customer and the applications most likely to be of interest to him. When we get to the plant, I talk shop with the plant manager and keep my eyes open for likely problems. If a plant has higher inventory levels than it needs, for example, I will probably notice it. Then, on the way back to our office, I discuss what I saw with my sales representative and suggest possible sales approaches. This helps the salesman choose a strategy for the account we have visited, and also trains him to do these things himself."

The GEM Region

The GEM region was responsible for marketing standard [31] data processing systems to the federal government, state and local governments, educational institutions, and medical accounts. GEM had been established in November 1965 by increasing the scope of the DPD Federal Region. Since 1963, the Federal Region had been responsible for sales to the federal government in the United States and those areas abroad where the U.S. Department of Defense had data processing installations.

The establishment of the Federal Region in 1963 had represented a significant departure from IBM's geographically oriented line sales organization. While individual salesmen and branches had specialized in certain industries, the regions and districts had remained unspecialized. In order to understand the reasons underlying the decision to depart from this organizational pattern in marketing to the federal government, it is necessary to be familiar with the historical context in which this decision was reached.

Prior to the Second World War IBM had marketed its products to the federal government through its regular branch organization. Although many sales to the federal government were made by the Washington, D.C. branch, this branch was essentially a conventional branch, which happened to be located in the national capital. In 1940, however, a resident vice president in charge of government activities was appointed, in recognition of the growing importance of the federal government as a data processing customer.

During World War II federal requirements for punched card tabulating equipment grew markedly, and there was a tendency for each of the armed services and federal agencies to centralize its equipment procurement in Washington. In order to market effectively in this new environment, the Washington branch was reorganized into a number of program departments, each responsible for sales to a particular military service or federal agency.

At the request of the government, IBM undertook certain nondata processing defense contracts during World War II and the Korean conflict. This experience led to the establishment of a separate Military Products Division (see Exhibit 3), which employed 13,000 people by the middle 1950s.

As it began to recognize the impact of defense technology on federal data processing requirements (1960), IBM established a new division combining the Military Products Division and the Washington Federal Marketing organization. Known as the Federal Systems Division (FSD) (see Exhibit 5), the new division was responsbile for the sale of both data processing and military products to the federal government.

FSD's marketing organization (essentially the Washington branch, and marketing personnel located in FSD's plants and certain branch offices) successfully accomplished this mission. In 1962 IBM still had a commanding lead in federal data processing and had improved its position with regard to defense contracts.

During this same period the Kennedy and Johnson administrations began to make significant changes in federal procurement policies. In general, these changes were in the direction of increased centralization of decision making, with major emphasis on standard specifications and competitive bidding. The new environment was not advantageous to IBM, since it de-emphasized customer experience and contact, two areas in which IBM was particularly strong. Moreover, some loss of market share seemed inevitable, since competition in the data processing industry grew steadily after 1960.

In response to these new conditions, IBM transferred responsibility for marketing standard data processing systems from FSD to DPD in early 1963. To handle this business, DPD established the Federal Region (Exhibit 9), which consisted essentially of those personnel who had concentrated on data processing in FSD.

The new Federal Region was assigned direct responsibility for sales to the federal government in the Washington area (through its old program departments) and staff responsibility for working with DPD geographic branches which had federal accounts in

---

[31] Special data processing equipment or programs (i.e., products which were not part of the IBM product line but had to be developed) were the responsibility of the Federal Systems Division. In general, GEM only bid on those specifications which could be met with standard IBM products, although some modifications (similar to those available to commercial customers) were permitted.

their sales territories. While the Federal Region had only one branch (Washington),[32] some Federal Region personnel were located in non-Federal branches that had heavy concentrations of federal business. These personnel worked with branch personnel on selling and servicing federal accounts in their territories.

In February 1965, 16 of these branches were assigned to the Federal Region on a line basis. In a few instances where Federal branches retained responsibility for some nonfederal accounts, but most nonfederal business was now assigned to the branches which remained in the geographic sales organization.

By mid-1965 it had become clear that several other customer groups had applications and procurement policies similar to those of the federal government. In particular, state and local governments, educational institutions and hospitals seemed more closely related to the federal business than to the commercial business.

Consequently, in November 1965 it was decided to expand the responsibility of the Federal Region to cover these industries, and the GEM (Government-Education-Medical) Region was formed. The industry managers responsible for state and local government, education, and medicine were transferred from the Market Operations Department to the GEM Region, as were 17 additional branches.[33] The GEM Region would now have direct line responsibility for sales to its industries in those places where it had branches, and staff responsibility (similar to that of the Market Operations Department) for sales in those areas where it worked through the geographic sales organization.

The GEM Region was headed by a vice president who supervised five district managers and three department heads. The five district managers were respectively in charge of the Eastern, Midwestern, and Western Districts, the Defense Programs Department, and the Non-Defense Programs Department. The three department managers were respectively in charge of marketing programs (industry marketing), finance and administration, and staff services.[34] The heads of the Defense and Non-Defense Programs Departments were considered "district managers" in order to preserve the distinction between "line" district managers and "staff" industry managers as it existed elsewhere in the DPD organization.

District Management

The Eastern, Midwestern, and Western District Managers were each responsible for about ten GEM branches. The districts were assigned geographic territories which did not coincide with the areas covered by the three geographic regions of DPD. The Midwestern GEM District, for example, had branches in Norfolk, Atlanta, Cape Kennedy, New Orleans, Houston, St. Louis, Topeka, Chicago, Detroit, St. Paul, and Huntsville. According to GEM executives, the Midwestern District's boundaries had been established in such a way that all responsibility for NASA Space Flight Centers could be assigned to a single district.

The districts themselves were operated in much the same way as the districts in the geographic regions. Each district manager received a quota that he divided among his branches. Reports of various kinds were submitted to the GEM district managers much as they were to district managers in the geographic regions. Like their geographic counterparts, GEM district managers spent the bulk of their time setting targets, monitoring performance, making key sales calls, and handling personnel matters.

Defense and Non-Defense Programs

These departments grew out of the World War II period, when separate sales organizations had been established to sell to each of the military services and government agencies. The Director of Non-Defense Programs was responsible for NASA, Scientific and Special Programs, and Civil Programs; the Director of Defense Programs was responsible for sales to the Department of Defense. Reporting to each of these men were a number of program directors, with responsibility for individual commands or agencies. In the Defense Programs Department, for example, program directors were responsible respectively for the Army, Navy, Air Force, and Joint Defense.

The program directors had line responsibility for sales to commands or agencies headquartered in the Washington area, and staff responsibility for sales to commands or agencies located elsewhere (whether or not served by a GEM branch). In practice, this meant that the program director and his staff functioned as a sales organization for accounts located in Washington and as a sales support organization for accounts located elsewhere. Consequently, the program director received both a line quota, which he was directly

---

[32] The Federal Region also had small offices responsible for DPD activities in Europe and the Pacific. As noted above, DPD was responsible for selling data processing equipment to the Defense Department for use overseas.

[33] In January 1966 two more branches were added.

[34] See Exhibit 16, Organization Chart of GEM Region.

responsible for meeting, and a memorandum quota, which he was charged with helping the branches to meet.

In selling to commands or agencies headquartered in Washington, the program directors answered requests for proposals (preparation of a proposal could require several man years or more), called on key government decision makers, and did all that they could to influence procurements at the Washington level. In cases where the sale was to be made to a command or agency headquartered elsewhere, the program directors attempted to use their expertise to help the field branches. In some instances they assigned assistant program directors to the branches, to carry out day-to-day marketing activities. In other cases, the program directors took an active role in the preparation of proposals to be submitted by outlying branches, or invited branch personnel to Washington to assist them in planning the strategy and mechanics of proposal preparation.

In commenting on his job, one program director pinpointed an interesting problem. He pointed out that federal business was highly prestigious and carried with it significant benefits in working with new technologies. IBM's greatest strength had always been in-depth competence throughout its widely dispersed sales organization. Yet, as the federal government increasingly centralized its procurement decision making, he noted, it was possible for smaller competitors to concentrate their resources against one or two key decision points. The program directors attempted to counter this tendency by assigning key personnel to major decision points.

The Marketing Programs Department

The Marketing Programs Department functioned within GEM in much the same way as the Market Operations Department functioned for DPD as a whole. Reporting to the director of marketing programs were four industry managers (state and local government, education, medical, and federal), a manager of scientific marketing, and a manager of marketing services.

In early 1966 the industry managers who had been transferred to GEM from the Market Operations Department (state and local government, medical, and education) functioned in much the same way as they had in their previous assignments. The state and local government and medical industry managers were still physically located in White Plains, while the education industry manager, who had recently moved to Washington, kept several of his staff at DPD headquarters.

Like their counterparts in the Market Operations Department, the three industry managers prepared marketing programs and industry sales forecasts, monitored sales results in their industries, and worked with the branches on particular sales opportunities. In working with the branches, the industry managers made no distinction between GEM branches and branches that were part of the geographic regions. According to one industry manager, however, GEM branches tended to cooperate more fully with his marketing programs than non-GEM branches. Moreover, at the time GEM was established there had been some confusion in the non-GEM branches concerning their industry contacts, since the industry managers now reported to a separate region rather than DPD headquarters.

The Federal Industry Manager's assignment differed somewhat from that of the other GEM industry managers. The federal government was a huge customer, whose applications covered an extraordinarily wide range. While some of these applications were peculiarly federal, many were similar to those in other industries. For example, many federal applications were concerned with payroll accounting and finance, and were similar to those in large manufacturing companies. Others were in the fields of industrial process control and logistics, and were similar to those in the manufacturing and distribution industries. In fact, according to the Federal Industry Manager, there was no industry in the Market Operations Department that did not have some relevance to the federal government's requirements.

For this reason, the Federal Industry Manager was responsible for interfacing between the federal marketing programs and the Market Operations Department. His seven industry representatives were each assigned several industries and/or applications, and were expected to work closely with their counterparts in White Plains. On the one hand, they were to find out what was going on in the industry departments — what programs, applications, and support materials were available. On the other hand, they were to try to influence the content of the various industry product and program development activities, representing the needs of the federal government to the greatest possible extent. According to the Federal Industry Manager, his assistants would do all that they could to become working members of the industry departments in White Plains.

Quotas in the GEM Region

Because of its dual sales responsibility the GEM Region was responsible for both line and staff (memorandum) quotas. Each year the regional manager asked each of his program directors to prepare a sales forecast (by account) for federal business during the following year. At the same time he asked each branch handling GEM business (whether or not a GEM branch) to forecast its GEM sales for the following year. Similarly, each of the four industry managers prepared a forecast for his industry, although the Federal Industry Manager relied heavily on the federal program directors in arriving at his forecast.

When the GEM regional manager received the various forecasts, he compared them and resolved any discrepancies through discussions with his industry and program directors. The final forecast he thus arrived at was used as a starting point for discussion with DPD headquarters.

Generally, the GEM quota did not differ significantly from the GEM forecast. When the regional manager received his quota, he assigned it to the programs and industries in roughly the same proportion as they had contributed to the forecast.

The program and industry managers then broke their quotas down by account, in order to determine how much of their quota should be assigned to GEM branches and how much should be assigned to the geographic regions. In the case of the federal quota, it was necessary to determine how much should be assigned to the program departments, the GEM districts, and the geographic regions. In the federal industry, it should be noted, GEM had line responsibility for meeting the quotas assigned to the federal programs *and* the GEM districts; and staff responsibility for quota assigned to the geographic regions.

The GEM district managers were free to assign their quotas as they saw fit, in much the same way as the geographic regional and district managers. In practice, however, the GEM district managers followed program and industry recommendations more closely than the geographic regional and district managers did.

Salesmen working on federal accounts were paid a straight salary. Prior to 1966 they were not eligible for incentive compensation or membership in the Hundred Percent Club. Because federal orders were generally of such great magnitude, a salesman was likely either to exceed his quota by a considerable amount, or fail to achieve even a small percentage of it. In 1965, even though the Federal Region exceeded its quota, only 29% of the federal sales force would have made the Hundred Percent Club if they had been eligible for membership. In contrast, more than 80% of all DPD salesmen qualified for the Hundred Percent Club in 1965. Nevertheless, all Federal salesmen would be eligible for the Hundred Percent Club (although not incentive compensation) in 1966.

Exhibit 1. Consolidated Statement of Operations, 1957–1966
(Dollar figures in millions)

	1966	1965	1964	1963	1962	1961	1960	1959	1958	1957
Gross income from sales, service, and rentals	$4,248	$3,573	$3,239	$2,863	$2,591	$2,202	$1,817	$1,613	$1,418	$1,203
Net earnings before income taxes	1,054	960	897	778	652	546	438	380	324	239
U.S. federal and foreign income taxes	528	483	466	414	348	292	233	204	172	128
Net earnings for year	$ 526	$ 477	$ 431	$ 364	$ 305	$ 254	$ 205	$ 176	$ 152	$ 110
Cash dividends	$ 231	$ 211	$ 166	$ 118	$ 83	$ 63	$ 55	$ 37	$ 31	$ 25
Stock dividends and splits								2½%+		
per cent	50%*	—	25%*	—	—	50%*	—	50%*	2½%	100%*
shares issued	17,645,985	—	6,990,140	—	—	9,204,515	—	6,402,610	288,737	5,251,119
Shares sold	1,577,301	176,655	136,297	114,212	116,604	94,794	43,401	44,769	7,826	1,050,223
*Per Share***										
Net earnings	$ 9.66	$ 9.03	$ 8.20	$ 6.96	$ 5.84	$ 4.89	$ 3.96	$ 3.41	$ 2.97	$ 2.16
Cash dividends	4.30	4.00	3.17	2.27	1.60	1.23	1.07	0.72	0.60	0.50
At end of year										
Net investment in plant, rental machines and other property	$3,099	$2,304	$1,748	$1,586	$1,534	$1,419	$1,204	$1,039	$ 962	$ 865
Long-term indebtedness	459	399	370	550	591	585	538	520	504	432
Net current assets	723	699	900	885	681	519	469	447	407	308
Number of shares outstanding	54,448,200	35,224,914	35,048,259	27,921,822	27,807,610	27,691,006	18,391,697	18,348,296	11,849,023	11,552,460
Number of stockholders	328,427	275,650	266,086	233,761	230,235	197,509	127,478	108,915	66,667	57,330

* Splits.
** Adjusted for all stock dividends and splits.

134 *Cases and Commentaries*

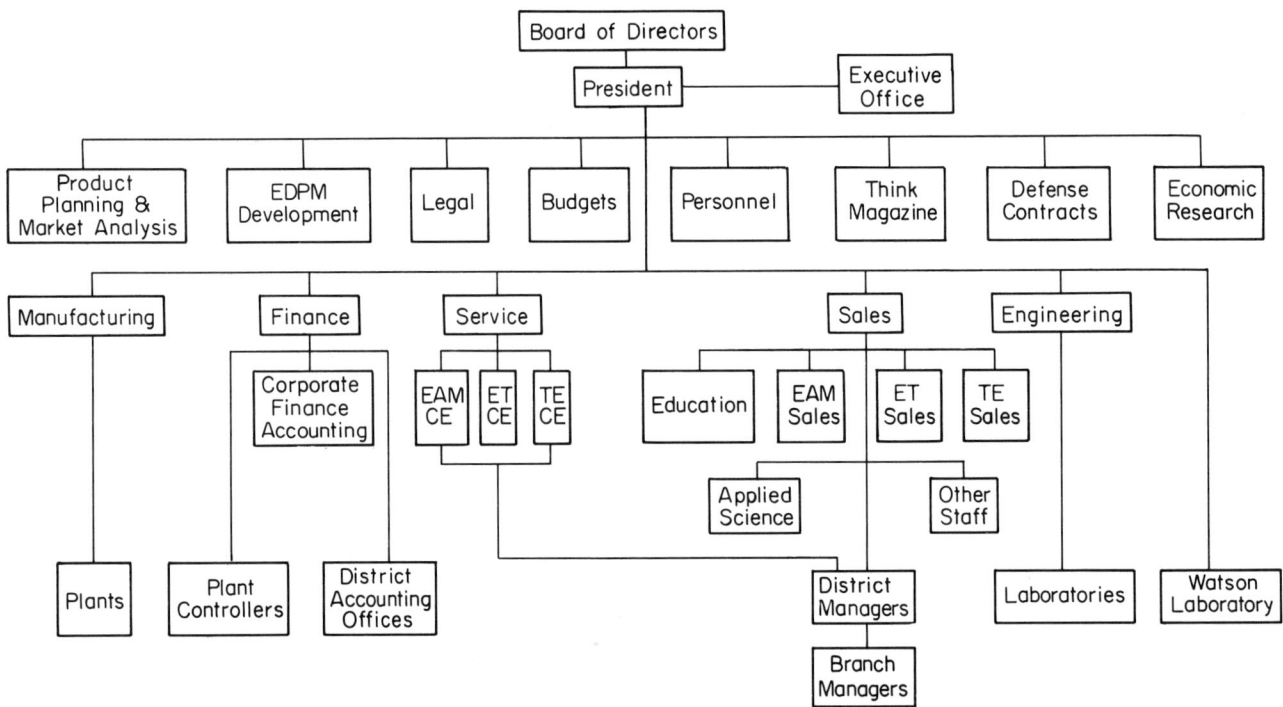

Exhibit 2. Corporate Organization Chart, May 1954

EDPM, CE = Electronic Data Processing Machinery, Customer Engineering
EAM, CE = Electronic Accounting Machines, Customer Engineering
ET, CE   = Electronic Typewriters, Customer Engineering
TE, CE   = Time Equipment, Customer Engineering

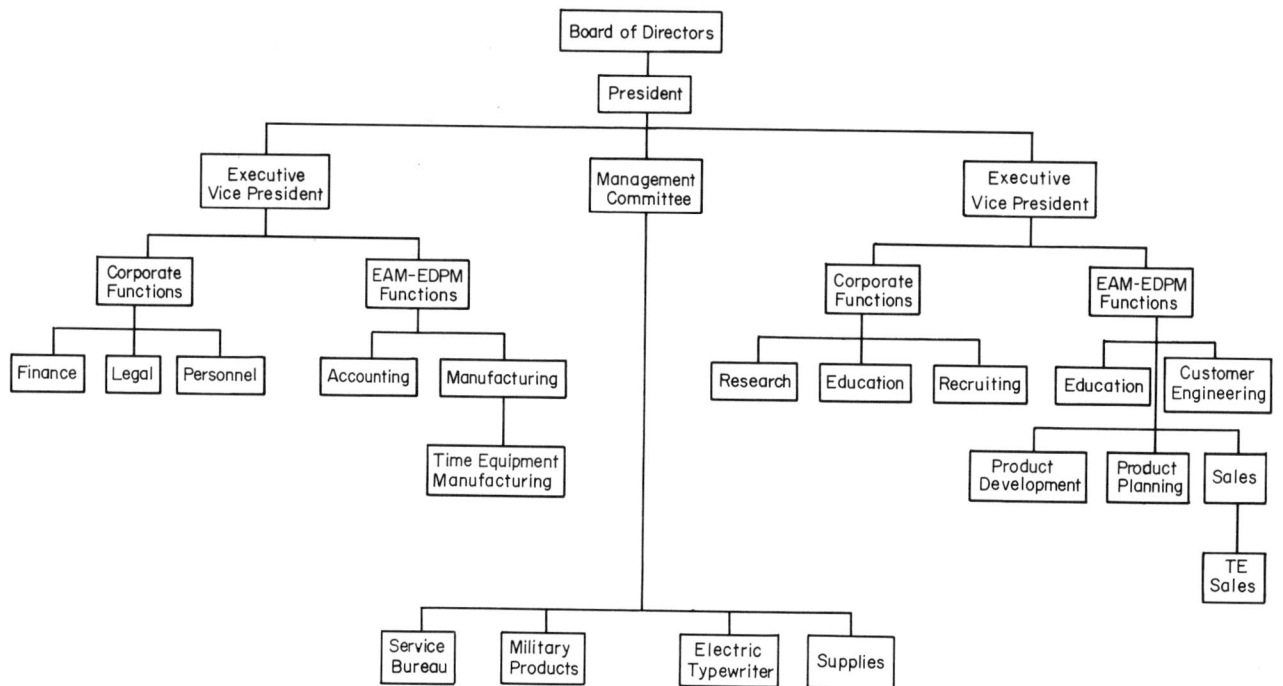

Exhibit 3. Corporate Organization Chart, June 1956

Exhibit 4. Corporate Organization Chart, November 1956

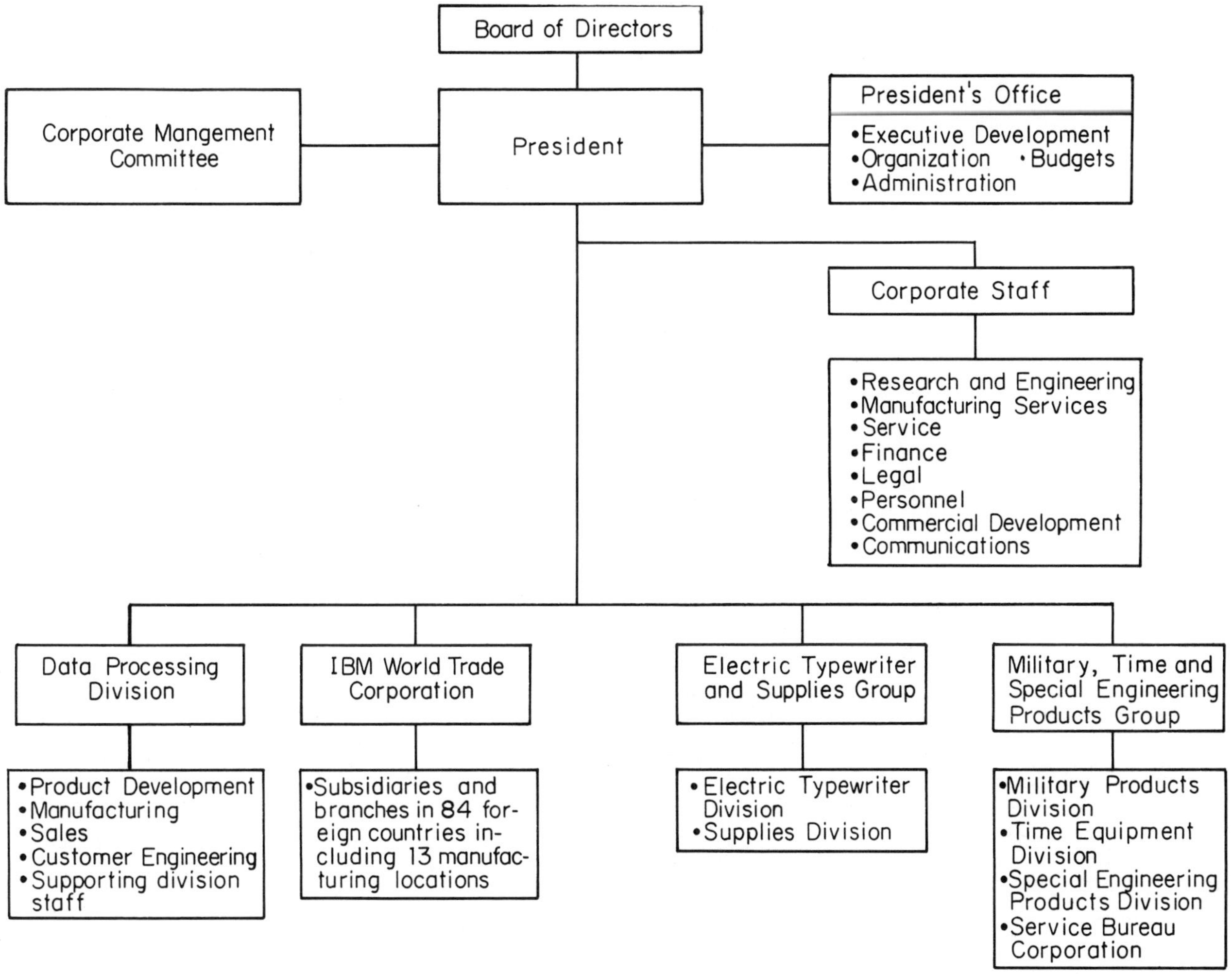

```
                          ┌──────────────────┐
                          │ Board of Directors│
                          └──────────────────┘
                                   │
┌──────────────────┐      ┌──────────────────┐      ┌──────────────────────┐
│ Corporate        │──────│                  │──────│ President's Office   │
│ Management       │      │   President      │      │ •Executive Development│
│ Committee        │      │                  │      │ •Organization •Budgets│
└──────────────────┘      └──────────────────┘      │ •Administration      │
                                   │                 └──────────────────────┘
                                   │
                                   │              ┌──────────────────────┐
                                   ├──────────────│   Corporate Staff    │
                                   │              └──────────────────────┘
                                   │              │ •Research and Engineering│
                                   │              │ •Manufacturing Services │
                                   │              │ •Service                │
                                   │              │ •Finance                │
                                   │              │ •Legal                  │
                                   │              │ •Personnel              │
                                   │              │ •Commercial Development │
                                   │              │ •Communications         │
                                   │              └──────────────────────┘
```

Data Processing Division	IBM World Trade Corporation	Electric Typewriter and Supplies Group	Military, Time and Special Engineering Products Group
•Product Development •Manufacturing •Sales •Customer Engineering •Supporting division staff	•Subsidiaries and branches in 84 foreign countries including 13 manufacturing locations	•Electric Typewriter Division •Supplies Division	•Military Products Division •Time Equipment Division •Special Engineering Products Division •Service Bureau Corporation

Exhibit 5. Corporate Organization Chart, December 1960

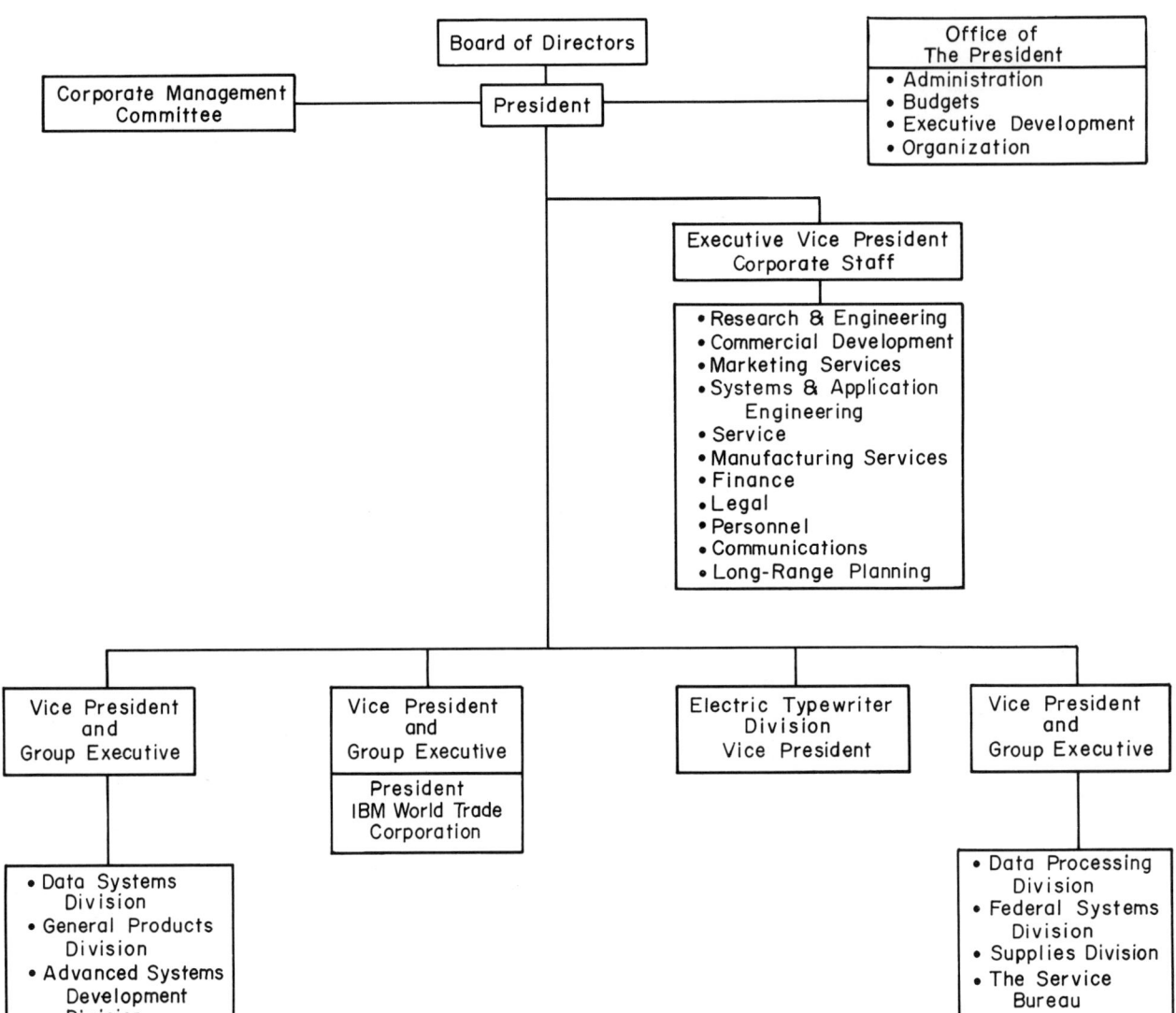

Exhibit 6. Corporate Organization Chart, July 1965

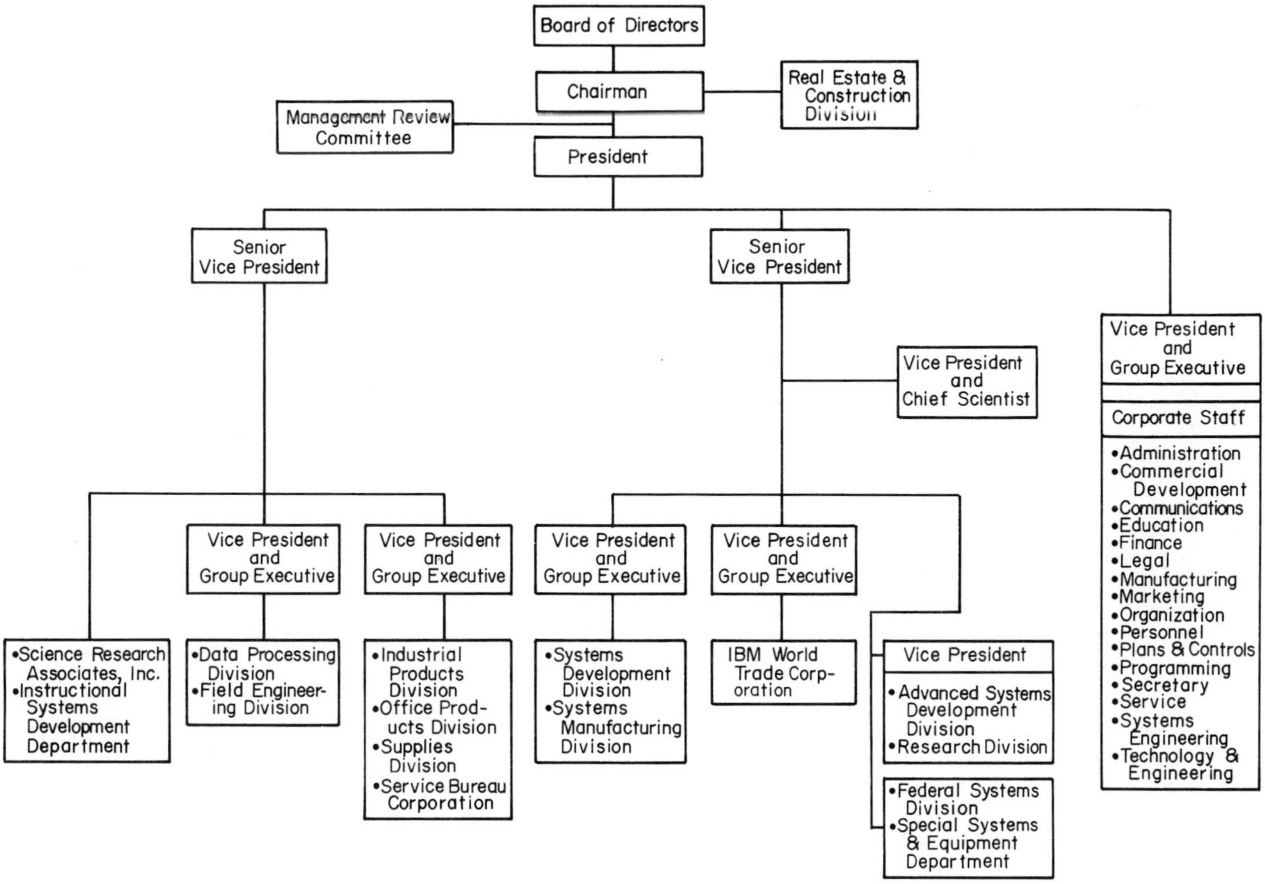

- Board of Directors
  - Chairman
    - Real Estate & Construction Division
    - Management Review Committee
    - President
      - Senior Vice President
        - Vice President and Group Executive
          - Science Research Associates, Inc.
          - Instructional Systems Development Department
        - Vice President and Group Executive
          - Data Processing Division
          - Field Engineering Division
        - Vice President and Group Executive
          - Industrial Products Division
          - Office Products Division
          - Supplies Division
          - Service Bureau Corporation
      - Senior Vice President
        - Vice President and Chief Scientist
        - Vice President and Group Executive
          - Systems Development Division
          - Systems Manufacturing Division
        - Vice President and Group Executive
          - IBM World Trade Corporation
        - Vice President
          - Advanced Systems Development Division
          - Research Division
          - Federal Systems Division
          - Special Systems & Equipment Department
      - Vice President and Group Executive
        - Corporate Staff
          - Administration
          - Commercial Development
          - Communications
          - Education
          - Finance
          - Legal
          - Manufacturing
          - Marketing
          - Organization
          - Personnel
          - Plans & Controls
          - Programming
          - Secretary
          - Service
          - Systems Engineering
          - Technology & Engineering

138 *Cases and Commentaries*

Exhibit 7. Corporate Organization Chart, April 1966

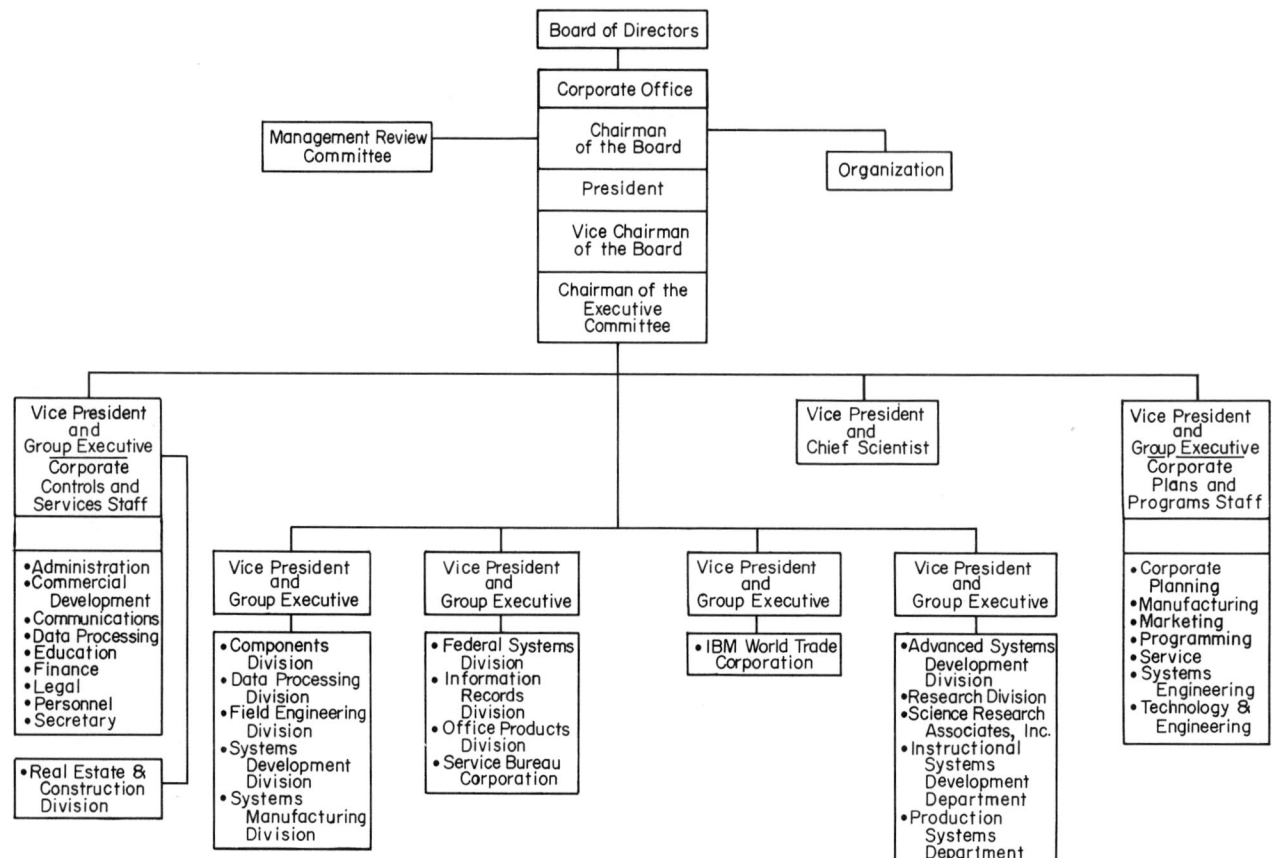

Exhibit 8. Organization Chart of Data Processing Division, September 15, 1959

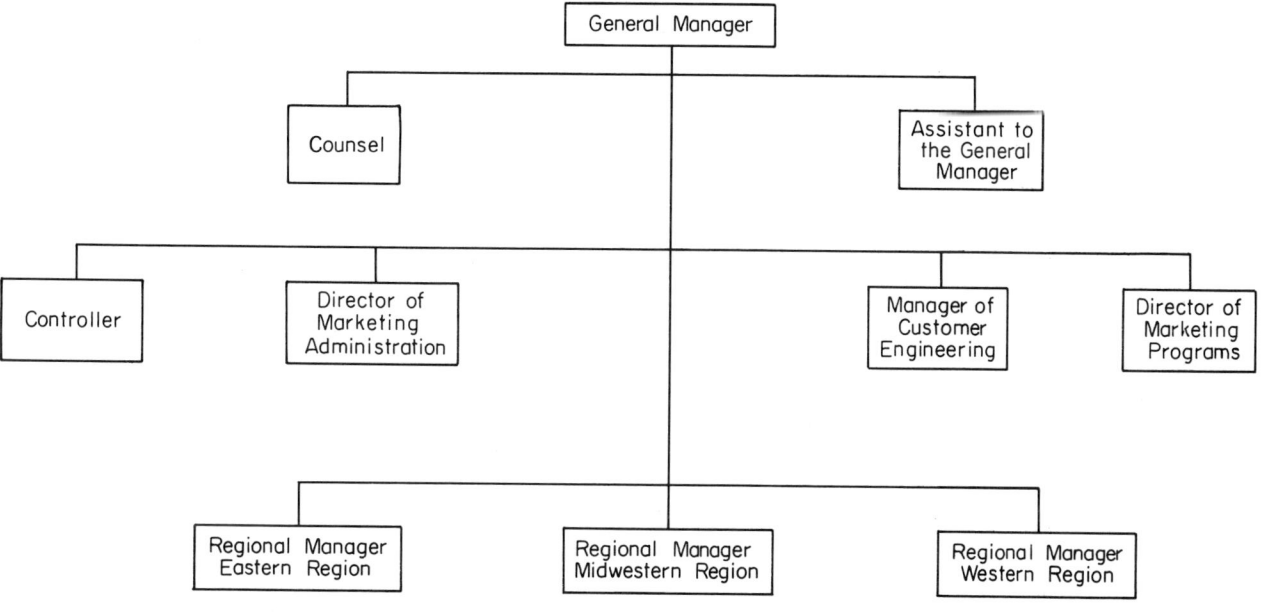

Exhibit 9. Organization Chart of Data Processing Division, October 1964

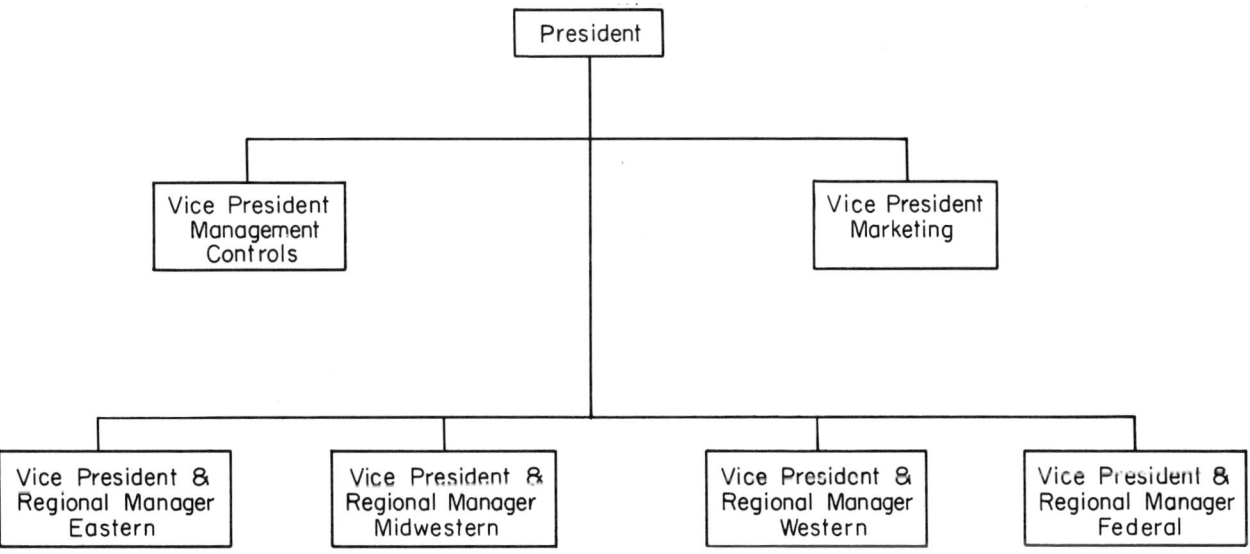

140   *Cases and Commentaries*

Exhibit 10. Organization Chart of Data Processing Division, March 1965

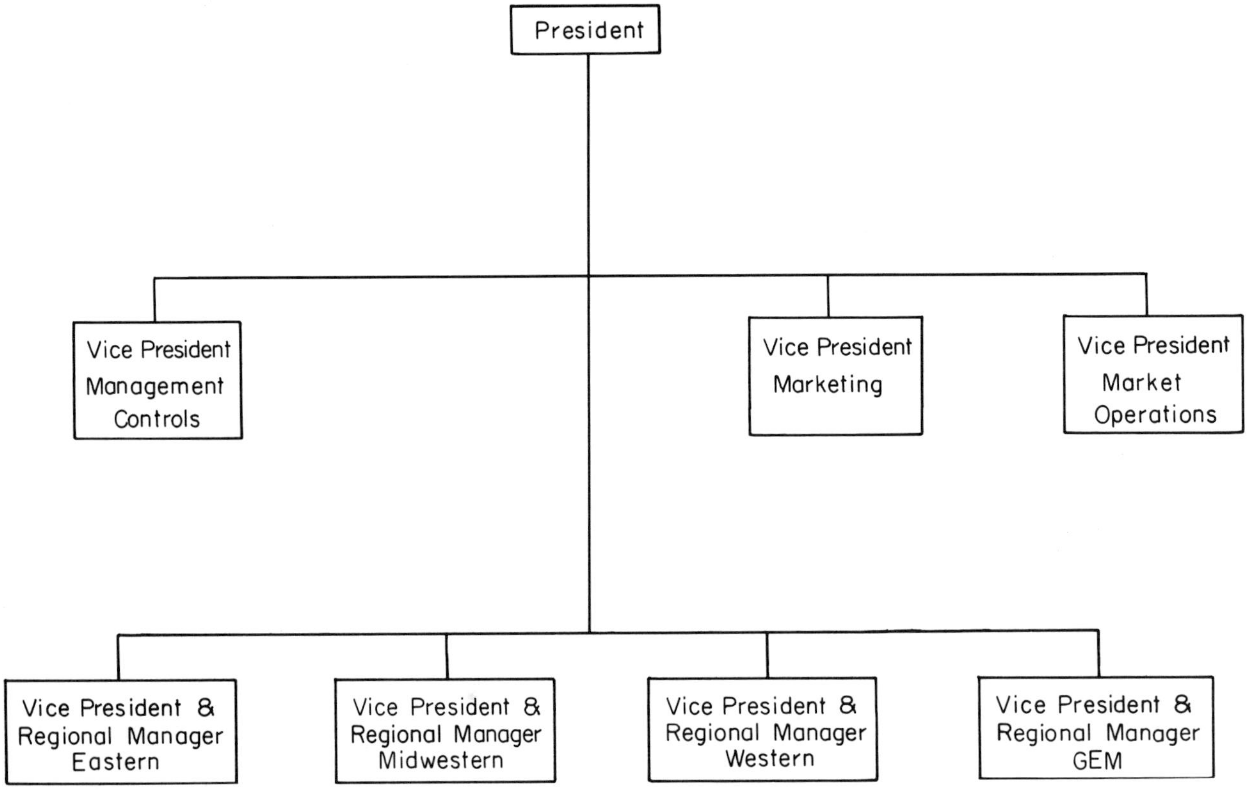

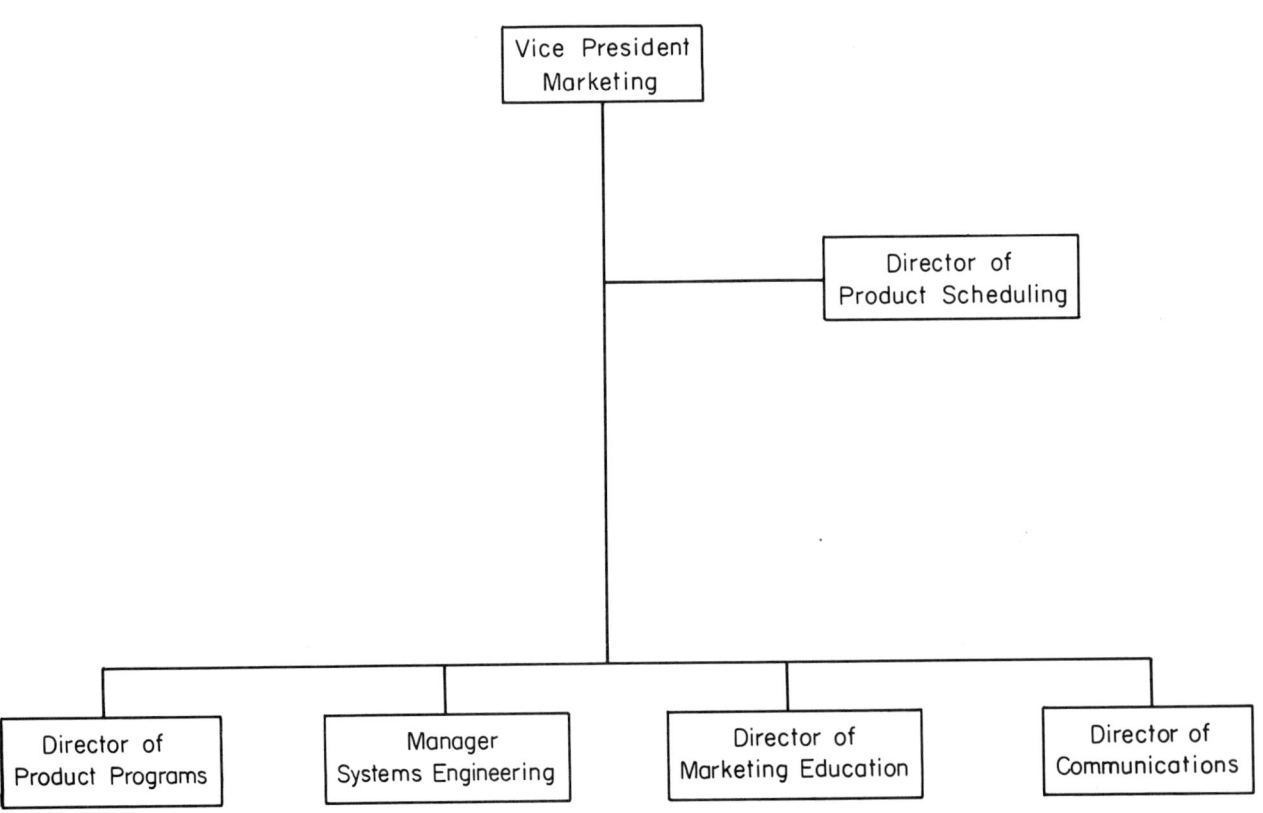

Note: The GEM Region was the Federal Region from 1963 to November 1965.

Exhibit 11. Organization Chart of Marketing Department, Data Processing Division, June 1965

IBM: Data Processing Division 141

Exhibit 12. Organization Chart of Product Programs Department, Data Processing Division, September 1965

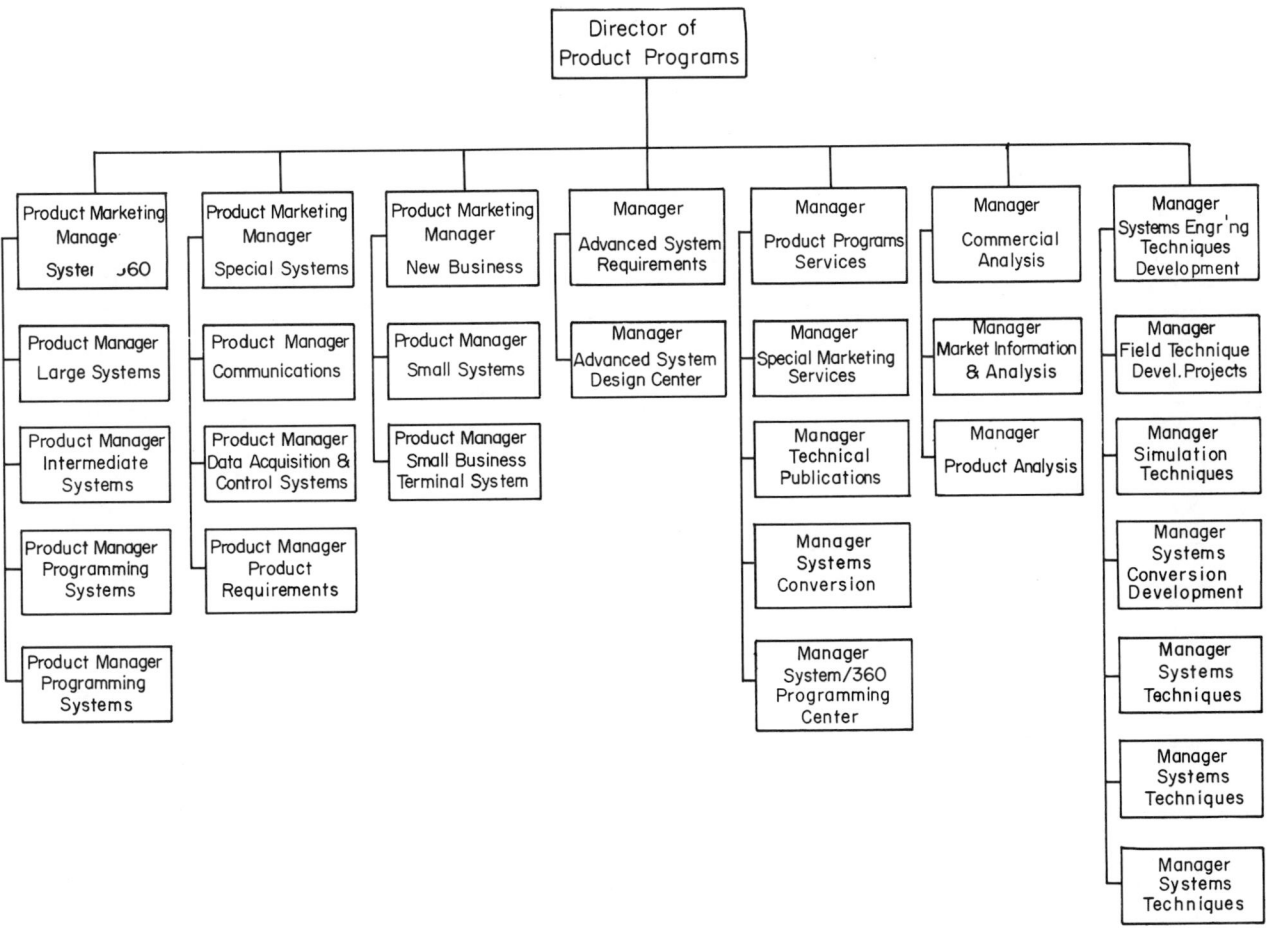

142 *Cases and Commentaries*

Exhibit 13. Organization Chart of Market Operations Department, Data Processing Division, September 1965

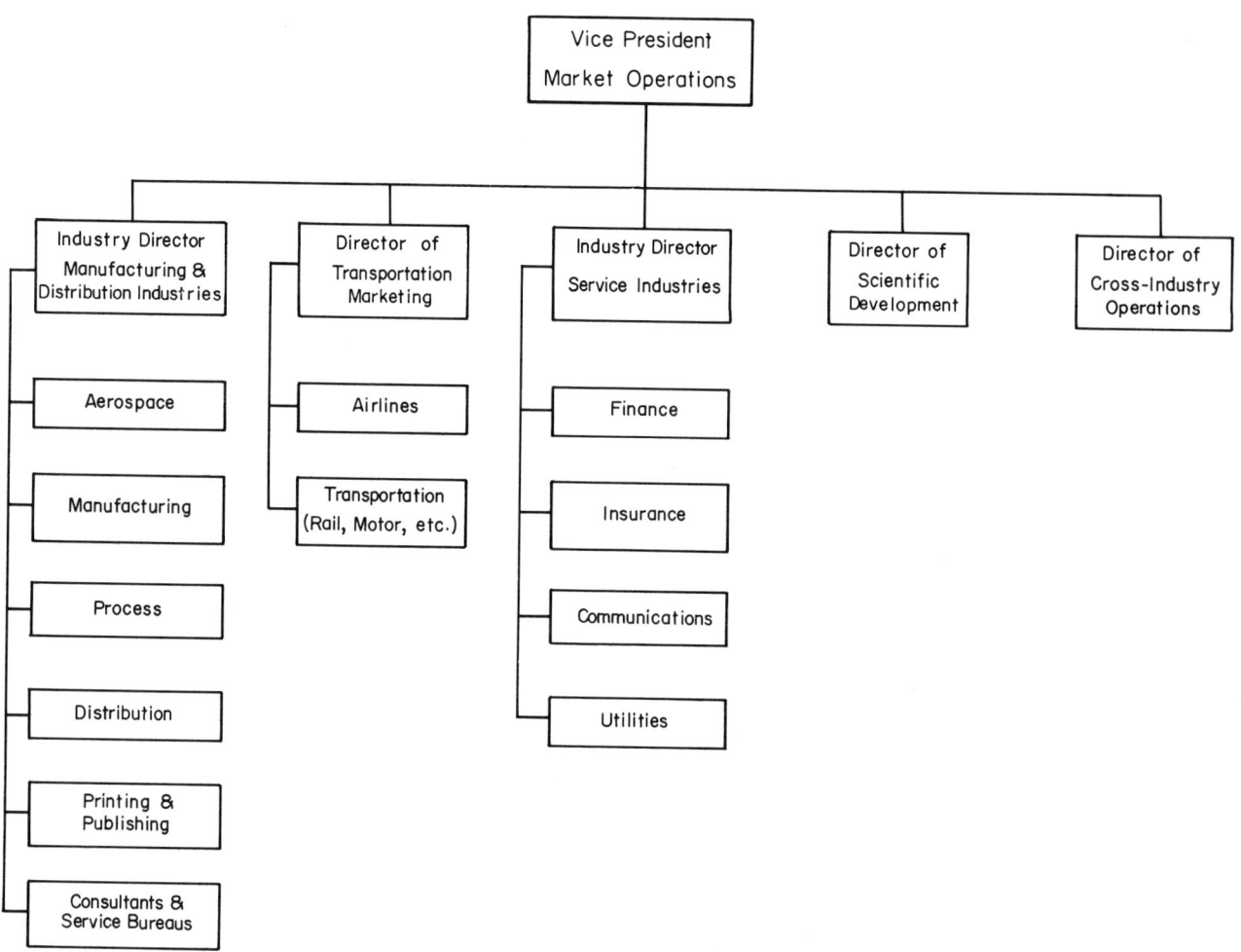

Exhibit 14. Organization Chart of Manufacturing & Distribution Department, Data Processing Division, August 1965

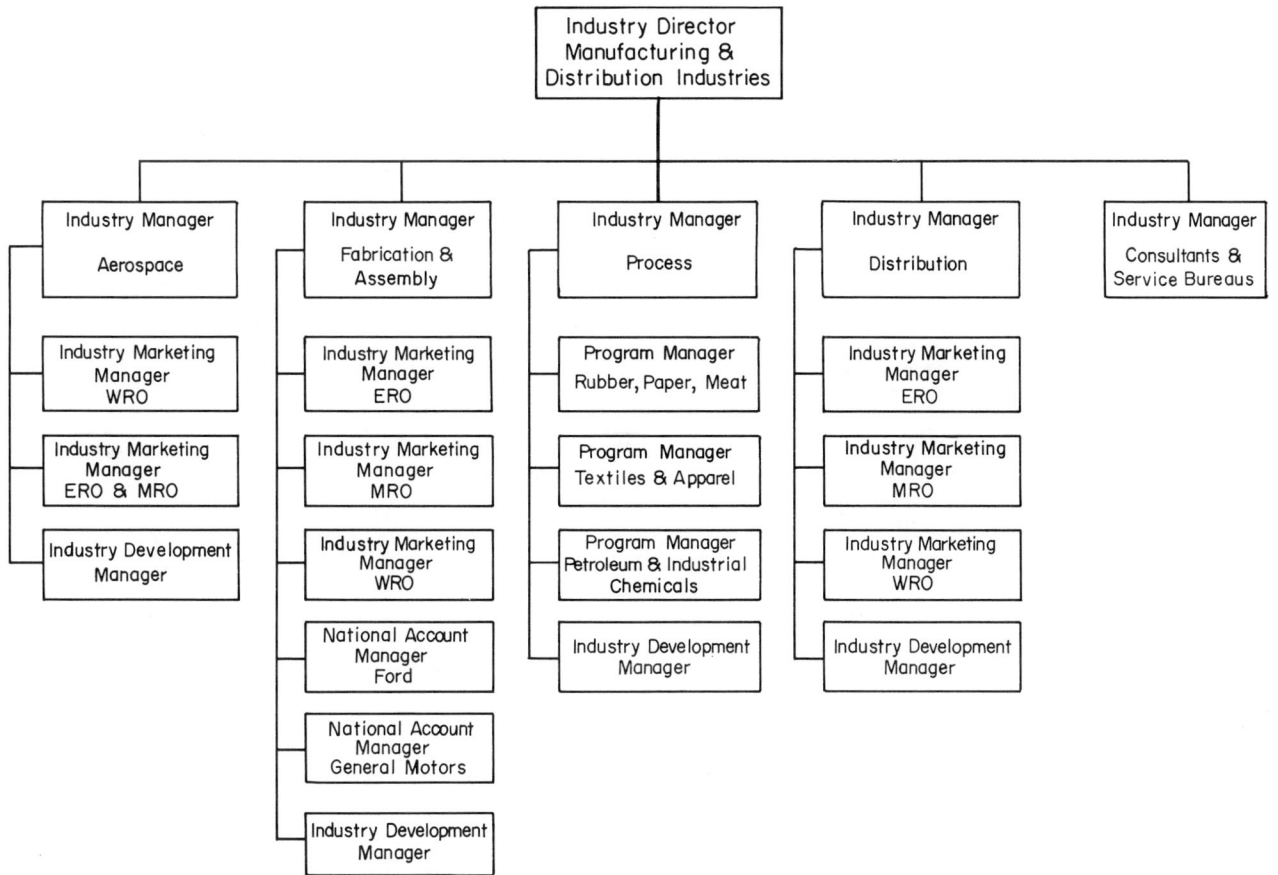

ERO = Eastern Region Operation
MRO = Midwestern Region Operation
WRO = Western Region Operation

144 *Cases and Commentaries*

Exhibit 15. Organization Chart of Midwestern Region, Data Processing Division, February 1966

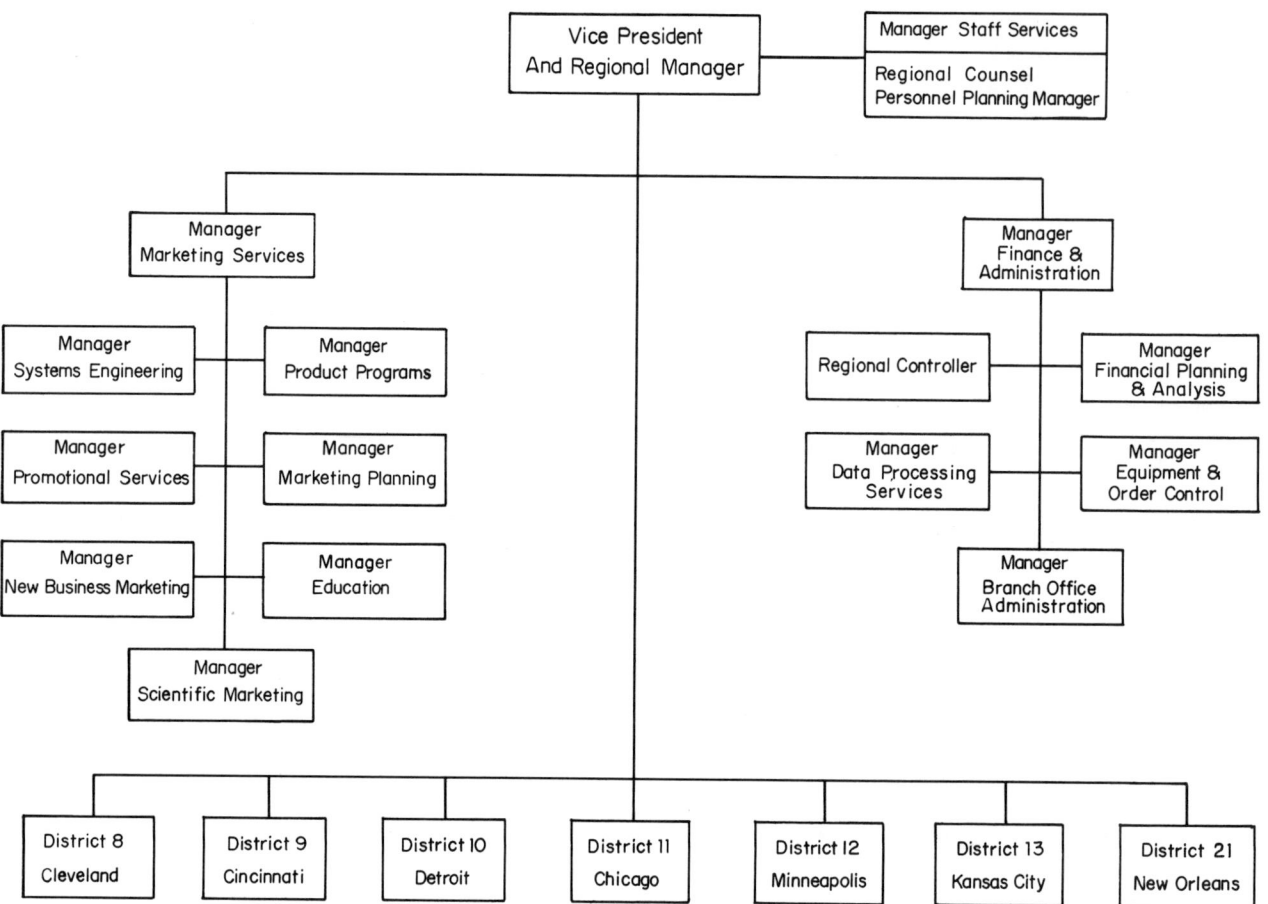

Exhibit 16. Organization Chart of GEM Region, Data Processing Division, February 1966

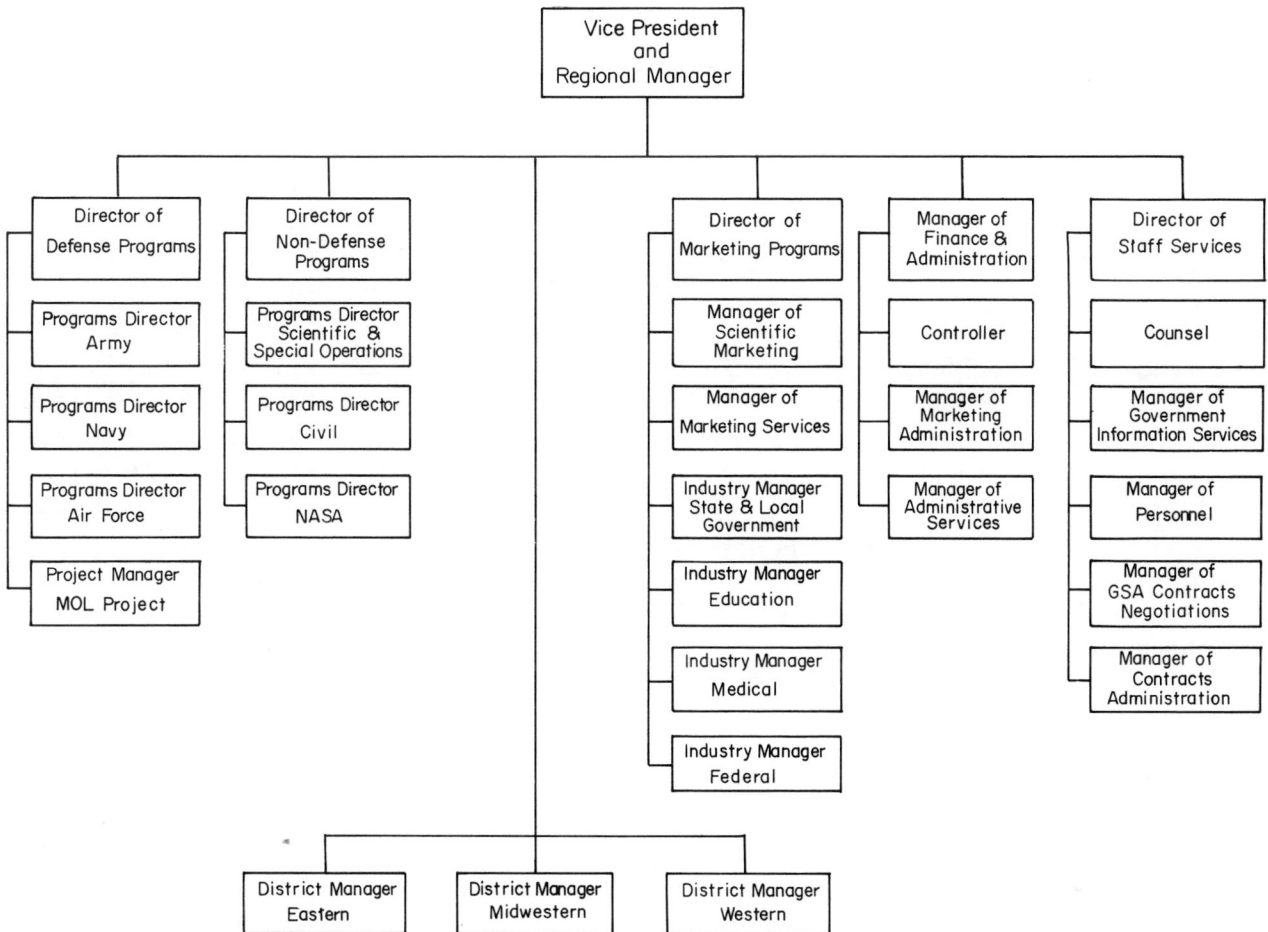

COMMENTARY

Between 1954 and 1966 the number of computers in place grew from less than 1,000 to 35,200.[1] In that period the sales of International Business Machines Corporation increased from $461 million to $4,248 million and its profits rose from $46.5 million to $526 million. A remarkable aspect of this growth is that the development of IBM's organization structure kept pace. It is relevant, indeed, that throughout this period IBM's organization was a matter of utmost concern for its president, Thomas Watson, Jr. He gave it his personal attention, and during the 1956–1966 decade a staff group for organization reported directly to him.

There is much to learn from IBM's experience. This statement will comment on four organizational aspects in particular: (1) the emergence of a data processing *business* and how its resource structure evolved; (2) the development of the industry marketing program structure — why this took place, how markets were segmented for organizational purposes, and how these units functioned; (3) the product program structure — how it supplemented industry programs, and how it functioned in new product development; and (4) the organization of field sales activities — the roles of regional and district offices and the development of field sales branches specialized by user industry. Finally it will be interesting to speculate as to the future direction of the growth of the organization of IBM's data processing business.

Structuring a Business

Lockheed-Georgia developed a business around a plant facility, building it up from government contracts to modify B-52 bombers. Mobil built an integrated business in the United States and Canada by putting together three corporate entities.

IBM structured a data processing business by stripping away unrelated activities.

In 1954 and 1955 IBM was organized as a single business; within major resource departments such as Sales, Service, and Manufacturing separate departments were established to handle the company's three major product lines: time equipment, electric typewriters, and electric accounting machines. By November 1956, however, IBM's management had organized the company into four separate businesses, one of which had responsibility for the design, manufacture, and sale domestically of data processing equipment (known earlier as the electric accounting machine line). This was a key organizational move. Self-contained and with separate identity, the data processing business grew rapidly. By 1959 IBM sales of data processing equipment exceeded total corporate sales for 1955.

Interestingly, the reasons given for establishing four business units are similar to those which prompted the Du Pont management to *consolidate* its five synthetic fibers operations into one business, and the Ford Motor Company to create a single North America Automotive Operations business. In each instance the new business provided a better framework for forward planning and for measuring performance.

The IBM experience also parallels that of Monsanto's Organic Chemicals Division, which was divided into six separate businesses. In both cases, organizational restructuring was undertaken to relieve the heavy management load imposed on top officers and to speed decision making at operating levels.

The Evolving Structure of the Resource Functions

The structure of the data processing business evolved gradually and was still changing ten years

---

[1] Source: The American Federation of Information Processing Systems.

later. The emergence of industry and product programs and the organization of field sales are reserved for later comment, but it is useful at this point to look at the overall structuring of the resource functions in the data processing business.

In 1959 data processing was divided into four divisions. Two of these divisions had both development and manufacturing responsibilities: the General Products Division for small systems and the Data Systems Division for large systems. The Advanced Systems Development Division was to identify new market opportunities and work on advanced designs. The Data Processing Division (marketing) was to report to a different vice president and group executive and to handle both domestic sales and the servicing of computers in use.

The distinction between large and small systems gave way with the development of System/360, a single product line covering the full range of applications. In 1965 the product development and manufacturing functions were separated in the Systems Development Division and the Systems Manufacturing Division respectively. The sales and customer engineering functions were segregated, with the Data Processing Division handling the first and the Field Engineering Division the second. As before, development and manufacturing divisions and the marketing divisions reported to different vice presidents and group executives.

In 1966, however, all these divisions were placed under one group executive, who was to coordinate their plans and activities and present integrated plans for the entire data processing complex to corporate management.

We can postulate that three factors may have led to the separation of the four functions organizationally. First, differences in time cycle. The case tells us that the Data Processing Division was heavily oriented toward day-to-day sales activities and therefore field engineering tended to receive inadequate management attention. Hence these two resource functions were placed in two different departments. In addition, systems development operated with longer time horizons than manufacturing, which was focused on meeting near-term production deadlines. Therefore, it was practical to have separate divisions for these functions.

The appropriate form of organization of the activity might be another factor. As the sales function developed, it became organized both in the field and at headquarters by market or customer industry group. In contrast, field engineering was best organized along product lines. Product specialization rather than specialization by user industry was the more critical dimension, then, along which to organize field engineering.

Having the sales and field engineering functions in separate divisions was also recognized as benefiting the professional growth of IBM field engineers. Probably the same consideration would apply in the case of systems development and manufacturing. The former function would call for more scientifically trained personnel. Their career paths and professional development would go along different lines from most manufacturing personnel.

Finally, the Ford Motor case tells us something of the reasons for separating product development and manufacturing functions: The development function needs to be positioned organizationally to give balanced consideration to market considerations, plant investment commitments, and manufacturing costs in planning and developing new products.

Almost ten years after Data Processing had been established as a separate business, systems development, manufacturing, sales, and field engineering emerged as segregated functions in the resource structure. The reasons that are suggested had to do with differences among these functions as to the time horizons of the work they did, the development and advancement of personnel in each function, and the way in which these functions should be appropriately organized internally. It also had to do, as in the case of systems development, with the range of considerations on which decision making in that function was based.

The Emergence of Industry Programs

In the late 1950s IBM began to establish industry marketing program management units at headquarters in the Data Processing Division. At the same time members of the field sales force began to specialize in specific user industries — utilities, financial institutions, manufacturing.

The pressures that led in this direction were several. First, user industry became the key dimension for forecasting sales. It was more accurate to predict the spread of computers by customer groups than to forecast sales of the product line as a whole.

A second major factor leading toward specialization by customer industry was that the *application* of data processing equipment varied widely from one industry group to another, but the same "hardware" could be used by all customer categories. System/360 was the common denominator. So-called Type II programs ("software") were designed for the different computer applications in the several industry groups.

In some cases, industry program management units served to place emphasis on highly critical markets: the government market, for example, where IBM was losing market share to competitors, and airlines, where a relatively few potential customers represented a large market.

Forecasting needs, differences in application technology among user groups, and the need for management focus on critical markets led to the development of an industry program structure in the Data Processing Division. But such a structure requires tremendous overheads in personnel specialized by user group. It must take a certain "critical mass" of sales volume to support such a structure. One cannot say exactly what this threshold level is; almost certainly IBM's sales of data processing equipment in the middle 1950s would not have supported such a degree of specialization. One might speculate that even in the middle 1960s no competitor was large enough to specialize by market to the extent that IBM had. A logical strategy, therefore, for smaller competitors would be to offer specially designed products and special applications skills in one or a limited number of market segments.

The Market Segmentation Scheme

As of 1966 IBM had divided its market into 16 major industrial classifications for purposes of organizing, forecasting, planning, and implementing marketing strategy. The scheme was based largely on differences among market segments in computer uses.

Application technology in the "airlines" market was markedly different from that in "distribution" and different again from data processing applications in "insurance" and "utilities." In addition, customer buying behavior tended to be relatively homogeneous within each segment. By contrast, the identification of "Federal Government" as a market segment for organizational purposes was predicated on *customer buying behavior* as opposed to application technology. "Federal Government" is a tremendously large customer group with a very wide range of applications. Many, if not most, of these applications — such as payroll accounting, process control, and logistics — were like those in such market segments as manufacturing, distribution, or insurance. The buying behavior of "Federal Government" is different, however, from that of other market segments, and centralized buying decision making and the use of competitive bidding procedures are key characteristics.

While decision making is centralized, it is also complex. In any one procurement, there are likely to be a number of decision-making influences at different locations (both geographically and organizationally) that need to be identified and addressed each in terms of his particular interests in the procurement. At the same time, IBM executives believed, the great use of competitive bidding procedures in the government discouraged customer appeals — service, reputation for reliability, systems design experience — that either cannot be expressed in dollar terms or, if quantified as part of the price, place the bidder at a competitive disadvantage.

In view of these considerations, marketing to the federal government is a field of its own. Government marketing expertise involves in-depth knowledge of government organization structure and procedures, a working knowledge of the people who participate in one way or another in procurement decisions. And unless it is kept current, such an expertise may quickly become obsolete because government organization and procedures change frequently and personnel turnover is rapid. In addition, skill in competitive bidding is based in part on a knowledge of competitors' strategies and pricing practices and of the bidding history on similar procurements. Finally, all of this will vary from one federal government organization to another and will lead to a program structure broken down by government agency.

Government marketing expertise is one factor. Another is that the regional sales organization, which was suited to commercial business, was not suited to government sales where the decision-making network is geographically dispersed. Hence, it is interesting to note, first, that in defining the field sales structure the geographic bounds of regions were bent to accommodate customer geography. Second, it may be noted that selling responsibility was lodged initially and primarily with program directors in Washington. They dealt directly with agencies headquartered in the Washington area and coordinated and supported sales activity in the branches.

While the DPD management decision to establish "Federal Government" as a program recognized that these customers had somewhat similar buying behavior patterns, the program organization was structured to account for similarities in computer applications with other market segments. It was designed to provide for close working relationships with all other DPD industry program teams so that program and product technology could be easily transferred from commercial to government markets.

"State and Local Government," "Education," and "Medical" were combined in 1965 with "Federal Government" as programs in the "GEM Region" because these four market segments were perceived as being related and also somewhat similar in buying characteristics. In many instances medical and educational data processing expenditures are financed by state, local, and federal agencies; and personnel in these agencies become involved in purchasing decision making. In addition, procurement in these markets is often (but not always) by competitive bid, and decision making is complex.

In a letter announcing the formation of the GEM Region in November 1965, the DPD President made the following statement:

Now — since "nothing succeeds like success" — we are extending the scope of the activities of the Federal Region to include State and Local Government, Education, and Medical industry marketing. Our studies and analyses have shown that the interests and data processing needs of customers and prospects in these fields are closely related to those of the Federal Government. By making them part of the new Government-Education-Medical Region we improve our ability to meet customer needs. We also help everyone concerned function more effectively in this interrelated marketing area.

Finally, the larger market base of the new GEM Region would indeed help to support the overhead structure which had to be put in place when the Federal Region was established. Thus, four programs, Federal Government, State and Local Government, Education, and Medical could share the field sales resources of the GEM Region. At the same time the state and local government, education, and medical programs might receive more management attention than previously. These might possibly have been considerations, if one is to speculate on why IBM's management made the move it did in November 1965.

There were, then, two basic criteria for segmenting IBM's market for organization and strategy purposes: application technology and differences in customer buying behavior.

The Role of Industry Marketing Management

Market Operations Managers were responsible for developing programs for their respective industry groups. A program might cover an industry or some specific data processing application within an industry. The program could describe the application and its potential market. It would suggest the amount of sales and systems engineering effort needed and schedule educational programs for IBM and customer personnel. The type and amount of sales support materials would also be delineated in the marketing program.

The program was implemented by field sales representatives, systems engineers, district education centers, and the headquarters communications department for promotional materials. Market Operations Managers did not exercise direct control over these resources but generally received their full cooperation.

Although Market Operations Managers depended on resources that they did not directly control to carry out their programs, they wielded considerable influence. This influence derived in large part from the fact that to meet their assigned quotas (by industry) it was essential for District Managers to pursue planned industry strategies. Similarly, the field branches, which included both salesmen and systems engineers, were dependent on the Market Operations Managers for soundly developed programs.

The influence of the Market Operations Managers seems to have increased as industry specialization of field branches spread. The industry-specialized branches were increasingly dependent on their respective Market Operations Managers for strategic planning. In addition Market Operations Managers were called on by the regional and district sales operations to advise in the staffing of specialized branches. Field sales personnel undoubtedly recognized, then, the influence that Market Operations Managers could exercise in their own career progress and were responsive to their guidance. Moreover, much of the education received by IBM salesmen and systems engineers was application oriented and stemmed from Market Operations units. Finally the influence of the Market Operations Managers was greatly extended in early 1964 when the 200 industry marketing specialists who had been on the staffs of the regional vice presidents were instructed to report directly to the Market Operations Managers in White Plains. These specialists continued to be located in the regional headquarters and disseminated industry marketing programs to the field sales force. The geographic extension of program management provided industry managers with the means for directly reaching IBM personnel who played a key role in implementing their programs.

It is interesting to note, however, that the functions of industry program management were not always perceived in the same way by those involved in it and their counterparts in field sales. Field sales managers wanted help in making individual sales; industry program managers wanted the time of field sales personnel to give them information on industry marketing programs and stimulate their interest in particular computer applications.

Industry program managers, then, did not directly control field sales resources but exercised a strong influence over field sales activities because (1) they developed the strategies which set sales tasks and against which sales performance was measured; (2) they had strong informal influence over program-specialized sales branches; and (3) their influence was extended through members of the program team who were in direct contact with field sales personnel.

Resource Units in the Programs

By contrast with Lockheed-Georgia where all the resource units were located in resource departments (i.e., engineering, manufacturing, materiel) and directly controlled by branch heads, certain resources were part of the industry marketing management organization. In particular, each industry manager had his own technically skilled personnel for developing Type II programs. Since "software" was an important part of what IBM sold to its customer, it may be said that each industry management team had its own product development group. Data processing applications varied greatly from one customer group to another, and it was logical that each industry program unit have its own "software" development resources. On the other hand, "hardware" product development, which was not unique for each user industry, was the responsibility of the Systems Development Division.

At least one program, the Airlines Industry, also had its own field sales and systems engineering personnel and did not draw on the regional organization. Because airlines reservations systems were highly specialized, because there were relatively few potential customers, and because each such customer was a potentially large user of IBM equipment, DPD management believed that specialized sales and systems engineering personnel should be attached directly to the program. Such an arrangement would be economical because a large force was not required to cover the potential market. Moreover, such an arrangement would facilitate the coordination of systems development, sales, installation, and servicing effort by individual customer. The concentration and coordination of effort that would be achieved would strengthen IBM competitively in this important market.

The Government, Education, and Medical group of programs shared a field sales organization and, like Airlines, did not utilize the resources of the regional selling organization. But unlike Airlines, there were a large number of large and small potential customers in these three categories. In the case of GEM, however, the reasons for having specialized field sales resources were twofold. First, customer buying behavior in these categories was different from that which characterized industrial purchasing behavior. It would be advantageous to have field salesmen who understood institutional customers and could develop experience in dealing with them. Second, the IBM regional sales organization was not well-structured geographically to deal in particular with federal government agencies. Hence, the GEM region had been delineated geographically to take account of customer locations. For example, the GEM Midwestern Region had been drawn so that the responsibility for NASA Space Flight Centers could be assigned to one district within the region. These considerations were important because buying decision-making influences were frequently dispersed geographically within the customer organization.

Another type of resource activity was found attached directly to the industry program organizations — designing industry-oriented training programs. These programs might then be conducted by the DPD Education Department for personnel in the district selling organizations. In addition, the case indicates, industry managers and their staffs also sometimes held seminars at headquarters or in the district or branch offices.

At IBM, then, certain resources were specialized by industry program and attached to the program organization. In all such cases, resource effort was specialized by market segment: the development of Type II programs, selling and systems engineering for Airlines and GEM, and designing and conducting industry-oriented training programs. In all cases, specialization was economically justifiable (the concentration of customers in the airlines industry made it feasible to have a specialized Airlines sales force). In one instance, Airlines, specialization by application was needed; in another, GEM, special expertise in customer purchasing patterns was required.

The Product Programs Organization

The IBM case introduces an organizational design providing for both industry marketing program managers and product marketing program managers. The Textile Fibers Department at Du Pont also used such a scheme. It may be useful to refer to this arrangement as a bilateral program structure and to see how the two functions interrelate.

The Product Marketing Manager in the Product Programs Department of DPD is concerned largely with product development, product introductions, product education for field sales personnel, and the identification of product marketing opportunities. He works to translate market requirements for new products and product features to the Systems Development Division. He gathers information from market and technical sources and takes initiative in proposing new product developments. Committed to the success of the products he manages, the Product Marketing Manager has the responsibility for moving his products into the on-going stream of sales and servicing activities. He works to make it as easy as possible for IBM sales representatives to sell his products, for field engineers to service them, and for customers to use them. A large part of his task is educational: to provide product training for IBM sales representatives, to identify market opportunities for them, to develop product brochures and demonstration films. An important part of his task is "internal selling": to persuade industry marketing program managers in the Market Operations Department and field sales personnel to devote time and attention to selling his products.

Is there a need for *both* industry program and product program managers? The two functions are complementary. Industry marketing focuses on the customer and is organized to deal with market segments. It is concerned with customer uses of computers. It works through the field sales organization. Its focus of attention is on on-going sales activities and the development of market potential for products in the line.

The product programs function is focused on new products, the process of maintaining a competitive product line, of developing new products at the leading edge of the state of the art, and moving them into the on-going stream of marketing activities. Product development cuts across, and involves integrating the efforts of such internal resources as sales, technical development, and manufacturing to a much greater extent than industry marketing. Product program activities have a longer time cycle than industry marketing program work. By providing for both product and market dimensions in its organization, the Data Processing Division seeks to assure balanced consideration for the needs of markets and for new technical advances in the development of its product line. The continued updating of the product line, although a competitive necessity, may be a source of disruption in sales and manufacturing activities. The role of product programs is both to take the initiative in product change and to facilitate the continued upgrading of the line.

It may be noted that the product program manager at IBM and in the Du Pont Textile Fibers Department plays a different role from that of product managers in organizations where there are not also market program managers. (This arrangement may be termed a *unilateral product program structure*.) Lockheed-Georgia and the General Foods Post Division are cases in point.

In these cases, "market" is defined essentially in terms of the market or markets for that product, and the marketing program is the strategy for developing and selling the product to all, or selected, potential customers. The product manager may also be deeply involved in initiating new product developments, or that function may reside in a separate product development department.

A unilateral product program structure, the statistical evidence in Chapter VI indicates, is usually found where there is not so much market diversity as in IBM and Du Pont Textile Fibers. It is also likely to be found where the size or "critical mass" of the business is not sufficiently great to support the overhead of a bilateral program structure.

The Product Development Process

The product development process at IBM, in which the product managers play a key role, is a very interesting one to study. It is useful to note, first, that new product development projects were initiated largely on the basis of, and supported by, market data (field sales requests, the perceived product needs of industry managers, and the analysis of competitive activities). Initially, then, the "burden of proof" resided with product managers in DPD. The Systems Development Division management could elect not to respond to a product development request if not satisfied on economic or strategic grounds that a convincing case had been made. But once SDD agreed to undertake development work, initiative then transferred to that department. SDD worked with product administrators to develop formal product specifications and visited IBM customers to appraise market response to the proposed new products. SDD then prepared sales forecasts and manufacturing cost estimates based on stated assumptions as to product features, price, and date of availability. Managers and staff personnel at the regional level then reacted to SDD forecasts, and the product administrator "negotiated" changes in specifications and forecasts with SDD. When DPD management formally concurred with SDD specifications and forecasts, then DPD program, product, and sales managers assumed sales responsibility for the new product.

Thus, while product administrators in DPD and SDD personnel had a close working relationship in the development process, *initiative* and *commitment* shifted back and forth from one group to the other. The process was designed to achieve a balance between market and technical considerations, assuring that products were developed in response to clearly identified market needs, that technical and manufacturing cost considerations were balanced against potential sales volume and profit estimates. Shifting the burden of primary responsibility between DPD and SDD at different stages also served to assure that each would contribute in a significant and timely way to product development.

It may also be noted that when a new product was completed and accepted by DPD, the product administrator, not industry marketing managers, took over the task of preparing promotional and educational materials. In effect, he prepared the way for market introduction, thus facilitating the task of the industry marketing managers.

The Field Sales Organization

IBM's field organization had three levels — regions, districts, and branches. There were three regional offices (East, Midwestern, and West), 20 districts, and within these districts 225 branches. The line selling and systems engineering work was done in the branches.

One might ask what functions were performed at the region and district level. First, the district managers served as reporting and performance review points for the branch managers. Approximately 10 to 12 branch managers reported to each district manager, making it possible for the latter to maintain a close surveillance of branch operations and to advise, counsel, and appraise his branch managers. This direct working relationship was an important link to DPD headquarters and served as well to maintain morale for branch managers at widely dispersed locations.

The district and regional offices also served as levels for developing and consolidating detailed sales and financial plans and budgets. In the other direction they translated overall quotas and sales objectives into goals for field branches.

A major concern of the districts and regions was personnel: recruiting, training, promoting, appraisal, and compensation. In this respect, the regional and district offices shared DPD headquarters responsibilities for developing resource competence in the field selling function.

Regional and district offices also served as the locus for certain specialized resource functions. In particular, there were education centers in each district for training IBM and customer personnel. While the needs of a single branch would not justify maintaining a complete educational unit for each one, the amount of training required for the several branches in a district could easily support a complement of skilled teaching personnel and physical facilities at the district level.

Regional and district offices provided an "outreach" for DPD headquarters Market Operations and Product Programs Managers. Their representatives, located at regional and district offices, disseminated industry market programs and product programs to the field and served as conduits for market information inputs to headquarters planning activities. Systems engineering managers in the districts similarly served as two-way conduits, disseminating information to systems engineers in the field sales organization, working on manpower planning and career development, and passing back information to the Systems Engineering Department at DPD headquarters.

Finally, district and regional managers participated directly in the selling function. They provided "high level" contacts with key customers, worked on critical competitive situations, and brought the resources of the field organization to bear on strategically important accounts. It is interesting, indeed, that the Vice President of the Midwestern Region spent time each week reviewing a "hot five" list with key members of his staff.

The region and district offices, then, (1) provided a reporting relationship for the branches, (2) were conduits for planning and setting sales objectives, (3) contributed importantly to resource development through sales recruiting, training, and promoting activities, (4) served as the locus for specialized resource units such as educational facilities, (5) provided program dissemination and field information points for headquarters industry marketing, product programs, and systems engineering, and (6) contributed directly to sales work.

Field Sales Specialization

A major factor in IBM's success has been the fact that it has planned and executed its marketing strategy in terms of categories of customers. The establishment of industry marketing programs at headquarters beginning in the late 1950s provided the planning vehicle. The development of specialized field sales branches facilitated the execution of industry programs by bringing customer-specialized skills to bear in selling.

What are the circumstances under which industry specialization at the branch level can be justified? The reorganization in 1964 of IBM's District 1 (the New England states) provides some useful clues. The district manager listed six criteria: (1) The geographic concentration of accounts in an industry group. (2) IBM's market penetration in that industry. (3) The travel costs of covering a geographic area using industry-specialized salesmen. (The first three considerations are interdependent in the respect that they relate the costs of supporting an industry-specialized field sales force to the volume of business available in the industry in a geographic area.) (4) The uniqueness of applications in an industry and the special selling skills required to work with customers on those applications. (5) The extent to which competitors offered applications-specialized talent to a particular industry. (These factors concern the relative competitive advantages of specializing.) (6) The amount of specialized talent available in a district that could be brought to bear on a given industry market. (The last is a matter of the effective utilization of scarce resources.)

To develop and maintain applications-specialized selling resources for 15 industry groups in 20 districts requires a large sales volume base. Because of its size IBM had a clear advantage over smaller competitors, whose sales could not support this amount of specialized talent. As stated earlier, competitors might then tend to specialize in certain industries rather than attempt to compete with IBM "across-the-board."

Industry specialization at the field sales level, it may be noted, would have one disadvantage. It reduces the flexibility the company has in moving sales personnel to different assignments. This is an inherent problem in the specialization of any resource. In the Lockheed-Georgia case, for example, the head of the Engineering Branch speaks of need to commit specialized resource units to programs but yet to maintain reserves of uncommitted personnel to give him flexibility in meeting urgent short-term needs.

Future Organizational Developments

As industry programs grew in size (sales volume), it became economical and competitively advantageous to add specialized resource units to industry marketing management organizations and to specialize field branches. Field representatives at the regional office level were also placed under the industry program management organizations, providing a communications outreach for gathering field information and giving guidance to the districts and branches. Probably the growing industry program organizations and their widening influence brought them into occasional conflict with the resource organizations. The case notes, for example, that there was some conflict between regional industry representatives and district managers in giving sales quotas to the branches.

Some industry program organizations had become more self-sufficient than others. Airlines and Government-Education-Medical, for example, had their own field sales resources.

Given no major change in technology, one would expect this trend to continue. The industry program organizations would become larger and more self-contained and might even in some cases approach the status of fully integrated businesses. Because of "hardware" commonality across all industry program lines, however, it is likely that common systems development and manufacturing resources would continue to be shared by most, if not all, programs.

Summary

Recognizing the potential in data processing, IBM's management stripped away other unrelated product lines to make this an integrated business in 1956. Over the next ten years the resource structure gradually took shape. The separation organizationally of marketing (Data Processing Division), product development (Systems Development Division), manufacturing (Systems Manufacturing Division), and customer service (Field Engineering Division) was based on key differences among these functions. These differences had to do with the appropriate form of organization of the work, time horizons which characterized the work, and the development and advancement of personnel.

As the business grew, there developed a bilateral program structure which included both industry marketing program units and product marketing program units. The first was organized by user industry segments. The segmentation scheme was based largely on differences among user industries in computer applications. In part, however, the scheme reflected differences in customer buying behavior. Thus there were marketing program management units for the Government, Education, and Medical markets because customers in these markets differed in purchasing behavior from those in the broad range of commercial markets.

An industry marketing program structure emerged because applications and Type II programs varied greatly from one user group to another, because it was easier and more accurate to forecast by product, and because management attention could be focused on critical markets. Finally, the industry program structure provided a vehicle for developing market-oriented selling strategies.

Industry marketing units worked largely through common basic resources: field sales and manufacturing, for example. But all units had their own resources for developing Type II programs; some (like Airlines and GEM) had their own field sales organizations. Where certain resources were found as part of the industry program structure, it was because (1) the work of that unit was specialized by user industry and (2) the specialization was economically justifiable; that is, the resource skills could be fully and profitably employed full time by a single program.

The function of product program management was to work across the business to develop new and improved products, to move them into the marketing stream, and to do all that was possible to encourage their sale.

The new product development process, in which product program management played a key role, is especially interesting for two reasons. It provided for balanced inputs of ideas and judgments from both market sources and technical sources. It was structured to shift initiative and commitment between DPD and SDD at different stages in the development process. The system thus sought to assure that each resource function would contribute in a significant and timely way to new product development.

IBM utilized a bilateral program structure because its markets were so diverse and it had a sales base sufficient to support such a structure. A bilateral structure, on the one hand, served to allow the business to focus on its individual markets, and, on the other hand, assured that attention would be focused on the continued development of a competitive product line.

IBM had a three-tiered field sales organization: regions, districts, and branches. The regional and district offices provided a reporting relationship for the branches and were conduits for setting sales goals at the branch level. They contributed to the development of field sales strength through recruiting and training. They served as the base for educational activities and provided program dissemination and field information points for headquarters managers.

At the branch level, IBM moved to a scheme of specializing field branches by user industry. The considerations relevant to such a scheme were economic in part: Were accounts in an industry group sufficiently concentrated so that the travel costs of covering these accounts did not preclude the idea of having the salesmen in a branch call on customers in only one industry? They were competitive in part: Did the applications in an industry call for special skills, and did competitors offer these skills to an industry user group? Finally, was such specialized talent available in the IBM organization?

Assuming no shift in IBM's strategy and no fundamental change in product technology, IBM's data processing organization is likely to grow in a predictable pattern. The formation of the GEM Region is a clue to future organizational developments. As IBM's sales grow in each of its markets, industry program management units will become increasingly self-contained, with more of them, like GEM and Airlines, adding their own field sales organizations.

Mobil Oil Corporation: North American Division

Between 1911, when it was established, and 1967 Mobil Oil Corporation grew from a regional marketer of kerosene and gasoline into one of the world's ten largest industrial organizations. By the latter date, Mobil had become a fully integrated producer, refiner, and marketer of petroleum and chemical products, with revenues and assets each approaching $6 billion.

In 1967 Mobil's corporate structure consisted of three line divisions and a number of staff departments (see Exhibit 1). The three line divisions were: (1) Mobil Chemical Company, responsible for chemicals on a world-wide basis; (2) the International Division, responsible for Mobil's petroleum business outside the United States and Canada; and (3) the North American Division, responsible for Mobil's petroleum business in the United States and Canada.

The North American Division was headed by a President, who had reporting to him two executive vice presidents and a number of staff departments (see Exhibit 2). One executive vice president was responsible for Exploration and Producing (crude oil and natural gas production); the other executive vice president was responsible for the "Complex."

The "Complex" consisted essentially of three major departments: (1) Manufacturing (refining); (2) Supply, Distribution, and Traffic; and (3) Marketing. Each of these departments was headed by a vice president. The Vice President-Supply, Distribution, and Traffic reported to the Vice President-Manufacturing and Supply. The Vice President-Manufacturing and Supply and the Vice President-Marketing reported to the Executive Vice President in charge of the "Complex."

NOTE: All financial information not publicly available and names of individuals have been disguised.

Historical Background

Mobil's corporate life had begun in 1911, when the old Standard Oil group had been split into 34 separate companies. One of these companies, Standard Oil Company of New York (Socony), was eventually to become the Mobil Oil Corporation. When it was established in 1911, Socony had been essentially a refining and marketing organization in New England and New York State, with some kerosene business in other parts of the world. It had no crude oil resources and no lubricating products business.

In 1912 Socony's refineries in Brooklyn and Buffalo produced more gasoline than kerosene for the first time. At this time, there were only 640,000 automobiles in the United States; the first service station would not be built until 1915. With assets of $90 million, Socony launched a program of acquisitions in order to obtain crude oil resources of its own and widen its marketing area.

In 1918 Socony acquired a 70% interest in the Magnolia Petroleum Company of Dallas, Texas, which had considerable crude oil production and reserves, owned refineries and pipelines, and marketed in Texas and nearby states. By 1925 Socony had purchased the remaining 30% of Magnolia, which became a wholly owned subsidiary.

In 1926 Socony acquired the General Petroleum Corporation of California, which had extensive producing properties and refineries in California, and marketing facilities in the Pacific Coast states. Magnolia and General Petroleum continued to operate independently, with largely the same management and personnel as they had had prior to being acquired.

The White Eagle Oil and Refining Company of Kansas City, Missouri, was acquired in 1930. White Eagle had refineries in Casper, Wyoming, and Augusta, Kansas, and marketed in all states north of Arkansas from the Mississippi River west through Colorado, Wyoming, and Montana.

In 1931 Socony merged with the Vacuum Oil Company, becoming the Socony-Vacuum Oil Corporation.[1] The two companies were highly complementary. Vacuum, a member of the original Standard Oil group, was a leading marketer of high-quality lubricating oils, with two-thirds of its business outside of the United States. It marketed its lubricating oils in every state and in most major countries of the world. It had its own tanker fleet, producing properties in Louisiana and Texas, and ten small refineries (six in the United States and four in Europe). Prior to the merger, Vacuum had acquired several companies, including the Lubrite Refining Corporation of St. Louis, the White Star Refining Company of Detroit, and Wadhams Oil Company of Milwaukee. Like Magnolia and General Petroleum, these companies operated with considerable autonomy.

By the early 1930s, then, Socony-Vacuum had become an international producer, refiner, and marketer of petroleum products. The next 25 years, punctuated by the great depression of the 1930s and World War II, were to be a period of "digestion" of the acquisitions.

Organization Structure in 1955

Between World War II and 1955 the petroleum industry experienced a period of increasing demand, product shortages, and good profits. The Socony-Vacuum Oil Company shared in this prosperity, marketing most of its products under the "Mobil" brand name. In 1955 the name of the corporation was changed to the Socony Mobil Oil Company, Inc.

At this time the corporation was organized on a functional basis, with Directors in charge of Production, Research, Manufacturing (refining), and Marketing. These Directors had line authority in the area served directly by Socony Mobil (the eastern two-thirds of the United States), and staff responsibility for coordinating their particular activities in the rest of the world (including the areas of the United States served by Magnolia and General Petroleum).

Under each of these functional Directors, a coordinating committee established broad policies to be followed by affiliates and subsidiaries. These committees were primarily concerned with coordinating the operations of Socony, General Petroleum, and Magnolia in the United States. The committees, however, were located in New York, and Magnolia and General Petroleum, whose presidents reported to the president of Socony Mobil, were relatively free from functional direction. According to Socony Mobil executives, many of the procedures and policies of the acquired companies had remained unchanged, and there was little uniformity among the three operations in the United States.

The Socony Marketing Department, which was responsible for marketing in the eastern two-thirds of the United States, was organized essentially on a product basis, with major headquarters staff departments responsible for gasoline and fuel oil, and lubricating products. Its marketing area was divided into two regions, which were, in turn, divided into ten divisions. The divisions had profit responsibility, and operated relatively autonomously.

The divisions were organized in much the same way as the headquarters Marketing Department, except that individual salesmen were generally assigned either to industrial accounts or to general territories. The territories of the "general" salesmen included retail service stations and commercial accounts using gasoline and motor oils (e.g., taxi cab companies; trucking fleets). Industrial accounts, requiring both industrial lubricants and motor fuels, were called on by industrial salesmen.

By 1955 Socony Mobil's management had recognized that the postwar sellers' market was coming to an end and that a general reorganization should be considered. Several studies were initiated, including a major study of manpower and organizational requirements by a member of top management.

The closing of the Suez Canal in 1956 added impetus to these studies. When the crisis ended, the industry was in an oversupply position. Earnings of all major oil companies were down. Socony Mobil had been particularly vulnerable, partly because it was not yet self-sufficient in crude oil in the United States. Earnings per share of Socony Mobil common stock fell from a high of $5.70 in 1956 to $4.63 in 1957 (and to $3.25 a year later). At this point, Mobil's management called in an outside consulting firm, to continue the studies begun before the Suez crisis.

1958–1959 Reorganization

In early 1958 the Socony Mobil Marketing Department was reorganized. As noted above, each division and subsidiary had been a profit center, responsible for much of its own planning and implementation. Under the new organization, planning and control

---
[1] The name was changed to Socony-Vacuum Oil Company, Inc., in 1934.

would be centralized, but the divisions would have more authority in carrying out the plans.

At the same time, it was decided that the Marketing Department would substitute "market orientation" for "product orientation." As one executive later explained: "The idea was first to orient our thinking to customer requirements, then to the products we had to sell." Specifically, the products departments at headquarters and in the divisions were to be replaced by departments responsible for "classes of trade." There were to be two classes of trade: Resale (i.e., accounts purchasing products for resale, such as service stations) and Commercial (accounts purchasing products for their own use rather than for resale).

Under this concept, two Marketing General Managers (one responsible for each class of trade) were to report to the Vice President-Marketing. The Marketing General Managers were to supervise staffs of specialists in their respective classes of trade. These specialists were to work with counterpart specialists in the divisions.

To carry out the principle of market-oriented direction in the field, individual salesmen would be assigned to either resale or commercial accounts, and would receive their direction from managers concerned exclusively with their own categories of customers.

As a further corollary, it was decided to eliminate the regions and to consolidate the field organization into a smaller number of divisions. As one executive explained: "We had to make up our minds to staff either headquarters or the regions. Since the major objective was to centralize control and planning, we decided to abolish the regions." Mobil's management was impressed by the opportunity to reduce costs under the reorganization. Smaller districts were consolidated; staff activities were evaluated and reduced at every level. Although cost reduction was vigorously pursued, management believed that marketing efficiency had not been compromised.

In early 1958, as the Marketing Department reorganization was being implemented, corporate management asked the consultants to study Socony Mobil's overall organizational structure. The second consultants' report, which was presented in late 1958 and implemented in 1959, recommended that the company's major operations be assigned to two new operating companies: the Mobil Oil Company,[2] which would include all operations in the United States and Canada (including those formerly assigned to General Petroleum and Magnolia); and the Mobil International Oil Company,[3] which would have cognizance over the activities of Mobil's foreign subsidiaries and affiliates. Socony Mobil[4] would become a parent company, concerned with long-range plans and policy matters rather than the day-to-day operations.

The new corporate organization had two major implications for operations in the United States: (1) nearly all Mobil activities were now assigned to one company, rather than three separate companies; and (2) management of the U.S. company no longer had responsibility for functional coordination of Mobil overseas subsidiaries and affiliates.

In commenting on the 1959 reorganization, Mobil executives cited four major advantages of the change:

(1) Division of the world between two equal organizational units considerably simplified the tasks of policy formation, planning, and appraisal of results.
(2) There had been major transfers of product among the three companies operating in the United States (Magnolia had operated the large Beaumont refinery, which served the eastern part of the United States). Placing related markets and refineries in the same organization would increase the efficiency of the supply and distribution function.
(3) It would now be possible to coordinate marketing approaches (marketing policies and strategies, sales programs and promotions, advertising, etc.) more effectively in the United States.
(4) Considerable cost savings would result from the elimination of the Magnolia and General Petroleum headquarters organizations, which had largely duplicated functions performed by Socony-Mobil in New York.

Establishment of the "Complex"

When the North American Division (initially the Mobil Oil Company)[5] was established, it was divided into three departments: Exploration and Producing (crude oil), Manufacturing (refining), and Marketing. Each department was headed by a vice president who reported to the North American Division President.

Each department was operated as a profit center.

---

[2] Later the North American Division.

[3] Later the International Division.

[4] Later Mobil Oil Corporation.

[5] The Mobil Oil Company became the North American Division in May 1966, when the name of the parent corporation was changed from Socony Mobil Oil Company to Mobil Oil Corporation. At the same time the Mobil International Oil Company, which coordinated petroleum operations outside of the United States and Canada, was renamed the "International Division."

Exploration and Producing sold crude oil to the Manufacturing Department at a "posted" price[6] and Manufacturing sold refined products to Marketing at "posted" prices. In each case, a department reported a profit equal to its gross margin minus operating expenses and overhead.

By 1961 there was considerable feeling in the company that splitting the North American Division into three profit centers had not been practical. The use of "posted" prices for crude oil transfers from Exploration and Producing to Manufacturing had not created significant problems, but the internal transfer pricing of products from Manufacturing to Marketing was considerably more complex and it was felt that undue management time was being devoted to establishing and arbitrating such prices.

In an effort to establish meaningful profit and loss responsibility at the operating level, the North American Division was reorganized in 1961. Two profit centers were established: Exploration and Producing, and the "Complex." The Complex included Marketing and Manufacturing, and the latter, in turn, included a newly structured Supply, Distribution, and Traffic Department. Thus, among other things, the establishment of the Complex minimized the difficult problem of transfer pricing of refined products. The Complex was headed by an Executive Vice President to whom the Vice Presidents of Marketing and Manufacturing reported (see Exhibit 2).

Case Organization

The remainder of this case describes the North American Division's marketing organization as it existed in 1967. It begins by describing the department's overall organization. It then describes the Commercial and Resale Marketing Departments, a typical field marketing division, and four headquarters staff departments (Planning and Financial Analysis; Pricing; Operations; and Advertising and Merchandising). Finally, it describes three processes (long- and short-range planning; supply and distribution; and product planning and development) which, although performed partially or wholly outside of the Marketing Department, had significant implications for its activities.

---

[6] The petroleum industry followed the practice of "posting" prices for crude oil and refined products at specified geographic locations (e.g., Gulf of Mexico, Arabian Gulf). These prices were widely reported on a daily basis by industry publications.

The Marketing Department in 1967

The organization of the Marketing Department in 1967 was similar to that established in 1957. The most notable development since that time had been the integration of the geographic areas previously served by Magnolia and General Petroleum. At first, these territories had been operated as separate divisions, increasing the total number of divisions from ten to twelve. Four of these divisions were subsequently consolidated with other divisions, in order to operate through a smaller number of larger divisions. Thus, in 1967 there were eight divisions covering the 43 states where Mobil products were marketed. (Mobil did not market in the five southeastern states, Hawaii or Alaska.)

The Marketing Department's 1967 organization chart is shown in Exhibit 3.

Four functional Department General Managers (Planning and Financial Analysis, Pricing, Operations, and Advertising and Merchandising) and eight Division General Managers reported to the Vice President and General Manager, G. B. Williams.[7] Two class-of-trade Marketing General Managers (Resale and Commercial) acted in a line capacity as deputies for the Vice President and General Manager of Marketing in the supervision of the marketing effort within the line divisions and the headquarters staff departments. This organizational arrangement was intended to reduce Mr. Williams' work load and provide specialized direction in both classes of trade.

The Commercial Marketing Department

The Commercial Marketing Department was responsible for sales to the commercial class of trade, which accounted for about a third of Mobil's U.S. sales volume. The Commercial Marketing General Manager was Mr. R. C. Harrington, to whom eight headquarters marketing departments reported.

The activities of these departments fell into three general categories:

(1) The Fleet Department and the Industrial Department provided staff services and guidance to counterpart sales units in the field marketing divisions.

---

[7] Until 1966, when Mr. Williams was named to his present position, the Division General Managers had reported to the General Sales Manager. When Mr. Williams became Marketing Vice President (he had been General Sales Manager), he combined the two positions to eliminate the layer of management between himself and the Division General Managers.

(2) The National Accounts and Wholesale Lubricants Departments carried out what were essentially "headquarters-to-headquarters" types of selling and coordinating activities.

(3) The Special Products, Marine, Aviation, and Railroad Departments were headquarters sales units, with their own sales forces, that marketed nationally and reported as line organizations to the Assistant Commercial Manager. Except for Special Products, they were large businesses with relatively few customers, spanning large geographical areas.

The following paragraphs describe six of these departments, which were selected to illustrate the range of activities carried out by the Commercial headquarters marketing departments.

The Industrial Department

The Industrial Department was concerned with a wide range of industrial lubricants. Purchasers of these lubricants ranged from small job shops to large manufacturing plants.

The Industrial Department's products were marketed by commercial sales representatives in the field marketing divisions. Within each of the eight marketing divisions, Industrial District Sales Managers (reporting to the division's Commercial Sales Manager) supervised the activities of specialized industrial sales representatives. These specialized representatives were supported by field engineers who reported to a Chief Engineer who in turn reported to the Commercial Sales Manager. They provided customer technical services, such as in consolidating the number of products used by the customer, product applications, and follow-up services.

According to the headquarters Industrial Manager, his influence on the field sales organization was largely the result of the services his department was able to provide that organization. These services fell into four general categories:

(1) *Sales Training.* As part of a 9-month training program, the Industrial Department conducted a 10-week industrial training program for all new salesmen.

(2) *Engineering Services.* Four senior staff engineers reported to the Manager of Engineering Services (who reported to the Manager of the Industrial Department). Each of these staff engineers was a specialist in a group of related industries (e.g., metalworking industries). These engineers were available to work on difficult problems and applications faced by the field.

(3) *Sales Programming.* The Industrial Department, working with the Advertising and Merchandising Department, created merchandising aids and advertising for its product lines. Among the merchandising aids distributed to the field in 1965–1966 was a kit for testing the hydraulic oils in machine tools.

(4) *Engine Builder Services.* A seven-man department worked closely with manufacturers of industrial machinery to arrange for the adoption and recommendation of Mobil lubricants in instruction and operating manuals. This group was frequently able to anticipate the need for new lubricants as new machinery was developed. The department also published the widely distributed *Industrial Engine Builders Book,* which listed Mobil's lubricating recommendations for most major types of machine tools, and was thought to give Mobil a significant competitive advantage.

The Manager of the Industrial Department explained that Mobil's approach to this market stemmed from the early history of the company. During the 1920s the Vacuum Oil Company had concentrated on high-quality products, backed up by strong technical service. Its sales strategy was to provide proved dollar benefits to the customer, rather than to enter the low-price commodity lubricants market. As a result of this continuing strategy, Mobil was able to command a premium price for its industrial lubricants and was the acknowledged leader in that market. The Industrial Manager added:

Our sales volume and market share have both been growing rapidly. Mobil should do more than $100 million in industrial products this year. Our field sales force also sells fuels — gasoline and diesel oil — to those industrial customers who have these requirements.

Fleet Sales and Service

The Fleet Sales and Service Department was responsible for sales to construction contractors, truck, bus, and taxi fleets, and other large consumers of fuel. Within each marketing division, there was a fleet district, whose manager reported to the Commercial Sales Manager. Fleet sales representatives, who reported to the Fleet District Manager, sold both fuel and lubricants to fleet accounts.

Like their counterparts in the Industrial Department, the fleet headquarters staff provided the field with training programs, engineering service, sales programming, merchandising aids, and advertising support. The strategy used to sell lubricants to fleet accounts was similar to that used by the Industrial Department for its accounts.

Special Products Department

The Special Products Department marketed petroleum products used by industry for applications other than lubrication and energy. In 1966 the department realized approximately $50 million in sales, divided among asphalt, process products, and petroleum coke.

Virtually all products marketed by the Special Products Department were manufactured by upgrading certain by-products of the petroleum refining process. Since without upgrading these by-products would have had to be sold at very low prices or destroyed, the incremental gross margins on special products were generally quite high. To realize these margins, however, it was necessary to invest moderately in plant and equipment, incur research and development costs,[8] and spend a higher-than-normal percentage of sales on marketing expense.

The marketing of process products required highly technical sales skills. As the Special Products Manager explained:

We do most of our business at the Ph.D. level. In order to make a sale we must study the customer's applications requirements, determine which product will fill those requirements, and — in many cases — arrange for the development, manufacture, and delivery of a specially formulated product.

To carry out its mission, the Special Products Department had its own sales force of chemical engineers selling process products, as well as coke and asphalt salesmen. While physically located in four of the eight field marketing divisions, these salesmen reported directly to Special Products District Sales Managers, who reported, in turn, to the Special Products Manager. According to the Special Products Manager, these salesmen were "guests" in the divisions; they used office space and staff facilities but were not considered part of the divisional organizations.

The Aviation Department

The Aviation Department was concerned with two broad product categories: lubricants and fuels. These products were sold to the military, airlines, airport dealers, and selected aviation equipment manufacturers. In 1966 sales of these products (mostly fuels) were less than $100 million. Most of this total was in sales to the military; next, in order of importance, were airlines, private airports, and jet engine manufacturers.

Prior to 1950 Mobil had been a major factor in the aviation market. As demand for aviation fuels rose in the postwar period, Mobil, faced with a short supply position and low profits on these products, gradually reduced its emphasis on the aviation market. By 1964 its share of the aviation fuel market had declined substantially, and the company was not a factor in the growing jet lubricants market.

In that year, however, Mobil reversed its strategy, and developed Jet Oil II, which was enthusiastically accepted by the airlines. With this stimulus Mobil had obtained a major position in the jet lubricants market by late 1966 and was increasing its share of the jet fuel market.[9]

Sales to the military,[10] airlines, and a major jet engine manufacturer were handled directly by the Aviation Department. According to the Aviation Manager, this procedure was used for several reasons:

First, the total number of customers is comparatively small. Second, specialized skills are required, whether on government bids or airlines' technical and service requirements. Finally, a contract to supply the military or an airline generally requires a major commitment of refining output and distribution facilities, and thus calls for top management approval of volumes and prices.

We handle the jet engine manufacturer directly, because it is an extremely large account, and our relationship with this account is crucial to our long-range jet aircraft lubricants and fuels development program.

Sales to airport dealers and other aviation manufacturers were made by the field marketing divisions, under the staff guidance of the Aviation Department.

The Marine Department

The Marine Department marketed Mobil marine lubricants and bunker fuel to the marine trade throughout the United States. There were three major categories of customers: ocean-going vessels, fishing fleets, and shipping using inland waterways.

In the marine lubricants market, Mobil was the leader by a wide margin. Helping to maintain this po-

---

[8] New special products were developed by the Technical Service Department, whose Manager reported to the Executive Vice President in charge of the Complex. Although not part of the Marketing Department, Technical Service worked very closely with the Special Products Department.

[9] This improvement in market share was attributed to the development of the nonpetroleum-based Jet Oil II, and to Mobil management's strategic decision to increase investment and emphasis in the growing jet fuel market.

[10] On military contracts, actual bids were prepared by the Pricing Department.

sition was the fact that an individual vessel generally used the same brand of lubricant throughout its life. Mobil's position in the marine fuel market was somewhat weaker, largely as a result of a management decision to limit product availability for this use.

The Marine Department was headed by Mr. P. F. Collins. According to Mr. Collins, marine sales strategy was based on a combination of product technology, quick service, and close contacts with shipping executives.

The department's functions were carried out by three sales districts, headquartered in New York (east coast), San Francisco (west coast), and Cleveland (Great Lakes and inland waterways). The Marine District Managers reported directly to Mr. Collins rather than to the field marketing Division Managers in whose territories they were located. According to Mr. Collins, the reason for this organizational arrangement was to permit servicing individual ships at any port where they needed service; if a vessel had been "sold" at New York, for example, it would require additional products at other points along its routes.

Marine sales representatives and engineers received daily anouncements of ship arrivals. If the arriving vessel was a Mobil customer, the sales engineer assigned to its berth scheduled the vessel's products requirements, arranged for speedy delivery, and provided any technical engineering service required.

Marine sales required close coordination between the North American Division and the International Division. For the most part, this was achieved through direct communication between the Marine Department and counterpart departments in foreign ports. For example, if a ship was sailing from New York to Rotterdam, and it was known that it would need an unusually large quantity of a particular product on arrival, the Marine Department cabled this information to the Mobil Marine Sales Department in Rotterdam, with a carbon copy to the International Division.

The National Accounts Department

The National Accounts Department had a staff responsibility for coordinating industrial sales activities with about 350 major national accounts. By definition, a national account was a company whose operations covered more than one Mobil marketing division. While far more than 350 companies fell into this category, the department concentrated its efforts on a preselected list of "major" companies.

The department acted as a focal point for the gathering and exchange of information concerning these accounts, and helped formulate and coordinate an overall sales approach to them. Department personnel worked through key executives at customers' corporate headquarters to maintain an overall favorable business climate. They supported district sales activity at the local plant level by making headquarters sales presentations, and by summarizing the benefits and savings obtained through Mobil engineering service.

The Resale Marketing Department

The Resale Marketing Department marketed Mobil products to retail service stations, car dealers, agricultural customers, and distributors. Resale accounted for approximately two-thirds of Mobil's U.S. sales. Because of a variety of channel arrangements, Mobil's immediate customer was sometimes a retail service station, sometimes a distributor (which then sold to service stations), and sometimes a fuel oil distributor. Some of the service stations to which Mobil sold were owned by Mobil and leased to dealers.

Mobil's resale market share varied considerably by geographic area, but was in general lower than the market share in industrial lubricants. According to resale executives, Mobil's position in the resale class of trade was due primarily to strategic decisions reached after World War II. At that time, it had been decided to concentrate Mobil's capital investments in crude oil exploration and production, and foreign marketing operations, rather than the construction of service stations in the United States. As a result of this strategy, Mobil's world-wide market position and profits increased considerably. Because several of Mobil's competitors chose to pursue different strategies, emphasizing service station construction in the United States, Mobil's relative share of the U.S. automotive gasoline market had declined.

Organization

The headquarters Resale Marketing Department was divided into five departments: Retail, Wholesale, TBA,[11] Training, and Real Estate. The managers of these departments reported to the Resale Marketing General Manager, Mr. J. J. Johnstone.

In the field marketing divisions, similar departments reported to the Divisional Resale Sales Managers, who also supervised the Resale District Managers. The Resale District Managers and their subordinates reported to division management, but they were expected to implement programs and policies developed by the headquarters Resale Marketing Department.

The following paragraphs describe the Resale Mar-

---

[11] Tires, Batteries, and Accessories.

keting Programs Council and the five Resale headquarters staff departments.

The Resale Marketing Programs Council

The Resale Marketing Programs Council was established in 1967. It consisted of the Resale Marketing General Manager (who acted as chairman), the Advertising and Merchandising General Manager, the Retail Manager, and the eight marketing division Resale Managers. The Resale Marketing General Manager was responsible for all final decisions of the Council; he had the authority to overrule a majority vote with which he disagreed.

The Council met every two months. Its primary responsibility was to review resale merchandising, cooperative advertising, and special promotional activities. It had full responsibility for planning and decision making in these areas.

A Marketing Programs Department was also established in 1967 to serve as a staff to the Council. The department was to gather information on local resale activities and ideas for new resale endeavors; in addition, it was to accumulate and analyze competitive information and prepare other materials at the request of the Council. Such other materials included: (1) alternative resale program development schedules, (2) summaries of existing and planned resale programs, (3) suggestions for new resale programs, (4) ideas for improving existing resale programs and procedures, and (5) analyses of resale budgets. According to the Resale Marketing General Manager, the primary purpose of the Marketing Programs Department was "to provide the resources needed to make the Council a capable planning and decision-making unit, and not simply a discussion group."

In commenting on the Resale Marketing Programs Council, the Resale Marketing General Manager explained:

> While specifically responsible for merchandising, cooperative advertising, and special promotions, the Council has a much broader mission. Because resale programs affect, or are affected by, almost all areas of the marketing mix, the Council must be informed of, and take into account, a wide range of plans and activities. For example, certain field marketing divisions might be requested to prepare, in advance of Council meetings, comments on field matters other than resale programs.
>
> The Council's primary purpose is to foster even greater cooperative effort in the use of Marketing's talents, and thus insure the best utilization of available staff, avoid duplication of effort, and achieve maximum results at minimum cost. It does this by bringing about a wide understanding of Marketing's total resale program activities, in order to give the various organizational units an appropriate unity of purpose.

The Retail Department

Mobil Products were sold by approximately 26,000 service stations in the United States. About one-third of these stations were owned or under lease by Mobil and leased to dealers. The others were owned by dealers or distributors, who had product supply contracts with Mobil.

The Retail Department assisted the Resale Marketing General Manager in his efforts to direct Mobil's relationships with these service stations. Departmental activities ranged from carrying out research projects to developing programs for use by field sales personnel or the service station operators themselves. As the Retail Manager explained:

> Almost everyone in Resale is concerned with service stations to a greater or lesser extent. It is our job to be the Resale Department's experts on service stations. We review marketing programs from the service station point of view and develop programs intended to strengthen our dealer organization. We are mainly concerned with short-range programs and increasing sales and profits for the dealer organization.

The Retail Manager cited two projects as typical of his department's activities. The first was concerned with the problem of attracting and holding dealers who owned and operated their own service stations. These dealers were an important factor in the petroleum business, representing two-thirds of Mobil's retail outlets (but a lesser percentage of sales volume). The major oil companies competed intensively for these dealers.

The Retail Department conducted a study of the factors that influenced a dealer's choice of supplier, and then prepared a program for use by field sales personnel. This program was mainly concerned with the "nuts and bolts" of locating prospects and selling the economic advantages of the Mobil franchise, including its impact on increased profits. Members of the department took the program to each field marketing division, and subsequently performed quarterly audits of each field marketing division's progress in signing up new dealers.

The second project dealt with the problem of turnover of dealers who operated leased stations. Mobil (and the oil industry as a whole) had been experiencing a turnover rate of 15% to 25% a year among these dealers in recent years.[12] These high turnover rates were considered an important problem because

---
[12] According to Mobil executives, turnover rates of this magnitude were not uncommon in small retail businesses.

of training and development costs and lost sales when a station was vacant or under new management.

In an attempt to reduce Mobil's dealer turnover rate, the department analyzed Mobil's experience in considerable detail. Characteristics of dealers who "turned over" were compared with those of successful dealers. At the same time, turnover histories of stations of various sizes and types of locations were analyzed to determine whether the station itself could be the cause.

The Retail Department also prepared programs intended to improve lessee dealer profitability. It had been determined, for example, that the first 30 days of a new dealer's operation were particularly critical to his success or failure. To assist him during this period, trained "money management specialists" were designated in the field marketing divisions. These specialists worked closely with the new dealers, helping them to establish bookkeeping systems, cash management procedures, etc. At the same time, the training of new dealers (at company-operated training stations) was intensified.

The department (working with the Advertising and Merchandising Department) also prepared programs intended to improve the quality of service station operations. The Friendly Way Dealer Contest in 1965 was typical of these programs.

In this contest, the dealers competed for prize points, which could be redeemed for a wide selection of merchandise and vacations (an electric razor "cost" 4,100 points, a hunting trip 25,000). Each station was visited several times during the contest by a "Friendly Way Mystery Shopper" who awarded points to the dealer on the following basis:

1. *Five Step Service*
   Was shopper greeted promptly, in a
      friendly way?
   Did service man suggest "Fill 'er up,"
      "Premium"?   1,000 points
   Motor oil checked voluntarily?
   Windshield and rear window cleaned?
   Did service man say "Thank you"?

2. *Solicitation of Motor Oil Sale*
   Suggest addition of makeup oil
                        or   400 points
   Inquire about or suggest oil change?

3. *Bonus Awards*
   Friendly attitude   400 points
   Answer travel information questions
      satisfactorily?   1,000 points
   Personal appearance   400 points
   Station appearance   400 points
                                                ──────────
   Total possible points   3,600 points

A dealer who scored a "grand slam" (i.e., earned all possible 3,600 points) became eligible for a district sweepstakes drawing through which he could win up to 50,000 additional prize points.

In addition to its various dealer programs, the department also arranged periodic field visits to check on the retail effectiveness of service stations in a particular area by comparing their appearance, services rendered, and physical condition with the standards of quality required by Mobil.

The Wholesale Department

The Wholesale Department was concerned with the portion of Mobil's business conducted through distributors, agents, and consignees.[13] Distributors accounted for approximately one-fifth of total resale gasoline sales and almost all fuel oil sales. Agents and consignees, who sold to farmers and customers in rural areas, were responsible for one-fifth of gasoline sales and a small volume of fuel oil sales.

These wholesale accounts were largely concentrated along the East Coast and in the Midwest. In the East, for example, Mobil sold to over 1,000 wholesale accounts; one-fourth of these accounts handled both gasoline and fuel oil; the others sold only fuel oil. In the Midwest most wholesale accounts handled the full line, with emphasis on gasoline sales.

Distributors operated their own bulk terminals and truck fleets. They purchased petroleum products from Mobil in bulk quantities and sold them to all classes of trade in their territories. In many cases, the distributors owned their own retail service stations.

The Wholesale Department performed several major functions. It prepared special wholesale programs, which included such elements as training programs for distributor personnel, management tools intended to improve distributor profitability, and special merchandising aids for use by sales personnel. In this latter category, gasoline programs were generally adapted from those prepared by the Retail Department. Fuel oil programs, on the other hand, were developed by the Wholesale Department with the assistance of the Advertising and Merchandising Department. Such programs typically included sales promotions, suggested advertising, salesman contests, etc.

The other major function of the Wholesale Department was to analyze proposals submitted by the field marketing divisions. All acquisitions, loans to distributors, and certain changes in operations (from con-

───────────
[13] These accounts were called on by the resale field sales force.

signee to a distributor, for example) required the approval of the Resale Marketing General Manager. The Wholesale Department analyzed proposals submitted by the field in these areas and made recommendations to the Resale Marketing General Manager. In most cases, it worked with the field marketing divisions *prior* to the submission of the formal proposals, in order to ensure that all relevant factors had been included and adequately evaluated before submission to headquarters marketing management.

The Tires, Batteries, and Accessories (TBA) Department

The TBA Department was responsible for the procurement and marketing of tires, batteries, and accessories. These products were manufactured by outside vendors according to Mobil specifications and were usually sold under the Mobil brand name.

In late 1967 the TBA Manager commented on his department's activities as follows:

Considering their numerous retail service station outlets (220,000), the major oil companies enjoy only a relatively small share of the tire and battery replacement markets (about 26% for tires and 35% for batteries). The remainder of these markets (74% and 65%, respectively) are enjoyed by other retailers, such as tire stores, accessory stores, department stores, and mass merchandisers, who, by comparison, have far fewer retail outlets.

Service stations occupy a most enviable position in the after-market. They have the most outlets. They have the most selling opportunities. All tire and battery buyers visit a service station some time or other to purchase gasoline. It would appear, therefore, that service stations should enjoy the bulk of the business. The reverse is true. Motorists have preconceived ideas about buying tires at service stations. They feel that

- There is an insufficient number of tires at service stations from which to make a selection.
- A service station is a high-priced place from which to buy tires.
- Credit terms are not available at service stations.
- Tires sold through service stations do not have the reputation of outstanding quality.

Service stations generally cannot stock a sufficient number of tires to satisfy customers' needs because of the many different sizes, types, and grades that are in demand. To do so would require a substantial investment in inventory on the part of the dealer. Mobil has made available to its dealers various credit plans to help alleviate this situation. However, credit plans by themselves do not solve the problem. Adequate physical space in which to store tires is lacking in most service stations.

Mobil has attempted to ease this problem by displaying tires attractively in outside tire merchandising cabinets and portable tire racks wherever permissible under local zoning ordinances.

Service stations do and should get a higher price for their TBA merchandise compared to other marketers of tires and batteries because of their convenience of location, hours of operation, and the many free services they render — more than any other type of retail outlet.

Motorists are usually not aware of the credit terms offered by service stations to the same degree that they are of terms offered by Sears and other mass merchandisers. Tires are a "big ticket" (high dollar) sale, and consequently a majority of them are sold on some form of credit arrangement. We are presently trying to increase awareness of Mobil's credit terms.

Motorists also do not know what particular brand of tire to associate with a particular petroleum company and, therefore, are apt to question the quality of tires sold in service stations. If they knew, for example, that a certain petroleum company marketed a Goodyear, or a Firestone, or even a Mobil branded tire, the problem of quality would be dispelled. More advertising appears necessary to correct this situation.

Inasmuch as the most profitable products for petroleum companies and service stations are gasoline and lubricants, effort is concentrated on these products to achieve gallonage targets. The careful selection of locations, the design of the station, the cleanliness of the station, the selection and training of operators, and the wholesale and retail programs are in the portfolio of the resale marketing representative. As a result, he does not have much time to devote to TBA merchandising. TBA, therefore, is generally relegated to a secondary position in the overall strategies of petroleum companies.

Most petroleum companies believe that by placing the greatest emphasis on the prime factors that influence gasoline sales, more traffic is created and, consequently, more TBA will be sold. TBA does contribute significantly to dealer profitability, and "rounds out" the line of services and products offered to his customers.

The Training Department

The Resale Training Department was responsible for the training of all Resale sales personnel and Mobil dealers.

The training of prospective resale marketing representatives, which covered a seven-month period, consisted of four phases. The first phase was conducted in the field marketing divisions and included orientation, some field work experience, and exposure to a one-month Dealer Training Course. This phase lasted approximately six weeks. The trainees were then sent to one of four Regional Training Centers for the next two phases which covered product knowledge, principles of retailing, and all aspects of sales territory management (fifteen weeks). The last phase, administered by the home division, consisted of additional field work experience, and exposure to various staff functions prior to assignment to a sales territory.

All Mobil dealers underwent a four-week training course prior to taking over the operation of a service station. Each Sales District had a training instructor,[14] who supervised a service station with classroom facilities. This facility was used to train new dealers and their employees in all aspects of service station operation. Dealer training was the responsibility of the local district, which received assistance and guidance from Training Department personnel.

The Resale Training Department also conducted a one-week sales management training program for first-line sales supervisory personnel and assisted in the development of specialized programs as required.

Real Estate Department

The Real Estate Department established policies and programs to implement marketing real estate investment plans established by Mobil management. In each field marketing division, a Real Estate Department did the actual work of acquiring service station sites. Although reporting to the divisional Real Estate Managers, it operated within policies and guidelines set up by the headquarters Real Estate Department. These policies included minimum economic criteria and site selection guidelines used in negotiating fee purchases and lease terms.

A Field Marketing Division

Exhibit 4 is the organization chart of a typical field marketing division. The division was headed by a General Manager, to whom reported a Resale Sales Manager, a Commercial Sales Manager, and several staff departments.

Resale

The Resale Manager had a staff similar to that of the Resale Marketing General Manager at headquarters. He also supervised the Resale District Managers, one of whom was responsible for all heating oil distributors in the division. The rest of the districts sold all other resale products in given geographical areas. One to three Area Managers, who were responsible for smaller areas, reported to each District Manager. The areas, in turn, were further divided into sales territories, each of which was assigned to a resale marketing representative.

The resale marketing representatives had annual sales objectives for each product line and called on service stations and other retail outlets in their territories regularly. They did not actually "sell" gasoline on a day-to-day basis since it was delivered under a contractual arrangement for a specific period, usually longer than a year. They did, however, sell tires, batteries, accessories, and lubricants. In addition, they tried to motivate the dealers in their territories to maintain their stations properly, follow Mobil marketing programs, and, in general, practice efficient business management techniques. Moreover, it was their function to insure that all stations in their territories were, in fact, being properly operated to maximize profits for both the dealer and the company. The resale marketing representatives recruited new dealers for lessee stations and arranged for the training of these new dealers. During the first few weeks of a new dealership, the resale marketing representatives worked closely with the dealers on all phases of service station operations.

One executive described the role of the resale marketing representatives as follows:

> I know that it has become fashionable to call salesmen by some other name, such as "resale marketing representatives." In our case I think that the title is appropriate. Our men do not really sell products; they are, in effect, marketing consultants to the dealers.

In carrying out their jobs, the resale marketing representatives received considerable assistance from the District Managers and the division Resale Manager's staff.

The Real Estate Manager and his real estate representatives worked closely with district sales management in acquiring or retaining service station locations. They not only assisted with technical matters but also negotiated sales prices and lease terms. *The Retail Manager* worked with the resale marketing representatives on retail programs and promotions. *The TBA and Lubricants Manager* performed a similar function for more specialized product programs and promotions.

Commercial

The Commercial Sales Manager did not have a staff broken down into subclasses of trade like those at Marketing Department headquarters. Instead, he had reporting to him a Chief Engineer who, in turn, supervised five or more engineers who worked closely with

---

[14] The district training instructors were trained at a school operated by Mobil in Garden City, New York.

sales representatives on specific applications, problems, and provided other technical services required by customers. Also reporting to the Commercial Sales Manager were District Managers who covered the territory of the entire division. One covered all fleet accounts; the others all industrial accounts. All other commercial business was handled by commercial marketing units reporting to departments at headquarters (Special Products, Railroads, Aviation, and Marine).

Each district had about 10 marketing representatives. In the industrial district, these representatives called only on industrial accounts; in the fleet district, only on fleet accounts. They received considerable staff assistance from the Industrial and Fleet Staff Departments at Marketing Department headquarters through written communications and field visits.

According to the Commercial Marketing General Manager:

> The industrial representatives are engaged in true selling. They isolate product needs, have good application knowledge, and can call on excellent technical assistance from engineering. Their major objective is to sell, through providing measurable dollar benefits to our customers.
>
> Fleet representatives have little opportunity to sell by this method. They mainly sell gasoline and diesel fuel, where price is the prime consideration. On these, they work closely with the Pricing Manager, since it is always possible to sell fuels in other ways (e.g., bid business with government bodies and other large consumers). Fleet representatives do, however, use the customer benefit approach when selling lubricants.

Headquarters Staff Departments

In 1967 there were four headquarters staff departments: Planning and Financial Analysis, Pricing, Operations, and Advertising and Merchandising. As staff departments these units served as advisors to the Vice President-Marketing, provided services for the Commercial and Resale Marketing Departments, and recommended policies and programs for implementation by the field marketing divisions.

Planning and Financial Analysis Department

The Planning and Financial Analysis Department was divided into three departments: Marketing Planning, Analysis and Control, and Marketing and Consumer Research. Marketing Planning prepared the Marketing Department's annually updated long-range plan and analyzed projects of a long-term and/or strategic nature. The Analysis and Control Department acted as controller for the Marketing Department, coordinated the preparation of the department's annual profit plan, and worked on projects with implications for the current year's operations. Marketing and Consumer Research carried out a wide range of marketing research activities, generally at the request of other departments.

The Marketing Planning Department was one of several long-range planning units in the Mobil Oil Corporation. At the corporate level, a Corporate Planning Department prepared long-range plans for the entire corporation. Each major division prepared divisional plans which served as inputs to the corporate plan. Finally, within the North American Division, each functional department (Exploration and Producing, Manufacturing, Supply and Distribution, and Marketing) had a long-range planning unit, which prepared functional plans as inputs to the individual plan.

The preparation of the annual long-range plan (described below) represented approximately 20% of the Marketing Planning Department's work. Most of its efforts were directed toward individual projects. These projects varied considerably in scope and objective, as shown by the following examples:

(1) A series of profitability studies of each segment of Mobil's market, followed by the preparation of a plan to increase profitability in that segment. One of these studies was based on a street-by-street analysis of major retail markets, with specific recommendations as to the strategy Mobil should follow in each of these markets. Data were, for the most part, collected by field marketing division personnel (following formats established by the Resale and Marketing Planning Departments).

(2) At the request of the North American Division planning unit, the department was studying the possibility of Mobil's expanding its resale marketing activities into additional markets.

(3) The department conducted post audits of major marketing investments, comparing actual cash flows with those forecast in the original discounted cash flow calculations.

(4) The department was presently engaged in a joint study with its counterparts in Supply and Distribution and Manufacturing concerning the appropriate strategy for Mobil to follow in the rapidly growing jet fuel market.

(5) The department worked on a large number of small projects at the request of the Vice President — Marketing and his staff.

The Analysis and Control Department functioned as the controller of the Marketing Department. It coordinated the preparation of the annual profit plan, monitored and analyzed performance, and made special studies at the request of marketing management. It did not, however, have responsibility for accounting and credit. These functions had traditionally been the responsibility of the Marketing Department, but they had been progressively assigned to the North American Division Controller between 1959 and 1963. The major reason for this change was that it had allowed Mobil to realize significant economies in the use of large computer installations and specialized data processing personnel.

The Marketing and Consumer Research Department made a distinction between market (i.e., industrial) research and consumer research. The former consisted primarily of forecasting growth potential for lubricants in various industries, largely at the request of headquarters personnel concerned with the commercial class of trade.

The department worked on two categories of research in the consumer (i.e., resale) area. One was a continuing series of studies of such factors as market share, company image, advertising effectiveness, and quality of service station facilities. The other was a series of specific projects, concerned with such questions as the effectiveness of a particular promotion or a new way of distributing credit cards. Studies in this latter category were carried out at the request of resale marketing executives. Field interviews and tabulation of results were generally "farmed out" to independent research organizations.

The Pricing Department

The Pricing Department was responsible for establishing pricing policies and schedules for automotive and aviation gasolines, jet fuel, diesel fuel, heating oil, certain residuals, and industrial and automotive lubricants and solvents. Final authority, however, rested with the Vice President-Marketing. The Pricing Department was not concerned with TBA or special products pricing, which were handled by personnel in the class-of-trade marketing departments.

Under delegated authority, the Pricing Department established posted price schedules for fuels in each terminal area. These could vary from area to area, depending on distribution costs and competitive conditions. Within each field marketing division, a Pricing Department reported to the Division General Manager, who had final authority on local pricing within guidelines set forth by headquarters. Since a change in posted prices for resale accounts could easily set off a chain of events affecting pricing over wide geographic areas, all price changes — up and down — had to be cleared with headquarters.

Although posted price schedules were also established for the commercial class of trade, discounting from posted prices had traditionally been common; prices often varied with volume, and competitive pressures existed with individual accounts. In the commercial class of trade the marketing divisions were allowed to raise or lower prices on their own authority, provided that they remained above a floor established by the Pricing Department. Any prices below the floor had to be approved by headquarters. According to Mobil executives, this procedure was intended to give field management enough flexibility to meet competition on the spot.

Lubricant prices for broad geographical areas were recommended by the Pricing Department and approved by the Vice President-Marketing. The divisions had the authority to reduce lubricant prices to a given floor to meet competition. Any reductions below the floor for a particular product had to receive headquarters approval.

The Pricing Manager, a long-service Mobil employee with considerable experience in the pricing area, commented on his job as follows:

> Rarely does a day go by when I don't have to make many pricing decisions.
>
> It's hard to overestimate the importance of these decisions in many cases. For example, a change of one cent in gasoline prices over a period of one year could represent a difference of $50 million in profits to Mobil.
>
> I am really the man in the middle. People out in the field frequently want lower prices; their main concern is with gallonage, and there is always some competitor nibbling away at the price structure. My boss — and his bosses — are primarily concerned with profits. You have to sell an awful lot of incremental gasoline to justify a reduction in price.
>
> Consequently, the field people occasionally feel that their inability to meet their gallonage quotas is caused by our reluctance to allow them to lower their prices. Obviously, there is a price level below which someone has to say, "No."

The Pricing Department also prepared bids for government business. According to the Pricing Manager, bidding on this type of business was pretty much an "educated guessing game." Prices tendered by individual companies varied with their supply/demand balances, incremental refining capacities, and refining costs. While the Pricing Department was cognizant of

Mobil's estimated costs and product availability, the "trick" was to bid the highest price that would win the award.

The Operations Department

The Operations Department prepared policies and guidelines for use by the Operating Departments in the field marketing divisions. These departments received products (delivered by tankers, tank cars, or pipelines) from the Manufacturing Department (in accordance with programs developed by the Supply, Distribution, and Traffic Department), stored these products in bulk plants (tank farms) and warehouses, and delivered them to service stations, distributors, industrial customers, and other users. In addition, they operated 15 plants where lubricants were blended from stocks supplied by the Manufacturing Department.

All operating facilities not located in refineries were under the control of the field marketing divisions. In practice, the divisional Operating Departments worked closely with the headquarters Operations Department.

The headquarters Operations Department functioned primarily by offering specialized services to the field marketing divisions. These services varied from establishing operating guidelines for bulk plants to conducting methods studies aimed at increasing the utilization of delivery vehicles. Staff members also designed service stations and provided technical assistance and guidance on service station construction to the marketing divisions.

The headquarters Operations Department worked closely with the Supply, Distribution, and Traffic Department to establish the most efficient source of supply for a given marketing area. If SD&T wished to supply an area from a refinery other than the one presently supplying the area, it was generally necessary to modify receiving facilities, storage depots, and delivery routes. The two departments worked together to determine the total investment needed, and to establish plans for carrying out the transition in an efficient and orderly manner.

The Advertising and Merchandising Department

The Advertising and Merchandising Department was divided into five departments: Advertising, Merchandising, Travel Services, Special Projects Development, and Customer Relations. Prior to mid-1966 there had been no Travel Services Department, and the merchandising function had been divided between a Marketing Programs Department and a Product Promotion Department. The two latter departments had been combined after a decision to curtail product promotions in special events such as the Indianapolis 500 race. The remaining functions of the Marketing Programs Department were assigned to the newly created Merchandising and Travel Services Departments.

The Advertising Department worked with two advertising agencies to plan Mobil's advertising programs. One agency, which was paid on a commission basis, handled Mobil's consumer advertising; the other, which was paid on a fee basis, handled Mobil's commercial, TBA, heating oil, and farm advertising.

The department was divided into two groups. A Commercial Advertising Manager headed the commercial advertising group, and the Advertising Manager himself headed the resale advertising group.

Within each group a number of program managers were responsible for the advertising of particular products (e.g., gasoline, fuel oil, packaging waxes). These program managers worked with the advertising agencies to develop copy and media plans for approval by higher management. In the gasoline and automotive oil fields (which represented the bulk of advertising expenditure), the Advertising Manager himself worked closely with the advertising agency in all stages of preparing a new campaign.

Prior to 1966 Mobil had used only one agency for both resale and commercial advertising. When it shifted its account to a highly creative consumer-oriented agency in late 1965, it had seemed desirable to assign the commercial account to a specialist in industrial advertising. It had then been possible to assign certain functions (e.g., direct mail) to the industrial agency and reduce the size of the Advertising Department's staff.

The advertising and sales promotion budget (about $17.6 million in 1966) was part of the Marketing Department's annual operating budget. The Advertising Department prepared a budget request, which was subject to modification or approval by successive levels of management. In general, Mobil was believed to spend a smaller percentage of its sales dollar on advertising than most of its major competitors.

The Merchandising Department planned and executed a wide range of promotional activities. The department was divided into four groups: retail promotions, wholesale promotions, project development, and special promotions.

Retail promotions were for the most part directed at the service station operator. The retail promotion group developed a program (such as the "Friendly Way" promotion described above), and then prepared dealer literature, sales kits, merchandising aids, and whatever other materials were necessary to implement the program. In addition, the group coordinated the logistics of local and national promotional activities.

The wholesale promotions group modified retail promotions for use by distributors and planned promotions directed specifically at wholesale markets (fuel oil, farmers). It might, for example, design a budget plan for use by fuel oil distributors or a display to be used at county fairs.

The project development group tested the feasibility of new projects, such as leasing vending machines to service station dealers. If the test was successful it would develop a program for national implementation.

The special promotions group was responsible for marketing publicity and special events, such as the "Economy Run" and certain other promotions of an image building nature. As noted above, Mobil's participation in this type of activity had been reduced considerably in recent years. In addition, this group was responsible for staging and coordinating large dealer conventions and meetings.

When several of Mobil's major competitors began to promote their credit cards extensively in the early 1960s, Mobil was forced to re-examine its credit card policies. In 1965 Mobil management decided to take an aggressive posture in the credit card field. *The Travel Services Department* was established in early 1966 to give direction to this program.

During 1966 the new department undertook several major projects. It experimented with several methods of increasing credit card distribution (e.g., direct mail, telephone solicitation), and negotiated with motel chains and car rental companies in an effort to increase the number of services for which a Mobil credit card could be used. By late 1966 several of these projects had been approved by higher management, and a significantly increased budget was in prospect for the following year. In addition, arrangements had been made with several credit cards companies to allow motorists to charge gasoline on general-purpose credit cards.

The Travel Service Department was also given responsibility for a number of other travel-oriented programs. These included the *Mobil Travel Guide*,[15] maps, the Mobil In-Station Travel Program,[16] and the Mobil Tour Service.[17] In assigning these programs to the Travel Services Department, marketing management hoped to give them unified direction and focus, as had been accomplished with the credit card program.

The Special Projects Department was responsible for the testing of major marketing innovations. It was a spin-off of the Market Development Department, which had been charged with the task of originating, evaluating, and implementing pilot marketing programs. The Market Development Department had been established in 1960 and abolished in 1965. The successor Special Projects group had no responsibility for programs as such. In 1967 its principal activity was the further refinement of the repair center concept, with which Mobil, a pioneer in this field, had been experimenting since 1963.

Marketing's Role in Planning and Forecasting

At Mobil, planning for the future was a continuous process. It was conducted at all levels and in all organizational units of the corporation. In order to integrate and communicate these plans both up and down through the organization, Mobil utilized a formal planning cycle in which short-term and long-term objectives were reviewed annually. Mobil executives believed that a formal planning cycle was particularly essential in an integrated and capital-intensive industry such as petroleum. The formal planning cycle was intended to ensure that all organizational units focused on contributing to the corporate objectives and to enable management to anticipate and plan future capital projects. It was within this company-wide planning framework that Marketing established its short-range and long-range plans.

The Marketing Planning Manager described Marketing's role in the long-range planning process as follows:

We primarily are concerned with identifying profitable business opportunities. This entails planning and forecasting product demands, capital requirements, expenses, and manpower requirements.

Two pieces of input to our planning effort are a statement of assumptions about the future and broad capital and earnings guidelines. These are prepared by the North American Division Planning Department. The guidelines define certain parameters within which our plan should

---

[15] The *Mobil Travel Guide* was a popular series of paperback books which rated restaurants, hotels, and motels throughout the United States. These books were sold at Mobil stations and book stores.

[16] A program intended to improve travel information available to the motorist at Mobil stations.

[17] A service that provided route information to motorists upon request.

fall. The assumptions essentially define the economic, technological, social, and political environment in which we should expect to operate over the longer term. We then interpret the implications which the assumptions hold for Marketing. A hypothetical example would be how we reflect the anticipated impact of inflation. If the planning assumptions indicate that cost of land is expected to escalate by some estimated percentage each year, we then would interpret its impact in terms of the future cost of service station properties. This would include the impact of inflation on the type and size of station we would build, the number of stations, and the capital necessary to carry out our desired program.

A second example of how we interpret the planning assumptions into Marketing terms is the use we make of forecast growth in total demand for various types of products. The planning assumptions include forecasts of industry-demand growth rates. We then relate our sales plans and programs to these forecasts to be certain that we are not unrealistic and do not underestimate the actions of our competitors who also seek to supply these demands.

Two additional inputs to Marketing's long-term planning effort are a review of key historical trends, and an evaluation of our resources and capabilities. We consider what and how we have done in the past, the competitive forces which have affected us, and the manpower and the skills we have. We then compare these to the programs we are planning for the future. If we find discrepancies between what we want to do and what we think we can do, we identify the additional resources (usually either men or money) we will need and include them in our plans. For example, if we wish to acquire more stations in a particular area, we evaluate how we and competition have operated there historically, and what we will need to achieve our objective. We then identify the capital which we will need, as well as the manpower, including first the real estate personnel to acquire the sites and then the sales and operating personnel needed to conduct our business.

During this entire planning cycle, we in Marketing Planning work closely with the Resale, Commercial, and Operating General Managers to advise them of our activities and to get their ideas, suggestions, and concurrence.

After Marketing translates these data into forecasts of product volumes, realizations, and expenses, we work with SD&T and Manufacturing to establish an integrated plan which maximizes profits for the Complex. This interface with other departments is coordinated by NAD Planning. We test different product mixes and strategies until we find the operating balance which we believe will achieve the overall objectives of the Complex. Marketing then modifies its long-term programs, objectives, and data to conform to the integrated strategy selected for the Complex. The revised Marketing data are combined by the Controller with revised plans from Manufacturing and SD&T into a P&L forecast for the Complex. The Complex P&L ultimately is included in a financial forecast for the North American Division, and in turn, in a forecast for the total Mobil Oil Corporation.

Once the integrated long-term plan is approved by the Executive Committee of the Board, the necessary steps are taken by each department to begin to implement the programs, plans, and strategies.

In Marketing, the first step is the formulation of a detailed, short-term profit plan and a capital budget. The profit plan deals with measurable specifics for each marketing manager. It includes volume forecasts for each marketing segment for our principal products, and it establishes manpower and expense budgets at the sales district level. The capital budget is broken down into individual markets and provides capital funds for each marketing segment to achieve its planned objectives: to open new stations, rehabilitate existing ones, modernize wholesale plants, add new motor vehicles, etc.

During the year each individual within Marketing is measured for his ability to perform against his particular objectives. For example, the marketing representative's success is evaluated by comparing actual volumes with his approved volume assignment for each product; the District Manager is measured against his district's volume and expense plans as well as for his success in implementing the capital program for his district and his ability to direct, train, and develop people.

Product Supply

Responsibility for product supply was divided between the Supply, Distribution, and Traffic Department[18] and the Marketing Department. SD&T drew up the schedule for the manufacture of products by the refineries and for the shipment of these products to primary terminals operated by the Marketing Department. The division Operating Departments then took over responsibility for the products, transporting them to secondary terminals (tank farms) if necessary, or directly to service stations and other customers.

Supply, Distribution and Traffic Department

An executive explained SD&T's function in this way:

The North American Division operates 9 refineries, 2 on the West Coast, 2 in the East, and the rest in between. It markets several thousand products in 43 states. In theory, any refinery could supply any market area with any product (up to capacity) at some cost. But making

---

[18] See Exhibit 2 for SD&T's organizational location; Exhibit 5 for an SD&T organization chart.

money in this business depends upon careful calculations. These calculations are the responsibility of SD&T.

Refineries are half the equation. A given refinery can produce various mixes of products. But costs depend on the mix. The cost/mix relationship in turn depends on the grade and type of crude oil being run and varies from one refinery to another.

Marketing is the other half of the equation. To some extent, Marketing can vary the mix of products which it sells and the geographic areas in which it sells them. At any given time there is some combination of discretionary sales, crude inputs, refineries schedules, and transportation methods which will maximize profits for Mobil. We're never perfect, but it is SD&T's job to get us as close to that optimum as possible.

SD&T's function is difficult to describe because it's hard to know where to break into the circle. I suppose it starts with Marketing's forecasts: what quantities of what products it expects to sell in which areas. SD&T then asks, in effect, how we can supply (i.e., make and transport) this demand most economically? And does it pay to supply this demand? Might Mobil make more money by selling some other product mix to some other group of customers?

I know it sounds awfully complex, but we've been in this business for quite a while, and have a pretty good idea of how it ought to go. And we've split up the job; no one piece is all that difficult.

Supply referred to the crude oil run through Mobil's U.S. refineries. Including its own quota imports of offshore oil, Mobil was less than 60% self-sufficient in crude oil in North America, and had to purchase the remainder of its requirements from other oil companies. Moreover, the crude oil produced by a particular oil company was not necessarily the best type of available crude oil to be used in that company's refineries, although this depended on the product mix a refinery was producing at a given time. Even if a company produced a crude appropriate to a particular refinery and product mix, it might be desirable to "swap" this crude for someone else's crude in order to save transportation costs.[19]

As a result, Mobil continually engaged in a series of crude oil purchases, sales, and swaps. This activity was the responsibility of SD&T's Crude Supply Manager and two regional crude supply managers located in Dallas and Los Angeles, respectively. Crude supply was, of course, closely related to questions of product mix and distribution. The quantity and grade of crude oil appropriate to a particular refinery depended largely on the product mix that refinery was scheduled to produce. Conversely, the optimum product mix for a particular refinery depended to a considerable extent on the grade of crude oil available to that refinery. For this reason it was considered important that crude oil supply be handled by SD&T rather than, for example, Manufacturing or Exploration and Producing.

Distribution referred to the process through which Mobil determined which refinery would supply which marketing areas with which product and, to some extent, what those products should be. This function was performed by several executives and their staffs.

The *Programs Manager* maintained a twelve-month supply and demand balance for light products.[20] The supply and demand balance compared forecast sales and refinery output for each month, to ensure that Mobil's refineries could profitably fill the demand forecast by the Marketing Department.

The Programs Manager received Marketing's forecasts at two-month intervals. The first two months of a year coincided with the first two months of the annual profit plan. Later months could deviate from the annual profit plan but did not change the approved sales objectives for the Marketing Department.

The Programs Manager had detailed current information concerning refinery capacities. He compared these data with marketing sales forecasts to establish a preliminary supply and demand balance. He then analyzed alternative refinery/product mix/market area combinations to determine whether forecast demand and supply could be balanced profitably.

There was generally a certain amount of flexibility in both supply and demand. On the demand side, certain types of government and fleet business were discretionary.[21] If Mobil chose to bid low enough, it could always get more of this kind of business. Conversely, if it did not want the business it could either bid high or not bid at all with no penalties the next time requests for bids were sent out. On the supply side, Mobil could generally make enough of a particular product, although possibly at a cost that made doing so uneconomical. If necessary, Mobil could purchase the product from another oil company.

The Programs Manager thus performed two key roles. On the one hand, he established the basic pattern through which normal demand would be filled by

---

[19] This type of "swap" arrangement was a common practice in the petroleum industry.

[20] Gasoline, kerosene, aviation fuel, fuel oil.

[21] In Mobil terminology, a discretionary sale was one that did not pass through regular channels (e.g., service stations) or go to a regular customer as a regular part of meeting his requirements. In practice, most discretionary business depended completely on price; Mobil could have the business if it bid low enough; otherwise another company obtained it.

normal supply. On the other hand, he established guidelines for use by the refineries and Marketing in making alternative decisions concerning discretionary production or sales. He might, for example, suggest to Marketing that it not sell Product A at a price lower than X, since it cost more than X to make the product, or because a price greater than X could be realized by making Product B, or by selling Product A through other channels. Or he might tell a refinery to make as much as it could of Product A, provided the cost did not go above Y (at which cost Product C, which had a higher price than Product A, could be produced).

The Programs Manager thus "drew up a road map" that he revised every two months. The *Operations Scheduling Manager* was responsible for "driving on the roadway" established by the Programs Manager. In practice the demand forecasts used by the Programs Manager rarely proved to be exactly on target. Demand for individual products might be higher or lower than had been forecast, or might follow a different geographic pattern from what had been expected. Similarly, the refineries were rarely able to produce exactly what had been forecast. It was the Operations Scheduling Manager's job to respond to short-term variations in supply and demand by making minor changes in the basic program to ensure that Marketing had an adequate supply of product at all times. In doing so, he generally stayed within guidelines established by the Programs Manager, but in certain cases (e.g., a strike or a very cold April) he found it necessary to deviate from them.

The *Product Purchase and Refinery Products Sales Manager* purchased and sold refined products as required by the supply and demand situation. If Marketing chose to sell more fuel oil than Mobil could produce (or found it economic to produce), for example, fuel oil was purchased on the open market. Similarly, if SD&T could sell refined products in cargo lots at a price higher than Marketing could realize through discretionary sales, refined products were sold on the open market. In essence the Product Purchase and Refinery Product Sales Manager was responsible for remedying (through purchases and sales) any imbalances in Mobil's short-term supply and demand situation.

The *Lubes and Allied Products Manager* was responsible for the distribution of all heavy products (lubricants, special products). For these products, he performed the entire distribution function (programming, operations scheduling, and product sales and purchases). Although he was concerned with many low-volume products rather than a few large-volume light products, he operated in much the same way as his colleagues in the light-product area. He worked out a supply and demand balance for each product, analyzed alternative distribution configurations, and expedited short-term programs as necessary.

The division of work in the distribution function was explained by one executive as follows:

The distribution of light products is very different from the distribution of heavy products. Considerations of manufacturing and transportation economics in the two areas are so different that you simply have to have different people working on them. Because there is more work in light products, we have split the job among several managers. In heavy products, one manager is enough.

Several other SD&T executives found it necessary to work closely with the Marketing Department. The *Distribution Facilities Manager* provided staff assistance to the terminals where products were transferred from Manufacturing to the Operations Department on receipt. The *Traffic* (or Marine) Manager arranged for the actual physical movement of products from the refineries to Marketing Department terminals, making short-term changes when market demands required. The *Planning Manager* prepared SD&T's annual long-range plan, which took into account Marketing's long-range demand forecast (from the Marketing Department long-range plan), and provided the Marketing Department with long-range cost data to be used as a basis in bidding on long-term sales contracts (e.g., a three-year jet fuel contract with an airline).

Balancing Act

SD&T added its own alternative forecasts to the forecasts received from Marketing. As an SD&T executive explained, "We have to have alternatives; if we don't have the product when it is needed, we're not doing our job."

Discretionary sales also called for the exercise of expert judgment. Marketing handled discretionary sales to government and large transportation accounts, and SD&T made such sales to other oil companies (i.e., cargo lots). In many cases, SD&T could sell products at higher prices than Marketing could, or distribution costs might make it more profitable for SD&T to sell a cargo lot than for Marketing to offer the product at a low bid.

Product Planning and Development

In its organizational manuals, Mobil made a distinction between long-range and short-range product planning and development. Long-range product planning and development included all new products and major changes in existing products; short-range product planning and development was concerned with minor adaptations of existing products to meet local or temporary market requirements.

Responsibility for long-range product planning and development was at the corporate level. The *Corporate Products Department,* after consultation with division marketing units, determined product requirements, transmitted these requirements to the *Corporate Research Department,*[22] and arranged for the introduction of the new product by the operating divisions.

Short-range product planning and development was located in the operating divisions. The North American Division, for example, had a *Technical Service Department* (reporting to the Executive Vice President in charge of the Complex) which worked on projects submitted to it by the Marketing Department (e.g., "We need a lubricant that will do everything that Lubricant X will do, but at minus-40 degrees F.").

Until 1966 the North American Division had also had a Product Planning Department, which had programmed the activities of the Technical Services Department.[23] The North American Division Product Planning Department had been consolidated with the Corporate Products Department in 1966. According to corporate executives, the North American Division Product Planning Department had been unable to do an adequate job of short-range product planning without being thoroughly familiar with the longer-range plans of the Corporate Products Department. It might, for example, devote considerable resources to upgrading a product to fit a particular application, only to have its work superseded by a totally new product developed by the Corporate Research Department. Consequently, beginning in 1966, the Corporate Products Department programmed the work of both the Corporate Research Department and the Technical Service Department.

Product Strategy Committees

In 1966, after the assignment of responsibility for product planning to the Corporate Products Department, two product strategy committees were formed, one for the North American Division and one for the International Division. The Manager of the Corporate Products Department served as secretary of both committees. Membership of each committee included the appropriate division's Commercial Marketing General Manager, Resale Marketing General Manager, Technical Service Manager, Research and Development Manager, and representatives from other departments as needed. The chairmanships of the Committees were to rotate among their members; the Commercial Marketing General Managers were serving as chairmen in early 1967.

The product strategy committees met about once a month. At these meetings the department managers determined what Mobil's approach to particular problems should be and, in effect, directed the Corporate Products Department to arrange for whatever product development was required (whether by Corporate Research or Technical Service). These research programs were reviewed by the North American Division and International Division Executive Vice Presidents every six months.

A member of the Corporate Products Department commented on the product strategy committees as follows:

From our point of view, these committees really have two purposes. First, they do give us guidance as to the direction our research activities should take. Second, and more important from my point of view, they give us an opportunity to obtain commitment from the operating managers. Now, when we come up with a new product, they can't say, "Who needs it?" If they do, we can say, "You need it! You told us so at a meeting last February."

It's still too early to tell how well the committees will work. On the basis of less than a year's experience, I believe that I can already sense a difference in the attitudes of operating personnel.

---

[22] The Corporate Research Department, through Mobil Research & Development Corp., a subsidiary, carried out both basic and applied research. It reported to the Senior Vice President-Research & Engineering (see Exhibit 1).

[23] The International Division had a similar department which was also abolished in 1966.

Exhibit 1. Corporate Organization Chart, 1967

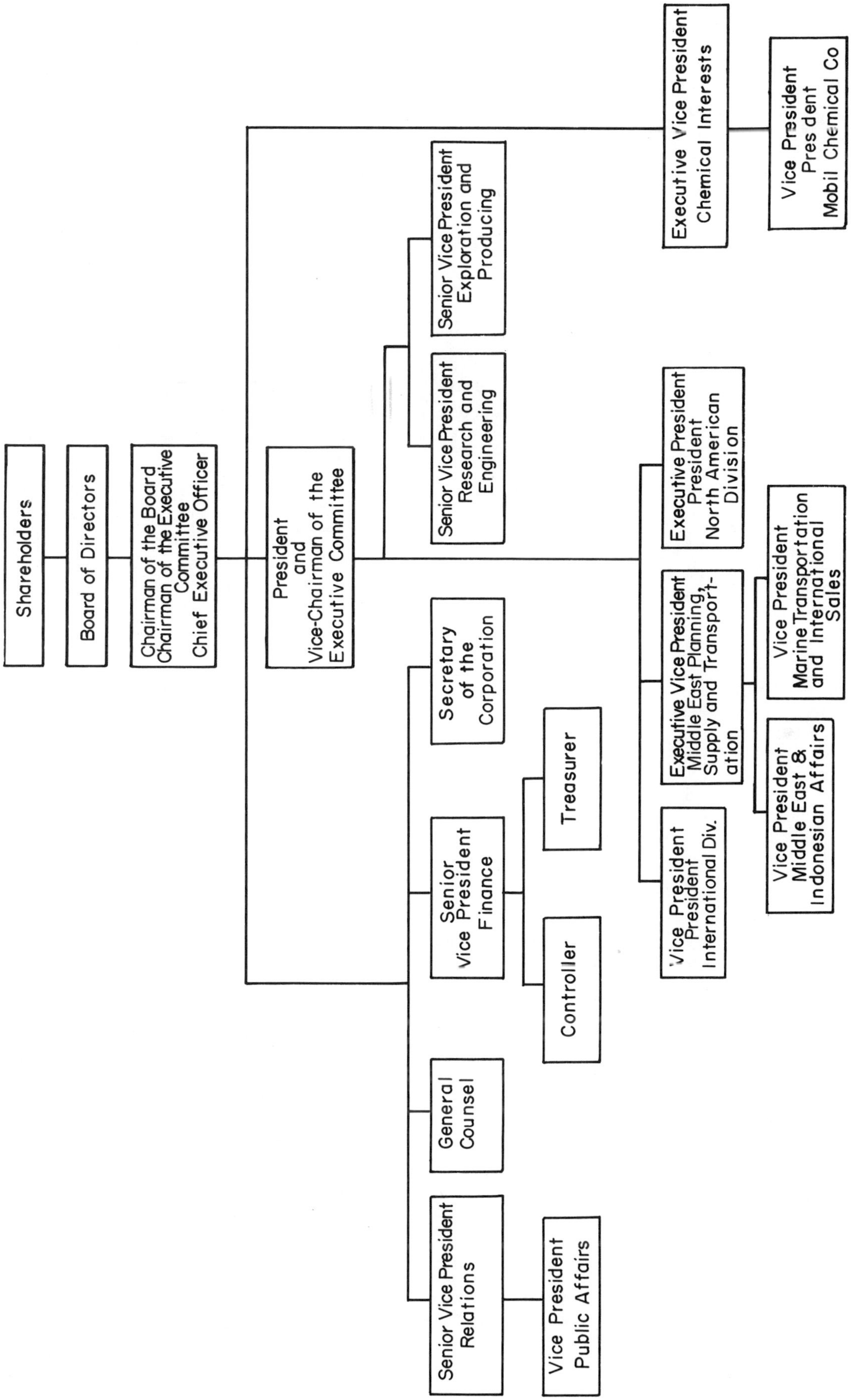

176   Cases and Commentaries

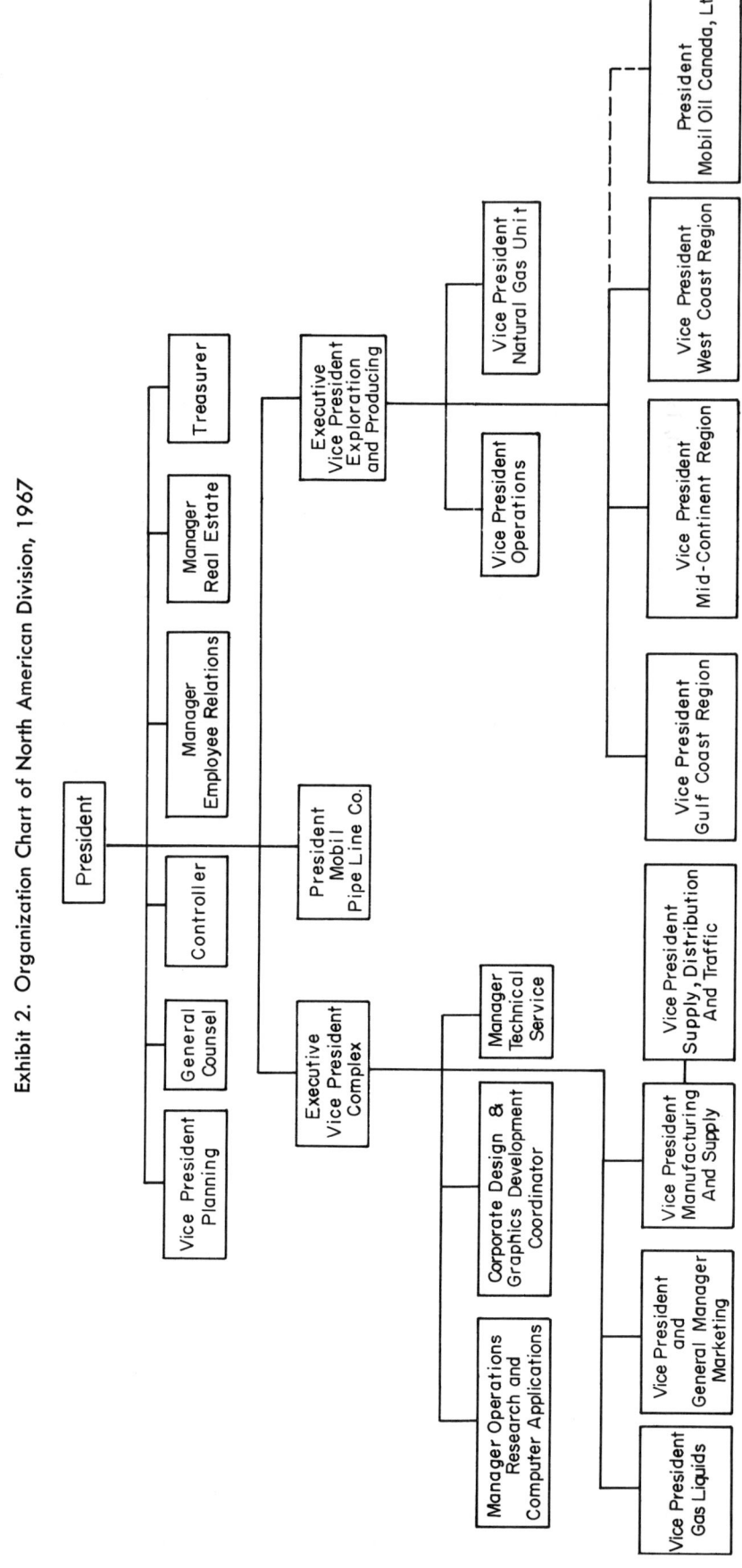

Exhibit 2. Organization Chart of North American Division, 1967

Exhibit 3. Organization Chart of Marketing Department, North American Division, 1967

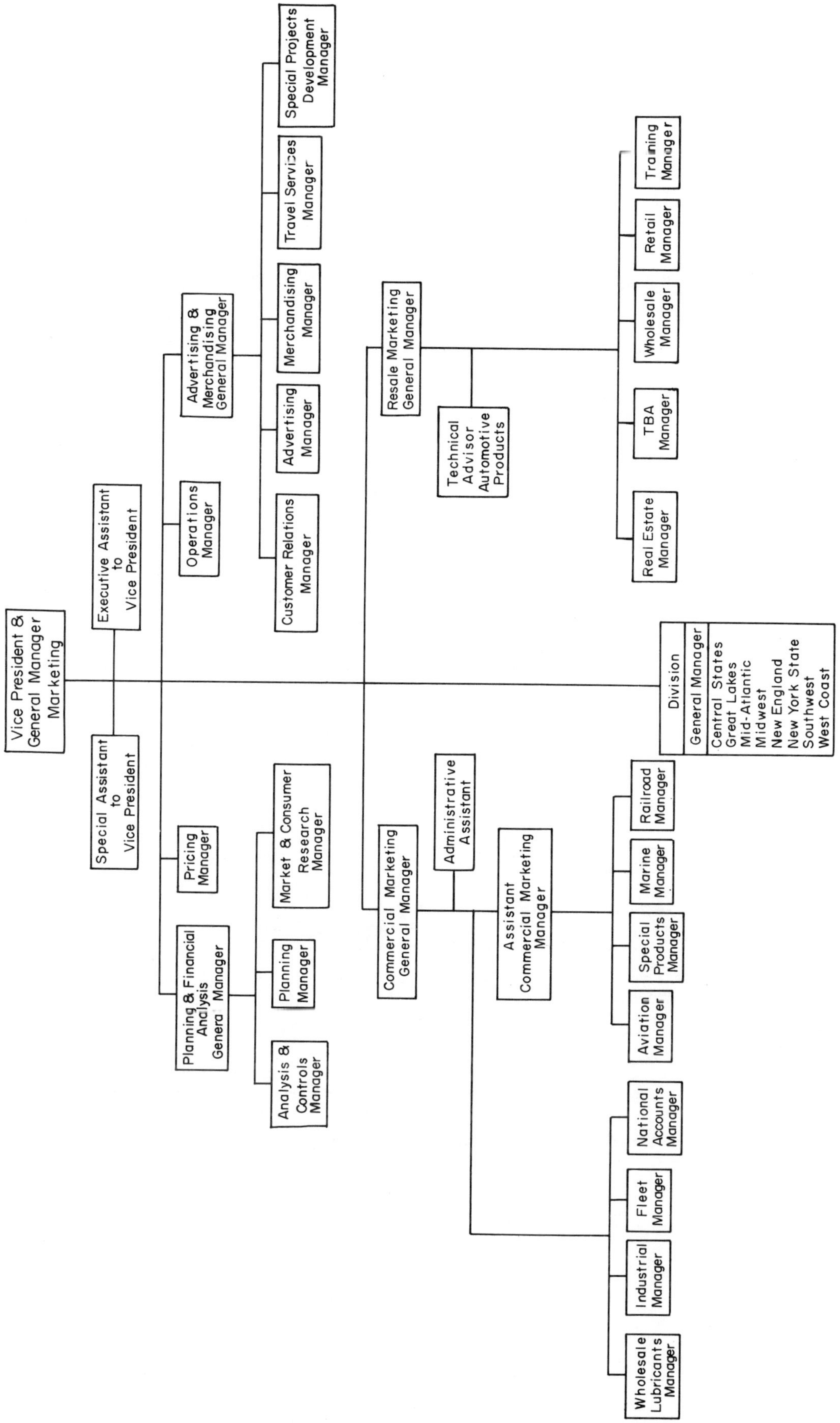

Exhibit 4. Organization Chart of Typical Division of Marketing Department, North American Division, 1967

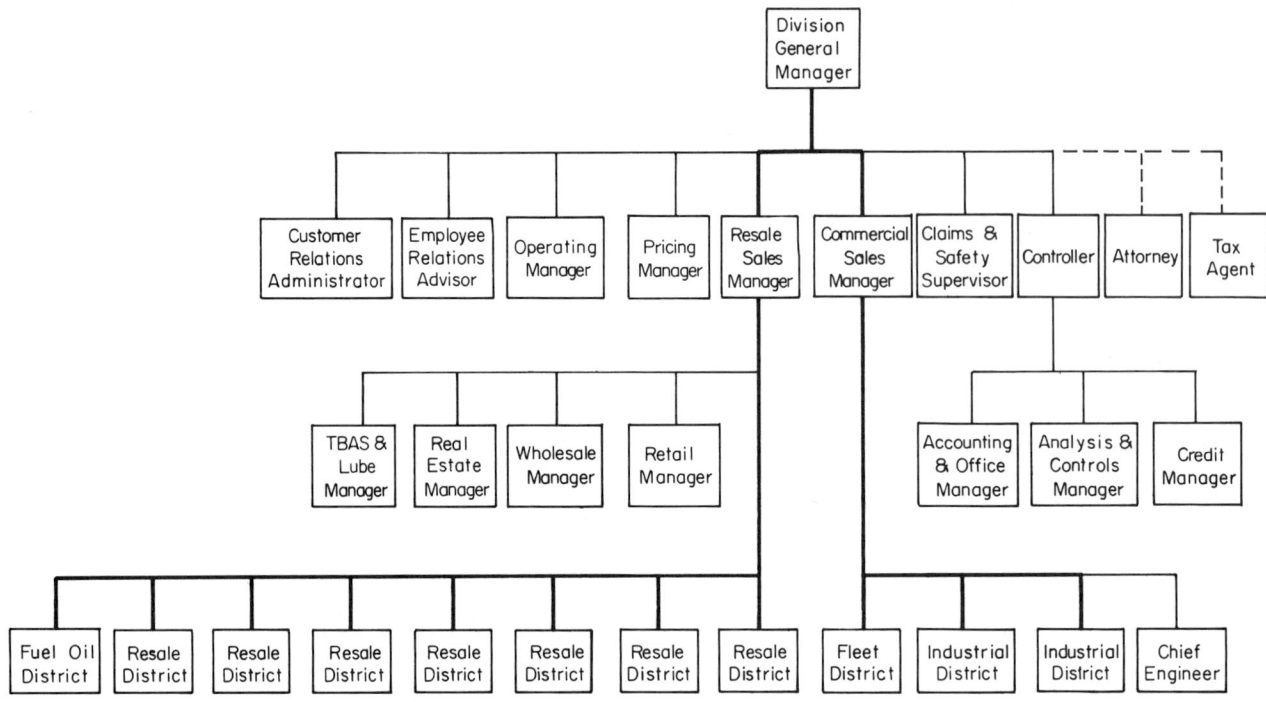

Exhibit 5. Organization Chart of Supply, Distribution, and Traffic Department, North American Division, 1967

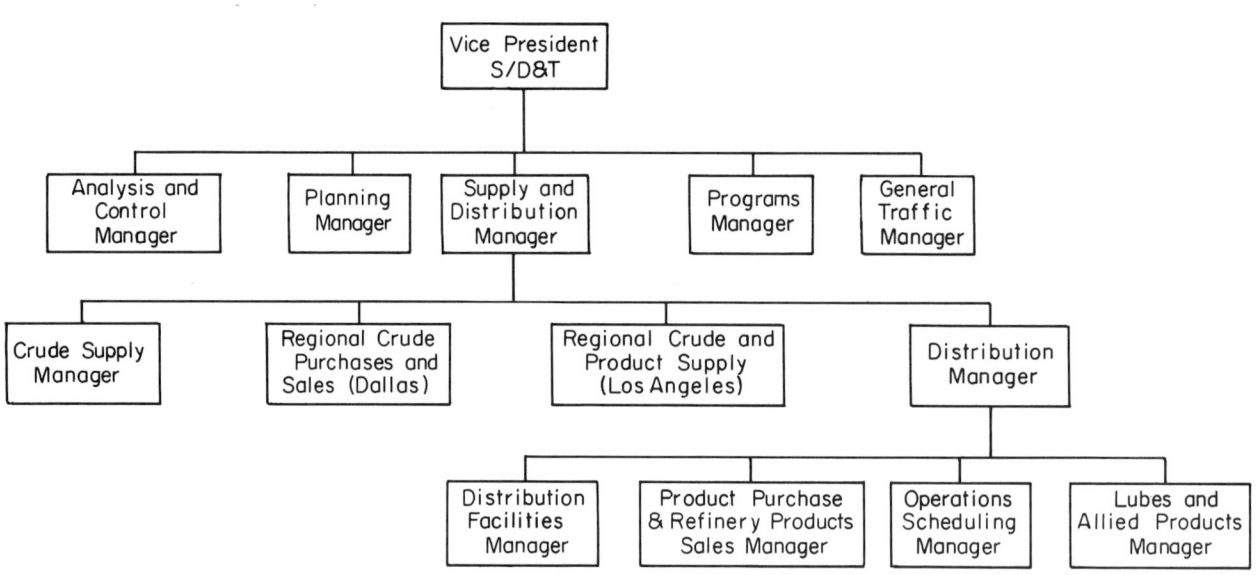

COMMENTARY

Mobil Oil Corporation in forming the North American Division from the old General Petroleum, Magnolia, and Socony Mobil companies put together a large business and a well-structured one. It was a business admirably organized to deal effectively with the vagaries of supply and demand in a highly competitive industry.

With large commitments in crude oil reserves, in refining and transportation facilities, and in retail stations, major oil companies are under constant pressure to produce crude oil in vast quantities and move it through the system. Supply often fluctuates widely and unpredictably; markets are tremendously diverse and subject to substantial shifts in demand; large crude oil producing areas are seldom located near large consuming areas; and the logistics system needed to match source and use is both vast and complex. The environment in which the major oil company operates is well described by one Mobil executive:

The North American Division operates nine refineries, two on the West Coast, two in the East, and the rest in between. It markets several thousand products in 43 states. In theory, any refinery could supply any market area with any product (up to capacity) at some cost. But making money in this business depends upon careful calculations. These calculations are the responsibility of SD&T.

Refineries are half the equation. A given refinery can produce various mixes of products. But costs depend on the mix. The cost/mix relationship in turn depends on the grade and type of crude oil being run and varies from one refinery to another.

Marketing is the other half of the equation. To some extent, Marketing can vary the mix of products which it sells and the geographic areas in which it sells them. At any given time there is some combination of discretionary sales, crude inputs, refinery schedules, and transportation methods which will maximize profits for Mobil. We're never perfect, but it is SD&T's job to get us as close to that optimum as possible.

The organization that was needed would have to be able to deal with the intricate problems of balancing supply and demand. It would at the same time have to plan and carry out strategies in such diverse markets as retail motorists, large and small industrial users, resellers of petroleum products, and federal, state, and local governments. It is useful to understand how Mobil evolved a workable definition of its domestic business; how within this structure it established marketing program organizations; how it developed a system for planning and allocating product to its several markets, and keeping demand and supply profitably in balance.

Definition of the Business

Although the signs of change may be in the wind, it often takes a crisis to precipitate a response. In this case, Mobil's management had recognized in 1955 that market conditions were changing and had initiated studies to assess the implications for organizational structuring. In 1956, however, the Suez crisis, which caused severe dislocations in the supplies of crude oil and refined products and extreme price fluctuations, created an urgent need for action. Mobil's earnings fell off sharply between 1956 and 1958. These events underscored basic weaknesses in the Mobil organization world-wide, and in 1959 the company was reorganized.

In the United States, prior to 1959, the operations of Socony Mobil (in the eastern two-thirds of the country), Magnolia (in the southwest), and General Petroleum (in the western United States) were coordinated through committees for Producing, Manufacturing, and Marketing. Coordination was needed particularly because there were large transfers of product among the three companies. Coordinating committees, however, were not an effective integrating device. While the presidents of Magnolia and General Petroleum reported to the president of Socony Mobil, Magnolia and General Petroleum operated relatively independently.

The formation of the North American Division (initially the Mobil Oil Company) to embrace all operations in the United States and Canada brought into one business unit all the related supply, refining, and marketing activities of the three companies. With a much greater operating scope than any of the three predecessor companies, North American Division's management controlled directly a large producing, transportation, refining, and marketing complex. It could deploy its resources quickly across this system to take account of shifts in market demand. It could absorb and adjust for changes in the supply picture. The broader scope provided a better basis for planning and greater control over the elements affecting profitability.

There were, in addition, significant advantages from a marketing viewpoint. In the retail motorist market, in particular, a unified approach for branding, advertising, service station design, and consumer credit was possible.

With the increasing mobility of the U.S. and Canadian populations, a single overall strategy for the U.S. and Canadian markets was indeed desirable. Economies could be realized, moreover, through the use of national television and magazine media. A single distribution system including retail stations, industrial agents, wholesalers, and distributors could be established.

The case speaks also of cost savings from eliminating Magnolia and General Petroleum headquarters, which had duplicated to a large extent functions being performed by Socony Mobil. Undoubtedly, there were savings that could be realized from replacing three headquarters marketing groups with one; from placing producing and refinery operations each under a single management. Consolidation probably made possible, as well, the development of larger, more finely articulated management units for each function than might have been feasible for any one of the predecessor companies.

Thus the interrelationships among the three companies on the supply end, the homogeneity of the markets they served, and the cost economies realizable from a consolidation of their operations led the Mobil top management to set up one business unit, the North American Division, to represent the company in the United States and Canada.

Defining Marketing Programs

When Socony Mobil (just prior to the consolidation) shifted from a product orientation to a market orientation, its management eliminated a series of product departments and established two "classes of trade" groups: Resale (primarily the retail motorist market and home heating market) and Commercial (industrial user accounts).

The initial breakdown by Resale and Commercial is a significant one. In serving the Resale market the stress is on building and maintaining immense distribution facilities, on conducting extensive advertising and promotional activities, and on monitoring and responding quickly to pricing behavior in the retail gasoline market. In the various Commercial markets the emphasis is often on technical service, on delivery commitments, on developing special products for particular applications, and on meeting competitive prices for large volume sales. Resale and Commercial markets are widely divergent, one from another, and it is interesting that in its new structure Socony Mobil distinguished between them organizationally, thus setting the pattern for the North American Division when it was formed.

Commercial Marketing Department

As in the IBM case, North American Division's program units were delineated in terms of market segments, each one of which might use a wide range of petroleum products. In the Commercial Marketing Department there were eight headquarter marketing departments, six of which are described in some detail in the case. Four of these, Special Products, Aviation, Fleet, and Marine, deal with distinct market segments characterized by well-defined buying patterns. A fifth one, Industrial, is a department whose markets consist of what remains of the commercial class of trade after these other markets are taken out. The sixth, National Accounts, is not a program in the same sense as the others but may be regarded as an organizational device for coordinating the selling efforts of the eight field divisions by major customers.

The Special Products Department prepared marketing programs for, and handled the sale of, products that were made by the further processing of certain basic refinery outputs. Two considerations favored the idea of having a separate marketing department with its own sales force for these products: First, many of the products were specially formulated to meet the requirements of individual customers. Second, the supply of "special products" fluctuated widely and close control had to be maintained over sales commitments and the direction of selling effort by products.

The sale of "special products," then, required technical expertise on the part of field sales representatives. A close coordination of sales effort was needed between field representatives and the Technical Service Department which developed new special products. Further, a tight manufacturing-selling coordination was needed so that sales effort could be directed according to current and projected supply conditions.

The Aviation Department sold lubricants and fuels directly to the military, airlines, and a major jet engine manufacturer. Sales to airport dealers and aviation manufacturers were made by the field marketing divisions. The markets for aviation lubricants and fuels were large and important to Mobil. In serving these markets, specialized knowledge and skills were needed to prepare competitive bids on large contract orders, both government and commercial. Finally, by having a separate Aviation Department, North American Division's top management could easily monitor the major product commitments that were being made in contractual arrangements with customers. The organizational arrangement was in part a device for allowing top management to focus on the company's aviation business.

The Marine Department served a "class of trade" that put great importance, the case indicates, on close personal contact between seller and buyer. In addition, it was essential for the seller to be able to provide customers with quick service in ports around the world. Potential customers were limited in number, easily identified and large in size. Finally, the market for marine lubricants was one in which Mobil was clearly the leader. For this combination of reasons, it was logical that the marine market be singled out organizationally for special treatment, that the head of the Marine Department make frequent calls on major customers, and that the department have its own field sales organization with district offices in New York, Cleveland, and San Francisco.

The customers of both the Industrial Department and the Fleet Sales and Service Department were not so neatly defined and were widely dispersed. Accordingly, they were reached through North American Division's extensive field organizations.

Inevitably field sales representatives dealing with a wide range of customers would have difficulty in selling to accounts needing technical help. To support field selling effort in these cases, the Industrial Department had four senior engineers each of whom was a specialist in a group of related industries. They worked with field salesmen on customer technical service problems and on the development of new products and applications for industrial markets. In addition, there were engineers in the field districts who worked closely with sales representatives on specific applications and provided technical service to customers.

Another inherent difficulty of having such a broadly defined group as "industrial" is that of coordinating marketing effort in large accounts. Mobil customers who buy and consume Mobil products at many different points, geographically, pose coordination problems. Buying decisions may be made at several points within the customer's organization, and the negotiation of contract terms may involve numerous members of his management at widespread locations. Similarly, delivery commitments on Mobil's part will often involve several supply points. The scope of the buyer-seller relationship would exceed the defined responsibility of any one salesman or division manager, and a number of Mobil representatives would have to work with any large customer in their respective territories. To achieve coordination and to provide a point for planning individual market strategies for large accounts, there was the National Accounts

Department. It is not to be regarded as a program management; it is instead an organizational device for coordinating marketing effort and for planning substrategies for large customers within an overall Commercial Marketing strategy.

Thus, it is interesting in the Commerical Departments to see what types of resources were attached directly to the programs. Special Products, Aviation, Railroad, and Marine each had its own direct sales force. The selling task in each case was specialized by technical know-how and by detailed knowledge of the industry and of individual customers. The markets were large, consisting of a relatively small number of large buyers, and easily reached with a small selling organization.

The Industrial and Fleet Departments utilized the field sales divisions to sell to their customers. But the Industrial Department included certain specialized resource units that facilitated and supplemented the field sales effort. There were specialists who conducted a ten-week training program for new industrial products salesmen. There was a cadre of senior engineers who worked with salesmen on technical application problems. A seven-man group prepared the widely distributed *Industrial Engine Builders Book* providing information on what lubricants to use with different machine tools. This team also worked with machinery manufacturers in preparing lubricating recommendations and instructions for operating manuals. Finally the Industrial Department had personnel who worked with the Advertising and Merchandising Department to develop promotional programs and create sales aids and advertising copy.

Resale Marketing Department

Unlike the organization of the Commercial Department, that of the Resale Marketing Department is not clear-cut and one must look closely to understand the logic of it. But it may be quickly added that the structure is well designed for its primary task: to build, nurture, and improve the distribution systems for reaching the motoring public, the home fuel oil consumer, and the agricultural user of Mobil products. Probably no element is so important in marketing strategies for these markets as a strong and extensive distribution system. Mobil's Resale Marketing Department is structured to build and maintain such a system.

The Retail Department developed programs for use by field sales personnel and service station operators. It was concerned with the problems of retaining existing dealers and attracting new ones. It prepared programs aimed at improving dealer profitability and programs intended to improve the quality of service station operations.

The Real Estate Department prepared policies and guidelines for the acquisition of new service station sites by the field marketing divisions. The Wholesale Department focused on building a fuel oil wholesaler organization and a distributor system for gasoline in areas where Mobil did not sell direct to retailers. The Wholesale Department analyzed proposals submitted by the field selling divisions involving acquisitions, loans to distributors, and changes in distributor status and recommended courses of action to the Resale Marketing General Manager. It prepared training programs for distributor personnel and management aids intended to improve distributor profitability. It prepared and supplied point-of-sale display materials, contests, and advertising copy.

The TBA[1] Department was not so concerned with the development of external marketing resources but did concentrate on developing a strong external supplier system for tires, batteries, and accessories. These were nonpetroleum products and Mobil did not manufacture them. Like the Retail Department, TBA was also concerned with devising strategies and programs for marketing its products to the motoring public through retail service stations.

Retail, TBA, and Wholesale, then, were centers for developing marketing programs. These three and Real Estate also played a central role in the development of Mobil's external distribution system and TBA supply system.

These departments worked through the field sales divisions. At each of the eight division offices there were personnel identified with these respective programs. They reported directly to the field division manager, but they had strong working relation-

---

[1] Tires, batteries, and accessories.

ships with their counterparts at headquarters. They worked with field salesmen in the geographic territories, advising, assisting, and providing direction which originated at Marketing Department headquarters in the several program management organizations. In this respect the Mobil organization was similar to IBM's, except that some program representatives stationed at field locations reported to program management units at headquarters. In practice, probably, this difference in reporting relationship was not a significant factor.

Marketing Staff Departments

In addition to the several program management units in the headquarters Marketing Department, there were several "staff" units which performed important coordinating functions.

It is significant, for example, that pricing was centralized for the broad range of Mobil products[2] and was the responsibility of a Pricing Department. All price changes on sales to resale accounts had to be cleared with this department. In the commercial class of trade the marketing divisions had authority to raise or lower prices, provided they remained above a "floor" established by the Pricing Department. Any prices below the "floor" had to be approved by headquarters. Similar procedures applied to lubricants prices.

There are several reasons why pricing should not, as a practical matter, be delegated to program units. First, pricing in the oil industry is complex. Prices on a wide range of products fluctuate constantly in different geographic areas and in different end-use markets. The pricing function then requires a continual flow of detailed market data, accurately interpreted. It calls for a degree of expertise that makes it a specialty function rather than one that could be effectively performed by program managers each responsible for devising and implementing the many dimensions of a total program strategy.

There are even more important reasons for centralizing pricing. Petroleum products are closely interrelated at the supply end. And in the market place, prices and pricing structures for different products, in different geographic areas, and in the wide range of end-use markets are inevitably related. Supply-demand shifts in any one product-market segment could, and would normally, affect others. If pricing responsibility was decentralized to the program management units, pricing action in any one area might easily have unanticipated, and probably adverse, effects on other areas. And on the supply end, shortages of some products and surpluses of others would result.

A related reason for centralizing pricing is that profitable operations are dependent to a large extent on the efficient utilization of plant. There must be an integrated pricing strategy devised to direct refinery output into the most profitable markets, both geographic and end-use. An integrated pricing strategy is all the more essential, and the more intricate to formulate, in view of the fact that product mix in a refinery can only be varied within relatively narrow limits. For every gallon of Product X that is made there may be two gallons of Product Y for which markets must be found.

Centralized pricing provides a better means organizationally for top management to focus on, and influence, price strategy. The importance to top management of pricing is caught in the statement of the Pricing Manager: ". . . a change of one cent in gasoline prices over a period of one year could represent a difference of $50 million in profits to Mobil."

Pricing in the oil industry, moreover, has long been a politically sensitive area. It affects competition among the corporate giants, as well as a very large segment of small business. It directly affects the consuming population. It is also of vital interest to the crude oil producing areas of the country. Pricing would then be a matter of vital concern to Mobil's top management, a function to be handled by specialists under top management guidance.

The delegation of pricing responsibility to program management units for two lines of products, TBA and Special Products, lends added weight to the logic of centralizing pricing for the high-volume basic lines such as automotive gasoline, aviation gasoline, jet fuel, heating oils, and industrial lubricants. Tires, batteries and accessories were pur-

---

[2] Except for Special Products and TBA.

chased outside and their supply was not at all related to that of petroleum products. Major oil companies had a relatively small share of the TBA market and the important competitive reference points in pricing included large retailers like Sears. TBA pricing, then, was based on an entirely different set of considerations from petroleum products pricing. It was better handled by those managers who were responsible for the procurement and promotion of TBA and who were knowledgeable in that area.

Special Products was also an area where the pricing reference points were very different from those in the higher volume lines. Many items were specially formulated to meet the particular requirements of individual customers. Marketing and product development costs were higher than might be incurred in the standard lines. Supply fluctuated and some special products were apparently manufactured as marginal items by the refineries. Under these circumstances, pricing was often done on an order-by-order basis with the dominant considerations being availability, technical development costs, and the value of the product to the individual customer. Pricing on Special Products was not likely to "impact" price structures in the high-volume product areas and, again, the pricing reference points were quite different. It was logical, therefore, to have program management units, rather than the Pricing Department, handle the pricing function in the case of TBA and Special Products. But in all other product areas it was essential that pricing be coordinated, centrally controlled and top management directed.

As in the case of pricing, the advertising and merchandising functions were centralized in one department to provide both a center of functional expertise and a vehicle for program coordination. The Advertising and Merchandising Department worked with two advertising agencies to develop copy and media plans. These plans were then submitted for approval to Mobil marketing management, including managers in the Retail, Wholesale and TBA Departments. The department worked with program management units in planning and carrying out a wide range of promotional campaigns.

Program management units were not delegating their responsibility for these critical aspects of program strategy. They were, however, utilizing the special skills of an Advertising and Merchandising Department. At the same time, a centralized department could assure that Mobil's advertising efforts had a common corporate identity. It could provide a single, professional point of interface with the company's two advertising agencies.

Basically, the Operations Department, like Advertising and Merchandising, was a point of interprogram coordination and expertise for a particular function — in this case logistics. At Mobil the field marketing divisions controlled and operated bulk plants (tank farms), warehouses, and vehicles for delivering petroleum products to service stations, distributors, and industrial customers. There were Operating Departments in each of the eight field divisions concerned with the product supply function.

The Operations Department at headquarters (1) prepared policies, useful operating data and guidelines for their use; (2) worked closely with the Supply, Distribution and Traffic Department on determining sources of products for each market; and (3) worked on plans for new storage and delivery facilities.

Again, it was a function that the several programs and the eight field marketing divisions could not handle individually. The technical knowledge required was one consideration. Another was the need for coordination of product supply and market demand between the refineries and the field marketing divisions. In this function (logistics) as in such others as pricing and advertising, interprogram coordination was essential because the programs were related one to another on these dimensions. In logistics as in advertising, it was useful to have one point of interface between the programs on the one hand and certain key resources on the other. In the case of advertising, the key resource was the two outside advertising agencies. In the case of Operations, it was the refineries.

The Planning System and Product Allocation

Given the constraints on supply — relatively fixed refinery capacity in the short run, limited flexibility in product mix — and the shifting demands of markets, the system by which Mobil allocated output to markets and balanced an immensely complex supply-demand situation was critical to its growth and profitability.

The annual profit plan was the initial step in the process. It was used by the Supply, Distribution and Traffic Department to plan refinery runs and shipment schedules. It was also the basis for setting volume and profit goals by market for the program management units and the field sales divisions.

With the year's programs underway, SD&T used current detailed information on refinery capacities and short-run market forecasts to revise the supply schedule every two months. Within that schedule changes were made on a day-to-day basis to respond to short-term shifts in market demand and to variations from planned manufacturing schedules.

A third element in the supply-demand balancing process was SD&T's work, on the one hand, to buy products from outside sources to meet demand that could not be filled internally, and on the other, to sell excess output in "discretionary" markets. SD&T also supplied Marketing with information that would be helpful in preparing bids on large government and commercial contracts, and the refineries with data on product profitability and volume-cost relationships to aid in scheduling refinery runs of different products.

These three elements of the product allocation process are worth further comment.

Annual Planning

The most interesting aspect of annual profit planning at Mobil was the relative contributions of operating management and top management. Annual planning began by the development and dissemination to operating units of certain basic assumptions as to economic growth and demand for petroleum products, and certain corporate objectives. The planning objective of operating management was to exploit any increase in market potential and to meet corporate volume and profit goals.

Plans Revisions

The annual profit plan provided only a first approximation of demand by markets for purposes of scheduling refinery output. The dynamic aspects of supply and demand made it necessary to refine these estimates every two months and then to adjust schedules from day-to-day. Plans and schedules went through successive degrees of refinement as the planning period became shorter and shorter. Annual plans provided the basis for making longer term commitments for raw materials, labor, and facilities. Shorter term plans provided the basis for shifting product from some end-use markets and geographic areas to others and adjusting refinery schedules accordingly.

Supply/Demand Adjustments

If Mobil could sell all that it produced — and no more — in markets that could be economically served from its refinery locations, the planning and scheduling process might end there. Instead, however, SD&T's work went beyond scheduling NAD refineries and included outside purchases, "swaps," and sales. It was in this way that NAD ultimately equated its supply with demand by product, by market, and by geographic area.

A central concept running through this phase of SD&T's activities is that certain market segments took priority over others and the needs of these markets would be satisfied first. The retail gasoline market, clearly, would be among those having high priority. Mobil had immense investments in service station facilities; thousands of dealers were depending on Mobil supplies; and any short-term failure to satisfy demand could result in a long-term loss of market share.

Some other markets were "discretionary." Generally, discretionary sales were made in large quantities on a bid basis. If Mobil had refinery capacity available, and there was no more profitable alternative, the output could be sold at a price that would cover costs and yield a small profit. These customers typically bought on a "spot" basis and NAD's management recognized no commitment to serve as a continuing source of supply.

SD&T, then, worked at the margin. It directed refinery capacity toward its most profitable utilization, recognizing at the same time NAD's commitment to serve as a reliable source of supply for certain channels of distribution and certain other classes of customers. It met these commitments by buying outside when and where necessary. Having done so, it sought to move excess output as profitably as possible in market segments that traditionally purchased on a price basis.

Summary

The consolidation of Socony-Mobil, Magnolia, and General Petroleum in 1959 to form Mobil's North American Division provided a broad framework within which the Division had the resources and the flexibility to balance product supply and market demand. NAD's territory embraced a series of relatively homogeneous markets for petroleum products. The Division, then, was a logical *business* unit for planning purposes.

It moved quickly to organize its marketing efforts by programs defined in terms of resale and user groups, not products. Program units became the focus of the planning effort, provided the initiative for promotion, supplied certain specialized technical services, and worked actively at field sales training. When it was economically feasible, certain resource units were directly attached to the programs — Aviation, Marine, Railroad, and Special Products had their own field sales forces; TBA did its own procurement. When the key to success in a market was a strong distribution system (as in retail gasoline or fuel oil), the programs management unit planned and carried out programs to develop these critical external resources.

Headquarters groups such as Pricing, Operations, and Advertising and Merchandising served three purposes. They were centers of expertise in their functional specialties. They coordinated and in some cases helped to shape program activity in these areas. They served in some instances as an interface between program management and their counterpart outside resources. In all three areas, program activities were inevitably interrelated and had to be coordinated.

Finally the planning system was a three-stage procedure for allocating refinery output to markets. Ultimately, however, the balancing of supply and demand was achieved by a series of outside purchases, exchanges, and sales of product in "discretionary" markets.

For large integrated oil companies, profitable operations will depend on moving at the greatest possible profit the maximum output of a fixed (in the short-run) refining capacity; building and maintaining strong distribution networks; serving as a reliable supply source; meeting individual needs for products and services in a wide range of markets. Mobil's organization was intricately and well designed for these tasks. The decentralization of programs and the centralization of certain key functions shows a fine degree of organizational sophistication. Paraphrasing a once popular cigarette commercial: "It's not how big you make it, but how you make it big."

E. I. du Pont de Nemours and Company: Textile Fibers Department

Between December 1951 and March 1956 some basic changes were made in the marketing organization of Du Pont's Textile Fibers Department. These shifts reflected changes in management thinking as to the approach that the company should take in adapting the organization to meet market conditions.

At the time of this study the Textile Fibers Department was one of 11 Du Pont industrial departments (see Exhibits 1 and 2). It manufactured and sold rayon, acetate, nylon, "orlon"[1] acrylic fiber, and "Dacron"[1] polyester fiber. These fibers were available in the form of short fibers and long filaments and in a wide variety of thickness and finishes. The company manufactured the fibers, but did no spinning or weaving. In the case of rayon, acetate, nylon, and acrylic fibers there were a number of other manufacturers. Dacron polyester fiber, on the other hand, was made and sold only by Du Pont and was a product on which the company held patents or patent rights.

The Textile Fibers Department sold through its field sales force to spinners and weavers. Weavers in turn sold cloth in semifinished form (greige goods) to finishers who bleached and dyed these materials themselves or who contracted to have this work performed by dye houses. The finished material was then sold to cutters to be made up in end-product form as articles of clothing, upholstery, curtains, and other household items. Du Pont fibers were also sold for industrial uses. Both rayon and nylon, for example, were used extensively in making tires and rubber belting. For such applications as these, fibers were generally sold directly to the end-product manufacturer.

Organization of the Textile Fibers Department in 1951

As of late 1951 the Textile Fibers Department included five divisions, one for each of the five fibers

---

[1] Du Pont trademark.

the department made and sold. Each division, under a Division Manager, had a Sales Department and a Manufacturing Department. A centralized Research Division existed. Individual Research Managers handled the specific fibers and received much guidance from the Division Managers. Each division also had its own field sales force. This type of organization had evolved over a long period of time as new fibers had been added to the company's line. The Rayon Division and the Acetate Division organizations had been established in 1936 and then, with certain changes, parallel sales-manufacturing-research organizations had been set up for each of the other three fibers when the product was developed for commercial use. Nylon was placed on the market in 1939, "Orlon" in 1950, and "Dacron" in 1952.

This type of organization had been workable up until the late 1940s, probably because the demand for synthetic fibers had been high and because only three fibers were involved. Synthetic fibers were consistently in short supply from 1940 to 1950, and the limiting factor in sales growth had been productive capacity rather than marketing effectiveness. Rayon and acetate had had phenomenal growth since they were introduced in the early 1920s. Similarly, nylon had achieved almost immediate acceptance when it was first offered in 1939. Its use for commercial applications, however, was sharply curtailed with the outbreak of World War II. During the war years almost the total output of nylon was used for applications related to the war effort. After the war, nylon continued to be in short supply as uses were found for it in a rapidly increasing number of end-products. Rayon and acetate sales volumes reflected nylon's impact on the market. Nevertheless, sales of rayon and acetate continued to grow and new uses were found, too, for these older synthetic fibers. In the late 1940s, for example, rayon, improved through Du Pont research, began to replace cotton as tire cord with the result that a very large new market was developed for this synthetic fiber.

When "Orlon" and "Dacron" were put on the market, demand for these new fibers was also strong. They had new and unique properties which appealed to the textile trade and to the public. Their immediate acceptance, however, was to be accounted for largely by a feeling on the part of the trade that one or the other might be a "new nylon."

Although demand continued high for synthetic fibers through 1951, the management of the Textile Fibers Department recognized the need for organizational changes. Some difficulties had been encountered, for example, in connection with making long-range plans for market growth and for new plant capacity. Each division manager exhibited a natural tendency to estimate a strong growth potential for his particular fiber at the expense perhaps of the other synthetic fibers. In fact, the combined estimates of market potential for each of the five fibers far exceeded the estimate of the total market potential for all synthetic fibers. Under these circumstances top management of the Textile Fibers Department was confronted with conflicting claims and estimates when it was faced with the problem of making plant investment decisions.

Other problems were evident. Some customers objected to the fact that they were visited, not by one, but by as many as five Du Pont fiber salesmen, each one making strong claims for his product. Customers also indicated that no one salesman could take up problems involving the use of two or more fibers — that salesmen did not get to know their customers well.

Consolidation of the Five Fiber Divisions

In December 1951 an organizational change was made that was intended to meet some, although not all, of these problems. The five divisions were combined so that there was just one Sales Division, one Research Division, and one Manufacturing Division. Each of these departments was organized, however, along product lines. In the Sales Division there continued to be individual sales forces for each fiber. Similarly, in the Research organization, one section was set up to do research work on each of the five fibers. Manufacturing was also organized along product lines, since each fiber was produced in separate plant facilities. Exhibit 3 is a chart of the basic organization as it existed from December 1951 until 1954.

In this organization the Sales Division had two sections, Direct Sales and Technical Sales. Under the Direct Sales Section there was one sales force for each of the five fibers, headed by a Product Sales Manager. This man had the responsibility for directing the field sales force, for working with the plant on production scheduling and inventory control, for promotional programs, and for long-range planning.

The Technical Sales Section included two groups. The Sales Development group worked with weavers, finishers, and cutters to find new uses for synthetic fibers. The Technical Service group worked on problems encountered by Du Pont customers in using Du Pont fibers.

Shortly after these organizational changes had been put in effect, the demand for synthetic fibers fell off very sharply. The difficulties which were then encountered under depressed market conditions indicated to the management of the Textile Fibers Department that the department's organization needed some further changes.

Further Organizational Changes

After about three years of experience with the organization that had been adopted in 1951, the Textile Fibers Department management again changed the marketing organization at the end of 1954. The fundamental change made at that time was to introduce a Merchandising Division headed by a Director of Merchandising who reported to an Assistant General Director-Marketing. Hence the merchandising function was on an organizational level with Direct Sales and Technical Sales.

There were six groups in the Merchandising Division: the Men's Wear Merchandising Section, the Women's Wear Merchandising Section, the Home Furnishings Merchandising Section, the Industrial Merchandising Section, the Advertising and Promotion Section, and the Marketing Research Section. Each of the first four sections was divided into subgroups along end-product lines. Thus the Men's Wear Merchandising Section had a Merchandising Manager for Boys' Wear, one for Furnishings and Sportswear, one for Tailored Outerwear, and one for Utility Clothing.

Each Merchandising Manager was responsible for developing marketing plans for the use of all five fibers in the product area for which he was responsible. His plans would then form the basis for direct sales emphasis, for promotional programs, for developing new fiber specifications and new fabrics, for production scheduling, and for long-range plans for plant facilities. The Merchandising Managers would be experts in their end-product areas and would develop close and continuing relationships with key people at all levels in the textile industry.

With the addition of the Merchandising Division, the Sales Development group under Technical Sales was disbanded, since its function would be assumed by the New Merchandising Managers. The Technical Sales group was then reorganized to include a Textile and Industrial Products Research Division in addition to the Technical Service Section. The Textile and Industrial Products Research Division had previously been included in the Textile Fibers Department's Research Division and was moved to the Sales Division in December 1954. This division was concerned primarily with research on the use of Du Pont fibers in specific end-products. The Technical Service Section, on the other hand, dealt with problems of processing Du Pont fibers and with problems of fiber specifications and fiber quality. In the Technical Service Section there was one manager for each of the five fibers, as well as managers for Fabric Development, Dyeing and Finishing, Industrial Technical Service, and Laboratory Service.

At this time, consideration was given to the possibility of having a single sales force with each field salesman selling all five fibers. An analysis was made, therefore, of the field selling job to determine the practicality of having a "multifiber" sales force. This analysis disclosed differences in the selling job for each of the five fibers. Technical service problems, for example, were of major importance in the case of nylon, "Orlon" and "Dacron" but minor with respect to rayon and acetate. Sales problems were different, too, because the new fibers were in short supply and had to be allocated to customers, whereas the older synthetic fibers were in plentiful supply. In the case of rayon and acetate, in fact, there was a large amount of excess production capacity, and consequently prices deteriorated and profit margins were low. As another point of comparison that made for differences in selling each of the fibers, the old fibers had much larger product lines than the new. There were 610 different putups of acetate fibers as compared to 62 for "Orlon" acrylic fiber. Again, the markets differed somewhat. While 50% of Du Pont's rayon was used for industrial purposes, over 60% of "Dacron" polyester fiber was used for men's wear and almost 70% of "Orlon" was used for women's wear. Hence, there was not a strong overlap among customer groups for each of the five fibers. Analysis disclosed that relatively few firms bought three or more Du Pont fibers and that the total number of customers for each fiber varied considerably.

This analysis indicated clearly the additional training problem that was necessary in order to change to a sales force in which each field salesman would be called upon to represent Du Pont's full fiber line. Because of the severe adjustment demands imposed upon the organization by the adoption of the "end-use" concept, it was decided not to take this further step at this time. Accordingly, the organizational plan adopted in December 1954 provided for continuing a field organization based on separate sales forces.

The desirability of a multifiber sales force became increasingly apparent, however, as the department gained experience in operating under the "end-use" concept. Accordingly, a multifiber sales force was established in March 1956 in order to improve service to customers.

In the consideration of the possibility of having a multifiber sales force it became apparent that there would be no group in the marketing organization with the responsibility for marketing and market development on a fiber basis. To provide for such a functional responsibility, therefore, a Sales Programs Division was added to the marketing organization in March 1956. Like the heads of the Sales Division and the Merchandising Division, the Sales Programs Division head reported to the Assistant General Director-Marketing. The Sales Programs Division included one Sales Programs Manager for each of the five fibers and a Sales Programs Manager for New Products.

The Sales Programs Managers were regarded as staff personnel. They kept in close touch with Merchandise Managers, the field sales forces, and Technical Sales Managers to assure that everything possible was being done to promote the uses of the fiber for which they had individual responsibility. Sales Programs Managers also maintained close and continuing contact with Du Pont fiber plants on production scheduling and inventory planning. The Sales Programs Managers, therefore, assumed many of the responsibilities held previously by the Product Sales Managers, but had staff rather than line authority in carrying out these responsibilities. Under this setup the Sales Programs Managers would be free to devote full attention to the "health" aspects of the fiber responsibilities without penalty to the selling effort. Similarly, Direct Sales Managers would be free to direct their attention to the direct selling aspects of the fiber responsibilities without penalty to the planning effort.

To do their jobs, the Sales Programs Managers had to work through other groups in the Textile Fibers Department. The organization that was developed as of March 1956 is shown in Exhibit 4. This organization included four functional groups: Sales, Merchandising, and Sales Programs, reporting to the Assistant General Director-Marketing, and Technical Sales, reporting to the Assistant General Director-Technical Sales. In the discussion that follows, the functions performed by each of these groups are described.

Sales Division

Sales to Du Pont's domestic customers were made through field sales personnel working out of five regional offices located in Charlotte, New York, Philadelphia, Providence, and Akron. Export sales were directed from Du Pont's Wilmington headquarters. For the most part, salesmen sold all fibers to assigned customers making a wide variety of end-products. In a few instances, salesmen were assigned to call on customers in a single industry. For example, Du Pont salesmen located in Akron sold only to rubber companies. One man working out of the New York office called only on rope and cordage accounts, while a salesman in the Philadelphia office called on all sewing thread manufacturers.

The sales Division Director and Assistant Director had three Sales Assistants. One of these men followed all sales of "Dacron" and rayon, and another was concerned with acetate, nylon, and "Orlon" sales. These two assistants worked in close contact with the respective Sales Programs Managers. The third Sales Assistant handled certain administrative matters and had particular responsibilities for keeping in touch with various merchandising programs.

The Sales Division Director had authority to price new products in the line and to set prices on obsolete items in inventory. On new product pricing, he solicited the recommendation of the Sales Programs Manager responsible for the fiber concerned. Basic price levels were determined by the top management of the Textile Fibers Department.

Merchandising Division

The Merchandising Managers in the Merchandising Division were intended to serve as the coordinating points for all information on their respective end-use markets. They were to evaluate market trends and, in the light of these trends, to forecast fiber consumption by end-use and to make long-range plans for the promotion of all Du Pont fibers. They were also responsible for making continuous evaluations of Du Pont's promotional and distributional programs in these end-use markets and the effect thereon of fiber prices. It was a requirement of the Merchandising Manager's job, therefore, that he maintain trade contacts as well as close relationships with Technical Service, Sales Programs, and Sales personnel in his company.

The Merchandising Manager had additional responsibilities for determining markets to be sought by Du Pont, the effect of fiber prices on penetration of these markets, and the advertising goals and themes. He was charged also with responsibility for developing specific plans to help Du Pont's direct customers move their products through trade channels.

Each of the four Merchandising Managers in the Merchandising Division had several managers reporting to him, each one responsible for Du Pont's programs in a group of end-product markets. For example, the Manager of the Industrial Merchandising Section had three Merchandising Managers reporting to him. As a group, they had responsibility for recommending programs in industrial end-use markets.

Sales Programs Division

As previously noted, the Sales Programs Managers held staff positions in the sales organization of the Textile Fibers Department. In general, each Sales Programs Manager was charged with looking after the "health" of his particular fiber and for serving as a clearing house for all information on it. Specifically, he worked with groups in the sales, research, and manufacturing organizations on scheduling production, allocating available supplies, planning new plant capacity, developing new plant capacity, developing new products and new applications, and promoting the use of his fiber in the market.

In planning production schedules, each Sales Programs Manager met with production personnel about the middle of each month to work on schedules for the month following the month immediately ahead. In the case of fibers that might be in short supply, the Programs Manager and plant personnel for that fiber established "grants" or "reserves" for each sales region. Estimates were made of the total supply by type of fiber and denier that would be available, and the amount reserved for each region was determined primarily by the historical sales patterns.

In the case of fibers not in short supply, Regional Sales Managers submitted forecasts of their requirements and production schedules were set accordingly.

The Textile Fibers Department used a 60-day order system. Orders scheduled for delivery in any given month could be taken both during that month and during the preceding month. Delivery was promised for a specific week. Orders were accumulated against reserves set for each region and copies of each order were sent from field sales offices to the mills and to the respective Sales Programs Managers.

Occasionally, because of specific needs of particular customers, Regional Sales Managers requested additional amounts over and above the original reserves. When these requests could be met, they were approved both by the Sales Programs Manager concerned and by headquarters Sales personnel. If, because of production delays, orders for a fiber were "carried over" beyond the month in which they were scheduled for delivery, the Sales Programs Manager was responsible for determining the order of priority in which these orders would be filled.

Another function of each Sales Programs Manager was to aid in planning new plant capacity for his fiber. He had the task of developing the long-range sales estimates on which plant investment decisions would be made. In doing so, he drew on the knowledge and judgments of Sales personnel and Merchandising Managers.

As new plant capacity was added, the Sales Programs Manager had the responsibility for determining the end-product markets in which efforts would be made to place the additional fiber output. These decisions were made in a way that would "build a sound market base" for the particular fiber. Sales Programs Managers were particularly interested, therefore, in building diverse end-product markets for their fibers and in avoiding excessive dependency on any one end-product application.

In determining the distribution of additional supplies of a fiber, the Sales Programs Manager relied heavily on the recommendations of both Merchandising Managers and Regional Sales Managers.

In addition to meeting with representatives from Manufacturing in connection with production schedules and plant expansion, each Sales Programs Manager had continuing contact with plant personnel on other matters. The size and pattern of inventories, for example, were determined by Sales Programs Managers and plant personnel with the Programs Manager taking major responsibility for such decisions. Problems having to do with the production of new fiber types were also handled by Programs Managers working with both plant and research personnel. As one means of maintaining close touch among men representing these three functions in the Textile Fibers Department, a Coordination Committee had been established for each fiber. This committee included the Sales Programs Manager, representatives from the plant making the fiber, and from those research groups concerned with the technical development of the fiber and its uses. This committee met weekly.

In addition to these activities, each Sales Programs Manager took an active part in the development of new fiber grades and new fabrics. He solicited ideas from field personnel, and estimated the potential sales volume for a proposed new fiber and the price it might bring. New ideas were discussed with Coordination Committee members. If the response was favorable, the Sales Programs Manager reviewed the idea with interested Merchandising Managers and requested their help in promoting the new grade of fiber in the specific applications for which it had been developed. Finally, Sales Programs Managers were responsible for recommending prices on new items in their line. Implementation of these recommendations required approval of the Sales Division Director.

Each Sales Programs Manager had several assistants. The Development Assistant worked to coordinate Direct Sales, Technical Sales, and Merchandising effort in developing and launching new and modified fibers in the market. In this job, he served essentially as an expediter, and he also helped to determine the nature and the timing of the market development program. He then worked on this program up until the point when the fiber became an established product on Du Pont's price list.

Each Sales Programs Manager also had a Sales Assistant. He maintained close direct contact with regional sales personnel and worked with them on any problems involving the sale of his particular fiber. Problems that could not be solved in the field were taken up by the Sales Assistant with headquarters Sales personnel.

The Sales Assistant was responsible each quarter for preparing short-range sales forecasts by months for the coming three months and by quarters for the next two years. These forecasts were based on sales estimates submitted by Regional Sales Managers.

The Programs Manager's Merchandising Contact Assistant was responsible for working with Merchandising Managers to plan detailed actions to implement those market development programs which had been recommended for his fiber. The Merchandising Contact Assistant then followed the progress being made on the various development projects. He also kept abreast, through the Merchandising Managers, of trends that would affect sales of his fiber.

Some Sales Programs Managers had Order Scheduling Assistants. These assistants kept records on orders received from the sales regions against reserves set for the regions. They also worked closely with the several plants to see that orders were shipped on schedule.

Technical Sales

The Technical Sales group included the Technical Service Section and the Textile and Industrial Products Research Division. Technical Service was concerned primarily with customer problems encountered in the use of Du Pont fibers, problems that could be handled without expenditure of very much research effort. This section included a Technical Service Manager for each of the five fibers, as well as Managers for Dyeing and Finishing, Fabric Development, and Industrial and Laboratory Service.

As noted previously, the Textile and Industrial Products Research Division had been "transplanted" from the Textile Fibers Department Research Divisions to the Sales Divisions in December 1954 at the time the Merchandising Division was established. Textile Research work related to developing new end-use applications for Du Pont fibers. Personnel in Textile and Industrial Products Research, for example, worked on designing new or improved types of fabrics or on ways of using fibers in industrial products such as tires and conveyor belts. Much of their work involved developing and improving the production processes for making products that used Du Pont fibers. Textile Research's work, then, involved creating new knowledge to be used in solving customer problems and in broadening the applications for Du Pont fibers. The problems on which this group worked were initiated either within Textile Research or by Technical Service Personnel, Merchandising Managers, Sales Programs Managers, or personnel in the Research Divisions of the Textile Fibers Department.

In the opinion of the Director of the Textile and Industrial Products Research Division, moving his group from the Research Divisions to the Sales Divisions had been highly constructive. He believed that, as a member of the Sales Divisions organization, he could evaluate more effectively the relative importance of problems on which his group was working. As a member of the Research Divisions, he had felt that his group was laboring under two handicaps. First, it was not aware, when technical problems were tackled and solved, of the new technical problems that frequently resulted. Hence, an individual piece of work was really only partially completed. Second, in presenting its ideas to Sales, his group labored under the obstacle of the "NIH (not invented here) factor." With Textile Research a part of the Sales Divisions organization, the ideas generated by this group seemed to be more favorably received by Sales than previously.

Textile Research personnel continued to work closely, however, with the Research Divisions. The Research Divisions worked primarily on new fibers, marked improvements in existing fibers, the use of new raw materials, and the development of processes for making fibers. The results of the Research Divisions' efforts often led to new capital investments.

Frequently, Textile Research personnel were loaned to the Research Divisions to work on new product developments and vice versa. They were expected to contribute information on problems relating to customer use of the new Du Pont product. If the development was successfully completed, these research men were moved back to Textile Research to work on the development of end-use applications for the new product.

A major responsibility of the Director of Textile Research was to set up a schedule of priorities for the research projects on which his organization would work. In determining the order of priority, he consulted various groups in the Sales Divisions to assess Du Pont's "stake" in each proposed project. Having made a list of projects in their order of importance, he assigned Textile Research manpower[2] and financial resources to the projects until these resources were exhausted. The amount of funds and the manpower allotted to each project were determined both by the magnitude of the project and by its urgency.

Once completed, the list of research projects had to be approved. Final approval for each project was obtained at various levels of Du Pont's management, depending on the estimated cost of the project and the nature of the work.

Having received authorization for the projects he would undertake, the Director of Textile Research then assigned "due dates" to each one. These dates were set after talking with the research man who would be in charge of the project. The list of priorities was revised quarterly.

Controlling the Operations of the Sales Divisions

The executive direction of the Sales Divisions

---

[2] In assigning manpower, the Director of Textile Research reserved 10% of each men's time to allow the man time for working on "bootleg" projects—projects which were not authorized but which related to the work of the Textile Fibers Department, and in which the man had a strong interest.

rested, by and large, in the hands of the Assistant General Director-Marketing. He directed sales activities through a system of regularly scheduled meetings at which division heads and key staff members reported on activities and trade information within their jurisdiction.

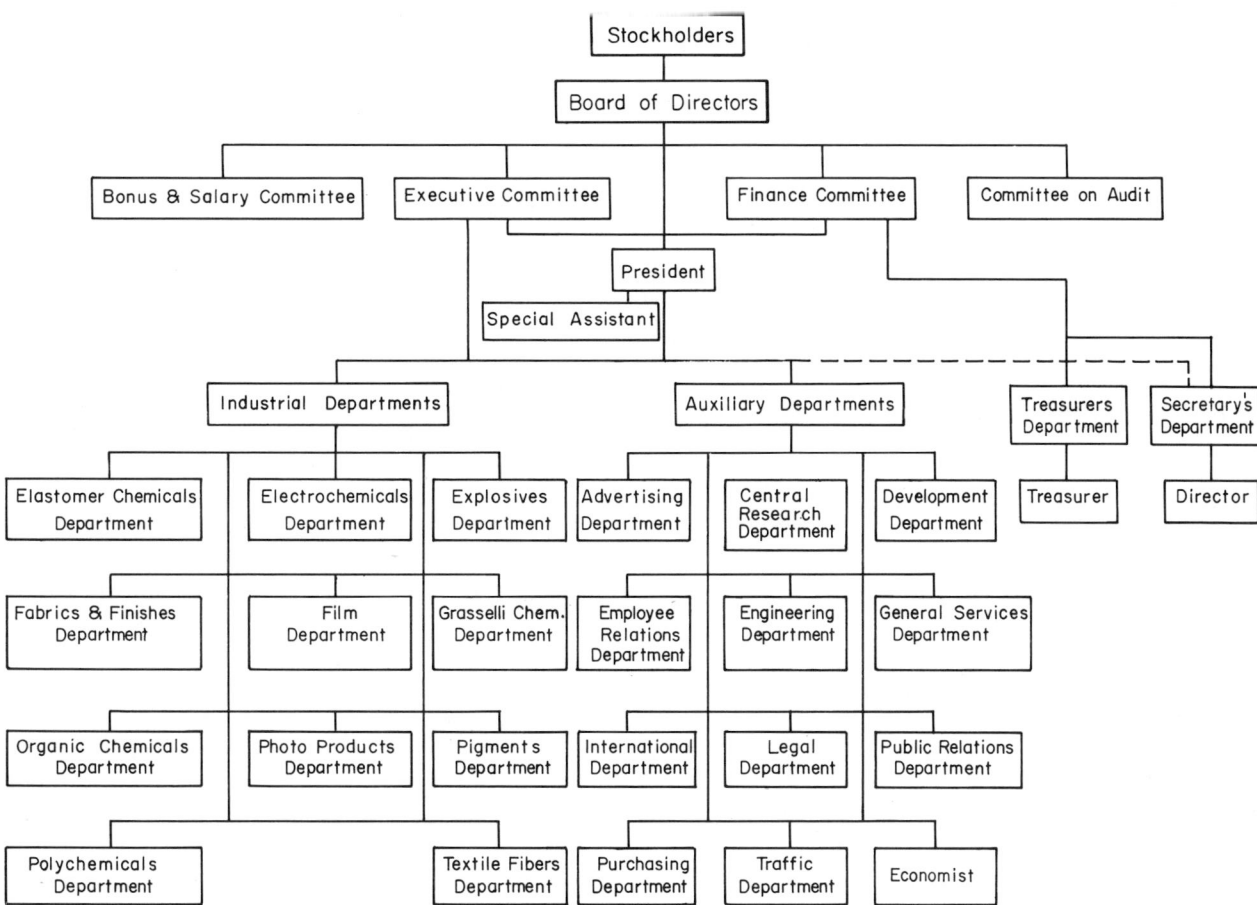

Exhibit 1. Corporate Organization Chart, March 1956

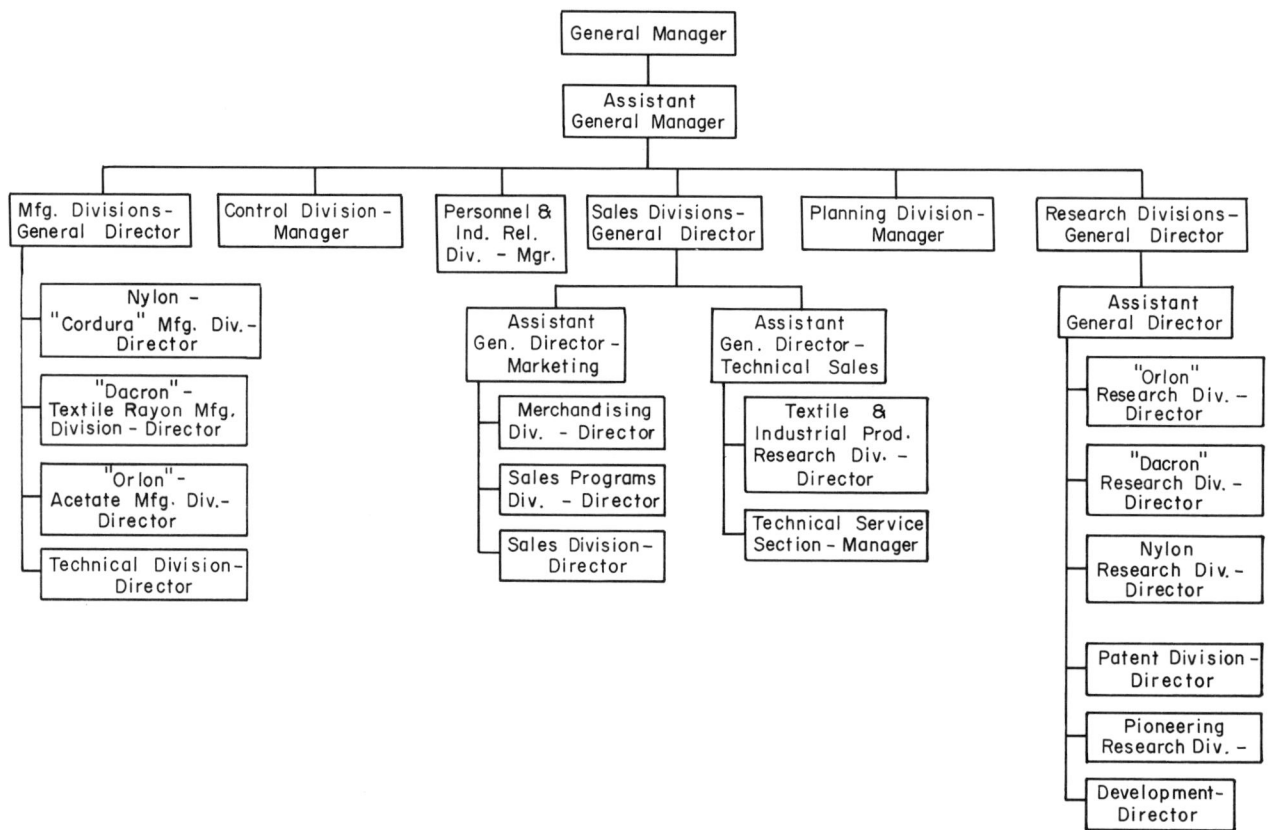

Exhibit 2. Organization Chart of Textile Fibers Department, March 1956

Exhibit 3. Organization Chart of Textile Fibers Department, December 1951–December 1954

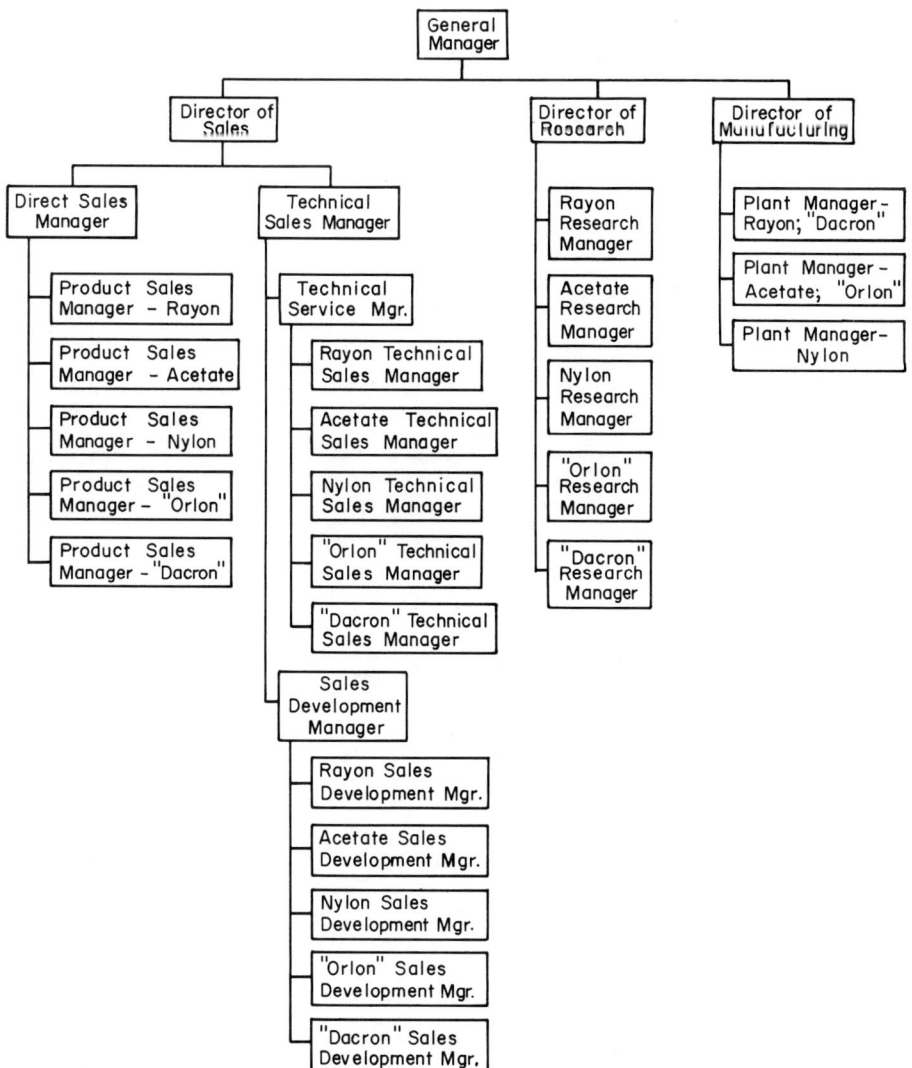

Exhibit 4. Organization Chart of Sales Divisions of Textile Fibers Department, March 1956

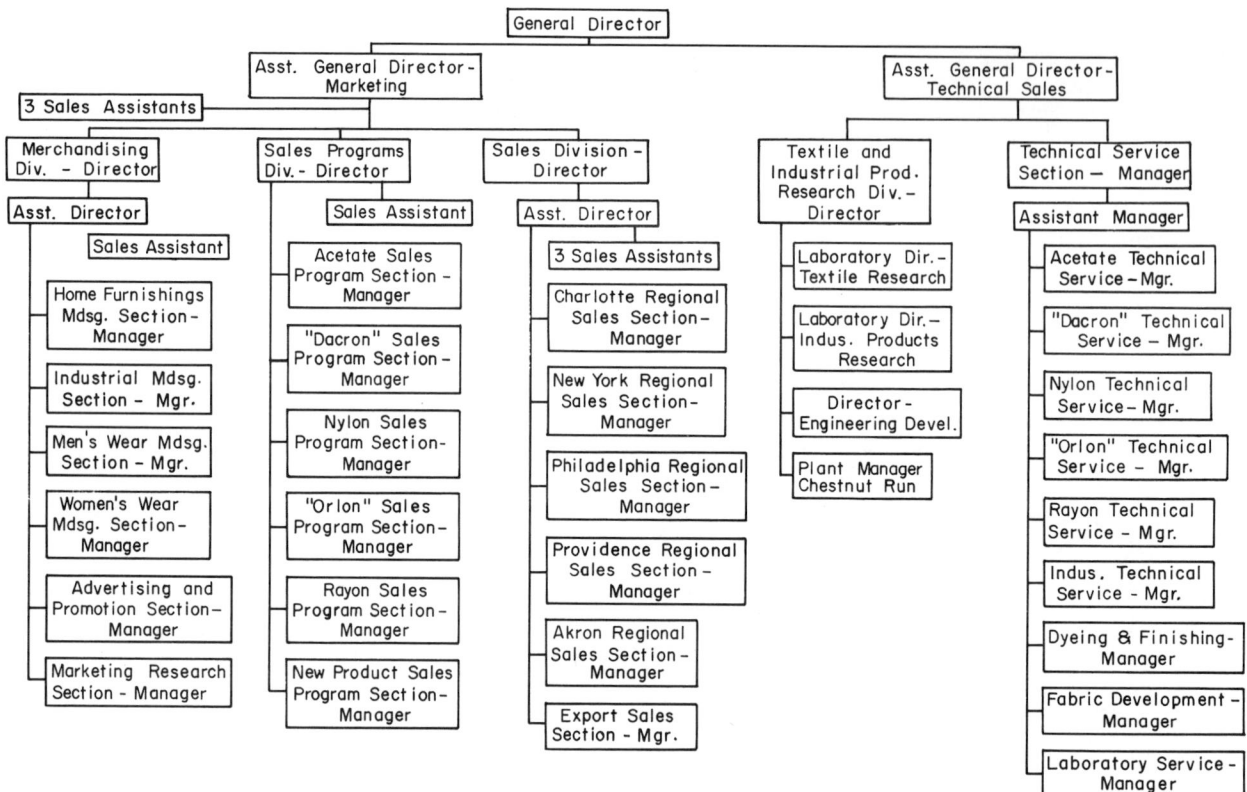

COMMENTARY

The organization of the Du Pont Textile Fibers Department changed radically between 1951 and 1956, going from five relatively independent product departments to a fully integrated multifiber business. In order to analyze the significance of these organizational changes, we will compare the structure that was in place before December 1951 with the one that had evolved by March 1956.[1]

Prior to December 1951 the Textile Fibers Department organization had five fiber divisions, each with its own sales and manufacturing units. Although there was a centralized Research Division, it was organized by fibers, which made it possible for the five product division heads to influence strongly the direction of research effort. In effect, then, the Textile Fibers Department operated as five separate businesses.

By March 1956 the Du Pont management had initiated some imaginative changes in the organization. There was now a single multifiber sales force with district offices in five important geographical markets. A Merchandising Division responsible for market development and promotion for all five synthetic fibers was established. This unit was organized, it should be noted, not by fiber but by broad end-use market. A Textile and Industrial Products Research unit was moved over from the Research Division and placed in the Sales Division because it worked extensively with Du Pont customers on their use of fibers in end-products.

Finally, a Sales Program unit, organized by fibers, was created. Sales Program managers for each fiber worked on scheduling production, planning new plant capacity, developing new products (items in the respective fiber lines), finding new applications, and promoting the use of these fibers in end-use markets.

It will be useful to comment first on the underlying reasons for organizational change. Then, we can look closely at the various units within the new organization to understand why each was structured as it was, how it functioned, and how it related to other operating units.

Strategy and Organization

Organizational change at the Du Pont Textile Fibers Department is to be understood against a background of changing market conditions, and of developing knowledge on the part of both users and suppliers about the markets for synthetic fibers and their use in various manufacturing processes. History played an important part in the evolution of the pre-1952 structure. The five fibers had been developed one after another, with rayon and acetate first, and then nylon, "Orlon," and "Dacron" following in that order. As each new fiber had been introduced into the Du Pont product line, a parallel sales-manufacturing-research organization had been created to develop and market it.

One might reason that such a structure is entirely appropriate for the early stages of market development. In this phase, the product is being improved with regard to its processing characteristics for a wide range of applications. Different "put-ups" are being developed to make the fiber available in various forms for different uses. Markets are being defined and staked out. Customers are being educated in how to use the fiber. Problems encountered in manufacturing are being solved by Du Pont and customer technicians working together. And, in the course of things, immense knowledge is being accumulated about markets, applications, fiber manufacture at Du Pont, and fiber processing in customers' plants.

In this stage, an integrated business developed around a single product has great advantages. Most

---

[1] The interim structure that was put in place in December 1951 simply replaced product department heads with resource heads (manufacturing, sales, and research) at the highest level, but left the product orientation intact below that level.

important, the tasks in the early stages of product and market development require close coordination among sales, research, manufacturing, and customers. Such day-to-day interfunctional relationships seem to work most smoothly within the context of a business with a narrow product focus.

Another advantage is the degree to which such an integrated business unit is committed to the task of market development. Since its success or failure is easy to measure, and its future opportunities are dependent on success in a single venture, the business group is highly motivated to devote intense effort to its task, without concern for the impact of its work on competing products. Russell W. Peterson, Director of the Research and Development Division of Du Pont's Development Department, comments as follows:

[The manager of a new venture] is provided with the necessary dollars, personnel, and facilities to make his group self-sufficient. He and all his people are put full-time on the new venture. Because they have no other assignment, they develop a strong vested interest in the project. Their morale and motivation are likely to be high.[2]

Such commitment is often a requisite for success, and it will tend to result in the greatest possible exploitation of the product. Thus, during the period when the task is to identify markets, to develop a product so that it can be used in a wide range of applications, and to educate potential customers as fully as possible, it is advantageous to have a number of separate, relatively autonomous integrated business units, each built around a single synthetic fiber.

In the late 1940s Du Pont's management recognized certain problems, some internal and some external. Internally, the Textile Fibers Department management found long-range planning difficult. Estimates of market growth for each fiber made by the respective product department managers tended to be overly optimistic. Externally, customers were complaining that several Du Pont fiber salesmen, each representing a different fiber, were competing against each other for their business. Customers wanted to deal with one Du Pont representative who could provide objective advice concerning which fiber or combination of fibers the customer should use for the particular end-products he manufactured.

Moreover, supply-demand conditions were changing. More large producers of synthetic fibers were coming into the market, industry capacity was increasing, and most synthetic fibers were no longer in short supply. The market environment for synthetic fibers had changed radically.

These conditions created the need for a change in strategy for Du Pont. The change in strategy, in turn, called for a change in organization. The interim (December 1951–March 1956) organization did not apparently meet the need; certainly, it did not resolve the problems customers encountered in dealing with Du Pont's competing sales representatives. We might, then, move quickly past this interim structure and consider the relationship between the March 1956 organization and Du Pont's change in market strategy.

To create *selective* demand for Du Pont fibers as opposed to competing products, and to develop further the *known* markets for synthetics, Du Pont needed to work at all levels of manufacture, distribution, and use of end-products made with synthetic fibers. In clothing, for example, this might include spinners, weavers, finishers, cutters, jobbers, retailers, and the consuming public. Du Pont could work at the manufacturing level, for example, to resolve technical problems, and at the retail and user levels to promote the use of synthetic fibers in a wide range of end uses. In fact, with its tremendous resources and its great stake in the growth of markets of synthetic fibers, it was practical for Du Pont to carry out an intensive consumer advertising campaign.

The Merchandising Division was organized in such a way as to provide a suitable structure for this effort. It was subdivided into units responsible for end-use markets. These units were to work directly at all levels in the supply chain. In particular, they were to ferret out new applications in their respective markets for individual fibers or combinations of fibers. In contrast, the pre-1952 organization was designed to deal primarily with Du Pont's immediate customers for synthetic fibers.

The new multifiber sales force was intended to

---

[2] Russell W. Peterson, "New Venture Management in a Large Company," *Harvard Business Review,* May–June 1967, p. 71.

meet the needs of customers for two or more fibers. It did not, however, foreclose the possibility of having sales representatives specialize in an individual fiber in sales districts where that fiber was the only Du Pont fiber used by certain large customers.

The March 1956 organization also provided a better framework for planning. Demand forecasts could be focused on end-use markets, making it possible to identify and appraise the factors affecting demand. Forecasts by markets could be cross-checked with forecasts by products. Forecasting and planning might then be less biased, since departmental plans could be based on estimates of growth of the total synthetic fibers markets.

The March 1956 structure attempted to compensate for the loss of close working relationships among manufacturing, sales, and research, through the creation of Sales Program managers. Each Sales Program manager was charged with the responsibility for the "health" of a particular fiber. It should be noted, however, that the need for close day-to-day inter-resource relationships probably diminishes over time, as the product line is developed and customers are educated in the uses of the product.

If Du Pont research laboratories should develop a completely new synthetic fiber, one that would replace existing synthetics for some applications but find broad new uses as well, it might be well to go back to a pre-1952 type of organization for that fiber. This form of organization would be well suited to product and market development, and would be expected to achieve maximum initial market penetration. The exploitation of the new product would likely be at the expense of existing products, however. If the new product was given to the existing organization, there might be a tendency to contain its growth, in order to prevent it from cutting into the sales of the older fibers in those markets in which it was directly competitive with them.

Understanding the Organizational Structure

If we are to understand fully the Du Pont Textile Fibers organization and compare it with the other studies in this book, we must look beyond position titles and examine the functions actually performed by specific units in the organization.

The Merchandising Division may be perceived as a program management center. Merchandising managers for home furnishings, industrial products, men's wear, and women's wear were responsible for appraising trends, making forecasts, developing plans, and preparing promotional programs for their assigned markets.

It is interesting to note, however, that in each of these program centers there were several sub-program management units each concerned with a specific segment of a broadly defined market. Programs in industrial markets were probably relatively independent of each other, ranging from tires to rope to parachutes. In other areas, such as men's wear, the programs for boys' wear, furnishings and sportswear, tailored outerwear, and utility clothing were clearly interdependent. These programs would share many of the same customers, and their promotional activities would benefit from being closely coordinated.

This is the first time we have seen a *pyramidal* program structure. While there were enough differences among the various markets in the men's wear category to warrant separate sub-program organizations, it was necessary to coordinate the activities of the sub-programs closely, especially at the market level. A pyramidal program structure would seem to be very well suited to these conditions.

The Sales Division in the new organization was different not only because it was a multifiber sales force, but also because its tasks were somewhat different. With many salesmen selling all five fibers, each salesman was not likely to have mastered as much technical product knowledge as sales personnel in a single fiber sales force. Salesmen in the new organization would thus have greater need for the technical back-up of product specialists in the Technical Service Section, and personnel in Textile and Industrial Products Research.

Moreover, with Merchandising managers developing in-depth promotional campaigns for each synthetic fiber market, sales representatives would be likely to deal almost exclusively with Du Pont's immediate customers. In the pre-1952 organization they almost certainly became involved in technical and promotional efforts beyond the immediate customer level, since no one else was available to do such work.

In the new organization, the Sales Division would tend to concentrate on the important functions of making the sale, and assuring that customers were supplied with a product as they needed it. Availability of fiber supply would be critical for customers whose continuity of production is dependent on it.

Sales Program managers were labeled as "staff" in the new organization — probably a designation intended to signal that the Textile Fibers Department would now be primarily market-oriented rather than product-oriented. Nevertheless, the functions of the Sales Program managers are most interesting. They were *product* managers in an organization where programs were not developed for individual products but for end-use *markets*. Looking closely at their functions, we might say broadly that they were responsible for developing and preserving the economic value of Du Pont's investments in synthetic fiber plants. Their work involved developing new product variations and new markets for their fibers, and working with fibers research laboratories to resolve technical problems that might inhibit customers from using their respective fibers.

They also worked with the Merchandising managers to assure that adequate emphasis was being given to their individual fibers in the several programs. They worked on production scheduling and inventory control to mesh market demand with output. (The Merchandising managers also became involved with allocating fibers in short supply, presumably with a view toward the long-run development of the most profitable markets for these fibers.) Finally, an important function of the Sales Program managers was the planning of new plant capacity, to assure that Du Pont would be able to satisfy, in the long-run, the demand created by the activities of the Merchandising managers.

Probably, because of the critical nature of these functions, because of the importance of return-on-plant investment measures at Du Pont, because of the product orientation of the old organization, these "staff" managers were highly influential in developing Du Pont's textile fibers strategy, and in making operational decisions. Moreover, it is interesting to observe that the inter-fiber competition, which had been conducted on the customer's doorstep in the old organization, now took place within the Sales Program Division.

The relative success of a Sales Program manager was likely to depend to a considerable extent on his ability to solicit the support of personnel in Merchandising, Sales, Textile and Industrial Products Research, and Technical Service. In almost all cases, it would be the efforts of these groups that would determine the sales and profit performance of each of the fibers.

Finally, it is useful to comment on the transplanting of Textile and Industrial Products Research (TIPR) from the Textile Fibers Department Research Division to the Sales Divisions. Although TIPR was a research unit, its work was with the customers. Located in the Research Division, it was one step removed from groups in direct contact with customers, and found it difficult to relate to Sales Division personnel. Under these circumstances, it must have been difficult to assess the relative commercial importance of solving alternative customer problems. This problem was probably compounded by the natural tendency of an autonomous research organization to give priority to the most technically intriguing problems rather than to the technical difficulties most inhibiting market growth. By transferring this unit to the Sales Division, Du Pont's management had placed TIPR in a different "value setting" for establishing work priorities, and had facilitated TIPR's working relationship with customers and with sales personnel.

In conclusion, let us emphasize the fact that the radical change in the organization at the Du Pont Textile Fibers Department between 1951 and 1956 did not take place in a vacuum, or in pursuit of some elusive organizational principles. As we have seen, the Textile Fibers Department's organization changed in response to a shift in marketing strategy — a shift triggered by the rapid technical maturing of the department's products and by basic changes in the competitive environment.

General Foods Corporation: Post Division

In 1966 General Foods Corporation was the largest manufacturer of packaged food products in the United States. Sales of $1.55 billion in fiscal 1966 [1] had placed General Foods 32nd in *Fortune*'s annual listing of the 500 largest United States manufacturing companies, and this represented an increase of 5.2% over 1965 sales of $1.48 billion. Profits had increased from $86 million to $94 million during the same period (See Exhibit 1 for a ten-year financial summary).

General Foods marketed a wide range of packaged food products (listed in Exhibit 2). Its U.S. consumer brands were assigned to five operating divisions. Maxwell House, Jell-O, Kool-Aid, Birds Eye, and Post. Each division was headed by a General Manager, who reported to a Senior Corporate Executive. Exhibit 3 gives the Corporate Organization Chart of General Foods.

The Post Division had traditionally been responsible for Post cereals and Postum beverages. In the late 1950s Gaines dog foods and Swans Down cake flour products were assigned to the Division. By early 1966 the Division was marketing 36 products. Of these, 18 were new products developed since 1958.

The Division was headed by a General Manager, who was also a Vice President of General Foods. Five department managers reported to the General Manager. These department managers were respectively in charge of Marketing, Operations (manufacturing), Personnel, Control, and Research and Product Development. An organization chart of the Post Division in August 1966 is given in Exhibit 4.

Development of the Post Marketing Organization

During the late 1940s and early 1950s, when the Post product line was limited to several cereals and Postum, three Product Managers were responsible for almost all marketing activities. The three Product Managers reported directly to the Post General Manager. They "purchased" products from the Post Operations Department and sales time from the General Foods field sales force. As long as they met the marketing objectives set by the General Manager, they were free to develop their marketing plans with little supervision by top management. As a result, there was little attempt to develop coordinated product line plans.

In 1954 General Foods replaced its field sales force with a separate sales force for each division. At this time the Post General Manager appointed a National Sales Manager (to supervise the new Post sales force) and a Marketing Manager (to supervise the three Product Managers and several headquarters marketing departments).

At approximately the same time Post management decided to modify the Division's basic marketing strategy. Instead of marketing each cereal brand as a "stand-alone" product, the Division would now present Post cereals to the consumer as an integrated product line. Advertising and promotion, for example, were to emphasize product features (especially through media advertising) rather than individual brand trade deals and in-pack premiums.

The new strategy required closer coordination of individual brand marketing plans. The Marketing Manager was responsible for coordinating the plans. By 1955 the autonomy of the Product Managers had been decreased considerably. Whereas previously each Product Manager had worked with his own advertising agency, for example, all cereal brands now used a single agency.

In 1956 the National Sales Manager was placed under the Marketing Manager, and an Advertising and Merchandising Manager (also reporting to the Marketing Manager) was appointed. The Product Managers

[1] General Foods' fiscal year ends March 31.

would now report to the Advertising and Merchandising Manager, rather than the Marketing Manager. According to Post executives, the new organization made it possible for the Marketing Manager to coordinate the activities of the product management organization with those of the field sales force.

When the Gaines and Swans Down product lines were assigned to the Post Division in 1959, the augmented product management organization was divided into three product groups: (1) Cereals, (2) Pet Foods, and (3) Beverages and Flour Products. Each product group was headed by a Product Group Manager, who reported to the Advertising and Merchandising Manager.

As the number of brands marketed by Post increased significantly in the mid-1960s, it became necessary to assign as many as four or five brands to each Product Manager. It soon became clear, however, that one Product Manager could not do a fully adequate job with so many brands. Consequently, it became necessary to increase the number of Product Managers. These new Product Managers were selected from the Assistant and Associate Product Managers within the Post Division and from other General Foods divisions. For the most part they were less experienced than the other Product Managers had been when they became Product Managers.

At the same time a Promotion Department was established to develop and coordinate promotion plans of the various brands following promotion objectives and strategies as determined by the Product Managers. In order to provide closer supervision for the less experienced Product Managers, and to train prospective Product Group Managers, Assistant Product Group Managers were appointed in the Cereals and Pet Foods product groups.[2]

---

[2] In late 1966 the Post Marketing Manager was promoted to Assistant General Manager of the division. Among his other duties, the Assistant General Manager was given responsibility for most aspects of the Post cereals business. The Cereals Product Group Manager and the Battle Creek Plant Manager (all Post cereals were manufactured in Battle Creek) now both reported to the Assistant General Manager, rather than to the Advertising and Merchandising Manager and the Operations (i.e., Manufacturing) Manager as they had previously.

According to Post executives, the establishment of a separate cereals business group, split out from the Marketing and Operations Departments, was attributable to three major factors:

(1) The Post cereals business had not been very successful in recent years, and it seemed desirable to give it increased top management attention.

(2) The new position of Assistant General Manager was

Marketing Organization as of August 1966

Exhibit 5 charts the organization of the Marketing Department of the Post Division in August 1966. Six departments carried out the Division's marketing activities: (1) the field sales organization, (2) the Marketing Research Department, (3) the Art Services Department, (4) the product management organization, (5) the Advertising and Promotion Department, and (6) the Marketing Accounting Services Department. The managers of the first three organizations reported to the Post Marketing Manager. The Product Managers and the Manager of the Promotion Department reported to the Advertising and Merchandising Manager. The Manager of the Marketing Accounting Services Department reported to the Post Controller, who reported to the Post General Manager, as shown in Exhibit 4.

The National Sales Organization

The Field Sales Organization: The field sales organization was headed by the National Sales Manager. Five Regional Sales Managers reported to him. Twenty-six District Sales Managers reported to the Regional Sales Managers. The National and Regional Sales Managers were located in White Plains. The District Sales Managers were located in the districts for which they were responsible.

Two types of personnel reported to the District Sales Managers: (1) sales supervisors, each responsible for training and supervising about seven salesmen, and (2) account managers, each responsible for selling to a limited number of major accounts. In early 1966 the field sales force consisted of the 26 District Managers and more than 400 sales supervisors, account managers, and salesmen.

The field sales force called on about 2,000 direct accounts, including wholesalers, small chains, and divisions or branches of the large national and regional

---

to some extent a training position, and management wished to give the former Marketing Manager exposure to all functional aspects of the business.

(3) The breadth of the Post product line had made it difficult for the Advertising and Merchandising Manager to give adequate attention to individual product groups. By removing the cereals business from his jurisdiction, Post management hoped to make it possible for him to give increased attention to Post's other (and more rapidly growing) product groups.

According to several Post executives, this organizational change was largely the effect of the current situation and did not represent a permanent structural change.

chains. Of these 2,000 direct accounts, 430 key accounts represented 70% of total national retail food volume.

An account manager was generally assigned two or three key accounts. He was responsible for local headquarters contact[3] and for a specified number of his chains' retail outlets. A salesman, on the other hand, might be responsible for one or two smaller direct accounts. In addition, he might be expected to call on some of the outlets of a chain for which an account manager, or other salesman, had headquarters contact responsibility.

The National Accounts Manager: Since 1963 the Post Division had experimented with national account management. The National Accounts Manager, who previously had been a Regional Sales Manager, reported to the National Sales Manager. He was responsible for contacts with the national headquarters of three large food chains. While most actual buying decisions were made at the division and branch levels of these chains, the National Accounts Manager attempted to presell key promotions and new product introductions at the corporate level.

The Regional Sales Managers were responsible for contacts with the corporate headquarters of major multibranch chains not covered by the National Accounts Manager. In general, each Regional Manager was assigned those multibranch chain headquarters located in his region.

The Sales Development Department: The Sales Development Manager also reported to the National Sales Manager. His department was responsible for preparing sales plans for implementation at the district level, including volume objectives for each product, local advertising schedules, promotion schedules, and new product introduction schedules. Although there was considerable similarity among the sales plans for the various districts, each was tailored to local marketing requirements.

The product management organization, which reported to the Advertising and Merchandising Manager, prepared marketing plans for each of Post's 36 products. Each product marketing plan called for various kinds of sales force support, whether to introduce a new product, sell a trade deal, secure customer merchandising cooperation, or modify in-store shelving arrangements. As part of its sales planning activity, the Sales Development Department translated the individual product marketing plans into an integrated set of objectives and sales plans for each district. At the same time, it represented the sales force in meetings with individual Product Managers, in order to assure that the sales support called for in the marketing plans was in fact feasible, that the product management objectives were compatible with sales objectives, and that no sales conflicts existed between one set of product plans and another.

By 1967 the roles of the field sales force and Sales Development Department in promotional planning were undergoing considerable change. The District Sales Managers were now asked to prepare a list of recommended promotional activities for their districts each quarter. The Sales Development Department used these recommendations in working with the product groups and Product Managers to establish a quarterly promotional plan for each district. Besides allowing the District Sales Managers to participate more fully in promotional planning for their districts, the new procedure was intended to facilitate Post's use of "target marketing," i.e., promotional activities tailored to the marketing requirements of individual districts.

The Product Management Organization

In mid-1966 the product management function was carried out by an Advertising and Merchandising Manager, three Product Group Managers, three Assistant Product Group Managers, fifteen Product Managers, and a number of Associate and Assistant Product Managers.

The Advertising and Merchandising Manager was responsible for three product groups (Cereals, Pet Foods, and Beverages and Miscellaneous Products) plus the Promotion Department. Reporting to each Product Group Manager were several Product Managers, each of whom handled several brands. In the Cereals and Pet Foods Product Groups, some of the Product Managers reported to Assistant Product Group Managers.

Each Product Manager was assigned one or more brands. The criteria used in assigning brands to Product Managers were different in each product group. In the Cereals Product Group, for example, a Product Manager was assigned either established brands *or* new brands, while a Pet Foods Product Manager typically had *both* new and established

---

[3] The meaning of headquarters contact varied among chains, but was generally directed at the lowest multistore decision point. In the case of a national chain, with divisions and districts, for example, an account manager was generally assigned to each district buying office. In the case of a regional chain, with only one buying office, the account manager was assigned to the chain's headquarters.

brands. Beginning in 1967, however, brand assignments in the Cereals Product Group were to be made on the basis of consumer category rather than whether a brand was new or established. Five cereals Product Managers were to be responsible for nutritional cereals, children's (pre-sweetened) cereals, family cereals, miscellaneous (e.g., bran) cereals, and cross-brand promotions respectively. According to the Advertising and Merchandising Manager, these new assignments were intended to reflect the Cereals Product Group's increased emphasis on market segmentation and — at the same time — give each Product Manager exposure to a greater variety of marketing situations.

Each Product Manager prepared an annual marketing plan for each brand to which he was assigned. These marketing plans included quarterly sales volume objectives, a general marketing strategy, analyses of competitive activity, and specific plans for advertising, promotion, packaging, pricing, product changes, and marketing research.[4] The marketing plan had to be approved ultimately by the General Manager of the Post Division, after a series of reviews and recommendations by lower level marketing management.

When a marketing plan had been approved, the Product Manager was responsible for its implementation. He worked closely with one or more advertising agencies and the various Post departments. He presented his marketing strategy to an advertising agency, for example, and asked it to prepare advertising copy and media plans. He then reviewed this material carefully and decided whether to recommend its approval by higher management. If his recommendation was approved, he then worked with the agency to execute the plan. In general, the Product Managers worked with Post staff departments in virtually the same way as they did with outside advertising agencies. They had no direct authority but were expected to make sure that the various elements of a brand's marketing plan were implemented effectively. According to the Advertising and Merchandising Manager, "Persuasion in the best interests of the business with strong emphasis on data, judgment, and logic [was] the Product Manager's best tool."

The Marketing Research Department

The Manager of the Marketing Research Department reported to the Marketing Manager. His department was organized in three product groups: Cereals, Pet Foods, and other products. Three men, ranging in experience from one to ten years, were assigned to each group. The senior member of each group reported to the Marketing Research Manager.

Marketing research personnel were assigned to individual brands. A marketing research project was generally proposed by the Product Manager for a particular brand. He and his marketing research counterpart then prepared a plan for carrying out the proposed research. In most cases outside research organizations did the actual research and tabulated the results.

All marketing research plans had to be approved by the Marketing Research Manager. When he and the Product Manager concerned agreed that a plan was feasible and would accomplish the desired objectives, they submitted it to the Product Group Manager for approval. After the Product Group Manager's approval, the plan was submitted to the Advertising and Merchandising Manager, and, in the case of very large projects, the Marketing Manager, for approval.

The Art Services Department

The Art Services Manager reported to the Marketing Manager. His department, which was staffed with eight commercial artists, was responsible for creating designs for Post packages and promotional materials. In most cases these designs were drawn in rough form; final art work was generally subcontracted to outside firms.

Members of the department worked with individual Product Managers and promotion specialists. In almost all cases work was done on request from one of these executives, but the department occasionally originated ideas for new packages and promotions.

The Advertising and Promotion Department

The Manager of the Advertising and Promotion Department reported to the Advertising and Merchandising Manager. The department was organized on a product group basis, with several promotion specialists assigned to each product group.

The Promotion Department worked with the Product Managers in designing promotions. In general, a Product Manager would ask the Promotion Department to design a promotion to achieve a given objective at a given cost. In some cases the recommended promotion would be a trade deal; in others an in-store display, media coupon, or self-liquidating premium promotion. To an increasing extent, several

---

[4] The brand marketing plans followed a prescribed format, developed by Post management. See Appendix A, "Content for Annual Marketing Plans."

promotional approaches were combined in a given promotion. For example, trade deals to encourage in-store merchandising efforts generally increased the effectiveness of a consumer promotion.

The Promotion Department had assembled extensive data concerning the results of different kinds of promotions. Consequently, it was able to predict, with a very small margin of error, what the results of a particular promotion would be. While most promotions were designed to meet a specific objective in a brand's marketing plan, promotions were sometimes kept "on-the-shelf," ready to be used in response to certain kinds of competitive situations.

The Marketing Accounting Services Department

The Manager of the Marketing Accounting Services Department reported to the Post Controller. His department carried out a wide range of routine accounting and control-type activities and prepared special reports for marketing personnel. According to the Marketing Manager, Marketing Accounting Services made it possible for product and sales managers to spend most of their time on planning, rather than on the thousands of calculations on which their plans were based.

The Product Managers, for example, were required to set volume objectives for each brand for each district. To a great extent, these objectives were based on historical data. A Product Manager was able to give Marketing Accounting his total volume objective for the year and information concerning variations in local marketing situations or marketing plans, and receive back, in a short time, a breakdown by quarter and district. Similarly, the District Sales Managers received a weekly report of their performance vis-à-vis their budgets.

The Marketing Plan

The Product Managers prepared an annual marketing plan for each of their brands. When approved by the top management of the Post Division, these marketing plans provided the basic structure for Post's marketing efforts during the following year.

Marketing plans differed significantly in the degree to which they were integrated into a product group plan. The Cereals Product Group, for example, published a product group marketing plan, which included all the cereal brands' marketing plans. For this reason, a cereal Product Manager had to coordinate his plans with his colleagues' plans, making certain that his marketing plan did not conflict with the overall product group marketing plan.

The Tang Product Manager, on the other hand, was responsible for a product that was not closely related to any other Post product. Consequently, he was able to write his plan with only a minimum amount of attention to the plans of other Product Managers. While his marketing plan had to be approved by his Product Group Manager and the Advertising and Merchandising Manager, he had considerable more autonomy than his counterparts in the Cereals Product Group.

Preparation of Marketing Plans

Sales forecasts, spending needs, and profit estimates were based on historical data, competitive trends, and judgment. When a Product Manager had made his first rough cut at these figures, and received concurrence from his Product Group Manager, he submitted them to the Advertising and Merchandising Manager for review. The Advertising and Merchandising Manager attempted to gauge the validity of the relationships on which the forecasts were based and at the same time to determine how well, in aggregate, the various marketing plans fitted with the division sales and profit objectives.

On the basis of his analysis and discussions with the Marketing Manager, the Advertising and Merchandising Manager frequently suggested changes in these preliminary forecasts. This generally occurred in late October. The Product Managers then prepared new forecasts, which they submitted upward for approval. Again, the Advertising and Merchandising Manager reviewed them, but now in terms of a firmer divisional volume plan on which other departments based their planning and forecasts. Volumes were modified as more current consumer data became available.

During this same period (October to December) the Product Managers wrote the other sections of their marketing plans. In doing so, they worked with the Promotion, Art Services, Sales Development, and Marketing Research Departments, and outside advertising agencies. The Product Manager generally presented a brand's marketing strategy to its advertising agency, for example, and asked the agency to prepare copy and media strategies. He reviewed these in detail, working with the agency to achieve modifications he considered appropriate. He then showed the strategies to his Product Group Manager, who might also suggest changes. When the strategies were approved, the agency began to prepare copy and media schedules. Again, the Product Group Manager reviewed these materials informally during preparation.

Similarly, the Product Manager presented his general objectives and strategies to the Promotion and Marketing Research Departments and asked them to prepare detailed plans. He worked with members of these departments in much the same way that he worked with account executives at the advertising agencies — reviewing alternative plans, suggesting changes, and consulting with his Product Group Manager.

In most cases the Advertising and Merchandising Manager reviewed the various sections of a brand's marketing plan informally, before it was formally presented to him for approval in December. When it was presented to him there were "few surprises," although he might request minor modifications.

When the Advertising and Merchandising Manager had approved the brands' marketing plans, they were brought together into a divisional plan. The Advertising and Merchandising Manager worked closely with the National Sales Manager, the Marketing Manager, and the General Manager to establish the final divisional plan. This plan was submitted to the corporate management of General Foods in late February or early March.

Plans Letters

After a brand's marketing plan had been "published," it was necessary to communicate elements of its content to the various departments responsible for implementing it. Although this was done in a variety of ways, the formal procedure was through the "plans letter."

A typical plans letter described what had to be done and by whom, to achieve a given objective. In many cases, this information was summarized in the form of a time schedule. Plans letters were written by the Product Managers, and signed by the Advertising and Merchandising Manager or the Marketing Manager. The product plans letter was an action document authorizing the commitment of resources.

In most cases, the Product Manager also communicated with the various departments on an informal basis, telling them when a plans letter would come out, and what it would contain. Similarly, he generally checked to make sure the plans letter had been received and was being implemented. Naturally, a Product Manager was more likely to follow up in these ways on a major or nonroutine matter than on one that continued an already existing arrangement.

Sales Planning

The marketing plans were tied in with the activities of the field sales force in a variety of ways. Before a brand's marketing plan was approved, the Marketing Accounting Services Department broke down its quarterly sales objectives into regional and district objectives on the basis of historical data. The National and Regional Sales Managers then reviewed these data, suggesting adjustments where called for by changes in local marketing conditions. When the divisional profit plan had been approved, the Sales Development Department consolidated the brand sales objectives for each district, thus establishing the district "sales budget" or quota.

It was more difficult to translate other elements of the brand's marketing plans. An account manager or salesman called on a given account once a week or once every two weeks. On his call, he generally was given only 10 to 15 minutes to make his sales presentation. An account would reorder merchandise already in stock without further effort by the salesman, but the salesman also had to accomplish a variety of specific objectives. For example, he might announce a new product, attempt to sell a trade deal, or try to improve Post cereal shelving. Since the product managers for a large number of brands each wanted the sales force to accomplish certain objectives, it was necessary to set priorities and schedule sales force efforts in such a way as to implement *all* marketing plans and maximize volume and profits for the Division as a whole.

To some extent the sales budget itself established priorities, since it was broken down on a brand basis. A District Manager who was below budget on a brand would naturally give priority to raising its sales, unless there was a good reason for him to give priority to accomplishing another objective.

Moreover, some objectives by definition received priority. New product introductions were scheduled for national or regional introduction on a specific date, which meant that the sales force had to devote its efforts to achieving distribution during a relatively short time period. Similarly, certain trade promotions were tightly scheduled, which meant that the sales force had to take advantage of them at a specific time.[5]

Scheduling of new product introductions and trade deals was coordinated by the Advertising and Merchandising Manager, in conjunction with the National Sales Manager and Sales Development Department. In general, new product introductions had to be separated, and trade deals were scheduled so as not to conflict with each other or new product introductions.

It was more difficult to establish and communicate priorities for other types of objectives. If a Product Manager wished to improve the shelving of a brand, for example, he might define his objective as "improved shelving in 80% of type A stores." Because an objective of this kind did not have to be accomplished at a particular time, the sales force worked on it on an opportunity basis rather than on a rigid schedule.

There were, however, a number of objectives of this kind. Both the Cereals Product Group and the Dog Food Product Group might want improved shelving, for example. Either of these objectives might be the more important in a particular account, depending on the current situation, relative volumes, and receptivity to change in each product area. It was thus necessary for individual salesmen to set priorities for each of their accounts. Post management used a variety of means to influence individual salesmen's decisions in these matters. The most important of these were sales meetings, bulletins, and reports; the incentive point budget; and the Division's sales force compensation plan.

Formal Communications and Reports

The National Sales Manager's Meetings: The National Sales Manager held a formal meeting with the Regional Sales Managers several weeks prior to the beginning of each quarter. During these meetings booklets containing promotion, advertising, and new product introduction schedules for the following quarter were passed out and discussed. These schedules, and the descriptive materials accompanying them, were prepared by the Sales Development Department. In some cases, Product Managers were present at these meetings to describe their plans for the coming quarter.

Regional Staff Meetings: Shortly after the National Sales Manager's staff meeting, each Regional Manager held a meeting with his District Managers. The quarterly schedules were passed out and discussed at these meetings, in much the same way as at the national meeting. Members of the product management organization were present occasionally to discuss their plans and listen to formal reports by the District Managers concerning the previous quarter's activities. This communications device was intended as another way of influencing future sales planning.

District Staff Meetings: When he returned from his regional staff meeting, the District Manager held a meeting of his sales personnel. At this meeting he presented promotion and new product introduction schedules and materials (tailored to his district), and discussed his plan for accomplishing the district objectives. He might, for example, suggest that efforts to increase the distribution of Tang be delayed until the end of the quarter, since a trade deal was scheduled for that time. Similarly, he might suggest that planned shelves be de-emphasized during the quarter, since heavy new product and promotion requirements would not leave adequate time for this activity. At these meetings stress was also placed on the "how to" aspects of implementing the plans.

Sales Bulletins: District Sales Managers received sales bulletins describing each promotion or new product introduction several weeks before the sales effort was to begin. These sales bulletins were prepared by the Sales Development Department after consultation with the Product Manager or promotion specialist who had planned the activity. In general, these sales bulletins described the activity, objectives, and any merchandising aids prepared by the Division, established timetables, and explained any special reporting procedure to be used. Exhibit 7 reproduces a typical bulletin.

Four-Week Assignments: District Managers gave their sales personnel new assignments every four weeks. An assignment was a district-wide list of objectives to be accomplished during the period. A major new product introduction, in itself, might be a four-week assignment for most sales personnel. In essence, an assignment was a list of objectives, ranked in order of priority. When a salesman had made every reasonable effort to accomplish objective #1 in an account, he was to move on to objective #2. In some cases, of course, a given objective was not applicable to a particular account.

---

[5] See Exhibit 6 for a schedule of promotional activities during Fiscal 1966. This schedule was prepared by the Promotion Department.

Weekly Sales Planning Report: The salesmen and account managers submitted a sales planning report to their supervisors each Friday. This report listed all the accounts in their territories and the opportunities existing in each account. An opportunity was defined as an assignment objective that had not yet been accomplished in that account.

On this form the salesman checked off the accounts he planned to call on during the following week and the objective or objectives he hoped to accomplish on each call. If his supervisor did not suggest a change, his plan was considered approved. According to one District Manager, when he approved a salesman's plan it became in effect an instruction.

On Friday, when he turned in his new weekly planning report, the salesman also turned in a copy of his previous week's plans. He circled the calls actually made, and the objectives accomplished. The supervisors reviewed these results carefully and generally required an explanation for any major deviation from plan.

The Incentive Point Budget

As noted above, the Division marketing plan was a composite of the product group marketing plans, which were, in turn, composites of the individual brand marketing plans. Each individual brand marketing plan included a breakdown of sales objectives for that brand by quarter and district. Consequently, the sum of the volume objectives for the various brands for a given district was the volume objective for which the District Manager was responsible.

The District Manager was also expected to achieve his quarterly incentive point budget. The incentive point budget, which was used to calculate the incentive compensation of the field sales force, differed considerably from the volume objective. The volume objective for each brand was stated in units, but a unit of one product was likely to be more important to the Division than a unit of another product. In some cases, a unit of a particular product might make a larger contribution to profits than a unit of another product. In other cases, Division management might want to give priority to a product for long-term strategic reasons.

In order to allow for variations in priority, a system of weights was used in establishing the incentive point budget. Under this system, the incentive budget for a district was equal to the sum of the unit objectives for each brand multiplied by their weights. For example, a district's incentive budget might be as follows:

Product	Units	Weighting Factor	Total
A	1,000	6	6,000
B	4,000	4	16,000
C	3,000	3	9,000
D	500	1	500
E	8,000	5	40,000

Quarterly incentive budget = 71,500

Before 1966 weights were established by the National Sales Manager, on the basis of a formula that took into account the relative profitability of the various brands. Beginning in 1966, however, the weights were established jointly by the National Sales Manager and the Marketing Manager. According to the Marketing Manager, this change would allow him to add strategic considerations to the profitability data previously used to determine weights.

Underlying this shift was the growing realization that Post brands differed in the degree in which sales force efforts could contribute directly to sales. Certain brands (Tang and Toastems, for example) responded well to consumer promotions aimed at maximizing impulse sales, while others (cereals, for example) faced different competitive pressures demanding fundamental sales activity with regard to distribution of shelf exposure.

Distribution of Incentive Earnings

The sales force was on an incentive compensation plan, which was closely tied to the incentive point budget. The plan consisted of two parts: (1) a quarterly bonus, based on overall district performance, and (2) an annual bonus, based on a combination of district and individual performance.

A district had to achieve 97% of its quarterly incentive point budget for established products to qualify for incentive compensation.[6] If it qualified, 10% of its new product incentive points were added to its established products incentive points to determine its incentive payment category. For example:

(1) Incentive Point Budget,
established products   100,000
(2) Incentive Points earned,
established products   99,000

---

[6] The incentive plan did not come into effect unless the Division achieved 97% of its incentive point budget. If the Division failed to do so, a district achieving 100% or more of its budget paid a quarterly bonus equal to 2.5% of quarterly base salary.

(3) Incentive Points earned,
   new products   14,000
(4) 10% of new product incentive
   points   1,400
(5) Line 2 plus line 4   100,400
(6) Incentive payment category:
   Line 5 ÷ Line 1 $\frac{100{,}400}{100{,}000} = 100.4\%$

Individual quarterly bonuses depended on the district's incentive payment category and the individual's base salary. Depending on the payment category, the bonus ranged from 1% to 13% of an individual's quarterly salary. The number of quarters in which a district qualified for incentive compensation during a fiscal year also influenced the size of the bonus paid.

The annual bonus was based on a combination of the percentage increase in a district's sales over its previous year's sales and the evaluation of an individual's performance by his superior. Annual bonuses ranged from 0 to 16% of annual salary.

In 1967 Post's entire system of sales force compensation was drastically altered. According to the National Sales Manager, the old compensation system had placed undue emphasis on the short-term sales results in a salesman's territory. Since short-term sales were at least as much a function of headquarters-prepared advertising and sales promotion efforts as of the salesman's own activities, the old system had tended to reward or penalize a salesman for results over which he had little real influence.

The new incentive system was designed to remedy this situation. Bonuses were now to be awarded on the basis of the District Manager's appraisal of the performance of the sales representatives in his district. The District Managers were to evaluate each man according to his performance in the following areas (maximum points to be awarded in each area are shown in parentheses):

   Distribution (10)
   Promotions (10)
   Shelving (10)
   Pricing (5)
   Customer Relations (5)
   Planning (5)
   Presentations (5)
   Teamwork (5)
   Records and Reports (5)
   Company Property (5)

The number of points a sales representative received were to determine the percentage of his salary he would receive as a bonus.

Relations with Advertising Agencies

In mid-1966 there was some feeling in the Post Division and its five advertising agencies that Post's organization and procedures were not as effective in stimulating agency creativity as they might be. In particular, it was felt that too many presentations and decisions were required before an agency's creative efforts were approved for implementation. Generally, an agency would present its copy recommendations to a Product Manager, then to his Product Group Manager, and finally to the Advertising and Merchandising Manager. In some cases, however, the agency also made presentations to an Assistant or Associate Product Manager (before making a presentation to the Product Manager) and to the Marketing Manager (after the presentation to the Advertising and Merchandising Manager).

Each presentation was, in effect, a decision point at which the agency's recommendation, approved at a lower level, could be rejected or sent back for modification. According to agency personnel, such occurrences, although infrequent, had an adverse effect on agency morale and tended to encourage "acceptable copy" at the expense of "creative breakthroughs."

In an effort to deal with this problem, Post management made several changes in its advertising review procedures. It limited the number of formal agency presentations to three, by insisting that the first presentation always be made to a Product Manager (rather than an Assistant or Associate Product Manager) and that when a presentation to the Marketing Manager was required, it was to be combined with the presentation to the Advertising and Merchandising Manager.

In commenting on these changes, the Advertising and Merchandising Manager explained:

> We really can't get by with fewer than three presentations. We want the Product Manager to review the copy and make a decision because it's his brand and he has to develop judgment in this area. We want the Product Group Manager to come in after the Product Manager has made his decision, because the Product Group Managers have had more experience with advertising, and are able to consider the effect of one brand's advertising over other brands in the category. Finally, the Marketing Manager and I need to be brought into the picture, since we are able to consider the agency's recommendations in the light of total Division objectives and resources. In addition, we have a continuing responsibility for relationships with the agencies, whose brand assignments often cross product groups.

In my view, the number of presentations is probably less important than the way we work. If each level of management makes its objectives clear at the start, there should be few instances where it is necessary to modify or reject agency recommendations which have been approved at lower levels.

Marketing-Manufacturing Relationships

The Post Division had three major manufacturing plants: Battle Creek, Michigan (cereals, Tang); Kankakee, Illinois (dog foods); and Evansville, Indiana (flour, cake mixes, Start, and Toastems). The managers of these three plants reported to the Division Operations Manager.[7]

According to the Operations Manager, relations between his Department and the Marketing Department were generally good. Because each plant worked with one product group, most problems were handled on a product group basis.

The Operations Manager did, however, cite two problem areas. There was some tendency, he thought, for the Product Managers to make unreasonable demands on Operations personnel. A Product Manager might telephone a plant, for example, and ask for an estimate of manufacturing costs at a given level of production. The plant might then spend three mandays preparing an estimate of unit costs to three decimal places, only to discover that the Product Manager needed only a rough estimate at that point to test the feasibility of a marketing approach.

The second problem had to do with promotions. According to the Operations Manager, the Product Managers sometimes did not fully assess the implications of their promotional plans for the Operations Department. Special label promotions, for example, frequently had very rigid dates. If a special label promotion was to begin at a time when the plant still had old label inventory, the plant had to hold the old label inventory until the promotion was over. This meant that at the end of a six-week promotion, the plant might be shipping products eight or nine weeks old. This problem could be easily avoided by building an outlet for the old label inventory into the marketing plan (staggering the date the promotion was to start in different areas, for example).

The Operations Manager summarized his view of Manufacturing-Marketing relationships as follows:

This is a marketing company. There is no question that we could schedule our plants more efficiently if we didn't have to worry about Marketing, but then we wouldn't be able to sell the product. I have no complaints on that score.

There is a tendency, however, for Marketing not to consider our needs adequately when preparing their plans. The two problems I have cited are typical; they are easily solved if only someone remembers to do so.

In discussing Marketing-Manufacturing relationships, the Advertising and Merchandising Manager agreed that relations were, for the most part, good. He alluded, however, to what he called the "chimney effect," which, he thought, often gave disproportionate importance to minor problems. As he explained:

Let's say one of the plants and one of the Product Managers have a disagreement. The plant guy then goes to his boss (the Plant Manager) who in turn goes to the Operations Manager. The Operations Manager then brings the problem up at the General Manager's weekly staff meeting (as he should), and the General Manager asks the Marketing Manager for his point of view. The Marketing Manager, as often as not, has no idea there is a problem, let alone what his point of view should be.

You might say that it's up to the Product Managers to keep the Marketing Manager informed. But how much of this sort of thing should the Marketing Manager be concerned with? These types of problems should be resolved at the product group—plant level (and they usually are), but there is no mechanism (or organizational arrangement) to make sure that they are.

Product Development

The Manager of Technical Research and Product Development was responsible for all Post product development activities, the bulk of which were split between two departments. The Technical Research Department, located in Battle Creek, Michigan, developed all new products and designed the manufacturing processes to be used in making these products. The New Products Development Department was essentially a marketing research organization, limiting its efforts to new products prior to the time when they were turned over to the product management organization.

Ideas for new products came from a variety of sources. Until recently, more than 90% of such ideas had originated in the Technical Research Department, as it sought to find applications for advances in food technology. In the last few years, however, the New Products Development Department had taken more

---

[7] In 1967 the manager of the Battle Creek plant was reporting to the Assistant General Manager, who was directly supervising the cereals business. See footnote 2.

of an initiating role, suggesting new products on the basis of apparent consumer needs. Although some ideas came from the product management organization and Post's advertising agencies, these sources had not historically been important inputs to the product development process.

The Technical Research Department received an annual budget (generally a fixed percentage of sales), which it allocated to specific projects intended to achieve the Division's "three-year objectives." If these objectives called for "two new cereals in test market in each of the next three years," for example, the Technical Research Department knew approximately how many new cereal projects it had to work on in order to develop the required number of new cereals for test marketing. The manager of the cereals group in the Technical Research Department made this decision (although it was reviewed by the Technical Research and Product Development Manager), and had almost complete authority to determine what kinds of new cereal to work on.

As a product was undergoing development in the Technical Research Department, the New Products Development Department conducted a series of consumer tests of the product's appeal. These tests ranged from simple concept tests in early stages of a product's development (e.g., "What would you think of a new children's cereal in the shape of automobiles?") to relatively large-scale consumer trials of prototype products. The New Products Development Department had had considerable experience in the use of these tests, and had developed data that made it possible to compare proposed new products with established products. The New Products Development Department could, for example, tell the Technical Research Department how a proposed new dog food compared (in the same test, and at the same stage in development) with Gaines Burgers, a very successful Post product.

When a new product was judged ready for test marketing, it was presented to the Post General Manager, who decided whether it should be turned over to a Product Manager for test marketing. According to the Research and Product Development Manager, this procedure generally worked well since his organization was expert in product development and consumer research, and the product management organization was expert in test marketing. There was some disagreement, however, concerning the state a new product should be in at the time of "turn over." The New Products Development Department frequently desired to turn over a product with a name, package,

advertising strategy — in effect, an entire marketing plan. The product management organization, on the other hand, preferred to receive just the product and develop its own marketing plan. In 1967 the Research and Product Development Manager was seeking to overcome this problem on a particular new product by physically transferring the man who had worked on the product in the New Product Development Department (an experienced Product Manager) to the product management organization.

The New Products Committee

In the late 1950s Post management had decided to place major strategic emphasis on the development of new products. In order to implement this strategy, the Post General Manager had established a New Products Committee, which consisted of the following members of Post's top management:

> General Manager (Chairman)
> Marketing Manager
> Controller
> Technical Research and Product Development Manager
> Operations Manager
> Advertising and Merchandising Manager

The New Products Committee met regularly to advise the General Manager as to whether (and when) new products proposed by the Technical Research and New Product Development Department should be turned over to the product management organization. In addition, it monitored test market results closely and helped the General Manager to decide whether a proposed new product should be introduced nationally.

In early 1966 Post management concluded that the Division's development efforts were overbalanced in favor of new products, and that opportunities to coordinate new and established product development were not being fully exploited. To correct this imbalance Post management replaced the New Products Committee with a Development Committee, responsible for both new and established products.

The Development Committee consisted of the following Post executives:

> Technical Research and Product Development Manager (Chairman)
> Advertising and Merchandising Manager
> Product Group Manager (assigned to product category)
> New Product Development Manager
> Assistant New Product Development Manager

Assistant Operations Manager
Marketing Accounting Services Manager

According to the Marketing Manager, the Development Committee was an improvement over the New Products Committee in three important respects:

(1) Because the Development Committee was responsible for both new and established products, better product line coordination could be expected. A proposed new product, for example, might better be introduced as an improved version of an existing product.
(2) The executives who made up the Development Committee were responsible for creating product line strategy. As a result, the assumptions on which new product proposals were based were likely to receive closer scrutiny than they had in the past. Therefore they could more readily influence the development of product concepts early enough in their creation to assure that they better fulfilled the strategic requirements of the product line.
(3) Top management could now concentrate its efforts on key decisions with long-range implications for the business, for which major resources had to be committed.

Exhibit 1. Selected Financial Statistics for Corporation, 1957–1966

Fiscal Years*	1966	1965	1964	1963	1962	1961	1960	1959	1958	1957
(All dollar amounts in millions, except assets per employee and figures on a share basis)										
INCOME										
Sales to customers (net)	$1,555	$1,478	$1,338	$1,216	$1,189	$1,160	$1,087	$1,053	$1,009	$986
Cost of sales	965	937	838	774	769	764	725	734	724	713
Marketing, administrative and general expenses	406	362	322	274	267	261	236	205	181	179
Earnings before income taxes	185	177	179	170	156	138	130	115	105	95
Taxes on income	91	91	95	91	84	71	69	61	57	51
Net earnings	94	86	84	79	72	67	61	54	48	44
Net earnings per common share	3.73	3.44	3.33	3.14	2.90	2.69	2.48	2.21	1.99	1.81
Dividends on common shares	53	50	50	45	40	35	32	28	24	22
Dividends per common share	2.10	2.00	2.00	1.80	1.60	1.40	1.30	1.15	1.00	.90
Earnings retained in business each year	41	36	34	34	32	32	29	26	24	22
ASSETS, LIABILITIES, AND STOCKHOLDERS' EQUITY										
Current assets	$527	$444	$436	$411	$387	$360	$357	$329	$313	$293
Current liabilities	219	173	202	162	142	123	126	107	107	98
Working capital	308	271	234	249	245	237	230	222	206	195
Land, buildings, equipment, gross	517	477	436	375	328	289	247	221	203	183
Land, buildings, equipment, net	308	283	264	223	193	173	148	132	125	112
Long-term debt	54	37	23	34	35	37	40	44	49	51
Stockholders' equity	569	527	490	454	419	384	347	315	287	261
Book value per common share	22.64	20.99	19.53	18.17	16.80	15.46	14.07	12.87	11.78	10.77
OPERATING STATISTICS										
Inventories	$261	$214	$256	$205	$183	$189	$157	$149	$169	$169
Capital additions	65	54	70	57	42	40	35	24	28	29
Depreciation	32	29	26	24	21	18	15	14	11	10
Wages, salaries, and benefits	218	204	195	180	171	162	147	138	128	126
Number of employees (in thousands)	30	30	30	28	28	25	22	22	21	22
Assets per employee (in thousands)	29	25	24	23	22	22	23	22	21	19

* Fiscal 1966 ended April 2, 1966. Other fiscal years ended March 31.

Exhibit 2. Principal Products of General Foods Corporation, with Special Reference to Those of the Post Division

COFFEES

Maxim Freeze-Dried Coffee
Maxwell House Coffee (regular)
Yuban Coffee (regular)
Sanka Coffee — 97% Caffein Free
Instant Maxwell House Coffee
Instant Sanka Coffee
Instant Yuban Coffee

DESSERTS

Jell-O Gelatin Dessert
Jell-O Pudding & Pie Filling
Jell-O Lemon Chiffon Pie Filling
Jell-O Golden Egg Custard Mix
Jell-O Instant Pudding
Jell-O Whip'n Chill Deluxe Dessert Mix
Jell-O Tapioca Pudding
Minute Tapioca
D-Zerta Dietary Gelatin Dessert
D-Zerta Dietary Pudding & Pie Filling
Dream Whip Whipped Topping Mix

BIRDS EYE FROZEN FOODS

Fruits, Vegetables, Southern Vegetables, Vegetable Combinations, Vegetables with Sauces, Potato Products, Awake, Concentrated Fruit Juices and Drinks, Prepared Fish, Fish Fillets, Onion Rings

*PET FOODS

Gaines Meal
Gaines Biscuits
Gaines Bits
Gaines Gravy Train Dog Food
Gaines-burgers
Gaines Prime
Gaines Variety

BAKING INGREDIENTS

Baker's Semi-Sweet Chocolate Chips
Baker's Peanut Butter Chips
Baker's Redi-Blend
Baker's Unsweetened Chocolate
Baker's Semi-Sweet Chocolate
Baker's German's Sweet Chocolate
Baker's Coconut products
Calumet Baking Powder
*Swans Down Cake Flour, Self-Rising Cake Flour
*Swans Down Cake Mixes

* Denotes Post Division Product.

*POST CEREALS

Alpha-Bits, Post Toasties,
Grape-Nuts, 40% Bran Flakes,
Grape-Nuts Flakes, Bran & Prune Flakes,
Raisin Bran, Sugar Crisp,
Corn Flakes and Fruit Cereals,
Honeycomb, Oat Flakes,
Sugar Sparkled Rice Krinkles,
Sugar Sparkled Flakes, Crispy Critters,
Post-Tens, Treat-Pak

OTHER GROCERY PRODUCTS

Baker's Cocoa
Baker's Instant Chocolate Flavor Mix
Certo and Sure-Jell Fruit Pectins
Good Seasons Salad Dressing Mixes
Good Seasons Open Pit Barbecue Sauce
— Original Recipe, Hickory Smoke and Mild Garlic Flavors
Good Seasons Shake'n Bake Seasoned Coating Mixes
— For Chicken and Fish
*Instant Postum Cereal Beverage
— Regular and Coffee Flavor
Kool-Aid Soft Drink Mix
Pre-Sweetened Kool-Aid Soft Drink Mix
Kool-Pops Ready to Freeze Pop Bars
Log Cabin Syrup
Log Cabin Buttered Syrup
Log Cabin Syrup — Maple-Honey Flavor
Log Cabin's Country Kitchen Imitation Maple Syrup
Minute Rice
Minute Spanish Rice Mix
*Tang Instant Breakfast Drink
*Toast'em Pop-ups
Twist Lemonade Mix
Twist Orangeade Mix

HOUSEHOLD PRODUCTS

S.O.S. Soap Pads
S.O.ettes Sponge-Back Soap Pads
La France Whitener-Brightener
Satina Ironing Aid
Tuffy Plastic Mesh Ball (Dishwashing Aid)

INSTITUTIONAL PRODUCTS

Institutional-size packs of GF and other products for food service customers — restaurants, hotels, schools, hospitals, etc. Individual-serving beverage envelopes and products for the vending machine industry, as well as Kernel-Fresh nuts and popcorn products.

General Foods: Post Division 215

Exhibit 3. Organization Chart of Corporation as of August 1966

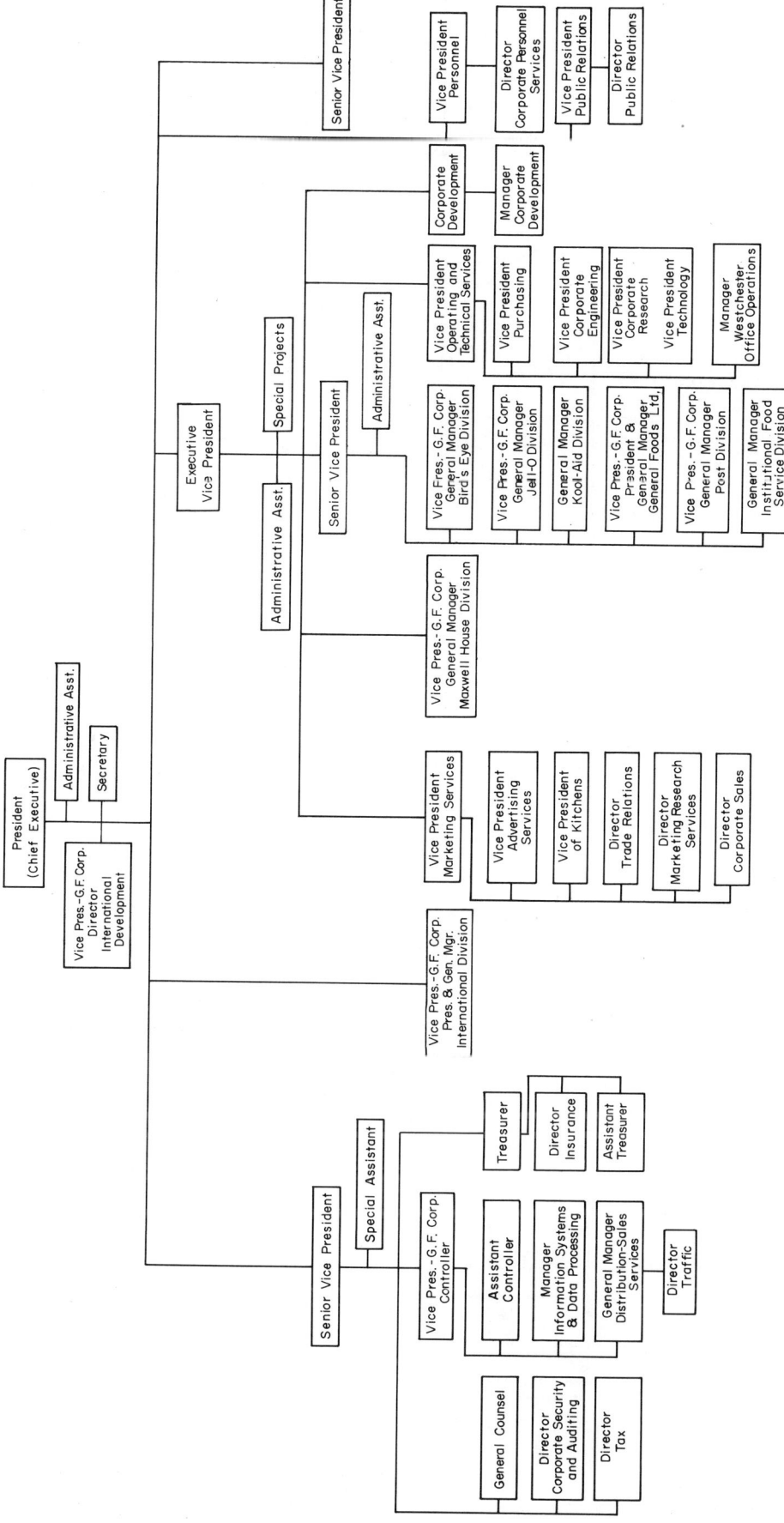

216   *Cases and Commentaries*

Exhibit 4. Organization Chart of Division as of August 1966

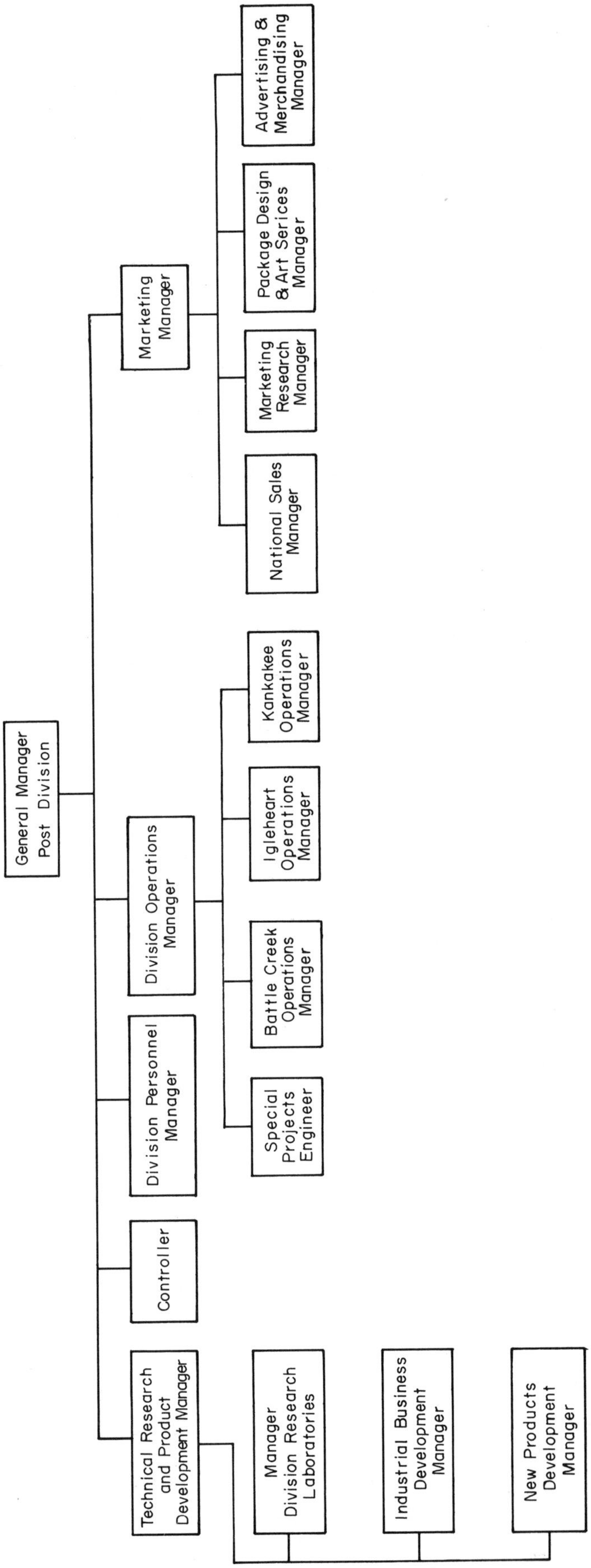

- General Manager Post Division
  - Technical Research and Product Development Manager
    - Manager Division Research Laboratories
    - Industrial Business Development Manager
    - New Products Development Manager
  - Controller
  - Division Personnel Manager
  - Division Operations Manager
    - Special Projects Engineer
    - Battle Creek Operations Manager
    - Igleheart Operations Manager
    - Kankakee Operations Manager
  - Marketing Manager
    - National Sales Manager
    - Marketing Research Manager
    - Package Design & Art Serices Manager
    - Advertising & Merchandising Manager

General Foods: Post Division 217

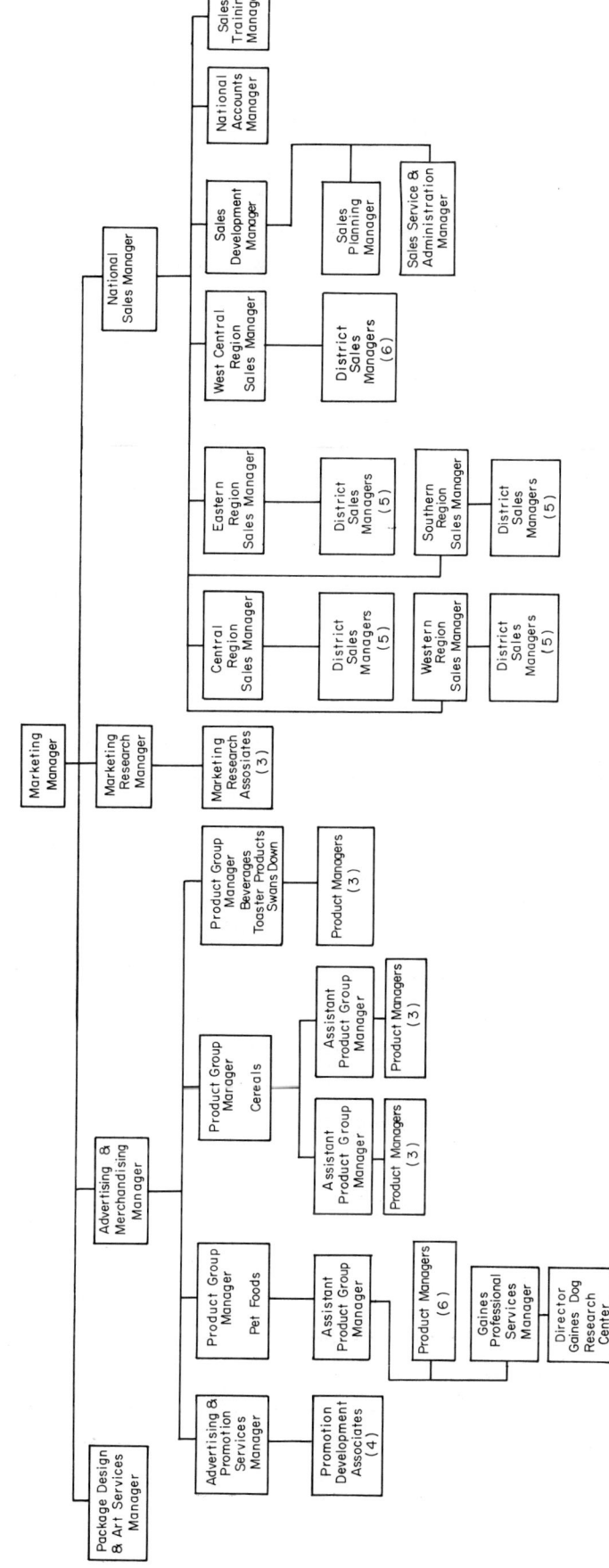

Exhibit 5. Organization Chart of Marketing Department of Division as of August 1966

Exhibit 6. National Promotion Schedule of Division for Fiscal 1966

	MONTH	APRIL				MAY				JUNE				JULY			
	ASSIGNMENT	#1				#2				#3				#4			#5
	WEEK BEGINNING	M 29	5	12	19	26	3	10	17	24	31	7	14	21	28	5	12	19	26
CEREALS	POST TOASTIES																		
	GRAPE-NUTS FLAKES																		
	RAISIN BRAN																	MATTEL TO
	BRAN FLAKES			25¢ S.L. SUGAR & CREAMER SET													
	GRAPE-NUTS							X 7¢ MC									
	POST-TENS																	MA
	TREAT-PAK																	
	SUGAR CRISP																	M
	ALPHA-BITS																	M
	SUGAR SPARKLED RICE KRINKLES					TABLE TOP RUNNER – PACK IN											
	SUGAR SPARKLED FLAKES																	M
	OAT FLAKES			25¢ S.L. SUGAR & CREAMER SET													
	CRISPY CRITTERS			$2.00 S.L. PINK ELEPHANT TOY													MAT
	BRAN & PRUNE FLAKES			$1.50 S.L. DECORATOR FRUIT						X 7¢ MC 14 DIST.					
	CORN FLAKES & STRAWBERRIES			BA-2 WK. PHASE I					X 7¢ MC (SEL. AREAS)		X 7¢ MC PHASE I		X
	CORN FLAKES & BLUEBERRIES			TRADE DELIVERY (TENTATIVE) (PH. I – AUG 2) (PH. II – JAN. 3) DEAL – 2 WK. BA, 5 WK. C/R												
	CORN FLAKES & PEACHES																	
	HONEYCOMB PHASE I - EAST. & CENT. PHASE II - WEST. REGION PHASE III - SOUTH., W. CENT.									BA – 40¢ CASE PHASE I						
	PUFFED CORN FLAKES PHASE I - SOUTHERN, DALLAS, HOUSTON PHASE II - WESTERN REGION													BA – 25¢ 15 OZ., 40¢ 25 OZ., PH. I	BA SIZ
PET FOODS	GAINES MEAL		OFF LABEL (6¢, 12¢, 25¢) NAT'L EXCEPT JAX			DAPPO JAX 1¢ PER LB.											
	GAINES BISCUITS/BITS		50¢ S.L. IRONING BOARD COVER														
	GRAVY TRAIN	DAPPO DISPLAY ONLY – 50¢ UNIT	25¢ – 50¢ REFUND OFFER – EXPIRES SEPT. 30, 1965, DISPLAY PIECE														
	GAINES. BURGERS									7¢ DM COUPON WESTERN REGION	50¢ DAPPO – EXCEPT 3 DIST.					
											X 7¢ MC PHOENIX		X	7¢ DM C EASTERN
	PRIME		7¢ PI, 10¢ MC, DAPPO, DAMPO, SELECTED AREAS			50¢ MEDIA RE-CERT. DENVER											
BEV.	TANG			7¢ PI PT, RB, SC						7¢-10¢-15¢ PI 11 DISTRICTS		7¢-10¢ BAL.
			XX 7¢ DM – 15 DISTRICTS.														
S.D.	SHORTENING MIXES		$1.00 C/R RUNNING			DAPPO-DAMPO – 20¢ SELECTED AREAS											
	ANGEL FOOD		CONTINUOUSLY NAT'L EXCEPT DENVER						DAPPO & DAMPO 50¢ SELECTED AREAS								
	CAKE FLOUR																	

CODE: X = COUPON DROP DATE BA = BUYING ALLOWANCE
       PI = PACK-IN   SL = SELF-LIQUIDATOR

General Foods: Post Division

	SEPTEMBER				OCTOBER				NOVEMBER				DECEMBER				JANUARY				FEBRUARY				MARCH		
	#7				#8				#9				#10				#11				#12				#13		
6	30	6	13	20	27	4	11	18	25	1	8	15	22	29	6	13	20	27	3	10	17	24	31	7	14	21	28	7	14	21

TEST

5¢ PI RAISIN BRAN

5¢ PI GRAPE-NUTS

5¢ PI CRISPY CRITTERS

ST

ST
ST

ACTION TOY PACK IN

ST

5¢ PI UNTIL 6/30/66   5¢ PI BRAN FLAKES & BRAN & PRUNE FLAKES

X 7¢ MC WESTERN LESS DENVER

BA – WK. PHASE II   X 7¢ MC (SEL. AREAS)   X 7¢ MC PHASE II   X 10¢ MC (PH. II) GOOD ON S OR B   7¢ PI–IN S,B,P, GOOD ON ALL 3, & 25¢ REF. OFF. (I)

GOOD (I)   7¢ PI – GOOD ON B & S (II)

TENTATIVE TRADE DELIVERY PHASE I

TENTATIVE TRADE DEL. PHASE II NOV. 15

TENTATIVE TRADE DEL. PHASE III

7¢ PI PHASE I

X 7¢ MC PHASE I   X 7¢ MC PHASE I   X 7¢ MC PHASE II
X 7¢ DM PHASE II

BONUS PACK 6#, 12#, 30# (EXCEPT CHARLOTTE DISTRICT) 7¢ OFF LABEL – 2 LB. (EXCEPT JAX DISTRICT)

OFF LABEL 6¢, 12¢, 25¢ (TENTATIVE)

10¢ PI PRIME

7¢ OFF LABEL, CELLOPHANE SLEEVE XMAS THEME (TENTATIVE)

TENTATIVE S. L. PREMIUM

X 7¢ DM COUPON, 60¢ S. L. DOG TAG

CROSS PACK 7¢ COUPON IN CEREALS (TENTATIVE)

X 7¢ DM COUPON SOUTHERN, CENTRAL, WEST CENTRAL

7¢ MC (TENTATIVE)

IECE WO 5

X 7¢ MC - READERS DIG. (SUBSC.)
X 50¢ RE-CERT. READERS DIG. (NEWSSTAND)   7¢ PI

RECIPE BOOK OFFER, PT & GNF, MAY 3- SEPT 3   X 7¢ DM COUPON

DEAL
DET.

MC = MEDIA COUPON
DM = DIRECT MAIL

July 1, 1965

Exhibit 7. Example of Sales Plans of Division, April 1966

Bulletin No. 188-66
April 21, 1966
Planning Guide Key B-3
Deletion Date: 7/31/66

TO SALES MANAGERS AT: New York and Philadelphia Districts
SUBJECT: *TANG JUNE QUARTER PROMOTION*

PURPOSE

To describe plans for a TANG refund offer promotion scheduled for the June Quarter.

DESCRIPTION AND TIMING

All sizes of Tang will be affected by the refund offer. Individual sizes will be flagged in red as follows:

	Estimated* Redemption	*Offer No.*
7 oz. — "30¢ IN CASH — FREE Mail in one 7 oz. label and one 1 lb. 2 oz. label — details inside"	2%	1064-7
1 lb. 2 oz. — "75¢ CASH — FREE — Details Inside Mail in three 1 lb. 2 oz. labels"	4%	1065-7
1 lb. 11 oz. — "$1.25 IN CASH — FREE Mail in three 1 lb. 11 oz. labels — Details Inside"	5%	1066-7

For identification purposes, cases for cash refund offer pack will be printed in blue color with the letter "R" appearing after the regular code number.

Target release dates for Tang cash refund pack are assigned to New York and Philadelphia as follows:

Size & Description	*Target Release Date*
27 oz. — $1.25 Refund Offer Pack	May 2, 1966
18 oz. — .75 Refund Offer Pack	May 16, 1966
7 oz. — .30 Refund Offer Pack	May 30, 1966

Substitution of refund offer pack for regular pack will be made on or following stated target date, depending on the availability of the pack at the DCs.

It is important that release dates for individual sizes of Tang remain staggered by the interval used for the target dates assigned. DSMs should coordinate with DSSMs the finalizing of actual product release schedules.

ALLOCATIONS

District allocations are outlined below:

	Cases 24/7 oz.	*Cases 12/7 oz.*	*Cases 24/18 oz.*	*Cases 12/18 oz.*	*Cases 12/27 oz.*
New York	3,517	418	2,446	2,923	5,206
Philadelphia	768	1,211	2,253	983	3,751
TOTAL	4,285	1,629	4,699	3,906	8,957
Estimated T/D	5/30/66	5/30/66	5/16/66	5/16/66	5/2/66

Regular Packs will be available for Military Sales and Direct Accounts who do not wish to handle the special packs.

OBJECTIVES

7 oz. — Promote trial of Tang with non-users of the brand; encourage repurchase of a larger size.

18 oz. & 27 oz. — Provide incentive for increased usage and repurchase of Tang by consumers who drink the product regularly.

* Based on allocated quantities.

Exhibit 7 (continued).

Obtain merchandising cooperation in the form of displays and/or advertisements for the refund offer pack.

MATERIALS

Sample refund offer labels will be forwarded to each district office the week of April 18, 1966.

REPORTING

None Required.

BASIC INFORMATION

Basic Information sheet is attached.

Distribution: Lists 1, 2, 3 & 4.

ATTACHMENT

Bulletin No. 188-66
ATTACHMENT

BASIC INFORMATION SHEET

PRODUCT NAME:	TANG	TANG	TANG	TANG	TANG
CASE DESCRIPTION:	24/7 oz. 30¢ Refund Offer Insert	12/7 oz. 30¢ Refund Offer Insert	24/1 lb. 2 oz. 75¢ Refund Offer Insert	12/1 lb. 2 oz. 75¢ Refund Offer Insert	12/1 lb. 11 oz. $1.25 Refund Offer Insert
PRICE:	---------PRICES ARE SAME AS REGULAR----------				
PRODUCT CODE:	10340-R	10350-R	10370-R	10375-R	10380-R
STANDARD UNIT:	10½ lbs.	10½ lbs.	10½ lbs.	10½ lbs.	10½ lbs.
CONVERSION FACTORS:					
UNITS	1.000	.500	2.571	1.286	1.929
DOZENS	2.000	1.000	2.000	1.000	1.000
APPROX. GROSS WGT.:	19.5 lbs.	10 lbs.	43.5 lbs.	22 lbs.	31 lbs.
APPROX. CU. FT. DISPL.:	.48	.24	1.03	.52	.73
PALLET PATTERN	16 OT	30 OT	8 OT	19 OT	15 OT
CS/PALLET	96	200	42	84	55
CS/TIER	12	25	7	14	11

Appendix

Content for Annual Marketing Plans of Division

A. What Does the Brand Believe Will Be the MAIN and MOST SIGNIFICANT *Characteristics of the Market Place in the Upcoming Year or Five Years?* (State it in one or two paragraphs.)
   For example:

   1. *Competition*
      — Type, number, location, spending levels, marketing intent, aggressiveness, promotional type, intensity, impact, product quality, pack sizes, labels, containers, advertising copy, media plan, pricing, trends-in-share, consumption, etc.
   2. *Pricing*
      — Raw material price levels and their impact on our own and competitive brands' marketing plans and executions.
      — Margins (our own and competition's) and the marketing significance inherent in these margin forecasts.
   3. *Trade — Distribution Channels*
      — Mergers, consolidations, buying practices, advertising/merchandising habits, etc. that will bear on our brand's marketing plans.
   4. *Major Media Trends*
      — Of significance to the brand's marketing success.
   5. *Total Market Consumption Trends*
      — Rates of change by regions, by user characteristics, store types, etc.
   6. Etc.

B. *What Is the Main Objective in Marketing the Brand Over the Next Five Years?* (State it in a paragraph as specifically as possible.)
   For example:

   1. Increase the profitability of the brand from ___ to ___% N.S.
   2. Increase the share-of-market from ___ to ___.
   3. Minimize the loss of brand share-of-market as new Division (competitive) products are introduced.
   4. Increase consumption of the product.
      — Nationally by ___% each year or a total of ___ units over five years.
      — Regionally by ___% each year or a total of ___ units over five years.
   5. Stabilize the business at present levels but with maximum profitability and efficiency of spending.
   6. Recreate or refurbish the brand's consumer image nationally/regionally, from one that is ___ to one that is ___ to be measured by before and after consumer research.
   7. Etc.

C. *What Is the Main Objective in Marketing the Brand in the Upcoming Fiscal Year?*
   For example:

   1. Hold present volume (@ ___ units), share (@ ___%) and profits (@ ___ unit rate), while a new business building marketing plan and/or product is developed and tested.
   2. Increase annual profits from ___ to ___.
   3. Increase consumption from ___ to ___ factory shipments from ___ to ___.
   4. Increase national or regional share of a static or diminishing market from ___ to ___.
   5. Recreate or refurbish the brand's image with all or selected consumers, from one that is ___ to one that is ___.
   6. Etc.

D. *What Is the Basic Marketing Strategy to Accomplish this Objective in the Upcoming Fiscal Year?*
   For example:

   1. Successfully introduce a new product, pack, label, advertising campaign nationally.
   2. Sample new users to the brand and/or category — switch users of competitive brands.
   3. Increase brand usage among current users through increasing the frequency, quantity, type of usage.
   4. Develop and test a new market plan.
   5. Increase the level of spending for advertising and/or promotion from ___ to ___ nationally/regionally.
   6. Etc.

E. *How Will the Brand's Product Compare with Competition during the Upcoming Fiscal Year?* (Show details in an appendix.) Consumer preferences by all the most significant stratifications — (sex, geographical location, light/moderate/heavy usage, etc.).

Appendix (continued)

F. *What Copy Strategy Will the Brand Follow in the Upcoming Year to Execute Its Basic Marketing Strategy?* (Show details of copy plan and samples of advertising in an appendix.)
Who are the prime prospects for the product category and the brand and what are their long-term basic reasons for using the product category and subject brand? What objectives will the copy strategy try to achieve with these prospects? What is the single idea about itself the brand wants to register on its prime prospects?

G. *What Media Strategy Will the Brand Follow in the Upcoming Year to Execute Its Basic Marketing Strategy?* (Show details in an appendix.)
What principles will be followed in delivering selling messages to prime prospects and what objectives will the media plan try to achieve?

H. *What Sales Promotion Strategy Will the Brand Follow to Execute Its Basic Marketing Strategy?* (Show rationale and details, especially regional variations in effort, in an appendix.)
What objectives will the sales promotion plan try to accomplish with the distributors and prime prospects for the product?

I. *What Spending Principles Will the Brand Follow in Executing This Basic Marketing Strategy?*
How much will the brand spend on what A & P (Advertising and Promotion), where (sales area, county size, etc.), and in what periods of time (quarter)?

J. *What Pricing Strategy Will the Brand Attempt to Follow to Execute Its Basic Marketing Strategy?*
What retail price objectives (by pack size) will the brand have geographically?
What gross profit margin objective does the brand have for the fiscal year?

K. *What Testing and Research Projects Will Be Initiated by the Brand to:*
   1. Gain information about the consumer.
   2. Evaluate the effectiveness of current elements of the market mix (copy, media, sales promotion, pack size, pricing, label, etc.).
   3. Improve the product quality or reduce cost of goods.
   4. Etc.

L. *What Will Be the Main Elements of the Measurement System to Determine Degree of Success the Execution of the Plan Achieves?*

M. *What Are the Specific Quarterly Marketing Financial Goals for the Brand in the Upcoming Year?* This will be the official financial "plan" (approved profit forecast) for the brand *as well as for the next four additional years* (to complete the "Long-Range Plan"). Volume, share, margin, advertising, promotion, total A & P and PBT (Profit Before Taxes).

Key Financial Controls for Marketing Planning

The Product Group will recommend and management approve the following key financial elements of the marketing plan for each quarter and for the fiscal year:

> Fiscal year volume — (base volume)
> Gross profit rate/unit — ("Bogey" or standard margin)
> Advertising expenditures rate/unit — (payout rate)
> Promotion expenditures rate/unit — (payout rate)
> PBT per unit — (payout rate)

Volume

The proposed fiscal year volume base must be reconciled with:

— historical trends for the brand (% change vs. year ago), share of market, and sales/M population trends.
— known and expected competitive activity.
— advertising and promotion expenditure, historical rates vs. proposed rates.
— anything else germane to the volume rationale.

Gross Profit Rate

The proposed fiscal year rate must be justified in relation to:

— "norms" for the company (as % net sales).
— historical trends for the brand or product group.
— retail pricing strategy past and proposed.
— manufacturing cost reduction possibilities.

When approved, this rate/unit becomes the "bogey" or "standard rate" objective for the entire Division (manufacturing as well as marketing) to achieve for this product.

Advertising and Promotion Rates

The proposed fiscal year rates must be justified in relation to:

— "norms" for the company.
— historical trends for the brand and/or product group.
— expected volume.
— expected PBT vs. "norms" for the product or product group.
— basic marketing objectives.
— known and/or expected competitive activity — advertising levels.
— etc.

Appendix of Historical and Supporting Data to Post Division Marketing Plans

I. *The Consumer*

Identify if possible the current "light," "moderate," and "heavy" user of the product in terms of:

1. Recent trends in % of brand's volume accounted for by each group.
2. The characteristics of each group as to sex, age, income, occupation, income group, geographical location.
3. Attitudes towards the product and category and copy appeals most persuasive to each group.

II. *The Product*

Identify the current consumer preference of the brand versus primary competition (and secondary competition if available), according to:

1. Light, moderate, heavy usage (if available).
2. The characteristics of each group as to sex, age, income, occupation, income group, geographical location, size of dog or size of family, etc.

III. *Shipment History*

Identify the recent shipment trends on the brand by total units and units/M population (brand development) according to districts, regions, and nationally.

IV. *Spending History*

Identify the recent spending trends on the brand by total dollars, dollar/M population, per unit sold for advertising, for promotion, and for total A & P by districts, regions, and nationally.

V. *Profitability History*

Identify the recent trends of list price, average retail price (by sales areas), gross profit margins, and PBT *in addition* to trends in:

— Gross profit as % of net sales.
— Total marketing as % of gross profit and per unit sold.
— PBT as % of net sales and per unit sold.
— ROFE (Return of Funds Employed) for each recent fiscal year.

VI. *Share of Market History*

Identify recent trends of:

a. The brands of share-of-market nationally, regionally, district-wide.
b. Consumption by total units and % gain/loss versus year ago nationally, regionally, district-wide.
c. Distribution by pack size nationally, regionally, district-wide.

Where applicable, trends in all of the above data should also be identified by store classification, chain versus independent (large, medium and small).

VII. *Total Market History*

Identify recent trends of the total market in terms of units and % gain/loss versus year ago nationally, regionally, district-wide, per M population, store type, county size, type of user (exclusive versus partial user), retail price trends, by user characteristics (age, income, etc.).

VIII. *Competitive History* (major brands), where available

Identify significant competitive trends in share, consumption levels by sales areas, store types; media and promotion expenditures; types of media, promotion; retail price differentials, etc.

COMMENTARY

At General Foods' Post Division a simple product management structure expanded into a complex one as the product line grew from several cereals and Postum in the early 1950s to 36 different food items by 1966. The structure became pyramidal, as in the case of the Du Pont Textile Fibers Department, because so many of the product programs were defined as segments of some broader groupings. As the product management organization was articulated, the resource structure also grew. Certain specialized functions were created to support the program managers and to relieve them of the necessity for being experts in promotion, packaging, marketing research, and accounting as well as strategy formulation.

The evolving pattern of the product program and resource structures at the Post Division is interesting to study. The planning procedures that the Division developed and used are also important to understand.

In particular it is useful to study the program-resource interrelationships. Managers in field sales, in manufacturing, and in Post's advertising agency encountered operational problems in their relationships with the program management organization. It is useful to know why. In addition, the Division seemed to have difficulty with new product development — first in getting enough new products, and later in coordinating the development of new products and existing ones.

The commentary deals with these four facets of the Post Division case: (1) the pattern of program and resource structure that emerged; (2) the planning procedures used; (3) the difficulties experienced in program-resource relationships; and (4) the problems in the product development process.

Program and Resource Structures

We can contrast the relative autonomy of the product manager in the early 1950s at the Post Division with the interrelationships of his 1960s counterpart. Product managers, 1950 style, were versatile entrepreneurs. They negotiated with Operations (manufacturing) for supplies of product and with the General Foods field sales force for selling time, and they had their own advertising agencies. Their responsibility to the Post General Manager was simply to meet objectives (sales and profits). Probably each one had some skills in the areas of promotional planning, display design, package design, market research, and advertising.

By comparison, product managers in the 1960s had to be team players operating in a pyramidal program management framework. Each was responsible for developing strategies and annual marketing plans for one or more products within a product group (such as Cereals or Pet Foods) for which there was a broad strategy framework. He drew on the expertise of a Marketing Research Department, an Art Services Department, a Promotion Department, and a Marketing Accounting Services Department. These resources aided him in studying his market, planning trade deals, in-store displays, and premium promotions, and monitoring the results to enable him to make quick tactical adjustments in his plans.

The reasons for the change are self-evident. The proliferation of Post product lines created many more product management jobs, and the limited supply of broadly skilled product managers was a real constraint. The expanded ranks of new product managers needed support in technical areas such as market research, promotion, and art. More to the point, these functions required considerable expertise and were likely to be handled more effectively by specialized resource units than by product managers who had to be "jacks of all trades."

The Post product management organization can also be described as unilateral; the assignments of its product/market managers were defined in terms of products. Each product was perceived as fitting into a segment of the packaged foods market. Post's experience indicated, for example, that there were several market segments for cereals and that different strategies had to be tailored for each. Hence there were managers for nutritional cereals, children's (pre-sweetened) cereals, and family cereals. These categories could be differentiated in terms of competition, consumer buying behavior, and relative sensitivity of sales volume to such strategy elements as media advertising, in-store displays, shelf location, premium promotions, trade deals, and consumer "cents-off" campaigns.

At the same time annual planning and strategy formulation had to be integrated for the several product groups — Cereals, Pet Foods, and Beverages and Miscellaneous Products. Each group was a family of brands going to the same customers and often promoted together. To provide this integration the program management organization was pyramidal with product group managers, assistant product group managers, product managers, and assistant product managers in each of the major groups. Annual marketing plans were prepared by product managers, integrated with other plans at that level, and consolidated into product group plans.

In contrast to Mobil and IBM, but like Lockheed-Georgia, the Post product management units did not include program-specialized resource units. At Mobil and IBM, some program organizations had their own sales forces, some their own engineering and technical service units, and one organization had a procurement function. At the Post Division the homogeneity of product, market, and manufacturing process made it practical for the many programs to draw on common resources.

One exception might well be noted: toward the end of fiscal 1967 the Battle Creek Plant, which manufactured cereals, became part of the Cereals Product Group. At the same time this group was placed directly under the Assistant General Manager of the Post Division. The reason was primarily to give Post cereals increased top management attention because this part of the business had not been very successful in recent years. With cereals product management and cereals manufacturing reporting to one man, better integration could be achieved between market planning and market supply.

Overall it was a sophisticated product/market program management structure. Product manager assignments were based on a fine segmentation of the markets for Post products. Yet the pyramidal grouping provided for the necessary integration of planning and strategy formulation of products that were related at the market level.

Planning: Form and Process

The Post Division case includes a useful description of a marketing plan and of the internal procedures by which plans are developed. In the plan, market strategy and sales volume objectives were established against a backdrop of historical data, current market trends, and competitive conditions. The strategy was elaborated in terms of specific programs and schedules for product development, packaging, pricing, advertising, and promotion. The Appendix of the case, "Content for Annual Marketing Plans," provides an excellent format, which might usefully be adapted for planning for other kinds of products as well as packaged foods.

As at Mobil, the process by which plans were prepared was characterized by a great amount of back-and-forth discussion between product management and Post Division top management. In the process, overall Division objectives were adjusted until the "whole" equaled a *workable* "sum of the parts."

There was, as well, considerable interchange between product managers on the one hand and resource managers on the other. In this way advertising, promotion, and field sales programs for each product took shape. In addition to helping product managers develop concrete plans for carrying out their strategies, the resource managers worked to adjust to the limits of the available resources the amount and timing of resource efforts called for in all the marketing plans. For example, a Sales Planning Manager in the field sales organization met individually with product managers "to assure that the sales support called for in the marketing plans was in fact feasible, that the product management objectives were compatible with sales objectives, and that no sales conflicts existed between one set of plans and another."

The procedure for approving marketing plans at different management levels was a formal one. When approved, each plan was translated into a "plans letter," which was described as an "action document authorizing the commitment of resources." The authority derived from the fact that each plans letter was signed by the Marketing Manager or his immediate deputy, the Advertising and Merchandising Manager. It set forth time schedules and detailed objectives and indicated the Post unit responsible for completing each piece of the plan. In the case of the field selling organization, sales volume objectives were broken down by district, and a schedule of promotions and new product introductions was prepared. Goals that could not be made explicit either quantitatively or by calendar days were communicated through regional and district meetings and in the planning that each district manager did with individual salesmen.

The planning system at the Post Division has much to commend it. We might, in particular, note the scope and detail of the annual marketing plans and the way product managers developed plans by working with resource managers. It is useful, too, to note the procedures by which the product plans in sum were made consistent with overall division objectives, on the one hand, and tailored to the limits of the available resources, on the other. We might also mark the well-developed procedures for translating plans into action schedules for implementation.

Program-Resource Relationships

In the case of each of the three major resources on which the product managers drew — field sales, manufacturing, and Post's advertising agencies — there is evidence of some friction in program-resource relationships. It is useful to understand why. And in each case the problems seemed somewhat different.

Advertising Agency Relations

The advertising agencies complained that the system tended to dampen creativity and encourage advertising mediocrity. Agency personnel made presentations of copy ideas at three, four, and sometimes five organizational levels at Post before the ideas were approved — whereas they could presumably be rejected at any one of these points. Post management responded by decreeing that the number of presentations in any case be limited to three, the first to the product manager, the next to the product group manager, and the final one to the Advertising and Merchandising Manager and the Marketing Manager. At each pass the recommendations were reviewed in a successively broader frame of reference to assure their consistency with an overall advertising program, and probably to bring to bear the greater judgment and experience of higher levels of management.

If the agency complaint is indeed a valid one — and it does in fact seem reasonable — it is doubtful that the intended solution would do much to increase agency creativity.

The problem is essentially one of developing an effective interface between the product programs, on the one hand, and the advertising agency, on the other. It is an important relationship because advertising is a very important element in Post's overall strategy.[1]

An alternative solution might be to establish an interface unit for advertising that would function like the Marketing Research Department. The Manager of the Marketing Research Department approved marketing research proposals, helped to prepare research plans, contracted with outside organizations to do the work, and then helped to interpret the results. A good Marketing Research Manager would need to have a grasp of product program research needs, an understanding of market survey design and research techniques, and a knowledge of the skills and qualifications of outside market research organizations.

An Advertising Manager, reporting to the Marketing Manager, could work with product managers and product group managers to determine

---

[1] In 1967 Post Division's expenditures on magazine, network TV, spot TV, and newspaper supplement advertising exceeded $30 million, and total General Foods advertising in these categories was more than $100 million. (Source: National Advertising Investments, Jan.–Dec., 1967, Leading National Advertisers, Inc., Norwalk, Conn.).

the allocation of advertising dollars among products in order to produce the maximum return. He could help to integrate advertising programs for the several product lines. It would be his responsibility to review, with the product managers, advertising agency presentations and to give final approval. On the other side, he could identify creative talent and ideas in Post's advertising agencies and work to have these resources applied to Post advertising programs. To work well, such an interface would need to understand how agencies operate so as to establish a working relationship in which the Post advertising agency could make its greatest possible contribution. At the same time, the function would need to have a clear sense of the objectives of advertising in Post's overall marketing strategy and its role in each product plan.

In this instance, there is evidence to suggest that resource productivity diminishes when the resource is subjected *directly* to the demands of a number of programs. A single point of interface can serve to lend order to the relationships, integrate program activities with regard to that element of strategy, modify program needs to fit resource capabilities, and assist the resource in scheduling its work by programs. (In the next case, General Electric's Housewares Division, we can observe this function in operation.)

Marketing-Manufacturing Relationships

Apparently, an effective interface was lacking, as well, in the relationships between the several product programs and Operations (manufacturing). Product managers had direct access to Operations personnel and made requests on Operations that were inordinately time-consuming to meet. In addition, special label promotions were often planned by product managers without their taking account of the possibility that the factory might be holding old label inventories that it could not move while the promotion was in progress. Thus the comment of the Operations Manager, "There is a tendency . . . for Marketing not to consider our needs adequately when preparing their plans. The two problems I have cited are typical. . . ."

For lack of an effective interface between Operations and the product programs, conflicts went "up the line" to top management for resolution, where there was a lack of background and factual information on which to base reasonable and constructive settlements.

In a bilateral structure (where there are both market programs managers and product programs managers) the product managers may represent manufacturing interests to the market programs. At the Du Pont Textile Fibers Department, for example, this function was handled by the Sales Programs (product) Managers. In a unilateral structure, such as the Post Division's the market programs-manufacturing interface must be provided for either in the Marketing department or in Manufacturing. The choice may not be critical, provided that the function serves the balanced best interests of the resource and the programs.

Field Sales Planning

In the case of field sales, problems in the relationship between programs and the resource were not caused by lack of an interface. Such a function was carried out by the Sales Planning Manager. Instead the evidence would suggest that, if anything, the sales force was "over-programmed" in the respect that it found it difficult to meet the multiplicity of specific objectives imposed on it by the programs. In addition to meeting sales targets and carrying out tightly scheduled promotions and new product introductions, the sales force had a number of nonquantifiable tasks to perform. These tasks might include better shelving for some products in certain classes of retail outlets, increased distribution, or improved customer relations. In addition, an incentive bonus system was intended to get increased emphasis on the most profitable products and those that were most sensitive to personal selling effort, as opposed to advertising outlays. The incentive system was a vehicle through which Post management could impose an "override" on the system to get sales effort placed where top management thought it would make the greatest contribution. The incentive system was an important motivation in the respect that sales performance against incentive budgets directly affected sales compensation.

Two developments suggest that the scheduling and motivating of field sales personnel became onerous indeed. First, the incentive point system was abandoned in 1967 in favor of a procedure by which sales representatives were subjectively evaluated by *district sales managers.* Incentive compensation was related then to district managers' appraisals. Second, Sales Planning, in 1967, gave up some initiative in programming field sales activities and district managers assumed the task of proposing promotional activities for their district each quarter.

These two developments, coming at about the same time, suggest that the field sales organization might have suffered under tight scheduling and a multiplicity of performance measures. Through Sales Planning, possibly, the ambitious plans of the product managers had been translated into overly detailed objectives, which gave the field district managers little flexibility in meeting the broader, more important targets in their own way. In this instance, it might have been well to provide an integrated time schedule for product promotions, but beyond that to prepare sales volume objectives by product and district.

The difficulties encountered by Post Division management in the relationships between product managers, on the one hand, and the advertising agencies, Operations, and field sales, on the other, indicate the need for effective program-resource interface functions. To perform well, interface managers need an understanding of program strategies and objectives as well as a good knowledge of the way the resource operates, its particular competences, and its limitations. Interface managers lend order to wide-ranging program demands; they may help to shape program strategies to make greatest use of the resource; they aid the resource to schedule its work to serve the programs effectively.

The Product Development Process

Product development at Post was the focus of considerable top management attention. For several years in the late 1950s and early 1960s a top level New Products Committee, chaired by the Post General Manager, worked to stimulate and to screen the flow of new product ideas. Then in early 1966 the committee was reconstituted and top management members were replaced with personnel from operating management ranks. The change was predicated on a belief that the development of existing (as opposed to new) products was getting insufficient attention; that the two areas of development could be better coordinated at operating levels.

By overlaying the normal product development process with a top management committee, the Post management recognized some deficiencies in the process — or at least signaled a dissatisfaction with the rate of new product development. Where might the weaknesses be?

If one compares product development procedures at IBM with those of the Post Division, two differences come immediately to attention. First, at IBM, which had a bilateral program organization, product programs managers in the Data Processing Division (marketing) took much of the initiative in new product development and introduction. Second, IBM used a formal "sign-off" system to transfer the development burden from marketing (Data Processing Division) to technical research (Systems Development Division) and back to marketing. This system served to commit each group in turn to the development effort and to draw forth its maximum contribution.

At Post 90% of the new product ideas originated in the Technical Research Department. Some ideas, the case tells us, came from the product management organization and Post's advertising agencies; these sources, however, did not provide important inputs to the product development process. This case, and others as well,[2] suggest that those who are preoccupied with planning and implementing marketing strategy for the existing line of products do not naturally play an initiating role in new product development. Although they may have ideas based on market responses to existing products, procedures need to be developed to elicit ideas from a variety of sources for product improvements, to screen them, to apply market research, and to determine technical feasibility.

The comparison with IBM suggests that what might have been missing at Post was a function in Marketing responsible for gathering, evaluating,

---
[2] For example, the General Electric Company: Housewares Division case.

and proposing product development ideas to Technical Research. The ideas might be drawn from product managers, field sales managers, the monitoring of competing product lines, and from new General Foods laboratory developments as well. While a top management committee can serve to stress the necessity for developing new products, operating procedures needed to be devised at Post to assure balanced technical and market inputs to the process.

Summary

At General Foods' Post Division, the role of the product manager changed markedly in a decade. The versatile entrepreneurs of the 1950s became the team players of the 1960s, developing interrelated strategies and drawing on skilled special resources. The program organization as of 1967 was a unilateral, pyramidal structure in which the program management units had none of their own program-specialized resource units. The organization was well structured to plan and implement programs in the market segments in which Post products competed.

The planning system described is a useful model. It provided for the development of market strategy and sales volume objectives against a backdrop of historical data, current market trends, and competitive conditions. Strategy was elaborated in terms of specific plans, schedules, and budgets for product development, packaging, pricing, advertising, and promotion. Product plans were adjusted to the limits of available resources, and were consolidated by group and for the Division. The overall Division strategy was the product of a great deal of informal discussion between Post Division operating and top management.

The case describes certain symptoms that might indicate weaknesses in the interface relationships between programs and resources. There was no interface between programs and advertising agencies, nor between programs and Operations (manufacturing). Product managers had direct access to these resources. Advertising agencies claimed that working procedures diminished their creativity. Operations management attributed some manufacturing inefficiencies to a lack of coordination between program planning and production scheduling.

It might have been useful to establish interface functions between the product programs and the advertising agencies and between programs and Operations. These interfaces could give order to the relationships, integrate program demands on the resource, and assist the resource in scheduling its work.

In the program-field sales relationship, there is evidence that Sales Planning (the interface function) may have erred on the side of "over-programming" the resource. In addition to meeting sales targets and carrying out tightly scheduled promotions and new product introductions, the sales force had a number of nonquantifiable tasks to perform. Through Sales Planning, possibly, the ambitious plans of the product managers had been translated into detailed objectives which gave the field district managers little flexibility in meeting volume, cost, and profit objectives in their own way.

Finally, the case registers some dissatisfaction on the part of Post Division management with the rate and effectiveness of new product development. Here, it was useful to compare the Post system with IBM's. In the latter case, new product development was the primary concern of product managers in the Data Processing Division. They gathered and screened ideas and requested the allocation of technical development resources. A comparable function was missing in the Post Division. Product managers, preoccupied with planning and implementing strategy for existing products, could not naturally be expected to assume initiative for developing new products.

The General Foods' Post Division case adds a great deal to our understanding of program definition and annual marketing planning procedures. It also provides an opportunity to apply some of the organization approaches observed in preceding cases in an effort to resolve some of the organizational problems experienced by Post Division management.

General Electric Company: Housewares Division

The General Electric Housewares Division (HD) manufactured and marketed a broad line of portable household appliances. Other General Electric divisions handled major appliances (e.g., washing machines, refrigerators), radios, television sets, and lighting products.

Prior to late 1964 HD had been divided into three decentralized product departments: Portable Appliances, Home Care and Comfort Products, and Clocks and Personal Care Products.[1] In September 1964 these product departments were consolidated into one division organized on a functional basis.[2]

In late 1966 HD marketed the following product lines (broken down by pre-1965 departmental assignments):

Portable Appliances

Steam and dry irons
Electric knives
Toasters
Electric coffee makers
Electric mixers
Electric can openers
Electric skillets
Electric grills
Electric blenders
Electric fire starter
Power tools
Rotisseries
Electric griddles
Warming trays
Electric kettles
Electric knife sharpeners

Home Care and Comfort

Floor cleaners
Electric fans
Electric blankets
Electric heaters

Clocks and Personal Care

Clocks
Electric toothbrushes
Hair dryers
Electric baby dish
Electric shoe polisher

New (post-1965) Products

Electric clothes brush
Electric cigarette lighters
Electric Christmas tree stand
Rechargeable flashlight
Electric food cooker
Electric manicure set
Electric massager

Many new products had been added to the HD product line between 1961 and 1966. According to HD executives, 40% of the products in the 1966 line had not existed in 1961, and virtually all HD products had been significantly modified during this period. In 1964 the division had introduced 33 new products; in 1965, 80 new products; and in 1966, 74 new products.[3]

In 1966 HD products were manufactured in nine factories, as shown in the following table:

Factory	Products
Brockport, Mass.	Knives, mixers, blenders, power tools.
Ashland, Mass.	Clocks, timers, motors, electric toothbrushes.
New Britain, Conn.	Manicure sets, shoe polishers, knife sharpeners, massagers, coffee makers.
Allentown, Pa.	Toasters, grills, rotisseries, warming trays, griddles, kettles, food cookers, coffee urns.
Asheboro, N.C.	Blankets, clothes brushes, heating pads, baby dishes, lighters, flashlights.
Bridgeport, Conn.	Fans, hair dryers, heaters, Christmas trees.
Cleveland, Ohio	Floor cleaners, floor polishers.
Ft. Smith, Ark.	Can openers, skillets, fire starters.
Ontario, Cal.	Irons.

HD marketed its products through approximately 900 independent distributors. Approximately 180 of these distributors carried the full HD line; approximately 370 carried all products except those in the home care and comfort category; and about 350 wholesalers oriented toward drug or jewelry stores carried only clocks and personal care products. In most geographic areas, several competing distributors carried all or part of the HD line.

---

[1] See Exhibit 1, HD Organization Chart (mid-1964).
[2] See Exhibit 2, HD Organization Chart (late 1964).
[3] Including new clock models, which were essentially styling changes (13 in 1964, 30 in 1965, and 26 in 1966).

In addition, HD operated its own distributor, General Electric Distribution (GED). GED carried the full HD product line, including several categories of products (power tools, price-maintained portable appliances) that were not carried by the independent distributors. As a matter of policy, GED operated under the same conditions and terms as the independent distributors did.

This case describes the evolution of HD's organizational structure. It begins by describing the old product department organization, then presents the reasons given by management for the late 1964 reorganization, and finally describes the 1966 organization in detail.

The Old Product Department Organization

As noted above, HD had been organized in three product departments prior to September 1964. Each product department had been headed by a General Manager, who reported to the Division General Manager. The Department General Managers had had profit responsibility and considerable freedom to operate their departments within policy guidelines established by divisional management. Each department had had its own product development, marketing (including field sales), manufacturing, and administrative organizations.

Although the departments differed somewhat in organization, the organization chart for the Portable Appliance Department (Exhibit 3) was fairly typical. The Portable Appliance Department operated three factories. Each factory had a Manufacturing Manager and an Engineering Manager, both of whom reported to the Department General Manager. The Managers of Advance Engineering,[4] Finance, Industrial Design, and Marketing also reported to the Department General Manager.

Exhibit 4 is an organization chart of the Marketing Section of the Portable Appliance Department. Reporting to the Marketing Manager were subsections responsible for sales planning, product planning, field sales, marketing administration, marketing research, merchandising (i.e., advertising and promotion), home economics, product service, and a marketing specialist.

Thirty-one district sales representatives worked exclusively for the Portable Appliance Department, although they frequently shared office space with sales representatives of other HD departments. Until 1962 these sales representatives had reported directly to the Field Sales Manager of the Portable Appliance Department. In order to improve sales training and supervision, which he believed to have been inadequate, the Department General Manager had appointed five Regional Sales Managers (reporting to the Field Sales Manager) in 1962.[5]

At the division level, the Division General Manager had had only a small staff before the reorganization in 1964. This staff was responsible for division-wide activities in such fields as overseas operations, legal matters, advanced development, business planning, and national distribution. (See Exhibit 1.)

HD's National Distribution Operation had carried out a wide range of divisional marketing activities. These activities included sales to premium companies (i.e., trading stamp companies) and certain large national accounts, division-wide advertising, field product service, and field relations. Eight Regional Field Relations Managers had represented HD in assigned geographic areas, but had not been responsible for meeting sales budgets.[6] As noted above, the district sales representatives had reported to departmental Sales Managers rather than to the divisional Field Relations Managers.

Proposed Reorganization

In early 1964 a major reorganization of the division was proposed in an internal memorandum:

The organizational boundaries which separate the three Product Departments of the Housewares Divisions are be-

---

[4] Most product development was carried out in the factories by engineers reporting to the Engineering Managers. The Advance Engineering Operation was primarily concerned with new technologies and products that would not be introduced in the near future.

[5] At the same time, the Clocks and Personal Care Department had appointed two Regional Sales Managers. The Home Care and Comfort Department chose not to appoint Regional Sales Managers; according to a high-level HD executive, this led to considerable difficulties when the sales forces were consolidated in 1964.

[6] The Field Relations Managers were expected to provide liaison between the division and the key customers in a geographic area and impart something of the "divisional philosophy" to HD activities in the field. The GEMD Field Sales Manager commented in 1967 that lack of responsibility and authority over field sales personnel had greatly reduced the effectiveness of the Field Relations Managers. Some had been more influential than others; but he believed that this function, in order to work at all, required men who were clearly the representatives of top management.

coming less and less distinct. Each of the Departments serves the same consumer, through similar distribution and by applying similar merchandising techniques.

This homogeneity has greatly reduced the need and desirability for specialized attention on a specific group of products. Only a short time ago it was necessary to break down these departmental walls for certain products, such as the hair dryer and baby dish, for more effective action in the market place.

While each of the plants has its own stable of engineering and manufacturing specialties, there remains much in common in many technologies, methods, and procedures under the general heading of mass production techniques.

Internal change because of new products and technologies and external change because of consumer and competitive developments have clearly signaled the need for the most effective action in these competitive areas. A common strategy, singleness of purpose, unity of action, are mandatory.

While these needs have been increasingly apparent in the market place for some time, it became even clearer when efforts were being made to produce a logical and comprehensive Division Business Charter. Our Consultant from Organizational Consulting Services observed at that time:

> "Keen merchandising and promotion judgment and timing, and knowledge of markets and market segments [are critical], so there is a need to multiply the unusual assets in this area that the Division now has, and also to nurture future added strengths. In this sense, the whole Division is like one big store."

From studies it was apparent the businesses of the Housewares Division and its three product departments included a compatible group of products and services bound together by many common customer needs, markets, and distribution channels. Thus, the businesses have melded together to form a *natural business unit* which lends itself to a functional type of organization structure similar to a number of our very successful corporate competitors.

It is consequently recommended that the Housewares Division be restructured to this type of organization.

We see many benefits in this proposal and would like to briefly review them. While the most important are in the general or marketing categories, there are likewise a number of important benefits that will accrue in the other functions.

I. MARKETING
1. Achieve better customer orientation and uniformity of approach as contrasted with the present departmentalized company-oriented structure. This would allow us to speak with one voice as we are attempting to do with College Bowl,[7] divisional space programs, and packaging.
2. Secure greater integration of total advertising and promotional efforts by our most knowledgeable man. This would also pave the way for utilizing a single advertising agency with its consequent savings in costs and valuable personnel time.
3. Develop common objectives and greater coordination of distributor franchising and distribution channels.
4. Take the initial step for the assumption of ultimate responsibility for GESCO [8] housewares *sales* operation.
5. Eliminate interdepartmental rivalry for distributor salesmen's time, and thereby control more prudently the money currently spent in this area. The present fragmented organization pits department against department within the Division.
6. Facilitate the adoption of sounder strategy in timing, planning, and introduction of new products — for example, not the three best products in each department, but the nine best for the Division with a minimum of wasted motion or ill-advised expenditures. In turn, this will permit acceleration of the important product development program, thus assuring greater sales volume and profit.
7. Accomplish complete coordination of sales programming and service policies.
8. Focus on competing for external customers and eliminate internal competition. Our competitors, both large and small, all operate in this manner — even when they promote two lines. Further, it gives better opportunity to re-evaluate overall distribution policy, such as a restudy of the entire private or secondary brand movement and its impact on the Division.
9. Allow business planning operation to study all areas of activities without concern for departmental scopes.

II. ENGINEERING AND MANUFACTURING
1. Accelerate and maximize pooled purchasing efforts through the establishment of a centralized purchasing operation for items common to all plants.
2. Engineer and manufacture products and parts in the plant most capable of handling in the best interest of the Division and Company.
3. Make possible the development of advanced engineering and manufacturing processes and tech-

---

[7] A popular television program sponsored jointly by the three HD departments.

[8] The General Electric Supply Company (GESCO) was a wholly owned distributor of General Electric housewares, radios, and electrical apparatus.

niques in a single plant, and the communication of this knowledge to the other plants, thus eliminating costly duplication.
4. Provide for the best use of facilities and resources; make-or-buy decisions; interplant manufacturing; and optimum sourcing.
5. Provide for the implementation of the most effective standardization program for all purchased or manufactured parts.
6. Provide cross-fertilization of both engineering and manufacturing techniques, as well as personnel.
7. Secure a lower total cost of quality by closer top level coordination of engineering and manufacturing.

III. FINANCE
1. Maximize use of electronic data processing equipment and procedures with resultant savings and profit.
2. Capitalize on benefits derived from standardization of basic routines, such as payroll, customer billing.

IV. GENERAL
1. Permit earlier development of young men and more appropriate placing of section and subsection level management due to elimination of product department boundaries. Also permit each function to be managed by the most highly skilled professional manager available.
2. Make possible faster and better decision making, oriented to overall customer and division requirements.
3. Increase the Division Manager's effectiveness by avoiding the time and effort required to integrate and counsel with regard to the programs for three separate product departments.
4. Facilitate integration with overseas subsidiaries — assistance required will be by function and will be more meaningful on division-wide functional basis, and much less costly.
5. Allow for a better organization to integrate total off-shore businesses, for example, export sales, Australia, and division-wide sourcing.
6. Eliminate job overlapping. Permit combining certain work elements to reduce expense.
7. Provide greater opportunity for more positive and direct teaching, advising and counseling on legal and patent matters relating to all functional areas.

. . . . .

Our position is unique in that we are now a world-wide integrated business, having recently received primary responsibility for overseas manufacturing and marketing. Moreover, in less than one year it is contemplated the entire distribution system could be radically altered. The proposed organization will help accomplish a more orderly transition, and materially aid in fulfilling the objectives listed above. It also will serve as a building block on which to grow dynamically in the highly competitive business climate forseeable in the years ahead.

We urgently request prompt approval of this recommended organizational structure.

The New Organization after September 1964

Corporate management accepted the recommendations contained in the memorandum, and the new organization was activated in September 1964. The new organization (Exhibit 2) was essentially functional with managers of marketing, finance, relations, production, advanced development,[9] business planning,[10] overseas housewares, and legal operations reporting to the Division General Manager, Mr. R. H. Gordon.

Between September 1964 and late 1966 only a few changes were made in HD's basic organization. In March 1965 General Electric acquired the Universal Manufacturing Company. Universal manufactured and marketed two major lines of portable appliances: (1) The Universal line, which was marketed under Fair Trade[11] on consignment, generally through department stores, and (2) Handy Hannah, a line of lower price portable appliances marketed primarily through drug stores. Universal's three factories were placed under the control of the HD Product Design and Production Operation. A separate Universal marketing organization was established (the Universal Marketing and Distribution Operation) at the same level as the already established marketing organization, now called the General Electric Marketing and Distribution Operation.

In January 1966 HD took over the housewares sales activities of the General Electric Supply Company, which distributed the products of several GE divisions, and established a separate unit called General Electric Distribution (GED) to handle this business. Within the Housewares Division GED was initially assigned to the General Electric Marketing and Distribution Op-

---

[9] The Advance Development Operation carried out research on technologies common to several product lines and on products that did not fit into an existing product line.

[10] The Business Planning Operation was headed by a longtime HD executive, with extensive experience in the control and financial areas. According to HD executives, this manager worked closely with the Division General Manager on special projects and problems of a general management nature.

[11] Many states permitted "Fair Trade agreements" between manufacturers and retailers. Such agreements provided that the products of a given manufacturer be sold by retailers at or above a specified list price.

eration, but was elevated to the General Manager's staff level within several months (see below).

Exhibit 5 is the organization chart of the Housewares Division in late 1966.

The General Electric Marketing and Distribution Operation

The Manager of the General Electric Marketing and Distribution Operation (GEMD), Mr. L. C. Davidson, directed the division's total marketing effort (except Universal and overseas sales). Each year, he presented a detailed sales forecast (by product and model) to Mr. Gordon.[12] When accepted (often with modification) by Mr. Gordon, this forecast became the GEMD sales target, which Mr. Davidson was responsible for meeting.

GEMD was divided into six sections: Sales, Advertising and Sales Promotion, Product Service, Industrial Design, Marketing Research, and Product Planning. (See Exhibit 6.)

Sales

The Sales Section sold all HD products,[13] whether to independent distributors, GED, or certain selected national or special accounts. The staff of the General Sales Manager of GEMD consisted of a Field Sales Manager, three Market Planning Managers, a Sales Administration Manager, three specialized sales managers (special accounts, timer and motor sales, and mail order distributor sales), and a manager of corporate buying office relations.

Market Planning: The market planning function was described by one executive as "the function which 'pushes' our products through distribution." As members of the Sales Section, the Market Planners developed sales promotions oriented primarily to distributors and retailers rather than consumers. Typical promotions featured quantity discounts, dating plans (i.e., "buy now, pay later"), and special incentives to distributor and retail sales personnel.

The three Market Planning Managers, who reported to the General Sales Manager of GEMD, handled home care and comfort products, clocks and personal care products, and portable appliances, respectively. Two Market Planners were under each Market Planning Manager. In the portable appliance group, for example, one Market Planner worked on coffee makers, food cookers, griddles, grills, kettles, knives, portable mixers, rotisseries, toasters, and warming trays. The other Market Planner worked on blenders, can openers, fire starters, irons, standard mixers, knife sharpeners, and skillets.

The Market Planners prepared marketing plans for their products, usually on a quarterly basis. The marketing plans did not follow a predetermined format, but generally included recommended price changes, planned new product introductions, planned closeouts, product "specials,"[14] and estimates of sales by product. These marketing plans were presented to the General Sales Manager of GEMD, the General Manager of GEMD, and the Division General Manager at separate meetings for approval.

The Market Planners received copies of production schedules, sales volume reports, and back-order position. As one Market Planner explained:

I worry about individual products. When I see something isn't coming off the line I try to influence production schedules. I am not allowed to go to the plant, but I do go to the Marketing Research Manager. I describe the problem, and get him to help me shift the schedule. He goes to the man in manufacturing who handles plant scheduling.

I also worry when sales start slowing down on an item. Then I might try to get Production to shut off the faucet.

In describing his function, another Market Planner explained:

I visualize this as a coordination job. We are the only ones with distribution experience. We are able to get the Product Planners, merchandising people, and advertising people together. We act as a catalyst. They look to us for experience, which is very much needed.

Most of the actual work is done by the staff marketing sections. The Advertising and Sales Promotion Section, for example, designs, prints, and distributes our spring and fall catalogues. I think it would be fair to say, however, that we influence every page of that catalogue. We

---

[12] The preparation of this sales forecast required approximately 10 man-months of work by marketing research personnel. The forecast itself took the form of a booklet containing more than 50 pages of detailed exhibits, including cost data received from the manufacturing plants.

[13] In 1966 the sales force for Universal products was placed under the Sales Section of GEMD. See p. 244 for a description of this development.

[14] A product "special" was typically a low-priced promotion, intended to move surplus inventory, take advantage of a competitive situation, or motivate the distributors to order a particular product line earlier than they otherwise would.

recommend prices and incentives, and even get into the details of presentation.

We also run the field sales meetings, presenting our programs to the field sales force. When a new product is to be introduced, it is our job to develop the complete program that will be used to sell it.

It would be fair, I think, to say that we are really product managers. While we are not responsible for profits, we are responsible for sales of the products assigned to us.

I believe that we should officially be designated product managers, and be given greater authority. It would make sense, for example, for product planning, manufacturing planning, engineering, and sales planning to report to us. These functions are organized on a product line basis anyway.

In a sense we would be like the old Department Managers, except that the field sales force and actual manufacturing facilities would not report to us. We are responsible for the total market planning job now; why not give us control of the resources we need to carry out our job?

At present, those of us at the working level, who are concerned with products, have to run around like crazy to put our complete program together.

The GEMD Manager claims that a functional organization works well — from his point of view. This may be true, but an awful lot of coordination is required at the working level. By the time he sees a program, the coordination job has been done. But blood, sweat, and tears have gone into putting that program together.

Field Sales: Prior to the 1964 reorganization, each department had had its own field sales force. Individual sales representatives had sold only those products manufactured by their department, and had received direction from their department's sales manager. In many cases, sales representatives from all three departments had called on the same accounts.

During this period several HD Regional Field Relations Managers had been responsible for assigned geographic territories. These Regional Field Relations Managers had confined their efforts largely to trade relations and had not exercised authority over the sales representatives.

At the time of the reorganization a new field sales organization was put into place. A Field Sales Manager was appointed, reporting to the General Sales Manager of GEMD. The United States was divided into nine geographic regions, each under a Regional Sales Manager reporting to the Field Sales Manager. All sales representatives were to sell all HD products and report to Regional Sales Managers. The new organizational approach was intended to provide better coordination and increased supervision at the field level, and to prevent several sales representatives from calling on the same account.

Within several months of the reorganization, it became apparent that the "full basket" [15] concept was not working out as planned. By early 1965 the sales force had returned to product specialization along the old departmental lines. The remaining significant change from the old organization was that they now reported to GEMD Regional Sales Managers, rather than to departmental sales executives.

According to HD executives, there were several reasons why the "full basket" concept had not worked. While some distributors had complained that they had to deal with too many salesmen under the old organization, there were more complaints about inadequate sales assistance under the new organization.

In particular, many distributors had explained that since their own salesmen carried the "full basket" (they could not afford product specialization), GEMD salesmen should have detailed knowledge of individual products and product features. One of the main functions of the GEMD sales force, these distributors believed, was to train distributor sales personnel. If the salesmen were not more specialized than distributor salesmen, there was relatively little they could offer in the way of assistance and training.

Equally important, the salesmen themselves did not like the new organization. As one salesman explained:

The basket was simply too full. It is impossible for one man to master such a wide range of products; you just don't sell clocks the way you do irons. There was too much; I could rarely get a distributor to give me enough time to go through my entire book.

Moreover, HD had franchised different distributors for its various product lines. Clock distributors were generally smaller and more numerous than portable appliance distributors, for example. As a result, GEMD sales representatives had to deal with a greater variety of distributors, and they complained that they had to work much harder to achieve a given level of sales.

The Boston Region: According to sales executives, the Boston Region was typical in most respects. The Boston Region covered all of New England plus upstate New York. Seven sales representatives reported

---

[15] A phrase used by the housewares industry to describe a salesman who sold a company's (or division's) full product line.

to the Regional Sales Manager. These sales representatives were assigned as follows:

Sales Representative	Assignment	
William Harris	Portable Appliances	— New England
John Dawson	Clocks, Personal Care, and Handy Hannah	— New England
Phillip James	Floor Care, Blankets, and Power Tools	— New England
Harold Williams	Universal[16]	— New England
Ray Lorring	Heaters and Fans	— New England and Upstate New York
	Blankets and Floor Care	— Upstate New York
Norman Smith	Portable Appliances and Power Tools	— Upstate New York
Ralph Markham	Clocks, Personal Care, and Handy Hannah	— Upstate New York

The Boston Regional Manager explained that his sales assignments were determined by a number of factors. Although geography was important, he had wanted Mr. Lorring to have some accounts in New England, since Mr. Lorring was a new man whom he wanted to supervise closely. He had assigned two men exclusively to portable appliances, because the training of distributor sales personnel (concerning product features and promotional tools) was particularly important in this area. Clocks, personal care products, and Handy Hannah products had been grouped together, since all required contacts with many small distributors, including drug wholesalers, who did not carry HD's other product lines. Where possible, he had placed heaters, electric blankets, and fans together, since these product lines tended to have counter-seasonal sales patterns.

Each Regional Sales Manager was assigned an annual sales budget, consisting of quarterly sales objectives for each product. The Regional Sales Managers divided this budget among the sales representatives in their regions. Individual salesmen's budgets were broken down by product, but they were paid commissions on percentage realization of their total budgets. These commissions varied from 1% of base salary at 62% budget realization to 40% of base salary at 130% budget realization. It should be noted that salesmen received commissions on sales *to* independent distributors and sales *by* GED. In other words, sales were applied to their quotas at the time goods were transferred from General Electric to an outside customer.

In late 1966 the Field Sales Manager was considering a new sales incentive plan. Under this plan, higher commissions would be paid on some products than on others. Such a plan could be used to emphasize the most profitable products. On the other hand, the greater complexity of the new plan might outweigh its supposed advantages, the Field Sales Manager believed.

Moreover, several executives believed that there was a basic conceptual defect in the incentive plan, and that this defect would not be corrected by increasingly complex refinements. According to these executives, it was not realistic to compensate a sales representative on the basis of sales in his territory, since HD advertising and promotions had at least as much effect on sales as the salesman's efforts did. These executives favored a different type of incentive plan, under which a sales representative would be compensated for the number of calls he made, his ability to service distributors, and his effectiveness in calling on retail accounts. While conceding that measurement of performance would be difficult under such a plan, these executives believed that this would be an appropriate task for the Regional Sales Managers.

The Field Sales Manager held a meeting with his Regional Sales Managers at least quarterly. These meetings covered a variety of topics and generally lasted three days. Exhibit 7 gives the agenda for a meeting held in October 1966.

The Regional Sales Managers sent Regional Activity Reports to the Field Sales Manager each month. These reports covered a wide range of subjects and were circulated among key executives at HD headquarters. Exhibit 8 is the report submitted by the new Cincinnati Regional Sales Manager in June 1966.

In commenting on the new organization, the Field Sales Manager expressed concern that the marketing function was becoming fragmented. Under the old organization, product planning, market planning, field sales, and advertising and merchandising had all reported to the Department Marketing Manager. All these functions were now part of GEMD, but there was little direct contact at the working level. As a result, communications tended to become formalized, which raised problems in interpretation and created significant delays.

Special Accounts: As described above, the Field

---

[16] Universal products were handled in upstate New York by a sales representative assigned to the New York Region. The Boston Regional Manager was responsible for Universal sales in upstate New York, however.

Sales Manager was responsible for sales by the field sales force to independent distributors and GED. The other sales managers were responsible respectively for timer and motor sales[17] (mainly to other General Electric divisions), mail order distributor sales, and sales to special accounts. This section of the case will describe the activities of the Manager-Special Accounts Sales, Mr. S. R. O'Neil.

HD used the term, "special accounts," to describe trading stamp companies, incentive plan companies, several large national distributors (mainly tire companies), and those companies (mainly banks) to which HD sold premium merchandise direct. Mr. O'Neil dealt with approximately 70 companies, of which 36 were trading stamp or incentive plan companies. These 36 companies represented over 90% of Mr. O'Neil's sales.

Mr. O'Neil's special accounts had several characteristics in common. For the most part, they merchandised their products through catalogues (Mr. O'Neil estimated that approximately 300 million incentive and premium catalogues were printed each year), and did not sell their products to the ultimate consumer for cash. According to Mr. O'Neil, the requirements of these special accounts differed markedly from those of HD's regular customers. For example, once a special account had printed its catalogue, it was "locked in" to a price and item for a full year. As a result HD had to guarantee the availability of those items that the special accounts agreed to carry. Moreover, it was often necessary to introduce new products to the special accounts prior to their national introduction, so that they could be photographed prior to the printing of a catalogue.

Appliance manufacturers competed intensely for space in the special accounts catalogues. Some manufacturers made special price concessions to obtain listings, but HD sold to special accounts at its standard distributor prices.

According to Mr. O'Neil, HD had had a Special Accounts Sales Manager for many years. When the premium and incentive companies first became important, it had been immediately apparent that they required service outside of regular selling channels. Even under the departmental organization structure, special accounts had been handled as a division-wide function. During that period, however, it had been necessary to obtain the concurrence of all three departments before a division-wide special accounts policy could be implemented. Under the new organization, according to Mr. O'Neil, it was much easier to respond to competitive moves and market conditions. One executive (the General Sales Manager of GEMD) was able to approve all plans, even if they cut across several product lines.

Advertising and Sales Promotion

The Advertising and Sales Promotion Section, which reported to the General Manager of GEMD, was divided into four subsections: Advertising, Merchandising (i.e., sales promotion), Visual Art Services, and Publicity.

The Advertising Subsection worked on both consumer and trade advertising in all media. At the time of the 1964 reorganization, HD had assigned all its advertising to one advertising agency, rather than using three agencies as it had under the old organization. The primary function of the Advertising Subsection was to work with this agency on advertising objectives, strategy, copy, and media plans.

Prior to 1966 a total advertising budget had been given to the agency (before 1964, to each agency). The agency had then allocated this budget among HD product lines, geographic areas, and types of media. Although HD had reviewed and sometimes changed the agency's recommendations, the basic proposal had historically come from the agency.

The 1967 advertising budget was being handled in a different way. The Advertising Subsection had made a careful study of the relative responsiveness to advertising of each of HD's product lines. It had found, for example, that fans were an impulse item ("When it gets hot, you run out and buy a fan"), which responded well to trade promotions ("Fans have to be on the shelf when it gets hot; the retail salesman has to have an incentive to sell our fan instead of someone else's") rather than consumer advertising.

The Advertising Subsection had also studied geographic and seasonal variances in advertising effectiveness for each product, identifying market areas where advertising had the most impact, and the months in which advertising would have the greatest effect on sales.

These data were used to prepare a detailed advertising budget, specifying the amount of money to be spent on each product in each market area each month. Of

---

[17] The factory in Ashland, Massachusetts, in addition to manufacturing clocks, also manufactured small electric motors (such as are used in clocks) and timing devices. These products were sold to other General Electric divisions (e.g., timers for automatic stoves and clock radios) and to outside manufacturers. In 1966 approximately 60% of timer and motor sales were made to other GE divisions, and 40% of sales were to outside manufacturers.

HD's 34 product lines, 7 were assigned high advertising budgets (as a percentage of sales), 5 were assigned medium advertising budgets, 9 were assigned low advertising budgets, and 8 were assigned no advertising budgets. Five product lines were split out as new products and assigned special advertising budgets. The criteria used in assigning advertising budgets are shown in Exhibit 9.

The new advertising budget was to be presented to Mr. Gordon, the Division General Manager. After his approval, it would be submitted to the advertising agency. The agency would then be expected to prepare its copy and media recommendations within the context of the advertising budget.

In commenting on this change, the Advertising and Sales Promotion Manager, Mr. P. Roudebush, explained that he expected some resistance from the Market Planners whose products would receive reduced advertising. Nevertheless, he was convinced that the new approach would significantly improve the effectiveness of HD's heavy expenditure on media advertising.[18]

The Merchandising Subsection developed trade and consumer promotions. Trade promotions included point-of-sale displays, merchandise catalogues, and a wide variety of incentives and contests aimed at independent distributors or their salesmen. These incentives ranged from special deals intended to increase distributor inventories ("buy" promotions) to incentives intended to obtain special efforts from distributors' salesmen ("sell" promotions). The Merchandising Subsection worked with the Market Planners in the Sales Section on those promotions, recommending approaches to meet specified marketing objectives. At the same time the Merchandising Subsection attempted to coordinate the various trade promotions, to ensure, for example, that several product lines were not offering incentives to the same salesmen at the same time.

Consumer promotions required a much heavier outlay of funds than trade promotions. They ranged from cash refunds on particular products during specified periods (e.g., "We will send you $2.00 if you purchase this GE steam iron") to premium promotions (e.g., "Four Freedom Prints with the purchase of any GE housewares product during July"). The Merchandising Subsection also worked closely with the Market Planners to coordinate and develop these promotions.

The Merchandising Subsection also handled the procurement and distribution of materials required for either type of promotion. Most art and design work was performed by the *Visual Art Services Subsection,* while fixtures and printed materials were produced by outside vendors.

The Publicity Subsection worked closely with the commercial and trade press. Press parties were given twice a year (prior to the spring and fall housewares shows), and various materials were given to leading editors and writers. These materials ranged from photographs and technical data on new products to suggested articles, radio interviews, etc. In addition, the Publicity Subsection sent out numerous press releases in the course of the year and worked closely with key editors, especially in the trade press.

In commenting on his organization, Mr. Roudebush pointed out that it worked closely with the Market Planners in the Sales Section. In general, the Market Planners were experts in distribution, while his section was most closely oriented to the consumer. Nevertheless, he thought that there might be some advantages (especially in communications) in combining the market planning and merchandising functions in a single section, since the work of these two groups (especially on trade promotions) was so closely related.

Industrial Design

The Industrial Design Section was responsible for the appearance-design of all HD products. Located in the Marketing and Distribution Operation, this section worked with engineers in the manufacturing plants to design the external cases for the products the engineers had developed. According to the General Manager of GEMD, centralizing appearance design in his operation had two advantages:

(1) It made available a pool of specialized talent, which would have been expensive to duplicate for each factory.
(2) To varying extents, it was now possible to achieve consistency in the "look" of HD products. This was particularly important as the division began to manufacture products in the same line in different factories.

Product Service

The Manager of the Product Service Section was Mr. M. H. Dolgin. His section operated 53 company-owned service centers and 5 spare parts distribution centers. In addition, it prepared parts lists, service manuals, repair techniques, and training programs, and was responsible for franchising and working with

---

[18] HD spent several million dollars on advertising annually, an amount greater than that spent by its competitors. HD had the largest advertising budget in the General Electric Company, even though other GE divisions had greater total sales.

167 independent franchised service stations. These independent service stations repaired products of other manufacturers, as well as those of General Electric. Between 1956 and 1966 HD opened 42 new company-owned service centers and franchised 58 new independent service centers.

Product service had been handled on a division-wide basis prior to the 1964 reorganization. According to Mr. Dolgin, the only major change in his function resulting from the reorganization was in the area of technical service. Previously each department had prepared its own parts lists, service manuals, and repair techniques. These functions were now performed for all products by a single subsection under Mr. Dolgin's direction. According to Mr. Dolgin, it was now possible to do a better job in these areas, since specialized talent was pooled in a single location and division-wide product service policies could be established. Moreover, a single unit could now handle all customer correspondence, and considerable savings could be realized through common purchasing of certain spare parts.

Besides operating the field service centers, and providing technical support to the field, the Product Service Section was responsible for establishing product service policies. For example, it was necessary to determine the length of the guarantee period for a product, whether the product should be replaced or repaired when brought to a service center, and how long to stock spare parts for a product. In establishing these policies, members of the Product Service Section worked closely with the product and market planners.

In discussing his function, Mr. Dolgin explained:

> We are really the ones in the middle. On the one hand, we represent the customer, trying to influence product design and development to insure that the product she buys requires as little service as possible. On the other hand, we *are* HD to many customers; our service centers are the only direct contact with HD most customers ever have. This job requires a certain kind of person; he must — really! — see both sides.

Marketing Research

The Marketing Research Section was headed by Mr. James Ross. It consisted of five subsections, three of which did marketing research on specific products.[19]

---

[19] Established products were assigned to these subsections in accordance with the old departmental breakdown, and new products were assigned on the basis of available skills and resources.

The other two subsections were responsible respectively for sales forecasting and production scheduling.

The Three Marketing Research Subsections made continual qualitative and quantitative surveys of the characteristics of the consumers of the products assigned to them. In essence, these surveys were intended to answer the questions: Who buys this product? Why does she (he) do so?

In addition, these subsections did marketing research on new products. Working closely with the Product Planning Section (see below), they assembled extensive data concerning such things as probable size of the market for the new product, consumer reactions to the new product, and the degree of market penetration HD could expect.

The Marketing Research Subsections used published sources, consumer panels, and field interviews in their work. To a considerable extent, outside agencies were used for field interviews and tabulating, although HD personnel drafted questionnaires, selected samples of respondents, and analyzed the data resulting from the interviews.

The Sales Forecasting Subsection used advanced mathematical techniques, computers, and other methods to arrive at forecasts of orders for each model in the HD line.

The Production Scheduling Subsection used these sales forecasts to place orders on the Product Design and Production Operation. Orders were placed one year in advance (broken down by month) and updated quarterly. Until early 1966 the Manager of the Production Scheduling Subsection had worked directly with the factories, recommending appropriate production levels for each product manufactured by a given factory. In arriving at his recommendations, he had taken into account forecast information received from the Overseas Housewares Department (exports), Product Service Section (spare parts), and Universal, as well as the GEMD forecast.

In January 1966 a production scheduling function was established in the Product Design and Production Operation. The new unit was to receive sales forecasts from each of the distribution channels (GEMD Sales, Export, GEMD Product Service, and Universal), and work with the plants to establish manufacturing schedules. The reasons for this change will be discussed below. As a result of the change, the Production Scheduling Subsection of the Marketing Research Section now submitted its forecasts to the Product Design and Production Operation, and was not directly involved in scheduling the plants.

Product Planning

The Product Planning Section was headed by Mr. T. C. Ardleigh. It was divided into five subsections: Home Economics,[20] Advanced Product Planning,[21] and three subsections concerned with product planning *per se*. These latter three subsections were each assigned several manufacturing plants and worked on products manufactured (or to be manufactured) by the plants assigned to them. According to Mr. Ardleigh, he had assigned his personnel to plants rather than, for example, product categories, in order to reduce travel time (Product Planners visited plant engineering departments regularly). In practice, plant assignments generally coincided with the old department breakdowns, and a Product Planner typically worked on the same products that he had under the old organization.

The job of the Product Planner was to do whatever was necessary to insure that the products assigned to him were as fully competitive as possible. He was to review competitive products, technological developments, marketing research findings, and salesmen's reports in an effort to identify requirements for change. In many cases the appropriate change was only a modification in color or style; in other cases a completely new product might be developed to replace one or more existing products.

When a new product or product modification had been approved (see below), the Product Planner acted as a coordinator. He established schedules, wrote specifications, set up meetings, and, in general, did all that he could to insure that the new product or product modifications would be ready on time and would meet the requirements of the marketplace. In describing the role of the Product Planner, most GEMD executives used terms like "coordinator" or "liaison." Most Product Planners seemed to prefer the term "catalyst," however.

HD used an elaborate procedure to screen and approve proposals for new products and product modifications (the same procedure was used for all changes, whether a simple change in color or an entirely new product). According to Mr. Ardleigh, this procedure had been used by the old product departments and was not attributable to the new organization. The only major difference under the new organization was that all new product ideas (regardless of type of product) were placed in "one pot" and measured against each other.

Ideas for new products and product modifications were collected by the Product Planning Section. These ideas came from a variety of sources, as shown in the following table:

Sources of Product Ideas (1966)

Source	Number of Ideas Submitted
Outside the General Electric Company	194
Other General Electric divisions	45
HD plant personnel	591
HD headquarters and field sales personnel	28
HD Advance Development Operation	192
Total ideas submitted	1,050

The Product Planning Section presented these ideas to the HD Advance Product Evaluation Council (APEC), which met approximately once a month. APEC consisted of representatives from product planning, marketing research, home economics, and other functions as required.

APEC considered each idea and determined whether it was a "good idea possibility." Good idea possibilities were transmitted to the various functional departments, which carried out their own appraisals. These appraisals were then submitted to the Advance Product Development Council (APDC), which had the same membership as APEC. APDC screened the ideas once more (using the appraisals received from the functional departments), and determined whether they should be rejected or submitted to the Product Programming Council (PPC).

The Product Programming Council consisted of the managers of GEMD, Financial and Commercial Services, Product Design and Production, and Advance Development. PPC reviewed APDC's recommendations, and determined whether each project should be rejected, accepted, or sent back to the functional departments for further study. An "accepted" idea was then submitted to the Division Product Review Council, which consisted of the same membership as the PPC plus the Division General Manager. The Division

---

[20] The home economists tested HD and competitive products, wrote instructions and recipe books, and provided a feminine point of view on many product matters. They were part of the Product Planning Section because, as one executive explained, there was nowhere else to put them.

[21] The Advanced Product Planning Subsection worked on proposals for new products that were not part of existing HD product lines. Much of its work was in the areas of economic and business analysis, rather than product planning *per se*. This function had not existed under the old departmental organization.

Product Review Council decided whether or not to go ahead with the new development, and assigned responsibility for design and production to one of HD's plants or, in a few cases, to an outside source. (See exhibit 10 for a product planning flow chart.)

In practice, most screening took place at the APEC level. Mr. Ardleigh estimated that out of 1,050 ideas, only 100 would be approved by APEC. Of these, perhaps 90 would be approved by APDC, 85 by PPC, and 84 by the Division Product Review Council.

In theory, all product line modifications or additions had to go through this entire procedure, which required between nine months and three years for completion. In practice, the procedure was rarely followed exactly ("four times in two years") because, as Mr. Ardleigh explained, "no two products are alike." Where a simple change (such as a change in color) was involved, a decision could be reached in less than a week. In many cases, proposals were "walked through" the various sections, rather than dealt with at formal meetings.

Nevertheless, there was a widespread feeling in HD that product development took too long, and many executives attributed long lead times to the new organization and overly formalized product planning procedures. Mr. Ardleigh disagreed with these contentions, pointing out that the new organization had coincided in time with the shift to a "war economy" in the United States, and that delays were attributable mainly to shortages of engineers, draftsmen, tooling capacity, and materials. Moreover, HD's record of 90% successful new product introductions (well above the industry average) was largely the result of elaborate review procedures, Mr. Ardleigh believed.

The Product Planner assigned to clocks[22] had a somewhat different point of view. As he explained:

Under the old organization, each department was headed by a closely knit management team. I was on the General Manager's staff, and knew what was going on at all times. Now, I frequently don't know why a decision has been made, or — worse — even that it has been made at all.

For example, we recently worked several months on a new product for introduction in 1967. Somewhere along the line a meeting was held, and it was decided to delay introduction for budgetary reasons. Nobody bothered to tell me, and I continued to push my people to meet the schedule. Finally, I checked the project's status, and found that the schedule had been changed. Under the old organization, I would have been at the meeting where the decision was made.

Moreover, it now takes an extraordinary amount of time to get a decision. Before we can go ahead with a new project, we have to have the General Manager's approval. Before we can even see the General Manager, we must first have meetings with the Product Planning Manager and the Product Programming Council. On something as simple as changing the plate on an iron to read "Permanent Press" instead of "wash and wear" it can take a month or more.

Under the old setup I would come up with a proposal for a new product. I would arrive at the office at 8:30 and call my boss (the Department Marketing Manager). I would ask if I could see him for a few minutes, and he generally said, "Yes." We discussed the idea, and if he liked it, we walked down the hall to the General Manager's office. It was not uncommon to have a decision by 10:00 o'clock.

The old Department General Managers really knew the products in their departments. It is impossible for the men at the top now to have that kind of knowledge concerning the division's 568 products. In the old Clocks and Personal Care Department, clocks were as important to the General Manager as they were to me. He knew how much money he had available for tooling (or advertising) and how much we could spend for clocks. Now, clocks have to compete for funds with every one of the Division's other products. If a new product needs funds, we get that much less advertising or have that many fewer clock models.

The GEMD Manager

In early 1967 Mr. Davidson commented on his Marketing and Distribution Operation as follows:

I realize that our organization is confusing to an outsider, particularly in the product planning area. As I see it, the Product Planners are essentially responsible for collecting information from the various functions, putting it together into a program, and establishing schedules so that all the elements which go into a new product are ready when they should be.

Naturally, the Product Planners aften have ideas of their own, and do influence the functional inputs to their plans, which is fine. But there is a tendency for them to think that they do the whole job, that the other sections do only what they tell them.

You have to divide a business somehow. I have divided GEMD on a functional basis: Product Planning is responsible for the product lines; Market Planning for moving the goods and distribution; Advertising for cre-

---

[22] This particular Product Planner had spent most of his business career working for the Telechron Clock Company, which had been acquired by GE in the 1930s but had not been consolidated with other GE activities until the late 1950s. Several HD executives expressed the opinion that this experience may have influenced his views concerning the new organization.

ating demand; Sales for calling on customers. Marketing Research is a resource function, giving information to the other functions and helping me with my forecasts.

Naturally there are other possibilities. Merchandising could be combined with Market Planning (rather than Advertising), but we would have to split an already small group into three pieces and lose much of our professional direction. I have thought of combining product and market planning, but Market Planners and Product Planners are different types of people; neither group could work for the other.

An organization such as ours is bound to cause conflict. There is some tendency for each group to want to take over other groups' functions, on the grounds that it knows all that there is to know. I don't agree with this approach. The Market Planners, with their distribution experience, know more about how to move products than the Product Planners ever will; and the Product Planners know more about what the products should be, in the future, than the Market Planners, who are oriented to immediate problems rather than long-range consumer needs.

The Product Design and Production Operation

The Manager of the Product Design and Production Operation, Mr. E. R. Jackson, reported to the Division General Manager, Mr. Gordon. The 1964 reorganization assigned to this operation the seven plants that previously had been divided among the three old product departments. Where previously each plant had had a Production Manager and an Engineering Manager, both of whom reported to the Department General Manager, each plant was now placed under a single Plant Manager, responsible for both engineering and manufacturing. When Universal was acquired, its two plants were assigned to the Product Design and Production Operation as well.

According to Mr. Jackson, the new organization was a significant improvement over the old. Having a single Plant Manager forced conflicts between engineering and manufacturing (e.g., "You made it wrong"; "No, you designed it wrong") to be resolved at the plant level. More important, it was now possible to allocate production among the plants on the basis of available capacities and skills, rather than departmental assignments.

According to Mr. Jackson, the new organization also had advantages in the area of product development. Where previously each department could develop only the products it could afford, new product decisions were now made for the division as a whole. Moreover, development work could be assigned to any plant, on the basis of available skills and resources, regardless of its present manufacturing assignment.

Another executive suggested, however, that the new organization had certain disadvantages in the area of product development. Under the old organization, development engineers in the plants were in close contact with departmental marketing personnel. As a result, they were closely "tuned in" to the market and were motivated to suggest new product ideas of their own. Under the new organization, the development engineers in the plants had little contact with Marketing (except through the Product Planning Section) and were beginning to view their job as working on projects assigned to them, rather than originating ideas of their own.

Production schedules were established by an executive reporting to Mr. Jackson. He received sales forecasts from each of the selling units (GEMD, Universal, Product Service, and Export) quarterly. These forecasts specified the quantity of each model or item that the unit expected to sell during each month of the following year. These forecasts were then consolidated and used to develop detailed manufacturing schedules.

Until early 1967 this function had been performed by an executive in the Marketing Research Section. According to manufacturing executives, the change had taken place for two major reasons:

(1) Marketing personnel had tended to "play it safe" by underestimating demand during the first half of the year, in the expectation that manufacturing "could always produce more if necessary." Manufacturing personnel had conducted several studies (based on historical data) to demonstrate the implications of this tendency for manufacturing costs and stock-outs. These studies had apparently carried considerable weight with the General Manager in his decision to transfer responsibility for production scheduling from GEMD to the Product Design and Production Operation.

(2) Universal, Product Service, and Overseas Housewares executives had preferred to submit their requirements to a "neutral" body, rather than one oriented toward a particular channel of distribution.

Universal Manufacturing Company

General Electric purchased the Universal Manufacturing Company in March 1965. Universal had marketed two major lines of products: (1) Universal portable appliances, which had been sold on consignment directly to retailers who sold them on a price-maintained basis, and (2) Handy Hannah portable appliances, which had been sold to retail drug stores through independent drug wholesalers.

Both product lines were believed to be complementary to HD's product lines. HD had gone off Fair Trade[23] in 1958, and was presently obtaining a large share of its volume from mass merchandisers, who sold HD products for prices below list price. In order to be able to sell at discount prices, the mass merchandisers accepted margins considerably below the standard 40% retail markup. As a result, department stores and other nondiscount merchandisers had to settle for reduced margins on HD products (which were readily identifiable and heavily advertised by the mass merchandisers). Although most major department stores carried HD products, there was a strong tendency for them to feature competitive brands, which were not sold by the mass merchandisers and thus offered higher margins. HD planned to use the Universal brand for a line of price-maintained portable appliances, which these retailers could sell at their standard markups.

The Handy Hannah brand provided a similar opportunity. Drug stores had traditionally been excellent outlets for inexpensive portable appliances, but HD had historically found it difficult to serve this market. Because individual drug stores could sell only a relatively small number of a given product, it had been customary to sell them (and the drug wholesalers who supplied them) combination packages consisting, for example, of three irons, two toasters, two coffee makers, and three skillets. HD, with its orientation toward large shipments of a single item (and volume discounts), had for the most part been unable to compete effectively in this market. Universal had had considerable success in this market with its Handy Hannah brand. HD planned to continue the distribution of Handy Hannah appliances through drug wholesalers and thus gain an entree into the lucrative drug store market.

After the acquisition, a separate Universal Marketing and Distribution Operation was established. Universal's three manufacturing plants were assigned to the Product Design and Production Operation. The manager of the Universal Marketing and Distribution Operation, Mr. A. A. Paulson, reported directly to Mr. Gordon.

Mr. Paulson supervised a staff responsible for such functions as product planning, market planning, marketing research, advertising, promotion, and field sales. In essence, his organization was the counterpart of Mr. Davidson's General Electric Marketing and Distribution Operation, except that it was much smaller and occasionally purchased services from the larger operation.

At first the Universal Marketing and Distribution Operation had had its own field sales force, which had reported to the Universal Field Sales Manager. This field sales force (most of whom had worked for the Universal Manufacturing Company) had been responsible for franchising retailers to handle the Universal line and drug wholesalers to handle the Handy Hannah line. Products in both lines were shipped directly to franchised retailers or drug wholesalers, without passing through GED or independent distributors.

It soon became apparent that the 11 Universal salesmen could not carry out the large assignment of franchising 2,000 accounts by 1967. To ease their work load, GED was given responsibility for servicing retail customers after they had been franchised by the Universal sales force. Universal customers would continue to order merchandise directly from HD (rather than GED), but GED would track down late shipments, accept returns of damaged merchandise, etc.

Several months later GED was given responsibility for calling on Universal accounts (to show merchandise and take orders). As the number of Universal franchises had increased, it had become obvious that the 11-man Universal sales force could not both set up new franchises and call on existing customers. Although Universal products would not technically move through GED distribution (Universal would maintain its own warehouses; GED would earn a commission rather than a markup), GED salesmen were expected to call on Universal customers in much the same way as they did their other retail accounts. The Universal sales force would, however, retain full responsibility for setting up franchises.

This change in responsibility caused some difficulty at the field level. In a given city, GED historically had not called on accounts serviced by independent distributors. In many cases, however, retailers franchised by Universal also purchased HD products from independent distributors. In calling on these retailers GED seemed, to some independent distributors, to be trying to steal their retail accounts.

While this was occurring, a change was made in the reporting channel of the Universal sales force. In order to achieve better administrative control and improved coordination in the field, the Universal sales force was placed under the GEMD Regional Sales Managers. Universal salesmen continued to report through the Regional Sales Managers to the Universal Field Sales

---

[23] See footnote 11.

Manager, however. The Universal Field Sales Manager, for example, approved all new franchises.

By October 1966 the independent distributors had apparently come to accept the fact that GED salesmen would sell Universal products to their customers, largely because GED salesmen had scrupulously avoided trying to sell General Electric products to these customers.

General Electric Distribution Company (GED)

Prior to January 1966 the General Electric Supply Company served as a distributor of HD products. The General Electric Supply Company (GESCO) was a company-owned distributor of housewares, radios, and electrical apparatus. GESCO functioned in much the same way as an independent distributor, having, for example, its own warehouses and field sales force. GESCO was headed by a Vice President, who reported to the same Group Executive as Mr. Gordon did.

During 1965 it was decided to split GESCO into three units, responsible respectively for HD products, radios, and electrical apparatus. The units responsible for HD products and radios would continue to share warehouse facilities and, temporarily, certain sales personnel, but each would have its own management structure and be part of the division that manufactured its products.

The part of GESCO assigned to HD was renamed the General Electric Distribution Company (GED). Its manager, Mr. P. J. Wilkinson, at first reported to Mr. Davidson, the manager of General Electric Marketing and Distribution. It soon became apparent that GED's management requirements differed significantly from Mr. Davidson's other responsibilities. Moreover, having GED report to Mr. Davidson seemed incompatible with HD's policy of dealing with GED at "arm's length." Consequently, GED was soon removed from Mr. Davidson's jurisdiction and placed under the direction of Mr. Gordon, the HD General Manager.

GED was organized in five zones, each having between four and seven sales districts. The Zone Managers reported to Mr. Wilkinson, as did staff members of distribution planning, merchandising, and national retail accounts.

Each district had eight to eleven salesmen, who called on retail accounts in much the same way as independent distributor salesmen did. These salesmen operated under the "full basket" concept, selling GED's full line of products. According to Mr. Wilkinson, geographic considerations prevented specialization of GED salesmen by product lines.[24] Selling to retailers required intensive coverage of a relatively small geographic territory. If a salesman handled only certain product lines, his territory would have to be enlarged to maintain his sales performance. In certain metropolitan markets this problem did not exist, and GED was planning to experiment with specialized salesmen in the near future.

GED districts were called on by salesmen in the GEMD field sales organization. According to Mr. Wilkinson, these calls were not really necessary, since GED personnel were as proficient at interpreting product "programming" as the salesmen were. Having GEMD salesmen present product "programming" to the GED sales force did have some advantages, however. For example, it was not necessary to have as many sales meetings as would have been required if GEMD salesmen did not call on GED districts.

---

[24] Mr. Davidson believed that industry practices were an equally important factor. Most distributors were relatively small and carried literally thousands of different items. Retailers had become accustomed to working with such distributors, who could not afford to specialize.

246 *Cases and Commentaries*

Exhibit 1. Organization Chart Before Reorganization in 1964

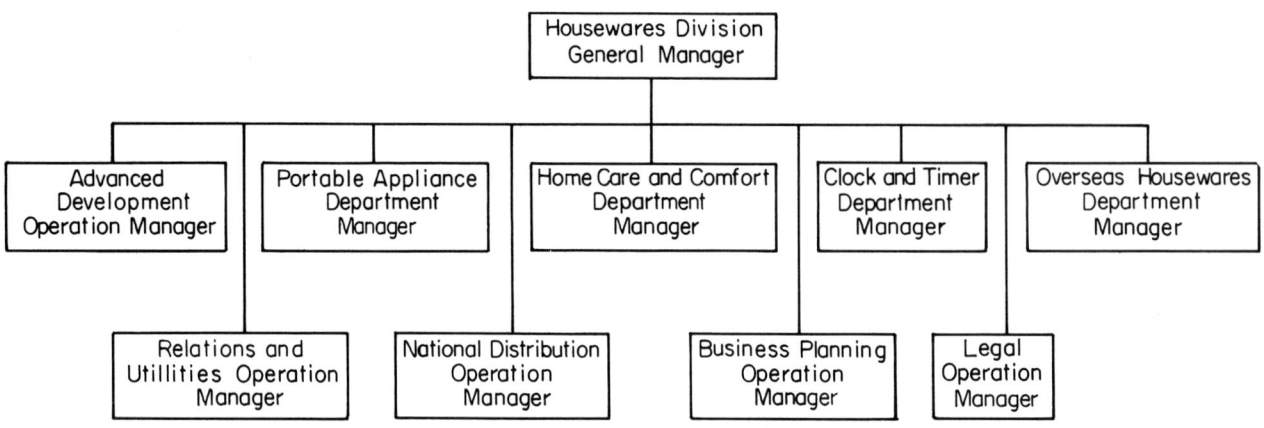

Exhibit 2. Organization Chart After Reorganization in 1964

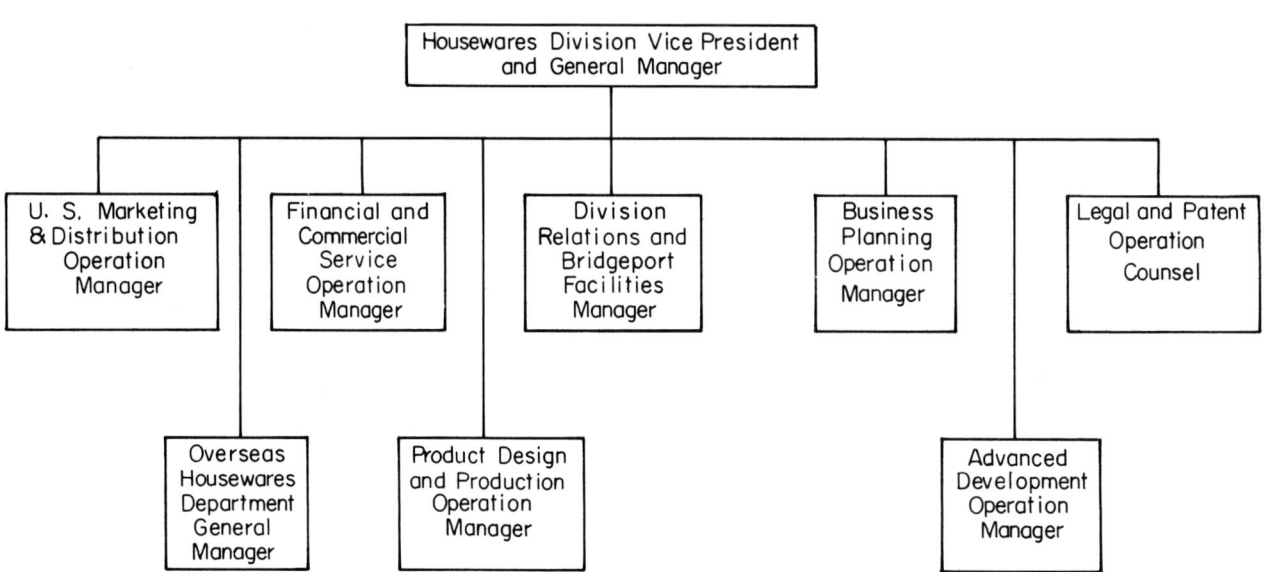

Exhibit 3. Organization Chart of Portable Appliance Department Before Reorganization in 1964

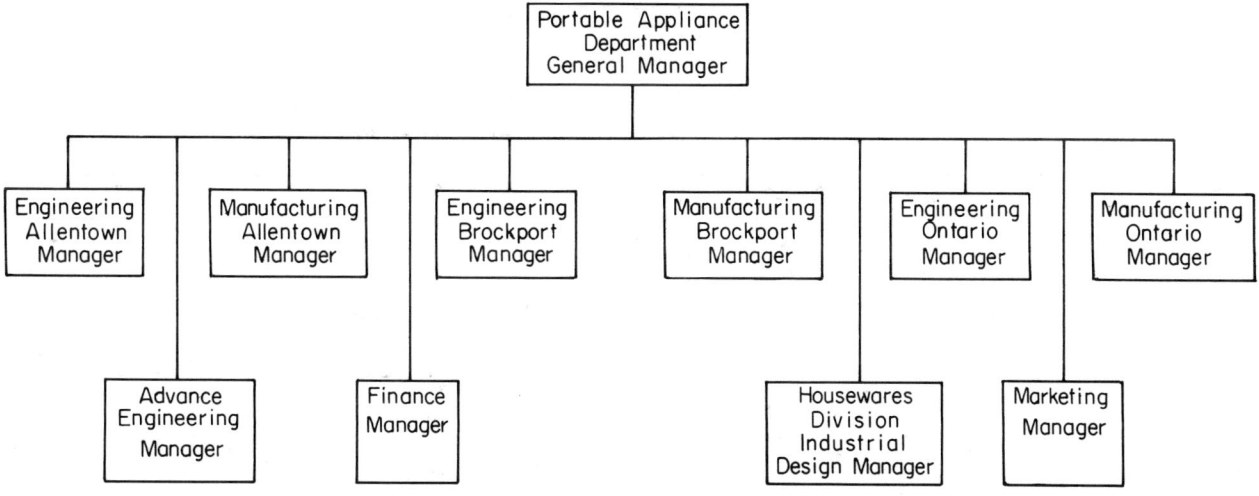

Exhibit 4. Organization Chart of Marketing Section of Portable Appliance Department Before Reorganization in 1964

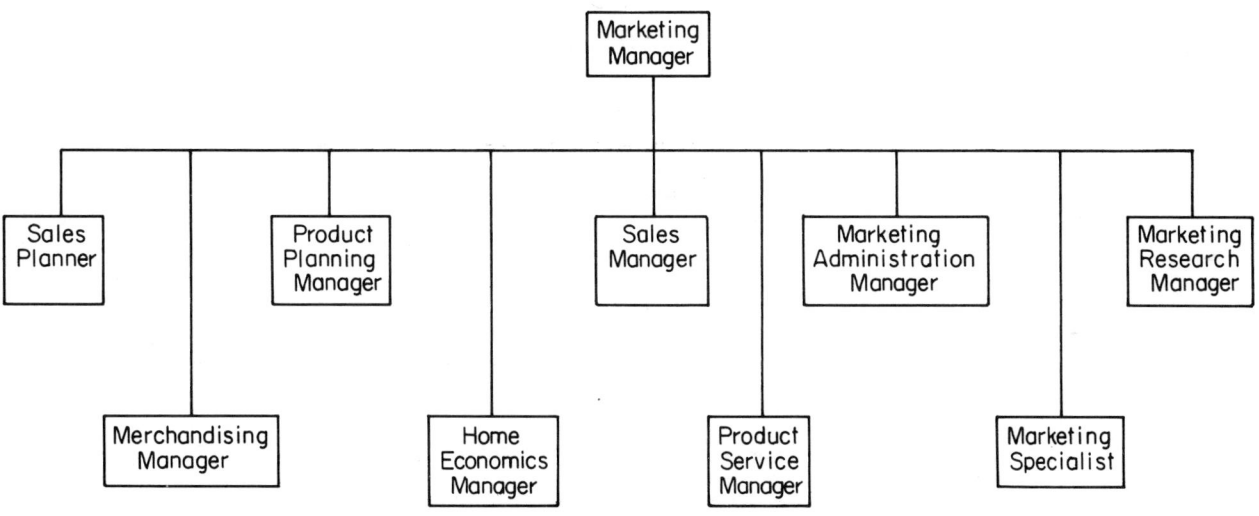

248 *Cases and Commentaries*

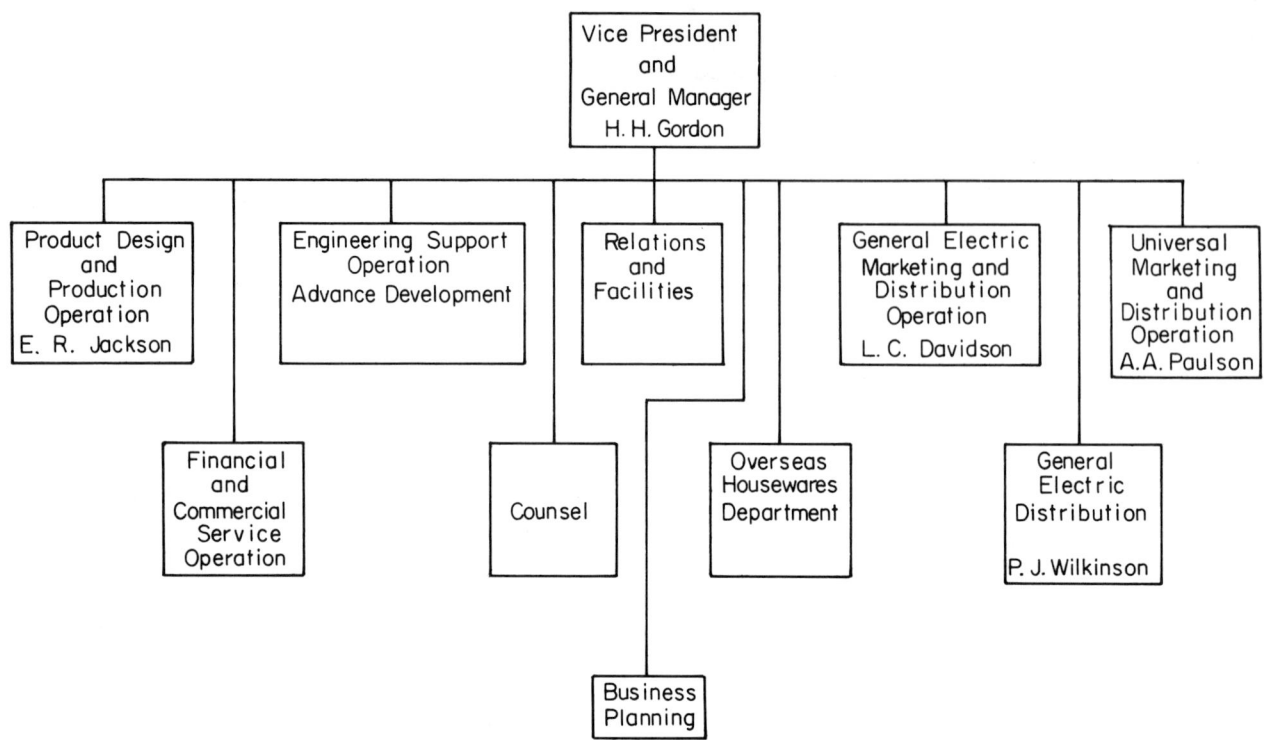

Exhibit 5. Organization Chart in Late 1966

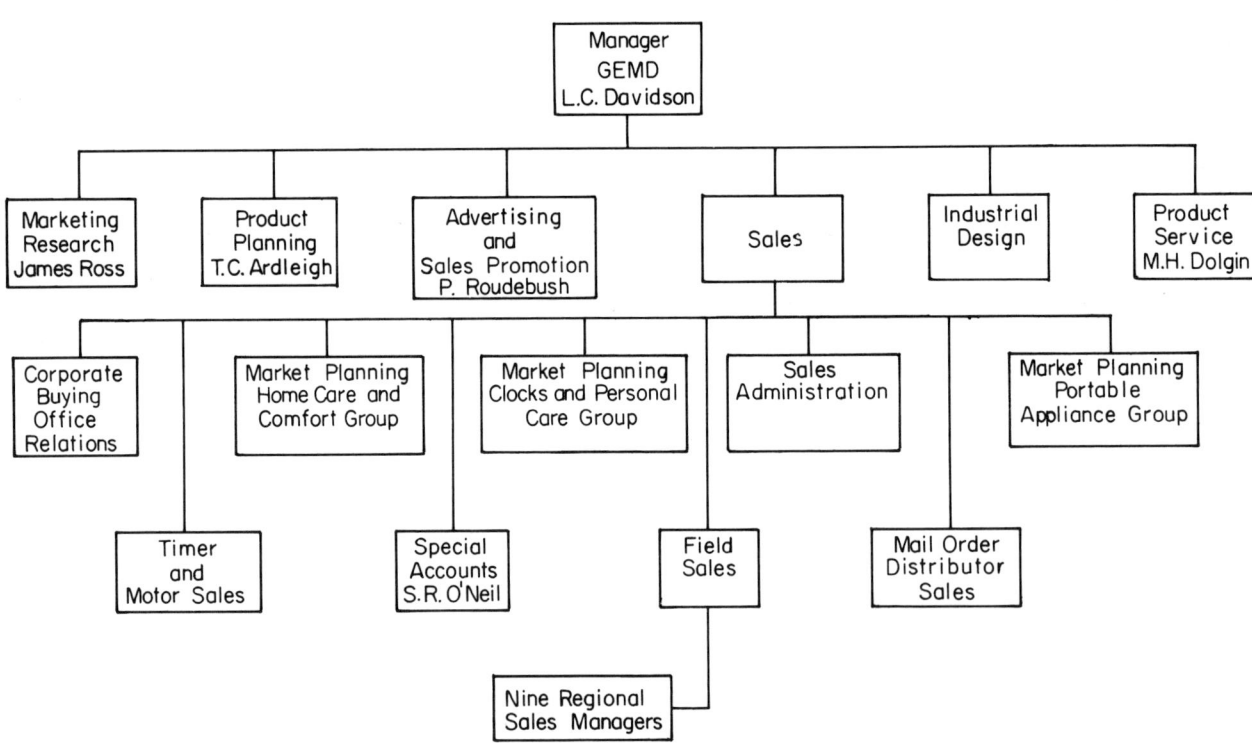

Exhibit 6. Organization Chart of GEMD in Late 1966

Exhibit 7. Agenda of Regional Managers Conference

DATE	TIME		LOCATION	SUBJECT
10/17	Monday	—	Bpt. Regional Mgrs. Arrive	
	Monday	1:30 PM	Conference Room 23D	*1966 Performance*
				a. Factory Sales & Sales Objectives 1966–1967 & Product Availability
				b. Distributor Sales
				c. Retail Sales
				1967 Manpower Review
				a. Territories
				b. Field Trainee Program
				c. Headquarters Trainee Program
				d. Personnel Improvement Program
				e. District Representative Review
				f. Regional Mgr. Objectives for 1967
				Universal Progress
				Handy Hannah Progress
				Distribution Requirements
				1967 Sales Office Expense
		4:15 PM		*Advance Information & Competitive Information*
		4:30 PM		*Commercial Service*
		5:00 PM		*Finance*
		5:30 PM		*December 5 Regional Sales Meeting*
		6:30 PM	Manero's Rest. — Dinner	
10/18	Tuesday	8:00 AM	Conference Room 23D	*Universal*
		9:00 AM		*Handy Hannah*
		9:30 AM		*Advertising/Merchandising*
		10:30 AM		*1967 Program Recommendations*
		12:30 PM	Fairway — Lunch	
		2:30 PM	Patterson Club	*GED Business Review*
		5:30 PM	Patterson Club — Dinner	
10/19	Wed.	8:30 AM	Conference Room 23D	*HC & CP Market Planning*
		9:30 AM		*Portable Appliance Market Planning*
		10:30 AM		*Clock & Personal Care Market Planning*
		11:30 AM		*Discussion*
		12:00 Noon		*Discussion*
		12:30 PM		*Discussion*
		1:00 PM		*Individual Conference & Departure*

Exhibit 8. Example of a Regional Manager's Activity Report, Cincinnati, July 1, 1966

Subject: *REGIONAL ACTIVITY REPORT — MONTH OF JUNE 1966*

Wholesalers, without exception, agree our programming is complete, hard-hitting, and should be very effective.

Retailers have a difficulty in conceiving the entire program, but there is so much available that they quickly land on several promotional activities. Follow-up contacts will result in getting retailers more involved in our complete market program.

NEW PRODUCT DEALER REACTION

The SV1 appears to have tremendous acceptance. All dealer reaction has been great. The full lineup of cleaners seems right with the price "step-up" story. We still need a good horsepower story. Even the female clerks ask about horsepower.

The percolator lineup is receiving excellent dealer reaction. This is especially true of the P12. Now we must deliver these in quantity if we want to keep ahead of competition. The P14 and P15 allocations appear meager. The Eternalum Percolators are considered nice, but no great volume builders. Dealers were generally less enthusiastic about this item than they were about any other.

The Mini-Basket should be a real "sales closer." Everyone thinks it's great and that it will supply the undecided consumer with the incentive to buy General Electric. The phrase "Mini-Basket" has been very quick to catch on and capture the imagination.

The FC1 Food Cooker: Dealer comments run the full spectrum from "great" to "gimmick." There is no doubt of the necessity for the demonstrational activities that we are planning in connection with this item. Television commercials should also feature demonstrations on the use of this product. We want early demonstrations, of course, but we should consider extending the demonstration activity date through December 25.

The new handle concept on our knives has been very well received. Knives in general appear slow at this time of the year and dealers are waiting for Fall before setting up promotions. Apparently, we are not out of the woods yet on the EK1 and EK2 problem. Distributor inventories have been cut in half in the last 30 days, but there are quite a few of these on hand at the retail level. The knife display is very well liked.

Our F91WT has been well received by dealers, but there was some concern about possible consumer reaction, the feeling being that the consumer today is well oriented to look for good steam patterns, regardless of the number of holes in an iron. Nevertheless, dealers were enthused. This iron is presently being stocked by dealers in addition to the balance of the line and represents a plus to us now, but it might hurt the sale of the F81T later this year when it gets in free supply. Dealers were unanimous in their acclaim of the iron display.

Reaction was skimpy concerning our new Electric Lighter line and our Manicure Set, primarily due to the lack of samples. I don't think this is a disadvantage since these products lend themselves to being carried by distributor salesman, and we will have an opportunity for specialized presentations.

Dealers in general like the total clock program. The Golden Series Display Deal is moving very well. Some comments were made to the effect that proper advertising on our Smokey-the-Bear Clock can focus consumer attention on the whole General Electric clock line.

Hair Dryers appear headed for another good season. The soft-bonnet type are being packed at a good pace for this Fall and dealers appear to be looking for specials to use in their ads. So far we have been pushing the HD50 because we had some small inventories, and our allocation on the HD51 and HD52 appears to be small. At this early stage, judging from dealer reactions, it would appear that the HD52 will be four or five to one over the HD51. From the looks of the allocation on these items, they were not forecast in this proportion.

The toothbrush line appears very complete. The display complete with replacement brushes appears to be just what the doctor ordered. Now that we say "take your choice," the general opinion is that our volume will come from the up-and-down action toothbrush. Dealers express the opinion that the Crest tie-in should attract excellent consumer attention.

On the flashlight we encountered more low-price competition than we expected. General opinion is that this is the first rechargeable flashlight to look like a flashlight, but it must get below ten dollars to move off the dealer's shelf.

Lots of "oh's" and "ah's" for the Christmas Tree, but sales have been modest. As of now, we should sell our quota, but no big demand for additional units is anticipated. The Tree, properly displayed on the Christmas Tree Stand, is helping the early sale of the Christmas Tree Stands.

COMPETITIVE FACTORS

The [Company A] program of no dealer co-op appears to be very well liked by distributor *management*, but there it stops. The distributor salesmen, the buyer in the store, and the store merchandise managers are not at all pleased with this type of programming. Usually a buyer has a responsibility to fill an ad or section in the paper with items tying in with a store activity, and it is the buyer's responsibility to literally sell this space to participating manufacturers. As a matter of fact, this sometimes takes precedence with certain buyers over the need to make a "good buy." Buyers have a tendency to buy items and run ads. They can't do this with [Company A]. I think this program is going to come home to roost for [Company A] in the months just ahead.

Exhibit 8 (continued).

COMPETIVE FACTORS (cont'd)

[Company B] appears to be beefing up their manpower and moving into more and more specialization in the marketplace. They have added several product specialists in the major cities within this region within the last few months. There is talk in the trade about a very heavy demonstration program for the Christmas holiday period, but I do not have the specifics on this activity at present.

Our Handy Hannah program looks great. It has been very well accepted and every drug wholesaler has indicated that this is exactly the type of programming that they want. We are geared up to work every individual drug wholesaler show to be run within this region, and I am very optimistic about the impact that we should make in the drug trade by the time these wholesalers' shows are over.

GENERAL COMMENTS

There has been no bad reaction to the fact that the GED organization is servicing Universal franchised retailers. As a matter of fact, I noted a definite attitude from the independent distributors of "Who cares?"

I am concerned that our full-bag concept of selling merchandise doesn't give us the flexibility and the speed to set the pace in the marketplace. I am firmly convinced that specialization by product line is a necessity if we are to continue forcing the pace.

There appears to be a buildup of retail demonstrational activities on the part of our major competitors to be used during the Christmas holiday period. It is my opinion that we should establish a key market holiday period demonstrational program of our own, and that we should put this into place as early as possible in order to secure competent demonstrational help, which should be at a premium this Fall. From my close work at the retail level last Fall with the Universal program, where we went all out with demonstrators, I observed their ability to *sell and switch* consumers during the last three feet of the sale, and I am very concerned that we must take an aggressive approach to retail demonstrations this Fall.

Our men have been working dealer shows practically every day, in addition to presenting our Fall programs and soliciting orders. We are going to have to shift gears in the next couple of weeks to start concentrating our efforts on retail calls and specialized sales meetings on specific product lines, and this should give us an opportunity to expose some of the new items as samples become available.

This has been an interesting month — attempting to get established here in a new area, digesting the new programs, picking up background on old programs still effective, meeting wholesale and retail customers, learning my way around the marketplaces, working some dealer shows, buying a new home, relocating my family, and establishing a regional office. I wish I could say all of these things have been accomplished, but I can say they are all being worked on.

Very truly yours,

Exhibit 9. Proposed Product Advertising Strategy

A. *Current Line Products*

1. *High Budget*

   Increase market share and maximize profits by concentrating advertising dollars on those products which are characterized by:
   a) High volume
   b) High profit
   c) High growth and/or profit potential
   d) Pull-thru characteristics
   e) Demonstrably different and/or exclusive features

2. *Medium Budget*

   Same as above but at lower level

3. *Minimum Budget*

   Provide support, primarily for broad range gift offerings, on products which are characterized by:
   a) Low volume
   b) Low profit range
   c) Limited growth and/or profit potential
   d) Push-thru characteristics

4. *No Budget*

   These products are characterized by:
   a) Low and/or declining value
   b) Low profit or loss
   c) Push-thru characteristics
   d) No demonstrably different features

B. *New Products*

Establish sizable market share quickly and build dealer support by expending abnormally high A/S % on those new products which have high growth and profit potential.

TIMING STRATEGY

1. COINCIDE TIMING AND WEIGHT OF ADVERTISING EXPENDITURES WITH RETAIL SALES RATES
   a) Budget approximately 60% of overall advertising dollars in second half, 40% in first half
   b) Place extra advertising weight against products with unique features
   c) Budget heavy expenditures for gift periods — especially Mother's Day and Christmas

2. SCHEDULE NATIONAL ADS FOR NEW PRODUCTS *ONLY* WHEN FACTORY STOCKS ADEQUATE TO HANDLE ANTICIPATED CONSUMER DEMAND

3. REVISE SCHEDULE PERIODICALLY TO CANCEL ADS FOR PRODUCTS IN SHORT SUPPLY, INCREASE ADVERTISING ON PRODUCTS IN HIGH INVENTORY POSITION

MAJOR MARKET STRATEGY

1. *PROVIDE EXTRA ADVERTISING SUPPORT IN MAJOR MARKETS*
   a) Top 25 markets account for 45% of retail sales
   b) Mass merchants and department stores concentrated in major markets
      1) Account for 35% of our sales
      2) Have poor retail sales personnel
   c) Retailers expect manufacturers to pre-sell

2. *INTRODUCE NEW PRODUCTS*
   a) Gain dealer support
   b) Obtain shelf space fast
   c) Build consumer support fast

General Electric: Housewares Division 253

Exhibit 10. Product Planning and Development Flow Chart

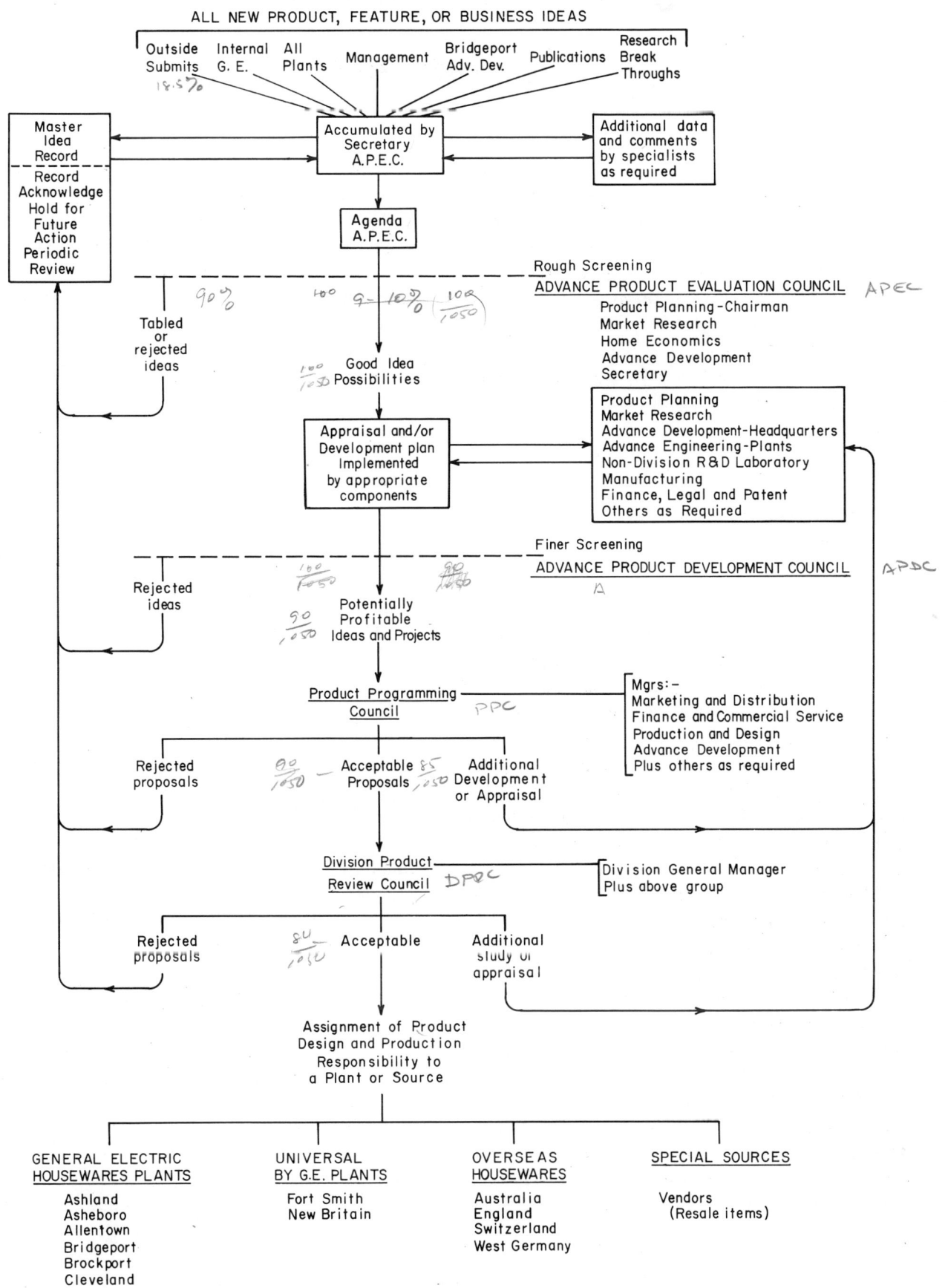

COMMENTARY

Similar to General Foods Corporation: Post Division in the respect that it sells a broad line of packaged goods through retail channels to consumers, General Electric Company: Housewares Division is a striking contrast in organization. Post had a well-articulated multiprogram structure, GE-HD was not structured by programs. The comment made by the Manager of the General Electric Marketing and Distribution Operation (GEMD) in the Housewares Division is particularly significant:

> You have to divide a business somehow. I have divided GEMD on a functional basis: Product Planning is responsible for the product lines; Market Planning for moving the goods and distribution; Advertising for creating demand; Sales for calling on customers.

The difference is important, and it is useful to understand why the Housewares Division operated with programs but not a program structure. It is useful, as well, to assess both the advantages and the difficulties of this organizational approach.

But before considering the Housewares Division organization we ought to look at the underlying reasons for consolidating three separate businesses into one. As at Ford, Du Pont, and Mobil, at General Electric clear gains could be realized from merging like businesses serving the same markets.

There is much to be learned, as well, from looking at two other dimensions of the Housewares Division case: the organization of the field sales function and the new product development process. Field sales organization is interesting because salesmen in GEMD Sales, selling to distributors, were specialized by product line while salesmen in the GED sales force, selling to retailers, carried the "full basket." Why was specialization appropriate in one case but not the other? As for the Housewares Division's new product development procedures, they are well worth studying. Product innovation was a key element in the Division's strategy and its success ratio was unusually high in marketing new products.

This commentary, then, will consider (1) the establishment of a single Housewares business, (2) its structure, (3) the organization of the field sales function, and (4) product development procedures.

The Case for Consolidation

The case for bringing together the Portable Appliances, Home Care and Comfort, and Clocks and Personal Care Departments to form a single GE Housewares business is a strong one. At the market level the three departments had strongly overlapping distribution. By merging they could deal as one business with these external resources — the retail and wholesale distribution systems. One set of procedures and criteria could be used in franchising distributors. Their selling efforts could be scheduled optimally for the several product lines, and the allocation of distributor effort would not be left to be determined by the outcome of an interdepartmental rivalry.

Advertising outlays could be planned for the entire line and advertising investments could be made in those lines where they would produce the greatest returns. There would be advantages, as well, in advertising that could cross the several product lines and thereby build an overall GE Housewares brand image.

In merging the three sales forces, the Housewares Division management then had a large enough sales base to afford to establish nine regional offices. Until the consolidation, one product department had five regional offices, one had two, and the third had none. Here was a notable gain. A strong regional reporting and control function for field sales is essential in recruiting, training, motivating, and compensating salesmen. It is essential in planning field sales strategy by product lines and customers, in carrying out new product introductions and special promotions, and in scheduling selling effort for each salesman.

Consolidating the three departments meant putting together product development resources and merging the streams of new product ideas. It became possible, then, to select the best of this pool of new product possibilities for development effort. Under the old arrangement it was possible that the best ideas might come out of one department, but the greatest resources for product development, both technical and financial, might be in another.

In long-range business planning a single Housewares Division management had the view of the total electrical household appliances market. Under the old arrangement each product department manager planned within a limited market scope — a piece of the whole. It had no meaning in terms of customers, or distribution channels, or production technology, or competition.

At the plant level the Housewares Division could begin to achieve economies through centralized purchasing of parts and materials. Manufacturing cost savings could be realized, too, by specializing production in the nine plants.

Other important gains were possible through the consolidation of the billing and payroll functions. Scarce managerial talent could be used most advantageously in handling division-wide managerial tasks. Moreover, the Housewares Division's overseas business would have strong central business direction. The Division had just been given responsibility by General Electric headquarters management for the overseas manufacturing and marketing of its lines.

Finally, the consolidation offered an opportunity for restructuring the business. As these three departments grew and their product lines proliferated, the logic of their separate identity would become increasingly tenuous. Any effort to distinguish the three departments in terms of products manufactured and sold or markets served would become a rationalization.

What was needed was a single business that could be organized internally according to some reasonable market segmentation scheme. Such a scheme might absorb new product developments and could be adapted to a changing strategy. The consolidation provided the opportunity for organizing to approach the total electrical housewares appliances market in a new and meaningful way.

Structuring the New Business

The logic of the consolidation contrasts with the *ex post facto* reactions of managers who had worked in the old departmental structures. There were three important types of reactions. Some of the managers felt that the decision-making process was far too long:

> . . . it now takes an extraordinary amount of time to get a decision. Before we can go ahead with a new project we have to have the General Manager's approval. Before we can even see the General Manager, we must first have meetings with the Product Planning Manager and the Product Programming Council. On something as simple as changing the plate on an iron to read "Permanent Press" instead of "wash and wear" it can take a month or more. (A Product Planner)

A second reaction was that communication among managers had become exceedingly cumbersome:

> Under the old organization, each department was headed by a closely knit management team. I was on the General Manager's staff, and knew what was going on at all times. Now, I frequently don't know why a decision has been made, or — worse — even that it has been made at all. (The same Product Planner)

Similarly, development engineers in the plants felt cut off from marketing personnel and from the market feedback that had stimulated their creativity on new product ideas. The Field Sales Manager in the GEMD Operation commented on the increased formality of communication under the new organization, a lack of direct contact at the working level among the several marketing functions, and the attendant difficulties of delay and misunderstanding.

A third reaction, among certain managers, had to do with a sense of incompleteness of job assignment and uncertainty about scope of responsibility and working relationships:

I believe that we should officially be designated product managers, and be given greater authority. It would make sense, for example, for product planning, manufacturing planning, engineering, and sales planning to report to us. These functions are organized on a product line basis anyway.

In a sense we would be like the old Department Managers, except that the field sales force and actual manufacturing facilities would not report to us. We are responsible for the total market planning job now; why not give us control of the resources we need to carry out our job?

At present, those of us at the working level, who are concerned with products, have to run around like crazy to put our complete program together.

The GEMD Manager claims that a functional organization works well — from his point of view. This may be true, but an awful lot of coordination is required at the working level. By the time he sees a program, the coordination job has been done. But blood, sweat, and tears have gone into putting that program together. (A Market Planner)

At the same time, the Manager of the General Electric Marketing and Distribution Operation spoke of the tendency on the part of product planners "to think that they do the whole job." Other executives described product planning as a "coordinator," "liaison," or "catalyst" function.

The basic causes of organizational uneasiness probably included a natural desire on the part of some Housewares Division managers to return to old, familiar working relationships. There may also have been some concern that for certain managers the responsibility scope of their assignments had been reduced, although the product scope had expanded.

Perhaps there was a more basic cause: *old organizational groupings* (the three product departments) *had been destroyed in the consolidation, but logical new groupings had not been developed.* The original *programs* still existed: one for portable appliances, another for home care and comfort products, and a third for the clocks and personal care lines. What was lacking was a clearly defined *program structure*. Market Planners for these three product lines came closest to filling the program management role and they reached out for it. They were positioned organizationally, however, so that they were an adjunct to Sales and their function was sales planning and strategy.

By contrast, General Foods' Post Division product managers were charged with developing total strategies for their lines. Their product plans provided for advertising, promotion, field selling, pricing, new product introductions, and manufacturing schedules. Although each plan was worked out with Post Division resource managers, it was fully integrated.

Had the Housewares Division management moved to establish a program management structure, rather than operating in effect as a single program, it would have been faced with the question of how to delineate the program organization. Actually, a good case could be made for a program segmentation scheme sketched out somewhat along the lines of the three predecessor departments, with some modifications. With one or two exceptions, such as the electric firestarter and power tool lines, portable appliances were kitchen-oriented. Home care and comfort products were mainly used out of the kitchen. Personal care products made a logical grouping, and clocks another. This is a product use delineation.

The way in which the Boston Regional Manager had made his sales assignments provides additional reasons in support of such a delineation. He specialized some of his men in portable appliances because the training of distributor sales personnel (concerning product features and promotional tools) was particularly important for these lines. Clocks, personal care products, and the Handy Hannah line were grouped for selling purposes, since all required contacts with many small distributors, including drug wholesalers, which did not carry Housewares' other products. Heaters, electric blankets, and fans made a logical grouping since these lines tended to have a counter-seasonal sales pattern. He also assigned the Universal line to one man. This line went through department store distribution while other lines went through mass merchandisers (discount houses) at lower retail margins.

Thus, if Handy Hannah products were grouped with clocks and personal care products and if the Universal line was handled separately, the original departmental breakdown apparently could be distinguished as well in terms of distribution channels and the different requirements of selling these products to distributors who in turn served different types of retail outlets. Probably these distinctions would lead as well to differences among the four product groupings (portable appliances; home care and comfort; clocks, personal care, and Handy Hannah; and Universal) in promotional and advertising techniques.

We might then conclude that the segmentation scheme provided by the way the three predecessor departments broke down the market could with certain modifications provide a basis for delineating a program management structure. These modifications would take account of the addition of the Handy Hannah and Universal lines. They would also take account of the fact that certain products might fit more logically in other product categories. (Should power tools, for example, be in with a line of electrical kitchen appliances? Should clocks, characterized by frequent styling changes, be in a separate category for product management purposes? Should the electric baby dish be part of the kitchen appliances group?)

Given a realistic segmentation scheme, a program management function might then have served usefully to develop total product strategies and to integrate resource effort in carrying out marketing programs. Housewares Division managers might then have sensed order rather than uneasiness. They might have had a feeling of being "tuned in" rather than being at remote listening posts.

Resource Domination

In the meantime, for lack of a clearly defined program structure, the key resources at GE Housewares Division — production, advertising, field sales, product planning — became the dominant influence in strategy formulation and implementation. Production took the initiative in determining production schedules on the grounds that a marketing-recommended schedule resulted in unnecessarily high manufacturing costs and stock-out experience.

Advertising and Sales Promotion allocated advertising funds by product line, giving some lines high advertising budgets relative to sales, some medium, some low, and some product lines were given no advertising. Budgets were based on a study of the relative responsiveness to advertising of HD's several lines. This section then worked directly with the GE Housewares advertising agency to develop promotional strategy and approve copy and media proposals. Similarly, the Product Planning Section exercised initiative and operated independently of the market planners in developing the product line.

We find here just the opposite of the situation at General Foods' Post Division. Certainly, the GE Housewares advertising agency could not complain because the process for reviewing advertising recommendations stifled creativity. Field sales did not suffer because its activities were too tightly programmed in order to meet the detailed objectives and schedules of the several programs. And Production could no longer object that marketing plans did not reflect a concern for manufacturing efficiency.

On the other hand, General Foods' Post Division had a structure that facilitated planning by market segment. Its organization was designed to coordinate resource efforts by product program in the execution of the strategies developed for each market/product segment. The business had been divided into manageable proportions for both strategy formulation and implementation.

An Evolving Scheme

There is a striking similarity between the Housewares Division organization as we look at it through this case study and the "Phase II" organization in the Du Pont Textile Fibers Department. The latter structure was in place in the December 1951–December 1954 period and was the first effort to consolidate organizationally what had been five relatively separate fiber businesses. In each case, there was no recognizable program structure and the key resource organizations were subdivided essentially along the lines of the old business units. At the Du Pont Textile Fibers Department, the rayon-acetate-nylon-"Orlon"-"Dacron" pattern was repeated in the field sales, technical service, research, and manufacturing functions. At GE

Housewares, functions such as market planning, field sales, product planning, and production tended to be aligned according to the old departmental breakdown: Portable Appliances, Home Care and Comfort, and Clocks and Personal Care. There were strong pressures at GE Housewares, however, as at Du Pont, which would be expected to lead either to a "Phase III" program structure or back to Phase I. These pressures include the Housewares managers' sense of uneasiness about the scope of their responsibilities and authority and about internal communications. Another pressure was almost certainly the rapidly expanding product line.

Phase II, in which the several basic resources are structured to represent the several business units from which the new business is built, seems inherently unstable. It is a compromise organization. The strains that seemed evident at GE Housewares are symptomatic of the instability. Housewares Division could return to the old product department arrangement but possibly retain a "pooled" sales force. Alternatively, it could remain as a single business and develop a program management organization.

Organization of Field Sales

The experimentation at GE Housewares with a "full basket" concept in organizing the field sales function is most interesting and deserves comment. The concept involved having each salesman, selling to distributors, carry the full Housewares Division line of products. Under the old organization, a salesman in any one of the three product departments sold the products of that department.

The "full basket" concept *was not* useful for salesmen selling to distributors. As one salesman explained:

> The basket was simply too full. It is impossible for one man to master such a wide range of products; you just don't sell clocks the way you do irons. There was too much; I could rarely get a distributor to give me enough time to go through my entire book.

The "full basket" approach *was* effective, however, for General Electric Distribution (GED) salesmen selling to retail accounts. Why was it workable for one and not the other?

History, of course, plays an important role. GED salesmen had traditionally carried a full housewares line when they worked in the GED predecessor organization, the General Electric Supply Company. By contrast, each member of the new HD sales force had had experience with selling only one of the three original product lines. He might find it difficult to learn about the whole range of HD lines and, even then, would tend to stress the old lines with which he was familiar.

This consideration is important, but other factors also are involved. Apparently part of the task of selling to distributors was to train distributor sales personnel. The training function requires some degree of product specialization, if sales representatives are to know their products well. For this purpose, the wider the line, the more superficial would be the training effort.

In addition, all distributors did not carry all three of the original product lines. Approximately 180 distributors were franchised for all three lines. Approximately 370 carried two lines: portable appliances, and clocks and personal care products. About 350 carried only clocks and personal care products. Therefore, in only about 180 accounts out of approximately 900 was there a sales potential for the full HD line.

The GED sales organization, on the other hand, apparently could not afford product-specialized salesmen. Selling to retailers required intensive coverage of a geographic area, and yielded far lower sales per account than selling to distributors. Specializing salesmen by product line would require either significantly increasing the territory each man covered or expanding the sales force, with attendant increases in selling costs.

The important development in GE-HD field sales under the new organization was that there was one "full basket" sales organization even though individual salesmen were generally product-specialized. By having responsibility for the full line, regional managers could use ingenuity in making selling assignments. In assigning products, accounts, and geographic areas to individual salesmen, regional managers could balance cost considerations, sales training needs, and the relative advantages of specializing salesmen either by type of account or by product line.

Moreover, by pooling the three original product lines and consolidating the three sales forces, a greatly strengthened regional management function could be supported. Until 1962, 31 Portable Appliance district sales representatives all over the country reported directly to headquarters. In 1962 the Portable Appliance Department General Manager had appointed five Regional Sales Managers, and one other department, Clocks and Personal Care, had named two. By contrast, the new Housewares Division had nine geographic regions, each with a Regional Sales Manager. As we observed in the IBM case, the regional (or district) sales management function is critically important in the supervision, training, and appraisal of sales personnel and in adapting selling strategy to local markets and individual customers.

Product Development Processes

Product innovation was a key element in the Housewares Division strategy and the Division had a remarkable record of new product successes. Product Planning generated a stream of new product ideas (1,050 in 1966!) and took the initiative in running them through a thorough screening procedure. Interestingly less than 3% of the new ideas came from headquarters and field sales personnel. At General Foods' Post Division, too, marketing personnel did not contribute greatly to the flow of new product ideas. One can only speculate that sales personnel, bent on selling the competitive advantages of the existing line, are not naturally sensitive to signals that suggest major product improvements.

The screening process exposed new product ideas to appraisal first by marketing research and product planning personnel. New ideas could be measured against a study of market needs and an estimate of cost and technical feasibility. This was the critical hurdle and 90% of the new ideas never passed over it. Further screening provided an opportunity for marketing, manufacturing, finance, and advanced development viewpoints to be brought to bear as well as the judgment of the division general manager. Another 2% of the ideas fell by the wayside and 8% then survived.

In the generation of new ideas and in the thoroughness of the screening, the system had much to commend it. But perhaps the new product development procedures at GE Housewares were too exacting. The 90% success rate for new product introductions leaves reason to wonder how many potentially successful ideas were screened out. Possibly the Division could sustain a lower success ratio and yet realize greater profits from new products overall, simply by introducing more new products.

In addition, there were complaints that the process was slow. That is understandable if one notes that the Housewares Division's top management was involved in the last two stages of the screening process. Because of heavy administrative burdens, it might be difficult for these managers to devote much time to new product reviews. Probably the process could have been accelerated if new product decisions had been relegated to Product Planning and Marketing Research after consultation with operating level managers in the resource departments. This would be equivalent to the first two stages in the procedure. It was at these stages that 90% of the new ideas were eliminated while the second two stages trimmed out less than another 2%.

Summary

The consolidation of the three product departments into one unified Housewares business had important advantages. Similarities in product line, customers, distribution, and merchandising techniques meant that the three departments used similar resources and skills. These resources could be pooled to offer operating economies and to make the optimal use of the best qualified personnel in each resource area. It provided the framework for developing a common strategy, a unified approach to distribution channels, and a single advertising program. Resources for new product development could be allocated rationally across the broad range of portable electrical household appliances.

The new business, however, had not developed

a clear program management structure to replace the old product department groupings. Managers, then, sensed difficulties and delays in decision making and implementation. But the new business was still in a formative stage and one would expect further organizational developments to evolve. Either a program management structure might emerge or the Division could revert to the earlier product department arrangement with possibly a single "pooled sales" operation serving all three departments.

In the new business the single sales force had, in fact, achieved substantial gains. It developed a strong regional organization. It gave regional managers flexibility in specializing field sales personnel by product lines and types of accounts. A "full basket" selling approach had been attempted and was found unsatisfactory. Different product lines and different types of distributor accounts called for varying sales skills and knowledge. And it was impractical for individual salesmen to cover the whole gamut. By contrast in the GE Distribution sales organization, selling to retail accounts, specialization was not suitable primarily for cost reasons. Sales per retail account were much lower than sales per distributor account and apparently could not justify the cost of having product-specialized salesmen covering large territories. Moreover, retailers were accustomed to working with full-line salesmen, whereas distributors wanted product specialists.

The Housewares new product development process was immensely effective. A rich stream of new product ideas was screened carefully through market research to evaluate sales potential. New product suggestions were then appraised by marketing, production, finance, and technical personnel to assess their feasibility from each of these viewpoints. Possibly, the 90% success ratio on new product introductions was achieved at the cost of eliminating some potentially profitable but more risky ideas. In addition, the process might have been accelerated if screening and decision making had been delegated to operating management levels rather than taking top management's time and attention.

Ford Motor Company:
North American Automotive Operations

With 1966 world-wide sales of more than $12 billion, Ford Motor Company (including consolidated subsidiaries) was one of the world's largest manufacturing enterprises. Ford had grown rapidly in recent years, approximately doubling its sales between 1956 and 1966. Earnings had also increased markedly, reaching a record $703 million in 1965.[1] Exhibit 1 presents selected financial statistics for the period 1957–1966.

Ford was a major participant in several industries, most notably automobiles, trucks, farm equipment, consumer electrical products, and military and industrial electronic products. In 1966 automobiles, trucks, and related parts and accessories were still Ford's most important business, accounting for approximately 89% of sales. Recent automotive sales data are shown in Exhibit 2.

The United States was Ford's largest market, but Ford products were also manufactured and/or sold in 123 countries. In 1966 overseas sales represented approximately 22% of Ford's total revenue.

The top management of Ford consisted of a Chairman (the chief executive officer) and a President. Reporting to these two men in late 1967 were a number of committees and central staff organizations, and three operating executives. These three operating executives were responsible respectively for (1) North American Automotive Operations; (2) Overseas Automotive and [World-wide] Tractor Operations; and (3) the Philco-Ford Corporation, a wholly owned subsidiary which manufactured and marketed Ford's consumer, industrial, and military electronic products, various home appliances, and training and technical support services.[2] (See Exhibit 4A, B, and C.)

---

[1] Earnings were $621 million in 1966.

[2] Ford acquired Philco Corporation, a manufacturer of consumer electronics products, in 1961, and subsequently assigned responsibility for several nonautomotive electronics businesses to the new subsidiary. According to Ford executives, Philco-Ford was operated as an autonomous subsidiary and had few direct operating relationships with the other

Evolution of the Ford Organization, 1957–1967

In the 10-year period, 1957–1967, the organizational structure of Ford Motor Company changed markedly.

At the beginning of the period — in the late 1950s — Ford's organization had reached the zenith of a trend toward decentralization that had begun in the early 1950s. In the United States, five relatively autonomous, functionally integrated divisions (Ford, Mercury, Lincoln, Continental, and Edsel) each designed, assembled,[3] and marketed its own line of cars (and, in the case of the Ford Division, trucks). In Europe, the two major Ford subsidiaries (Ford Motor Company, Ltd. in Dagenham, England, and Ford-Werke, A.G. in Cologne, Germany) each designed, manufactured, and marketed its own products, competing with each other (and with Ford-U.S.) for sales to Ford assembly and/or sales affiliates in third countries. Ford tractors were manufactured and sold in the United States by the Tractor and Implement Division, while a separate line of tractors was made and sold in Britain by the Ford Motor Company, Ltd. As in the case of cars, the two tractor organizations competed for sales to Ford affiliates in third countries.

By 1967 Ford's organizational structure had changed radically. In the United States, all cars and trucks were designed, manufactured and sold by a single, functionally organized unit — North American Automotive Operations. A new organization — Ford of Europe — was to coordinate all automotive activities in Europe. And Ford Tractor Operations, which had been established in 1962, had world-wide responsibility for the design, manufacture, and distribution of

---

parts of the company. Consequently, this case will not deal with the Philco-Ford Corporation, except to note that it sold a few components to the automotive divisions (e.g., car radios) and had its own international division.

[3] The Edsel Division did not assemble cars.

Ford tractors and equipment for the farm and industrial markets.

These organizational developments are reflected in Exhibits 3 and 4 (Ford Motor Company organization charts dated May 23, 1959, and November 1, 1967, respectively), and described below.

Case Organization

This case begins by describing the organizational development of Ford's North American automobile and truck businesses between the early 1950s and 1967. It then describes the organization of North American Automotive Operations in early 1967 in considerable detail, with particular emphasis on the Ford and Autolite-Ford Parts Divisions. After briefly describing the reorganization of North American Automotive Operations in late 1967, the case concludes by tracing parallel organizational developments in Ford's tractor and overseas operations.

The Development of North American Automotive Operations

By the late 1940s it had become clear to Ford management that the company's traditional highly centralized organizational structure had become increasingly cumbersome as the company had grown. In particular, the top executives seemed to have too much responsibility to manage the various aspects of the business effectively. What was necessary, these executives believed, was to divide the total business in such a way that a lower level of management would have reasonably full responsibility for distinct organizational units. In keeping with the organizational pattern that had become common in the automotive industry, Ford was thus divided into several operating divisions, each of which was responsible for designing, assembling, and marketing one of the company's automotive lines.

At first, there were two such divisions: Ford and Lincoln-Mercury. As the company planned or introduced new automotive lines (the Continental in 1955; the Edsel in 1957), new divisions were established to operate these businesses. Lincoln and Mercury were separated and a division was formed to market each car line. Thus, in 1956 there were five integrated vehicle divisions, each operated as a profit center. In addition, there were a number of basic manufacturing divisions, also operated as profit centers, which supplied components to the assembly plants serving the five vehicle divisions.

According to a corporate executive in 1967, the mid-1950s had been a period of "fragmentation" in Ford's organizational history. Ambitious marketing objectives had led to the establishment of new vehicle divisions, and the proliferation of vehicle divisions had led to a similar tendency in manufacturing.

By late 1956 it had become apparent that there would not be enough business to justify separate Lincoln and Continental Divisions, and the two divisions were merged to form a single Lincoln Division responsible for both lines of cars. For similar reasons the Lincoln and Mercury Divisions were merged in late 1957, and the Edsel Division was combined with the Lincoln-Mercury Division to form the MEL Division in 1958.[4] These moves were made primarily because none of the three smaller divisions had sufficient volume to justify the high overhead expenses of an autonomous divisional organization.

In 1959 and 1960 a number of additional organizational changes were made in order to reduce overhead expenses further. In 1959 Lincoln-Mercury assembly operations were transferred to the Ford Division. In 1960 Lincoln-Mercury purchasing, engineering, and warehousing activities were consolidated with these functions in the Ford Division. This latter change, it should be noted, facilitated the design and use of interchangeable parts by the three car lines, thus reducing engineering, purchasing, and manufacturing costs as well as overhead expenses.

In 1960 Ford and Lincoln-Mercury assembly operations were transferred from the Ford Division to a newly formed Automotive Assembly Division. As a result, neither the Lincoln-Mercury Division nor the Ford Division was now a fully integrated product division, although the Ford Division did perform certain functions (purchasing, engineering, and warehousing) for both divisions. In addition, the Ford Division had primary responsibility for the 1,200 dealers franchised by both the Ford and the Lincoln-Mercury Divisions. Lincoln-Mercury continued to have primary responsibility for the 1,400 Lincoln-Mercury dealers not holding Ford franchises.

In discussing Ford's organization during the early 1960s, one Ford executive commented in 1967:

Our organization was sort of a half-way house. On the one hand, the Ford and Lincoln-Mercury Division had

---

[4] When the Edsel was withdrawn from the market (1960), the MEL Division became the Lincoln-Mercury Division.

far less autonomy than they had had in the late 1950's. On the other hand, the Company tended to treat them as if they were still autonomous, as profit centers with control of their own destinies.

To some extent, the vehicle divisions never had been really autonomous. In this business, there are several really big decisions each year: the product program including styling, the marketing budget, and the capital budget. These decisions could never have been delegated entirely to the divisional General Managers. They are simply too important!

Transfer prices have also been a problem. It was extremely difficult to establish meaningful transfer prices for parts and assemblies "purchased" by the vehicle divisions from the manufacturing divisions, since reliable "market" prices for many of these items could not be obtained.

I am not suggesting that these problems were new in the early 1960s. They were not. But as the product divisions became less and less integrated, the basic weaknesses of our organizational structure became more and more apparent.

By the mid-1960s Ford's top management had concluded that the half-centralized, half-decentralized operation of the automotive business ought to be modified. As a first step, an organization known as North American Automotive Operations was established in late 1964. This organization, which was headed by an Executive Vice President, consisted of all divisions that manufactured, assembled, or marketed cars and trucks in North America. When it was formed, it was divided into three groups: Car and Truck (i.e., the vehicle divisions); Engine, Transmissions, and Parts; and Stamping, Assembly, and Steel, each headed by a Vice President or Group Executive. The Car and Truck Group initially consisted of the two vehicle divisions, Ford and Lincoln-Mercury, plus Ford of Canada's domestic marketing operations.

Between late 1964 and 1967 the major impact of the new organization was in the manufacturing and assembly areas, where further integration took place. Operation of the vehicle divisions was largely unchanged.

In July 1967 top management completed the implementation of the 1964 decision to establish the North American Automotive Operations by restructuring it as a centralized, functionally organized business unit (see pages 274–277). North American Automotive Operations would now consist of three groups: (1) Manufacturing, (2) Product Development, and (3) the vehicle divisions (now without product planning and engineering) as a Sales Group.

The most notable aspect of the new organization was the establishment of the Product Development Group, which took over the car and truck product planning and engineering functions from the vehicle divisions, and the advanced product research function from the Engineering Staff at the central office level.

North American Automotive Operations in Early 1967

By early 1967 North American Automotive Operations was divided into four groups: Basic Products; Engine, Transmission, and Parts; Body and Assembly; and Car and Truck (Exhibit 5). The first three of these groups performed manufacturing functions. The Basic Products Group manufactured steel, glass, and other basic materials for use in Ford products. The Engine, Transmission, and Parts Group engineered and manufactured components for later assembly into cars and trucks. The Body and Assembly Group engineered and manufactured body parts for cars and trucks, and "purchased" components from the Engine, Transmission and Parts Group and outside vendors. It then assembled these components into finished vehicles, which were sold by the vehicle divisions in the Car and Truck Group.

The Car and Truck Group consisted of four operating divisions—Ford, Lincoln-Mercury, Ford of Canada, and Autolite-Ford Parts—plus Product Development and Marketing Services. The Ford and Lincoln-Mercury Divisions were considered vehicle divisions; as such they were responsible for the product planning, engineering, and marketing of their respective lines of vehicles. As noted above, the Ford Division performed certain functions (engineering and warehousing)[5] for both itself and the Lincoln-Mercury Division.

In order to illustrate how the Car and Truck Group operated in early 1967, the following pages describe the organizations and major activities of the Ford Division and the Autolite-Ford Parts Division.

The Ford Division

The Ford Division marketed five lines of automobiles (Ford, Fairlane, Falcon, Mustang, and Thunderbird) and several series of trucks through a net

---

[5] Responsibility for purchasing was assigned to the Automotive Assembly Division in 1967.

work of approximately 6,100 franchised dealers in the United States. In 1966 the Ford Division sold 2,062,588 cars in these lines and 568,129 trucks and buses. Its sales approximated 85% of the Ford Motor Company's U.S. automobile sales; 100% of the Ford Motor Company's U.S. truck sales; 22.2% of industry automobile sales; and 29.5% of industry truck sales.[6]

The scope of activities carried out by the Ford Division had been reduced considerably in recent years. In particular, the Division's purchasing and assembly functions and parts business had been assigned to other organizational units between 1960 and 1967 (see above).

Organization

The Ford Division Organization Chart as of April 12, 1967, is shown in Exhibit 6. The Division was headed by a General Manager and an Assistant General Manager, each of whom directed certain functions.

The Truck Operations Manager, Car Product Planning Manager, Chief Engineer-Car Product Engineering, Personnel and Organization Manager, Controller, and managers of public relations, marketing research, cost estimating and special vehicles (i.e., racing) reported to the General Manager.

The General Sales Manager, National Service Manager, General Fleet and Leasing Manager, Dealer Development Manager, Advertising Manager, and Merchandising Manager reported to the Assistant General Manager.

The Truck Operations Manager was responsible for truck product planning, truck product engineering, and heavy truck sales and marketing.

The Division was thus organized on a functional basis, with several exceptions. Truck product planning and product engineering were handled separately from automobile product planning and product engineering, and a separate organization was responsible for the sales and marketing of heavy trucks. All other functions were concerned with both automobiles and trucks, although separate car and truck departments generally operated below the functional office level.

Automobiles

In 1966, 78.7% of the Division's dollar sales were accounted for by passenger cars, a percentage that had increased by 4% since 1963.

The great majority of Ford Division personnel was directly concerned with the automotive side of the business. The Ford dealer organization, while selling trucks and parts, was also oriented mainly toward automobile sales.

Product Line

The Ford Division marketed five lines of passenger automobiles:

Ford: The Division's basic entry, available in 18 models (convertibles, sedans, station wagons, etc.) with a wide range of engine choices and other options. Depending on the model and options, suggested retail prices for the Ford ranged from $2,440 to about $5,300. In 1966, 960,905 Fords were sold.

Fairlane: Introduced in 1961, the Fairlane was somewhat smaller and less expensive than the Ford, but was nevertheless a family-size automobile; 295,419 Fairlanes were sold in 1966.

Falcon: A compact car, introduced in 1959, primarily to compete with European imports. Gradually, the Falcon has become somewhat larger and more expensive than when initially introduced; 169,558 Falcons were sold in 1966, compared with a high volume of 505,137 units in 1960.

Mustang: A highly successful sports-type automobile introduced in 1964. The Mustang was designed to appeal primarily to the youth market; a wide assortment of options made it possible for the purchaser to "design his own car." There were 566,367 Mustangs sold in 1966, but sales declined somewhat in 1967 as other manufacturers entered the sports-type car market.

Thunderbird: Originally introduced in 1955 as a two-passenger sports car, the Thunderbird had become by 1958 a luxury five-passenger sports-type car. With suggested retail prices beginning at $4,600, 70,339 Thunderbirds were sold in 1966.

Most observers believed that the single most important trend in recent years was the proliferation of automobile car lines and models, and of the number of options available for each model. Where the Ford Division had sold only 22 basic models in 1960, for example, its product line included 47 basic models in 1967.

Virtually all functions for passenger cars were performed by the undifferentiated functional offices. The only notable exceptions to this pattern were product planning and product engineering.

Product Planning

The Car Product Planning Office developed plans which, when approved, shaped the Division's automobile product line. These plans were quite comprehensive, ranging in scope from broad product

---
[6] See Exhibit 2.

policy matters (e.g. Should there be a Mustang?) to the very minute details of a car's design.[7]

The office consisted of a manager and a number of product planners. These planners were, for the most part, assigned to individual car lines (e.g., Mustang, Fairlane), rather than specialties within the product planning function.

The formal product planning cycle for a model year spanned several years. The first period of this cycle was known as the "pre-program period." During this period, the product planners established the basic structure and features of the product line. They worked closely with advanced engineering groups to ascertain the nature of any technological developments that would become available; with Marketing Research to probe consumer attitudes and preferences; and with Product Engineering and Manufacturing to determine the costs and feasibility of product proposals.

The pre-program phase culminated in the submission of a formal proposal to corporate management outlining the changes planned for the model year, their rationale, and the economics underlying the plan. When the proposal was approved by corporate management, expenditures were authorized for tooling and manufacturing start-up during the final program period.

At the end of the pre-program period, certain features of the product line were firmly established. For the most part, these features required long lead times or were major constraints on the work of the automotive stylists and engineers. While styling was not yet determined, for example, decisions concerning the extent of change (a "face-lift" or an entirely new car) had already been made. Similarly, decisions concerning the width of doors and angle of window panes had to be made early, in order to give engineers and suppliers adequate time to design and develop tooling for these components.

When these basic features had been approved by corporate management, the corporate Design Office (Exhibit 4A) began to develop styling alternatives for review by the product planners. Preliminary sketches and models were generally developed during the pre-program period, but final styling decisions were delayed as long as practicable in order to have the benefit of reasonably current data concerning consumer attitudes and sales results for new models.

A major portion of the product planners' work was devoted to economic analysis of alternative product features and styling approaches. In performing this function, the product planners worked closely with the Cost Estimating department, a separate function reporting to the Division General Manager. Cost estimating provided the product planners with rough cost estimates during the pre-program period and more refined cost estimates as the model year approached.

Product Engineering

The Car Product Engineering Office of the Ford Division was responsible for translating the plans developed by the Product Planning Offices of the Ford and Lincoln-Mercury Divisions into detailed cost and performance specifications. The specifications were then transmitted to a design office, where they were used as the objectives for detailed engineering development. In general, the design office that worked on a particular part or component was located in the manufacturing division that would manufacture the part. A notable exception to this pattern was the Chassis Design Office, which was a part of the Ford Division Product Engineering Office. Prior to production start-up for a given model year, the design offices submitted engineering prototypes to the Car Product Engineering Office, which reviewed the prototypes to make sure that they met specifications.

The major portion of the Car Product Engineering function (as the term has been used above) was performed by four groups reporting to the Assistant Chief Engineer—Vehicles. These groups were responsible respectively, for (1) Falcon, Fairlane, and Mustang; (2) Ford and Thunderbird; (3) Comet and Cougar; and (4) Lincoln and Mercury. Within each group

---

[7] A Ford publication listed some typical questions in the product planning area:

Should the planned model be completely new or should it be a re-styled car with components carried over from the previous model?

If the basic design is to be all new, should engine, transmission, and chassis components also be new? Would improved designs result in enough of an increase in efficiency and customer appreciation to offset the fixed costs and possible increases in variable costs?

What changes should be made in offerings of optional equipment? Are current designs as modern and efficient as competitive offerings? Should some current options be offered as standard equipment on the model?

If the basic car is to be a carry-over, what components should be changed to provide a distinctive, improved appearance?

Should the car size be changed in any important dimensions?

What mechanical features would attract customers and better serve their needs?

What body types and series should be offered? What sales volume estimates are reasonable for each?

Source: Ford Motor Company, Educational Aids Series, Vol. 1, *Product Planning and Development*, p. 2.

there was a Vehicle Design Department, divided into two sections, one responsible for chassis and power train and the other responsible for body and electrical. These sections did most of the actual translation of product plans into product specifications.

Trucks

The Ford Division was a major factor in the U.S. truck industry, which had been growing very rapidly in recent years, with a 70% sales increase since 1960. A considerable portion of this increase was attributable to general economic trends. In addition, better equipment, use of light trucks for recreational applications, and an improved road system had enhanced the competitive position of trucking as a form of transportation.

The truck industry made a sharp distinction between light trucks and heavy trucks. The usual point of demarcation between the two categories was approximately 10,000 lbs. gross vehicle weight. Extra-heavy trucks had a capacity as great as 80,000 lbs. gross combination weight.

The light truck market consisted essentially of pickup trucks, delivery vans, and utility vehicles. Ford and Chevrolet had approximately 75% of industry sales between them. In general, light trucks were designed, manufactured, and marketed in much the same way as passenger automobiles.

Heavy trucks were a different matter. The three leading manufacturers of heavy trucks were International Harvester, White, and Mack, with Ford and GMC in fourth and fifth places respectively. The purchasers of heavy trucks were generally business-oriented users who required trucks for hire, construction, agricultural, or general purpose uses. They made their buying decisions primarily on the basis of cost-benefit analysis, rather than styling or taste. A large percentage of the heavy trucks sold were built to special order with many modifications.

In summarizing the difference between light trucks and cars, one Ford executive stated:

> The light truck business is an off-shoot of the passenger car business, although there are enough differences to justify giving it specialized attention. The heavy truck business, on the other hand, is like the machine tool business. They really are two different ball games.

Truck Operations

Prior to 1964 the Ford Division made little distinction, organizationally, between the car and truck businesses. At that time the Division was organized functionally, with truck specialists located in the various functional offices such as engineering, product planning, and sales. The General Manager of the Ford Division had cognizance over the entire truck business (with the exception of manufacturing), and it was treated, in effect, as another car line. During this period the great bulk of Ford's truck business was in the light truck field.

In 1958, however, Ford developed a new gasoline engine suitable for heavy trucks and soon afterward entered the heavy truck business in earnest. At this time (1958–1963) Ford established in its various functional offices organizational units concerned exclusively with heavy trucks. It also established in 1958 a separate heavy duty truck sales franchise for its largest models. Approximately 260 dealers located throughout the country held this franchise. Heavy trucks dealers, it was believed, needed facilities and skills not available in the average automobile dealership. Lighter trucks remained part of the normal automobile franchise, however.

By 1964 Ford had developed a more competitive line of heavy and extra-heavy trucks and was beginning to have considerable success in the marketplace. In order to expand efforts in this field and give the truck business as a whole more direction, it was decided to appoint a Truck Operations Manager, reporting to the General Manager. The truck business was to be treated as a separate profit center, and the Truck Operations Manager was to have profit responsibility.

Certain functions, such as light truck sales, advertising, and programming, were performed by personnel remaining in other line operations such as the General Sales Office. Truck product planning and product engineering were established as separate offices, however, and assigned to the Truck Operations Manager. It was reasoned that there was little similarity in these functions between cars and trucks, and that the Truck Operations Manager should have complete control over the product with which he went to market.

A separate Heavy Truck Sales and Marketing Office was also established reporting to the Truck Operations Manager. At the same time, the truck merchandising departments in the district sales offices were split into two departments, heavy and light. While reporting to the District Sales Manager, the heavy truck merchandising specialists received their functional guidance from the Heavy Truck Sales and Marketing Office. The light truck merchandising personnel continued to receive their functional guidance from the

General Sales Office and the General Marketing Office.[8]

The Truck Operations Manager thus had direct control over product planning for all trucks; product engineering for all trucks; and substantial influence over the sale and marketing of heavy trucks. In commenting on the split between light and heavy trucks in the latter function, one executive explained:

What we are saying, in effect, is that light trucks and heavy trucks have more in common with each other than either has in common with cars in the product planning and product engineering fields. We believe, however, that light trucks have more in common with cars than they do with heavy trucks from a sales and marketing standpoint.

Truck Product Planning

The Truck Product Planning Office was divided into three groups: (1) light truck planning, (2) heavy truck planning, and (3) advanced programs and special studies. The latter group was a recent innovation, established in August 1966. Its function was to carry out advanced product planning for both light trucks and heavy trucks through the preparation of future product "want lists" and the correlation of advanced planning with advanced engineering.

The Truck Product Planning Manager described the truck product planning process as follows:

The first thing to be considered is the difference between truck product planning and car product planning. For one thing, truck cycles (i.e., period between completely new models) range from 6 to 7 years on light trucks to about 10 years or more on heavy trucks, versus 3 to 4 years in the car business. Moreover, especially on heavy trucks, we are dealing with much smaller unit volumes, which requires a different viewpoint in trading off higher unit costs to achieve lower tooling costs.

Product changes which coincide with our major cycle changes tend to be more dependent on formal marketing research and inputs from the research and development programs than in-cycle changes. We regularly survey our customers and dealers in an attempt to ascertain their attitudes, preferences, and wishes.

We work closely with our larger customers to determine what they want. Heavy truck buyers generally have a good idea of what they want in the future.

We also watch custom orders very closely. If enough customers want something badly enough to place a special order, there's a good chance it should be a regularly available option.

---

[8] Until early 1967 the Ford Division had a General Marketing Office. Then it was eliminated and separate offices for advertising and merchandising were set up. See page 271.

All of our plans require corporate approval, in much the same way as the car product plans.

Truck Product Engineering

The Truck Product Engineering Office was divided into three activities: (1) light trucks, (2) heavy trucks, and (3) common design services. Design services performed a support function, supplying drafting and other technical services to the two engineering activities.

The Truck Product Engineering Office prepared designs and engineering drawings to meet product requirements. According to the Chief Engineer-Truck:

The establishment of these requirements is formally in Product Planning's domain; however, all elements of the Truck organization, including engineering and sales, contribute to this process.

The engineering design activity is clearly and deliberately separated between light and heavy trucks. Light truck design deals in the main with fairly high volume units and has some basic similarities to the design function in Ford car operations. Heavy truck, on the other hand, is generally involved in much lower volume segments of the market and requires somewhat different design and testing techniques. One of the problems peculiar to heavy truck is the tremendous number of special orders. This results in a sort of "custom building" activity which puts a premium on a combination of ingenuity and experience in order to keep engineering and tooling costs at reasonable levels. As an example, one of our fleet customers might specify a rear tandem suspension system which he has particular reasons for wanting in his fleet. It might happen that we have never built a truck with this suspension. If his order is for say 50 units, we are faced with the problem of doing a design and testing job that will result in a satisfactory truck without spending the kind of time and money we would devote to a new suspension that might be required for light truck where the volume would be in the hundreds of thousands.

Heavy Truck Sales and Marketing

The Heavy Truck Sales and Marketing Office had been established in 1964 to give direction to the Division's heavy truck marketing efforts. At headquarters, the office had departments responsible for national accounts, product recommendations, and field operations. In the field, all heavy truck specialists reported to their district managers but received their functional guidance from the Heavy Truck Sales and Marketing Office.

The national account managers were primarily responsible for helping dealers to sell to large trucking companies. For example, they frequently assisted a selling dealer in preparing formal bids for large orders.

Such bids were often quite complex, including, for example, provisions for the trade-in of used trucks.

The Heavy Truck Field Operations Department worked closely with Ford's 260 specialized heavy duty truck dealers, 230 of whom also held Ford car franchises. The Department implemented basic policies related to the heavy duty truck franchises, prepared training programs and manuals for heavy truck retail salesmen, provided business management guides, and, in general, working through district sales offices, looked after the heavy truck dealer organization.

The Ford Dealer Organization

In June 1967, 6,100 dealers sold Ford Division cars and light trucks in the United States. With very few exceptions these dealers were independent businessmen who had agreed to perform certain functions in return for a franchise to sell Ford products. Fifteen hundred of these dealers were also franchised to sell Lincolns and Mercuries, mainly in small towns, but the Ford Division had primary responsibility for these dealers.

Certain dealers were also franchised to sell heavy duty trucks and/or Ford's Cortina, a compact car imported from England. In addition, a limited number of dealers specialized exclusively in trucks and were not franchised to sell passenger cars.

Dealerships varied considerably in size of investment, sales, and profitability, with the larger dealerships generally located in or near major cities.

Several components were primarily concerned with the Ford Division dealer organization. Within the General Sales Office, the Market Representation Activity was responsible for the selection and franchising of dealers; the Field Sales Organization (divided into 7 regions and 37 districts) was responsible for dealer contact; and the Programming and Distribution Activity was responsible for filling dealer orders. Supporting the General Sales Office in these tasks were Dealer Development, which provided financial assistance to selected dealers; the National Service Office, which provided guidance to the dealers and monitored performance in the automotive service field; the Fleet and Leasing Office, which assisted dealers in their contacts with large accounts and administered a rental and a leasing program; and the Merchandising Office, which developed promotions and point-of-sale display pieces to aid (or encourage) the dealer organization in its sales efforts.

Market Representation

The Market Representation Activity[9] was described by its manager as the "long-range side of the General Sales Office." Its function was to plan the number, size, and locations of Ford dealerships, establish franchises, build facilities, recommend purchase of real estate, coordinate dealer signs, and, in general, provide assistance to the dealer organization. In most districts a Market Representation Manager and a Business Management Manager served as local arms of the market representation function. In the largest districts an Assistant District Manager was given responsibility for market representation, heading a task force of analysts and specialists. Under either organizational approach, district market representation personnel made continuing studies of their markets, seeking to determine the optimal number and locations of dealerships. Having thus established market representation objectives, they encouraged existing dealers to relocate or upgrade their facilities and, when necessary, established a new dealership or arranged for a new dealer to buy out an existing dealership. In addition, they served as troubleshooters, working with individual dealers on problems (generally of a management nature) which affected their profits.

The market Representation Manager commented on his activity as follows:

A lot of people in the Ford Division are concerned with specialized aspects of the dealer organization. We are concerned with the whole picture, with making sure we have the right number of the right dealers in the right facilities, doing what they should be doing to achieve their profit potential.

We have used the franchise system for more than sixty years. We feel that it is the best way to go to market because of the entrepreneurial energy it creates at the local level. Many of our dealers have done extremely well and have provided excellent service to the consumer. One of our prime responsibilities is to see that our market representation plans and actions provide the basis for continued profitability of the franchise.

A major problem facing dealers is the upward pressure on the costs of doing business. Wages, fringe benefits, taxes, and facility costs are all increasing, while the dealer must continue to sell in a highly competitive environment.

We are encouraging our dealers to place greater emphasis on all revenue-producing aspects of their business. Service is, of course, one area, but so is used cars. And

---

[9] An "activity" was a nonstandard organizational entity, at a lower level than an office, but at a higher level than a department.

we have instituted leasing and rental programs, to give our dealers an opportunity to get a share of those markets.

Dealer Development

The Dealer Development Activity was responsible for those dealerships in which the company had a financial investment: for example, (1) dealerships purchased from a retiring dealer or his estate, which were operated temporarily by the company until a suitable purchaser could be found; and (2) dealerships falling directly under the dealer development program.

The dealer development program was intended to make it possible for qualified individuals to become dealers even though they lacked adequate financial resources. As the Dealer Development Manager explained:

It takes more money today to start a dealership than it ever did before. Operating investment requirements have gone up, with the result that it is very difficult for a relatively young man to save enough capital to buy a dealership. The dealer development program allows us to select the best qualified man for a dealership and to put him in business at a young enough age for him to spend twenty or thirty years as a Ford dealer.

Dealer Contact

Day-to-day contact with the dealer organization was carried out by the Ford Division field organization. This organization was divided into seven regions, which were, in turn, divided into 37 districts. The districts were the focal point of dealer contact. Within each district, Field Managers were responsible for smaller geographic areas, known as "zones."

The Field Managers called on their dealers at least once a month to obtain orders and also worked with them on problems within the dealership. In addition, they had a continuing longer range responsibility for their zones, recommending changes in market representation, for example, as appropriate.

The districts also had specialists concerned with specific aspects of the dealer organization. While there were some variations among districts in specific assignments (large districts tended to have more fully elaborated specialist organizations), all districts had specialists concerned with car merchandising, light trucks, heavy trucks, business management, fleet and leasing, customer relations, and service. These specialists (there were generally several within each specialty) normally worked through the Field Managers but called on dealers when specific problems arose.

All districts also had a sales planning and analysis department and a distribution department, both of which were essentially inside activities.

The larger districts had an Assistant District Manager responsible for market representation and service. Most districts had market representation departments. Large districts had retail management specialists (essentially a consulting function). Some larger districts had Ford Authorized Leasing System (FALS) managers, who worked directly with FALS dealers. Districts with relatively strong imported car sales had imported vehicle specialists.

Programming and Distribution

The Programming and Distribution Activity served as the interface between the Ford Division and the Automotive Assembly Division (AAD).[10] Since 1964 the activity had been part of the General Sales Office, reporting to the General Sales Manager. Prior to 1964 it had reported to the Division General Manager, on the grounds that it would thus be able to preserve its neutrality between sales and assembly. The change was made in order to facilitate closer day-to-day working relationships between Programming and Distribution and Sales.

The function of the Programming and Distribution Activity was, in simple terms, to determine the mix and quantity of automobiles and trucks required by the market, to communicate these requirements to the Assembly Division, and to program the distribution of vehicles to the districts and individual dealers. This function was performed with varying degrees of refinement for different time periods to serve a variety of different purposes.

Dealer orders provided the major input to the short-term programming process. Approximately one month before the beginning of a sales month, the Field Managers called on each of their dealers. The Field Managers brought with them Ford's forecast of industry sales and Ford penetration for the month in question, and worked out a sales forecast with the dealer. The dealer then used this forecast in conjunction with his working stock level to determine how many vehicles he would want during the month in question. He then gave the Field Manager a "basic order" for a specific mix of lines and models or equipment.

These orders were then consolidated and reviewed at the district, regional, and divisional levels. Historical mix data (corrected for current trends) were applied to the orders to determine how many of each

---
[10] See Exhibit 5.

model each district was to receive. Each district was then "sourced"; i.e., it was determined which assembly plants would ship each model to each district. Although source patterns were relatively stable, they could vary considerably if, for example, seasonal demand for installed air conditioners in one district required that that district be sourced from a plant with adequate air conditioner capacity during that season.

The dealers then ordered specific vehicles. When a dealer ordered a vehicle, he specified whether it was a "retail order" (i.e., had already been sold) or a "stock order" (i.e., for inventory). Stock orders were generally placed at ten-day intervals, while retail orders were submitted daily.

As the orders came in from the dealers, the district distribution departments compared the totals with the program established for the district. The total number of units ordered could generally be expected to agree with the program (which was itself derived from basic orders), but it was not unusual for the mix of vehicles to deviate from the program. In cases of this sort, the districts requested a change in their program. Most such changes were easily handled by the Assembly Division by balancing them against changes in other districts or modifying assembly schedules, but this was not always possible. When it was not possible, the dealers were informed that they had to change or defer their orders, with preference generally given to "retail orders" over "stock orders."

The program for heavy trucks was not handled in this way. Because the great majority of heavy truck orders were for custom modifications, it was considered essential that the interface between sales and assembly be even closer than it was for cars and light trucks. For this reason, the Louisville plant, where all heavy trucks were assembled, had its own programming and distribution department. This department received all orders for heavy trucks, reviewed the specifications submitted, established assembly schedules, and notified the district submitting the order when delivery could be expected. Truck Operations management in Dearborn visited Louisville once a month to review and approve the program planned for the next month.

Fleet and Leasing

In 1963 the Ford Division had established the Fleet and Leasing Office to direct the Division's efforts in five important market segments. These market segments and their respective shares of the car and truck markets for 1966 and 1967 are listed in the following table:

Market Segment	% of Industry Car Sales		% of Industry Truck Sales	
	1966	1967	1966	1967
Commercial fleet	2.4%	2.1%	10.5%	9.7%
Leasing	3.3	3.8	4.4	3.9
Rental	2.2	2.9	—	0.4
State & local government	0.8	1.0	3.9	4.3
Federal government	0.2	0.2	3.4	2.5
	8.8%	10.0%	22.2%	20.8%

Prior to 1964 Ford's marketing programs in these areas had been formulated by a Fleet Manager and a FALS Manager on the General Marketing Manager's Staff. The new office, reporting to the Assistant General Manager, had been established to give high-level direction to the Division's fleet and leasing efforts.

Commercial Fleet: All sales of Ford Division products (except sales to the federal government) were made by or through the Ford dealer organization. Nevertheless, a considerable number of major fleet accounts wished to have a single contact within the Ford Division, or required a level of expertise frequently not available at the dealer level. To provide the required expertise at the local level, Fleet Merchandising Managers (generally with one or more assistants) were appointed in each district. These specialists, who were highly knowledgeable concerning the kind of economic analysis necessary to sell to major fleet accounts, helped the dealers to sell to Fleet accounts by assisting them to plan their sales strategies and by calling on the accounts.

Leasing: The Ford Division had two approaches to the leasing market. Independent leasing companies were handled in the same way as other fleet accounts. In addition, since 1958 the Division had operated the Ford Authorized Leasing Systems (FALS), a network of participating Ford dealers. Dealers who qualified could receive a FALS franchise, provided that they had adequate capital and resources to be in the leasing business and were located in accordance with the Division's representation plan. In 1967 FALS had approximately 120,000 units in operation and was the largest leasing system in the United States. Franchised FALS dealers operated within policies established by the Fleet and Leasing Office, and received assistance from FALS specialists in the district offices.

Rental: The rental market in the United States consisted essentially of two segments: (1) large national "primary" rental companies (Hertz, Avis, National), whose facilities were generally at airports, and (2) smaller "secondary" rental companies, which generally served local markets and charged rates lower than the primary companies. Since 1965 the Ford Division had pursued different strategies in dealing with these two markets.

Ford sold cars and trucks to the primary rental companies through its dealers, in the same way that it sold to fleet accounts and leasing companies (except that the volume was, of course, much greater). Ford executives emphasized the importance of the primary rental market as a means of exposing potential purchasers to Ford vehicles.

In dealing with the secondary market, Ford pursued a different strategy. While Ford dealers were encouraged to sell cars to the secondary car rental companies, Ford was in the process of developing its own Rent-a-Car System to compete in the secondary market. Under this system, approximately 2,000 Ford dealers had available approximately 20,000 cars for daily and weekly rental. Ford executives pointed out that the Ford Rent-a-Car system (already the third largest in the United States) would provide a significant boost to dealer profits, besides offering a real benefit to the customer who left his or her car for service.

Ford's fleet and leasing business was thus handled by the dealer organization, with assistance from specialized personnel located in the district offices. The Fleet and Leasing Office established monthly objectives (by market segment) for each district, and measured the performance of district personnel against these objectives. Each month, the Fleet and Leasing Office published a document ranking the 37 districts on their accomplishment of the previous month's objectives. According to office personnel, this document was useful for appraising and motivating fleet and leasing personnel in the district offices.

Advertising and Merchandising

Until early 1967 the Ford Division had had a General Marketing Office reporting to the Assistant General Manager. The General Marketing Office had been divided into four major components: Advertising (subdivided into car advertising and truck advertising); Car Merchandising; Truck Merchandising; and Used Vehicle Promotion.

In early 1967 the General Marketing Office was eliminated, and separate offices responsible for advertising and merchandising were established (reporting to the Assistant General Manager). While each office would have car and truck components, it was hoped that there would be more "rub-off" between car and truck advertising, and car and truck merchandising, than there had been under the old organization. As one executive explained:

We are not denying that there are differences between cars and trucks in these areas. It is obviously necessary to split this job up somehow. You can do it on a product basis (our old setup), or you can do it on a functional basis (our new setup). Either way, people in the two areas have to talk to each other, to assure that we go to market with coordinated programs.

Advertising: the Advertising Manager was new in his job, having recently been associated with Ford's advertising agency. He commented on his approach to advertising as follows:

Advertising, while very much a factor in automobile merchandising, is relatively unimportant compared with toothpaste, beer, and cigarettes. In the case of low-priced rapid-turnover items, the consumer buys the advertising as much as or more than he buys the product. With automobiles, styling, past product experience, price, and relationship with a dealer can all be deciding factors. Advertising can set the stage, display the styles, and point out features, but it is only one factor when it comes to closing the deal. For example, you would have to really work hard to lose a Mustang buyer through bad advertising. Price, style, quality, distribution — we had everything going for us.

Advertising can create a favorable predisposition, but it is largely the dealer that pulls the customer in. When you are working with product loyalty that can reach 70%, there is a limit to what advertising can do. We do know that people tend to pay increased attention to automobile advertising after making a purchase; they want to justify their buying decision.

Features are more important in truck advertising, where style is not as great a factor. We have done extremely well with our Twin I-Beam suspension, for example.

We have a corporate advertising activity, in the Marketing Staff [Exhibit 4A]. Their job is to provide a backdrop against which the divisions can sell. In essence, they sell Ford-the-Company, using quality, engineering, safety, and features common to both vehicle divisions as appropriate. We sell the cars and trucks.

Our biggest job is at announcement time, when we run heavy campaigns to make sure everyone knows that we have a new, better car, and what it looks like. During the rest of the year, we provide continuous advertising support which we peak during key periods: the January slump, the Spring build-up, the July-August phase-out period.

The rest of the job is up to the Ford Dealer Associations[11] and local dealers. For the most part, we advertise styling and product features; they advertise events and price. The closer you are to retail, the more direct you have to be.

Merchandising: The Merchandising Office was divided into four departments: Car Merchandising, Truck Merchandising, Used Vehicle Sales/Promotion, and Display & Exhibits. The Car Merchandising Department was divided into three components: Car Sales Promotion, Car Sales Training, and Special Promotions.

The Car Sales Training component was concerned primarily with product training, rather than job training, which was the responsibility of the Ford Marketing Institute.[12] The unit prepared fact books, films, and pocket pieces to train retail salesmen on the products they were selling.

In addition, this component had developed a job training program for "new hires." According to the Car Merchandising Manager, this program was a supplement to the Ford Marketing Institute, intended to combat the high turnover rate of retail salesmen during their first 90 days of employment.

The Car Sales Promotion component was primarily concerned with short-term sales and marketing situations. It had, for example, developed an annual "January White Sale," in which a special low-priced car was offered to the dealers during January. More recently, it had developed the very successful "Mustang Sprint" promotion:

In 1966 demand for eight-cylinder Mustangs had proved considerably greater than had been expected, and the Division found itself unable to fill orders, even though it had excess six-cylinder capacity. In an effort to turn this situation to Ford's advantage, the Car Sales Promotion unit had developed the "Mustang Sprint" promotion, which was implemented in the field within two months of its inception.

The "Mustang Sprint" was a special product, essentially a standard six-cylinder Mustang with additional chrome, wire wheel covers, and a special package of options. It was sold to dealers at a reduced price and was believed to offer customers significant savings.

Advertising was directed at consumers who traditionally had expressed a preference for six-cylinder cars. "Six and the Single Girl," for example, was one of the advertising themes used in the promotion.

A Mustang objective was established for each dealer and retail salesman received a $25 cash incentive for each six-cylinder Mustang they sold.

The Car Merchandising Manager cited the "Mustang Sprint" program as an example of a successful short-term promotional effort. Sales of six-cylinder Mustangs had been increased from 30% to 45% of Mustang sales, and the rate had remained high after the sale was over.

Service

Service has always been a difficult problem to resolve in the automobile industry. The customer expects his car to run perfectly all the time, but there just is no such vehicle. The dealer knows that service is important (it represents 60% to 65% of his assets), but he generally has less experience in this area than in merchandising.

Service is a very important part of the dealer's business. Besides representing a large investment for the dealer, it has a significant effect on new car sales. On the average, about 65% of Ford owners will buy another Ford when they buy a new car. Among those dissatisfied with our service, this percentage drops considerably. Needless to say, that difference represents a lot of business for both the dealer and the Company.

The National Service Office, whose manager made the above statement, was responsible for the Ford Division's efforts in the service field. It planned and implemented (through the service departments in the districts) programs intended to improve dealer service, conducted service training in the field, and worked with Product Planning, Product Engineering, and Design on service-related problems. In addition, it administered the Ford warranty program and handled service-oriented communications between the Division and its customers.

The office maintained records of all customer complaints received by the Division. Those dealers having the most complaints were singled out for special attention, including a letter from the Assistant General Manager of the Ford Division. Moreover, field service specialists in the districts called on these dealers in an attempt to help them locate and solve their problems.

These problems generally fell into two areas:

(1) Inadequate service, from the customer's point of view.

---

[11] The Ford Dealer Associations were company-sponsored associations of Ford dealers in the same geographic area. They were used as forums for the discussion of common problems, and to provide a vehicle for shared local advertising.

[12] A formal training program for dealer personnel operated by Marketing Services, a function reporting to the Vice President, Car and Truck Group (Exhibit 5).

(2) Low-profit operations of a dealer's service facility.

The National Service Manager commented on these problems as follows:

We need to become more familiar with the dealer's service problems so we can provide direction. We have an experimental service facility, and have instituted a program of thorough analysis of the service operations of certain selected dealers. When this program has matured, we will expand it to cover all dealers, or, at least, the 2,000 largest dealers.

Moreover, we are adding to our retail knowledge by actually operating two retail facilities, utilizing the most sophisticated diagnostic equipment and techniques. These are pilot projects designed to assist the dealer through development of better service techniques, etc. We have no intention of getting into the retail service business on a continuing basis.

I am optimistic. We are giving service a higher priority and have organized to do something about it. We are beginning to get some answers, and we think we have found a way to disseminate them to the dealer organization.

The Autolite-Ford Parts Division

The parts business for Ford trucks and cars had traditionally been handled by Parts and Service Offices in the Ford and Lincoln-Mercury Divisions. For the most part, Ford and Lincoln-Mercury parts had been sold to Ford and Lincoln-Mercury dealers by the district sales organization. The Ford dealers then used these parts to repair vehicles and also sold them to independent garages, repair shops, and service stations.

The parts market was highly competitive, with independent parts manufactures having a considerable share of the market. While Ford had a reasonably "secure" market for certain parts, such as fenders and body panels, this was not the case with other parts, especially electrical parts. In the late 1950s Ford had a very low share of the independent "aftermarket." [13]

In April 1961 Ford acquired certain assets of the Electric Autolite Company. Electric Autolite was a major manufacturer of electrical automotive parts and accessories, somewhat oriented toward Chrysler Corporation products. According to published reports, Ford had acquired Autolite in order to achieve increased penetration of the aftermarket, especially in spark plugs, batteries, and other electrical parts. The Autolite business was to be operated as a separate division.

Thus, in 1961 Ford had three separate parts businesses:

(1) The Autolite parts business, going exclusively through the independent aftermarket.
(2) The Ford Division parts business, through franchised Ford dealers.
(3) The Lincoln-Mercury parts business, through franchised Lincoln-Mercury dealers.

Between 1964 and 1966 Ford management directed that a number of studies of the overall parts business be made. During this period, several major decisions were made:

(1) It was decided to broaden Autolite's product line to compete directly with full-line parts manufacturers in the automotive aftermarket.
(2) At this time, Ford was selling parts under six brand names. It was decided to reduce this number to two basic brands: Ford for the Dealers, and Autolite for the independent market. In addition, it was decided to brand more original equipment parts (e.g., filters, electrical parts) as "Autolite."
(3) It was decided in 1966 to consolidate all parts activities in a single division: the Autolite-Ford Parts Division. The Division General Manager would report to the Vice President, Car and Truck Group (Exhibit 5), and have full responsibility for the parts business.

In discussing this organizational change, Ford executives pointed out that the formation of a new division concentrated parts marketing in one place, in the hope that conflicts between the different distribution channels could be reduced.

The job of the Autolite-Ford Parts field representative was cited as an example of how the new organization would work. The field representative would be assigned a geographic territory containing both Ford dealers and independent distributors, jobbers, and garages. He would be given a sales quota, derived from the number of Ford vehicles registered in his territory. His objective would be to maximize the use of Autolite-Ford parts in his territory, using the best balance of dealers and independent outlets.

Autolite-Ford Parts executives did not believe that the new organization would create problems at the dealer level. Although the dealer would now be called on by two Ford salesmen (Ford Division and Autolite-Ford Parts), the parts salesmen would, in almost

---

[13] The "aftermarket" consisted of the market for all repair and replacement parts. The *independent* "aftermarket" referred to all parts sold through channels other than dealers franchised by the major automobile manufacturers.

all cases, deal directly with the dealer's parts manager.

The General Manager of Autolite-Ford Parts believed that the advantages of the new organization could best be understood in broader context. He said:

> Both service and parts are becoming increasingly complex. In recent years, we have seen a great increase in the number of two-car families, and a proliferation in the number of lines and models needed to serve these families. You never see two "family cars" in a two-car garage. Because of this proliferation of models, we now must stock 180,000 parts, as compared to 88,000 in 1957. And the automotive mechanic has to be able to deal with a much wider range of repairs.
>
> We have also seen increased governmental concern with safety and air pollution. But original equipment is only a minor part of these problems. We can manufacture nonpolluting exhaust systems and safe brakes, for example, but what happens after the car has been in service to the point where normal maintenance calls for a tune up, or a brake job?
>
> Given this set of considerations, we have two major objectives. First, we know that the substantial majority of Ford Motor Company's sales and profits come from new cars and trucks; we need an efficient service and parts supply capability to build and maintain customer loyalty. Second, we know that parts and service are a sales and profit opportunity — for us and for our dealers.

North American Automotive Operations in Late 1967

As noted above (page 263), North American Automotive Operations was significantly restructured in July 1967, according to a new organizational concept and framework. Instead of four groups (three of which were primarily concerned with manufacturing and/or assembly operations — Exhibit 5), there were now three groups: Manufacturing, Product Development, and Sales (Exhibit 4A). The Sales group, consisting of the two vehicle divisions, Ford of Canada, the Autolite-Ford Parts Division, and Marketing Services, was not operationally a Group, since no Vice President-Group Executive had been appointed to direct its activities. The former Vice President-Car and Truck Group had become Executive Vice President-North American Automotive Operations when the preceding Executive Vice President retired. The new Executive Vice President continued to supervise the divisions in the Sales group directly. Nevertheless, there was general agreement that a Vice President-Sales Group would eventually be appointed, as North American Automotive Operations moved toward a tri-functional, or "troika," form of organization.

The most significant immediate effects of the new organization were the loss by the vehicle divisions of their car and truck product planning and engineering functions; and the establishment of the new Product Development Group, which would take over these functions from the vehicle divisions and also the advanced product research function from the Engineering Staff at the Central Staff level (Exhibit 4A).

The following pages describe the Ford Division and the new Product Development Group after the reorganization.

The Ford Division

The organization chart of the Ford Division after the reorganization (October 16, 1967) is shown in Exhibit 7. The most significant changes from the Division's previous organization were:

(1) The transfer of the Car Product Planning and Car Product Engineering Offices to the new Product Development Group.
(2) The elimination of Truck Operations as an organizational entity.
(3) The transfer of Truck Product Planning and Truck Product Engineering from Truck Operations to the Product Development Group.
(4) The shift in the reporting relationship of the Heavy Truck Sales and Marketing Office from Truck Operations to the Assistant General Manager.
(5) The transfer of the Marketing Research Activity to the Corporate Marketing Staff.
(6) The establishment of a Marketing Product Plans Office, to serve as an interface between the Ford Division and Product Planning in the new Product Development Group.

The Marketing Product Plans Office was divided into three components: (1) Market Analysis, (2) Light Truck Plans Analysis, and (3) Car Plans Analysis. The Market Analysis Activity was to develop forward product strategies and needs as marketing inputs to the Product Development Group. The Light Truck Plans and Car Plans Activities were to review the Product Development Group's product plans after they had been formally submitted to top management, in order to make sure that the Ford Division could, in fact, "live with" the planned vehicles. As one executive explained:

> It [the Marketing Product Plans Office] is really a device to assure that we in the Ford Division have the capability to get our 2 cents in. As we look ahead, from

a sales point of view, we get strong indications as to what the market will want in terms of features, options, and accessories. It is important that we have a way of collecting and transmitting this information [to the Product Development Group] and of making sure that they give us a car that we can sell.

Product Development Group

The Product Development Group was headed by the former Vice President and General Manager of the Ford Division. It was divided into three major units: (1) Car Product Planning, which was responsible for the conceptual design of Ford, Lincoln, and Mercury automobiles; (2) Car Engineering, which was to establish engineering specifications for all automobile lines; and (3) Truck Product Development, which was responsible for both product planning and engineering for the Ford line of trucks (Exhibits 4C and 8).

In a letter of July 12, 1967, announcing to Ford executives the formation of the Product Development Group, the Chairman of the Board, Mr. Henry Ford II, wrote in part:

> ... The Product Development function which is being activated today will assume the responsibility for product planning, product engineering, program timing, and related financial controls for all North American automotive products that were previously assigned to the vehicle divisions. It will further assume appropriate coordination responsibilities for products of Ford Motor Company of Canada, Ltd. Although the selling divisions no longer will have direct line responsibility for product development, they will be expected to provide significant marketing inputs into the product development process and to participate in all key product decisions, through both continuing liaison during the development process and membership in key advisory committees.

Ford executives cited several anticipated advantages of the new group:

(1) The new group would be in a position to give balanced consideration to market appeal, plant investment commitments, and manufacturing costs in planning and engineering new products.
(2) The new group would be able to integrate planning for new models (previously done in the vehicle divisions) with advanced vehicle concepts (previously coming from the Central Engineering Staff) more effectively than had been possible under the old organization.
(3) It would be possible to organize the new group in terms of engineering vehicle systems (i.e., body, chassis, power train, electrical systems) rather than just component parts, and thus achieve improved performance, greater reliability, and cost economies.

Mr. Ford placed particular emphasis on the advantages and necessity of a systems approach in his letter of July 12.

The assignment of engineering design responsibilities to manufacturing divisions has proven effective in achieving the desired coordination between product engineering and manufacturing personnel. We plan to continue this pattern of engineering design responsibility. It is believed to be essential, however, that we improve the systems coordination and control over component design. To achieve this result, the present vehicle engineering functions will be reorganized along systems lines. The new systems engineering organizations within Product Development will continue to establish product acceptance specifications and carry out the engineering sign-off procedure before the start of production. In addition, the systems engineers will have concurrence responsibility in both advanced and final engineering releases. We anticipate that this will improve the participation of the systems engineers through the product development process. They will be in a position to assure that the necessary compromises in component design to satisfy multiple objectives will be made in the best interest of the total vehicle system.

Car Engineering

Car Engineering consisted of two major offices: Car Systems Engineering and Product Research. The Product Research Office was transferred intact from the Corporate Engineering Staff and worked on research in a number of automotive-oriented areas (e.g., gas turbines). Car Systems Engineering represented a new concept, replacing the vehicles engineering function in the old Car Product Engineering Office of the Ford Division.

Car Systems Engineering (Exhibit 9) was essentially responsible for translating product planning concepts into detailed specifications, much as the Ford Division Car Product Engineering Office had been. Rather than being organized along car lines, however, the new function was organized along two related dimensions:

(1) There were two car systems engineering groups, one concerned exclusively with light cars (Mustang,[14] Falcon,[14] Fairlane,[14] Montego,[15] Cougar[15]) and one concerned exclusively with "custom" cars (Ford,[14]

---

[14] Ford Division product.
[15] Lincoln-Mercury Division product.

Mercury,[15] Lincoln,[14] Thunderbird[15]). These groups did much the same kind of work as the old vehicle product engineering groups, except that they were organized by type of car (e.g., Mustang and Cougar; Lincoln and Thunderbird) rather than by vehicle division.

(2) There were four major functional systems engineering groups, responsible respectively for body, chassis, power train, and electrical systems. These major systems groups, which were in turn divided into smaller systems groups, took their respective sections of the basic vehicle specifications (which had been developed by the vehicle systems engineering groups), refined them further, and transmitted them to the appropriate design office.[16] In addition, they were to work with their respective design offices to ensure that resulting designs did, in fact, meet specifications.

In discussing the new organizational concept, the Vice President-Car Engineering pointed out that he now had a vertical organization (vehicle systems engineering) and a horizontal organization (body, chassis, power train, and electrical systems engineering). The former organization was designed to provide a smooth interface with Car Product Planning (which was organized by car lines) and the latter to provide a smooth interface with Manufacturing (which was organized by subsystems).

As an example of how the latter interface worked, he explained that each design office had appointed one or more persons to work directly with the systems engineer responsible for its product line. In effect, the systems engineer and design office representative working on a particular subsystem were to act as a team, to ensure that specifications, designs, and trade-offs between the two were made with maximum efficiency.

This new organizational arrangement had two major implications: (1) The systems engineers, working across car lines, would be able to specify designs with maximum advantage to the company as a whole (rather than individual car lines); and (2) the systems engineers in effect, took over direct responsibility for the implementation of their specifications, thus relieving Product Planning of follow-up work it had formerly been required to carry out.

Product Planning

The new Car Product Planning Activity (headed by the former manager of the Ford Division Car Product Planning Office) was divided into three activities: Ford, Lincoln-Mercury, and Advanced Car Product Planning (see Exhibit 10). In general, it was staffed with personnel from the old vehicle division product planning offices.

The most significant feature of the new organization was a greatly expanded advanced product planning function. This function was to work on all aspects of advanced planning for all company car lines preceding program approval. According to the Car Product Planning Manager, it had been possible to establish this function and still operate with fewer personnel because of the reorganization in Car Engineering. Under the new organization, it would be possible for Product Planning literally to "sign-off" a program (leaving implementation to the systems engineers) and thus focus its attention exclusively on planning.

In discussing his organization, the Car Product Planning Manager explained that he had had a choice between organizing by vehicle division or organizing by type of car (i.e., the light car and custom car). Although organizing by type of car would have facilitated communication with Car Systems Engineering, he had decided to organize by division and car lines, since executives in the vehicle divisions felt strongly that there should be readily identifiable product planning components working on their respective divisions' car lines.

The Ford and Lincoln-Mercury product planning groups were divided into groups working on light cars and groups working on custom cars. These groups provided a direct link between Product Planning and the light car and custom car systems engineering groups in Car Systems Engineering.

Truck Product Development

Truck Product Development was headed by the former Ford Division Truck Operations Manager. In his new position, he had reporting to him the same functions which had reported to him in his old position, except that the Heavy Truck Sales and Marketing Manager now reported to the Ford Division Assistant General Manager.

Under the new organization, the truck program continued to function much as it had under the old. While the Truck Product Development Manager no longer had direct responsibility for marketing, in many ways he continued to function as the individual most closely identified with the overall truck program. The expanded role of truck engineering (through the new systems approach) had, in fact, increased his re-

---

[16] As noted above, the design officers, with the exception of chassis, were located in the basic manufacturing divisions.

sponsibility for the "cradle to grave" implementation of product programs, particularly in the manufacturing area.

Organizational Changes in Other Ford Operations

The following section briefly describes the recent organizational histories of Ford's tractor and overseas businesses. As will be seen, developments in the organizations of these businesses paralleled those of North American Automotive Operations in a number of interesting respects.

Overseas Operations

In 1957 the Ford International Division (FID) provided staff support for Ford's far-flung operations outside the United States. Staff services in such areas as finance, industrial relations, marketing, manufacturing, product planning, and engineering were offered to Ford companies in Europe, Africa, South America, and Australia. FID had regional managers for (1) European manufacturing, (2) European sales and assembly, (3) Latin America, and (4) a manager for Ford's "direct franchise" dealers. The first three managers served in a liaison capacity between FID and Ford's foreign subsidiaries. The fourth was essentially the sales manager for Ford products, regardless of origin, sold through direct franchise dealers.

At this time Ford's overseas operations could be classified into four types of activities:

(1) There were large, fully integrated design-engineering-manufacturing-sales companies in England and in Germany. These companies were strong in their respective domestic markets and also sold in other countries.
(2) There were assembly-sales complexes in such countries as Holland, Belgium, Denmark, South Africa, Brazil, and Australia. They imported car and truck subassemblies (in "knock-down" or "KD" form) from U.S., English, and German companies and assembled them for sale.
(3) There were sales subsidiaries in countries such France, Uruguay, and Chile.
(4) There were Ford franchised dealers in many other countries where Ford did not have subsidiaries. These dealers accounted individually for relatively small volumes, and were supplied by export from the United States, England, and Germany in response to their orders.

In early 1959 Ford established an office in Brussels. This office had a resident director and was to supply staff services to Ford's assembly-sales complexes in Europe, excluding England and Germany. Shortly thereafter, the resident director was given coordinating authority over the assembly-sales complexes. By this time, however, Ford was in the process of closing many of its European assembly plants. Because of the establishment of the European Economic Community (EEC) tariff rates were falling, and it was becoming more economical to ship finished units (rather than parts and components) across national borders.

In 1965, FID's staff operations were consolidated with Ford's Central Office staff groups. The reason for this move was that top management was to an increasing extent viewing the company as a world-wide organization, and wanted its key staff groups to develop a multinational orientation. As part of this change in thinking, FID was renamed Overseas Automotive and Tractor Operations.[17]

In mid-1967, after an intensive study of its European operations, Ford's top management created Ford of Europe. Ford of Europe was organized in "troika" form with three function groups: Product Development, Manufacturing, and Sales (see Exhibits 4B and 11). British and German concerns continued to function as legal entities within their countries under the coordination of Ford of Europe.

In the meantime, Ford's operations in other parts of the world had grown. In some parts of the world, Latin America in particular, restrictive laws had forced the creation of national automobile industries. In some of these countries, Ford had made substantial capital commitments in order to stay in the market, and had built assembly and manufacturing plants. In Mexico, Fords and Mustangs were manufactured largely from locally manufactured parts and components, including engines. In Brazil, Ford Galaxies were produced. In Australia, the Ford subsidiary made a version of the Falcon. And there was still a growing export business through direct franchise Ford dealers.

In 1967 several groups reported to the Executive Vice President-Overseas Automotive and Tractor Operations (Exhibit 4B). Ford of Europe coordinated the company's activities in Europe. The Latin American Group supervised Ford affiliates in Argentina, Brazil, Mexico, Chile, Peru, Uruguay, and Venezuela. The Canadian Overseas Group supervised af-

---

[17] The world-wide Tractor Operations reported to the Executive Vice President-Overseas Automotive and Tractor Operations, but was operated independently of the overseas automotive business.

filiates in Australia, New Zealand, Singapore, and South Africa (all of which were technically subsidiaries of the Canadian company) but not Ford of Canada itself, which was part of North American Automotive Operations. As a matter of organizational convenience, Overseas Distribution Operations, which handled exports from the United States to franchised dealers in a large number of countries and the shipment of KD units to affiliates throughout the world, was operated as part of the Canadian Overseas Group.

Tractor Operations

Long interested in a "farm locomotive," Henry Ford had developed a workable, lightweight tractor by 1907, four years after he had founded Ford Motor Company. Almost from the beginning, then, Ford was in the tractor business. Under the stimulus of wartime conditions, mass-produced Fordson tractors began coming off the assembly line in 1917, mainly for shipment to England. Manufacture of Fordson tractors began in Cork, Ireland, in 1919. Then in 1933 tractor production began in Dagenham, England, following the closing of the Cork line in 1932.

The U.S. and British companies emerged as the two sources of Ford tractors, with each supplying both domestic and export markets. In the United States (circa 1957), the Ford Tractor and Implement Division mainly sold gasoline-powered tractors. Ford Motor Company, Ltd., in England, however, had converted to a diesel-powered line in order to be competitive in European markets. The British tractor line achieved a major market position in other European countries. It grew to be as large as Ford's U.S. tractor business and, in fact, supplied diesel units to Ford in the United States.

In 1961 Ford Tractor Division was formed to coordinate the activities of the United States and British tractor operations. In 1962 the Division was given world-wide line responsibility for the design, manufacture, and distribution of Ford tractors and equipment for farm and industrial use.[18]

There were several reasons for creating a worldwide tractor business. First, world market needs were perceived to be relatively homogeneous, although sales mix might vary widely from one country to another. Second, markets outside the United States were growing faster than the U.S. market. Finally, there would be significant cost savings from establishing a single world-wide manufacturing and distribution system.

Ford Tractor Division was organized as a "troika." Product development activities were carried on in Birmingham, Michigan, and in Basildon, England. Major manufacturing points were Highland Park, Michigan; Antwerp, Belgium; and Basildon. These manufacturing facilities were specialized, operating as "single sources." There were 27 assembly points throughout the world, building complete units from parts and components made in Highland Park, Antwerp, and Basildon. The marketing function was organized regionally, with three regional managers (U.S., European, and Overseas[19]) directing sales branches in various countries.

In 1967 Ford Tractor Division reported to Ford's Executive Vice President-Overseas Automotive and Tractor Operations.[20]

---

[18] The name of the Division was changed to Ford Tractor Operations in 1967.

[19] I.e., the rest of the world.

[20] For additional information see Ford Motor Company. Tractor Division case, beginning on p. 412.

Exhibit 1. Ten-Year Financial Summary of Ford Motor Company and Consolidated Subsidiaries, 1957–1966
(Dollar amounts in millions)

	1966	1965	1964	1963	1962	1961	1960	1959	1958	1957
Sales	$12,240.0	11,536.8	9,670.8	8,742.5	8,089.6	6,709.4	6,797.6	6,648.8	5,280.9	6,839.3
Income before income taxes	$ 1,166.8	1,305.3	992.1	1,026.2	1,003.7	828.4	885.0	958.0	272.2	650.4
Provision for income taxes	$ 539.6	595.6	482.2	529.7	513.4	407.0	426.4	464.6	126.3	331.2
Net income	$ 621.0	703.0	505.6	488.5	480.7	409.6	427.9	451.4	116.2	294.0
Retained income	$ 356.4	470.0	284.2	289.8	282.5	244.7	263.3	291.9	6.8	163.3
Capital expenditures for expansion, modernization and replacement of facilities (excluding special tools)	$ 692.5	629.1	463.1	352.1	279.9	267.0	229.7	143.3	169.4	414.5
Depreciation	$ 307.9	267.5	242.5	232.9	228.3	210.5	208.4	211.6	223.2	208.1
Expenditures for special tools	$ 358.9	366.6	324.7	220.4	171.1	174.3	202.1	190.9	178.4	249.6
Amortization of special tools	$ 322.5	276.4	234.6	188.9	170.1	184.1	177.7	217.9	246.0	231.8
Stockholders' equity at year end	$ 4,782.0	4,490.8	4,011.0	3,717.9	3,418.4	3,127.7	2,879.6	2,614.8	2,312.9	2,300.3
Employe data										
Worldwide										
Payroll	$ 2,807.8	2,613.0	2,252.1	1,983.1	1,822.2	1,491.8	1,495.3	1,400.6	1,172.8	1,413.7
Average number of employes	388,016	364,487	336,841	316,568	302,563	262,066	266,027	251,451	229,777	277,330
U.S. Operations										
Payroll	$ 2,203.8	2,062.8	1,750.9	1,552.4	1,452.3	1,173.4	1,193.9	1,151.6	954.5	1,204.6
Average total hourly labor costs per hour worked, including employe benefits*	$ 4.81	4.56	4.29	4.11	3.92	3.73	3.59	3.44	3.33	3.09
Average number of employes	233,849	217,741	197,578	187,428	186,640	154,659	160,181	159,541	142,076	191,759

* Excludes data for Philco-Ford and other subsidiary companies.

Per share (in dollars)										
Net income	$ 5.63	6.33	4.56	4.42	4.36	3.72	3.90	4.12	1.06	2.70
Cash dividends	$ 2.40	2.10	2.00	1.80	1.80	1.50	1.50	1.40	1.00	1.20
Stockholders' equity	$ 43.51	40.39	36.17	33.61	30.99	28.42	26.22	23.83	21.12	21.11

Exhibit 2. Ten-Year Summary of Vehicle Factory Sales, Ford Motor Company and Consolidated Subsidiaries, 1957–1966

U.S. and Canada — cars and trucks*										
Cars	1966	1965	1964	1963	1962	1961	1960	1959	1958	1957
Ford U.S.										
Ford	960,905	1,044,066	878,353	909,886	721,848	711,847	916,073	1,352,110	985,166	1,506,469
Fairlane	295,419	251,222	233,177	318,291	385,138	58,795	—	—	—	—
Falcon	169,558	204,803	279,627	341,261	380,530	485,302	505,137	99,304	—	—
Mustang	566,367	564,999	293,807	—	—	—	—	—	—	—
Thunderbird	70,339	74,102	89,045	65,643	74,496	86,463	85,337	74,475	52,401	15,532
Mercury	152,220	189,967	125,482	118,577	108,454	109,394	160,049	156,253	129,088	274,521
Mercury Comet	127,195	161,982	194,568	149,683	145,018	185,419	196,876	—	—	—
Mercury Cougar	42,356	—	—	—	—	—	—	—	—	—
Lincoln Continental	51,374	43,921	37,231	32,858	32,962	32,538	19,998	29,248	26,319	36,336
Total**	2,435,733	2,535,062	2,131,747	1,959,579	1,929,100	1,685,015	1,884,023	1,741,855	1,221,909	1,883,045
Ford of Canada	181,426	184,169	161,688	142,887	120,967	99,679	95,855	101,669	92,135	110,472
Cars, total	2,617,159	2,719,231	2,293,435	2,102,466	2,050,067	1,784,694	1,979,878	1,843,524	1,314,044	1,993,517
Industry	9,288,835	10,009,712	8,308,462	8,167,464	7,363,164	5,868,179	7,000,217	5,891,219	4,555,648	6,452,953
Percent of industry	28.2	27.2	27.6	25.7	27.8	30.4	28.3	31.3	28.8	30.9
Trucks***										
Ford U.S.	568,129	543,339	448,431	425,527	372,893	335,654	338,311	347,042	242,703	338,728
Ford of Canada	54,021	40,795	37,414	32,906	25,747	19,902	19,883	18,587	17,539	24,652
Trucks, total***	622,150	584,134	485,845	458,433	398,640	355,556	358,194	365,629	260,242	363,380
Industry	1,926,533	1,893,721	1,650,372	1,560,761	1,321,089	1,197,387	1,263,490	1,205,539	939,098	1,177,965
Percent of industry	32.3	30.8	29.4	29.4	30.2	29.7	28.3	30.3	27.7	30.8
Cars and trucks, total	3,239,309	3,303,365	2,779,280	2,560,899	2,448,707	2,140,250	2,338,072	2,209,153	1,574,286	2,356,897
Industry	11,215,368	11,903,433	9,958,834	9,728,225	8,684,253	7,065,566	8,263,707	7,096,758	5,494,746	7,630,918
Percent of industry	28.9	27.8	27.9	26.3	28.2	30.3	28.3	31.1	28.7	30.9
Outside U.S. and Canada — cars and trucks										
Cars										
Britain	441,128	501,653	517,167	492,361	357,561	341,057	383,392	321,399	292,019	240,401
Germany	441,950	464,279	355,573	348,982	269,548	230,352	181,771	133,055	109,017	69,248
Australia	50,135	40,311	36,214	36,705	45,029	26,572	14,361	—	—	—
Argentina	16,198	15,442	11,966	2,043	—	—	—	—	—	—
Mexico	17,743	7,842	—	—	—	—	—	—	—	—
Cars, total	967,154	1,029,527	920,920	880,091	672,138	597,981	579,524	454,454	401,036	309,649
Trucks										
Britain	110,982	84,676	91,121	83,542	87,909	92,568	91,327	85,367	69,948	52,618
Germany	45,630	32,346	38,479	36,096	35,831	31,682	27,552	21,858	16,831	20,799
Brazil	13,783	11,905	11,842	12,819	21,622	14,044	19,037	—	—	—
Australia	7,009	7,656	7,051	7,603	7,746	4,328	—	—	—	—
Argentina	13,536	13,233	9,862	—	—	—	—	—	—	—
Mexico	9,379	4,624	—	—	—	—	—	—	—	—
Trucks, total	200,319	154,440	158,355	140,060	153,108	142,622	137,916	107,225	86,779	73,417
Cars and trucks, total	1,167,473	1,183,967	1,079,275	1,020,151	825,246	740,603	717,440	561,679	487,815	383,066
Worldwide tractors										
Ford U.S.	38,620	31,047	25,880	26,046	27,489	24,319	26,806	45,014	45,685	44,874
Overseas	79,768	76,978	68,292	85,198	74,696	71,962	71,474	65,817	59,375	45,127
Tractors, total	118,388	108,025	94,172	111,244	102,185	96,281	98,280	110,831	105,060	90,001
Total worldwide factory sales	4,525,170	4,595,357	3,952,727	3,692,294	3,376,138	2,977,134	3,153,792	2,881,663	2,167,161	2,829,964

* Factory sales are by source of manufacture, except that Ford U.S. exports to Canada are included as factory sales of Ford of Canada and Ford of Canada exports to the United States are included as factory sales of Ford U.S.

** Includes an aggregate of 229,888 units of car lines no longer produced by the Company.

*** Includes buses.

Source of Industry Data: Automobile Manufacturers Association

Exhibit 3. Corporate Organization Chart, May 23, 1959

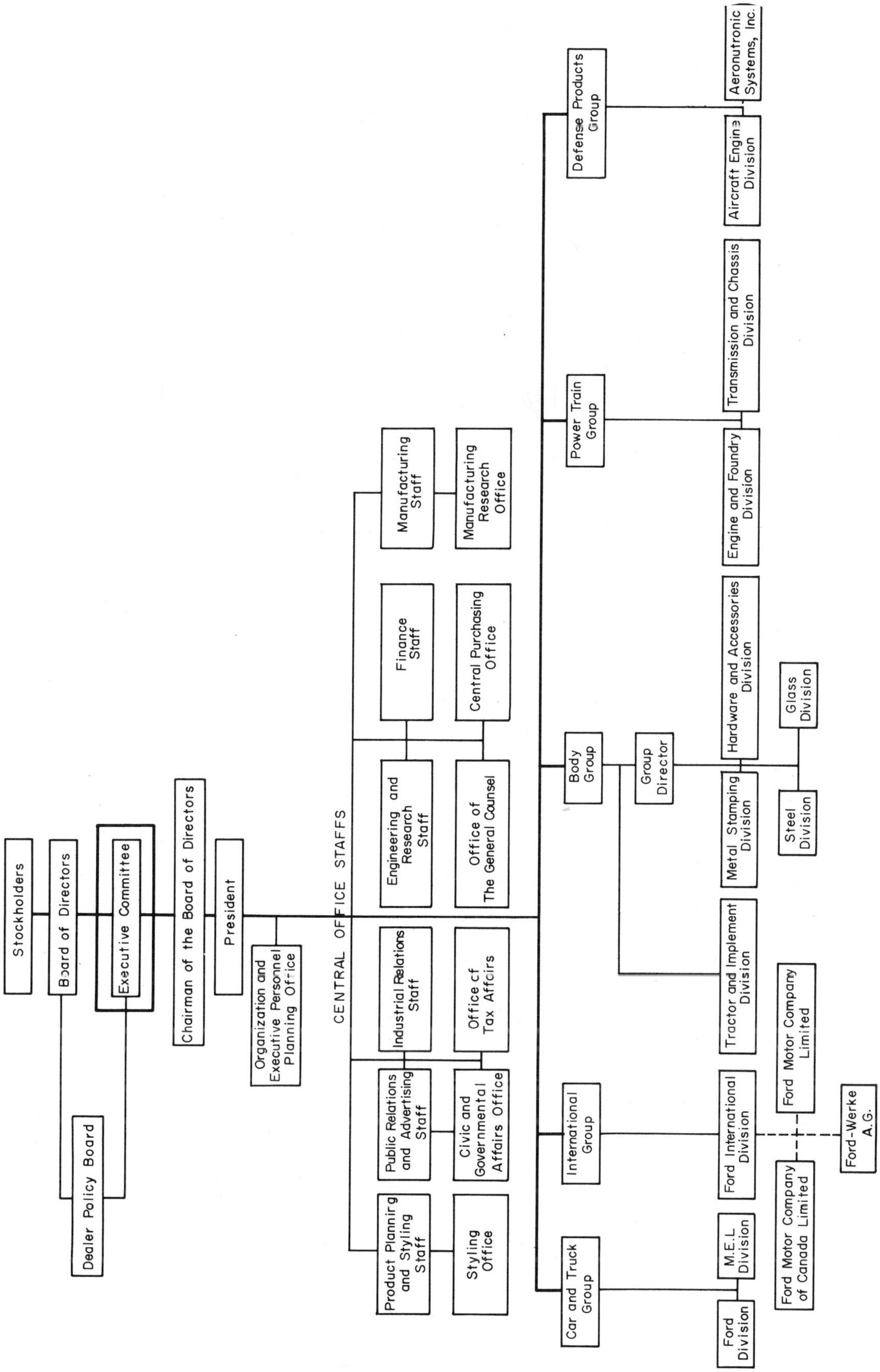

282 Cases and Commentaries

Exhibit 4A. Corporate Organization Chart, November 1, 1967

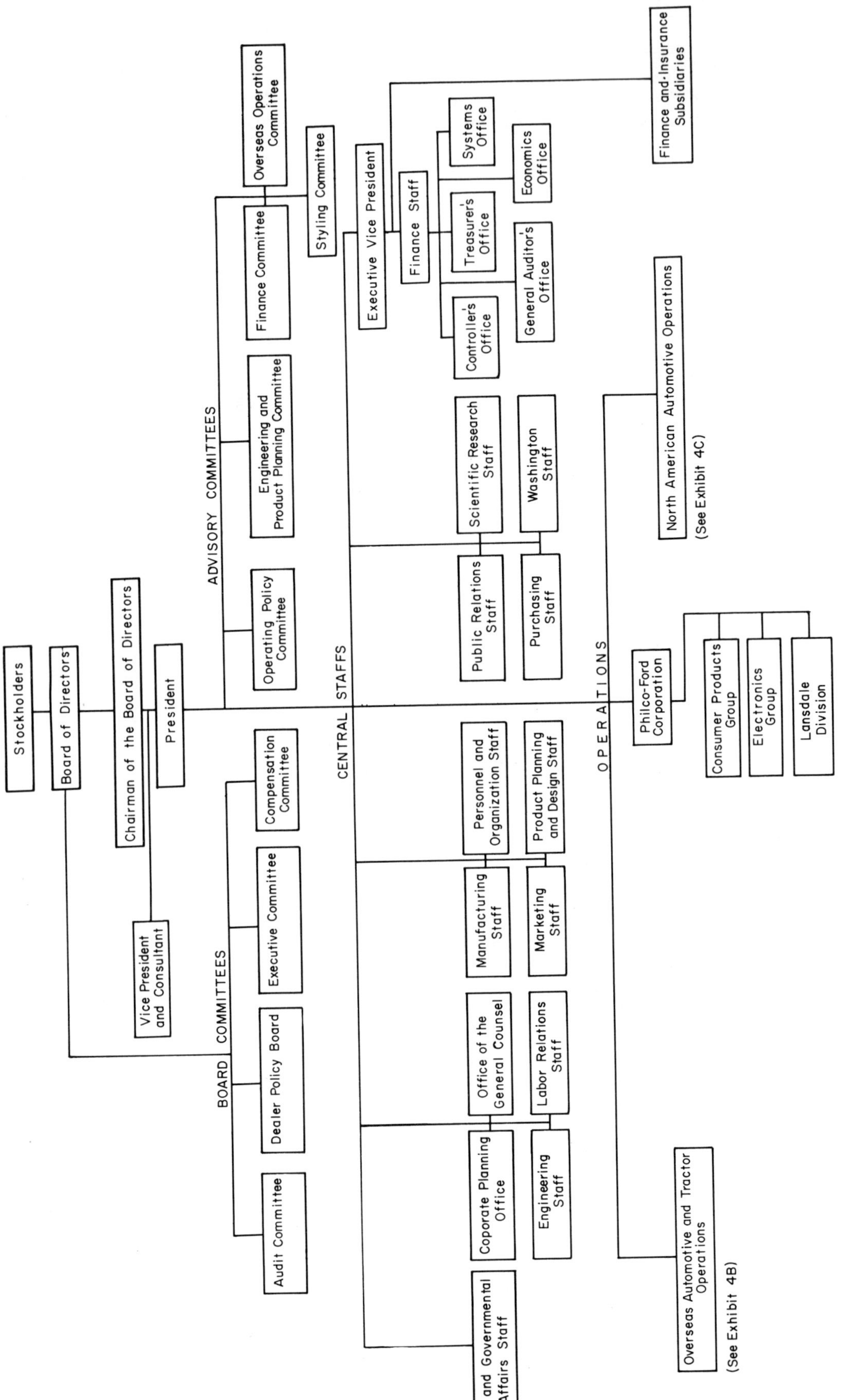

- Stockholders
- Board of Directors
- Chairman of the Board of Directors
- President
- Vice President and Consultant

BOARD COMMITTEES
- Audit Committee
- Dealer Policy Board
- Executive Committee
- Compensation Committee

ADVISORY COMMITTEES
- Operating Policy Committee
- Engineering and Product Planning Committee
- Finance Committee
- Styling Committee
- Overseas Operations Committee

CENTRAL STAFFS
- Civic and Governmental Affairs Staff
- Corporate Planning Office
- Engineering Staff
- Office of the General Counsel
- Labor Relations Staff
- Manufacturing Staff
- Marketing Staff
- Personnel and Organization Staff
- Product Planning and Design Staff
- Public Relations Staff
- Purchasing Staff
- Scientific Research Staff
- Washington Staff
- Executive Vice President — Finance Staff
  - Controller's Office
  - Treasurer's Office
  - Systems Office
  - General Auditor's Office
  - Economics Office

OPERATIONS
- Overseas Automotive and Tractor Operations (See Exhibit 4B)
- North American Automotive Operations (See Exhibit 4C)
- Philco-Ford Corporation
  - Consumer Products Group
  - Electronics Group
  - Lansdale Division
- Finance and-Insurance Subsidiaries

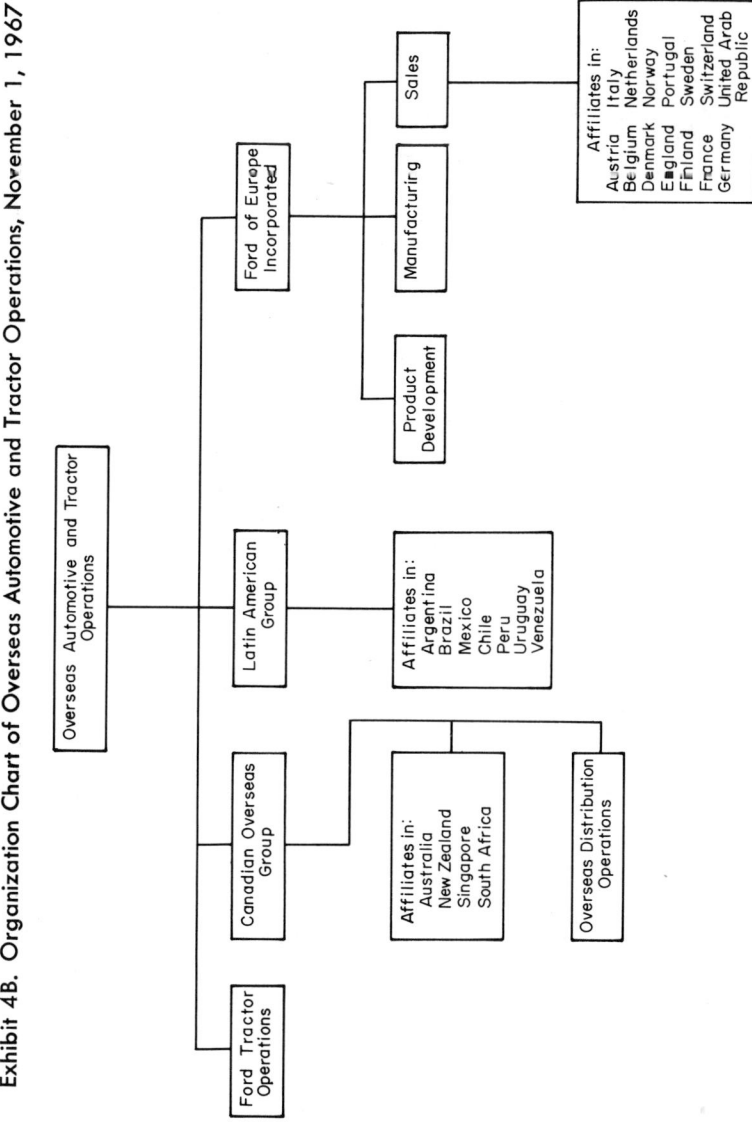

Exhibit 4B. Organization Chart of Overseas Automotive and Tractor Operations, November 1, 1967

284   Cases and Commentaries

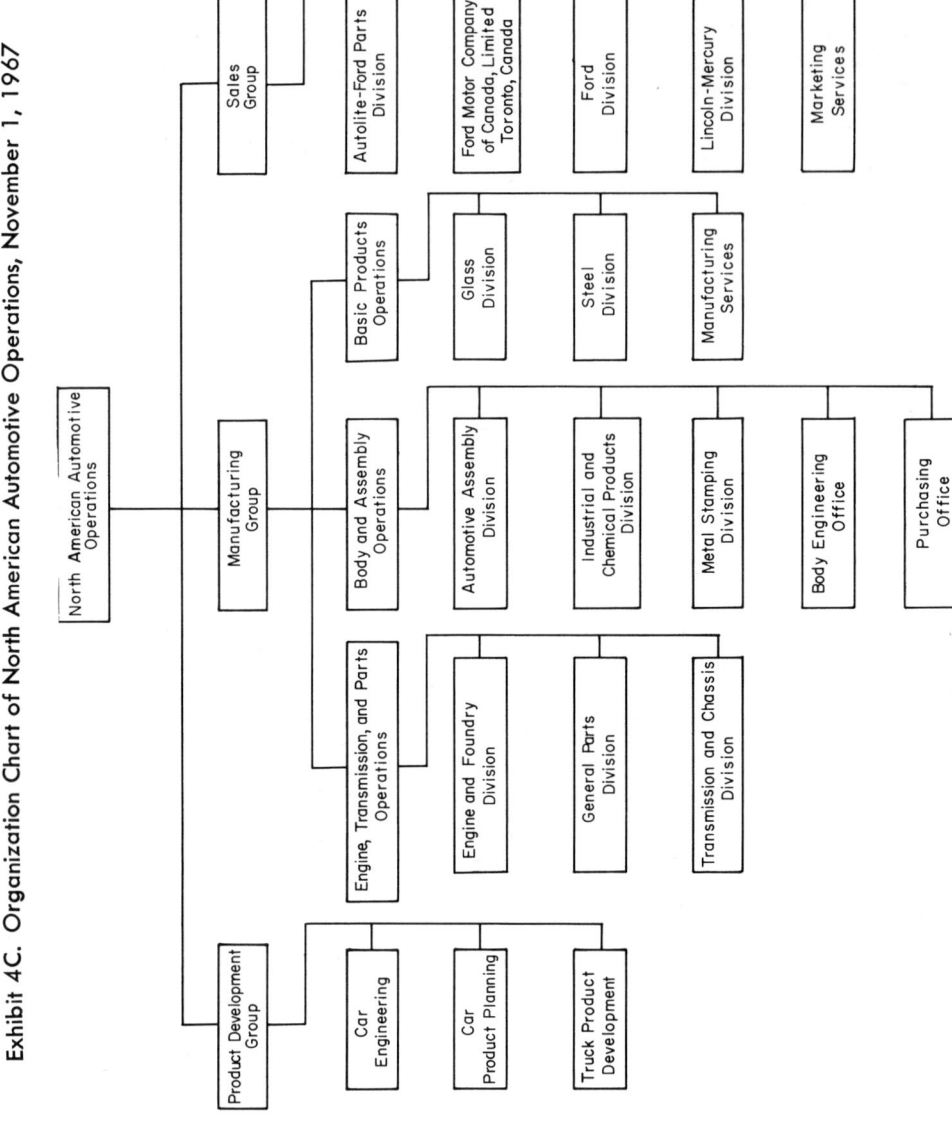

Exhibit 4C. Organization Chart of North American Automotive Operations, November 1, 1967

Exhibit 5. Organization Chart of North American Automotive Operations, May 1967

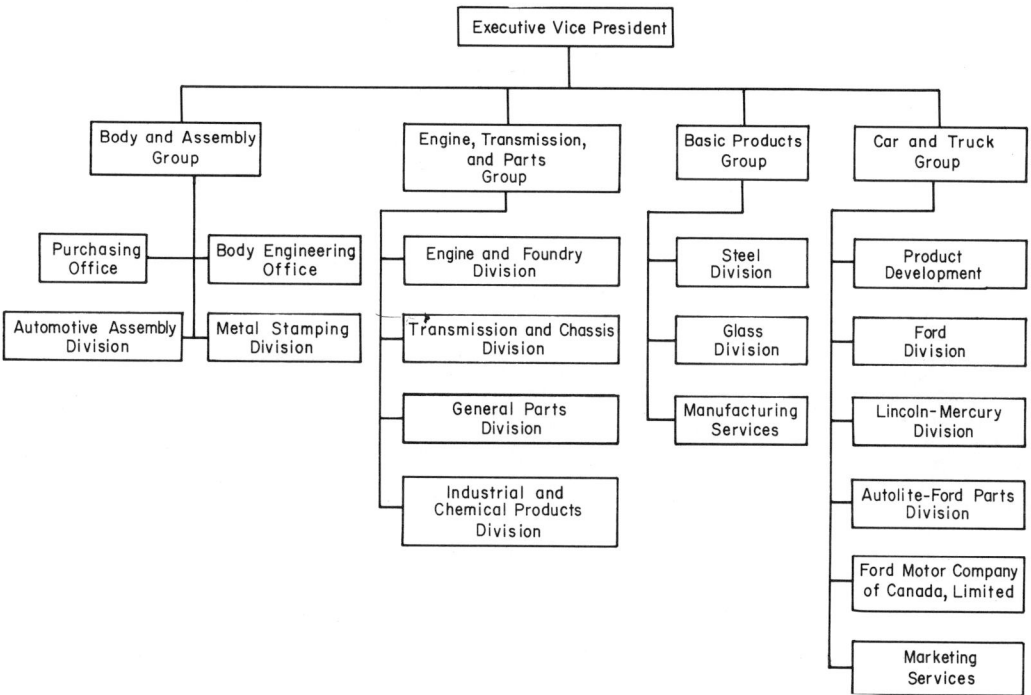

Exhibit 6. Organization Chart of the Ford Division, April 12, 1967

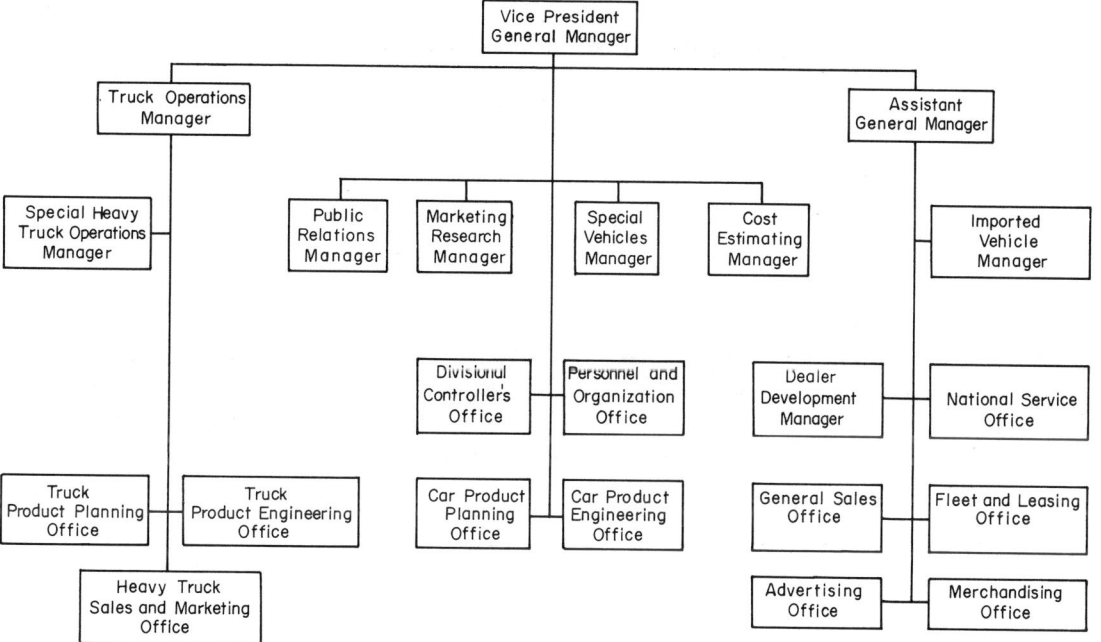

Exhibit 7. Organization Chart of the Ford Division, October 16, 1967, After Reorganization

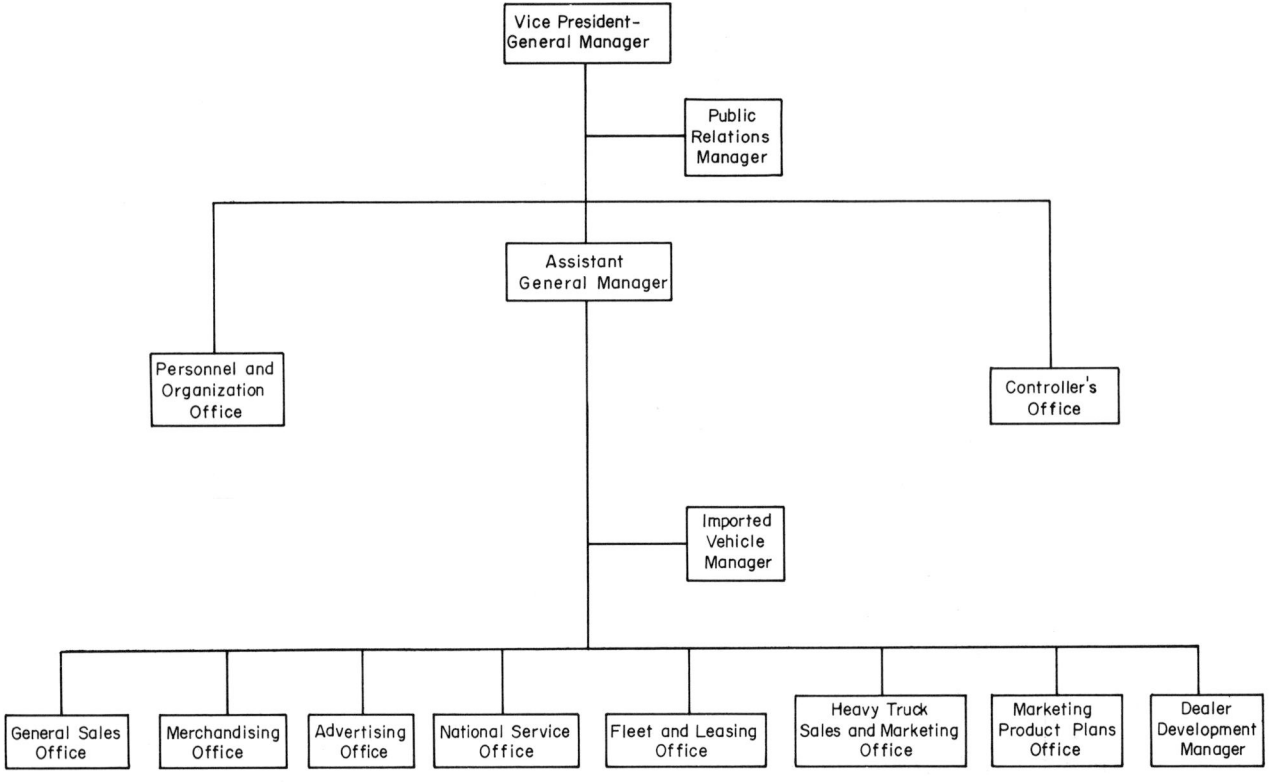

Exhibit 8. Organization Chart of Product Development Group, July 12, 1967

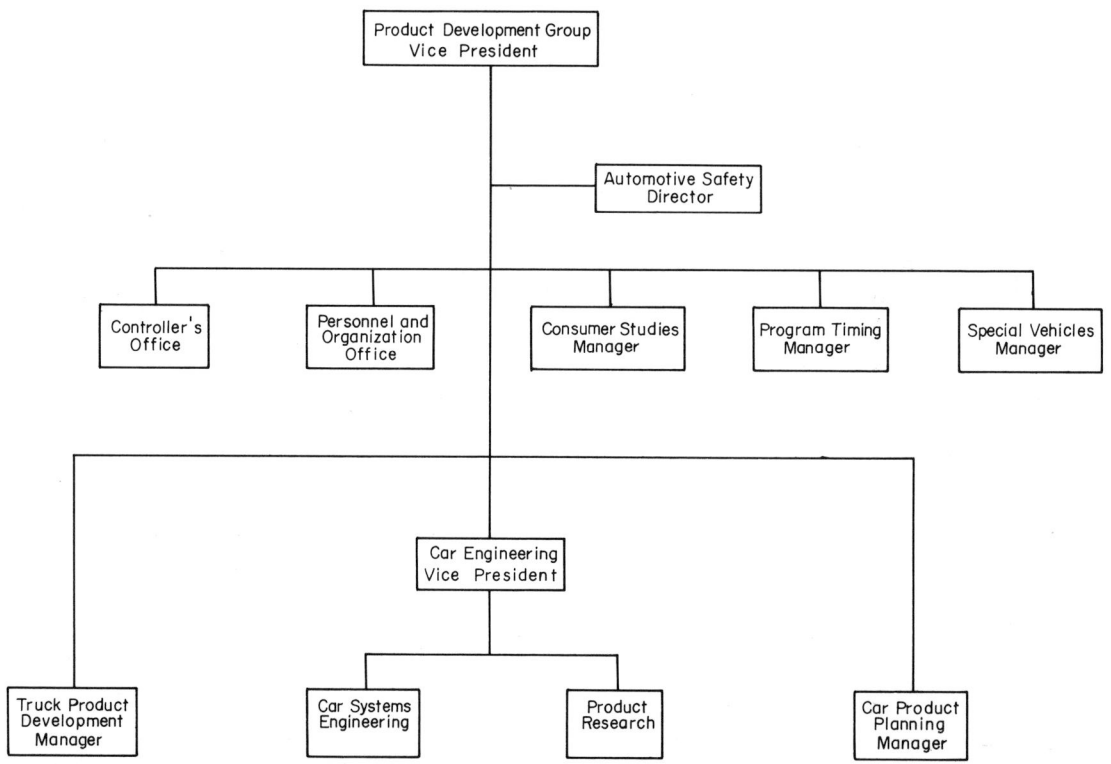

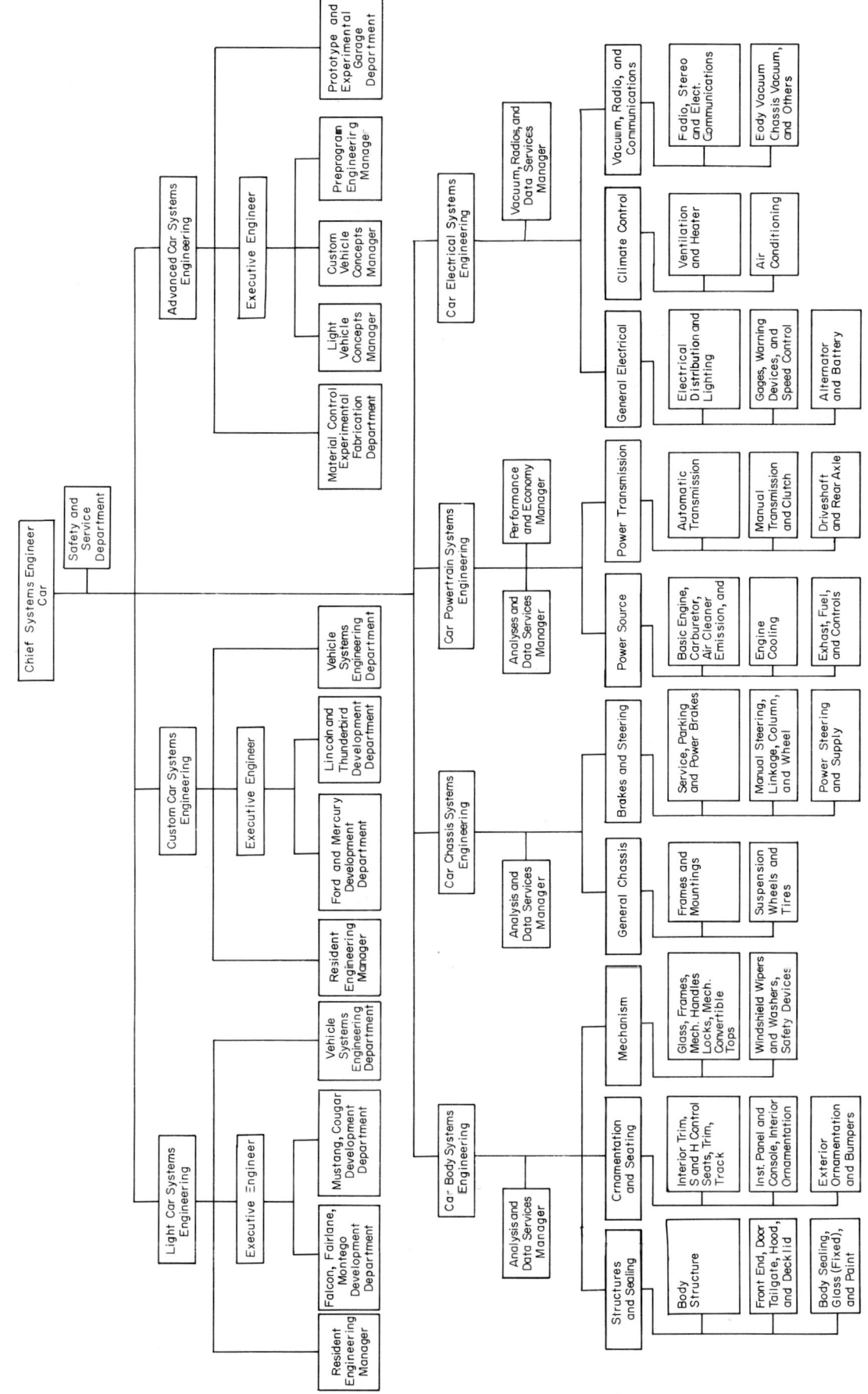

Exhibit 9. Organization Chart of Car Systems Engineering, August 16, 1967

288 Cases and Commentaries

Exhibit 10. Organization Chart of Car Product Planning, August 16, 1967

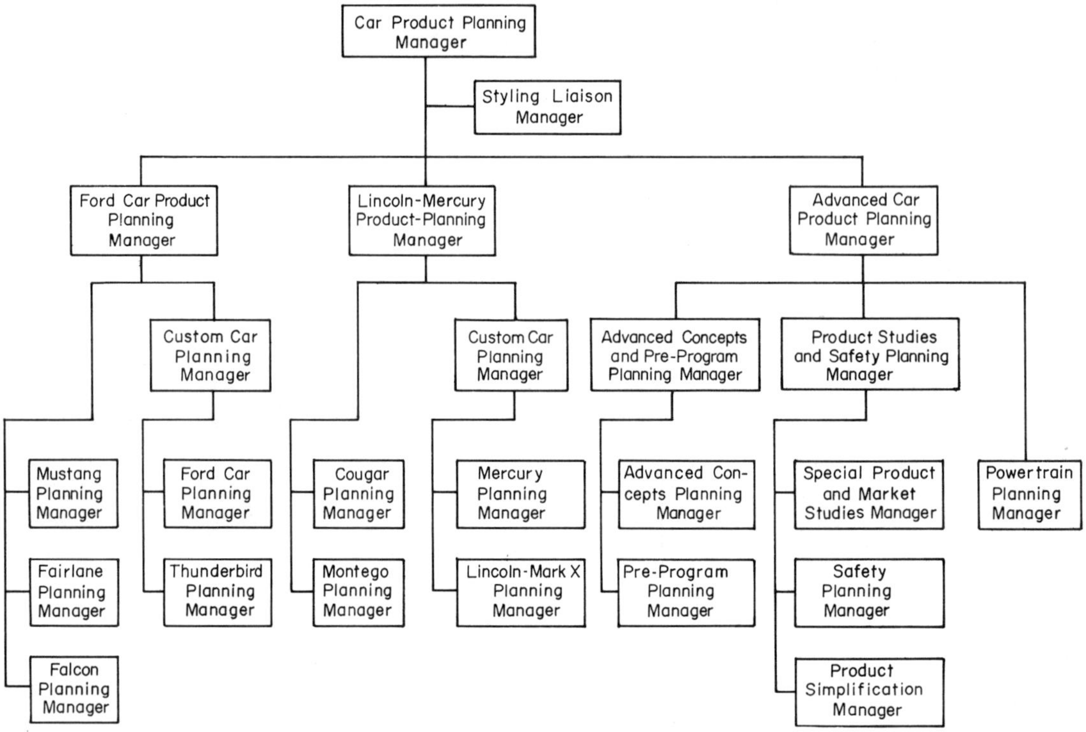

Exhibit 11. Organization Chart of Ford of Europe, Incorporated, Mid-1967

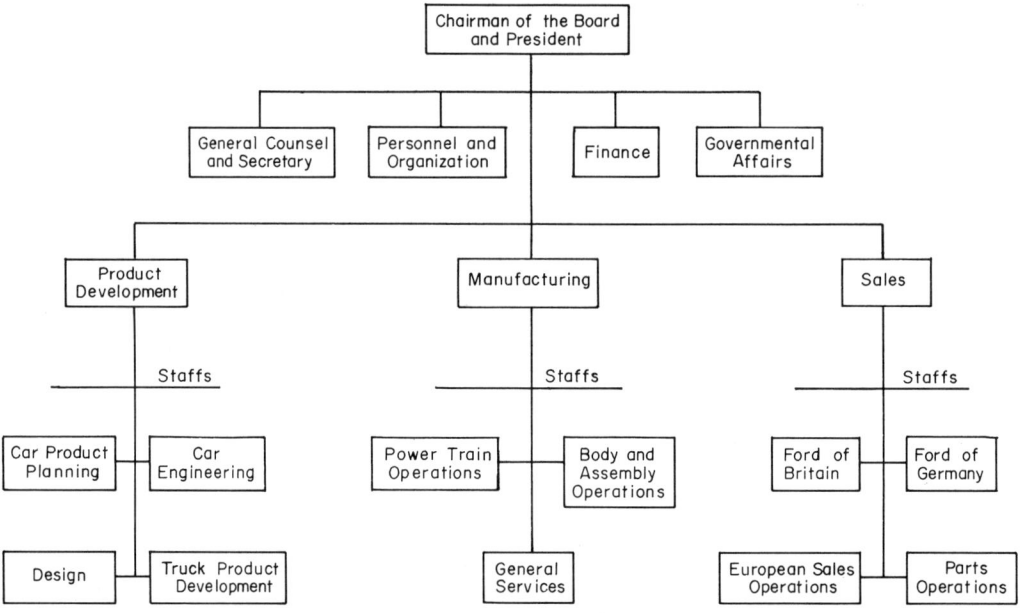

COMMENTARY

The Ford case history describes more than a decade of moving by stages from decentralization by product line in the middle 1950s to the establishment of a single North American "business" by 1968. During these years the structure was somewhere in between. The framework was probably a difficult one in which to operate in a growing, changing, highly competitive industry.

In the 12-year period, 1956–1968, Ford's domestic operations moved in three stages from an organization decentralized by product line (Ford, Lincoln, Continental, Mercury, and Edsel) to a single business structure for all cars and trucks. In the first stage, the smaller divisions were consolidated into the Lincoln-Mercury Division. In a second phase, basic resources (assembly, purchasing, engineering) for the two divisions (Ford and Lincoln-Mercury were merged, with the Ford Division managing these functions for all car and truck product lines. In stage three, the several manufacturing units were consolidated into one group. A Product Development Group was formed from product planning and engineering units in the two vehicle divisions plus a unit from the Central Engineering Staff responsible for advanced vehicle concepts. Ford, Lincoln-Mercury, Autolite-Ford Parts, and the domestic marketing operations of Ford of Canada then constituted a third wing, the Sales Group. By 1968, then, Ford's North American Automotive Operations had arrived at what its management called the "troika" form of organization: Manufacturing, Product Development, and Sales. It was structured as one business embracing the sale and leasing of all Ford cars, light and heavy trucks, and repair parts in the United States and Canada. Within this framework a program structure had developed and was still evolving.

In the same period the Ford top management had also completely restructured its overseas operations. Ford of Europe, put together from the British and the German companies, was organized in a "troika" form as a single business for cars and trucks in Europe. Ford Tractor was established as a single world-wide business from tractor operations in the United States and Britain.

The discussion which follows will focus mainly on North American Automotive Operations. It will be useful (1) to ask why the decentralization scheme of the middle 1950s did not work and what advantages derive from creating a single domestic car and truck business. Then, of particular interest are (2) the formation and structuring of the Product Development Group in late 1967; (3) the program-resource structure in the Sales Group; and (4) the implications for strategy. Given the history of the Ford domestic organization it may be useful, next, (5) to speculate as to future organizational developments. Finally, in an effort to broaden our understanding of the range of factors that are relevant in defining the scopes of integrated business units, the commentary considers the establishment of Ford of Europe and Ford Tractor as businesses.

E Pluribus Unum

The move in the early 1950s to establish several operating divisions, each responsible for designing, assembling, and marketing a Ford automotive line, was in accord with an organizational pattern common in the industry. Undoubtedly, the General Motors structure was a strong influence. From 1925 on General Motors had had operating divisions for Chevrolet, Pontiac, Oldsmobile, Buick, Cadillac, and General Motors Truck. In the words of Alfred Sloan each division would:

> . . . manufacture and sell complete motor cars — purchasing part of the component parts from outside sources, part from other divisions of the Corporation and manufacturing part with their own facilities.[1]

---

[1] Alfred D. Chandler, Jr., *Strategy and Structure* (Cambridge, The M.I.T. Press, 1962), p. 135.

The General Motors structure was designed to carry out a marketing strategy of having a car in each market-price bracket from lowest to highest. As Sloan described it:

> It seemed to me that the intelligent approach would be to have a car at every price position, just the same as a general conducting a campaign wants to have an army at every point he is likely to be attacked.[2]

Hence, in the original scheme, Cadillac was the General Motors offering in the highest-price category and Chevrolet in the lowest. Oakland, Buick, and Oldsmobile were at intermediate points and the Pontiac was brought out in 1925 to fill the price bracket between Chevrolet and Oldsmobile.[3]

Another important element in the Sloan organization concept was the autonomy of operating division managers coupled with the coordination and control of division activities by a headquarters management. In his book, Mr. Sloan elaborated:

> . . . good management rests on a reconciliation of centralization and decentralization, or "decentralization with co-ordinated control."
>
> Each of the conflicting elements brought together in this concept has its unique results in the operation of a business. From decentralization we get initiative, responsibility, development of personnel, decisions close to the facts, flexibility — in short, all the qualities necessary for an organization to adapt to new conditions. From co-ordination we get efficiencies and economies. It must be apparent that co-ordinated decentralization is not an easy concept to apply.[4]

Indeed, it was not an easy concept to apply at the Ford Motor Company. In an intensively competitive industry, the volume base of business in all but the Ford line was apparently insufficient to support the overhead of separate, integrated division structures. It is interesting in this regard, that all the consolidation moves described in the case stressed cost economies as the primary motivating factor.

At Ford the decentralized structure was also an inadequate framework for planning, strategy formulation, and measuring division performance. Key strategic decisions on styling and on marketing budgets were made at top management levels and not in the operating divisions. In addition, need to use common resources made the divisions less autonomous and somewhat interdependent. There was a high degree of overlap in the dealer organizations for the several car and truck lines. Then from 1956 on key resources such as assembly, purchasing, engineering, and warehousing were consolidated under Ford Division management. Transfer prices had to be negotiated between the manufacturing divisions and the vehicle divisions since both types of divisions had profit responsibility. When market prices do not exist to provide a useful benchmark, transfer prices become difficult to establish and are determined largely by negotiation. What, fundamentally, is being negotiated is the split of corporate profits among marketing and manufacturing units. Division profits, then, may become more a measure of negotiating skill than of overall business performance.

In this "half-way house," division performance would be difficult to measure and division profitability would lose meaning as a guide to performance.

One would also expect that as car and truck markets developed and product lines proliferated, the original price bracket segmentation scheme for organizing purposes (Ford, Mercury, Edsel, Lincoln, Continental) would not be in accord with actual market segmentation. By the 1960s the car and truck market might more usefully be segmented into such categories as "small or light cars," "sports cars," "family cars-utility," "family cars-prestige," "light trucks," "heavy trucks," "fleet sales," and "leasing." This classification of market segments would bear considerable refinement. Its purpose is to suggest that such a scheme is more in accord with buyer behavior than a "price bracket" definition. Moreover, the price delineation by which car divisions were established at General Motors and at Ford no longer seems to be the factor distinguishing one division from another. Price lines have become considerably blurred as each brand offering has been expanded.

In forming a single domestic car and truck business, North American Automotive Operations,

---

[2] Ibid., p. 143.
[3] Ibid.
[4] Alfred P. Sloan, Jr., *My Years with General Motors* (Garden City, New York, Doubleday & Company, Inc., 1964), p. 429.

the Ford management recognized, first, that the decentralized structure had inherent weaknesses which made it difficult to plan, to operate, and to measure performance. Beyond that, Ford's management seemed strongly motivated by a need to effect cost economies. The Lincoln, Mercury, and Edsel divisions were consolidated in 1957–1958 "primarily because none of the three smaller divisions had sufficient volume to justify the high overhead expenses of an autonomous divisional organization."

Changes made in 1959–1960 were intended as well to reduce overhead expenses. In particular, the consolidation of purchasing, engineering, and warehousing activities facilitated the design and use of interchangeable parts across car lines. Clearly important manufacturing and inventory scale economies were to be achieved through parts commonality.

Then in 1967 the establishment of one Product Development Group organized to develop vehicle systems (i. e., body, chassis, power train, electrical) for all cars and trucks was a major step in the direction of achieving even further cost economies. It was also a significant move in the direction of integrating product planning across vehicle lines, and of coordinating near-term model changes with planning advanced vehicle concepts.

Finally, a single Product Development function could be organized and specialized in a way that was not possible for the much smaller units in the Ford and Lincoln-Mercury Divisions. Because of its structure, it had the potential for being much more effective in the product development function. It could be more effective, too, in relating to other key resources, Manufacturing and Sales.

In summary, Ford's structure in the early 1950s seemed to take a page from the General Motors book in the respect that it was organized into five autonomous car divisions. This approach did not work because it was an inadequate framework for planning, strategy formulation, and measuring performance. Division managers did not control critical variables affecting their performance; nor did they have control over their own basic resource units. In particular, the negotiation of transfer prices between marketing and manufacturing departments tended to reduce the significance of profitability measures. For these reasons it may well be said that Ford was never really organized as a series of autonomous divisions.

In consolidating its domestic car and truck activities into a single business, North American Automotive Operations, the Ford management achieved important cost economies, provided a more suitable framework for business planning, and created a potentially more powerful, more effective product development function.

The New Product Development Group — Concept and Structure

The consolidation of vehicle product planning and product engineering into the new Product Development Group was the culminating step in the formation of a "troika" organization in NAAO. Ford's management found it impractical to maintain separate functions for each of the two vehicle divisions and an advanced product planning function in the headquarters organization. Both external and internal factors probably pressured Ford's top management in the direction of creating a single large Product Development organization.

Keen price competition, the proliferation of models, and the rapidly escalating number of vehicle parts and components created an urgent need for parts commonality across vehicle lines. Parts commonality would be difficult to achieve as long as there were car product planning functions in each of two vehicle divisions. Probably, too, the growing public concern over car safety features created important design problems that could be resolved most economically by a single Product Development function for all car lines.

Among the internal factors leading to the change was the need in Product Development "to give balanced consideration to market appeal, plant investment commitments, and manufacturing costs. . . ." As functions had been stripped away from the vehicle divisions, they became to an increasing extent marketing organizations. The product planning and engineering process would tend, then, to be dominated by market appeal considerations. Annual model changes, however, require heavy investments in new tooling and increased manufacturing costs. These were the dimensions that were apparently not being considered adequately in product planning decision making. Furthermore, the case suggests that the old organizational arrangements did not facilitate the coordination of planning in the vehicle divisions with the development of advanced vehicle concepts in the Central Engineering Staff. In the evolution of vehicle design the annual model changes should be conceived as shorter range implementing steps toward longer range design concepts. These concepts are both aesthetic and functional. The consolidation of planning for annual model changes and of advanced design in the Product Development Group was an important step, then, in strengthening the relationship between short-term and advanced design objectives.

The internal organization of the Product Development Group is worth noting as well. It was divided into three units, Car Product Planning, Car Engineering, and Truck Product Development (which included both product planning and engineering for trucks). These units were organized to facilitate close working relationships with the vehicle divisions at one end and the design offices in manufacturing at the other. Thus, Car Product Planning had a Ford and a Lincoln-Mercury unit. Car Systems Engineering had groups for light cars (in both the Ford and Lincoln-Mercury lines) and "custom" cars (again, Ford and Lincoln-Mercury). These units translated plans into detailed cost and performance specifications. These specifications were further refined within Car Systems Engineering by four major functional engineering groups (body, chassis, power train, and electrical systems). These organizational units then worked with design offices in the manufacturing divisions to see that designs were carried into engineering drawings for manufacturing.

Product Development was a larger unit than either of its predecessor organizational units. It was elevated in status organizationally. It was headed by the former vice president and general manager of the Ford Division. A letter from Henry Ford II announcing the Product Development Group indicated that it was charged with carrying out important responsibilities. These factors *ab initio* would give the new group power in its relationships with manufacturing on the one hand and the vehicle divisions in the Sales Group on the other.

Thus, the organization of the new Product Development Group was based on the concepts that vehicle systems were the common denominator in the design and development of the Ford car lines; that advanced product planning should be carried out for all lines together. The Group was structured to interface with the Ford and Lincoln-Mercury Divisions in the Sales Group at one end and with Manufacturing (which was organized by subsystems) at the other. At the same time a single Product Development function could afford a greater degree of specialization in design and engineering functions than any of the smaller predecessor units could have afforded. Finally, Product Development was positioned independently of both Sales and Manufacturing to assure that "balanced consideration" would be given to "market appeal, plant investment commitments, and manufacturing costs" in the product development process.

Program-Resource Structure in the Sales Group

The Sales Group in NAAO housed program management units as well as certain resources. The program-resource structure, however, is not easy to sort out. It may be understood best, perhaps, in terms of historical development. The two vehicle divisions had been shaped through the process of consolidating five relatively integrated business units (Ford, Lincoln, Mercury, Continental, Edsel) and then transferring key functions (such as assembly and product planning and engineering) to the newly formed Manufacturing and Product Development Groups. Essentially marketing functions remained.

It might be said that in the Ford Division of the Sales Group there were program "clusters." There was one program for Ford cars sold to private owners. Fleet and Leasing mounted two programs. One was for fleet sales to commercial buyers, leasing companies, and car rental companies. The other was the Ford Rent-A-Car program and the

Ford Authorized Leasing System, both through Ford dealers. Truck Operations planned and implemented programs for light and heavy trucks. As the case stresses, there were marked differences between the two truck programs in terms of customer behavior, product planning considerations, and distribution channels.

The programs were represented in each of the 37 districts; specialists concerned with car merchandising, light trucks, heavy trucks, and the fleet and leasing programs worked through field managers and sometimes directly with dealers.

The programs shared a wide range of marketing resources. All the programs utilized the Ford dealer system. Although a separate franchise was issued for heavy truck dealers, 230 out of 260 heavy truck dealers also held Ford car franchises.

Three resource units at headquarters were concerned with the all-important task of building the Ford dealer organization. Marketing Representation planned the number, size, and locations of Ford dealerships, established franchises, built facilities, recommended purchases of real estate, and provided assistance in a variety of ways to dealers. Dealer Development kept a watchful eye on dealerships in which Ford had a financial interest. The National Service Office planned and carried out programs for improving the quality of dealer repair and maintenance service.

The Advertising Office planned advertising for cars and trucks. The Merchandising Office planned promotional campaigns and developed programs for training retail salesmen in product features.

Like the program units, the resource groups also had representatives at the field district level, implementing resource activities with the dealer organization.

Strategy and Organization

The restructuring of Ford's domestic operations has important implications for strategy. The establishment of a single Product Development Group suggests that Ford's product strategy will be to have tightly coordinated lines and yet to provide for styling differentiation by brand name.

In distribution, Ford's organization suggests increasing reliance on a single dealer system, even though all dealers are not franchised for all brands. The case suggests, too, that Ford's distribution strategy is shaped with a strong concern for preserving the strength of its dealer organization. In this respect, Ford's several marketing strategies might be said to be "resource constrained." All programs went through the dealer organization, although in certain instances (for example, large fleet sales) much of the work might have been done by Ford marketing personnel. The Ford Authorized Leasing System and the Rent-A-Car program were carried out through Ford dealers at least in part "to give our dealers an opportunity to get a share of those markets" and "to provide a significant boost to dealer profits." Marketing strategy, then, in some of the Ford Division programs was shaped with a concern for the Ford commitment to its dealer organization and a concern for maintaining its strength in the face of severely rising dealer investments and operating costs.

It is useful also to note the strategic implications of establishing a separate Autolite-Ford Parts program in the Sales Group. The marketing of parts had been essentially a subprogram of new car sales and servicing, with parts going through Ford and Lincoln-Mercury dealers. With the establishment of an Autolite-Ford Parts organization in the Sales Group, the marketing of parts became an independent program. Under the Autolite-Ford Parts arrangement, parts sales would be channeled directly to the various segments of the automotive aftermarket: other-make vehicle dealers, independent garages, gasoline service stations, mail-order houses, and parts specialists, as well as Ford and Lincoln-Mercury dealers. The objective was to raise the relatively low share that Ford had in the aftermarket. The case refers to conflicts among the different distribution channels reaching the several segments of the parts markets. These conflicts might arise in part from a complex discount structure, which characterized this business. The case suggests that a single division could deal more effectively with these conflicts at operating levels.

The strategic implications of Ford's organizational developments, then, had to do with the product line strategy, the preservation of a strong dealer organization, and the establishment of the marketing of parts as a separate program independent of the Ford and Lincoln-Mercury marketing programs.

An Evolving Structure

It took more than ten years for Ford's operations in the United States to evolve from a decentralized product line organization to a single car and truck business. There is no reason to believe that it will not continue to evolve. What are some possible organizational changes that might take place? At least three possibilities can be projected from organizational trends that are clearly evident.

First, the heavy truck business could be established as a separate business. Heavy trucks are different in all critical respects from light trucks and cars with regard to the length of the planning cycle and the economic considerations of investing in new tooling. A different type of dealer organization for heavy trucks is required. The change may likely occur when the Ford management considers the volume of heavy truck business to be sufficient to support fully an integrated set of resources. In all the key functions of product planning, engineering, manufacturing, field sales, advertising, and promotion, there are now heavy truck-specialized resources. The step to a separate heavy truck business would probably not be a difficult one.

Second, one can see the possibility of some rearrangement in the two vehicle divisions. The Ford and Lincoln-Mercury Divisions are themselves the result of the consolidation of five separate vehicle divisions. There might be some advantages in consolidating these two organizations and then restructuring the whole along market program lines. Factors that might lead in this direction are (1) the tremendous proliferation in car models and the overlap of car lines, (2) the current overlap in dealer organizations, (3) the transfer of car product planning and engineering functions from the vehicle divisions to the new Product Development Groups — leaving the vehicle divisions completely free to organize according to marketing considerations. The shape of a new program management structure is not so easily predicted, but it is likely to follow some new market segmentation scheme more in tune with current categories of car and truck buyers.

Third, one can see the dealer organization changing and evolving. Increasing cost and investment levels for dealerships, more complex service demands, and increasing competition point in the direction of having a smaller number of larger dealers. In addition, dealer revenue may be derived to an increasing extent from service, leasing, and rental programs, and from having a broader line of cars.

Ford of Europe and Ford Tractor as "Businesses"

In addition to establishing NAAO as a business, the Ford management also created Ford of Europe (from the British and German companies) and Ford Tractor (from British and U.S. tractor operations) as businesses.

High on the list that led to establishing Ford of Europe were the potential economies that could be achieved through having parts commonality across the automotive lines of the two companies. In addition car planning, engineering, manufacturing, and distributive resources could be employed with increased efficiencies. The development of the European Economic Community and the reduction of tariff rates had already made it economical to close a number of small assembly plants established to supply local markets. It was possible that tariffs between England and the Continent would also be reduced, facilitating the establishment of a single supply system for Europe. Such a system would presumably have a smaller number of larger manufacturing plants.

In addition, European markets were apparently perceived as becoming increasingly homogeneous — another reason for creating Ford of Europe.

One might ask, however, why it might not be logical to create a world-wide, or even a U.S.-European, vehicle business. Apart from the management and legal difficulties of consolidating such large entities as NAAO and Ford of Europe, the potential gains in terms of further cost economies might be slim indeed. Moreover, the needs of domestic and foreign markets would not be seen as identical. The narrower roads, the shorter normal travel distances, the higher price of gasoline, and high taxes on both automobiles and gasoline are factors contributing to the demand for small cars with small engines in European markets as compared with the domestic market, for example. This consideration would be one important deterrent to creating a world-wide automotive business if such a business was to appeal to mass markets in major countries.

By contrast, world markets were perceived as relatively homogeneous with common needs in the case of tractors. The Ford management's third important move, then, was the establishment of a world-wide tractor business from units in both the United States and England. The lines were basically complementary. Important cost savings could be realized by developing a single world-wide manufacturing and distribution system.

Finally, Ford was forced, probably, into establishing integrated business units in countries such as Mexico and Brazil where restrictive legislation on imports made it necessary to establish integrated manufacturing and distribution facilities. In such instances, the product lines were very limited and probably manufacturing and selling costs were high by comparison with those of NAAO. Even so, establishing integrated business units was the price of continued participation in markets in which all competitors were faced with similarly high operating costs.

What, then, have seemed to be the factors that have tended to define business units at Ford? First, market homogeneity has been an important consideration. The domestic market for cars and trucks, the European market for cars and trucks, and the world market for tractors have been perceived as having common needs in a broad sense.

Economies of scale are a second major consideration. Where the consolidation of units has promised lower costs, the Ford management has made the move.

Third, where nationalistic laws aimed at developing local industry have forced the establishment of a business unit to serve a country, it has been necessary to choose between doing so or vacating the market.

Sears, Roebuck and Co.

Sears, Roebuck and Co. was the world's largest general merchandise company, with 1966 sales of slightly more than $6.8 billion. Approximately 77% of Sears' 1966 sales volume was derived from Sears retail stores; the remaining 23% represented sales through the Sears catalog.

Sears operated 801 retail stores in the United States as of January 31, 1967. The Sears 1966 *Annual Report* segregated these stores into three categories:

Complete Department Stores	199
Medium-sized Department Stores (carrying extensive assortments of general merchandise)	363
Hard Lines Stores (carrying major household appliances, hard lines, sporting goods, and automotive supplies)	239
	801

Between 1962 and 1966 Sears had opened 164 new retail stores, some of which were relocations of smaller obsolete units, increasing total retail selling space by 37%. In 1966 alone 46 new stores were opened; 37 additional stores were planned for 1967.

Sears catalog order business was serviced by 11 catalog order plants, each serving a geographic area. A considerable portion of Sears catalog orders were placed at catalog, retail, and telephone sales offices, rather than sent through the mail. In January 1967 Sears operated 1,653 such offices, an increase of 60% since 1961, and over 20% from the previous year.

Organization

A simplified organization chart describing reporting relationships as they existed in early 1967 is shown in Exhibit 1.[1] The company was headed by a Chairman and a President, to whom reported Vice Presidents of Merchandising, Personnel, Public Relations, Credit, Law, Factories, Real Estate, and Operations; the Corporate Comptroller and the Corporate Treasurer; five Territorial Vice Presidents; and a Vice President of International Operations.

All field operations in the United States were under the control of the five Territorial Vice Presidents. Each territory was divided into retail groups, zones, and catalog order regions. A group consisted of a number of stores in a single metropolitan market. A zone covered a fairly wide area and included the stores in smaller one-store cities and towns. The key difference, according to Sears executives, was one of media usage. In a metropolitan market, where all customers could be reached by metropolitan newspapers, it was considered essential that all stores have the same merchandise available at common prices. In a zone, however, there was much less need to coordinate the pricing policies of individual stores. A catalog order region covered the area served by a catalog order plant and included the catalog order offices located in that area. In the Eastern Territory, for example, there were 14 groups (containing 113 stores), 3 zones (containing 91 stores), and 2 catalog order regions.

Each group and zone was headed by a Group or Zone Manager, who reported to the Territorial Vice President. Retail Store Managers reported to the Group and Zone Managers. The catalog order plants were headed by Plant Managers, who also reported to the Territorial Vice Presidents. The managers of the catalog order offices reported to the Plant Managers, generally through several layers of field administration.

Each territory, group, zone, catalog order plant, and store was operated as a profit center. Managers at each level had considerable freedom to operate their organizational units as they wished, subject to policies established by the headquarters departments or higher levels of territorial management.

Sears employees generally made a distinction between the "Parent" and the "Field" when discussing the company's organization. The Field consisted of

---

[1] This organization chart and all other charts included in the case were prepared by the casewriter. Since the founding of the company, Sears managements had made it a point *not* to have formal organization charts.

the five territories, and the Parent included the various headquarters departments.

The largest Parent department was the Merchandising Department (Exhibit 2), which was responsible for the development, procurement, and promotion of all merchandise sold in Sears stores or catalogs. The Merchandising Department was divided into 51 Buying Departments and several merchandising departments.

The 51 buying departments were each assigned a line of merchandise (e.g., hardware; children's clothing).[2] The retail stores were also divided into 51 departments, known as "divisions." A retail division sold the merchandise bought by a Parent buying department. In the Cambridge, Massachusetts, retail store, for example, Division 26 (home laundry appliances) sold the merchandise bought by Buying Department 626 (home laundry appliances).

Each buying department was headed by a National Merchandise Manager, who reported to the Vice President-Merchandising. The retail divisions were headed by Division Managers, who reported to their Store Managers (generally through one or two layers of store management).

The National Merchandise Managers had no authority over the Field. The stores generally did not sell merchandise that had not been bought by a buying department, but they were not required to order particular merchandise items. If a buying department purchased 100,000 pink toasters, for example, and the Division Managers did not wish to order pink toasters, the buying department found itself with an inventory of 100,000 pink toasters.

Two important exceptions to this pattern should be noted. Each buying department received a specific number of pages in each Sears catalog. Having received these pages, the buying department was free to place whatever items it wished in that catalog, subject only to page limitations and catalog staff approval. The catalog thus differed from retail in that a buying department could select the merchandise to be displayed in a catalog, but could not specifically select the merchandise in the retail stores.

The other exception concerned merchandise items designated "basic-basic items." If a buying department designated a line "basic-basic," all retail stores with over 32,500 square feet of selling space were required to carry that line. "Basic-basic" items accounted for more than 46% of Sears retail dollar sales, but a much smaller percentage (6%) of the items sold by Sears. Even in the case of "basic-basic" items, the Division Managers had considerable autonomy. One Division Manager might order 12 of a "basic-basic" item, for example, while another Division Manager (in a similar store) might choose to order 12 dozen, in expectation of a different rate of sales.

The Field had similar autonomy vis-à-vis the other Parent departments. A Parent department could develop a training manual with the aid of the personnel department and distribute it to the Field, but it could not require the Field to use it. Similarly, a given territory or group might choose to follow policies and procedures different from those set forth in a Parent department operating manual. If a Parent department believed that such deviations from its policies were not in the company's best interests, it could go to the President or the Chairman, but this was rarely done.

The Comptroller's function was an important exception to this pattern. Unlike the other Parent departments, the Parent Comptroller's Department had direct authority over controllers in the Field, even though they reported to Field management. The Comptroller's Department reviewed all Field operating budgets and statements, and had the authority to direct that its policies be implemented. According to Sears executives, the Comptroller's Department needed this authority because of its responsibility as custodian of company assets.

One Sears executive commented on the concept of Field autonomy as follows:

It is impossible to understand Sears' organization without fully understanding our concept of autonomy. Everything we do at Parent takes the form of a recommendation when sent to the Field. We spend a lot of money on advertising mats for use by the Field, for example, but a group or store is perfectly free to prepare its own advertising if, taking the costs of local advertising preparation into account, it feels it can make more money that way.

In practice, the Field does follow most Parent recommendations. With few exceptions, it orders the merchandise selected by the buying departments, uses Parent-prepared advertising in one way or another, and follows the procedures established by the various Parent departments.

You should not, however, allow this willingness to follow Parent recommendations mislead you. The important thing about autonomy is that it exists — as a right! — not that it is used. The right of the Field to reject our recommendations is the best possible way to insure that our recommendations are correct and practical. There is no critic more severe than a retail store executive!

---

[2] Exhibit 3 lists many of the Buying Department assignments.

Recent Developments

In discussing the company's organization, Sears executives cited two developments as having particular significance for the future. The first was a fundamental change in the nature of the catalog order business, bringing it much closer to the retail store business. The second was related to fundamental changes in consumer buying behavior; from "need" buying to "want" buying.

The Catalog Order Business

Sears had historically operated the retail stores and the catalog as two separate businesses. In general, the catalog customer had lived in a small town or on a farm and had not had access to a Sears retail store. He had received a Sears catalog in the mail, and had then mailed his order to the catalog order plant serving his area. The catalog order plant had then shipped the merchandise to him, generally by mail.

Since World War II, the catalog order business had changed markedly. To an increasing extent, catalog customers now had access to Sears retail stores. There were several reasons for this change:

(1) The shift in population from small towns to cities placed more customers of all kinds (including catalog customers) in big cities, where Sears had retail stores. There were simply fewer people in rural areas than there had been prior to the war.
(2) Sears' executives store building program (277 new retail stores were built and 310 stores were relocated between 1945 and 1967) provided many more people with access to Sears retail stores than previously.
(3) Increased affluence and improved roads made it possible for many rural families to shop in urban centers, rather than the small towns where they had previously made most of their retail purchases.

By 1967 these trends had gone so far that Sears executives believed that it was no longer possible to differentiate between retail customers and catalog customers. As one executive explained:

> They are really the same people. The same customer will buy some items from the catalog; others from a retail store. It depends on the kind of item, how busy she is when she decides to "shop," local traffic conditions, and a host of other factors.

The change in the characteristics of the catalog order customer contributed to a major change in the nature of catalog order shopping. By 1967 only 10% of catalog sales were received through the mail. The remaining 90% of catalog sales were placed in one of three ways:

(1) At catalog order desks in retail stores. These desks had all Sears catalogs available and were able to provide merchandise not available in the store. The large Sears General Catalog, it should be noted, contained approximately six times as many items as were stocked by the largest Sears stores.
(2) At catalog order offices, which were essentially like catalog order desks, except that they were in separate facilities (generally in small towns), rather than a Sears retail store. A customer typically came into a catalog order office to place an order, and then picked up the merchandise at the office approximately 48 hours later.
(3) By calling a telephone sales office to order merchandise from a catalog in the customer's possession.

The implications of these changes for the Sears organization were described by one executive as follows:

> It is clear that the old distinctions between the retail business and the catalog business are breaking down. For the most part, we are now dealing with the same customer in both businesses, and there is little difference between shopping in a retail store and shopping in the catalog. In some cases, the customer finds it more convenient to choose from merchandise on physical display in a store; in other cases, she finds the catalog more convenient.
>
> What this means is that we have to improve coordination of the two businesses. There have always been slight differences in price between retail and catalog due to differences in transportation and services supplied. This was especially true, for example, if one of the businesses was running a sale on a particular item. I wonder whether this will be possible much longer.
>
> Or, to take another example, we now have separate departments working on copy writing and art work for the catalog and on retail advertising. To a great extent, we use a different promotional approach in the catalog from the one we use at retail. If it's the same customer, and the same merchandise, does this make sense? I'm not saying that it doesn't, mind you; I just think that we sometimes get so set in our ways that we don't see (or understand) what is happening — even if we are the ones who are making it happen.

The Boston Experiment: One unmistakeable effect of these developments was that the catalog order plants were now in the retail business. In 1967 there were twice as many catalog and telephone sales offices (under catalog plant management) as there were retail stores. In many ways, operating catalog and telephone sales offices was more like operating retail stores than like operating catalog plants. There were common problems of field supervision, retail sales personnel management, store maintenance, sales tax, real estate, and cash management. It seemed possible, therefore, that it might be more appropriate for the catalog and telephone sales offices to report to the retail organization than to the catalog plants.

In an attempt to test this possibility, all catalog and telephone sales offices in the Boston catalog order region were assigned to the groups and zones in whose territories they were located. This organizational change permitted the Boston catalog order plant to dispense with its field sales organization, and was intended to facilitate coordination between retail stores and catalog and telephone sales offices in the same geographic area.

In early 1967 the experiment had been in progress for less than a year, and Sears executives believed that it was still too early to assess results. Although sales had been encouraging and expenses had been reduced somewhat, many executives believed that the critical factor was the separate identity of the catalog order business. As one executive explained:

We believe that it *might* be better to have these offices report to the retail field organization. We may, to some extent, save money through elimination of dual coverage of some territories, but coordination and quality of management strike me as more important considerations.

There is another side to this question, however, and we really haven't decided which way to go. To some extent, the catalog business is different; some lines sell better in the catalog and others sell better in the stores. Moreover, the catalog business is smaller than the retail business and might not receive adequate management attention without its own field organization.

It really comes down to a single issue. The catalog stores would undoubtedly benefit from professional retail management and closer coordination with the retail stores. On the other hand, they presently benefit from a specialized field organization, whose performance is measured solely on the basis of catalog sales. We are trying to find out which of these considerations is more important. The Boston experiment is an attempt to answer this question.

"Need Buying" vs. "Want Buying"

The other major change in Sears' way of doing business was related to a fundamental change in consumer purchasing behavior. With greater affluence, a growing proportion of U.S. consumer expenditures were for merchandise the consumer "desired" or "wanted" rather than merchandise that she "needed." According to Sears executives, the consumer engaged in "want buying" and the customer engaged in "need buying" were susceptible to different merchandising approaches. If a customer "needed" an item, these executives reasoned, she would scan advertisements and search for it in a catalog or a store. If she only "wanted" it, however, she was unlikely to make a purchase unless the item was brought dramatically to her attention. In merchandising to the "want" market, therefore, it was necessary to present the consumer with advertising and displays that drew her attention. Having seen the advertisement, or entered the selling area, she was likely to purchase the item that she found she wanted; she would not, however, search for that item, as she would in the case of "need" merchandise.

This shift toward "want buying" had significant implications for advertising, display, and merchandising in general. Sears' advertising had traditionally been highly item-oriented, for example. A single page of newspaper advertising (circa 1950) contained advertisements for brassieres, lawn mowers, and teen-age fashions, to take an extreme example. This advertising had been appropriate to "need buying"; if a man "needed" a lawn mower, he would find it even if it was positioned between lingerie and beauty aids. If he only "wanted" the lawn mower, however, he was more likely to find it if it was positioned with other items in the same merchandise category (e.g., garden tools and lawn fertilizers).

By the early 1960s "want buying" had had an impact on virtually all areas of Sears' operations. All advertisements, for example, now featured related lines of merchandise, rather than many unrelated individual items. Division locations in the stores were realigned, to group related lines of merchandise together. Category promotions, such as "National Hardware Week," offered reduced prices on broad categories of merchandise.

Nevertheless, in late 1966 the Vice President-Merchandising believed that Sears had not yet gone far enough in adapting to changed consumer purchasing behavior. Each of Sears' 51 buying departments was highly independent, procuring and merchandising its product line with little regard for the activities of related buying departments. In women's clothing, for example, separate buying departments were responsible for lingerie (Dept. 638), brassieres and girdles (Dept. 618), and nylon hosiery (Dept. 675). Although the National Merchandise Managers heading these departments often met in the corridors or at lunch, they rarely conducted business together. In at least one case, two National Merchandise Managers in a single category had never been in each other's offices, even though both had been in their present positions for several years.

Coordination, where it existed, had been largely due to the efforts of personnel in the Retail General Merchandising Office. A number of Category Merchandisers reported to the Divisional Vice President-Retail Merchandising. These Category Merchandisers had each been responsible for overseeing (but *not* directing) the advertising and promotional programs of several related buying departments. In many cases, they had worked with the buying departments assigned to them and with the advertising and sales promotion staffs, to develop programs featuring merchandise from several buying departments.

In early 1967 the Vice President-Merchandising decided to make major changes in Sears' retail promotional planning procedures (see below). As part of this change, he established 15 merchandise categories: home fashions, home appliances, automotive, recreation, men's apparel, shoes, notions and fashion fabrics, women's apparel, intimate apparel, children's apparel, hardware store, home improvement (installed), toys, candy, and specialties (miscellaneous).

Each category consisted of several related buying departments. A senior National Merchandise Manager was elected Chairman of each category. The categories were expected to develop joint category plans for presentation to Parent executives and the field. To aid them in this task, several Parent departments (e.g., Advertising, Display, Retail Merchandising) realigned their organizations to assign specific individuals or work groups to each category.

In commenting on this change, the Vice President-Merchandising explained:

Category merchandising began in Parent in our marketing effort directed by our retail merchandise staff. What I am trying to do is to modify our organization and procedures to conform to what has already happened, in order to maximize the value of what we offer the Field, and — ultimately — the consumer.

I am trying to do this without changing our basic structure. We have Category Chairmen, but they have no authority over the other National Merchandise Managers in their categories. In fact, the Chairman is elected by the other National Merchandise Managers in the category. All National Merchandise Managers still report to me! The job of the Category Chairman is to preside at meetings and to give me one person to talk to when I want to know what is happening in a particular category.

It's still too early to know how well the new approach will work. It all depends on the National Merchandise Managers. I have, in effect, told them to start working together. Now it's up to them!

Merchandising

On November 8, 1966, the Vice President-Merchandising, had called a meeting of all Sears buying personnel. No such meeting had been held for some time, and interest was heightened by the fact that he had recently been promoted to his present position. In his "remarks" to the buyers, the Vice President-Merchandising described the buyers' responsibilities:

YOU, the BUYER, are responsible for everything that has to do with your lines of merchandise. As buyers you have been assigned to the narrowest product line responsibilities possible commensurate with the known potentials of those lines.

This structure enables YOU to learn and master YOUR lines and be responsible for an understanding of your consumer — your market — the product, research and development — where to have it made — what costs you generate — under what contractual arrangement it will be produced — what assortments you will have — what prices — what packaging — when it will be offered — what type of display and advertising — what guarantee — how it will be promoted — what training, servicing, etc., is required.

There is nothing as it relates to a line that the buyer is not responsible for, including the inventory (old and new) — sales — the growth — and, above all, the profit.

This is an overwhelming responsibility — an awesome assignment.

But interestingly enough I have never known the perfect buyer — that buyer who incorporates in his education, experience, or aptitudes all of the characteristics necessary for the perfect buyer. I have met, and have personally known, some who indulge themselves with the fantasy that somehow they were blessed with special powers — not so for those of us less gifted.

Do our talents lie in creativity — that sensitive area which transforms a consumer want, desire, or need into physical product?

Do they lie more in the economic structure of the buying arrangement, or perhaps in the special gifted area of selling and promoting? Usually our aptitudes include one or two of the areas, but I have yet to see, for example, the strong figure-oriented aptitude be creative in merchandise, or vice versa.

Each of us has talents that predominate, and each of us has weaknesses that are evident.

Fortunately, we, in Sears, do not have to be perfect, *but we do have to be good administrators* — because for every talent we might lack — the company, in its infinite wisdom, has made up for it — there is — today — no area of your responsibility where the company does not provide the services of a gifted specialist to advise and counsel you. From industrial engineers to any fanciful named designer, to the most exotic testing equipment . . . from cost accountant to home economist . . . to controller . . . from attorney to promotional specialist . . . services have been and are available to the buyer.

The Vice President-Merchandising was responsible for all Parent merchandising activities. Reporting to the Vice President-Merchandising were 51 National Merchandise Managers (each heading a buying department), Divisional Vice Presidents in charge of Source Development, Retail Merchandising, Catalog Merchandising, and New York Buying, a staff administrator for overseas and domestic buying, a Manager of Merchandise Research, a General Merchandise Controller, and the Director of the Merchandise Development and Comparison Laboratory.[3]

The Buying Departments

Each of the 51 buying departments was headed by a National Merchandise Manager. Reporting to each National Merchandise Manager were a Retail Sales Manager, a Catalog Sales Manager, a Merchandise Controller, and from 6 to 25 buyers. The Retail Sales Manager and the Catalog Sales Manager developed programs to promote their department's merchandise through their respective channels of distribution. The Merchandise Controller was responsible for preparing inventory budgets and for keeping track of commitments to sources, inventories, and other control-oriented data.

Each buying department was appraised on the basis of its contribution to profits. Buying department personnel received a significant portion of their compensation in the form of a bonus, which was closely (although not systematically) related to their estimated contribution to sales and profits.

The buying departments arranged for the availability of products, which the stores could then order; they were not able to place the merchandise automatically in the stores.[4] The method used to inform the stores of product availability was the "merchandise list," which contained all necessary information as to how to merchandise a line. This list was issued at least every two years. Division Managers in the stores ordered merchandise from this list, generally directly from manufacturing sources.

---

[3] See Exhibit 2, Organization Chart of Merchandising Department.

[4] In most retail merchandising chains the buyers purchased merchandise for shipment to specific stores and thus had considerably more authority than Sears buyers. Most Sears executives believed that this procedure would not be practicable for Sears — because of the large number of stores in the chain.

In addition, each buying department offered merchandise in the monthly "Combo." The Combo listed merchandise that would be promoted during the month in question, generally at reduced prices to both the stores and consumers. An advertising layout book and display recommendations were sent to the stores at the same time as the Combo, to be used in support of the promotions planned for the month.

Merchandise was placed in the catalog through a different process. Each buying department was allotted a specific number of pages, which it was relatively free to use as it wished. In practice, however, the amount of space allotted to a department was at least partially determined by what the department planned to do with it.

A significant percentage of Sears merchandise was bought on a basic known-cost basis. Under this type of arrangement, Sears specified the quantity and type of merchandise it wished to receive over a relatively long time period, and the source agreed to supply Sears with cost data, which was subject to audit. Sears then paid the source the cost, plus an agreed-upon profit margin. In these cases, Sears absorbed certain costs directly, such as tooling or R&D, and sometimes procured materials (such as fabrics) for the source concerned.

Four Buying Departments

This section of the case describes four of Sears' 51 buying departments: Home Laundry Appliances, Hardware, Infants' and Children's Wear, and Junior Clothing (i.e., dresses and sportswear for teen-age girls and younger women). These buying departments have been selected to illustrate differences in source arrangements, buying techniques, logistics patterns, and merchandising approaches.

Home Laundry Appliances

The Home Laundry Appliances Buying Department (Department 626) bought and merchandised Sears' Kenmore[5] line of washing machines and dryers. These products were manufactured exclusively by the Whirlpool Corporation. Whirlpool sold home laundry equipment to other retailers under the Whirlpool brand name, but Sears was estimated to take 65% of Whirlpool's laundry equipment production in 1967.

Sears was exceptionally strong in the home laundry field, having an estimated 32% of the total United

---

[5] A brand name used by Sears for a wide range of home appliances.

States market (vs. 7% of total retail sales). According to Sears executives, their strong position was attributable to three major factors:

(1) Sears' excellent working relationships with Whirlpool, which had begun in 1911 and had never been formalized by more than a "hand shake."
(2) Sears' extensive product development expenditures and distribution economies, which gave it a competitive advantage in quality, features, and price.
(3) Sears' "big ticket" selling techniques, which were considered by the industry to be Sears' most significant advantage.

In early 1967 the National Merchandise Manager of Department 626 commented on his department as follows:

Our buyers' job is to stimulate and work with Whirlpool in product development, manufacturing, and service to our stores. Because we work with just one source — Whirlpool — we do not get involved in many of the things other departments do. We have to do all that we can to keep Whirlpool's costs down; they are, after all, really our costs.

Product Development: We are continually engaged in two kinds of product development. One is an evolutionary process: new features or designs for the products we are currently selling. The other is a revolutionary process — a search for entirely new ways to give the consumer clean, finished clothing and linens. With PERMA-PREST,[6] and our new Combo washer-dryer,[7] the housewife's laundry day has changed markedly. In the future — who knows — we may launder clothes with radio waves or lasers.

Our buyers work closely with Whirlpool's engineers on both types of product development. Some of the ideas come from us; some from them. We agree on what we want in the way of product or features, and they tell us what it will cost (both development and manufacturing costs). Then, if we still want it, they move through the normal sequence of prototypes, manufacturing models, and regular production series. Our testing laboratory works closely with the Whirlpool testing laboratory, to assure that their procedures give us the kind of quality we require. We try to keep our management and the Field informed concerning new developments, but have to be careful to avoid pressure to bring out a new product before it is ready.

Product Line Structure: In structuring our product line we pay close attention to the selling strategy used in the stores. We begin with the top of the line, the very best product we can make, with all the most advanced features. We then build a low-priced machine, of the same quality as the top-of-the-line, but with fewer features. Our advertising covers various models but usually emphasizes the lower-priced machine. If a customer wishes to buy the machine we have advertised — fine. But, depending upon her needs, she will usually do better (and we will do better) if she buys a machine with additional features.

After we have established the top-of-the-line and the bottom-of-the-line (our opening price point) we ask, "How many models do we need to fill the gap?" On the one hand, each price point must give the consumer real benefits as compared to the price point immediately below it. On the other hand, the jump between price points must not be so great that the consumer will be unwilling to move up. And we do not want to have too many price points, since every increase in stock keeping units increases inventories. On automatic washing machines, we have six basic price points: $119, $149, $169, $189, $219, and $239. Approximately 60% of our sales are between $189 and $219.

In the stores, our salesmen are experts at "trading up by trading down." A good salesman (who follows the manual we give him) will start a customer at the top of the line, and work down from price point to price point, explaining which features have been deleted at each step. If he goes the other way — from the bottom of the line to the top of the line — the customer soon feels that every step she takes costs her $20. It is essential, of course, that our merchandise be displayed in such a way that this selling pattern is practicable. For the most part, the stores stick to the Merchandise Arrangement Guide[8] on our products.

The Catalog is not the most important medium for us, probably because of the nature of our product. Most rural communities have some sort of appliance store, selling brand name appliances on credit. In urban areas (where most of the catalog business is anyway) people generally want to see a major appliance before buying it. We do display our products in the catalog sales offices, and sell a large number of appliances this way, but these are really retail sales — not catalog sales. In this department, retail runs the business and the catalog follows. It is important, for example, that the catalog not anticipate retail promotions.

Logistics: In most group operations our merchandise is handled through pool stocks. The stores stock only display models; merchandise is actually shipped to the customer from a central warehouse. The Division Managers in the group stores thus do not actually order merchandise, except floor samples. It is a group function to maintain inventories at an adequate level. In zone

---

[6] A process used in manufacturing clothing, which permitted the clothing to be washed, tumble-dried, and then worn without ironing.

[7] An appliance that washed and tumble-dried in a continuous operation.

[8] A document prepared by the Visual Merchandising Department; see below.

stores, on the other hand, the Division Managers order directly from Whirlpool.

We have worked with Whirlpool to establish the "Gateway" program. The Gateways are essentially bulk warehouses, to which the various Whirlpool plants ship their products. The Gateways then mix products to form carload lots, which are shipped to the stores and groups. As a result, we are able to give our smaller stores better service (at lower cost) and are able to keep close control over finished goods inventory.

Retail Merchandising: Our Retail Sales Office consists of a Sales Manager and four assistants. Each assistant has assigned functional responsibilities (e.g., advertising, display) and a product assignment (automatic washers, dryers, combos, and wringer washers respectively). All members of the Retail Sales Office visit the stores regularly (although one has special responsibility for zone stores) and work on the basics of the business. While we are a very large department in terms of sales, we are a small department in terms of personnel. We assign responsibilities, but everyone is constantly aware of what the others are doing.

The monthly promotional offering is one of our key retail merchandising tools. We prepare a promotional program at least eight months in advance and give the Field a package to work with. This package includes a description of the promotions we have planned for the month, a suggested advertising schedule, a mat service, display ideas, selling ideas, and a work sheet for the Field to use in its own planning. The work sheet, if used properly, allows the Field to determine which products should be promoted on which days. In general we believe in promoting items that people want to buy at a particular time, rather than trying to create demand.

Most of our advertising is directed toward getting the customer to come into the store. Field personnel frequently ask us to place greater advertising emphasis on top-of-the-line merchandise; they really want us to trade the customer up for them. We are now studying and experimenting with such an approach.

Our Retail Sales Office works closely with the buyers to prepare and disseminate product information to the Field. This is particularly important on a new product, such as the combination washer-dryer.[9] When appropriate, we prepare a film strip to introduce a new product to our people, as well as product manuals, training manuals, and sales aids. It is not unusual for our training manuals to contain a quiz,[10] to allow the salesman to determine how well he has learned his lesson.

[9] The combination washer-dryer was not technically a new product. Sears had introduced a washer-dryer some years before, but had run into serious service and maintenance problems. In 1965 Sears reintroduced a greatly improved washer-dryer, the "new product" referred to here.

[10] Sample question: "To clean the pump protector, customer must open the little access door inside the wash cylinder. True or false."

Within our department, each buyer operates quite autonomously, as he must if he is to fulfill his complete responsibility. My Retail Sales Manager and I do occasionally get involved in product decisions, however. I recently felt that a particular color was going to be important next fall. My Retail Sales Manager was quite excited about the color; the buyers, for the most part, were not. We presented our case as strongly as we could, but made it clear that the decision was the buyers'. They ended up agreeing with us, but they certainly did not have to.

Category Merchandising: There has been a lot of talk lately about category merchandising — I am the Category Chairman for major appliances. As I see it, category merchandising is basically a communications device, to facilitate communications between the buying departments and the Retail Merchandising Department and between the Retail Merchandising Department and the stores. In major appliances, where we use the same source and obviously have to have the same colors, we have always worked closely together anyway.

Hardware

The Hardware Buying Department (Department 609) bought and merchandised power tools, hand tools, lawn and garden tools, lawn mowers, snow blowers; welders, cabinet hardware, builders' hardware, and a wide variety of general hardware ranging from nails and screws to mail boxes. Department 609 was one of Sears' largest departments in sales, number of stock keeping units (6,372), and number of sources (411).

At one time the Hardware Department had been responsible for product lines presently assigned to Departments 606 (recreation and sporting goods), 611 (housewares), 630 (paints), 634 (small electrical appliances), 642 (plumbing, heating, and cooling), and 664 (building materials), but these departments had been spun off from Department 609 as the hardware business grew.

Department 609 had 13 buyers, each assigned a reasonably narrow product line. (See Exhibit 4 for a summary of buying assignments). The Retail Sales Office consisted of a Retail Sales Manager and five Assistant Retail Sales Managers. Each Assistant Retail Sales Manager had functional responsibilities (e.g., shopping reports, sales contests), a product line assignment (e.g., hand tools), and responsibility for liaison with one of Sears' five territories. The department also included a Catalog Sales Manager, a Merchandise Controller, and approximately 65 clerical personnel. The Catalog Sales Manager, besides being responsible for the selection of merchandise and preparation of copy for the catalog, also prepared the retail merchandise lists and retail catalogs for hand and power tools.

One of Department 609's buyers was responsible essentially for buying flat wrenches and socket wrenches (*not* adjustable wrenches). He described the buying function as follows:

Source Relationships: I took over this line two and a half years ago. When you come onto a line, there are existing products and sources. You constantly look at these sources, to make sure that product quality and service of supply are what they should be. Price is also important, but it is really secondary to the other two factors.

I work with five sources. We take about 50% of one source's production; about 10% of another's. Several other Department 609 buyers are dealing with these same sources.

We occasionally have to consider a change from a source if it has not been able to keep up with our growth; or if quality and service of supply have fallen off. We bring the problem to their attention well in advance, and offer to give them any help needed. We don't just drop a source; Sears' success depends on good source relations.

Commitments: I decide how much production to contract for. My lines are pretty much staples, and I can learn a lot from last year's sales pattern. I read a lot of business periodicals concerning the state of the economy and watch our monthly sales figures pretty closely. We are currently on an uptrend; I'm looking for a 15% to 20% sales increase.

We have various kinds of contracts with our sources. Some have known cost contracts, where we agree to take a certain percentage of production for a specified time period. Others have unit contracts, where we agree to take a certain quantity of a specified product. In addition to the contract the important thing is to schedule the production and the flow of materials to effect the most economies.

We regularly fill in a contract balance report, so that the General Merchandising Office knows how much Sears is committed for. This is really a tool to help them with their financial planning.

Product Development: I have full responsibility for selecting items within my line responsibility. I watch the trade journals and automotive magazines; I go out and talk to automotive mechanics concerning what they would like if they could get it. Inventors come to us with ideas for new products; if an idea seems promising we send it to a source for a cost evaluation, and to the Sears laboratory for testing.

It's up to the buyer to decide whether or not to go ahead with a new product, although he may check with the National Merchandising Manager or Retail Sales Manager on a really big thing.

The National Merchandising Manager of Department 609 had been in his present position for many years. He commented on his Department, and its organization, as follows:

Each of our buyers has full responsibility for the lines assigned to him. It is up to him to make sure that we have the right quantities of the right products at the right time. Our Retail Sales Manager, Catalog Sales Manager, and I are then responsible for pulling the whole thing together.

Retail Promotions: Because most of our products are staple items, we are able to freeze our retail promotions six months in advance. We set our targets for a season and ask the buyers to give us their candidates for promotion. The buyers send their spec sheets to me and the Retail Sales Manager. We both review them and then call each buyer in individually, and do all that we can to get him to do an even better job.

We then call all the buyers together and vote on what to include in the promotion. This is better than if the Retail Sales Manager and I just chose. It gives us an idea of how the buyers are thinking, and helps to create internal competition within the department.

The Catalog: Our Catalog Sales Manager then develops catalog pages compatible with what retail has decided to do. The catalog is very good for us on some items, because it allows us to describe an item fully. The average retail salesman does not want to sell electric arc welders, for example. A customer who wants an electric arc welder probably knows more about the product than the salesman does, and this makes him insecure. In the catalog we can say, "Here it is; here are its specifications; here's what it can do." Hand tools and other impulse items do better in the retail stores, of course.

Store Relations: We do not get all the volume we should in the stores. If we know we could sell 100,000 of an item in our 800 stores, we are likely to cut our target down to 65,000. We simply know that all the stores are not going to do everything right based upon differences in personnel, promotions, etc.

I cannot put enough stress on internal selling. We have great products (a totally new kind of lawn mower, for example), but just don't get through to the customer. The lawn mower is just one of 6,400 items; we don't push it as a lawn mower company would.

In 1964 we visited all Sears retail stores. I personally was on the road 80% of the year. We spent eight to twelve hours on a thorough analysis of our department in each store. We presented a written report to the Division Manager and his Store Manager, and a summary to the Territorial Office. I don't think you can do what we are trying to do with paper. We need belly-to-belly confrontations with the Division Managers and Store Managers. One day in a store is better than tons of paper.

I have also instituted a "work-a-week" program. All Department 609 personnel (except the clerks) spend one week a year in a store selling. Besides selling, they are to handle all customer complaints concerning our products. It's just a device, but a darn effective one!

Logistics: The stores order some of our products direct from source; others from the control stores.[11] They pay a handling fee to the control stores for this service, but, on many items (especially small ticket items), this fee is cheaper than ordering direct.

I participate in the selection of Department 609 Control Buyers (in the catalog plants) and try to influence the choice of Division 9 Managers in the retail stores. On my store visits, I do not hesitate to call attention to a weak Division Manager, or to point out to the Store Manager that he should have strong men in the hardware area, since it produces so many profit dollars for him.

Junior Clothing

The Junior Buying Department (Department 619) was one of ten buying departments located in New York City. These buying departments (see Exhibit 3 for specific assignments) were responsible for buying women's and girls' clothing and accessories, luggage, and jewelry. They were located in New York rather than Chicago because these particular industries were concentrated in New York City to such a great extent that it would have been impractical to operate out of Chicago.

The New York office was headed by a Divisional Vice President who reported to the Vice President-Merchandising. In addition to the ten buying departments, representatives of other Parent departments (e.g., Chicago-based buying departments, Retail Merchandising, Catalog Merchandising, Merchandise Control, Merchandise Comparison, Operations, Merchandise Laboratory) were located in the New York office. While these personnel reported functionally to their respective Parent departments, it was generally understood that they were under the administrative control of the Divisional Vice President, New York. The National Merchandise Managers of the ten buying departments headquartered in New York reported directly to the Vice President-Merchandising, but they consulted on a day-to-day basis with the Divisional Vice President, New York, on most policy matters.

Department 619 was responsible for buying and merchandising "Junior" clothing. Junior was a term used by the fashion industry for many years to describe a range of sizes and styles oriented primarily toward teen-age girls and women "with a young outlook."[12] In recent years the Junior category had been increasingly associated with "Mod" styles and exciting brightly colored fashion merchandise. The so-called "Junior Look" had become extraordinarily popular in the mid-1960s, with the result that Junior merchandise was accounting for a steadily increasing share of the women's ready-to-wear market.

Department 619 had been established in late 1965. Prior to this time, Junior merchandise had been bought by Department 607 (women's sportswear), Department 617 (ladies' coats and suits), Department 677 (girls' and teens' wear), and Department 631 (women's dresses). Although each of these departments had been moderately active in the Junior field, Sears had never really tried to go after the Junior customer in a big way. An exception was Department 677, which had begun to "push" Juniors in about 1963, primarily in an effort to make up for the vanishing subteen market.[13] Department 677 had had unusual success with its Junior program, which represented 25% of departmental volume in 1965. It had begun to work with the leading manufacturers of Junior merchandise, and had made significant inroads into the women's sportswear and dress fields. The decision to establish a separate Junior department was made by top management, "to bring Sears into line with what had happened in the department stores five years before."

When Department 619 was established, it took over responsibility for merchandise lines that had repre-

---

[12] Sears executives estimated that the Junior market was divided according to age as follows:

Age	% of Junior Customers
12–15 years	33%
16–19 years	36
20–24 years	14
25–29 years	5
30–39 years	8
40 and over	4
	100%

[13] According to Sears executives, the subteen market was disappearing because girls were going directly from children's clothing to teen-age clothing, without passing through a subteen style phase.

---

[11] The catalog order plants (control stores) were used as retail warehouses for some items, at the discretion of the buying departments. See below, p. 318.

sented 15% of the Girls' Department's volume, 25% of the Dress Department's volume, 10% of the Coat and Suit Department's volume, and 20% of the Sportswear Department's volume. In its first year, Department 619's sales were approximately as planned, being held back mainly by delays caused by the physical problem of establishing the new department in all stores. Nevertheless, all the departments, except the Girls' Department, performed near or above their prior volume levels. The Girls' Department's volume was almost exactly as expected.

The National Merchandise Manager of Department 619 had been in charge of the Girls' Department during the period when it had begun to "push" Junior merchandise (1963–1965). When he took over the Girls' Department, he said: "I will have succeeded when this department is split in two." As the driving force behind the Junior program, he had been, according to Sears executives, the logical choice to head the new department.[14] In early 1967 he commented on his department as follows:

Ours is a fast-moving fashion business. Dress manufacturers are coming out with new styles every day of the week. While we plan ahead as much as we can on our relatively more stable merchandise (e.g., outerwear), we have to retain considerable freedom to be where the action is. A young designer in a loft down the street can revolutionize this business overnight.

That is actually an overstatement. A certain amount of lead time is required before an item can really take off, particularly with regard to fabrics. There is sort of a pulse in this industry: textile mills, fabric houses, manufacturers, designers, and buyers somehow all get moving in the same direction at more or less the same time, but a certain number of items — the items that give you a fashion image — do have an aura of spontaneity about them.

Buying Assignments: We have ten buyers, most of whom are responsible for a particular type of product (e.g., outerwear, or skirts, blouses, and sweaters). There are two major exceptions to this pattern. We have three dress buyers, each responsible for a particular price range. This is the way the industry is organized; one manufacturer makes lower price dresses, another makes higher price dresses, and so forth.

We also have one buyer who buys all dresses for the catalog. This is a high risk business. We need to buy nine months ahead, and yet be right with regard to fashion. We buy for the Christmas catalog in March; for the retail Christmas season in September and October. Although we can move a catalog item which doesn't sell into the stores (or fill in a "hot" catalog item with merchandise we bought for retail), we can do this only to a limited extent.

Product Line Breakdown: Most of our planning is done by "Box Code" rather than line. A Box Code is generally a category smaller than a line. We now have nine Box Codes for dresses, for example: Junior Petite Dresses, Junior Dresses, Junior Petite Knits, Junior Knits, Junior Dressy Dresses, Junior Petite Dressy Dresses, Long Formals, and Graduation Dresses. Several buyers may buy merchandise in a single Box Code; in the case of dresses, buying assignments are based on price ranges rather than Box Codes.

We vary the Box Codes from season to season, as particular types of merchandise become more or less important. In spring and summer we have nine Box Codes for swim wear; in fall and winter only one or two. Similarly, when a new type of merchandise becomes important, we break it out of its existing Box Code and give it a Box Code of its own. Right now, for example, pants dresses are the hottest item on the market. When pants dresses began to take off, we gave them their own Box Code.

Despite our best efforts, there's bound to be some confusion. When an item gets hot, everybody gets into the act. There are some pants suits that are unmistakably pants suits, for example, and certain pants dresses that are clearly pants dresses. But there are an awful lot of garments which could be one or the other. It's not unusual for a dress buyer and the suit buyer to bring in virtually identical samples — one made by a dress manufacturer and the other by a suit manufacturer.

Logistics: The Box Codes form the basis of our central merchandising setup. With very few exceptions (mainly staple items and coordinated separates), our products are merchandised and distributed through the fashion centers.[15] These fashion centers handle merchandise for all the New York departments except luggage and jewelry, and a few items for the Children's Department in Chicago.

We have a Fashion Merchandiser for our department in each fashion center. While he works for the territory, he is concerned only with our lines of merchandise.

---

[14] Before taking over the Girls' Department, he had been National Merchandise Manager of the Luggage Department. He smiled as he explained (in 1967), "It was the joke of the year in the fashion industry when Sears put a luggage merchant in charge of girls' clothing."

[15] There were five fashion centers, one in each territory. The fashion centers were intermediate warehousing facilities, which ordered and received merchandise from manufacturing sources and then shipped the merchandise to the stores.

Each fashion center was headed by a manager, who reported to the Territorial Vice President. Within each fashion center, a "Fashion Merchandiser" was assigned to each buying department using the fashion centers. The Fashion Merchandiser was responsible for placing orders on the sources and for distributing merchandise to the stores.

The Fashion Merchandiser works out a merchandising program with each store in his territory. The program in essence says that a given store should have a specified quantity of items in inventory and "in sight"[16] in each of our Box Codes during each week of the year. Generally speaking, the proper program for a store depends on its size, although other factors are important. Suburban stores require a balance of merchandise among Box Codes (and within Box Codes) that is different from the balance in urban stores, for example.

The Division Managers in the stores do not order merchandise, although they do help to establish the merchandising program for their division. All of our fashion center merchandise is ticketed with punched tickets. When an item is sold, the punched ticket is torn off and retained by the person writing up the sale. These tickets are collected and mailed to the fashion center daily. At the fashion center, they are run through a computer which prepares a sales summary by Box Code for the week. The Fashion Merchandiser then uses this summary to determine how much merchandise in each Box Code to ship to the store during the following week. The Division Managers can, of course, short-cut the system when necessary. They might enclose a note with their tickets, for example, saying, "For God's sake, don't send me any more red dresses."

Generally, merchandise is shipped to the stores in predetermined size, color, and style assortments within a Box Code, unless a Division Manager has requested an exception. In practice, however, the Fashion Merchandisers must exercise a considerable amount of judgment. If a Fashion Merchandiser receives a shipment of a particularly "hot" dress, for example, he could send the whole shipment to one large store or group; he could divide it among all the stores in his territory; or he could divide it among a certain category of stores (e.g., suburban stores, suburban stores in New England, or suburban stores in New England but not around Boston). Needless to say, his judgment is equally important with merchandise that is something less than "hot."

Central merchandising of fashion merchandise makes a lot of sense. We feel that we have a better understanding of the direction styles are likely to take than our Division Managers do. If nothing else, we have learned that *our* taste (as compared with the customer's) is relatively unimportant. If we let the Division Managers do the ordering, we would run into situations where a key store would not be stocking pants dresses because the Division Manager didn't like pants dresses.

Markdowns: We do make mistakes, of course; it's part of the fashion business. Our problem is to get the stores to take markdowns, and take them fast. The Division Manager is faced with conflicting pressures in this area. On the one hand, if she doesn't move the merchandise she doesn't get new merchandise. On the other hand, markdowns erode margins (but increase profits by increasing turnover), and some Store Managers simply hate to see a markdown. We work with the Field constantly in this area.

We take back certain seasonal merchandise (such as outerwear), crediting the store with the selling price less 35%. We collect returned merchandise of this sort in the fashion centers until we get a meaningful inventory (i.e., a reasonable assortment of sizes and colors). We then make a deal with a big group, which thus is able to buy enough merchandise at reduced cost to justify a promotion.

Promotions: In the promotional area we have not yet really made our mark. I am convinced that cut price advertising, "Combos," and newspapers in general are just not the way to move our lines of merchandise. Our customers read the teen-age fashion magazines; that's where they get their ideas and that's where we ought to advertise.

We have been held back from doing as much of this sort of thing as we should by a couple of factors. There are still a lot of people in Sears who refuse to let go of the price impression approach, for example. One of the territories still insists on stocking $5.98–$7.98 dresses, even though we have dropped these price points in the other territories.

Infants' and Children's Wear

The Infants' and Children's Wear Buying Department (Department 629) bought and merchandised four lines of merchandise: infants' clothing and accessories, little boys' clothing, little girls' clothing, and children's staples (e.g., underwear), which were generally the same for both sexes. Department 629 had been part of the Girls' Clothing Buying Department in New York until 1949, when it had been spun off and moved to Chicago.

The National Merchandise Manager of Department 629 commented on his department as follows:

The children's clothing industry has changed markedly in recent years. This used to be a staples business, with little difference in style (as distinct from color) between little girls' clothing and little boys' clothing. We sold a few party dresses, of course, but mainly jeans, tee-shirts, and underclothing. Now, it is a fashion business with emphasis on style, fabric, and color. Trends in teen-age apparel are having a tremendous impact on children's clothing — style has become the name of the game.

You can speculate all you want about the sociological implications of the trend; the fact is that industry sales have shot up enormously. And our sales — I am happy to say — have grown at a rate much faster than that of the industry.

---

[16] I.e., on order or in transit.

Buying Assignments: These changes have had a marked impact on our departmental organization. We have twelve buyers, each of whom is responsible for particular lines of merchandise. One buyer buys girls' sweaters, tights, tops, suits, jumpers, skirts, and blouses; another buys boys' dress and sport shirts, slacks and slack sets, and playwear. Until several years ago buying assignments were quite different. One buyer bought all slacks, whether for boys or girls. Another bought all sweaters. The industry was (and to some extent still is) set up that way, but it was the wrong way to merchandise fashion goods. Now, we have buyers who can coordinate slacks *and* sweaters, who are experts on style and color.

Our buying assignments [see Exhibit 5] are established according to four criteria. First, we think it is important to separate boys, girls, and infants; they are simply different markets. Second, we try to assign buyers so that they will deal with a limited number of sources. Third, we want each buying assignment to be large enough to warrant a top quality buyer. Fourth, we take account of the seasonal factor; it would be wrong for one buyer to have nothing but swimwear and beach accessories.

Our new buying assignments make it possible to coordinate certain lines of merchandise: boys' slacks and sweaters, for example. But we are also interested in coordination among lines. We have a fashion coordinator who works with leading designers to select colors and styles for a particular season. He then works with the buyers to make certain that their lines "work" together. This is difficult to do, but we have done it. Our top-of-the-line "Winnie the Pooh" collection is the talk of the industry. For the first time we are able to compete successfully (and *are* competing successfully) with the leading specialty and department stores.

We have one buyer who buys nothing but piece goods. He works closely with Department 833 (textiles, trimming, and converting) to take advantage of quantity prices, and, more important, get us the fabrics we want. We then have these fabrics dyed, and ship them to our sources for manufacture into finished garments. We tell our sources what we want, and they make it for us. This is a tremendous advantage; other retailers generally don't do this and therefore have to take what the industry offers. This is one reason why we have been able to move into children's coordinates faster than our competitors.

We have buying representatives in New York and on the West Coast. They visit sources and actually buy merchandise when we ask them to. We do very little regional buying, except for outerwear on the West Coast, where styles are quite different from the rest of the country.

Retail Display: Emphasis on style has also changed our approach in the retail stores. Where we used to divide our department into types of merchandise (e.g., sweaters, slacks), we now try to have separate boys', girls', infants', and "neuter" areas. Our Retail Sales Promotion Managers are each assigned a territory to work with. During the last several years they have spent most of their time on the road, selling the new concept to the stores. As a result, we probably have a more fully elaborated retail sales promotion organization than most other departments do.

The Catalog: We are probably one of Sears' strongest catalog departments; the catalog accounts for 36% of our business, as compared with 23% for the company as a whole. There are two major reasons for this. First, the catalog is a very convenient way to shop for children's clothing, especially since we are in a position of style leadership. Second, and probably more important, we have been able to expand our space in the catalog much faster than in the stores. We have gone from 40 pages to 100 pages in the Fall catalog, for example.

Catalog sales management is willing to give us increased space, because the revenue and profits are there. The stores are unable (or unwilling) to move as fast. But the retail business will come; it's the same customer and the same merchandise.

Category merchandising has been a real asset for us. I am Chairman of the Children's category, which includes Department 629 (except infants), part of Department 640 (boys' clothing and furnishings), and Department 677 (girls' and teens' wear). While category merchandising may have some effect on buying — we may extend the Winnie the Pooh concept into girls' clothing — its main impact will fall in the promotion area.

By working as a category, we will be able to take advantage of the fact that our sales peaks do not come at exactly the same time. We will plan our advertising so that each department gets strong advertising support when it needs it. Instead of running separate small newspaper ads for each department, the Field will be encouraged to run full-page ads or double-truck ads. These ads will in some cases feature merchandise from one department; in other cases the whole category. As a result, our total impact will be much greater than it has been in the past.

Moreover, we will no longer run into situations where we are promoting children's underwear at six for $2.88 (against a regular price of $3.00) while the Boys' Clothing Department promotes boys' underwear at six for $1.39 (regular price $1.99). Situations of this kind, while rare, are confusing to the customer — to say the least.

Retail Merchandising

The retail merchandising function was described by one Sears executive as follows:

The buying departments are responsible for selecting the merchandise to be sold in the stores. The territories are responsible for assuring that we have an adequate number of well-run stores in the proper locations. And the Retail Merchandising Department is responsible for providing the stores with advertising, promotions, and displays which will bring customers into the stores and motivate them to buy.

The retail merchandising function was headed by the Divisional Vice President-Retail Merchandising. Reporting to the Divisional Vice President-Retail Merchandising were eight Category Retail Merchandisers, and the heads of the Visual Merchandising Department (display and packaging), the Retail Merchandise Lists Department, and the Retail Sales Promotion and Advertising Department.[17]

The Category Retail Merchandisers were each assigned several buying departments, generally with related lines of merchandise. Prior to early 1967 these assignments had been somewhat flexible, depending as much on the availability and experience of retail merchandising personnel as on the desire to group related lines of merchandise together. Beginning in 1967, however, retail merchandising assignments were standardized to conform to the new merchandise categories.

The Retail Merchandisers performed two major functions. On the one hand, they coordinated the work of the departments reporting to the Divisional Vice President-Retail Merchandising (e.g., display, advertising) with that of the buying departments. On the other hand, they represented the Field to the buying departments and the buying departments to the Field. In addition, they had been performing the *de facto* function of coordinating the promotional activities of the various buying departments to which they were assigned, particularly if their buying departments had related lines of merchandise.

One Retail Merchandiser described his function as follows:

Our job description, if we had one, would say that we were responsible for coordination. I think that "catalyst" would be a better word. We are in close touch with our buying departments, and with the various merchandising specialists with whom they work. We know what these people are thinking and what the Divisional Vice President-Retail Merchandising is thinking. Our job is to make sure that everyone knows what everyone else is thinking, and that good ideas do not get lost in the shuffle. We call meetings when necessary, but spend most of our time "communicating." I'll spend an hour with a buying department's Retail Sales Manager, an hour with the Advertising Department, and a few minutes with the Divisional Vice President-Retail Merchandising, for example, just to make sure that everybody is moving in the same direction at the same time.

We also take the lead role in certain types of activity. Several buying departments in my category, for example, have been quite successful with a joint rotogravure supplement program. I have, from the beginning, taken the lead in calling meetings to determine when a supplement should come out, what its theme should be, and how many pages each buying department should get. After these things have been decided, I sort of "ride herd" over the artists and copywriters, to make sure it's what we want, and, at the same time, "sell"[18] the supplement to the Field. In general I would say that my role is more direct in joint efforts of this kind than in activities confined to a single buying department.

The Visual Merchandising Department was responsible for making recommendations to the Field in the areas of display, point-of-sale advertising, and merchandise arrangement, and to the buying departments concerning packaging. Two documents prepared and distributed by the Visual Merchandising Department were of particular importance. The Merchandise Arrangement Guide, which was updated regularly, contained recommendations concerning the location and amount of space for each buying department in various types of stores (i.e., depending on size, whether urban, suburban, or rural). While Store Managers were not required to follow the Merchandise Arrangement Guide, most Sears stores were in fact laid out approximately as suggested by the Guide. As one Sears executive explained:

If a buying department wants more space or a better location (and what department doesn't?), it does two things. It tries to convince the visual merchandising people to change the Merchandise Arrangement Guide, and it tries to convince individual Store Managers to deviate from the Guide. The visual merchandising people are concerned with company-wide profits. The Store Managers are concerned with store-wide profits. Both serve as checks on the understandably parochial objectives of the individual buying departments.

The monthly "Spotlite Service" was a bulletin containing recommendations for display and fixtures. It was distributed to all stores each month, as part of the monthly "Combo." While concerned primarily with items to be promoted during the month in question, it also contained ideas of a longer term nature. The

---

[17] See Exhibit 6, Retail Merchandising Organization Chart.

[18] The Field was not required to buy and distribute the rotogravure supplements prepared by Parent. Because Parent subsidized about 75% of the true cost, however, it was difficult for the Field to refuse to take a supplement.

stores generally adopted most of the recommendations in the Spotlite Service, using local sources or their own personnel to construct and set up the displays.

The Retail Merchandise Lists Department was responsible for the review and distribution of the merchandise lists and various promotional offerings to the stores. As its manager explained:

> Our form of organization requires a constant flow of paper from Parent to Field. Our job is to make sure that everything arrives at one place on time, to put it together, and to actually ship it to the stores.

The Retail Sales Promotion and Advertising Department worked with the buying departments on the physical design and preparation of advertising and promotional materials. In addition, it was responsible for the preparation of data used to plan Sears' monthly promotional strategy (see below). Because of the long lead times, it was necessary for the department to work on different stages of several months' promotions at the same time.

Promotional Planning

The major task of the departments and individuals reporting to the Divisional Vice President-Retail Merchandising was to prepare the monthly Combo (see page 301). The Combo consisted of special merchandise offers to the stores (i.e., opportunities to buy merchandise at reduced prices), an advertising mat service, a display recommendation service, and various kinds of historical sales data to be used as a planning aid at the local level.

The preparation of a monthly Combo was a complex process, beginning many months before it was to take effect. In particular, the buying departments required long lead times for promotional merchandise, since a full-scale Sears promotion could easily double or triple the short-term sales of the manufacturer concerned. As one executive explained:

> We are too big to operate by the seat of our pants. If a typical department store buyer wants to have a promotion, she goes to New York, buys the merchandise, and gets someone to draw up an ad. We just can't work that way. The quantities we need are so big that no manufacturer can supply us from inventory. And our Advertising Department is a large organization in its own right. It has to be able to schedule its work, like a manufacturing plant, if it is to be able to operate efficiently.

In an effort to systematize Sears' promotional planning procedures, Retail Merchandising developed the "Master Retail Promotion Planning and Procedures Timetable" in early 1966. This document listed 30 major steps to be followed in planning and implementing a monthly Combo.

Planning for a particular Combo began approximately thirteen months prior to the month in question, with a preliminary seasonal calendar review. Based largely on extrapolations from detailed historical sales data, this review was used to highlight the types of merchandise likely to be susceptible to promotional support during the month in question.

The buying departments used the data to select merchandise for promotion. After a series of meetings with the Divisional Vice President-Retail Merchandising, the Retail Merchandisers, and the Visual Merchandising and Advertising and Promotion Departments, tentative promotional offerings (with promotional themes) were presented to representatives from the Field at "Tote Board" Meetings.

The "Tote Board" was a device initiated by Sears in 1959 to promote communications between Parent and Field. A four-day Tote Board Meeting was held in Chicago every two months. Selected representatives of the Field (generally Store, Group, and Zone Managers) came to Chicago to listen to Parent department presentations and offer reactions. In theory, the buying departments presented their tentative promotional offerings for the seventh and eighth months following the Tote Board[19] and used Field reactions to guide them in preparing their final offerings. In practice, buying commitments were often made *prior to* the Tote Board Meeting, and changes generally could not be made by the buying departments when requested by the Field.

After the Tote Board Meeting the various departments worked toward a series of deadlines, culminating in the mailing of the Combo to the Field approximately three months prior to the beginning of the promotional month. In commenting on these procedures, the head of planning in the Sales Promotion and Advertising Department explained:

> I know our Timetable sounds awfully formal, but there is really no other way to get the job done. We have literally hundreds of promotions each and every month; each promotion requires inputs from a buying department, visual merchandising, and several different types of advertising personnel [i.e., copywriters, artists]. We simply have to have a way to make sure that everybody's contribution is there when we need it.

---

[19] I.e., the Tote Board Meeting held in February 1966 dealt with September and October 1966.

By early 1967 a number of merchandising executives had come to the conclusion that Sears' promotional planning procedures were deficient in several respects:

(1) There was inadequate coordination of promotional planning among buying departments with related lines of merchandise (see above, pp. 299–300).
(2) The all-store Tote Board meetings had not been as effective as had been hoped. While they had improved Parent-Field relations somewhat (through face-to-face contacts), the Field had not really provided useful inputs to Parent merchandising decisions. For the most part, this deficiency was attributed to the fact that Field representatives were generally Store, Group, and Zone Managers, who were not adequately familiar with individual lines or specific items of merchandise.
(3) The Field was not doing an adequate job of promotional planning. Field personnel had a natural tendency to be concerned with "this week," or, at best, "this month," and did not devote enough attention to longer range planning. Existing procedures called for such planning at the Field level, using the "monthly sales planning guide," but Parent executives were not, in general, satisfied with the resulting plans.

In order to remedy these deficiencies, the Vice President-Merchandising announced a new promotional planning procedure in early 1967. Known as the "New Corporate Direction," the new procedure had the following major elements:

(1) Fifteen merchandise categories were established, and changes were made in the organizations of the departments reporting to the Vice President-Merchandising (see above, p. 300).
(2) The Tote Board meetings were to be replaced by a series of category "Totes," each limited to the merchandise offerings and promotional plans of the buying departments in a single category for a specific period (3 to 6 months). Field representatives were to be Category Merchandisers, familiar with the lines of products to be discussed, rather than executives with general management responsibilities.
(3) The category "Totes" were to be followed by territorial quarterly marketing reviews (held in the Field), at which the Category Merchandisers and the territorial merchandising staffs presented their promotional plan for a quarter to Field representatives.

In commenting on the New Corporate Direction, the Vice President-Merchandising pointed out that it was intended to improve planning at all levels of both Parent and Field. While the new procedure was designed to remedy certain defects of the old system, its most important contribution would be increased emphasis on careful, coordinated planning — with adequate provision for review to make sure the planning job was being carried out.

Catalog Merchandising

The Catalog Merchandising Office and its subordinate departments were responsible for the planning, execution, and distribution of Sears catalogs. The Divisional Vice President-Catalog Merchandising supervised a group of Catalog Merchandisers (essentially responsible for planning), an Advertising Department (layouts, art work, copy writing), and a department that planned and did research in the fields of catalog circulation and distribution. In addition, he worked closely with the eleven catalog order plants, even though they reported to the Territorial Vice Presidents. The Divisional Vice President-Catalog Merchandising explained that he was able to work directly with catalog management in the Field, as there were only eleven catalog order plants.

Catalog planning began with the appropriation of funds for the catalog by corporate management. In making this appropriation, management compared the probable return on investment in the catalog with other investments available to it (e.g., new stores). In general, the Catalog Merchandising Office did not materially influence the size of the catalog budget.

Once the budget had been established, the Catalog Merchandising Office determined how it should be spent. In simple terms, there were three major considerations:

(1) How many separate catalogs should there be?
(2) How many pages (and how many color pages) should each catalog contain?
(3) How many copies of each catalog should be distributed?

These questions were studied in minute detail, using exhaustive historical data on return per page, return per catalog, return per type of customer, etc. In practice, it was very difficult to change the number of separate catalogs (there were always two big general catalogs, for example), somewhat easier to change the number of pages in a catalog, and easiest to change the number of catalogs to be distributed and the categories of customers who were to receive catalogs.

Once these decisions had been made, it was necessary to allocate pages to the buying departments. The spring and fall general catalogs each contained 1,600 pages. The Catalog Merchandising Office had to determine whether a buying department should, for example, receive 50, 70, or 100 pages. This decision could not be made for the individual department, since a change in one department's allocation necessarily affected other departments.

In theory, the buying departments did not have to accept the full number of pages allocated to them. They were charged with the cost of each page they used, and might find that an incremental page would not be profitable. In practice, virtually all departments wanted more pages than were available to them and competed vigorously for more pages each year.

Early in the planning process, the Catalog Merchandising Office asked each buying department to present a request for catalog pages and its plans for their use. On the basis of these requests and historical data concerning return per page, the Office then made its page allocations. According to the senior Catalog Merchandiser responsible for making this allocation, the major blocks of catalog pages fell into place without difficulty. The problem was generally at the margin, when a department had submitted a justifiable request for more space and it had to come from some other department's allocation. In cases like this, all he could do was to examine all relevant data, reach a decision, and stick to it.

No matter what I do, [he explained,] I can't please everyone. I simply have to exercise my best judgment as to how the company's interest will best be served. For the most part, the buying departments recognize what I am up against, and do not complain too loudly when they do not get what they want. After all, they have much the same problem with getting selling space in the stores.

After the allocation of catalog pages, the buying departments determined what merchandise would be included in the catalog. Catalog copywriters were physically located in each buying department, although they were formally part of the Catalog Merchandising Office. These copywriters made rough layouts of their departments' catalog pages and submitted them to the Catalog Merchandising Office for review. When they were approved, artists in the Catalog Merchandising Department, working with outside photographic studios, prepared the art work, while the copywriters wrote the final copy. An elaborate system of checking and rechecking catalog pages was followed, to prevent errors and violations of Sears' stringent advertising policies.

The catalogs were distributed to Sears customers who had met criteria concerning such factors as total purchases, number of purchases, and use of credit during the previous year. These criteria were changed frequently and varied among geographic areas and types of catalog. In some cases (e.g., the opening of a catalog order store in a town where Sears had not previously had an outlet), catalogs were sent to persons who were not presently Sears customers.

The Field

The Field was divided into five territories, each headed by a Vice President who was usually a member of the Sears Board of Directors. The territories, in turn, were divided into groups, zones, and catalog regions (each containing one catalog order plant). In general, individual stores were part of either a group or a zone, and catalog sales offices reported through several layers of field administration to the manager of the catalog order plant in their region.

This section of the case describes the organization and activities of the Eastern Territory. It begins by describing the territorial office, and then describes a group (Boston), a zone (Mid-Atlantic), and the Philadelphia Catalog Order Region.

The Eastern Territory

The Eastern Territory included the states of Maine, New Hampshire, Vermont, Massachusetts, Rhode Island, Connecticut, New York, New Jersey, Pennsylvania, Delaware, Maryland, Virginia, and West Virginia; the District of Columbia; and a portion of Ohio. This geographic area contained approximately 40% of the population of the United States, but represented a considerably smaller percentage of Sears sales volume. According to Sears executives, the company's relative weakness in the East was attributable to two major factors: (1) Sears had fewer stores (and less square feet of floor space) per capita in the East than it did in its stronger territories; and (2) Sears had not yet overcome its hard-goods image in the East to the same extent as it had in the newer territories.

In this territory there were 14 groups, 3 zones, and 2 catalog order regions. In addition, one large "A" store (Harrisburg, Pennsylvania) reported directly to the Territorial Vice President. At the end of 1965 the territory contained 204 retail stores, 113 of which were in groups. The largest group (New York) consisted of 37 stores, of which 10 were large stores. The smallest groups had only 2 or 3 stores. In 1965 retail sales represented approximately 75% of the territorial total. The 14 groups accounted for approximately 70% of retail sales; the 3 zones for approximately 29%; and the independent "A" store for slightly more than 1%.

Catalog order sales represented 25% of territorial sales. There were two catalog order plants in the territory, one in Philadelphia and one in Boston. Each catalog order plant served a catalog order region; the regional boundary was a more-or-less straight line between lower Connecticut and Rochester, New York. Sales in the Philadelphia Region were almost three times as great as those in the Boston Region in 1965, but the Boston Region had been growing more rapidly than the Philadelphia Region in recent years.

Only 10% of catalog order sales were traditional mail-order sales. The majority of sales were made by catalog sales offices, telephone sales offices, and catalog order desks in the retail stores. In recent years the trend away from straight mail order had been accelerating rapidly, as Sears expanded the number of its telephone sales offices and catalog sales offices. At the end of 1965 there were 211 catalog sales offices and 35 telephone sales offices in the Eastern Territory.

In late 1966 the territory was engaged in a major expansion program. Twelve new stores had been opened in 1965; almost 30 additional stores were to be opened in 1966 and 1967. For the most part these were large full-line department stores in suburban locations. The expansion program, which represented a large share of Sears' total capital budget for new stores, was intended to bring Sears' penetration of the eastern market up to the level the company enjoyed in the rest of the country.

The territorial office was located in Philadelphia in an office building adjacent to the Philadelphia catalog order plant. Reporting to the Territorial Vice President were an administrative assistant and 12 managers of staff departments (see Exhibit 7, Organization Chart of the Eastern Territorial Office). The 14 Group Managers, 3 Zone Managers, 2 Control Store Managers (the Catalog Order Regions), the independent "A" Store Manager, and the Fashion Center Manager also reported to the Territorial Vice President but were not considered part of the territorial office.

The Territorial Vice President had virtually unlimited authority to make operating and policy decisions for his territory. As one executive explained:

The Territorial Vice Presidents are really like presidents of their own companies. Each territory, by itself, would easily make *Fortune's 500,* and our Territorial Vice Presidents are equal to their counterparts [i.e., the presidents of other large companies] in compensation, responsibility, and authority. At Sears, there's no question that the Territorial Vice Presidents run the show.[20]

In practice, the Territorial Vice Presidents generally operated within policies, guidelines, and procedures established by the various Parent departments. In theory, they were free to reject or alter most[21] of these policies but in fact rarely did so.

The formal relationship between the Territorial Vice Presidents and the Executive Office was limited to such matters as budget and performance reviews and requests for capital appropriations. In practice, the relationship was somewhat more complex. When a Territorial Vice President requested funds for store expansion, for example, he was required to submit a list of store sites and pro forma operating statements. After he had received the allocation of funds, and approval for specific stores, any major enlargement in plans or change in location required the approval of the President or the Chairman.

Moreover, the President and the Chairman took a keen interest in operating data which they received regularly. If a catalog order plant's omissions rate[22] had increased, for example, it was not unusual for the President to telephone the Territorial Vice President or Catalog Order Plant Manager to ask why. Similarly, a Group Manager, or even a Store Manager, might receive a call from the Chairman if there was something he wanted to know. As one executive explained:

The members of our top management have been with Sears for a long time. It's amazing how many Store Managers (and even Division Managers) they know on a first name basis. They visit the Field a great deal and have worked with a lot of these people on the way up. It would be ridiculous for them to sit stewing in their offices, or go through a chain of command, if there's something they want to know. Our Territorial Vice Presidents are extremely jealous of their prerogatives, but this sort of thing doesn't bother them at all.

The twelve staff departments making up the territorial office varied widely in size, authority, and relationships with their Parent counterparts. Although all these departments had a Parent counterpart de-

---

[20] Of Sears' four Chairmen and Presidents in recent years, three had been Territorial Vice Presidents immediately prior to their promotions to top management.

[21] Limitations on the Territorial Vice Presidents' authority included budgets and buying on merchandise, which had to be approved by Parent; capital expenditures, which required a Parent allocation of funds; and accounting and personnel policies, which were closely administered by Parent.

[22] The percentage of orders received that could not be filled because of an out-of-stock condition.

partment, some (e.g., control, legal, personnel) were more strongly influenced by Parent than others. Moreover, the relationship between the territorial staff departments and groups, zones, and stores varied considerably. For example, some departments had counterparts at the group and zone levels; and some had counterparts in large stores but not small stores.[23]

In general, the staff departments performed several distinct types of functions. They disseminated Parent policies to the stores, established territorial policies (often by modifying Parent policies), and provided direct assistance to the stores when unusual problems arose. In addition, most of these departments had line responsibility for certain activities at the territorial level. The Personnel Department, for example, established personnel policies for the stores and also handled directly most "check list" [24] personnel matters, recruited college graduates for the entire territory, and ran an executive training program. Similarly, the Display Department gave display guidance to the stores and also planned the layouts for all new stores.

The following paragraphs describe two staff departments in further detail. These staff departments have been selected because their activities are of particular relevance to this case; they are not necessarily typical of other departments.

The Comptroller's Department: Within Sears, the comptrollership function was handled somewhat outside the regular line organization. While the Territorial Comptroller reported to the Territorial Vice President, it was quite clear that he also reported to the Parent Comptroller. As he explained:

I work for the Territorial Vice President. When he wants me to do something, he tells me to do it. I am the comptroller for the territory; it is my job to give the Territorial Vice President whatever information, data, or advice he wants.

At the same time, I am custodian of corporate resources in the Eastern Territory. If something doesn't look right, I must report it to the Corporate Comptroller.

My Territorial Vice President understands this fully; he wouldn't want it any other way.

It's the same way at the store level. A store controller works for his Store Manager, but also reports to me through his Regional Controller. Occasionally we have problems when a Store Manager violates company policy to increase his profits and I hear about it, but this happens — at most — once a year.

The Comptroller's Department performed three major functions:

(1) It prepared figure-oriented special reports and analyses at the request of the Territorial Vice President or his administrative assistant.
(2) It worked with the groups, zones, and catalog order plants to develop the semiannual seasonal budget. (This process is described below, p. 317).
(3) It performed, through its regional accounting centers, a regular audit of each store in the territory at least once a year. These audits were *not* primarily financial audits. Although financial statements and cash handling procedures were analyzed, the greater proportion of the traveling auditor's time was devoted to an analysis of the store's conformity to Parent and territorial operating procedures and policies.[25]

3010. Use two boards (current and previous month) [to maintain receiving records]. At the end of the month remove the papers for the oldest month, place 9" x 12" cardboard at the front and back of the papers, and bind the covers with a fastener. Label the package with month and year file. Destroy after three years.

The Merchandising Department: This department consisted of a Manager, a Merchandise Controller, and approximately 20 Territorial Merchandisers. The Merchandise Controller worked with the groups, zones, and stores to prepare "sales and inventory budgets" (this process is described below, p. 317). The Territorial Merchandisers were responsible for assisting the groups and stores with specific lines of merchandise.

Each Territorial Merchandiser was responsible for one or more divisions. These assignments did not generally correspond to the new category breakdown, but would probably be brought into line with the category concept in the near future. In the past territorial merchandising assignments had been made on the basis of need, as perceived by territorial manage-

---

[23] Some departments were divided on a geographic basis that did not correspond to the groups and zones. The Comptroller's Department, for example, had eleven Regional Controllers, headquartered in the catalog order plants, who worked with individual stores (some of which had controllers). The control regions varied from the store areas somewhat because of work load and travel time; a control region would contain stores in several groups and zones, and an individual zone might be served by more than one control region. Similarly, the Public Relations Department was organized around political jurisdictions rather than the retail store organization.

[24] "Check list" was Sears' term for "exempt" personnel.

[25] These policies could get quite detailed. The "Receiving and Shipping Manual," for example, contained over 350 pages divided into nine chapters; e.g., "Maintenance of Facilities," "Packaging for Shipment," "Receipt of Merchandise," "Marketing," "Control of Papers." Each chapter was divided into numbered paragraphs, for example:

ment. Several Merchandisers were assigned to certain lines, some lines did not have a Merchandiser assigned to them, and some Merchandisers were headquartered in Boston rather than Philadelphia. In a few cases, the salaries of the Merchandisers were paid (or shared) by the Parent buying departments on whose lines they worked.

The Territorial Merchandisers were primarily responsible for disseminating Parent-sponsored programs to the store organization. In some cases such programs were basically advertising programs, and it was the Merchandiser's job to encourage the groups and stores to use Parent-prepared advertising programs in their local markets. In other cases emphasis was on display or selling techniques, and the Merchandisers concentrated on these areas.

The Merchandisers also worked with Parent to develop local promotions tailored to the Eastern Territory (e.g., a Washington's Birthday sale). The Merchandisers asked the buying departments for "special deals" on merchandise for such sales and arranged for the Parent Advertising Department to prepare advertising mats. While most of Sears' promotional efforts were national in scope, it was generally believed that local promotions (at the territory, group, *and* store levels) were necessary to give Field personnel "a feeling of belonging to something a little bit smaller than a $7 billion plus corporation."

The Parent buying departments used the Territorial Merchandisers as sounding boards for new products and promotional programs. The Merchandisers visited Chicago (or New York) frequently, at the request of the Parent departments, and attended all category "Totes." In some cases, when dissatisfied with a line or a promotional approach, the Territorial Merchandiser invited Parent personnel to attend a meeting of group and store merchandising personnel.

In a few cases the Territorial Merchandisers also performed a regional buying function. There were considerable advantages in using local sources for some products (e.g., nursery stock;) and the buying departments found it desirable to delegate day-to-day buying responsibility to the Territorial Merchandisers. Selection of sources and specification of merchandise remained a Parent function, but was often done on the basis of recommendations by the Territorial Merchandisers.

The Boston Group

The Boston Group contained 17 stores at the end of 1965. Of these, four were A stores, five were B1 stores, one was a B2 store, and seven were B3 stores.[26] These stores were located within a geographic area circumscribed by a highway network forming the limits of what was generally known as "Boston and its suburbs." As highway facilities had improved in recent years, and the suburbs had moved outward, the Group's boundaries had been broadened to include outlying stores that had previously been part of the New England zone.

Like the rest of the Eastern Territory, the Boston Group was engaged in a major facilities expansion program. By June 1967 the Group expected to have nine A stores in operation and planned to build an additional five or six A stores in the next few years. As new A stores were opened, small B and C stores in surrounding towns were being closed. The downtown Boston store (a large old store known affectionately as the Ark) had recently been extensively remodeled as had an older A store in Cambridge.

According to the Group Manager, Sears' image in the Boston area had traditionally been somewhat weak, largely as a result of the facilities through which it had been doing business. The major objective of the store expansion program, besides extending Sears' coverage, was to present the consumer with a better, more modern image of Sears as a retail chain.

The group office consisted of the Group Manager, Controller, Operating Manager, Sales Promotion Manager, Service Manager, Personnel Manager, Advertising Manager, three Group Merchandisers (responsible for soft lines, hard lines, and "big tickets" respectively), and about a dozen merchandising assistants (responsible for narrower product lines, such as home fashions or men's and boys' wear).

The Group Manager and his staff had considerable freedom to operate their Group as they saw fit. They selected the sites for new stores (subject to territorial approval), established group policies, and were free to accept, modify, or reject the various policies, promotional programs, and merchandise offerings emanating from Parent. While most such programs were accepted and implemented, a group was more likely

---

[26] Sears stores were classified as A, B1, B2, B3, or C stores according to several criteria. An A store was the largest type, a full-line department store, uusally located in a large city. A B1 store was the smallest type to include all selling divisions. A B2 store carried fewer lines of merchandise than a B1 store and was usually located in a small town. A B3 store carried hard lines and appliances on a broader scale than a C store and was usually located in or near a metropolitan area. C stores, which were the smallest type, carried hard lines and appliances and were usually located in small towns in rural areas.

to reject or modify a program than a territory was. As the Group Manager explained:

> The Boston market is really quite different from other markets. Discount and basement merchandising were born here, and the consumer is exceptionally price conscious. Somehow, "getting a bargain" is more respectable here than it is in other places.
>
> As a result, we tend to promote price more than most of the other groups do. We use some Parent-prepared advertising, and create some of our own. In general, I would say that we use most of what Parent sends us, but we have to be selective. If we don't tailor our programs to our local market, we are bound to miss some pretty good opportunities.

Most merchandising decisions for the stores in the group were made by the group office. The Group Merchandisers (in consultation with Store Merchandisers and/or Division Managers) determined which specific items were to be stocked by each store, and at what prices they should be sold. The group Advertising Department prepared and placed all advertising for the Group. The Division Managers in the stores were responsible for ordering the merchandise selected for them at the group level, and for making certain that it was displayed and sold effectively.

The Group operated a "pool stock" and a number of central repair service facilities. The pool stock delivered all major appliances directly to customers from its central warehouse, thus relieving the stores of the necessity to maintain inventories of these items. Similarly, a customer requiring repair service for a Sears product telephoned a central repair service office which scheduled the service call, thus relieving the local store of responsibility for repair service.

The Mid-Atlantic Zone

The operation of a *zone* was quite different. By definition, a zone comprised a number of stores that were *not* linked together by common media, road networks, etc. Consequently, individual stores in a zone operated with considerably more autonomy than stores in a group. The Division Managers, for example, not only ordered merchandise, but also selected the items that they would sell and established the retail price at which they would be sold. The Zone Manager and his staff (which was smaller than a group staff) visited most of the stores in the zone regularly, and tried to provide as much direction as their group counterparts did. They concentrated mainly on providing a communications channel among the Parent departments, territory office, and retail stores.

The Mid-Atlantic Zone was typical in many respects. Its territory included New Jersey, Delaware, Maryland, Eastern Pennsylvania, and parts of New York. It did not, however, include the metropolitan areas of New York City, Allentown, Philadelphia, and Wilmington, all of which were group operations.

The zone contained 27 stores (14 B1, 3 B2, 4 B3, and 6 C). Located in smaller cities and towns, these stores ranged from large full-line B1 stores, which would have been A stores if located in a group, to small agency outlets, which carried only a few lines of merchandise. The catalog sales offices within the zone's territory were operated by the Philadelphia catalog order plant, rather than by zone management.

The Philadelphia Catalog Order Region

The Phildelphia Catalog Order Region consisted of a large catalog order plant and approximately 150 catalog and telephone sales offices. Sales of almost $300 million in 1965 made it Sears' second largest catalog order region.

The Region was headed by the Philadelphia Control Store Manager, who reported to the Territorial Vice President. Reporting to the Control Store Manager were an Operating Superintendent, a Merchandising Superintendent, a Sales Superintendent, a Comptroller, a Customer Service Manager, a Catalog Manager, and a Personnel Manager.

The Operating Superintendent was responsible for the operation of the Philadelphia plant and all activities having to do with the physical movement of merchandise (receiving, storing, assembling orders, packing, and shipping).

The Merchandising Superintendent supervised the activities of 11 Merchandise Managers and 92 Control Buyers. The Merchandise Managers developed promotions and other merchandising tools for use by the catalog and telephone sales offices. In recent years, the growth of telephone selling had made short-term catalog promotions feasible. Where previously it had been necessary to wait passively for mail orders to come in, it was now possible to institute telephone campaigns at the local level. Such campaigns in some cases entailed telephone calls to Sears' customers to inform them of a special catalog sale; in other cases telephone operators were instructed to mention the sale to customers calling in to make regular orders. Similarly, promotions were often featured in point-of-sale advertising at the catalog sales offices.

The Control Buyers were responsible for forecasting sales, ordering merchandise, and keeping inventory records. In many ways their function was similar to that of the Division Managers in the retail stores, except that they were assigned narrower lines of merchandise and did not supervise retail sales personnel. In recent years, as computers had eliminated some routine record keeping, the Control Buyers had begun to work closely with the Merchandisers on catalog promotions.

The Sales Superintendent directed the activities of 7 District Managers, each of whom was responsible for approximately 20 catalog and telephone sales offices. The District Managers provided line supervision to the managers of the offices assigned to them. A customer service specialist and a sales promotion specialist worked for each District Manager, assisting the offices in these areas.

Planning, Logistics, and Product Development

Planning, logistics, and product development were three areas of particular concern to Sears management in early 1967. The following pages describe these processes from a company-wide, rather than departmental, point of view.

Planning and Budgeting

For planning purposes, Sears divided the year ino two six-month periods. Several months before the beginning of a new period, the Parent Economic and Marketing Research Department prepared economic and business forecasts, which it submitted to corporate management. Using these data, corporate management developed a forecast of company sales for the next six-month period. The forecast was stated in the form of a percentage change over the same period during the previous year; for example, "Sales in existing facilities should increase 3.5%; total sales (including new stores) should increase 5%."

This forecast was sent with a covering letter to the buying departments and territories. While both were required to develop their own forecasts, it was expected that these forecasts would not deviate markedly from the company forecast. In practice, any major deviation from the company forecast had to be supported with strong reasons, and management was reluctant to approve forecasts above the company forecast.

Management's reluctance to approve forecasts higher than the company forecast was due primarily to its strong concern with inventory control. The "sales and inventory budget" prepared by each store and the store's forecast, were, in fact, tied closely together.

The forecast sales for a given division, for example, when divided by the appropriate inventory turnover for that division, gave the average inventory level for the division during the period in question. Thus, the greater the territory forecasts, which were composites of group, zone, and store forecasts, the higher the level of inventory the stores were authorized to carry.

Pressures were placed on the buying departments to keep their forecasts low for much the same reason. A buying department that succeeded in obtaining approval for a high forecast could use that forecast to encourage the stores to carry disproportionately high inventories of its merchandise.

Buying department forecasts were used to guide the Field in preparing its sales and inventory budgets, not to determine how much the buying departments should buy. As one executive explained:

> The concept is really a simple one. If we make mistakes, we want to make them at the Parent [buying department] level. Our buyers are experienced merchants, who are much closer to what is happening nationally than the people in the stores. If they buy too much, they have a whole country in which to move the goods.
>
> The stores are a different matter. Store personnel think about today and next week, not about next year. If they make a mistake, they're stuck with the merchandise; they simply do not have the options that a Parent department does.
>
> Thus we are very tight on sales budgets. If a buying department expects more demand than we allow it to budget for, it buys accordingly. If its service of supply is set up properly, and the increase in demand materializes, we end up with increased sales, increased turnover, and increased profits.

Logistics

The distribution pattern for a given line of merchandise was established by the buying department responsible for that line of merchandise. The merchandise lists used by the stores to order merchandise contained detailed instructions as to how specific items should be ordered. The buying departments attempted to weigh considerations of transportation economics against the need for rapid delivery or special handling in choosing among four basic logistics systems in use in early 1967.

Direct Source Shipments: Under this procedure, the Division Managers ordered merchandise directly from the source, which shipped directly to the store placing the order.

Pool Stocks: Most large groups operated pool stocks, which were essentially warehouses for "big ticket" lines of merchandise (e.g., washing machines, television sets). The pool stocks ordered directly from the sources, attempting to maintain an inventory adequate to cover all of the needs of the group. The sources shipped the merchandise directly to the pool stocks, which in turn delivered the merchandise directly to the customer. Under this system, it was not necessary for the stores to maintain inventories, except for floor samples.

Control Stores: Certain high-volume merchandise (e.g., hardware items) were shipped by the sources to the catalog order plants, where they were held in inventory. In some cases where packaging was the same, these items were mingled with catalog order inventories; in other cases, they were not. The stores then ordered these items from the control stores, which were able to deliver small quantities on short notice. The control stores charged the stores 7% of the cost price of the merchandise for this service. (The stores paid freight costs under the other logistics procedures.) In some cases a buying department specified that A stores were to order a given line of merchandise direct, while B and C stores were to order from a control store.

Fashion Merchandising Centers: Certain lines of volatile fashion merchandise (e.g., dresses) were ordered and stocked by five fashion merchandising centers (one for each territory). These fashion centers shipped merchandise to the stores according to a computerized automatic inventory replenishment system (see above, pp. 306–307).

Each of the four methods of merchandise distribution had advantages and disadvantages. Direct source shipments were generally the least expensive way to distribute merchandise, but required relatively long lead times and standard quantities. Pool stocks were efficient for lines of merchandise requiring delivery and installation, but were otherwise not economic. Use of the control stores facilitated shipment of nonstandard quantities of merchandise, but it was expensive from the point of view of the stores.[27] The fashion centers were very expensive, and were only warranted when justified by merchandising (as distinct from logistical) considerations.

By the mid-1960s Sears management had concluded that there was a significant opportunity to increase profits through the rationalization of Sears' distribution system. The current approach, while providing the buying departments with some options, had grown up through the years without adequate attention to the overall company-wide implications of decisions made for individual lines of merchandise. In particular, the practice of using the catalog order plants as retail warehouses was controversial, as was the arbitrary 7% charge to the stores for this service.

Several groups in the company were working on this problem in early 1967. The Operations Department had recently been given responsibility for both logistics and data processing and was working on a computerized system that was expected to revolutionize Sears' entire logistics pattern. This system was not expected to become operational, except on a test basis, for several years, however, and there was a general feeling that "something ought to be done now." In early 1967 the Vice President-Merchandising appointed an "assistant on distribution" to review the procedures being followed by each of the buying departments and recommend changes when appropriate. In making this appointment, the Vice President-Merchandising pointed out that he was confident that there were considerable opportunities for savings, even before the new computerized system went into operation.

Product Development

In early 1967 the Vice President-Merchandising was particularly concerned with Sears' efforts in the area of product development. As he explained:

Our Chairman has publicly stated the goal of $10 billion in sales by 1970, a $3 billion increase in three years. Some of this increase will come from new facilities, but only a relatively small part of it. If we are to achieve our goal, we must develop new products — unique to Sears — which will draw new customers into our stores and motivate them to spend a larger share of their disposable income with us.

Speaking frankly, I must admit that we have not done all that we should in this area. Our buyers, merchandise laboratory, and sources have developed a great many new or superior products, but, considering the number of products we carry, we have really only scratched the surface.

Historically (with some very major exceptions), we have let the leading manufacturers of branded consumer goods develop new products and introduce them to the public. We have then refined their developments, to give the consumer a higher quality product for less money.

I strongly believe that product development is the area of greatest potential growth for Sears. The buyers are responsible for product development — let there be no doubt of that! — but we will review their lines more frequently (asking continually, "What's new?") and give them more help. I hope that the new product categories, with more resources than the individual buying departments, will be able to increase our efforts in this area.

---

[27] The 7% charge was generally higher than that for direct shipment. It should be noted, however, that this was not Sears' true cost, which may have been higher or lower. Moreover, the control store system absorbed a considerable amount of catalog order plant overhead.

Exhibit 1. Corporate Organization Chart, 1967

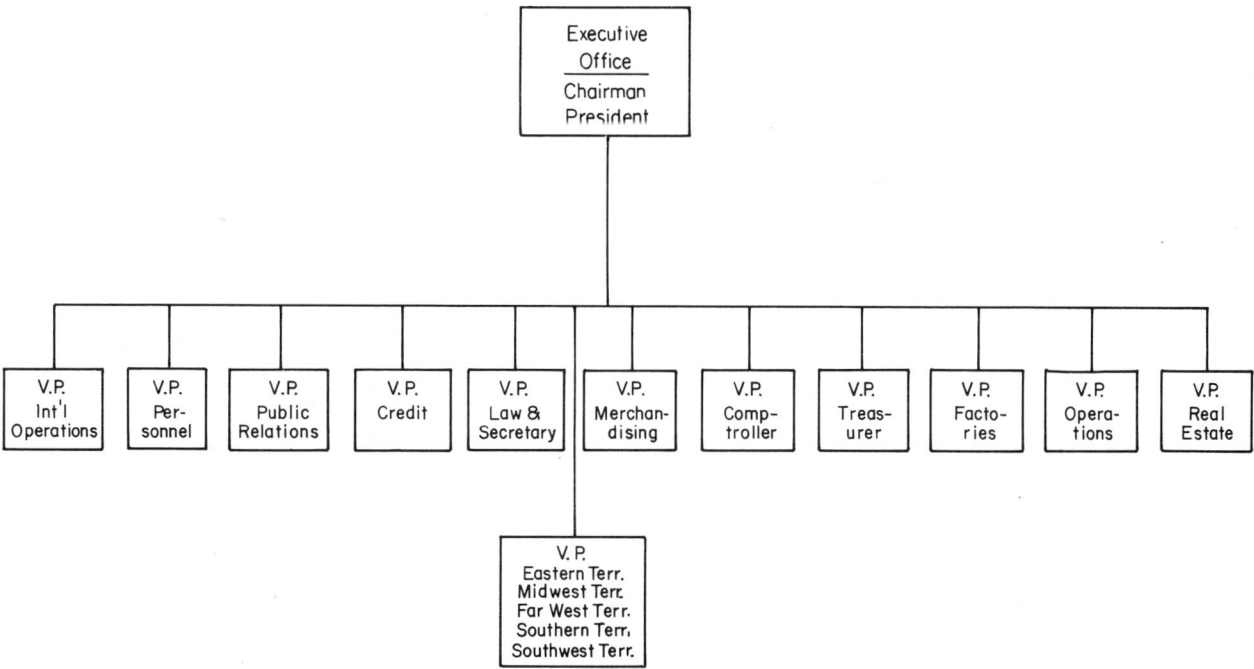

Source: Prepared by case writer.

Exhibit 2. Organization Chart of Merchandising Department, 1967

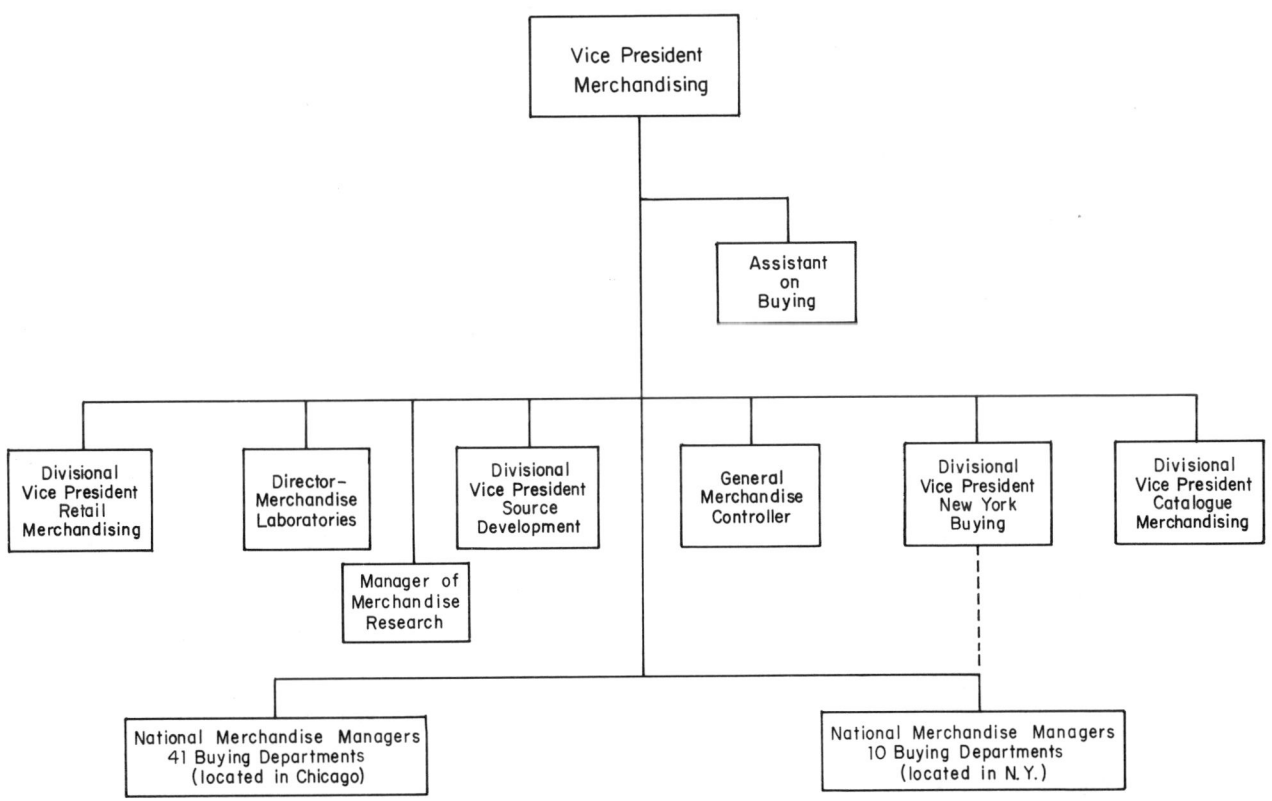

Source: Prepared by case writer.

Exhibit 3. Buying Department Assignments

CHICAGO BUYING DEPARTMENTS

Department	Assignment
601	Furniture
603	Photographic equipment, business equipment, educational and general stationery
606	Family recreation, sporting goods
608	Drugs and cosmetics
609	Hardware
611	Housewares
615-54-67-76	Shoes and rubber footwear
618	Women's support garments
620	Sewing machines, vacuum cleaners, floor polishers
621	Home fashion accessories
622	Stoves
624	Curtains, draperies, bedspreads
625	Notions
626	Home laundry appliances
628	Auto accessories
629	Infants' and children's wear
630	Paint, ladders, and accessories
632	Fencing
633	Men's furnishings
634	Electrical appliances and lighting fixtures
636	Yard goods
637	Floor coverings
638	Women's lingerie, loungewear, and robes
640	Boys' clothing and furnishings
641	Men's work clothing and sportswear
642	Plumbing and central heating/cooling apparatus; lawn sprinkling systems; swimming pools
644	Tailored-to-measure clothing
645	Men's dress clothing
646	Refrigerators
647	Freezers, air conditioners, and dehumidifiers
649	Toys
657	Televisions, radios, phonographs, musical instruments, phonograph records
664	Building materials
665	Kitchens
671	Lawn and garden
687	Confections, food service, food products, and smoker's needs
695	Tires and tubes
696	Bath — slumber — linen
698	Repair parts

NEW YORK BUYING DEPARTMENTS

Department	Assignment
604	Tradition jewelry
607	Women's sportswear
614	Luggage
617	Ladies' coats, suits, rainwear, and furs
619	Junior clothing
631	Dresses
675	Women's and children's hosiery
677	Girls' and teens' wear
678	Millinery
688	Accessories

Exhibit 4. Buying Assignments of Hardware Department (609)

BUYER A

Line #1 — Electric Motors & Electrically Driven Hand Tools

1. Electric Hand Saws
2. Electric Hand Saw Accessories
3. Electric Drill Kits
4. Electric Drills
5. Electric Drill Accessories & Attachments
6. Drills, Twist & Stands, Jigs & Sharpening Stands
7. Circle & Gasket Cutters
8. Power Wood Bits & Accessories
9. Electric Impact Wrenches
10. Pneumatic Tools
11. Pneumatic Tool Accessories
12. Sabre Saws
13. Sabre Saw Accessories & Blades
14. Electric Sander/Polishers
15. Electric Sander/Polisher Accessories
16. Electric Grinder (#2584)
17. Electric Grinder Accessories
18. Electric Routers
19. Electric Router Accessories
20. Electric Planers
21. Tool Cases

Line #2 — Power Tools & Accessories

26. Roto Trowels & Midget Vibrators

Line #7 — Lawn & Garden Tools

16. Electric Edgers & Accessories
17. Electric Hedge Trimmers & Accessories

BUYER B

Line #1 — Electric Motors & Electrically Driven Hand Tools

22. Motors
23. Electric Bench Grinders

Line #2 — Power Tools & Accessories

1. Bench & Floor Model Saws
2. Bench & Floor Model Saw Accessories
3. Radial Saws
4. Radial Saw Accessories
5. Band Saws
6. Band Saw Accessories
7. Jig Saws
8. Jig Saw Blades
9. Drill Presses
10. Drill Press Accessories
11. Thickness Planers, Jointer Planers & Accessories
12. Sanders
13. Wood Lathes
14. Wood Lathe Accessories
15. Wood Shapers, Cutters & Accessories
16. Belt Driven Grinders, Mandrels & Polishing Heads
17. Metal Lathes
18. Metal Lathe Accessories
19. Metal Lathe Chucks
20. Machine Stands & Accessories
21. 6–12″ Circular Blades
22. Dado Sets
23. Molding Heads & Cutters
24. Power Hack Saws
25. Line Shafts, Shaft Hangers, Coupling, etc.
27. Tool Lights
28. V-Belts & Accessories
29. V-Pulleys
30. Flexible Shafts & Accessories
31. Publications
34. Furniture Kits

Line #3 — Carpenters' & Masons' Tools

33. Work Benches

Line #5 — Shop Tools & Supplies

1. Shop Vacuums
2. Shop Vacuum Accessories

BUYER C

Line #1 — Electric Motors & Electrically Driven Hand Tools

24. Arc Welders
25. Arc Welder Accessories

Line #2 — Power Tools & Accessories

32. Gem Makers & Accessories
33. Misc. Hobby Supplies & Publications

Line #3 — Carpenters' & Masons' Tools

30. Surveying Instruments
31. Brushes, Wire
32. Hand Grinder & Grinding Wheel Dressers

Line #5 — Shop Tools & Supplies

3. Oxy-Acetylene Welders
4. Oxy-Acetylene Welder Accessories
5. Buffs, Buffing Wheels & Compound
6. Sanding Discs
7. Wire Wheel Brushes
8. Sanding Belts
9. Glue & Adhesives
10. Coated Abrasive Products
11. Karbo Grit Products
12. Steel Wool
13. Stones, Grinding Wheels & Points
23. Dowels
24. Respirators, Goggles, Glasses & Shields

BUYER D

Line #3 — Carpenters' & Masons' Tools

1. Auger Bits, Expansive Bits, Countersinks & Screwdrivers

Exhibit 4 (continued)

2. Axes
3. Bow Saws
4. Braces & Drills
5. Brackets & Saw Horses
6. Brick Hammers & Masons' Tools
7. Chisels, Wood
8. Clamps, Woodworking
9. Combination Squares
10. Coping Saws & Blades
11. Hand Sanders
12. Files & Hasps
13. Hammers, Ball Peen
14. Hammers, Carpenter
15. Replacement Handles
16. Hand Saws
17. Hatchets
18. Levels, Carpenter & Mason
19. Misc. Carpenters' Tools
20. Miter Boxes
21. Planes & Rasplanes
22. Pouches, Tools
23. Putty Knives & Scrapers
24. Rules & Tapes
25. Squares, Rafters, Miter & Sliding T Bevel
26. Stapler & Staples
27. Vise, Bench
28. Wrecking Bars, Wedges, Sledges
29. Magnate, Magnetic Pencils & Stud Finder
34. Import Tools

Line #10 — Precision Tools

1. Linear Measuring Tools
2. Linear Measuring Tool Accessories
3. Gauges
4. Indicators & Accessories
5. Miscellaneous Precision Tools

BUYER E

Line #4 — Automotive & Mechanics' Tools

1. Craftsman Sockets
2. Sears Sockets
3. Wrenches — B.E., O.E., Combination
4. Nut Drivers
5. Set Screw Wrenches
35. Import Tools

BUYER F

Line #4 — Automotive & Mechanics' Tools

6. Soldering Guns
7. Soldering Irons
8. Electric Engraving Tools
9. Stencils & Steel Letters
10. Glass Blowing Kits & Accessories

Line #5 — Shop Tools & Supplies

14. Solder

Line #8 — Plumbers' Tools

1. Wrenches, Pipe
2. Pipe Stocks & Dies
3. Vises, Pipe & Stand
4. L.P. Torches
5. Blow Torches
6. Taper Reamers
7. Taps, Dies & Related Items
8. Miscellaneous Plumbers' Tools
9. Import Tools

BUYER G

Line #4 — Automotive & Mechanics' Tools

11. Craftsman Screwdrivers
12. Sears Screwdrivers
13. Punches & Chisels
14. Arc Joint Pliers
15. Cutting Pliers & Nippers
16. Slip Joint Pliers
17. Tin Snips
18. Belt Cutters
19. Wrenches, Locking Pliers
20. Wrenches, Adjustable
21. Creative Precision Tools
22. Convertible Retaining Ring Pliers & Wire and Cable Strippers
23. Plier Grips
35. Import Tools

BUYER H

Line #4 — Automotive & Mechanics' Tools

24. Body and Fender Tools
25. Wheel, Brake Muffler, Battery and Filter Tools
26. Leaf Feeler and Gap Gauges
27. Specialty Engine Repair Tools
28. Auto Creepers
29. Torque Wrenches
30. Craftsman Tool Truck Item Development
31. Hack Saws
32. Saw Blades, Hack
33. Tool Boxes, Chests and Cabinets
34. Oilers

BUYER I

Line #5 — Shop Tools & Supplies

15. Belting & Accessories
16. Rope
17. Rope Hoists & Blocks
18. Wire Rope & Accessories

Exhibit 4 (continued)

19. Chain Hoists, Lever Hoists & Winches
20. Conveyors
21. Jack Screws
25. Chain & Accessories

Line #6 — Builders' Hardware

10. Mending Plates & Brackets
11. Barn Door Hardware
12. Nuts, Screws, Bolts, Washers, Tacks, Brads, Wire Nails, Rivets, Wire Goods, Springs
13. Weatherstrip
14. Stove Accessories
15. Casters & Glides
16. Screw & Bolt Dispensers
17. Peg Boards & Hooks
18. Do-It-Yourself Aluminum
19. Adjustable Screens & Ventilators
20. Screening
21. Nails
22. Hardware Cloth
23. Sash Cord
24. Twine

BUYER J

Line #5 — Shop Tools & Supplies

22. Miscellaneous Lubricants

Line #6 — Builders' Hardware

1. Locksets
2. Door Closers
3. Padlocks & Night Latches
4. Cabinet Hardware
5. Standards, Brackets, Particle Boards & Shelves
6. Hinges, Butts & Hasps
7. Sash & Door Hardware
8. Mail Boxes
9. House Numbers & Metal Signs

BUYER K

Line #7 — Lawn & Garden Tools

1. Push-type Rotary Mowers
2. Self-Propelled Rotary Mowers
3. Riding Power Mowers — Medium Duty
4. Riding Power Mowers — Heavy Duty
5. Reel Type Power Mowers
6. Hand Mowers
7. Lawn Vacuums & Accessories
8. Power Edger-Trimmers
9. Hand Edger-Trimmers
10. Lawn Sweepers (Hand & Power)
11. Snow Throwers & Snow Plow Attachments
12. Lawn Mower Accessories
13. Grass Catchers
14. Gas Cans
15. Blades

BUYER L

Line #7 — Lawn & Garden Tools

18. Garden Hose
19. Hose Reels
20. Sprinkler Hose & Soakers
21. Laundry Hose
22. Hose Nozzles
23. Hose Accessories
24. Sprinklers
25. Grass Whips, Hooks & Scythes
26. Lawn Rakes
27. Shovels
28. Grass Shears
29. Pruning and Hedgecutting Equipment
30. Edgers
31. Hand Garden Tools
32. Steel Goods
33. Wheelbarrows — Carts & Wheels
34. Garden Carts
35. Wheels
36. Lawn Rollers
37. Hand Trucks
38. Post Hole Diggers
39. Snow Tools

BUYER M

Line #9 — Pocket Knives & Shaving Supplies

1. Men's Electric Shavers
2. Ladies' Electric Shavers
3. Imported Mens' Shavers
4. Imported Ladies' Shavers
5. Electric Shaver Parts
6. Razor Blades & Razors
7. Clippers & Clipper Sets
8. Misc. Barber Supplies
9. Pocket Knives

Exhibit 5. Buying Assignments for Infants' and Children's Wear, Department 629, Chicago

BUYING ORGANIZATIONAL CHART

```
                              ┌─────────────────────┐
                              │      National       │
                              │ Merchandise Manager │
                              └──────────┬──────────┘
                                         ├──── Secretary
```

Merchandise Controller		BUYING STAFF					
		Buyer	Buyer	Buyer	Buyer	Buyer	Buyer
•Coverage Policy	•Fashion Co-ordinator and Quality Control	Asst. Buyers		Buyer's Asst.	Asst. Buyer	Asst. Buyer	
•Service of Supply		Buyer's Asst.				Buyer's Asst.	
•Office Manager	•Asst. Fashion Co-ordinator and Quality Control	•Nightwear	•Infants Sleepwear	•Anklets	•Boys Accessories	•Feeding Items	•Piece Goods
		•Girls Sweaters	•Bootees	•Denims	•Boys Dress and Eton Suits	•Nursery Items and Drugs	
	•Merchandise examiner and inspector	•Stretch Tights/Tops	•Infants Sweaters	•Westernwear	•Sport Coats	•Gifts and Toys	
		•Girls Suits	•Layettes		•Knit Headwear	•Mites and Toddlers Playwear	
		•Jumpers	•Gift Sets		•Scarf Sets and Mittens	•Mites Swimwear	
		•Skirts	•Shawls		•Boys Ski Pants	•Topper/Tight Sets	
		•Blouses	•Cotton and Tricot Underwear		•Boys Rainwear and Toppers	•Buntings	
			•Slips		•Boys Coats and Coat Sets	•Carriage Suits	
					•Boys Snowsuits		
					•Boys Jackets		
					•Boys Headwear		

BUYING STAFF					Pacific Coast	New York Office
Buyer	Buyer	Buyer	Buyer	Buyer	Buyer	
Asst. Buyer	Asst. Buyer		Asst. Buyers	Asst. Buyer		•New York Market Liason
•Boys Dress and Sport Shirts	•Girls Playwear	•Diapers	•New Born Sets	•Knit Shirts	•All Lines of Merchandise	
•Boys Slacks and Slack Sets	•Girls and Boys Swimwear	•Accessories	•Baby Dresses	•Girls Knit Blouses		•New York Market Liason
•Boys Playwear	•Beach Accessories	•Bedding	•Diaper Sets	•Boys Sweaters		
		•Padding	•Christening Sets	•Polo Shirts		
		•W/P Pants	•Dresses	•Colormates		
		•Shoes	•Girls Headwear	•Fleece Clothes		
		•Slippers	•Girls Coats and Coat Sets			
			•Girls Snowsuits			
			•Girls Jackets			
			•Girls Ski Pants			
			•Girls Rainwear and Toppers			

Exhibit 6. Organization Chart of Retail Merchandising, 1967

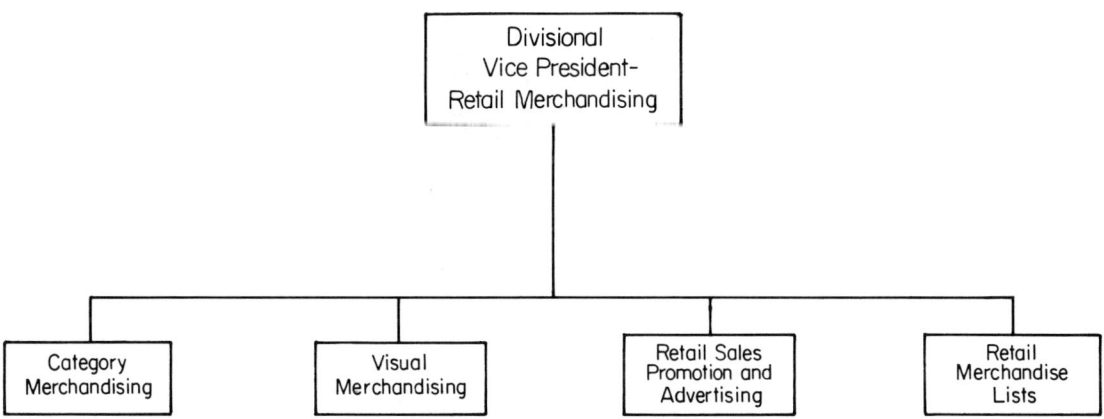

Source: Prepared by case writer.

Exhibit 7. Organization Chart of Eastern Territory, 1967

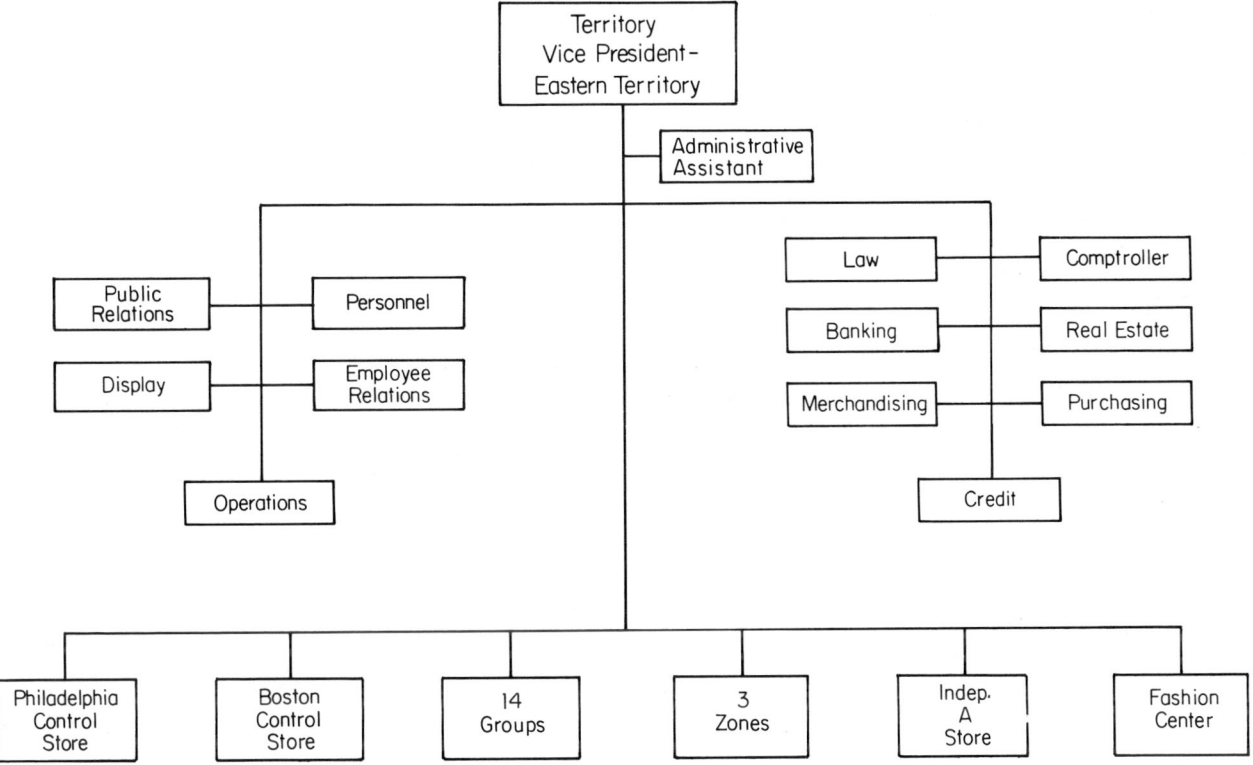

COMMENTARY

The basic framework of Sears' present organization was put in place between 1941 and 1948, based on a concept that was devised in 1929, implemented early in 1930, and abandoned two years later. The concept was the organization of the business into autonomous field divisions (the five territories), on the one hand, and the centralized functional departments in Chicago, on the other.

Until 1925 Sears had operated solely as a mail-order business. In that year Sears built its first retail store and then moved rapidly to expand this new dimension of its business. By 1929 Sears had 324 such outlets, and the new stores accounted for 40% of the company's sales.

Much of the impetus for Sears' new retailing strategy came from General Leonard Wood, who joined Sears in 1924 and became its president four years later. Wood came to Sears after a distinguished military career, first in Panama, where for 10 years he worked on the construction of the Panama Canal, and later in World War I. After leaving the Army in 1918, Wood went to Montgomery Ward as General Merchandise Manager. According to Chandler's history of the Sears organization:

> At Montgomery Ward, Wood began to advocate a new business strategy. More than any other mail-order executive of the time, he (General Wood) was aware of the impact of increasing urbanization and of the coming of the automobile on the national and, particularly, the mail-order market. This awareness apparently came from an odd passion for reading the *Statistical Abstract of the United States,* developed during his off hours in Panama. Such statistics emphasized, Wood told his colleagues at Ward's, that the United States was rapidly becoming an urban nation. Since the mail-order buyers lived in the rural areas, Ward must adjust itself to these changes. Moreover, the mass-produced automobile was making it possible for the farmer to get to town more easily and to buy from a much broader assortment of goods than was available at the crossroads general store.[1]

But the Montgomery Ward management failed to respond to Wood's urging to build retail stores. Wood left Montgomery Ward in 1924 to join Sears as Vice President in charge of Factories and Retail Stores, where he found strong support for his ideas.

Wood began to plan a retail store system almost immediately. Eight stores were opened in 1925; one in 1926; and sixteen in 1927. By the end of 1928, the year in which Wood became President of Sears, there were 192 retail stores in operation.

Although Sears now had a dual strategy for reaching consumers, its top management did not immediately see the need for a major organization change. The managers of the ten mail-order houses were given responsibility for managing the stores in their respective areas. Regional Retail Managers in the mail-order houses supervised the day-to-day operations of the retail stores.

Severe administrative difficulties soon developed, however, particularly with regard to obtaining personnel for the new stores. The problems of recruiting and training store managers and other store personnel were acute and could not be handled effectively with such thin staffing of the retail store administration function in the field.

In 1929 Wood engaged George E. Frazer, the senior partner of a Chicago firm of certified public accountants, Frazer and Torbet, to take charge of reorganizing the Sears management structure. Frazer was to chair a Committee of Reorganization, which would study the emerging problem areas and recommend organizational changes.

Chandler speaks of the Frazer Committee Report as a "landmark" in the history of Sears, Roebuck and Co.[2] It resulted in both a restructuring

---

[1] Alfred D. Chandler, Jr., *Strategy and Structure* (Cambridge; The M.I.T. Press, 1962), pp. 233–234.
[2] *Ibid.,* p. 241.

of headquarters departments and the creation of four new territorial divisions for the management of mail-order houses and retail stores in the field. The new scheme greatly altered the centralized pattern of management, in which the buying departments had exercised considerable autonomy. According to the Frazer Report:

> The Territorial Officers are on the executive line of authority, reporting directly to the Senior Vice-President. Such officers are authorized and instructed to stop or change any or all orders affecting their territories if, in their judgment, the best interests of the Company are served.[3]

The four Territorial Officers and 33 District Managers were given wide responsibilities. They were "responsible to the President and the Senior Vice President for the activities of the Company in the territory, including assets, profits, expenses, inventories, sales, personnel, and good will of the Company." The managers of the retail districts were to report directly to the Territorial Officer "when and as requested" by that officer. The Territorial Officers were not, however, given the necessary personnel or information to discharge their responsibilities. Moreover, the managers of the retail districts maintained direct lines of communication with headquarters personnel in Chicago.

The new scheme was ambiguous and at the same time violated old and established patterns. Consequently, conflicts between headquarters and Territories — between Parent and Field — soon emerged. The Territories and headquarters departments each sought to direct the retail stores and mail-order houses.

These conflicts were aggravated by the deepening Depression. Territorial managements became more directly involved in the running of retail stores and mail-order houses as their concern about profits mounted. Headquarters managers, on their part, asserted that Territorial Officers were assuming duties that belonged to the functional departments in Chicago. To add to the heightening tension, there was increasing concern at both levels over administrative costs.

---

[3] *Ibid.*, p. 248.

In May 1932 General Wood abolished the Territories and reverted to "centralized" management. The retail stores then came directly under the Vice President in charge of Retail Administration in Chicago. The mail-order houses reported to the Vice President of Operations.

Although the Territories had been abolished by decree, local informal administrative units gradually emerged in the field. Managers were added, especially in merchandising, to build sales by tailoring merchandise lines to local consumer tastes and demands, to develop advertising and displays for their lines, and to appraise store performance. "Soft lines," in particular, had to be responsive to local consumer wants. Merchandise Managers serving in an advisory capacity for the large A stores, Groups, and Zones kept both the retail stores and the Chicago buyers tuned to changing local patterns of demand. In an A store, for example, there were Merchandise Managers for hard lines, soft lines, "big tickets," and home furnishings.

In the meantime the Sears growth trend was renewed. Sales increased from $337 million to $744 million between 1935 and 1940. The number of retail stores went from 428 at the end of 1935 to 520 by the end of 1939.

Unplanned organizational development and the resumption of business growth after 1935 led the Sears top management to turn once again to the Frazer Committee's scheme. This time the changes were made more slowly. A Pacific Coast Territory was set up in early 1941. Describing the role of the Pacific Coast Territorial Manager, the Chandler study states:

> ... All managers of Group, Zone, independent A stores, and mail-order plants in his area were to report to him. He had full responsibility for the functional activities of the company as well as administration of store personnel. Unlike the former Territorial Officers, he had a staff of officers responsible for the performance of the various functional activities. His merchandise was ordered through Chicago, for the Merchandise Department remained the only source of supply for all Sears stores. A close liaison continued between the sales promotion experts at Chicago and the Merchandise Superintendents and field men in the offices of the Group, the Zone, and the independent A stores. Aside from this vital contact, [the Territorial Manager] looked to Chicago only for

policy guidance and for a budget under which he had to operate.[4]

The new unit worked well, and other Territories were established in the South and East in 1945; and in the Midwest and Southwest in 1948.

At headquarters, the buying departments procured merchandise which the retail stores could order and prepared promotional materials for their use. The buying departments could suggest prices, stock plans, and sales promotions techniques but had no authority to implement these ideas in the Field.

An Interpretation of History

Interpreting the organizational change that began with the Frazer Committee Report, we might usefully see the moves as shifts in the locus of responsibility for the management of both marketing programs and of field sales resources. When Sears was solely a mail-order business, the buying departments in the Merchandise Department planned and executed the programs for their respective lines and became, as might be expected, highly autonomous. The mail-order houses (merchandise distribution points) were under the centralized control of the Vice President in charge of Operations.

The move into retail stores created a need for local resource administration to manage the development of retail properties, to recruit and train large numbers of store personnel, and to operate the retail store system. These tasks could not be handled effectively from Chicago, as later experience proved.

The new retail store strategy also called for a tailoring of merchandise offerings and promotion to local market needs. Merchandise that appealed in one part of the country would not necessarily appeal in another. This was particularly true of the soft lines carried by the large A stores and the medium-sized B stores. Selling space in stores was a greater constraint than sales pages in catalogs. Therefore the right selection of merchandise *by geographic area* became critical to the success of the retail store strategy. Until 1930 the Parent buying departments selected, bought, and established the lines to be sold by the retail stores, but had no method of supervising these lines at the point of sale.

What the Frazer Committee Report established, in effect, were Territories that exercised decentralized control over the retail selling resources. In making the Territorial and District Managers profit responsible, however, the Report did not at the same time provide for the decentralized development of merchandise programs at the district or retail store levels. Personnel were not available for this purpose. Moreover, store managers received their instructions on merchandise lines from Chicago, with which they retained direct lines of communication.

The abolishment of the Territories in 1932 cleared the ambiguity somewhat, but was hardly a constructive step forward in organizational growth. Nevertheless, the organization continued to develop in an unplanned way to meet the urgent need for tailoring merchandise and promotional programs to local market conditions.

In re-establishing the Territories, Sears management recognized that the Field should manage the retail and catalog field warehousing and selling resources. It should also have responsibility for tailoring its own retail store marketing programs by selecting from merchandise purchased by the Parent buying departments, and from promotional materials prepared in Chicago. It would be an oversimplification, however, to say that the locus of program management had shifted to the Field. The Chicago buying departments did much to develop marketing program strategy through the choices they exercised as buyers. They, in effect, set the merchandise policy framework within which local Merchandise Managers and division managers worked.

Understanding Sears Today

The commentary seeks now (1) to "sort out" the Sears structure of today in terms of the organizational concepts that have emerged from our study of preceding cases. We then look in more

[4] *Ibid.*, p. 270.

detail at (2) the buying departments — how they are structured and how they operate. We turn, next, to study (3) the changing roles of Parent and Field in developing strategy and (4) the implications for organization of the new emphasis at Sears on product development. It will, then, be useful (5) to assess the significance of growth and of some of the current developments in both organization and strategy for the future of the Sears structure.

A Concept of the Sears Organization

In basic concept, Sears, although a "retailing" as opposed to a "manufacturing" enterprise, yields to the same analytical scheme that we have used to study companies such as Mobil, IBM, and Ford. We can define a business and we can identify and describe a program structure within that business as well as its resource structure. We can understand how programs and resources relate — the interface functions, the resource allocation process, and the procedures.

At Sears, the "business" may be seen as the total retailing operations, including retail store and catalog. Retailing is a self-contained business in the respect that it has a full complement of resources with which to operate. Its basic resources are its retail store system, its catalog channels (both internal resources), and its supplier system (external). It has a wide range of specialized resources available, such as the Retail Merchandising Department with its highly skilled units for developing advertising, display, and promotional materials for retail stores. There is a Catalog Merchandising Office with its creative specialists. In addition the Sears organization includes such information resources as the Comptroller's Department, with its strong and immensely elaborate control system extending throughout the business, and the Parent Economic and Marketing Research Department. In an organization as large as Sears the list of specialized resource units is long.

The locus of program management is in the 51 buying departments. The National Merchandise Managers serve as program managers. The task of strategy development is divided by product groups within each of the 51 departments. Buyers function, then, as sub-program managers. Their work is coordinated within the buying department by the Retail Sales Manager (for retail stores) and by the Catalog Sales Manager (for catalog). Thus the sub-program structure is essentially delineated by *product* while sub-program coordination is by *market*, with the initial market segmentation scheme based on the type of distribution channel used by buyers (retail, catalog).

The primary external resource, Sears' elaborate system of suppliers (largely independent), may be perceived as being a resource that is attached to, and part of, the program structure. Each buyer has a number of sources with which he contracts for merchandise.

Although some internal units are specialized in certain aspects of product development (test laboratories, design consultants, and industrial engineers), supply sources, in effect, function as product development resources. Buyers work with suppliers on new product development in much the same way that the Product Program Managers at IBM work with the Systems Development Division, suggesting market-generated ideas and monitoring the development process.

In the field selling resources, there are program-specialized units. The retail store selling function is organized by "divisions," which correspond to the buying department breakdown in the respect that a division sells the merchandise bought by a Parent buying department. The catalog might also be said to be a program-specialized resource in the respect that its pages are divided among buying departments.

Resource Allocation Procedures

As in the case of other companies included in this study, annual planning was an important device for allocating resources to programs. At Sears, top management in effect set the level of available resources and the buying departments worked within these guidelines. Retail selling space was a function of the building program. The level of commitments to sources was determined every six months when top management accepted economic and business forecasts (prepared by the Economic and Marketing Research Department) and, in effect, asked buying departments and territories to plan within those parameters. Corporate management determined the level of mail-order selling resources when it appropriated funds for catalog preparation and distribution.

Each buying department then established, in effect, its own manufacturing capacity by making contract commitments with sources. The Catalog Merchandising Office in the Parent organization allocated catalog space. The Visual Merchandising Department in Retail Merchandising effectively controlled the allocation of selling space in the stores through the Merchandising Arrangements Guide.

The Buying Departments

As Sears sales have grown dramatically since 1940, the number of its National Merchandise Departments has increased from 20 to 51. Within each department, the number of buyers has tended to grow steadily. What are the implications of such a proliferation? Can Sears continue to grow indefinitely by the same process of accordion-like expansion at the headquarters level?

The Merchandising Organization

At the buying department (program) level, the delineation of the structure was developed originally by grouping similar lines of merchandise. The proliferation of buying departments seems to have resulted mainly from efforts to maintain "manageable" units. Thus, for example, the case indicates that the Hardware Buying Department (609) had at one time been responsible for the product lines now assigned to Departments 606 (recreation and sporting goods), 611 (housewares), 630 (paints), 634 (small electrical appliances), 642 (plumbing, heating and cooling), and 664 (building materials). Even though Department 609 was no longer responsible for these lines of merchandise, it remained one of Sears' largest buying departments in number of stock-keeping units (6,372) and number of sources (411).

A heavy burden of program planning falls on the National Merchandise Managers and their Retail and Catalog Sales Managers. As volume grows and product lines become longer, it would become difficult for this team to respond to market growth and change. Hence, it becomes administratively practical to split large National Merchandise Departments into smaller ones.

Nevertheless, the proliferation of buying departments has apparently been at some cost when it comes to maintaining the integrity of strategically related merchandise lines. Thus in women's clothing, for example, separate buying departments were responsible for lingerie (638), brassieres and girdles (618), and nylon hosiery (675). These are lines that might logically be styled, priced, promoted, and grouped together at the point of sale.

"Category merchandising" seems to be an effort to preserve the "manageability" of the buying departments while maintaining the strategic integrity of related lines of merchandise. Under this concept, the 51 buying departments were grouped into 15 categories. Each such category included buying departments with lines that were closely enough related at the market level to make it feasible to coordinate their advertising and promotion.

The categories, however, appear to be structured essentially as "federations" of buying departments. This organizational device serves to integrate one element of strategy. It was not designed, apparently, to cut across the full range of strategic planning, including product line planning and development and pricing.

Buying Department Organization

If we can identify the 51 National Merchandise Managers at Sears as program managers working with their respective Retail and Catalog Sales Managers, then the buyers are sub-program managers. They play a key role in the respect that they exercise initiative in product line planning and are involved, therefore, in marketing strategy formulation. They are the interface between program (buying) departments and external manufacturing sources both for supply and for new product development.

The role of the buyer is depicted in these words of the Vice President-Merchandising:

YOU, the BUYER, are responsible for everything that has to do with your lines of merchandise. As buyers you have been assigned to the narrowest product line responsibilities possible commensurate with the known potentials of those lines.

This structure enables YOU to learn and master YOUR lines and be responsible for an understanding of your consumer — your market — the product, research, and development — where to have it made — what cost you generate — under what contractual arrangement it will be produced — what assortments you will have — what prices — what packaging — when it will be offered — what type of display and advertising — what guarantee — how it will be promoted — what training, servicing, etc., is required.

There is nothing as it relates to a line that the buyer is not responsible for, including the inventory (old and new) — sales — the growth — and, above all, the profit.

This is an overwhelming responsibility — an awesome assignment.

Fortunately, we, in Sears, do not have to be perfect, *but we do have to be good administrators* — because for every talent we might lack — the company, in its infinite wisdom, has made up for it — there is — today — no area of your responsibility where the company does not provide the services of a gifted specialist to advise and counsel you. From industrial engineers to any fanciful named designer, to the most exotic testing equipment . . . from cost accountant to home economist . . . to controller . . . from attorney to promotional specialist . . . services have been and are available to the buyer.

At the sub-program level, the definition of the assignment (the scope of the buyer's product line) is determined to a large extent by two factors: (1) the number of suppliers with which a single buyer can work effectively; and (2) the structure of the supply industry. Thus, for example, in Department 619:

. . . We have three dress buyers, each responsible for a particular price range. This is the way the industry is organized; one manufacturer makes lower price dresses, another makes higher price dresses, and so forth.

The buyer structure also matched market segments *if* market segmentation and the structure of the supply industry corresponded to each other

Thus, for example, in Department 629 (Infants' and Children's Wear):

. . . We have twelve buyers, each of whom is responsible for particular lines of merchandise. One buyer buys girls' sweaters, tights, tops, suits, jumpers, skirts, and blouses; another buys boys' dress and sport shirts, slacks and slack sets, and playwear. Until several years ago, buying assignments were quite different. One buyer bought all slacks, whether for boys or girls. Another bought all sweaters. *The industry was (and to some extent still is) set up that way.* . . .

Our buying assignments are established according to four criteria. *First, we think it is important to separate boys, girls, and infants; they are simply different markets. Second, we try to assign buyers so that they will deal with a limited number of sources.* Third, we want each buying assignment to be large enough to warrant a top quality buyer. Fourth, we take account of the seasonal factor; it would be wrong for one buyer to have nothing but swimwear and beach accessories. [Italics added.]

In another department (619: Junior Clothing) buying assignments were defined to facilitate close working relationships with suppliers but strategic planning was done by "Box Codes," product groupings based on a market segmentation. Most buyers were responsible for a particular type of product (outerwear, skirts, blouses, sweaters) or a price range (in the case of dresses) because "this is the way the industry is organized." On the one hand, a buyer's line of products would normally cut across several Box Codes; on the other a single Box Code might include items purchased by several buyers. Planning by Box Code was probably the joint effort of the buyers in the department, working with the National Merchandise Manager, and the Retail and Catalog Sales Managers.

Buyers, then, had immensely broad responsibilities for the lines they managed. The product scope of their assignments, however, was limited by the number of source contacts they could effectively manage. Moreover, the delineation of the buying structure in a department tended to be shaped by the structure of the supply industries with which it dealt.

One cannot help but wonder whether a buying structure shaped by these considerations is also an optimal framework for planning and implementing marketing strategies. Certainly, it would not always be so. In the case of Department 619 (Junior Clothing), for example, buying assignments, on the one hand, and Box Codes for strategic planning, on the other, were not identically delineated; in fact, they represented two different dimensions of the departmental structure.

These considerations suggest that Sears should perhaps establish a finely articulated *market* program structure in the buying departments in addition to a *product* program (buying) structure. Such a structure would be similar in basic concept to the IBM scheme of Industry Program Managers and Product Program Managers; and to the Du Pont Textile Fibers organization which provided for both Merchandise (market) and Sales Programs (product) Managers.

In a Sears buying department the market program structure could be broken down initially into retail and catalog elements[5] as at present. It could then be divided into groupings of products which are perceived by consumers as being related in the buying process and in use, and could thus be logically planned, priced, advertised, and promoted together. Market program managers might then focus on the strategic planning of their product lines, and on pricing, advertising, promotion, and display. Buyers (product program managers) would then be responsible for source development, source relationships, and product supply. Under such a scheme, one buyer is likely to be concerned with the supply of items going into several market programs. Similarly, an individual market program would be likely to cut across the lines of several buyers.

If the burden of market program management is relegated to a lower level in the organization, Sears may be able to operate through a smaller number of larger buying departments, thus restoring the integrity of strategically related lines for organizational purposes.

The Roles of Parent and Field in Formulating Marketing Strategy

As we have seen, a major reason for establishing autonomous territories was to facilitate the tailoring of merchandise lines, promotions, and pricing strategy to local market conditions. Division managers in retail stores could select the merchandise that would sell in their market areas. They could adapt promotional campaigns designed at headquarters to suit the needs of local retailing strategies or design their own. In effect, the buying departments offered product lines and promotional programs, and the retail stores were free to select from among these offerings.

This concept is an important article of faith in the Sears *modus operandi*. As one Sears executive commented:

It is impossible to understand Sears' organization without fully understanding our concept of autonomy. Everything we do at Parent takes the form of a recommendation when sent to the Field. We spend a lot of money on advertising mats for use by the Field, for example, but a group or store is perfectly free to prepare its own advertising if, taking the costs of local advertising preparation into account, it feels it can make more money that way.

In practice, the Field does follow most Parent recommendations. With few exceptions, it orders the merchandise selected by the buying departments, uses Parent-prepared advertising in one way or another, and follows the procedures established by the various Parent departments.

You should not, however, allow this willingness to follow Parent recommendations mislead you. The important thing about autonomy is that it exists — as a right! — not that it is used. The right of the Field to reject our recommendations is the best possible way to insure that our recommendations are correct and practical. There is no critic more severe than a retail store executive!

In recent years, however, the changing market environment seems to have led to a shifting balance in the respective roles of the retail stores and the

---

[5] It is significant that by 1967 only 10% of catalog sales were mail order and 90% were handled through catalog order desks in retail stores, catalog order offices, and telephone sales offices. There were 1,543 such offices as of January 1967, an increase of 60% since 1961. These facts support the greatly reduced significance of "mail order" v. "retail" as a *geographic segmentation* of Sears' markets and its increasing importance as a *buying behavior segmentation*. On these grounds, it would seem that significantly different marketing strategies should be developed for the catalog and retail portions of the business.

buying departments in designing retailing strategy. With the development of a dominantly urban population in the United States, the domestic market has become increasingly homogeneous. There is, then, less need for tailoring merchandise programs to local market conditions — although the need still exists especially in soft lines. In the meantime, the buying departments have been given the responsibility for designating certain items as "basic-basic." All retail stores with over 32,500 square feet of selling space were required to carry items that were so designated. While "basic-basic" items represented only 6% of the items in the Sears line, they accounted for more than 46% of Sears' retail store sales.

In the case of a few fast-moving lines, buying departments are in a position to exercise additional influence on local merchandising. An example comes out of Junior Clothing (Department 619). According to the Department manager:

. . . With very few exceptions (mainly staple items and coordinated separates), our products are merchandised and distributed through the fashion centers.[6] These fashion centers handle merchandise for all the New York departments except luggage and jewelry, and a few items for the Children's Department in Chicago.

We have a Fashion Merchandiser for our department in each fashion center. While he works for the territory, he is concerned only with our lines of merchandise.

The Fashion Merchandiser works out a merchandising program with each store in his territory. The program in essence says that a given store should have a specified quantity of items in inventory and "in sight"[7] in each of our Box Codes during each week of the year. Generally speaking, the proper program for a store depends on its size, although other factors are important. Suburban stores require a balance of merchandise among Box Codes (and within Box Codes) that is different from the balance in urban stores, for example.

The Division Managers in the stores do not order merchandise, although they do help to establish the merchandising program for their division. All of our fashion center merchandise is ticketed with punched tickets. When the item is sold, the punched ticket is torn off and retained by the person writing up the sale. These tickets are collected and mailed to the fashion center daily. At the fashion center, they are run through a computer which prepares a sales summary by Box Code for the week. The Fashion Merchandiser then uses this summary to determine how much merchandise in each Box Code to ship to the store during the following week. The Division Managers can, of course, short-cut the system when necessary. They might enclose a note with their tickets, for example, saying "For God's sake, don't send me any more red dresses."

Generally, merchandise is shipped to the stores in predetermined size, color, and style assortments within a Box Code, unless a Division Manager has requested an exception. In practice, however, the Fashion Merchandisers must exercise a considerable amount of judgment. If a Fashion Merchandiser receives a shipment of a particularly "hot" dress, for example, he could send the whole shipment to one large store or group; he could divide it among all the stores in his territory; or he could divide it among a certain category of stores (e.g., suburban stores, suburban stores in New England, or suburban stores in New England but not around Boston). Needless to say, his judgment is equally important with merchandise that is something less than "hot."

Central merchandising of fashion merchandise makes a lot of sense. We feel that we have a better understanding of the direction styles are likely to take than our Division Managers do. If nothing else, we have learned that *our* taste (as compared with the customer's) is relatively unimportant. If we let the Division Managers do the ordering, we would run into situations where a key store would not be stocking pants dresses because the Division Manager didn't like pants dresses.

The increasing homogeneity of the market, the use of computers for rapid information collection, and the growing importance of styled merchandise in the Sears line are factors tending to establish the buying departments as the primary source of marketing program strategy. Under these circumstances, Merchandise Managers and Division Man-

---

[6] There were five fashion centers, one in each territory. The fashion centers were intermediate warehousing facilities, which ordered and received merchandise from manufacturing sources and then shipped the merchandise to the stores. Each fashion center was headed by a manager who reported to the Territorial Vice President. Within each fashion center, a "fashion merchandiser" was assigned to each buying department using the fashion centers. The fashion merchandiser was responsibel for placing orders on the sources and for distributing merchandise to the stores.

[7] I.e., on order or in transit.

agers in the Field might usefully be regarded as extensions of the Parent buying departments, working on program implementation and, importantly, feeding back data that will be useful in future planning.

Product Development Strategy and the Implications for Organization

As indicated by the Sears Vice President-Merchandising, growth objectives for the future will need to be satisfied to an increasing extent through new product development. The expansion of retail selling space would not, by itself, be sufficient to achieve the goals set by the Sears management.

> Our chairman has publicly stated the goal of $10 billion in sales by 1970, a $3 billion increase in three years. Some of this increase will come from new facilities but only a relatively small part of it. If we are to achieve our goal, we must develop new products. . . .
>
> Historically (with some very major exceptions), we have let the leading manufacturers of branded consumer goods develop new products and introduce them to the public. We have then refined their developments, to give the consumer a higher quality product for less money.
>
> I strongly believe that product development is the area of greatest potential growth for Sears. The buyers are responsible for product development — let there be no doubt of that! — but we will review their lines more frequently (asking continually, "What's new?") and give them more help. I hope that the new product categories, with more resources than the individual buying departments, will be able to increase our efforts in this area.

It is useful to recall that in such businesses as Ford's North American Automotive Operations and General Electric's Housewares Division product development has been organized as a single integrated resource. At Ford (NAAO) a Product Development Group was established in 1967 to complete the "troika" resource structure.

At General Electric (HD) the product development process provided for generating a flow of new product ideas, having these ideas screened through market research and appraised by manufacturing, engineering, and marketing personnel. Special sales and promotional programs were then planned for introducing new product offerings.

At Sears, however, the locus of responsibility for initiating, screening, and passing judgment on new product ideas rested with the individual buyer. The buyer in Department 609 (Hardware) for flat wrenches and socket wrenches stated:

> I have full responsibility for selecting items within my line responsibility. I watch the trade journals and automotive magazines; I go out and talk to automotive mechanics concerning what they would like if they could get it. Inventors come to us with ideas for new products; if an idea seems promising we send it to a source for a cost evaluation, and to the Sears laboratory for testing.
>
> It's up to the buyer to decide whether or not to go ahead with a new product, although he may check with the National Merchandising Manager or Retail Sales Manager on a really big thing.

One might well ask, however, whether the individual buyer would have the time (and expertise) to carry out a significantly stepped-up new product development program. Moreover, such day-to-day responsibilities of the buyer as negotiating and administering procurement contracts, new source development, and planning promotional strategies might result in relegating new product development to a lower order of priority than would be desirable.

We might expect, then, that Sears' increased stress on product development may well lead, as at Ford, to the establishment of specialized product development resources, possibly within each buying department.

An Overview — and the Future

The Frazer Committee concept proved to be eminently sound as a framework for Sears' great growth and expansion. It created a structure that, as the business grew, could be subdivided to create manageable units for program management and for the buying (sub-program) function.

Several factors suggest the need for a further evaluation of the buying department structure.

The sensed need to improve strategic coordination among market-related product lines through "category merchandising" is one. Second is the emerging recognition that catalog selling, as a form of market segmentation based on patterns of consumer buying behavior, requires its own program. Finally, the "want buying" idea suggests that changes in the market environment have led to a shift in Sears' advertising strategy and, possibly, an upgrading in Sears' lines. Undoubtedly, growing consumer affluence and style consciousness have strongly influenced the development of Sears' product lines. Advertising might well become a more important element of strategy than in the past.

All these developments suggest an increasing need for a program structure based on market segmentation and not necessarily tied to the buying structure. To fill this need, Sears may choose to establish *market* program management units in the buying departments side by side with the existing *product* program (buying) organization.

If product innovation does in fact become an increasingly important element in Sears' strategy, we might see specialized product development resources emerge.

Looking further ahead, it is not unlikely that large buying departments (of "category" size and product scope) could develop as relatively self-contained businesses. Each might have a full range of resources, except that all would probably continue to share the common retail store and catalog sales systems.

By way of prediction, then:

(1) The category groupings may emerge as the key unit for marketing program planning, buying, and new product development. Instead of being an informal confederation of buying departments, the category would be an integrated organization having central direction.

(2) Within the category a structure may emerge for developing and implementing marketing programs for the several market segments served by the category. The category would have separate program units for retail and catalog, in addition to cadres of buyers. The buyers would be responsible for source development, source relationships, and product supply. Program managers would be concerned with merchandising (determining the content of the product line), advertising, promotion, and pricing.

These developments, along with additional growth, would create pressures toward further specialization; and away from the concept that the buyer is "responsible for everything that has to do with [his] lines of merchandise."

(3) Product development might well become a specialized function within each category. Product development managers could generate a flow of ideas from buyers, program managers, sources, the Field, and competitive intelligence. Procedures could be designed for screening ideas. In addition, the product development managers might be responsible for working with Sears' technical development resources and outside suppliers to assure that products are designed and engineered according to specifications derived from marketing research.

(4) Each category would be of sufficient size to support its own advertising and promotion specialists. They would work with program managers in their category; and with their counterparts in Retail Merchandising.

Monsanto Company:
Organic Chemicals Division

Monsanto's Organic Chemicals Division in 1967 was one of the largest and most profitable of the company's eight divisions. Its 1966 sales volume of more than $250 million was accounted for by a very wide range of chemicals (grouped into ten broad product lines) going to many different customers in different industries. The Organic Division, for example, made a line of chemicals for the rubber industry and another for the paper industry. It made and marketed food ingredients, fine chemicals used in pharmaceuticals, petroleum additives, and plasticizers and resin materials used for making plastics. One large and profitable line was the functional fluids developed for use in aircraft hydraulic systems, heat transfer processes, steel quenching, electrical transformers, and die casting — all applications where oil was inadequate because it was combustible.

Organic's customers ranged widely in size, but approximately 75% of the Division's sales volume came from customers each of whom purchased more than $500,000 of chemicals a year from Monsanto. In the United States, Organic served these customers with 19 manufacturing plants, 43 nonplant warehouses and bulk terminals, and a fleet of 1,400 tank cars.

Organization in 1967

The Division was functionally organized in 1967 and had four Product Directors, each of whom was responsible for planning (longer range) and pricing on two or three of Organic's ten product lines (see Exhibit 1). These four and an Assistant General Manager reported to the Division Vice President and General Manager. The Directors of Marketing, Manufacturing, Research and Development, Commercial Development, Personnel, and Business Systems and Planning, and the Division Controller reported to the Assistant General Manager.

Product Directors

Product Directors were profit responsible. They were charged with pricing and long-range planning for their assigned product groups — with determining broad strategic objectives for each group, the need to add new products to these lines and to eliminate others, the requirements for plant facilities, and the kinds of markets and customers that would be served.

An Informal Business Group (IBG) had been constituted for each of the ten product groups; it was chaired by the Product Director and became the vehicle through which much of the long-range planning was carried out. Each IBG included representatives from Marketing, Manufacturing, Research, Accounting, and Commercial Development. Working together under the Product Director, the members of each IBG prepared plans by product line. Each IBG member then reviewed with his functional head that portion of the plan which pertained to his function. The resulting revisions were checked by the Product Director, and if he approved, the plan was submitted to the General Manager. With the General Manager's approval, the several functions were then committed to carrying out the stated objectives. *How* the objectives were to be met was determined within the functional areas. Progress against plan was reviewed periodically both in the functions and in the IBG, and periodically, too, revised plans were prepared.

The exact nature of the Product Directors' role was still evolving. The Division General Manager regarded them as being equal in organizational status to the functional heads, and he judged their performance to an important extent by the return on the gross investment allocated to their product groups. Appendix A is a position description for a Product Director in early 1967.

One functional head referred to the Product Director as the "profit center delegate of the General Manager" and stated that he should have responsibility for setting objectives, ratifying the plans made to achieve those objectives, and then reviewing progress. Another functional head indicated that the Product Director was an "extension of the General Manager" and ran his product groups as "sub-companies." A third commented that "Product Directors should be planners; some of them unfortunately get into day-to-day operations and keep the water muddy. A strong Product Director will tend to use the IBG as his staff and that creates problems."

Another member of management pointed out that how the Product Director worked was to a large extent a function of his own personality and background experience, and also depended on the character of the General Manager. (There had been three different General Managers in the Organic Division since the Product Director job had been created.)

Marketing Department

Organic's Director of Marketing supervised a department that included a Director of Sales-Field (with 12 District Sales Managers reporting to him); three Directors of Sales-Products and Markets (who, among them, directed seven Market/Product Group Managers, called Product Managers); and a head of Marketing Administration, who supervised five managers of staff srevices. (See Exhibit 2.)

The seven Market Product Group Managers took care of the seven product groups and served as Marketing representatives on the IBGs for these product groups. Each supervised a team of several market managers and technical service representatives who gave "business direction" to field sales representatives and provided them with technical service back-up at the customer level. The Product Managers spent much of their time in the development of plans by product and market. They became directly involved in customer problems, especially in the larger accounts. Within limits they could make pricing decisions and usually exercised initiative in making more fundamental pricing recommendations to their respective Product Directors. Appendix B is a position description for a Product Manager.

In the field, District Sales Managers gave administrative direction to the Organic Division's sales representatives. In the smaller districts, one District Sales Manager[1] exercised direct supervision over the salesmen. In a larger district, such as New York, the District Manager might delegate supervisory responsibilities to as many as three Industry Sales Managers, each one of whom had one to three of the seven product groups.

District Sales Managers and the Industry Sales Managers were concerned with sales training, performance reviews, salary increases, and sales expense accounting. They reviewed customer strategy plans and sales objectives prepared by field sales representatives and consolidated these plans into district plans. The assignment of sales personnel to the districts and transfers out of the districts were determined, however, by the Directors of Sales-Products and Markets at Division headquarters.

The Organic Division's marketing effort was also aided by three Regional Vice Presidents. These men were part of the Monsanto Marketing Staff organization and their activities cut across the divisions. The Regional Vice Presidents, who were senior men by age and experience, coordinated selling activities by major customer, working within their territories. They also represented Monsanto with local government organizations, trade associations, and civic groups.

The Directors of Sales-Products and Markets to whom the Product Managers reported served as a part of the Marketing Director's immediate "team." A large amount of their time was spent on the selection, development, and evaluation and promotion of Product Managers and their key subordinates. These Directors of Sales made sure that product strategies were kept up-to-date, but participated in strategy formulation only to the extent that the strategy plans for one product or market impinged on those of other products and markets. In particular, the Directors of Sales were careful to see that strategies were coordinated with regard to the way they might affect relations with key customers.

Manufacturing Department

The Organic Division operated five plants, whose managers reported to the Director of Manufacturing. In addition, its products were manufactured at 14 other locations. At these points Organic was the "guest" of other "host" divisions. At the guest locations, Organic was responsible for capital investment (which was carried on the Organic Division's books), process technology, inventory control, and distribution. The host division took care of personnel, labor relations, maintenance, in-plant warehousing, plant services, and administration. In each case the guest operation was run by a superintendent who reported administratively to the plant manager but whose salary and promotion were governed by the guest division.

---

[1] Appendix C is a position description for a District Sales Manager.

These superintendents were given direction by a Manager of Interdivision and International Operations who reported to Organic's Director of Manufacturing.

The immediate team of the Director of Manufacturing also included Managers of Production Planning and Distribution; Manufacturing Technology; and Maintenance and Utilities. The Manager of Manufacturing Technology had under him three Technical Production Managers who divided among them the seven product groups and served on the respective IBGs. (See Exhibit 3.)

The Technical Production Managers (TPMs) were concerned with plant capacity problems and with all of the dimensions of the technical work done in the plants on their respective product lines. With regard to the former, the TPMs made forecasts of production capacity needs five years ahead for their assigned products. Appropriation Requests for new capacity were usually prepared at the plants, but the TPMs reviewed these requests for accuracy and completeness, and prepared themselves for any questions that might be raised by the Organic Division's management as these requests moved up the review and approval chain. A TPM could, himself, approve capital investments up to $5,000.

TPMs worked with plant personnel to initiate programs for cost and quality improvements. Their main point of contact in each plant was the Technical Service Department, which reported to the plant manager but with which the TPM had a strong "dotted line" relationship. The Technical Production Manager was the link between the plant and Marketing and the plant and the IBG. Product Directors, Product Managers, and field salesmen could not deal directly with the plant on matters involving major or minor changes in product specification and deliveries. Requests for such changes went through the Technical Production Manager, and he decided whether a proposed change would be advantageous based on cost, profit, and customer considerations. He was described by the Director of Manufacturing as 'an umbrella over the plant to keep the plant from having its energies drained off on things we really shouldn't do."

The Production Planning and Distribution function (Exhibit 4) focused primarily on logistics supply and was concerned with the "marketing-manufacturing interface in the on-going business." Initially, sales forecasts, supplied by Product Managers, by product and by month were used as the basis for planning production schedules. A forecast was completed by November 15 for the following year by months. This forecast was revised as of February 15 for the April–December period, as of May 15 for the July–December period, and again on August 15 for October–December. When necessary, shorter term revisions could also be made. The production schedule allocated plant capacity by products and planned for the sequencing of different runs through the process equipment.

When a field salesman placed a customer's order on a plant (usually by teletype), a copy of that order was sent to the Customer Services group in the Production Planning and Distribution Department. Customer Services monitored the order to make sure that it was placed correctly, that the product was available, and that the transportation specified was correct. In these respects Customer Services were a direct link between the field salesmen and the Organic Division's plant-warehouse-transportation complex to assure that orders were filled quickly and efficiently.

Computer systems were used to keep a daily "fix" on inventory levels, product receipts, and shipments at each stocking point. Computer programs were also used to establish maximum-minimum inventory levels and reorder quantities for each product and each stocking point. Computer-generated information then served as the basis for Production Planning and Distribution to place orders on plants.

Research and Development Department

The Research Department worked on developing new products and improving existing product offerings in response to customer needs as defined by the Commercial Development and Marketing Departments. Going beyond, Research put stress on product development where market needs had not yet been articulated but might be anticipated through new technical developments. Hence many of the new developments on which Research worked were initiated by the Department itself as it translated internal and external technical advances into new product ideas.

The Research Department, working on budget allocations from the Marketing Department, also provided customer technical service support for field sales. And working on annual budget allocations from Manufacturing, Research assisted process design, plant start-up, and process cost and quality improvements.

As in the case of Marketing, a basic dimension of the Research Department was the product group organization. Five Product Group Managers assumed the responsibilities for research and development for Organic's ten product groups. The total annual research budget and the Research Department's technical manpower resources were divided among the research projects managed by the Product Group Managers.

The Research Department's technical personnel were organized into approximately 35 teams, each with a group leader. Some of these teams specialized in exploratory (or basic) research, others in product definition, others in product development, and others in process development. These teams were assigned to projects and to Product Group Managers; about two-thirds of the teams (those working primarily on product development) were permanently assigned to specific Product Group Managers and the remaining third were temporarily assigned, depending on the nature of the project. There were, in addition, technical personnel whose special skills were of such a nature (for example, physical analytical instrumentation distillation technology, crystallization, or pilot plant engineering) that they gave support to a number of projects rather than being assigned to any one.

Two other key members of the Research Department were the Manager of Operations and the Manager of Administration. The first was concerned with the assignment, evaluating, and compensation of all personnel; the second handled the budgeting and control functions and was responsible for the operation, allocation, and expansion of physical facilities.

The Product Group Managers served on the IBGs and worked there on the formulation of plans for product development. Through IBG discussions, research and development programs were planned for each major product group. These programs were then submitted for review to the Director of Research. If he felt that Research did not have the resources to do all that was asked, he indicated that cutbacks would have to be made in certain of the programs. Product Group Managers from Research then met with Product Directors and recommended specific changes in their respective research programs.

With proposals for the utilization of research manpower and dollars coming from several sources, the Director of Research had final authority in the allocation of his technical resources to research projects. If his judgment in any case should be disputed, the difficulty would be resolved in conference with one or more Product Directors and the General Manager.

A major task, then, for the Director of Research was the selection of research projects and the allocation of research and development funds and manpower to each such project. To assist in this effort, he had a staff Project Selection Group working to develop data on which he could base his decisions. This group, working with Product Group Managers, attempted to assess such factors as potential market volume and profitability, level of research effort required in time and dollars ("optimistic," "most likely," and "pessimistic" estimates were made), and the probability of success related to level of research expenditure. In the Project Selection work, a computer program was used to assist in determining the optimum allocation of research resources among projects. The Research Director, in speaking of this computer program, commented, "I use it mainly in the 'what-if' area: what would happen if I stretch this project out for three years instead of two and accelerate another one. We are still working to develop a more sophisticated system for project selection."

Research funds were allocated to four classes of projects. Approximately 10% of the budget went to *exploratory* work. The rest was about equally divided among *regenerative, expansion,* and *venture* research. "Regenerative" projects related to development of improvements in product or process on products currently in the line and helped Monsanto to maintain its market position. Projects undertaken with the purpose of increasing market share were classed as "expansion," and "venture" projects were generally designed to penetrate new market segments. "Generally speaking," commented the Research Director, "venture research calls for large chunks of money and requires top management approval. Regenerative projects are usually much smaller in scope and do not need to be approved by our General Manager. Division management, though, is very much interested in how our total budget breaks down among regenerative, expansion, and venture."

The system called for continuing reviews of projects in process through Project Analysis reports, and Product Group Managers were required continually to re-estimate the probability of success and the time and dollars needed for completion.

Commercial Development

Although it was at one time a part of the Research Department, Commercial Development (CD) in Organic Chemicals was split out in 1957 to become a separate functional department reporting to the General Manager. It was charged with the responsibility for defining new market opportunities, proposing research and development projects, monitoring these projects at every stage, and then introducing new products to the market in the initial stages of commercial development. Initially, CD prepared a Pre-Research Appraisal (PRA) which identified a market need, specified the kind of product required and the market potential (estimates of market potential were developed jointly by CD and Marketing) for such a product at given price levels; and indicated the technological skills needed to develop and support the product, the nature of existing competition, and the advantages Monsanto might have against the competition. The PRA was then sent to the Research Department with a request for technical appraisal of the proposed product. A technical appraisal included an assessment of the "state of the art," technical disciplines required beyond the Research Department's existing capabilities, facilities, manpower, and time needed, and the probability of success.

If the proposal survived the technical appraisal stage, it was submitted formally along with the PRA to a Product Director for approval. With his approval, both CD and Research became committed to undertaking the project.

During the research stages, Project Analysis reports were issued jointly by CD and Research to keep the top management informed on the status of the project. The Project Analysis reports covered both research and commercial progress.

As research neared completion, CD worked on the preparation of a business strategy, identifying key customers, targeting a market position for the new product, indicating price levels, and preparing plans for any new capital investment that would be needed.

At a point in time — if Research had succeeded — the new product was transferred from Research to Commercial Development. At this point, Research prepared a report detailing the performance of the new product against the "ideal" and against competitive offerings, and estimated full-scale production costs. CD at this juncture either accepted or rejected the new product and, if the former, issued a Project Analysis report detailing a Commercial Development program.

CD then began initial market introduction of the product. Promotional devices such as technical bulletins and visual aids and an advertising program were prepared, prices were set with the cognizant Product Director, calls were made on customers, and feedback on customer reactions and their experiences in using the product was obtained and analyzed. On the basis of these results, commercial development was extended to obtain broad customer acceptance, and forecasts were made of sales and of plant capacity needed to satisfy demand. As the commercialization effort progressed, CD began working closely with Marketing, first to work out a detailed strategy plan based on early market feedback and then to set a time for transferring the new product to Marketing.

At the time of transfer, a Transfer to Sales report describing the total commercialization effort and its results was prepared jointly by CD and Marketing in the form of a total product strategy for the new product, including a detailed Sales Plan showing how the new product would be integrated into the full product line and promoted.

The organization of the Commercial Development Department was relatively simple. There were five Managers of Development, each reporting to the Director of CD — one for functional fluids, one for rubber chemicals, one for paper chemicals, one for food additives, and another for all the rest (fine chemicals, intermediates, plasticizers, resins, petroleum additives, and heavy chemicals). Each Development Manager had a team of three to seven men, technically and commercially skilled, and each Manager worked on one or two projects.

The Director of Commercial Development believed strongly that this function should be separate from Research on the one hand and from Marketing on the other. He said:

Commercial Development is the "patient money" department. Normally we work on a project for three or more years. In Marketing, every Product Manager has a lot of products to worry about and focuses on short-range budgets. If CD were part of Marketing, the longer range development projects would have to take second place. Moreover, Marketing tends naturally to think that if the customers want it, it should be done — and that is not always the case.

Commercial Development needs also to be separate from Research. It works best as an independent market place, a voice able to take issue with Research. Research people develop something and then want to take it out to the market, and Commercial Development has to be free to contribute a commercial judgment on projects.

The Director of Commercial Development explained that CD's function was to work on major new opportunities.

The little product improvements are taken care of directly by Marketing working with Research. The growth of existing products in existing markets is strictly a Marketing function. Each Product Manager should have technical specialists who can do this job. About 5% of our time is spent on regenerative activity — and I try to keep it down to this. The rest of our time is split roughly between expansion and venture projects.

Cutting it another way, about 40% of our time is spent on PRA work; that is the staff part of our function. About 60% is spent on product and market development — following a product through the research phases and taking it into the market place. This is our line function and CD's sales range each year from $5 to $15 million. This effort has paid off; 32% of Organic's sales in 1965 were represented by products introduced since 1952. And this does not include the entire agricultural chemical development, which we spun off as a separate division.

In the case of one large project, CD and Research were not completely separated. Dr. Holloway[2] was both a Development Manager in Commercial Development and a Product Group Manager in Research. He was concerned in both capacities with a major paper chemicals project. This project had developed out of a 1959 study made by a corporate study group. The study had identified five major paper chemicals product opportunities. Between 1961 and 1963 the paper chemicals research group (working on all five projects) had been expanded from four persons to thirty persons, and three persons (two of whom were recruited from paper companies) had been assigned to paper chemicals in CD.

By late 1965 it was apparent that one of the projects was encountering significant difficulties. Despite considerable effort it had not proved possible to achieve the technical breakthrough necessary to reach the cost/performance target. In early 1966 Dr. Holloway, who had had prior experience in both the Research Department and Commercial Development and who had not previously been associated with paper chemicals, was given full responsibility for paper chemicals — both Research and Commercial Development.

In commenting on the early difficulties, Dr. Holloway said:

> The CD-Research interface becomes acute when a program runs into trouble, and it is difficult to assign responsibility for the particular problem. Actually, though, the fact that we have an IBG can go a long way toward facilitating this interface; the IBG tends to offset the dominance of the line departments. I deal more with the Product Director than I do with my line bosses in CD and Research and turn to the latter only on administrative matters or when I need a sounding board to go over some of the technical or commercial approaches we are considering.
>
> When I first took over this program, I moved the three CD men to the research building in with the Research personnel assigned to the program. This was very helpful. CD kept day-to-day touch with the research effort and the Research team was kept in close touch with market considerations. CD contributes a lot on "how it's done in a paper mill." They help in making alternative choices regarding the direction of the research effort, and they project research results in terms of market potential as we go along. CD is responsible, too, for preparing a total business plan — plant size and capabilities, manufacturing cost projections, cost-volume-profit estimates, and so forth.
>
> There are some potential disadvantages in having CD and Research under one head. We lose the check-and-balance factor, and the IBG can't effectively serve as a check because the Marketing and Manufacturing representatives on the IBG don't know that much about what we're doing.
>
> Actually when we get to the market testing stage it might be better to separate CD and Research again. At that point the CD-Marketing interface becomes very important. It would become difficult for me to continue to supervise the research and run the marketing tests and market introductions, and I wouldn't want to delegate any of this.

Plans and Budgets

In the Organic Division, marketing plans were prepared for each of 60 product lines, for each market and for each major customer. Thus, for example, there was a product strategy for a particular plasticizer (which had flooring applications), a market strategy for the floor tile market, and a customer strategy for a major customer who was a large flooring manufacturer. Inputs to these plans came from such functions as Field Sales, Manufacturing, Research, and Commercial Development. They were based initially on plans developed by the Product Managers, and they took shape under the leadership of the Product Directors working with the IBGs. These plans were reviewed and revised from time to time.

Then each year in June the Product Managers submitted product "budgets" based on their sales forecasts for the coming calendar year. The budgets constituted a marketing commitment and were used as a base for purchasing and production planning and for making cost estimates.

In September the district offices submitted their sales forecasts by product, by customer. Product Managers on reviewing these estimates might then ask the districts to make either volume or product mix adjustments.

By December each Product Manager had prepared an annual Product Group marketing plan for each of his product lines. These plans were based on the longer run strategies and the shorter run sales forecasts and customer strategies prepared through the efforts of headquarters and field personnel. The plans set forth annual sales goals by product and by customer. In addition, they provided advertising and sales promotion programs worked out with the help of advertising specialists on the Monsanto central headquarters Marketing staff.

---

[2] Disguised name.

The districts also prepared their final plans for the year ahead. These plans detailed overall sales goals and expense budgets. For each product they described problems and opportunities in the larger accounts. For each salesman they showed his goals, his expense budgets, the frequency of his calls on customers, and any revisions he wished to make in individual customer strategies. The district plans also described personnel development and training programs to be undertaken, as well as proposed changes in organization and manpower utilization.

International Organization

The General Manager of the Organic Chemical Division commented that "organizing for overseas business is one of our most pressing problems at the moment." And members of this management team agreed with him.

In 1964 profit responsibility for business abroad had been given to the several operating divisions. Prior to that time, Monsanto's operations outside the United States were the concern of an International Division. After the issuance of the 1964 directive, the Organic Division began working with International to arrive at an organizational pattern by which Organic could assume return on investment responsibilities abroad, but still leave the administration of overseas operations to International. Under the scheme worked out by the two divisions, there would be an Organic Director of Sales in each of the four areas overseas — Europe, Canada, Latin America, and Asia-Pacific. These men would report administratively to the International Division Area Managers, and would have a dotted-line reporting relationship to the Organic Director of Marketing in the United States. The appointment of these Sales Directors, their compensation, and performance would all be subject to review by the Director of Marketing.

Reporting to the overseas Sales Directors there would be counterparts for each of the Product Managers in the U.S. Marketing Department. These counterparts (to be called Market Managers) would work with the U.S. Product Managers to develop product/market strategies by area. In each geographic area, too, there would be Organic Chemical specialized District Managers.

The Plasticizer Product Group

This section of the case illustrated the way in which the Organic Division operated by describing the Division's program for one of its major product lines, plasticizers. The case provides some background description on the plasticizer industry, Monsanto's posture in that industry, and the way it was organized both at headquarters and in the field to serve its customers.

Plasticizers are high boiling liquids or solids used to improve the processing of plastic resins and to impart flexibility and softness to the finished plastic material. Important properties of various plasticizers are compatibility with the resin and fusibility (how fast and how well the plasticizer fuses with the resin), toxicity, stain resistance, impact resistance, fire retardant characteristics, electrical insulating qualities and heat resistance, or high temperature characteristics. From the beginning, plasticizers had a tendency over time to leach out of the finished material and to be extracted in the presence of certain materials. Hence, another important product quality was its degree of "permanence." All of these characteristics were more or less important depending on the end application for which the plastic material was intended. Large markets for plasticized materials were vinyl flooring, vinyl film and sheeting, covering for electrical wire and cable, surface coating, adhesives, and molded, dipped, and coated products made with plastisols (plastic materials in liquid form).

There were several classes of plasticizers: the phthalates, the adipates, and the polymerics. They were made from such basic materials as alcohols, acids (both monobasic and dibasic), hydrocarbons, and glycols. Plasticizers and the basic materials used in their manufacture were produced in large plants. In 1967 the largest plasticizer plants enjoyed significant manufacturing scale economies over plants of lesser size. It was believed that even larger plants would soon be built in which unit manufacturing costs would be even lower than the costs in any existing plant. Industry production capacity tended to be added periodically and in large chunks. There were alternate periods, then, of oversupply and undersupply with pronounced effects on market prices.

There were several distinct segments in the market for plasticizers. First, it may be noted that approximately 70% of all plasticizers were used with polyvinyl chloride resin (PVC). So-called general-purpose plasticizers accounted for 65% of this amount, which went for a great range of expendable plastic products like shower curtains, notebook covers, and plastic bags. The remaining 35% of the PVC plasticizer market was made up of applications calling for better product quality and a great deal of technical work with customers. Vinyl flooring was one large application; here it was important that the plasticizer be stain resistant, that it provide flexibility characteristics at low temperatures, and that it be compatible with floor wax. Upholstering materials was another application, and in furniture and automotive applications length of product life was important. Electrical wiring was a third large market; in this case electrical insulating characteristics were critical as well as the ability of the plasticizer to withstand high temperatures without deteriorating or being extracted from the plastic material.

About 30% of all plasticizers were used with resins other than PVC for such applications as hot melt adhesives, fluorescent pigment carriers, and hot dips plastisols where high viscosity, fast fusion, and fast jell were the qualities with which customers were concerned.

Monsanto was a major supplier of plasticizers and had a complete product line of over 80 different kinds of plasticizers. It was not a major supplier, however, of the large general-purpose plasticizers such as dioctyl phthalate (DOP). Alcohol was the major raw material in DOP manufacture, and Monsanto was not a basic producer of alcohol.

Monsanto was especially strong in those markets where its technical skills and the quality of its products gave it competitive advantages. It was, for example, strong in the vinyl flooring market and here its largest selling product was a branded item. This plasticizer was also made by one other large supplier in the United States and three in Europe. For every other plasticizer application, Monsanto also had tailored products to meet market requirements and was widely recognized for its technical competence in each application.

While prices on all plasticizers had declined over the long term, the prices of general-purpose products had suffered the greatest declines and were the most volatile.

Monsanto's marketing strategy for plasticizers was planned to focus particularly on those markets where the company's branded items could be used to customer advantage and where the company's technical competence gave it a competitive advantage. At the same time, an important element in its strategy was to serve its markets as a full-line supplier. Finally, to maintain its market position, to develop new markets, and to meet the challenge of declining market prices, Monsanto had committed large investments. Sizable capital expenditures had been made periodically for large plants, and large allocations had been made each year for process and product research.

Marketing Organization — Headquarters

The Product Manager (in Marketing) for plasticizers had structured his unit by establishing a Market Manager-Vinyl and a Market Manager-Specialty Resins. This was both a market and a product classification. These two managers prepared business plans for their markets, gave business direction to field sales representatives, and reviewed the customer strategies the latter prepared. The Market Manager-Vinyl had three men under him. One focused entirely on large flooring accounts, developing a business plan for that market and providing technical back-up for field sales in these accounts. The two other men were concerned with technical service for such vinyl plasticizer applications as wire and cable, film and sheeting, plastisols, and flooring (the smaller accounts). Each was assigned a geographic territory to cover. In addition, each was responsible for preparing technical literature, contributing to business plans, and developing ideas for advertising copy.

The Market Manager-Specialty Resins did all that his counterpart for Vinyl did; in addition, he had cognizance over the plasticizer distributor program and performed customer technical service work. He had one assistant for technical service.

The Product Manager had experimented somewhat with the organization of his unit. He had, for example, gone through a stage in which he had three Marketing Specialists, one for flooring, one for film and sheeting and wire and cable, and a third for plastisols, adhesives, and surface coatings. The flooring specialist had been effective because he could concentrate on a single industry with a limited number of accounts. The second man covered too many applications to develop the expertise he needed and too many customers to meet all the demands placed on him. The third man found plastisol applications of particular interest and tended to work more in this area than on adhesives and surface coatings. The current organization had the advantage of evening work loads, providing technical men with broader experience, and separating technical service responsibility for plastisols from that for adhesives and surface coatings.

The Marketing Director for the Organic Division and the Product Director of Plasticizers looked to the Product Manager for the marketing strategy on this line, and for recommendations on customer strategy and on pricing. Within broad limits, the Product Manager could himself handle pricing questions.

In the New York District, the Organic Division's largest, there were three sales representatives who accounted for the great bulk of the sales of plasticizers in that territory. But since the New York District was organized by "market" rather than "products," a few salesmen, other than these three, also sold plasticizers to their assigned accounts.

The three main plasticizer salesmen did not specialize by market segment; instead each was given a number of accounts in each major user industry. Their supervisor believed that it would be disadvantageous for them to specialize because as salesmen were promoted and transferred in and out of the district, he needed to have some flexibility in covering accounts. In addition to his accounts, each salesman also had a geographic area assigned to him in which he was to develop new customers for all Organic Division products. It was clear, however, that his first responsibility was his large plasticizer accounts. (In one instance, five customers accounted for 75% of a salesman's volume.)

In the course of his work a Monsanto plasticizer salesman faced a variety of customer problems. The following are illustrative:

(1) A large flooring account began using a low cost "extender" material, which enabled it to reduce its use of a Monsanto plasticizer. The salesman on this account got in touch with the Product Manager who, in turn, called in Research Department personnel. Research developed a modified product to meet the customer's need better than the combination of the original plasticizer and the extender material, and began tests in the customer's plant.

(2) A carpet manufacturer wanted information on how to make a plastisol-backed carpeting. The salesman requested information from technical personnel in the Product Manager's organization. He was supplied with complete data on materials and a manufacturing process for this product, and transmitted it to the carpet manufacturer. As this new customer began production, the salesman continued to give him such technical assistance as he could and to call on technical service back-up support from Division headquarters in St. Louis for additional help.

(3) The purchasing agent in one large account asked for a one-half-cent-a-pound price reduction on plasticizer in return for a significantly larger share of his business. After several telephone conversations with the Product Manager, the salesman was instructed to tell the customer that Monsanto would not shade its price. Shortly thereafter Monsanto began losing this account's business to a large competitor.

(4) Several of the flooring accounts in the New York District had developed a sheet flooring material which had a hard, stain-resistant vinyl top layer, a thin foam layer underneath for cushioning, and a felt or asbestos backing material underneath. This product had entered the market first as an inexpensive floor covering at about $2 a square yard. It had been upgraded, however, to $6 to $10 a square yard. The higher priced product called for a plasticizer with high stain resistance that could sell at a relatively high price per pound.

Monsanto did not have a product suited for this particular application, but one large competitor did. The New York salesmen urgently requested the Product Manager to arrange to have a research project launched to develop this product.

Division Reorganization

In early December 1967 the General Manager of the Organic Division announced a major reorganization of the Division. As he explained the new organization represented a shift from the Division's "traditional structure of horizontal, division-wide operating departments for research and development, commercial development, and marketing to one of vertical, operationally distinct business embracing each of the six major product areas of the Division."

In the new organization the Division was to be divided into six Business Groups (Food and Fine Chemicals, Petroleum Additives, Functional Fluids, Rubber Chemicals, Paper Chemicals, and Plasticizers and General Chemicals), each headed by a Business Group Director. Reporting to each Business Group Director would be personnel responsible for sales, research, commercial development, and manufacturing liaison. The old Marketing, Research, and Commercial Development Departments would no longer exist, although a limited amount of inter-Business Group coordination would be carried out by functionally oriented divisional staff personnel. While the Division's manufacturing plants would continue to report to the Division Director of Manufacturing, plant components producing particular products would be considered part of the appropriate Business Group.

The following paragraphs are excerpts from an internal memorandum describing the new organization and its rationale:

Up to now the Organic Division has been organized as though it were one business — organic chemicals. The line departments have been in the traditional functional pattern of Manufacturing, Marketing Research, Development, and the various administrative functions. As the size of the Division increased, product directors were introduced to assist the General Manager on a staff basis to coordinate the functional groups with respect to an emerging number of different customer groups or "businesses."

The Division has been quite successful in continuing its total growth as well as growth in its several businesses. In addition, new and different businesses have been developed within the Division charter.

With greater size it has been increasingly burdensome to maintain the past high standards of customer service and quick response to the many different business interests. The general management burden has been further aggravated by the stepped-up rate of developing new products and obsoleting old products and the related changes in manufacturing processes in each of the several businesses.

With this situation in mind, the Division conducted an intensive study of its functions, markets, and system of operation with particular emphasis on its methods of planning and executing the wide variety of programs called for.

As a result of its study, the Division has concluded that it is no longer just an organic chemical business; instead, it is a number of separate businesses who happen to employ organic chemicals, for the most part, to meet the requirements of distinctly different markets. Furthermore, by orienting itself to market requirements, a much wider vista for future growth opens up. Under this concept, for example, future products may not necessarily be limited to chemicals. In turn, this may lead to better earnings on investment than is possible in the capital-intensive general chemical manufacturing.

To agree with this conclusion, the Division has been completely reorganized. It will operate as a conglomerate of separate businesses rather than as a group of functions.

Under the new organization, line authority will flow from the General Manager to the director of each of the six businesses. Each director will have line authority over those portions of the former functional departments which relate to his business. He will thus directly supervise his own managers of research, development, and marketing, including product and field personnel, and he will supervise a manufacturing liaison function.

The Marketing Department will become the Sales Administration Department, which will be concerned only with administrative activities in this area.

The prime function of the General Manager is to lead the Division into expansion or new business opportunities rather than referee decisions about the conduct of the present business. He is still, however, required to assure the Corporation that management of the six businesses is effective; that the total budget is valid; and that the functional and business departments operate well together; generally that the Division develops and meets goals for both its own and corporate purposes.

The directors of the businesses have general management responsibility for their own business as assigned. They have a profit responsibility and full authority to carry approved programs out as line managers. Their responsibilities include:

— Planning and developing programs for approval;
— Budget development;
— Organization, personnel, and operating concept;
— Effective management and execution;
— Cost, price, volume, and profit.

Exhibit 5 contains additional information from this memorandum.

346 Cases and Commentaries

Exhibit 1. Organization Chart, March 1967

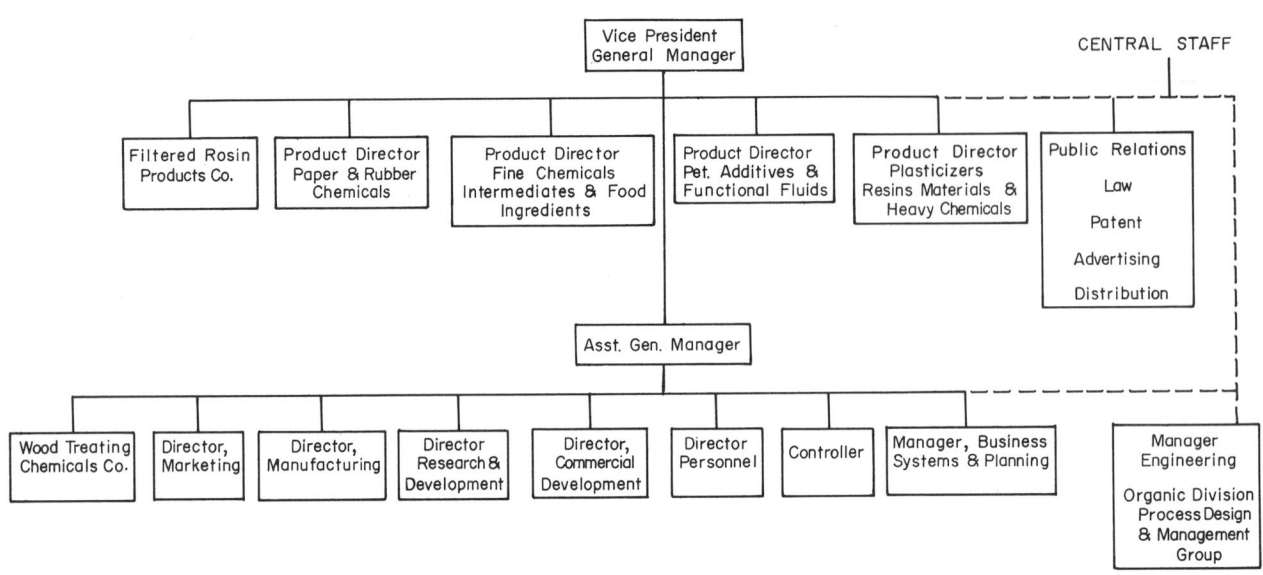

Exhibit 2. Organization Chart of Marketing Department, March 1967

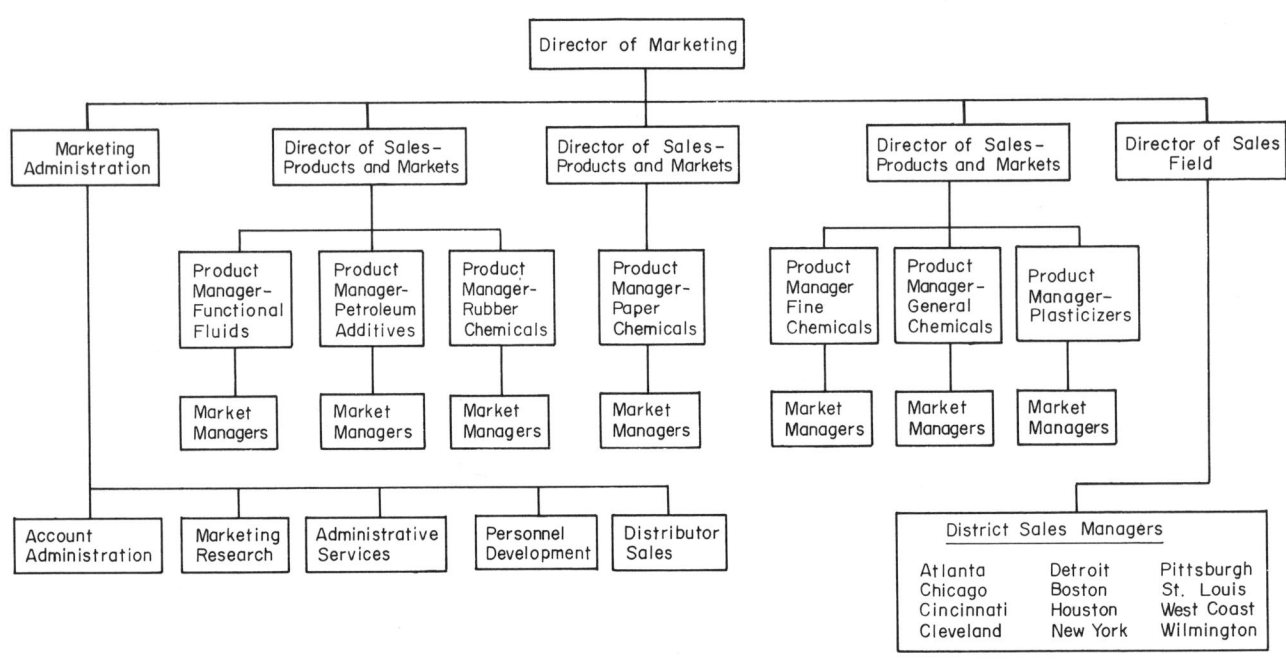

Exhibit 3. Simplified Organization Chart of Manufacturing Department, March 1967

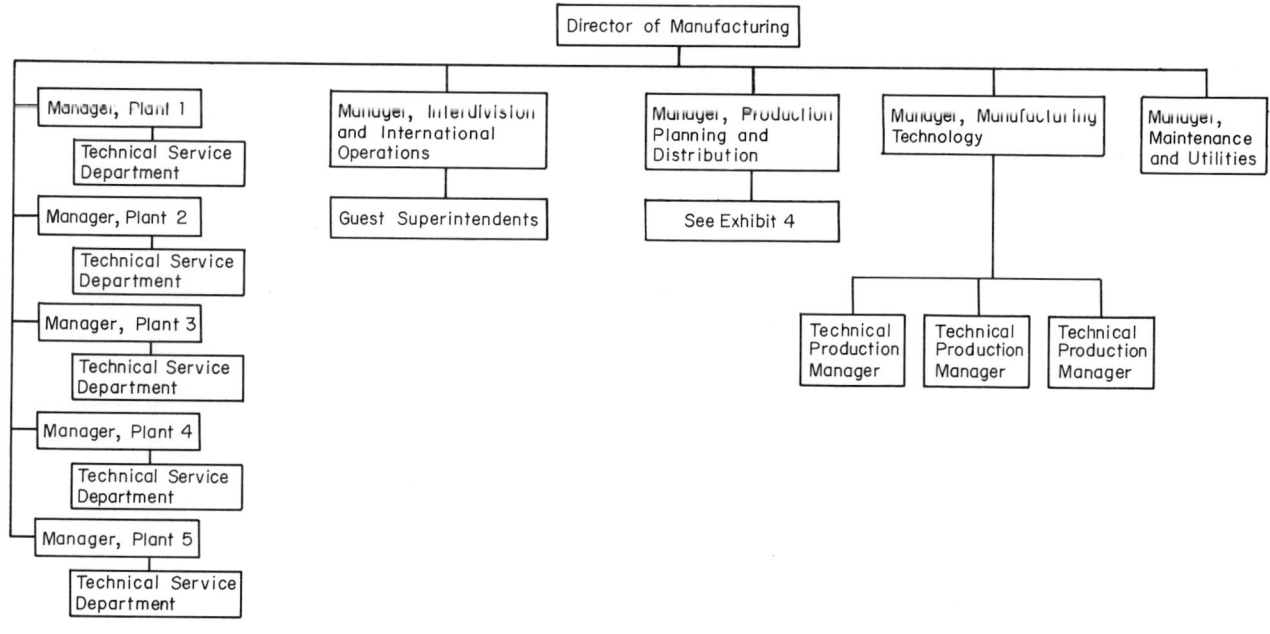

Exhibit 4. Organization Chart of Production Planning and Distribution, April 1967

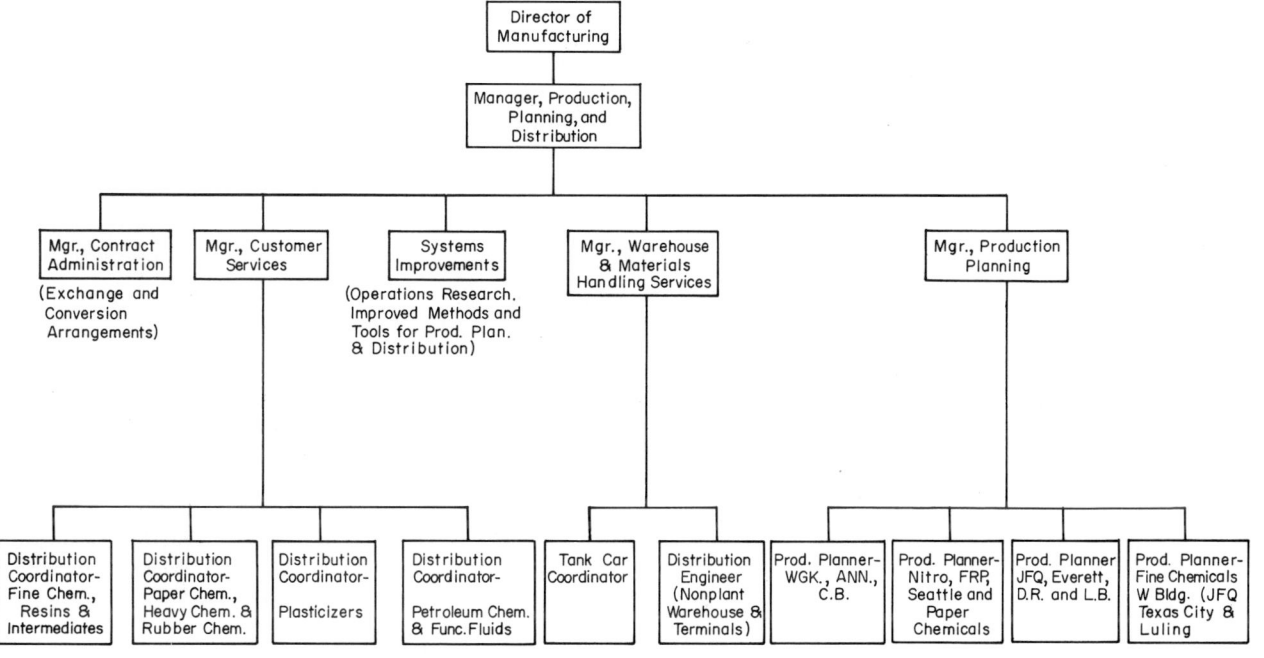

Exhibit 5. Simplified Organization Charts of Division Before and After Reorganization of December 1967

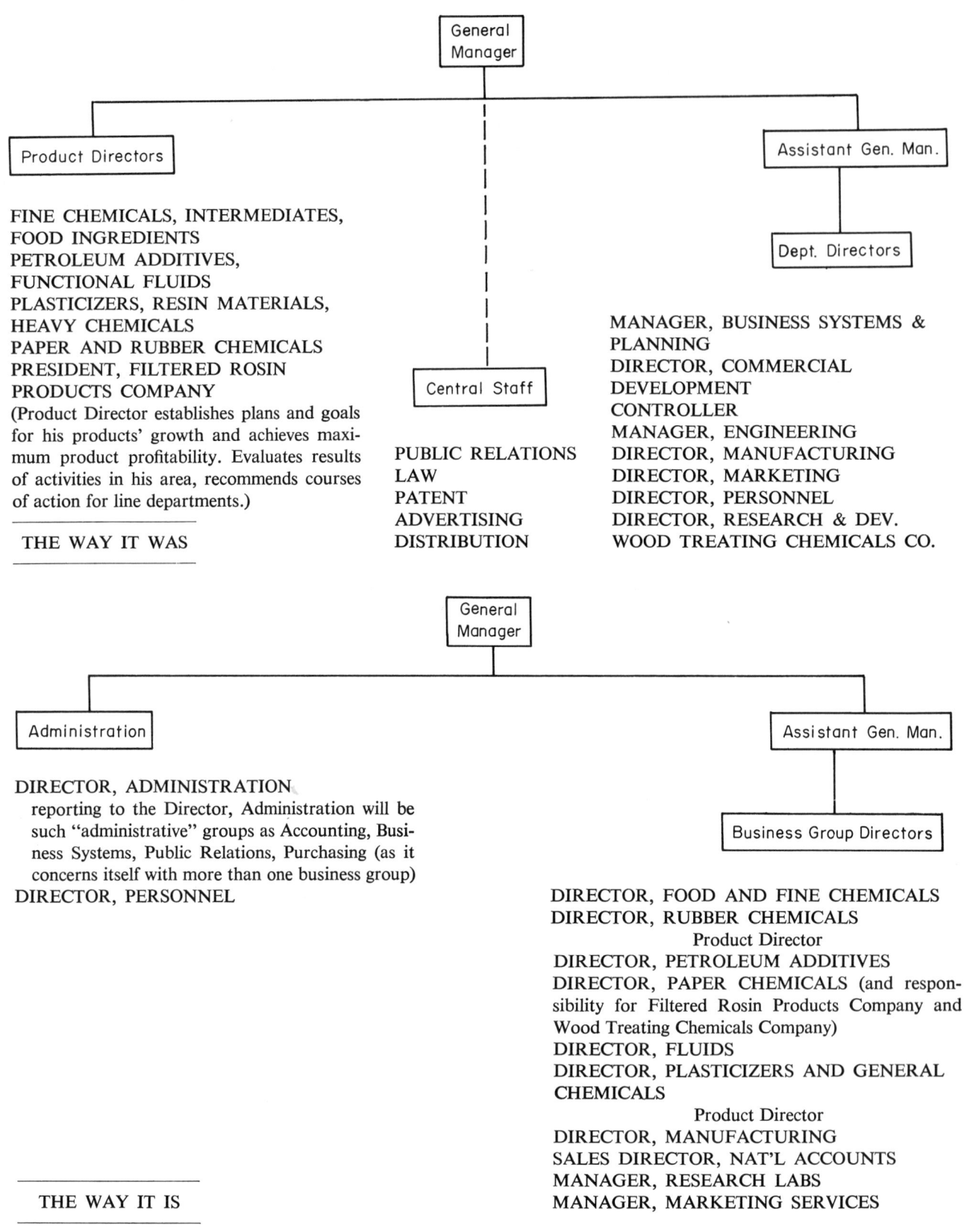

Exhibit 5 (continued).

SOME ANSWERS

WHAT HAS HAPPENED? As a general statement, under the "old" organizational setup, the department directors (of Manufacturing, Marketing, Research, etc.) were considered "line" managers . . . responsible for their *functional* groups. The product directors could be categorized as "staff" managers . . . with staff responsibility for product groups. Thus, line authority was associated with functional responsibility . . . staff responsibility was divided by product groups.

Again as a general statement, under the new organizational setup, line authority is now associated with product groups (as they're now called, "business groups"). Thus, a line manager is now responsible for, say, Fluids, for Rubber Chemicals, etc. Staff responsibility is now with the "functional" administration groups reporting to the Division General Manager, and with the manager of research laboratories and the manager of marketing services.

WHAT'S GONE, WHAT REMAINS? In essence, there is no more Marketing Department, no Commercial Development Department, no Research Department. There are two staff managers, for research laboratories and for marketing services, who will be responsible for administrative/personnel matters which are common to marketing or research people in all six business groups.

WHAT ABOUT DISTRICT OFFICES, LINE AUTHORITY IN MARKETING? A field salesman, who has been specializing in selling rubber chemicals, for example, will *not* be reporting to the district manager of that office, but rather will be part of the business group in Rubber Chemicals, and will ultimately report to the director of sales in that business group, and to the business group director. Thus, he will not be a member of a district office . . . he will be a member of a business group.

HOW WILL THE BUSINESS GROUPS BE ORGANIZED? This will be at the discretion of the director of each group. In one form or another, however, *each* director will have individuals in his group who will be responsible for the marketing, research, and development of the products *within* that business, and will also have a manufacturing liaison man. As an example, a business group organization may look like this:

        Director, _____ Chemicals
           Director of Sales
           Research Manager
           Commercial Development
           Manufacturing Liaison

ANY ADDITIONAL ADVANTAGES? In the area of personnel development, for example, there will now be *six* general managers (the business group directors, with delegated authority for their products), *six* directors of sales, etc. . . . with each acquiring valuable experience and training in managing a business. A significant advantage involves this: within the division, financial reporting is done on a product-group basis. You probably recall reading in our communications media, for example, that rubber chemicals were over (under) budget, fluids were ahead (behind) last year's performance, etc. With the new organization, there is *one* group where decision making, responsibility for marketing, development, profit, and growth of that product group, can be pin-pointed and coordinated to improve performance.

Appendix A

Position Description for Product Director

I. *Function*

As a staff member of management and a delegate of the General Manager, the Product Director is responsible for the overall profitability and dynamic growth of assigned products and product group(s). Secondarily, the Product Director is responsible for overall Organic Division activities in serving specific "markets."

He shall develop specific plans for continued profitability and growth for such products and groups and see that the necessary customer, product and market strategies are prepared and implemented by the proper line organizations. He will recommend the implementation of these plans to the General Manager and Department Directors. He will assist the Department Directors by suggesting appropriate action to achieve the effective coordination and integration of department efforts and activities to accomplish these plans. For specific assigned "markets," he will be responsible for the coordination of all Division activity concerned with the serving of this market.

He will follow activities in all departments and recommend to Department Directors such action as may be necessary to continue and maintain the maximum coordination of departmental activities to achieve maximum results. He will represent the General Manager in important customer and industry contacts with respect to product groups and/or specific markets.

The primary function of the Product Director is product administration, i.e., planning, recommending, coordinating, and appraising action and results. The secondary function of the Product Director is to specific markets — the coordination of all Division activity in such markets and the determination of the extent of the Division penetration into such markets.

The Product Director establishes "what" is to be done, and the timing — not "how" work is handled.

II. *Responsibility and Authority*

Within the limits of Corporate and Divisional policies and the program as approved by the General Manager, the Product Director is responsible for, and has commensurate authority to accomplish the following duties:

A. Overall responsibility for the profitability and growth of assigned products and product group(s).
B. Overall responsibility for product group budgets and forecasts.
C. Develops and keeps current a long-range plan for profitability and growth of assigned products.
D. Overall responsibility for Division activities in specific markets. Prime product responsibility stays with the appropriate Product Director regardless of the product use in a specific market assigned to another Product Director.
E. Develops recommendations to assist the line departments in the implementation of the long-range plan.
F. Conducts a continuous, critical analysis and appraisal of all activities which affect the profitability of the product group or groups involved. Assists the line departments in developing and maintaining the most effective policies and plans for the product group or groups concerned. Based on the results of such an analysis, recommends appropriate action as necessary to the General Manager and the Department Directors.
G. Conducts a continuous, critical analysis and appraisal of all Division activities within a specific market(s). Assists the line department in developing and maintaining the most effective policies and plans for such markets. Recommends appropriate action as necessary to the General Manager and the Department Directors.
H. Division responsibility for specific assigned raw materials. Reviews and approves raw material purchase contracts.
I. Reviews and approves Appropriation Requests related to his areas of responsibility. Writes, edits, and sponsors Appropriation Requests which require approval at levels of authority above the General Manager.

   Sponsors individual Project Summary projects; coordinates and expedites progress against Project Summary schedules. Enters projects in the Capital Forecast and obtains necessary approvals. Writes or edits Appropriation Reviews.

   Works closely with the line departments and other Product Directors where there is a mutuality of interest in the development of capital projects.
J. Establishes sales prices for individual products (including prices for sales of goods overseas), and sets price boundaries, or parameters, in which the Director of Marketing may move as dictated by competitive action.
K. He will act as Chairman of the Ad Hoc Informal Business Group not only with regard to domestic business, but also for total international business as defined in the International Division Charter. As such, he will represent the Organic Division for policy matters affecting his product groups with the International Division.
L. Works closely with the line departments in the development, for General Manager approval, of contracts with outside individuals or firms covering research and development efforts, joint operation, purchase, sale or exchange of know-how pertaining to his assigned products. Administers such contracts that cut across several functional departments or as designated by the General Manager.
M. He shall be alert for acquisition which would widen product lines, broaden specific market coverage, and enhance total Division profitability.
N. He will continually re-assess market goals in terms of customer needs.

Appendix A (continued)

III. *Relationships*

The Product Director will observe and conduct the following relationships:

A. General Manager/Assistant General Manager

   He is responsible to the General Manager for fulfillment of his functions, responsibilities, authority, and relationships.

B. Department Directors
   1. The Product Director will work closely with the Directors and other personnel of the line departments in the development and follow-up on the overall plan for profitability and growth of assigned products.
   2. He shall work closely with, and be guided by, the Product Director having prime product responsibility in the handling of such products in his specific assigned market areas.

C. Others
   1. He shall maintain liaison with Division Accounting and through them Corporate Accounting, R&D, Advertising, Patent, Legal, and other supporting activities which are involved in the growth of operation of the respective product groups.
   2. He will conduct such other relationships outside the company as are necessary to the accomplishment of his functions.

Appendix B

Position Description for Product Manager

I. *Function*

To provide business direction from a marketing viewpoint on a world-wide basis for his products and markets toward the end of achieving maximum sales and minimum selling expense. To develop marketing strategies and plans, and to implement them through the field sales forces.

II. *Major Responsibilities*

1. Formulate market strategies for the markets and sub-markets of significant concern to his group.
2. Formulate total product strategies for all major products and product groupings.
3. Review and approve all total customer strategies of concern to his group and to participate personally in the formulation of the strategies for the major accounts.
4. Develop a Product Group Annual Marketing Plan for the purpose of transmitting to the field sales forces the essence of the market strategies and total product strategies and the detailed annual marketing program.
5. Participate in the appropriate ad hoc informal business groups provided by the corporate policy procedure for international operations.
6. Direct all customer technical service activities for his products including the provision of back-up help for field sales, preparation of bulletins and literature, direction of laboratory technical service work, and the selection and justification of application research projects.
7. Make calls on sales offices and customers so as to interpret the strategies and plans, assist in the development of key total customer strategies, to help train sales representatives in product and industry knowledge, to assist in selling customers, and to maintain a firsthand knowledge of the market conditions for his products.
8. Develop new markets, new uses, and new models for our present products using market strategies and total product strategies as the means of securing action by other departments.
9. Keep the director of sales advised of the marketing effectiveness of the district offices for his products and recommend appropriate changes in such areas as territorial coverage, account assignments and personnel assignments.
10. Participate with Marketing management and the product director in developing pricing strategies and policies that will achieve maximum long-range profits. Recommend product list price moves and take appropriate action on Requests for Specific Price Change received from field sales.
11. Maintain complete technical knowledge of his products and their applications in industry and continually appraise their competitive advantages and disadvantages so as to help develop improved products and to keep the sales force up to date on product knowledge.
12. Forecast sales of his products both short term and long term to enable the planning of production rates, inventory levels, and raw material requirements.
13. Communicate, as the hub of the communications network for his products, both commercial and technical information among the field sales force, customers, Development, Research, Manufacturing Marketing management, the product director, and other divisions.
14. Direct the marketing efforts of the division at conventions and represent the marketing interests of the division in appropriate trade associations.
15. Approve, plan, and supervise customer visits to the General Offices, plants and laboratories of the division.
16. Define specific sales objectives, pressure points, audiences, and market potentials to the Advertising and Sales Promotion Department. Counsel and guide in the development of promotion programs, then approve and finally implement with appropriate field action the advertising and sales promotion programs for his product group.
17. Act on package changes, product quality specification changes, credits and claims, complaint settlements, and minimum inventories.
18. Develop and submit for approval an annual selling expense budget for his product group and supervise the expenditure of funds to insure effective utilization of the money in the approved budget.
19. Establish and direct an objectives program within the product group which will include overall group objectives and personal objectives for himself and for each of his men.
20. Supervise and be responsible for the development of all personnel in his department.
21. Maintain adequate security for the safeguarding of confidential information so as to prevent its release to outsiders or to Monsanto personnel not authorized to receive it and train his department employees to do likewise.

III. *Organizational Relationships*

He is responsible to a director of sales-products/markets. He has supervisory responsibility for assigned technical service representatives.

In giving business direction to the field salesmen and industry managers, he keeps the district managers informed.

He has commensurate authority to carry out his responsibilities in keeping with company and division policies, procedures, and standards and within the limits of approved budgets.

Appendix C

Position Description for District Sales Manager

Function:

Manages the Organic Division's sales activities in a district in terms of the number and complexity of accounts, dollar volume, and personnel supervised; supervises district personnel to ensure the achievement of sales objectives; plans, coordinates, and implements sales strategies; directs and trains sales representatives and specialists; analyzes the market place for profit improvement; creates and maintains favorable Company-community relationships.

Duties:

1. Analyzes customer and prospective customer requirements as well as competitive activities to establish district sales objectives and plans and implements necessary strategies to meet these objectives.
2. Reviews and develops annual district budgets and forecasts and submits them to the Field Sales Director for approval.
3. Provides work guidance to district personnel including the evaluation and review of performance.
4. Reviews manpower requirements and sales representative and specialist assignments and recommends organizational changes as necessary.
5. Plans and conducts district sales meetings, strategy and communication sessions.
6. Develops and maintains high level contacts with personal accounts, other key customers, and distributors.
7. Directs the district office clerical activities.
8. Reviews and approves requests for staff assistance from the Division Marketing Department; approves and arranges customer visits by Divisional personnel.
9. Develops and maintains a high degree of cooperation and coordination with other Monsanto divisions to ensure the continuity of favorable customer relations.

Supervision:

Direct — Supervises the activities of the following personnel:
Sales Representatives and Specialists
Sales Correspondent Supervisor
Secretaries/Clerks

Functional — None

COMMENTARY

Organizational design in successful companies reflects, and is shaped by, the company's market environment, the nature of its business, and its strategy. In the case of Monsanto's Organic Chemicals Division organizational design responded significantly to (1) the size and diversity of the business, (2) the industry's high rate of technical development, (3) a high level of customer need for technical service, and (4) the fact that the bulk of the business came from a limited number of large buyers.

The Organic Chemicals Division had to be structured, then, to develop and implement a series of *interrelated* market strategies — interrelated by product for different market segments and interrelated by customer (the larger ones) for different products. It had to have short lines of communication with customers to respond effectively to their technical service needs. It needed procedures for gathering and screening product development ideas from a range of sources, both market and technical. It had to be structured to develop new products that would meet market needs and move them efficiently into the on-going marketing stream.

Organization and processes had to meet these specifications. In addition, if the Division was to grow profitably it had to have a sharp top management focus on its markets to respond quickly to competitive conditions and market opportunities. It was because of this condition that the Organic Chemicals management in December 1967 created six businesses out of what had been one.

The commentary, then, analyzes (1) the program-resource structure, (2) the planning procedures, (3) new product development processes, and (4) the realignment of the business structure in late 1967.

Program-Resource Structure

The locus for strategy formulation and implementation was at the Market/Product Group Manager level. These men (called Product Managers) were responsible for developing plans and for exercising considerable direction in their execution.

It was a pyramidal structure delineated initially by product and then broken down by market. There was, for example, a Plasticizers Product Manager. Under his direction Market Managers prepared plans for marketing plasticizers to a range of plastics end-product manufacturers: vinyl flooring, wire and cable, film and sheeting, adhesives, and surface coatings. Different types of plasticizers were used in these markets and application technology varied widely from one user industry to another.

Product program organizations often had their own program-attached technical service resources to help customers solve production problems and to work with them on product modifications. For technical work of a more advanced, specialized nature Product Managers could draw on Research Department talent.

Field sales personnel were program-specialized but not program-attached. Product (and Market) Managers gave "business direction" to field sales representatives. And, in fact, the assignment of sales personnel to the districts was determined by Directors of Sales-Products and Markets at headquarters (to whom Product Managers reported). District Managers gave "administrative direction" to field salesmen. They were concerned with sales training, performance reviews, salary increases, and sales expense accounting. They reviewed salesmen's objectives and customer plans.

As the description of the selling problems of the New York plasticizer salesman indicates, he had frequent and direct contact with the Plasticizers Product Manager at headquarters. That was essential if the Product Manager was to respond quickly to the threat posed by competitive pricing moves and new technical developments.

On both pricing and technical service, then, the organization was structured for fast responses and close headquarters-field relationships.

Research and manufacturing resources were program-specialized, as well, in the respect that there were research units allocated to each product group and identifiable manufacturing facilities for each. Product Managers had a much different relationship with these resources, however, from that with technical service and field sales. They influenced the direction of the effort far less. In the case of research, the Director of Research had final authority in the allocation of his technical resources to projects. Product Managers, as members of the Informal Business Groups, could only formulate market needs and opportunities calling for research.

The Director of Manufacturing, as well, kept close control over the utilization of production resources. Technical Product Managers (TPMs) were the link between plants and Product Managers. Product Managers and field salesmen, the case tells us, could not deal directly with the plant on matters involving major or minor changes in product specification and deliveries. Requests for such changes went through the TPMs, and they decided whether a proposed change would be advantageous based on cost, profit, and customer consideration. A TPM was described by the Director of Manufacturing as "an umbrella over the plant to keep the plant from having its energies drained off on things we really shouldn't do."

Technical service and field sales were easily divisible resources and required specializing by product. Manufacturing and research resources were not easily divisible and had to be managed as tightly integrated units. As for the latter, Product Managers would not be expected to provide long-range direction for research investments. Their concern is selling today's product, serving today's customer, and meeting today's competition.

Planning

The case describes what seems to be — and undoubtedly is — a complex planning procedure. It was necessarily complex because plans had to be integrated by product, market, and customer.

The organizational provision for integrating planning is the most interesting aspect of the process. Individual *market strategies* (prepared at the Market Manager level) were the building blocks for formulating a *total product strategy* (developed by Product Managers). It was important that product rather than market be the critical dimension for planning. Pricing strategy had to cut across markets. Product supply had to be allocated to markets according to market growth potential and relative profitability.

At the level of the Directors of Sales (to whom the seven Product Managers reported) product strategies were coordinated as they might affect relations with large customers.

The four Product Directors contributed in two ways. Primarily responsible for long-range product and market policy, the Product Directors were concerned that overall Division objectives were implemented in the form of shorter-range product strategies. In addition, the Informal Business Groups, chaired by the Product Directors, were the vehicle through which product/market programs were adjusted to fit the Division's available manufacturing and research resources.

Thus planning procedures, starting with the development of market strategies, were intended to provide for the integration of these plans into total product strategies, the adjustment of product strategies to eliminate marketing conflicts, the coordination of plans by major customers, and the implementation of long-range Division plans through short-range programs.

Product Development Processes

In the development of its product line, the management of the Organic Chemicals Division was exposed to three types of influences and had well-established channels for responding to each. These were the Division's customers, new technical developments generated by Research, and the perceived market needs for new organic chemicals.

Development projects undertaken in response to customer needs were generally classified as "regenerative" — to maintain market position. The response channels, here, went directly from the customer and the field sales representative to technical service personnel in the Product/Market

Groups. When the project required more sophisticated technical effort, Research personnel became involved.

"Exploratory" research projects not based on articulated market needs but on new technical advances were initiated in the Research Department. Here, the stimuli might well come from the exposure of Research personnel to developments in the scientific community and from laboratory experiments.

The Commercial Development Department was charged with covering the third area — product development to meet the challenge of identifiable new market opportunities. The Director of Commercial Development credits his department's success in part to its independence from Research, on the one hand, and from Marketing, on the other. Commercial Development could play its role most effectively if it kept Research effort sharply focused on meeting defined market needs. At the same time it could not act effectively as a part of Marketing because Commercial Development effort was characterized by much longer time cycles than was Marketing work. According to the Director of Commercial Development:

Commercial Development is the "patient money" department. Normally we work on a project for three or more years. In Marketing, every Product Manager has a lot of products to worry about and focuses on short-range budgets. If CD were part of Marketing, the long-range development projects would have to take second place. Moreover, Marketing tends naturally to think that if the customers want it, it should be done — and that is not always the case.

Commercial Development needs also to be separate from Research. It works best as an independent market place voice, a voice able to take issue with Research. Research people develop something and then want to take it out to the market, and Commercial Development has to be free to contribute a commercial judgment on projects.

There are other factors, too, which probably contributed to CD's effectiveness. There was, for example, the same kind of formal commitment and monitoring procedures here that we observed at IBM. At each stage, as a project moved from the identification of a market need, through technical appraisal, technical development, and commercialization, there was a clear transfer of responsibility from one department to another.

Even so, the process was such as to provide for continually close working relationships between the Commercial Development and Research Department teams during the technical development stages. Similarly close working relationships were maintained between CD teams and Marketing units as the new product entered the commercialization phases. These relationships were built around a single project. When team effort was spread across several projects simultaneously, the success of any one project was jeopardized.

It is also worth noting that Commercial Development carried each successful technical development through the initial commercialization stages — preparing sales programs and promotional materials, calling on customers, and making sales. In this way, the Commercial Development team could test the product, identify sales obstacles, plan production facilities based on estimated market demand, and prepare a marketing strategy. It is likely that if the product was transferred prematurely to Marketing personnel, it would not receive the detailed attention that it needed in the early stages of market development. Nor is it likely that information on product advantages and weaknesses, on customer problems and selling obstacles would be fed back quickly to permit modifications in the product and in the marketing strategy.

The Organic Chemicals Division had well-developed channels for screening and responding to product development ideas from customers, from the laboratory, and from chemical markets broadly. The channels were short and workable. The product development process was structured in such a way that market needs would strongly influence technical development. It was characterized by formal commitment procedures and by close working relationships among Commercial Development, Research, and Marketing teams, around a sharply focused new product idea.

Division Reorganization

The split-up of the Organic Chemicals Division into six businesses was a logical development, stemming directly from rapid growth and product line proliferation. Key considerations are clearly indicated in the internal memorandum announcing the change. In particular, there was the difficulty that a single management had in making strategic decisions and formulating policies for such a wide range of products going into many markets. The Division's management had found it "increasingly burdensome to maintain the past high standards of customer service and quick response. . . ." In addition, the natural growth of the Division to take advantage of market opportunities was apparently being constrained as these opportunities led in the direction of nonchemical products, new technical disciplines, and different manufacturing processes. As a single business, Organic Chemicals would tend to seek its growth through the expansion of existing resources. As six different businesses, the Division might well go beyond the existing framework of manufacturing resources and technical skills.

The split was facilitated by the fact that the Marketing, Manufacturing, and Research Departments were already divided organizationally into product groups. And in Manufacturing, plant facilities were specialized broadly by product lines.

In retrospect, the use of Product Directors may be seen as an interim step intended to aid a single management in coping with the problems posed by a high rate of new product development. Product Directors, however, could provide only limited relief. Their role was described as "planning," "assisting," "recommending"; it tended to be ambiguous, changing under a succession of General Managers. The General Managers were still called on to make strategic decisions and to be quickly responsive to customer needs.

Summary

As in each of the preceding companies that have been studied, Monsanto's Organic Chemicals Division had developed a structure and organizational processes designed to cope with the conditions of its industry environment. It supplied a wide range of products to diverse markets. A limited number of big customers accounted for a large percentage of its sales. These customers required considerable technical assistance. And to meet market needs and opportunities there was a high rate of new product development.

Market programs were integrated by product line, coordinated by customer, and implemented with strong direction from Product/Market Group managements. The structure facilitated close technical relationships between individual customers and the Division's technical service and research resources.

The Division was well organized to respond to the stimuli of new product ideas from customers, from chemical markets broadly, and from exploratory scientific research. Its procedures were such as to bring to bear the influence of identifiable market needs in guiding research efforts. Research and development processes provided for close working relationships among Research, Commercial Development, and Marketing teams and for obtaining the commitment of each to the work at each stage of project development.

Finally, the division of Organic Chemicals in December 1967 into six businesses was a logical development. It was no longer possible for a single management to respond adequately to needs and opportunities in so many markets. Moreover, the natural growth of Organic Chemicals was apparently being held within the capacities of a set of resources designed for chemical products. Its management believed that opportunities outside of chemicals might exist in the markets presently served. To take advantage of these growth possibilities, line responsibility had to be delegated to several business management teams.

Monsanto Company: Agricultural Division

The Agricultural Division was one of eight operating divisions of the Monsanto Company, an integrated manufacturer of chemicals and related products.[1] In 1966 Agricultural Division sales accounted for approximately 10% of Monsanto's total sales of $1.6 billion. The Division's sales had increased 27% over 1965 and 153% over 1961, a rate considerably greater than that achieved by any other division.

The Agricultural Division had been formed in late 1960[2] to consolidate the agricultural activities of two older Monsanto divisions, Organic Chemicals and Inorganic Chemicals. At that time Monsanto management had believed that the Company's growth would be increased by having an operating division which concentrated exclusively on the agricultural market. Several manufacturing facilities had been assigned to the new Division, and a management team had been formed from executives in the older divisions.

In 1967 the Agricultural Division manufactured four major groups of products:

Plant Foods (fertilizers), including anhydrous ammonia, ammonium nitrate, diammonium phosphate, and several other less important products. In general, these products were characterized by an ammonia base (Monsanto was a leading producer of ammonia), and were commodities in the sense that at least several manufacturers made identical products.

Blasting Agents, which were various mixtures of ammonium nitrate (a fertilizer) and fuel oil, used mainly as substitutes for dynamite in mining and quarrying.

Animal Feed Additives, including MHA[3] (a poultry feed supplement), Santoquin[3] (an animal feed additive used to retard oxidation), feed grade urea (a protein source), and several less important products. Urea was a commodity, MHA was produced by three U.S. manufacturers, and Santoquin[3] was proprietary to Monsanto in the United States.

Pesticides, including several proprietary herbicides (Avadex,[3] Rogue,[3] Ramrod,[3] and Randox[3] were the most important) and a number of commodity pesticides (of which Parathion was the most important).

Of these product groups, Plant Foods and Pesticides accounted for the greatest sales volume, and proprietary herbicides made the greatest contribution to profits.

The Agricultural Division operated three manufacturing plants and used facilities in several plants operated by other Monsanto divisions. The Division sold some ammonia to the Textiles Division. It did not purchase a significant amount of its raw materials or final products from other Monsanto divisions.

The various plant foods and blasting agents were closely related, since all used the same basic material. In simple terms, ammonia could be sold as ammonia (as either a raw material or a fertilizer) or it could be upgraded to form nitric acid or ammonium nitrate. Ammonium nitrate, in turn, could be sold as a fertilizer, or it could be combined with fuel oil to form a blasting agent.

The feed additives and pesticides were each relatively independent. The capacity to produce a particular product was constrained by the manufacturing capacity for that product rather than by a common raw material or manufacturing process.

From a manufacturing point of view it was also useful to differentiate between commodity products and proprietaries. In general, it was necessary to produce commodities at full capacity on a year-round basis if costs were to be kept low enough to realize a profit. Price levels for proprietaries, on the other hand, were high enough to allow considerable flexibility in manufacturing scheduling. As one executive explained: "On

---

[1] Monsanto's eight divisions were Agricultural, Hydrocarbons & Polymers, Inorganic Chemicals, International, Organic Chemicals, Packaging, Plastic Products & Resins, and Textiles.

[2] The year 1961 was the first full year of operations for the new division.

[3] Monsanto trademark.

commodities we have to sell all that we can make. On proprietaries we have to make all that we can sell."

Until 1960, when the Agricultural Division was formed, virtually all of Monsanto's sales of agricultural products were to other manufacturers. These manufacturers (generally other chemical companies) used the Division's products as ingredients in manufacturing fertilizers, feed additives, and pesticides. It soon became apparent, however, that it would be only a matter of time before these manufacturers were themselves self-sufficient in the products manufactured by the Division. As a result, Division management had decided to follow a program aimed at getting closer to the consumer.

By the end of 1966 this program had been largely implemented. The Division had opened its own retail outlets and also was selling a substantial percentage of its production through wholesalers and independent dealers. Nevertheless, the Division's distribution mix varied markedly from product to product. Because the Division was not able to distribute its full production of commodity fertilizers and insecticides through its usual channels, it also sold these products to resellers or upgraders. Individual pesticides varied in their distribution channel, depending on the geographic area in which they were used. The Division had retail outlets in some areas but not in others. Feed additives were sold to resellers and large feed mills, although plans were being made to extend distribution to premixers who sold, in turn, to smaller feed mills. Blasting agents were sold direct to mines and quarries, although the basic material, ammonium nitrate, was also sold to resellers.

While the Division's pattern of distribution was moving closer to the consumer on several fronts, the most notable development was the establishment of Monsanto Agricultural Centers. As noted above, Monsanto had sold ammonia and ammonium nitrate primarily to other chemical companies in the late 1950s. In the very early 1960s distribution was broadened in some geographic areas to include independent fertilizer dealers. In order to obtain many of these dealers Monsanto had found it necessary to invest in ammonia storage tanks and fertilizer blending plants and to underwrite local bank loans. By 1963 Division management had decided that this program did not provide an adequate return on investment, and it was curtailed.

Division management had then decided to experiment with company-owned retail outlets known as Monsanto Agricultural Centers (MACs). These outlets sold fertilizers, pesticides, and a variety of agricultural services. By early 1967 the Division operated approximately 150 MACs, located primarily in the corn belt of the Middle West. In commenting on the MACs, one executive explained, "The farmer has been taught that 'fertilizer is fertilizer,' to be bought wherever he can get the best deal. We are trying to change this, to differentiate our products on the basis of service and availability."

Organizational Structure

The Agricultural Division was headed by a Vice President and General Manager and an Assistant General Manager. Reporting to these two executives were seven Directors, responsible respectively for Administration, Research and Development, Commercial Development, Process Engineering, Wholesale Marketing, Retail Marketing (the MACs), and Manufacturing.[4] In addition, the Division had personnel assigned to it in a number of Monsanto central departments (Engineering, Advertising, Distribution, Law, Patent, Public Relations, Treasury).

Wholesale Marketing

Four Sales Directors reported to the Director of Marketing (Wholesale). Two of these Sales Directors were responsible for product lines, each supervising the work of a number of product managers. The third Sales Director was responsible for the field sales force, and the fourth was responsible for the Division's international marketing activities.

Product Management: The two product Sales Directors were responsible respectively for plant foods and blasting agents, and for pesticides and feed additives. Until early 1967 the Field Sales Director had been responsible for product management of blasting agents, but this responsibility had been combined with plant foods in order to facilitate trade-offs among the Division's various ammonia-based products.

Several product managers reported to each product Sales Director. In the Plant Foods and Blasting Agents group there were product managers for direct-application liquid fertilizers,[5] bulk blenders,[6] other plant

---

[4] See Exhibit 1, Organization Chart of the Division.

[5] Essentially anhydrous ammonia, a gas which becomes a liquid under pressure. Anhydrous ammonia was applied to soil by means of equipment which inserted it (under pressure) several inches below the surface.

[6] The product manager for bulk blenders was responsible for a particular category of independent retail outlets (bulk blenders) rather than a line of products.

foods,[7] and blasting agents. In the Pesticides and Feed Additives group there were product managers for proprietary pesticides, technical (i.e., commodity) pesticides, crop technology, and animal nutrition. Each product manager (except the product manager for bulk blenders) supervised the work of several product supervisors, each of whom was responsible for one or two individual products.

Each level of product management was concerned with sales, forecasting and budgeting, pricing,[8] marketing channels, and marketing programs for the products assigned to it. These functions varied considerably among products, as illustrated by the following examples.

In the Plant Foods and Blasting Agents product group, most product managers and supervisors were primarily concerned with sales, forecasting, and marketing channels. Because demand for fertilizer peaked markedly during the spring and varied sharply depending on the weather, it was virtually impossible not to be in short supply in some geographic areas, even though the industry as a whole or Monsanto might have excess capacity for a particular product. Moreover, price levels tended to increase considerably toward the end of the planting season, and then drop precipitously as summer approached.

The key to plant food profitability was to have an adequate supply of the right product in a given geographic area at the time when farmers needed it and prices were high. To some extent, the planting season varied from one geographic area to another and it was possible to schedule shipments to coincide with historical climate patterns. Because the plants were producing at full capacity for immediate distribution (rather than inventory) during the peak season, there was little room for error. Despite a company's best efforts, it would inevitably be faced with surpluses in some areas and stock-outs in others.

Compounding the problem was the need to make constant trade-offs among products and channels of distribution. Depending on price levels, it might at a particular time be more profitable to produce anhydrous ammonia rather than ammonium nitrate, for example. Similarly, it was possible to ship a product to the MACs, to independent dealers, to distributors, to co-producers, or abroad at a given point in time. Decisions in these areas were influenced by transportation costs, price levels, historical relationships, and a variety of other factors.

As a result, product personnel in the Plant Foods group spent most of their time in the peak season working with the group in the Administration Department (see pages 364–365) which actually scheduled shipments, and most of their time in the off-season planning for the peak season.

The product manager for blasting agents was also concerned with product supply, since he "competed" for ammonium nitrate during the peak season; but his main responsibility was "to oversee a business within a business." Unlike the Division's other product lines, blasting agents were sold by specialized salesmen, rather than salesmen responsible for the entire product line. The blasting agents product manager worked closely with these salesmen and their key accounts, conducted studies of potential locations for new blasting agents facilities,[9] and worked with research and development personnel on product improvements and new applications.

The product manager for feed additives also ran "a business within a business." The Division sold its feed additives to about 50 feed millers and 15 pre-mixers. The product manager and supervisors made most sales to key accounts themselves, and spent a great deal of time developing individual accounts. According to the product manager, it was difficult to obtain sufficient attention for his products from the field sales force, since his was essentially an industrial business; i.e., sales were to manufacturers. In the future he hoped to have specialized feed additive salesmen, in much the same way as the blasting agents product manager did.

In the pesticides field, product management was primarily concerned with sales, forecasting, product policy, and development. Most of the Division's proprietary pesticides were currently in short supply, and it was necessary to decide, for example, whether to saturate a particular geographic area while neglecting others, or to attempt to market a product on a limited availability basis over a wider geographic area. Product managers in the pesticides group were also very much concerned with developing specific marketing programs, such as a series of seminars intended to introduce a new pesticide to farmers in a particular area.

As noted above, the bulk blenders product manager

---

[7] Essentially ammonium nitrate, and various blends in which ammonium nitrate was a major ingredient. These fertilizers were in the form of dry pellets or a dry powder, and were easier to apply (although more expensive) than anhydrous ammonia. In general, some soils and crops lent themselves to dry fertilizer and others to liquid fertilizer.

[8] Final authority for pricing was retained by Division top management.

[9] Small blasting agents plants, where blasting agents were blended and packaged, were located at or near the sites where the blasting agents were to be used.

had a somewhat different type of job, in that he was concerned with a distribution channel rather than a product line. He had been assigned to his present position at the time when the Division was in the process of deciding to phase out the independent bulk blender business in favor of the MACs. As a result, he had had little to do, but had realized that he would have to develop a program if he was not to find himself out of a job. He had, in fact, designed a new type of facility for use by bulk blenders (a sort of "low-overhead" MAC), and had then arranged with outside vendors to manufacture the components and actually build the new type of facility. He had then traveled extensively, selling the facility to entrepreneurs who wished to enter the fertilizer business. By early 1967 he had sold (and had had constructed) nine plants and was about to close deals on two more. He had not, however, received much support from Division management, which was "MAC-oriented," and he was in doubt concerning the future of his program.

In commenting on product management, both product Sales Directors expressed concern with regard to the proper role for the product manager as the MACs became increasingly important. Historically, the product manager had been primarily concerned with product allocation, marketing channels, and pricing. As a greater percentage of the Division's sales began to move through the MACs, the product manager's job was changing. In investing in the MACs, the Division had, in effect, committed itself to supplying them with the products they needed to serve their markets.

One product Sales Director suggested that product assignments might be realigned, with each product manager becoming responsible for the sale of a broader product line through a particular channel. One product manager might be responsible for *both* solid and liquid fertilizer sales through the MACs, a second for all pesticide sales through the MACs, a third for sales to distributors, and a fourth for sales to independent dealers. Blasting agents and feed additives would, however, continue to be operated as separate businesses.

Field Sales: Reporting to the Sales Director (Field Sales) were 9 District Sales Managers, who supervised a field sales force of 46 men. Ten of these salesmen were specialized in blasting agents, and the other 36 were responsible for the remainder of the Division's product line. Each salesman was responsible for an assigned geographic territory. The salesmen were compensated by straight salaries and were not paid commissions.

The selling job varied considerably from one geographic area to another. In the Midwest an increasing percentage of the Division's business was handled by the MACs, which were not the responsibility of the field sales force. The field sales force was responsible for calling on pesticide distributors, feed millers, and independent dealers located in areas not served by the MACs. In the South much of the Division's fertilizer business was still conducted through independent dealers, with whom the salesmen spent a great deal of time. In the East there was little fertilizer business, and the salesmen spent most of their time selling pesticides to independent distributors and feed additives to industrial accounts.

There was a considerable amount of competition among the product managers for the time of the field sales force. As one of the product managers for fertilizers explained:

There's not much glory or excitement in selling fertilizers. The challenge is in selling pesticides and feed additives, where a great deal of technical expertise is required. About all I can expect is that the salesman will ask for a fertilizer order at some point in his selling presentation to a dealer.

Big accounts are a different matter. Generally, the District Sales Managers handle these accounts themselves, or we will visit them ourselves. It is important that the salesmen keep in touch with these accounts, to see that they get proper service, but they do not do the real selling.

The feed additives product manager was particularly concerned about lack of support by the field sales force. At one point he had asked the salesmen to take a survey of the leading feed mills, receiving a premium for every ten questionnaires returned. According to this product manager, the real purpose of the survey had been to motivate the salesmen to become familiar with key industrial accounts, not to gather information.

In two districts an experiment in field organization was under way in early 1967. In these districts a single district manager had been placed over both the field sales force and the MACs. This organizational experiment was intended to facilitate the Division's newest distribution strategy, which was to fill in the area between MACs with independent dealers. According to sales management, the proposed organization would avoid overlapping sales efforts between MAC managers and the field sales force.

The managers in the experimental districts continued to report to the Sales Director (Field Sales), who, in turn, reported to both the Director of Marketing and the Director, Monsanto Agricultural Centers, since the latter was responsible for the MAC business now under his direction. According to Division executives, this organizational arrangement was clearly temporary, and would have to be modified if the experiment was to be implemented over a broader geographic area. Moreover, some provision would have to be made for the blasting agents and feed additives businesses, "which would be lost in a retail-oriented field organization."

Monsanto Agricultural Centers

In 1963 the Division had established a separate department to build and operate the new MAC business. While this function might have been performed by personnel in the Marketing Department, management believed that the new business required concentrated management attention if it was really to get off the ground. The MAC Department was headed by a Department Director, who was on the same organizational level as the Director of Wholesale Marketing.

During the first three years of the MAC program the new business had grown at a rapid rate:

Year	Number of MACs	Sales Index
1964	35	100
1965	88	400
1966	118	900
1967	150	—

Profits, however, had been far from satisfactory. The Division earned a profit on products transferred to the MACs (at market prices), but most MACs were not yet doing sufficient business to break even at retail. Individual MACs increased their sales rapidly from season to season, however, and most had been able to break even by their third year of operations.

Each MAC was managed by a Monsanto employee, known as a branch manager. These branch managers were generally recruited in the local community, and were the only non-hourly personnel on a MAC's payroll. In addition to the branch manager, a MAC's employee complement included a plant operator, a bookkeeper, and temporary truck drivers and laborers as required. The branch manager generally did most of the selling himself and frequently made deliveries as well.

Branch managers were paid a base salary, ranging from $600 to $800 a month. In addition, they were paid an annual bonus based on operating profits before taxes but after a monthly charge of one-fourth of 1% on average accounts receivable and a 6% annual charge on investment in plant and equipment. There was no charge on investment in inventories. No bonus was paid on the first $5,000 in annual profits. The bonus increased on a sliding scale from 10% to 30% on profits above that amount.

Products were sold to the MACs at a bookkeeping price determined by Division management for each product at a level related to prices to independent dealers. There had been a number of problems in this area because it was often difficult to determine the bookkeeping price. Retail prices were established by the MAC regional managers, on the basis of recommendations from the MAC area supervisors and branch managers.

Five to eight branch managers reported to each MAC area supervisor. The area managers in turn reported to four MAC regional managers. The regional managers, who were headquartered at the Division headquarters in St. Louis, reported to the MAC Director.

In March 1967 the MAC Director commented on his organization as follows:

Our Department was set up to give the MACs an identity of their own. While this concept made a lot of sense, we have certainly had our share of problems.

At first, the Wholesale Marketing Department didn't know what to make of us. We had a lot of conflicts particularly in the area of product supply. It's not just a question of who gets the product allotments; it's also a question of who gets the box cars to move the products. This is one of the reasons why we established a planning and logistics function over in the Administration Department, which is neutral. In many areas we are taking business away from the wholesale salesmen. While the dollars (and more of them) go into the same pot, the wholesale salesman — somehow — just doesn't see it as his pot.

Our real problem comes from the simple fact that our business is really different. No one else in the company thinks the way we do. The company is used to selling to big national companies, not to Joe Smith, farmer.

The engineers, for example, just won't put their best people to work on our plants. They like to build multimillion dollar facilities, not a whole lot of small plants. But the cost of a MAC plant times 150 is an awful lot of dollars.

We have a similar problem with accounting. It took us a full year to get them to let us put "Thank You" on the bottom of our invoices. We just aren't a retail company — yet!

We have problems that no one in this Company even heard of. In one town we found that our plant operator was the town drunk. So we fired him. But it turned out that he was a "good drunk," very popular with the townsfolk. We still haven't got our business back in that town.

Or take liquid ammonia spreaders. Most spreaders have five rows, but one of our plant managers found a manufacturer who made seven-row spreaders. He bought two and hitched one to his truck and one to a friend's truck and drove around town after church one Sunday. By one o'clock he had a line of prospective customers outside his plant. Which was fine. But it turned out that the seven-row spreader was an inch wider than the gates in that part of the country.

The point I am making is that we really are different. Having a separate organization certainly creates problems, but it is the only way until the rest of the Division gets to be retail-oriented. Eventually, we'll have to pull the whole thing back together. Our current experiment in two districts may be a step in the right direction.

International Sales

In 1966 Monsanto's international sales accounted for slightly more than 20% of the company's total revenue. The company operated manufacturing facilities in a great many foreign countries and did a great deal of export business as well. Historically, the Agricultural Division had been less active internationally than the company as a whole. Proprietary pesticides were exported in considerable quantities, but fertilizers were exported only as a last resort. By 1966 three small insecticide blending plants had been established in Central America.

In September 1964 corporate management had announced that the company's product divisions would henceforth have full responsibility for world-wide profits on their respective product lines. Prior to this time products had been sold to the International Division, which had operated the company's foreign manufacturing facilities and had earned a margin on export sales. To a greater or lesser extent the product divisions had always provided counsel and technical support to the International Division, but the new corporate directive was widely interpreted as a method of forcing the product divisions to pay greater attention to non-U.S. business.

The product divisions responded to the corporate directive in a variety of ways. Some divisions were content to allow the International Division to retain responsibility for sales, for example. Other divisions insisted on having greater authority over activities that would influence their measured performance. The Agricultural Division fell into the latter category; as one executive explained, "If we're going to be responsible for world-wide profits, you can be darn sure that we're not going to rely on someone else to make them for us."

The International Division was organized in three geographic areas: Europe and Africa, Asia-Pacific, and Western Hemisphere. Each area was headed by an Area Manager, who reported to the General Manager of the International Division. Reporting to each Area Manager were functional directors of Marketing and Manufacturing.

Between September 1964 and January 1967 the Agricultural Division arranged for experienced marketing personnel in the Division to be appointed Area Agricultural Marketing Managers, reporting to the International Division's Area Marketing Directors. The International Division management had been happy to go along with this move, since it increased the Division's product competence in the field.

Then, in January 1967, the Agricultural Division's most experienced product Sales Director was appointed Sales Director (International). According to Agricultural Division executives, the Area Agricultural Marketing Managers would now take their direction (especially concerning pricing and product policy) from him, although they would continue to report administratively to the International Division's Area Marketing Directors. In March 1967 the nature of the relationship between the International Division and the Agricultural Division had still not been fully worked out, particularly with regard to the reporting relationships of the Area Agricultural Marketing Managers.

Within the Agricultural Division, there were still a number of unresolved problems as well. The product managers had been given responsibility for world-wide pricing and so, in effect, had the Sales Director (International). In March 1967 it was still not clear whether he would make pricing decisions (keeping the product managers informed) or whether the product managers would make pricing decisions (keeping him informed).

Product Development

Product development was the shared responsibility of the Commercial Development Department and the Research and Development Department. The Research and Development Department received an annual budget, which it allocated among projects. Several times each year, members of the two departments met to discuss new ideas and agree on priorities. Some ideas came from the Commercial Development Department;

others from research personnel. According to the Director of Research and Development, ideas rarely came from the Marketing Department, although Marketing personnel were making more suggestions as the Division moved closer to the consumer.

In addition to defining product needs, the Commercial Development Department was responsible for establishing requirements for new products (through market studies, discussions with agronomists, etc.), for field-testing new products developed by the Research and Development Department and for assisting marketing in the first two years of commercial sales. It was also responsible for the very time-consuming process of obtaining government approval for new products. As a new product approached commercial introduction, the Commercial Development Department prepared product brochures, technical manuals, and pricing recommendations in collaboration with the product manager responsible for the product.

Most commercial product development activity was currently concerned with proprietary pesticides. The Division General Manager approved the allocation of the research budget to the four product groups ("to assure a balance between the Division's strategy and R&D expenditures"), but he was not primarily concerned with individual projects. As the Director of Research and Development explained:

The General Manager and Marketing want to be sure that we're working in enough areas to hit at least a few by chance. But it's up to me how I spend the money! We generally work on eight or nine big projects and a number of small ones. We have to resist pressures from Marketing and Commercial Development, in order not to five-and-ten-cents ourselves to death.

Pricing

Pricing was the responsibility of the product management organization. Each product supervisor recommended prices for his products to his product manager, who, in turn, made a recommendation to his Sales Director. On major products the approval of the General Manager or Assistant General Manager was required for all price changes.

One executive commented as follows concerning pricing:

In theory, the product manager is responsible for pricing. This is a myth. If you think the product managers at [a major auto company] set prices, you are out of your mind. You can be sure that [the president of the auto company] sets every price in the line. It's the same way here.

Except for a few minor products (where nobody cares anyway!), pricing is a top management function!

Scheduling

Scheduling was the responsibility of the Planning and Operations group in the Administration Department. The manager of the group explained his function as follows:

We are the traffic cops. We determine which products we *should* make, who *should* get the product, and how to get it there. While the actual decisions are made by the product managers, we tell them what their decisions *ought* to be — from a strictly economic point of view.

Our function could be in the Marketing Department or in the Manufacturing Department. It is better where it is, because of our neutrality. A marketing man has one objective — to sell. Some are more profit-conscious than others, but this is not necessarily a good thing. If he worries too much about profits, a marketing man may be too cautious.

We have one, and only one, concern: Where can we make the most money? We are doing our job right when most people are dissatisfied with what we are doing.

On plant foods, the product managers develop sales plans on a day-to-day basis. We look at the sales requirements and the plant capacities, and compute a nitrogen balance. If there is not enough product to go around, the product group must decide which product it wants to make. But we tell them which product mix will make Monsanto the most money.

Similar decisions must be made with regard to customers. Some customers (because of location and quantities taken) are simply more profitable than others. We run the numbers and make a ranking, but it's up to the product group to decide. Some customers will still be around next year; others will not.

An awful lot of planning goes into this process. During the off-season, we and the product managers work out detailed plans as to who will get what under which circumstances. But we look at the weather when we get up each morning. It's just that kind of business.

We have a computer model which we use in our basic planning and to evaluate our performance after the fact. During the peak season, the computer is not much use. You can't get data into the computer fast enough.

But our people are good — and experienced. If one of our plans is going to fall behind schedule today, we know it almost as quickly as the plant manager does. We can then shift schedules — to make sure that the customer who needs it first gets it first.

The MACs have a man assigned here who tells my men which MACs to ship to. He also buys products for the MACs from outside sources. We generally give the MACs service, but we will let their inventories run down if it's in the Company's best interest.

Planning and Budgeting

The product management organization was responsible for preparing five-year sales forecasts for each product manufactured by the Division. These forecasts were largely based on industry trends, for example, expectations concerning acreage under cultivation and industry manufacturing capacity. The forecasts were used primarily for capital budgeting purposes and, according to several executives, tended to be vague in the later years.

Annual plans were a different matter. The product managers forecast sales on a monthly basis, updating their forecasts at least once a month. During the peak season, these plans were divided into shorter time periods and were updated weekly or, in many cases, daily.

The Division distinguished beween a "forecast" and a "budget." A "forecast" in effect answered the question, "How much can you sell if *everything* goes right?" A "budget," on the other hand, answered the question, "How much do you actually expect to sell?" Both a forecast and a budget were prepared for each product for the current (or next) year. In general, the "forecast" was used to plan production, and the "budget" was used to establish profit targets, cash budgets, and the like.

The planning process for the following year began in July or August (after the peak season). Each product supervisor estimated sales for his products to each major account. Each field salesman did the same thing. According to Division executives, the product supervisors knew some accounts better than the field salesmen did, and vice versa. During this period the MAC branch managers also estimated their sales.

Then, generally in late August, the District Sales Managers and Product Managers came together for a three-day meeting. During this meeting, according to one executive, "We fight it out, account by account, product by product. By the end of the meeting a few heads may be bloody, but we have agreement — in at leats 99% of the cases."

The forecast and budget were then consolidated with the MAC forecast and budget, and submitted to Divisional management for approval. When approved, the consolidated forecast and budget were sent back out to the Districts, where they were distributed to individual salesmen. The sum of the budgets of the individual salesmen did not necessarily agree with the total Division budget. If an individual salesman had forecast sales higher than finally agreed upon, he was generally encouraged to "shoot for the higher target."

The Division budget, once established, remained the budget for the year. Although changes in product and customer mix were made on a day-to-day basis during the peak season, these changes did not affect the Division's profit and revenue targets. The targets were established on the basis of detailed analysis and plans; the actual achievement of the targets could deviate markedly from the original plans.

Exhibit 1. Organization Chart of the Division, November 1966

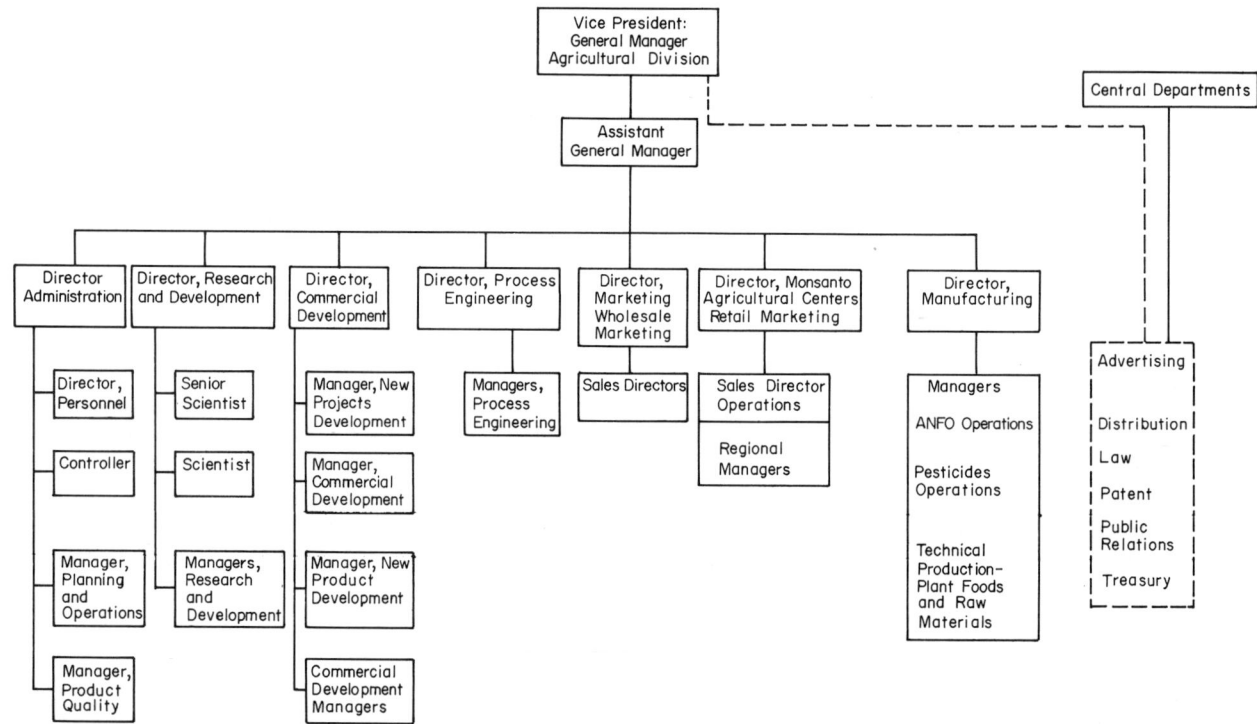

COMMENTARY

Between the 1950s and 1966 Monsanto's strategy for selling to the agricultural market changed radically. In the 1950s Monsanto sold chemicals to manufacturers of fertilizers, pesticides, and other agricultural products in much the same way that it sold rubber chemicals to tire manufacturers. During this period Monsanto was not in the agricultural products business to any greater extent than it was, for example, in the tire business. For the two divisions involved (Organic and Inorganic), the agricultural market was essentially another industrial market.

During the late 1950s, however, many of Monsanto's major customers for agricultural products began to manufacture their own raw materials or expand their production capacities. As a result, Monsanto management concluded that Monsanto would have to integrate forward toward the ultimate consumers of its products if it was not to lose its share of the agricultural products market.

The Agricultural Division was thus established in response to changing market conditions. Management believed that Monsanto would have to develop a new marketing strategy — oriented toward the consumer rather than other manufacturers — if it was to continue to play a major role in the agricultural products market. A new Division was established to develop and carry out this strategy because of management's belief that a consumer-oriented marketing strategy would be incompatible with the basic missions of the Organic and Inorganic Chemicals Divisions, both of which sold primarily to other manufacturers.

The Agricultural Division case thus provides us with an excellent example of how a change in a company's environment leads to a change in its marketing strategy; and how the new marketing strategy, in turn, leads to a change in organizational structure. In establishing the Agricultural Division, Monsanto management created a new organizational framework within which to develop and implement a new marketing strategy.

Agricultural Division Organization

In some respects, the organization of the Agricultural Division was similar to that of the Organic Chemicals Division. Both Divisions had pyramidal product/market program structures, for example, and separate Commercial Development Departments. There were, however, a number of important differences between the organizations of the two Divisions. These differences reflect the distinctive characteristics of the agricultural market and the marketing strategy that had been developed by the Agricultural Division.

The most readily apparent difference between the two Divisions was the presence, in the Agricultural Division, of separate wholesale and retail (MAC) program organizations. Unlike the Organic Division, the Agricultural Division had structured its program organization at the highest level on the basis of distribution channels, rather than products.

It is not difficult to understand why the program organization was structured in this way. As the MAC program manager explained, the processes through which the MAC business was carried out were fundamentally different from those used for the Division's other programs. While having a separate MAC program organization created some problems of coordination (primarily in product supply and market coverage), these problems were judged to be less important than those which would arise from trying to run a retail business through a wholesale-oriented program organization.

The second major difference between the two divisions was the tendency in the Agricultural Division to attach program-specialized field sales units to the program management organizations. The MAC and blasting agents program organizations each had their own sales resources, and the feed additives program was seeking to have its own sales organization as well. In all three cases, program managements believed that their programs required attached specialized field sales resources if they were not to receive short shrift from an unspecialized field sales organization. Because of the wide variations in the *types* of customers with which it dealt (large manufacturers; small mixers and blenders; mines and quarries; individual farmers), the Agricultural Division apparently found it impractical to operate through a common sales resource.

The third, and perhaps most important, difference in the organizations of the two divisions was that the Agricultural Division had a centralized unit, the Planning and Operations Group, which was responsible for recommending what the Division's manufacturing plants would produce, and which markets (and customers) would receive products during periods of short supply. Having a strong function of this kind was essential in an industry characterized by wide fluctuations in demand from one market to another, and from one geographic area to another, especially since many of the Division's markets required the same products (or raw materials). As the Manager of the Group explained:

We are the traffic cops. We determine which products we *should* make, who *should* get the product, and how to get it there. . . . Some customers (because of location and quantities taken) are simply more profitable than others. We run the numbers and make a ranking, but it's up to the product group to decide. Some customers will still be around next year; others will not.

In other words, the independent Planning and Operations Group was able to optimize product allocations to markets and customers on the basis of short-term profit considerations. It was not, however, able to take into account other important marketing considerations, such as how a customer would react if his order was not filled, or how competition might respond if Monsanto decided to neglect a particular market segment. For this reason, the Group's conclusions took the form of recommendations, which could be modified by the product-market program management units. Presumably, the program managers would be able to use their market "feel" in making the final decisions, but would do so in full awareness of the short-term economics of the situation.

This procedure may be viewed as a compromise necessitated by the organizational structure of the Division. Division management apparently believed that the scheduling function should be independent of the various programs and resources, in order to assure its objectivity and neutrality in suggesting allocations of a limited supply of products to market segments with competing demands. In giving the scheduling function an independent organizational position, however, there was some risk that it would carry out its function in a vacuum, without adequate analysis of nonquantifiable marketing considerations. The product-market program managers were thus given final decision authority, acting, in effect, as a market-oriented fail-safe mechanism.

It is interesting to note that all three of these distinctive organizational features of Monsanto's Agricultural Division were also present in Mobil's North American Division. The Agricultural Division's Planning and Operations unit was very similar to Mobil's Supply, Distribution, and Traffic Department; its wholesale and MAC program organizations were similar to Mobil's Commercial and Resale Classes of Trade; its program-attached field sales resources were similar to those in certain Mobil programs (e.g., Marine; Special Products).

These similarities would seem to stem directly from the fact that the environments and marketing strategies of the two businesses also had a great deal in common. The Agricultural Division and Mobil each had product lines including both undifferentiated commodities and differentiated proprietary products; each sold to markets characterized by greatly fluctuating demand patterns; each had at least some freedom to shift production capacity from one product form to another; and each had a strong commitment to supply a retail distribution system in which it had a large investment.

By 1966 the Agricultural Division had embarked on a marketing strategy more similar to that of Mobil than to that of the Organic Chemicals Division. It is understandable, therefore, that its organizational structure had also come to resemble Mobil's more closely than it did that of the Monsanto divisions from which it had been spun off.

Monsanto Company: International Division

Monsanto Chemical Company made its first foreign investment in 1920 when it purchased a half interest in the Graesser Chemical Company in Ruabon, Wales. Monsanto acquired the remaining half interest in Graesser in 1928 and renamed the company Monsanto Chemicals Ltd. (MCL). In 1948 shares amounting to a third interest in MCL were sold to the British public. While this move served to raise capital for the rapidly growing company, the primary reason for the sale of stock was to identify MCL as a concern partly owned by British interests, thereby helping to create a favorable local environment for its business activities.

In the meantime Monsanto Canada Ltd. (Mocan) had been formed in 1932 with other interests (later bought out by Monsanto). And in 1940 Monsanto Chemicals (Australia) Ltd. (MC(A)L) was established by merging holdings that Monsanto had obtained in 1928 in the Southern Cross Company of Australia.

Monsanto founded or acquired interests in a number of other companies abroad in the years that followed,[1] but the first three continued to be among Monsanto's most important subsidiaries. In 1967 MCL had a larger sales volume than any other overseas member company by a considerable margin. Mocan was the second largest and MC(A)L the fourth, after the Mitsubishi Monsanto Chemical Company, a 50%-owned joint venture in Japan, which was started in 1950.

Monsanto also exported to foreign markets during this period, although this business was of very modest proportions before World War II.

In 1939 a Foreign Department was formed in the company primarily for the purpose of handling all export sales. The department worked quickly to establish a world-wide network of approximately 90 agents. MCL acted as Monsanto's agent in England and assumed primary responsibility for setting up agents in Europe, the Middle East, and most Commonwealth countries. The Canadian and Australian companies served as agents in their respective countries. Export sales were made by the Monsanto Chemical Company, the Monsanto Overseas Corporation, and in many countries in the Western Hemisphere through the Monsanto Export Corporation, a Western Hemisphere trading corporation. For accounting purposes, profits on export sales were divided between the Monsanto Export Corporation and the domestic divisions. In the early 1950s, just prior to the establishment of the Overseas Division, the Foreign Department had a cadre of almost 100 people, including sales personnel and sales correspondents in St. Louis and New York, department management personnel, sales personnel in overseas assignments, product managers located in the operations divisions, and order and billing personnel.

The Overseas Division

In 1954, as part of a company-wide reorganization, the Foreign Department became the Overseas Division. Export sales grew rapidly after World War II, and the Overseas Division's organization for handling export sales grew commensurately. In addition to handling exports, the Division was given the responsibility for managing Monsanto's growing investments in overseas member companies. In the 1950–1960 decade Monsanto made investments in 19 foreign companies.

From 1954 through 1960 the marketing operation in the Overseas Division was organized primarily on an area basis (see Exhibit 1) with a Director of Sales for the Western Hemisphere and one for the Eastern Hemisphere. Each of these directors supervised an organization that was structured along product lines corresponding to the operating divisions then existing (Organic and Inorganic). The organizational arrangement for plastics sales was an exception to this pattern; there was a Director of Sales, Plastics-World-Wide.

By 1961, however, the Overseas Division's market-

---

[1] For example, in Mexico (1950) and Argentina (1954).

ing operations were organized completely by product line (see Exhibit 2), and there were Directors of Sales for Organic, Inorganic-Agricultural, and Plastics. Each Director of Sales had world-wide sales responsibility for his respective product line. But within the product-oriented groups, there were field sales representatives with sales responsibilities defined by geographic area.

Monsanto Europe

In early 1963 Monsanto Europe was created as a separate entity independent of the Overseas Division. Monsanto Europe was to act as a European headquarters operation, reporting directly to Monsanto management. According to an internal memorandum:

> Monsanto Europe will have as its principal responsibility the providing of management assistance to the parent company's interests in the European area. In addition, the new company will be responsible for the marketing in Europe of those products made by the parent company in the United States and by its wholly owned subsidiaries elsewhere....
>
> This new organization will add greater emphasis to our success and growth. Whereas the various companies in the Monsanto Europe area will retain the same status they have had all along, they will now, at whatever times they deem advisable, be able to call upon a group of specialists not far away, in Brussels....

MCL and Monsanto's large synthetic fibers operations in Europe[2] were specifically excluded from Monsanto Europe. Consequently, Monsanto now had three large organizational entities in the European area, and it was not clear how each was supposed to relate to the others, to the domestic operating divisions, and to the Overseas Division.

Emerging Problems

With the great growth of Monsanto's international business, certain basic problems emerged. For example, some member companies began competing with each other and with the domestic divisions in third-country markets. In the case of polystyrene, Monsanto manufactured this plastic in the United States, Canada, Argentina, Australia, Spain, Japan, England, France, and Mexico. Monsanto's agents in third countries were free to buy from any of these sources, and in a few cases would whipsaw one against the other on price.

Monsanto encountered difficulties, too, in dealing with large international customers. Both MCL and Monsanto's Organic Chemicals Division, for example, sold rubber chemicals to the large rubber companies, most of which operated tire factories all over the world. These sales efforts, as well as product development programs for rubber chemicals, were uncoordinated and often in conflict.

Furthermore, the development of markets abroad, according to Overseas Division executives, was impeded because the domestic divisions tended to give first priority to domestic customers in periods of short supply and to become interested in export trade primarily when supplies were ample.

Appraisal and Restructuring

In 1964 the head of the Overseas Division and his two assistant general managers made an intensive study of Monsanto's international operations and recommended significant changes to the company's board of directors. The most important proposal was that the domestic divisions be given profit responsibility for their respective product lines world-wide, and responsibility for planning and executing world-wide product strategies. A new International Division would "administer" overseas activities and would contribute foreign market expertise in formulating investment plans and market strategies. As one executive described it:

> The idea was that there would be strong area groups to monitor the political climates, to study the emerging market needs and shifting trade balances, and to supply these inputs for product division planning. Through its knowledge, the International Division would help greatly to reduce the political and economic uncertainties of doing business abroad and to anticipate political, economic, and competitive developments (in Europe, alone, we have over 800 competitors). International would also help us evaluate opportunities by country and by product line and would take the lead in bringing these opportunities to the attention of the domestic product divisions. Finally, International would look after personnel and manning and would administer the resources for our overseas operations — sales, manufacturing, and research.

On their part, the product divisions headquartered

---

[2] Monsanto's synthetic fibers business in Europe was part of its Chemstrand Division (later, Textiles Division). Chemstrand had originally been formed as a joint venture with American Viscose, and Monsanto had purchased American Viscose's 50% interest in 1960.

in St. Louis would provide "business" direction to the marketing managers abroad. They would provide technical direction and set standards for manufacturing plants, and initiate or approve any research and commercial development efforts undertaken abroad. In addition, the product divisions would direct the physical distribution of their products world-wide. Appendix A contains excerpts from a May 1964 memorandum entitled "Charter of International Division."

The International Division (ID) came into being in 1964, based on these concepts. Late in that year a new ID General Manager was appointed. He moved quickly to help the domestic divisions prepare to take on an enlarged role abroad. He also appointed two area directors, for Latin America and Asia-Pacific. These area directors were to serve as "delegates" of the ID General Manager, provide him with area information, and help him plan overall area strategies. The member companies in Latin America and the Asia-Pacific area reported formally to the ID General Manager, but in fact they received most of their immediate guidance from their area directors.

In 1965 the ID General Manager established in Europe a Chemicals and Plastics-Europe organization with the managing director of MCL as its head. He also created a Textiles-Europe organization, which would manage Monsanto's textile businesses in Europe, taking "product and market guidance" from the General Manager of the Textiles Division (formerly Chemstrand) in the United States.

In late 1964 the new head of the International Division brought personnel together from MCL and Monsanto's Organic Chemicals Division to plan a world-wide product strategy for rubber chemicals — a plan that would embrace market and customer strategy, product supply, and research and development.[3] It was hoped that this effort, called Project Nova, would set a pattern for similar planning for other product lines. In particular, similar planning was needed for

---

[3] It is of interest to note that the new ID General Manager came into this position after serving in the Organic Chemicals Division as Director of Commercial Development, then Director of Research, and then Director of Marketing. He had experienced personally from all three vantage points the world-wide conflicts in Monsanto's program for developing and marketing rubber chemicals.

He had also been instrumental in starting the concept of the Informal Business Groups in Organic Chemicals and had seen the great effect of this organizational device on product development, sales, and profits in the product lines for which IBGs had been established. Finally, he had participated in the 1964 review of Monsanto's Overseas Division and its international operations.

such widely sold high-volume products as nylon and acrylic fibers, polystyrene, polyvinyl chloride, and petroleum additives.

In early 1965 the job of the Directors of Sales was changed. They became Commercial Directors, responsible respectively for Organic, Inorganic-Agricultural, and Plastics products. Their scope of activities broadened. These managers became responsible for searching out new markets for their products, initiating proposals for plant expansion abroad,[4] and locating new investment opportunities. A Project Evaluation group at the Overseas Division headquarters made studies of these proposals, estimated investment and manufacturing costs, projected sales volume, prepared business plans, calculated profits and return on investment, and prepared appropriation requests for approval by Monsanto's board of directors.

In late 1965 the new ID General Manager moved to Brussels and set up his offices there, with staff groups for legal, financial, control, public relations, and purchasing. Personnel and office services staff functions were located in London. In St. Louis there were also staff offices concerned with International Division control, personnel, and information and planning functions.

At the same time Monsanto's management acted to restructure its burgeoning investments abroad. Twenty-four new foreign investments had been made between 1960 and 1965. In each country in which Monsanto had an affiliated company, the affiliate became both a supply point and an ID district office. Monsanto also negotiated the termination of its agency agreements in many European countries. Key personnel from these agencies were often kept on as sales managers and sales representatives in the new district offices.

With this restructuring, Monsanto had seven "member company" operating units abroad, each one having profit responsibility:

Chemicals & Plastics-Europe (which included Mofran, Monsanto Europe headquartered in Belgium, and MCL)
Textiles-Europe
Mocan (in Canada)
MMSA (in Mexico)
MARG (in Argentina)
MC(A)L (in Australia)
Central America (with operations in El Salvador, Guatemala, and Nicaragua)

As profit centers, these operating units purchased chemicals from the Monsanto Company at the com-

---

[4] Member companies also initiated proposals for plant expansion during this period.

petitive prices prevailing in the receiving country. In most cases, the member company also acted as an agent for Monsanto products, receiving a commission sufficient to cover selling costs and to provide a profit on which it could pay taxes.

The Evolving Organization — Structure and Interfaces

In late 1966 the ID organization was still evolving and ID executives were working to define and structure the relationships between this division and the product divisions. During 1966 the Chemicals and Plastics-Europe organization had been perhaps more fully articulated along the new lines than other ID organizational units (see Exhibit 3). Reporting to a Director, C&P-Europe, were a Marketing Director, a Planning and Control Director, two Executive Group Directors, two Manufacturing Directors, and the heads of the European member companies. The Marketing Director's organization included five Directors of Sales (Organic Chemicals, Inorganic Chemicals, Polymers, Hydrocarbons & Plastic Products, Agricultural) and a Director of Field Sales. The Directors of Sales in turn supervised the work of three to five Marketing Managers — one for each major product line. The Director of Field Sales had eight district offices.

The interface between C&P-Europe and the domestic operations divisions was to take place on three levels, as shown in the following diagram (using the Organic Division as an example):

C&P-Europe		*Organic Division*
Executive Group Director (Chemicals)	↔	Product Directors[5]
Area Director of Sales-Organic Chemicals	↔	Director of Marketing
Marketing Manager, Plasticizers	↔	Product Manager-Plasticizers (i.e., Market/Product Group Manager)

Thus, the Marketing Manager-Plasticizers in Europe took "business direction" from the Product Manager-Plasticizers in the Organic Chemicals Division. He then gave "business direction" to plasticizer sales representatives in the European district offices. Management levels above the field sales representatives in C&P-Europe consulted with their counterparts in the product divisions on all personnel appointments, promotions, and salary increases. In addition, the Marketing Managers worked directly with their counterparts (the Market/Product Group Managers in the case of Organic Chemicals) to formulate area customer and product strategies as part of the world-wide strategy plans.

The two Executive Group Directors in the European C&P organization were to "act as extensions" in Europe of the comparable operating division product directors. In the planning phase, they would contribute all European information that could affect world-wide product line profitability including raw material costs, manufacturing costs, and selling prices. In the execution phases, they were responsible for monitoring all European department activity to see that objectives and profit goals were achieved for their respective product lines, and were responsible for initiating appropriate remedial action through European line departments.

Customer orders originating in Europe were transmitted directly to London or Brussels and from there were sent to plants and warehouses in Europe, the United States, or elsewhere in accordance with overall supply plans developed by the production planning groups in the product divisions. When deviations from anticipated order or production patterns created supply problems, the problems were to be resolved by the product division whose products were involved.

Similarly, a Director of Research-Europe would manage all laboratory facilities and the administration of laboratory personnel, but the directors of research of the operating divisions would establish overall technical administrative policy for their respective product lines and would approve European research budgets and their objectives. In the same fashion, the directors of commercial development in each operating division related directly to the Commercial Development Director-Europe. The general direction of commercial development projects would come from the product divisions, and in both Research and Commercial Development the operating divisions would contribute guidance and assistance out of their experience.

In November 1966 a new General Manager-International Division was appointed, and he gave further thrust to the development of the ID organization. In the Latin American area and Asia-Pacific, marketing organizations similar to that of C&P-Europe were established during 1967, when an Area Marketing Director was appointed for each area (see Exhibit 4).

Later, in 1967, the Area Director-Latin America was given line responsibility for all operations in that area. In the future, the Area Marketing Director and the general managers of the member companies in Latin America would report directly to him. Simultaneously, the Mocan organization in Canada was

---
[5] See Monsanto Company: Organic Chemicals Division, pp. 336–337.

transformed into an area organization, and its Managing Director was appointed Area Director-Canada.

As the structure emerged and organizational roles were defined, there was considerable discussion concerning what would happen to one of the roles performed by the former Commercial Directors. The four Commercial Directors, who had been both product and internationally oriented, had exercised considerable initiative in spearheading market development projects and new product development projects, and had taken a leading role in investigating certain corporate acquisitions and new business ventures overseas. Some ID executives thought a similar function should be provided for in the newly reorganized International Division. ID managers, they contended, would be sensitive to new opportunities, to the need for adjusting product strategies, and for devising new packaging and supply tactics to capture new customers. The product departments headquartered in St. Louis might not be easily persuaded to capitalize in a timely fashion on these opportunities either because they did not fit in with domestic business patterns, or because they were relatively small compared to domestic opportunities, or because the domestic division was fully occupied simply with gaining a grasp of international operations. As one ID executive stated the case:

Lots of deals are being made in my area. How do we bring these to the attention of the operating divisions? We're the trigger, but how many shots do we have to fire? How far can we go if we have to pull the operating divisions kicking and screaming into a new opportunity? We need strong commercial development groups that can take the initiative.

Another ID manager expressed the concern that as world-wide *product* strategies were developed the need for maintaining strong *country* organization should be an important consideration. He noted, for example, that in one country a significant portion of its volume was made up of sales of a chemical imported from one of the operating divisions. There were indications that the government in that country was about to close the border to the imported chemical in an effort to stimulate local manufacture of this product. Because the Monsanto operating division had not yet made plans for local manufacture, the Monsanto organization in that country was in danger of suffering a sharp drop in its sales and profits. This manager noted: "What's best for the product strategy is not always best for Monsanto in each country. Part of ID's responsibility is to see that the country organizations remain strong as product strategies are developed and implemented."

A Revised Charter for the International Division

In early 1967 the new General Manager of the International Division prepared a new international policy statement (Appendix B), which took account of Monsanto's three years of experience in working under the 1964 ID charter. He had played a key role in formulating and supporting the new organizational approach. In commenting on major differences between the 1964 and 1967 documents, the new General Manager noted first that ID would no longer have responsibility for providing "the initiative and coordination" for world-wide product strategies; this responsibility would reside with the operating divisions. In the past, in "initiating" product strategies ID had, as a practical matter, often become actively involved in product strategy formulation, while the operating divisions took a somewhat passive role. Under the 1967 charter the operating divisions were called on to "prepare market and customer strategies using data, information, and area market strategies provided by the International Division for the ex-U.S. portions." For its part, ID was responsible for developing "total business plans and profit goals for each member company based on the product plans established by the operating divisions."

The new policy statement clearly placed responsibility on the operating divisions for initiating and making capital investments abroad. On the other hand, the statement explicitly charged ID with controlling organization structures and manpower outside the United States and with personnel development.

The 1967 policy statement also called on ID to safeguard the investment in member companies abroad. In practice, then, ID would be concerned that operating division product strategies were such that the viability of the member companies would not be jeopardized and that the profitability of individual investments in countries abroad would be watched carefully and not lost sight of as increasing attention was focused on world-wide product strategies.

The new General Manager believed that ID now had to work to make sure that: (1) the viability of investments in every country was maintained; (2) the marketing effort abroad was put where the greatest market opportunities existed; and (3) the operating divisions moved up quickly and effectively to their responsibilities for developing world-wide product strategies.

Exhibit 1. Organization of Monsanto Overseas Division, April 1960

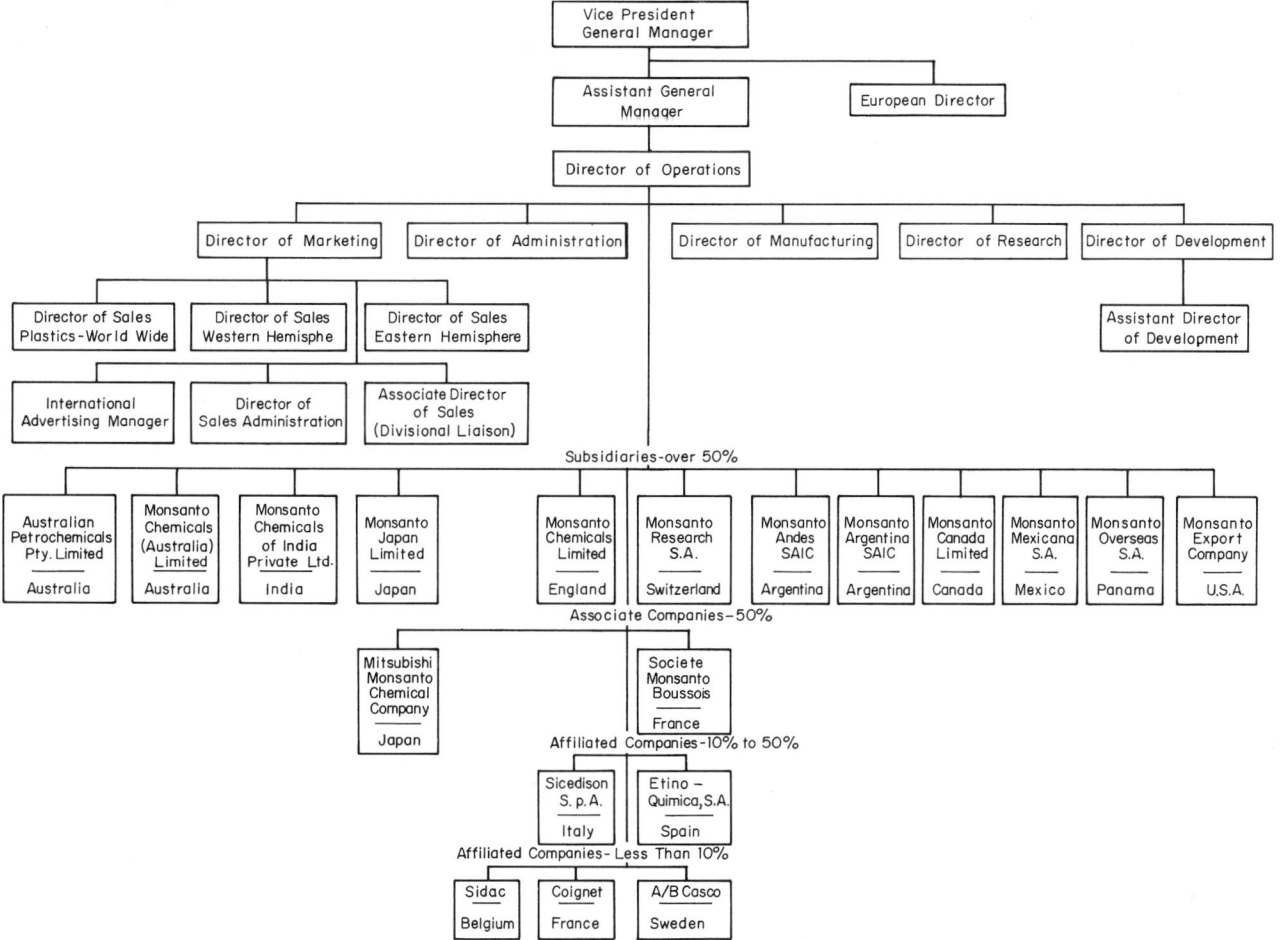

Exhibit 2. Organization of the Monsanto Overseas Division, April 1962

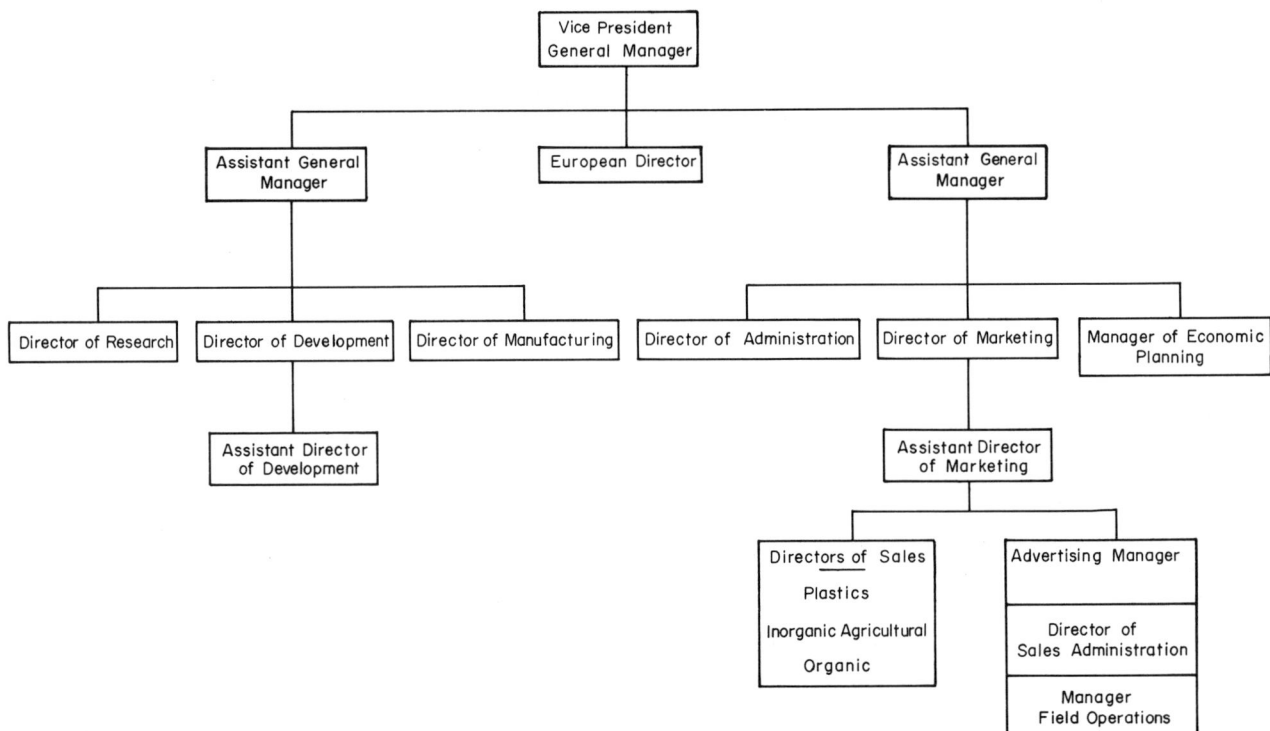

Exhibit 3. Organization for Chemicals and Plastics — Europe, May 1967

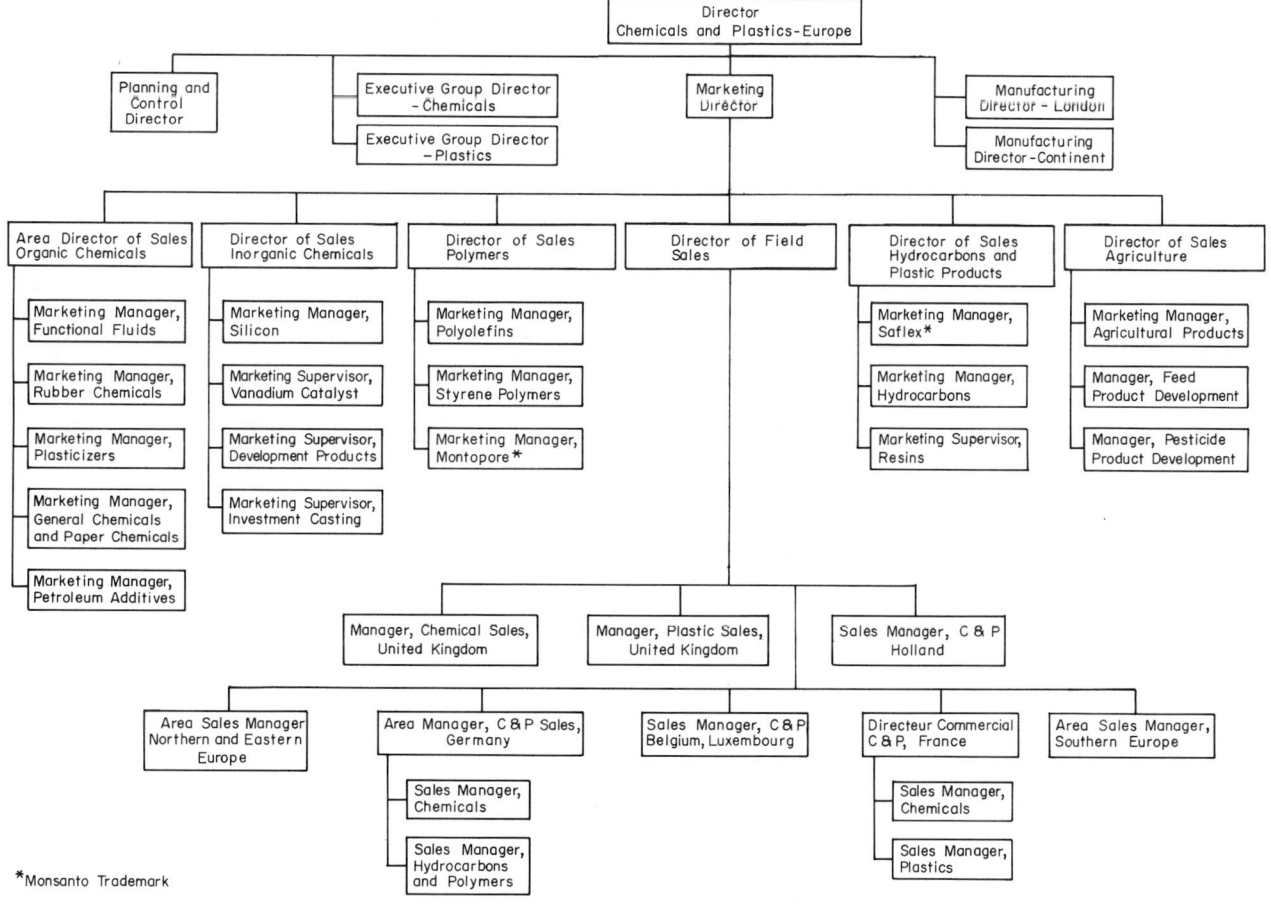

Exhibit 4. Organization for Latin America and Asia — Pacific, May 1967

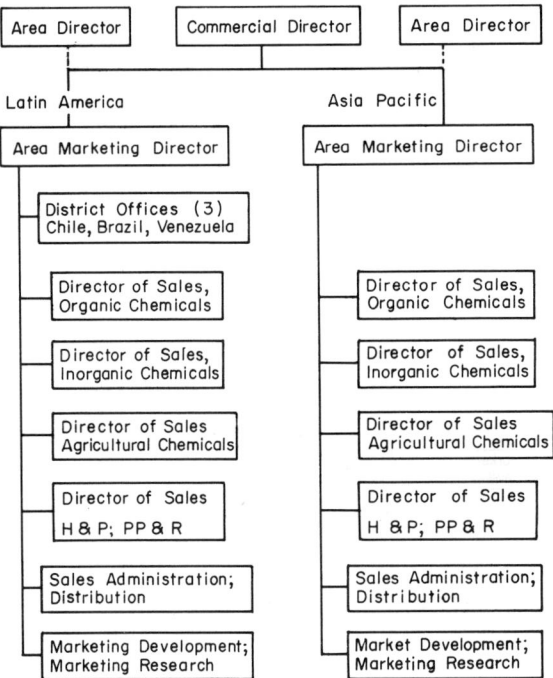

Appendix A

Excerpts from Charter of Division, Effective May 26, 1964

The International Division, as a delegate of the President, is a business management group knowledgeable and sensitive to rapid changes in world areas. Additionally, it has broad responsibilities for foreign investments — excluding Monsanto Europe — and coordination of world markets and services. The Division will coordinate Monsanto's interests world-wide in order that the company can and will act decisively, consistently, and rapidly to enhance its business performance in world markets.

On a Corporate Basis:

The President places with the International Division:

1. A responsibility to provide the initiative and the coordination for centrally controlled strategies which describe the interacting relationships among:
   (a) common products manufactured or sold in world markets,
   (b) key international customers,
   (c) selected world markets.
   In order to carry out this responsibility, the Division through means of intense world commercial and political intelligence assembles from reliable sources the bases to provide initiative and coordination essential for the development of such interacting world-wide strategies.
2. A responsibility for collecting, correlating, and disseminating broad knowledge of *all* Monsanto activities outside the U.S. to assure that no unilateral action is taken which would adversely affect the corporate interests.
3. A responsibility for management of subsidiaries and associates and a safeguarding responsibility for Monsanto investment in affiliates.
4. A responsibility for export marketing of products from U.S. and European (ME) manufacturing plants.
5. A responsibility for searching out and implementing new enterprises based on Monsanto products/services, or on new and unrelated know-how.

* * * * *

PURPOSE:

To establish the means for implementation of Monsanto policy regarding world-wide product, market, and customer strategies. This procedure sets forth the authority and responsibility for the development of such strategies and establishes the general sequential steps required in their development.

PROCEDURE:

Joint contributions by the operating divisions, International Division, Monsanto Europe and foreign subsidiaries are required for maximization of world-wide opportunities. Operating divisions furnish technical and business know-how to create and update the strategies. International Division, by delegation from the President, carries responsibility to provide initiative and coordination essential for development of world-wide strategies for interaction of markets, products and customers.

A. *World-wide Total Product Strategy* is the long term product business plan, with alternatives, set to achieve a pre-set goal or objective based on the best available knowledge within Monsanto. World-wide product strategy governs activity related to a product manufactured and/or marketed in the United States and at least one other country.

Development of world-wide total Product Strategy is the responsibility of the operating Division General Manager assigned that product. Work is accomplished through an ad hoc informal business group with the chairman appointed by the operating division general manager. Other members of the ad hoc group include selected participants from the concerned Division together with participants from International Division, Monsanto Europe, and other subsidiaries as required. Informal business group participants are selected by the chairman with the approval of the concerned organizational units. Members selected for participation must have the experience and authority within their respective organizations to make decisions and commitments. The ad hoc informal business group:

1. Analyzes present Corporate position, world-wide, on profitability, sales volume, competition, discrete markets, technical and economic trends.
2. Determines what forces are, or will be, at work to change the position of the product in world markets it serves — together with an idea of their magnitude.
3. Assesses key characteristic of the product (or service) which, if improved, will most dramatically improve sales and profits; determines capabilities of doing same.
4. Works out a statement of general strategy, together with alternates, and including offensive and defensive strategy of pricing.

Appendix A (continued)

5. Makes decisions on specific actions needed to achieve goals.
6. Lays out timetable of sequence of actions — who, what, when.
7. Works out a follow-up system to measure improved sales and profits.

B. *International Market Strategy* is the long-term plan of action, with alternatives, which covers a market or a sub-market important to the company now and/or in the future. International market strategy is a base for both world-wide total product strategy and (see C below) customer strategy serving to ensure understanding and cohesive action on the part of all pertinent groups in the Company as they discharge their respective responsibilities.

Development of international Market Strategy is the responsibility of the operating Division General Manager assigned that market. Work is carried out through an ad hoc informal business group with the chairman appointed by the operating Division General Manager. Other members include selected participants from the concerned Division together with participants from International Division, Monsanto Europe, other subsidiaries, where required, and appropriate Corporate staff groups. Informal business group participants are selected by the chairman with the approval of the concerned organizational units.

The ad hoc informal business group:

1. Classifies (present) business in markets or market segments in such a way that it can be seen how direction of effort toward individual segments might result in more business than present gross product group treatment.
2. Analyzes total Company's present posture in serving the market, world-wide.
3. Assesses prime characteristics of each major segment of the market, world-wide.
4. Determines what forces are, or will be, at work to change the character of the market — and determines their direction and size.
5. Draws objective conclusions to define total Company's future posture to serve the market and the consequences of not achieving such posture.
6. Defines what kinds of information needed beyond that presently available anywhere (technical, commercial, political, customer, product) for possible assistance in redirecting total Company effort in serving the market.
7. Describes a statement of General Strategy, with alternatives of Monsanto action and competitor reaction.
8. Defines necessary integrated, total Company effort which, on balance, will achieve desired future posture predicted by the General Strategy.
9. Estimates total cost of redirected effort and compares with expected profit gains long term.

C. *International Customer Strategy* is the long-term overall marketing plan for United States-based customer companies having their own international organizations, transnational companies, and very large special distributors and general franchise agents. Customer Strategy is to achieve customer perception of a consistent corporate Monsanto approach to serve his needs world-wide.

In addition, customer strategy ensures and enforces better coordination, consistency, and speed of reaction for changes in prices or products and thereby provides distinct competitive advantages.

The Marketing Director of the operating Division, or his delegate, handling most of a given customer's business serves as chairman of an ad hoc business group with other Marketing Directors from concerned Divisions, including International Division, Monsanto Europe and subsidiaries, as necessary, who serve the same customer, as participants in the group.

* * * * *

RESPONSIBILITIES:

A. *Operating Divisions*
 1. Assume overall responsibility for development of product strategy; provide input business and technical information necessary such as emerging technology, productive capacity data, competitive technology position, etc.
 2. Assume overall responsibility for development of market strategy; provide input business information such as definition of the market itself, competitive pricing data, the market needs, competitive market position, scope and quality of technical marketing services, percentages of market penetration; and other forces at work.
 3. Provide technical support to ensure implementation of strategy by concerned overseas subsidiaries.
 4. Assume leadership for development of customer strategy; provide input information on customer needs and plans as known, customer's requirements for technical service, customer's international activities and markets, etc.
 5. Execute portions of overall strategy to be carried out by their respective divisions.

B. *International Division*
 1. Determines need for new or modified world-wide market, product, and customer strategies.
 2. Draws together and correlates market, product and customer strategies, as developed, to ensure compatibility among all company segments and interrelation to one another in describing the changing world-wide nature of the Company's several businesses.

Appendix A (continued)

3. Keeps abreast of the course of development of the various world-wide strategies; aids concerned divisions, Monsanto Europe and other subsidiaries, as necessary to ensure completion and updating of required strategies.
4. Coordinates strategies adopted and implemented by monitoring progress and ensuring compliance by concerned foreign subsidiaries.
5. Contributes directly to the development of strategies, where appropriate, by:
   — seeking out and identifying opportunities abroad
   — providing background data on economic climate
   — providing necessary information on governmental aspects, including appropriate data on local law and customs
   — furnishing information on the currency stability
   — assessing conditions of local labor market
   — evaluating uniqueness of business conditions in the general marketing areas

* * * * *

D. *International Subsidiaries*
   1. Implement their roles in product, market, and customer strategies.
   2. Request technical and management support necessary to carry out their roles in implementing strategies.
   3. Feed back to International Division and parent Operating Division information on business climate, competitor reaction, and other data for incorporation into world-wide strategies.
E. *Corporate Staff Departments*
   1. Participate in the development of world-wide strategies from their functional areas of responsibility.

Appendix B

Policy Statements and Position Description for General Manager, March 1967

INTERNATIONAL POLICY STATEMENTS

Scope of International Operations

Monsanto, as an international company, utilizes its resources and technology in any free world area where desirable return can be expected for the shareowners and where the shareowners' equity is reasonably secure in keeping with company objectives.

The International Division, operating divisions, and the central departments have assigned responsibilities for Monsanto's activities outside the United States. In those member companies where Monsanto has management responsibility, the activities will be carried out by the indicated groups. For those member companies where Monsanto does not have management responsibility, the activities will be carried out as appropriate in accordance with the contractual and legal arrangements applying to Monsanto's relationship with that company.

Operating Divisions' International Responsibilities

Products are manufactured and marketed world-wide and each operating division is accountable for the profit results of its product lines. In discharging this responsibility, the operating divisions:

(a) develop product strategies to maximize world-wide profitability.
(b) prepare market and customer strategies using data, information, and area market strategies provided by the International Division for the ex-U.S. portions.
(c) provide technical support to all operations.
(d) develop expansion programs and projects in keeping with identified commercial opportunities.

International Division

The International Division is a business management group knowledgeable of commercial, political, financial, and socio-economic conditions in areas outside the United States. The International Division:

(a) determines the corporate structure and the business arrangements for ex-U.S. enterprises.
(b) develops personnel in ex-U.S. operations ensuring the optimum contributions of personnel regardless of their country of national origin.
(c) provides personnel administration for all employees outside the United States.
(d) collects, correlates, and disseminates knowledge from abroad; provides counsel and support to operating divisions on ex-U.S. matters for the development and implementation of centrally controlled strategies for products, international customers, and world markets.
(e) analyzes and correlates the various operating division product, market, and customer strategies in order to establish effective business plans and goals for ex-U.S. activities.
(f) directs ex-U.S. business activities to achieve optimum profits in keeping with requirements of local business, public, government, customer, and tax considerations based on the world-wide product plans of the operating divisions.
(g) guards against unilateral product line action which would adversely affect Monsanto's interests.
(h) represents Monsanto's interests in associated and affiliated companies outside the U.S.

Business planning and decisions and management of investments ex-U.S. pertaining to oil and gas production and exploration are the responsibility of the Hydrocarbons and Polymers Division.

Management of ex-U.S. Member Companies

International Division, through area management groups, guides ex-U.S. member companies and in discharging this responsibility:

(a) develops total business plans and profit goals for each member company based on the product plans established by the operating divisions; grants approval to total budgets of the member companies consistent with plans approved by the operating divisions.
(b) safeguards the investment in member companies.
(c) initiates action necessary to achieving the established member company profit targets.
(d) ensures the provision of professional and specialist business assistance as requested or required.
(e) controls member company organization and manpower costs in both line and staff functions.

Central Department Responsibilities

Central departments work directly with ex-U.S. member companies, as appropriate, in provision of the necessary support and control. International Division approves staff organization requirements in its area management groups.

Appendix B (*continued*)

Commercial Development ex-U.S.

Commercial development abroad is the responsibility of the operating divisions in their assigned product areas working through the appropriate local management structure. Development of new, unrelated products (new ventures) are undertaken and managed as determined by the Executive Committee upon recommendation of the New Ventures Committee. International Division supports commercial development through the continuous search for profitable business opportunities in areas outside the U.S.

New Investments Abroad

Operating divisions prepare capital appropriation requests for new or additional product line investments outside the U.S. International Division supplies pertinent data and reviews the resulting appropriation request for concurrence prior to further management approval. International Division initiates and prepares capital appropriation requests for ex-U.S. manufacturing sites, plant services and utilities, and site development projects as appropriate to the company's product plans.

Export Marketing

The export marketing activity of the International Division functions as an extension of the operating divisions' marketing efforts while providing a centralization of the special services required and a unified relationship with the field group — either member companies, field offices, or agents. Pricing for exported products is set by the strategies prepared by the operating divisions.

Marketing Practices

Marketing management of ex-U.S. member companies employ local or regional distribution channels. Implementation of marketing strategies, including advertising and sales promotions, is consistent with the Corporate Identity Program and utilizes personnel as deemed appropriate to business practices in the countries of operation.

Research Conducted Outside the U.S.

Research activity outside the U.S. may be carried out in product or process areas as agreed with concerned operating division or the Central Research Department.

Contacts with Agencies of Foreign Governments

All contacts with agencies of foreign governments are made by, or coordinated with, the International Division.

POSITION DESCRIPTION
POSITION TITLE   General Manager, International Division
REPORTS TO   Senior Vice President, Operations

FUNCTION

Serves as the company's chief executive responsible for the surveillance and monitoring of current business activities and potential business opportunities outside the United States, including management and profit analysis of Monsanto's international activities and interests.

DUTIES

1. Directs the activities of the division as a business management group knowledgeable and sensitive to rapid changes in world areas.
2. Provides unified action within national and geographic trading areas via business management direction to ex-United States activities; supports and aids the product direction provided by the operating divisions or the New Ventures Committee through maintaining area management structures which permit the operating divisions to carry out their product responsibilities in ex-United States areas.
3. Assists concerned divisions in the development and implementation of centrally controlled strategies for products, international customers, and world markets. Assists in determining need for new or modified strategies in ex-United States areas and aids concerned divisions as necessary, to permit completion and updating of required strategies.
4. Establishes broad guidelines and major procedures vital to the successful achievement of assigned international objectives.
5. Collects, correlates, monitors, and disseminates broad knowledge of all company activities outside the United States to ensure against unilateral action that could adversely affect company world-wide interests.
6. Coordinates Monsanto's interests ex-United States to ensure consistent and decisive action to enhance its business performance in world markets.
7. Directs, and/or monitors, export marketing activities as an extension of operating division marketing.

Appendix B (continued)

8. Brings central departments into full participation in ex-United States activities without duplication of effort.
9. Supplies to concerned operating divisions the pertinent data required for preparing capital appropriation requests for ex-United States product line investments; reviews the resulting appropriation requests for concurrence before their submission to the Executive Committee for approval.
10. Initiates and prepares capital appropriation requests for ex-United States manufacturing sites, plant services and utilities, and site development projects as appropriate to the company's product plans.
11. At the direction of the New Ventures Committee, provides data required for and/or prepares appropriation requests and provides the management organization to execute ex-United States the business plans formulated and directed by this committee.
12. Ensures the provision of technological, manufacturing, and marketing expertise and support for ex-United States operations from the appropriate divisions and central departments.
13. Provides broad and essential ex-United States economic, political, and cultural intelligence.
14. Seeks out and identifies expansion or new marketing opportunities abroad; provides background data on economic climate, governmental aspects, currency stability, labor market conditions, cultural factors, and uniqueness of business conditions in the general marketing area.
15. Plans, coordinates, and provides for the development of personnel to assure optimum contributions of individuals regardless of their country of national origin.
16. Establishes new corporate entities ex-United States utilizing and coordinating the expertise of corporate departments and operating divisions.

COMMENTARY

In 1940 Monsanto's operations included its domestic businesses, three subsidiaries abroad, and an export business. By 1967 Monsanto's management had developed the framework for a series of fully integrated world-wide businesses. In the process the organization moved through five stages of growth.

In Stage I (about 1940) Monsanto's interests outside the United States consisted of three relatively self-contained businesses (in Canada, Great Britain, and Australia) and a limited amount of export sales handled through a Foreign Department. In Stage II (1954) the Foreign Department was given added responsibilities for managing Monsanto's investments in a rapidly growing number of overseas member companies and was renamed the Overseas Division. Stage III (1963) saw the creation of Monsanto Europe as a vehicle for providing management assistance to the managements of European operations. In Stage IV (1964) the domestic operating divisions were charged with responsibility for formulating worldwide strategies for their product lines. At the same time an International Division was formed to "administer" overseas activities and to contribute foreign market expertise in formulating investment plans and market strategies.

A revised charter in 1967 for International brought on Stage V by redefining the International Division's role. It made clear that strategy initiative did, in fact, rest with the operating divisions. International would contribute to strategy formulation, but its primary function was the administration and maintenance of Monsanto's resources abroad.

What led from one phase to another and what might Stage VI be? It will be useful to review the unfolding of the structure for Monsanto's rapidly growing operations outside the United States and to speculate about future developments. The case study provides an opportunity to look, as well, at how the Stage V (current) structure of the International Division was designed to interface with the domestic divisions to carry out integrated world-wide strategies.

Stage I: In the early phase of the development of international business opportunities, Monsanto's acquisitions in Great Britain, Canada, and Australia might best be regarded as three separate businesses. The relationship between each of these and the domestic divisions was primarily on a technical level involving licensing and the interchange of technical information. The export business conducted by the Foreign Department and its worldwide agency system was operated independently of these foreign interests, although the British, Canadian, and Australian companies served as export agents in their respective countries. The domestic divisions were not vitally concerned about markets abroad. The Foreign Department was the domestic divisions' marketing arm outside the United States.

The suitability of this system hinged critically on the size and complexity of the business and on the fact that these several overseas interests could be operated in relative isolation. As more interests were acquired, as volume grew, as numbers of products marketed abroad increased, problems of conflict and interdependency would inevitably arise.

Stage II: In the decade of the 1950s Monsanto's business abroad did expand greatly. Export sales grew rapidly. Monsanto made investments, as well, in nineteen foreign companies. In 1954, then, Monsanto's management established an Overseas Division, replacing the old Foreign Department. The new Division handled exports and managed Monsanto's investments in overseas member companies.

Here was a single vehicle that might usefully serve to coordinate a series of businesses that would inevitably impinge on each other. The complexity of the business led the Overseas Division to organize at first on an area basis. This would reduce the amount of detailed decision making forced up to Division headquarters for action. The area approach suggests, too, that coordination problems were perceived as being regional in nature; that marketing strategies, too, had to be regional in nature, responding to geographic environmental influences.

The shift to organizing by product line, around 1961, suggests that markets for the kinds of products Monsanto made were becoming worldwide in the respect that Monsanto's customers and competitors were both operating on a multinational basis to an increasing extent. Prices in different areas of the world would undoubtedly affect one another. Moreover, Monsanto's domestic divisions were becoming increasingly involved in ex-United States markets. By organizing on a product line basis, the Overseas Division could better coordinate foreign and domestic operations.

Stage III: Subsidiaries that have developed successfully as independent enterprises with little control on the part of the parent company are not easily drawn into interdependency. The creation of Monsanto Europe, then, in 1963 gives the appearance of being a probing step toward a unified organization. Monsanto Europe did not challenge, for example, the autonomy of the largest European member company, Monsanto Chemicals Limited. Nor did it include the Chemstrand Division's European operations. Moreover, Monsanto Europe was presented as a vehicle for "the providing of management assistance to the parent company's interests in the European area." Even then the internal memorandum describing the role of Monsanto Europe was careful to say:

> Whereas the various companies in the Monsanto Europe area will retain the same status they have had all along, they will now, at whatever times they deem advisable, be able to call upon a group of specialists not far away in Brussels. . . .

In retrospect, Monsanto Europe may be seen as a transition step toward a much greater integration of Monsanto's interests abroad than had existed hitherto.

Stage IV: The pressure of mounting conflict left no time for a leisurely transition to the establishment of world-wide businesses. The types of problems that developed are useful to note:

1. Some member companies began competing sharply with each other and the domestic divisions in world markets.
2. Sales and technical relations with large customers operating internationally were uncoordinated and often in conflict.
3. In periods of short supply, domestic divisions tended to give first priority to domestic customers and to become interested in export trade primarily when supplies were ample.

The 1964 move was the clear break with the past. The domestic divisions were given worldwide profit responsibility for their respective businesses. Investments abroad were grouped to centralize operations by geographic area. Export agents were terminated and their key personnel were given opportunities to work in member company organizations. In particular, domestic divisions and overseas affiliates began planning world-wide product strategies with Project Nova as a symbolic first step.

As would be expected, however, the domestic divisions were not prepared to take on suddenly the planning and execution of world-wide strategies. In the meantime the International Division and its predecessor organizations had traditionally assumed the initiating role in developing and managing Monsanto's investments and operations abroad. The domestic divisions were charged then with world-wide profit responsibility, but they were not prepared to take it on. Nor was the International Division, at least in spirit, prepared to give it up.

This was apparently the underlying issue in the debate about the role of International Division's Commercial Directors. The Commercial Directors of Sales had operated from 1964 on as initiators. They searched out new markets for existing products, spearheaded new product development projects, and took the lead in proposing plant expansions and in investigating corporate acquisitions and new business ventures abroad. Some International Division executives believed that such a role should be preserved. As one executive stated the case:

> Lots of deals are being made in my area. How do

we bring these to the attention of the operating divisions? We're the trigger, but how many shots do we have to fire? How far can we go if we have to pull the operating divisions kicking and screaming into a new opportunity? We need strong commercial development groups that can take the initiative.

The fact was that the 1964 International Division charter was somewhat ambiguous. While it placed *responsibility* for strategy development on operating Division General Managers, it placed squarely on the International Division:

> A responsibility to provide the initiative and the coordination for centrally controlled strategies which describe the interacting relationships among:
> (a) common products manufactured or sold in world markets,
> (b) key international customers,
> (c) selected world markets.

That would seem to mean that the International Division would play a leading role in seeing that world-wide strategies were developed and that International Division inputs would have a significant influence on strategy content.

In addition, International had:

> A responsibility for management of subsidiaries and associates and a safeguarding responsibility for Monsanto investment in affiliates.

Stage V: The significance of the 1967 revision in the International Division Charter is that it stressed the second of these two kinds of responsibility. The revised charter emphasized the Division's role as resource builder and custodian for personnel, area management structures, and investments abroad, and as a source of information on which world-wide strategies might be based. The 1967 document lists as the first three duties of the General Manager, International Division:

1. Directs the activities of the division as a business management group knowledgeable and sensitive to rapid changes in world areas.
2. *Provides unified action* within national and geographic trading areas via business management direction to ex-United States activities; *supports and aids the product direction provided by the operating divisions* or the New Ventures Committee *through maintaining area management structures* which permit the operating divisions to carry out *their* product responsibilities in ex-United States areas.
3. *Assists* concerned divisions in the development and implementation of centrally controlled strategies for products, international customers, and world markets. *Assists* in determining need for new or modified strategies in ex-United States areas and *aids* concerned divisions as necessary, to permit completion and updating of required strategies. [Italics added.]

In practice, the new International General Manager would interpret his duty to safeguard Monsanto's investment in member companies as including a responsibility for reviewing world-wide product strategies to assure that the viability of the member companies abroad would not be jeopardized. This would mean, undoubtedly, that he would seek to assure that world-wide strategies provided for the economic utilization of plants, sales forces, and research laboratories overseas. To maintain ex-United States resource strength, it was important that these assets be used.

The shift in emphasis from an International Division that *initiated* strategy to one that developed and preserved the resources for *carrying out* strategy came probably with the growing readiness of the operating divisions to take on the responsibility for developing and executing world-wide business plans for their respective product lines.

There is another significance in the 1967 clarification of the International Division's role. It reaffirms directly the idea that Monsanto would pursue a set of world-wide business strategies, rather than establishing a series of different businesses in various parts of the world. International Division Commercial Directors, pursuing corporate acquisitions and new business ventures overseas, might easily have launched Monsanto into businesses only tangentially related to those of the domestic operating divisions.

A Structure for World-Wide Strategies

In understanding the organization in 1967 of the International Division, it is important to distinguish between Europe, on the one hand, and Latin America and Asia-Pacific, on the other. The size of the European market and its proximity to the United States are factors which led to the development of a somewhat intricate organization structure, integrated closely with the operating divisions in the United States.

The basic concept, however, is not complex. Each Marketing Manager in C&P-Europe may be regarded as a member of the marketing program management team for his product, a team headed by a Market/Product Group Manager in a headquarters operating division. The Marketing Manager abroad provides information on his markets as inputs for world-wide marketing strategy formulation. Once plans are made, he is then responsible for directing sales representatives for his products in European district offices. He provides the geographic "outreach" for program managements at headquarters. He translates overall world-wide strategies for his area, and he may make modifications to meet the particular environmental conditions in his markets.

In theory, he is like the division manager in a Sears retail store who tailors the merchandise programs of the headquarters buying departments to suit the demands of local customers. His function also bears similarities to that of the IBM Industry Marketing Specialist located in a regional office. These men serve, in concept, as "extensions" of the program managements at headquarters.

An Area Director of Sales in C&P-Europe functioned like a Director of Sales in a headquarters division, a role that included strategy coordination as well as selection, development, appraisal, and promotion of Product/Market Managers and their key subordinates.

As for resource management, C&P-Europe's Director of Field Sales administered a direct sales organization which served all European markets for chemicals and plastics, very much like a regional organization in the United States. Following the U.S. pattern, too, many of Monsanto's field representatives in Europe were specialized by product line and took "business direction" from the Marketing Managers for those products.

The Research, Manufacturing, and Commercial Development organizations were not regionalized resources in the same way as the Field Sales organization was. The supply system would apparently be world-wide in character with European markets being sourced from manufacturing points in Europe, the United States, and elsewhere. Similarly, both Research and Commercial Development were parts of a world-wide system, since projects in Europe might have potential payoffs not only in local markets but outside Europe as well. Thus, Manufacturing, Research, and Commercial Development activities in Europe are to be perceived as branch operations in a multinational system, serving European needs primarily, perhaps, but not exclusively.

In C&P-Europe the role of the Executive Group Director is not clear, perhaps because the role of his domestic counterparts, the Product Directors, was unclear, too. (As seen in the case on Monsanto's Organic Chemicals Division, the Product Director's role was eliminated when that division was split into six different businesses.) Probably, the Executive Group Director coordinates program management and resource management in Europe; sees that marketing plans fully utilize resource capacity; serves as a high-level interface with domestic operating divisions on matters of strategy, availability of supply, and key personnel moves. He is largely an extension of the general manager of a business.

By contrast, Latin America and Asia-Pacific seemed to be structured much more like the old Overseas Division, since these markets had probably not developed to the same extent as European markets. Member companies received direction from the Area Director. Area Marketing Directors and the Directors of Sales for the several product lines maintained communication with Market/Product Group Managers at headquarters. Member company activities could be coordinated through the Area Directors.

Stage VI: There is little reason to believe that Monsanto's structure for conducting world-wide businesses will cease to evolve. The critical question is the direction of further change.

In his study of multinational companies, Stopford notes:

An increasing diversity of products abroad demands an increasing amount of communication between the international division and the United States product divisions, which may lead to conflicts between the international division and the United States product divisions. These conflicts would be greatly lessened if the international division were abandoned in favor of giving each product division world-wide product responsibilities.[1]

In 1964 Monsanto's domestic divisions *were* given world-wide product responsibilities for reasons that are broadly suggested by Stopford. As the operating divisions assumed these responsibilities, the role of the International Division changed from *initiating* strategies to *developing and maintaining the resources* to carry out strategies. Although they were part of the International Division, the Marketing Managers abroad began to function as geographic extensions of Market/Product management teams at headquarters when it came to formulating and implementing strategy.

A clear possibility, and Stopford's analysis would suggest it, is the dissolution of the International Division. If so, it might come about in stages with the operating divisions assuming complete responsibility for more highly developed markets (such as Europe) and International functioning in less developed market areas (Latin America and Asia-Pacific). Alternatively, International may continue to serve most usefully by providing a geographic framework for resource management and local administrative structures for personnel development, supervision, and appraisal. Like the Sears retail store management system, the International Division would be the vehicle for implementing total strategies on a local level.

In the authors' opinion, the latter is the more likely possibility. The resource management functions in areas abroad call for expertise of their own. It would not be easy for managers of domestic resources to administer plants, laboratories, and field sales forces all over the world. The International Division performs important management functions not easily assumed by headquarters and is likely to remain in place for some time to come.

---

[1] John M. Stopford, "Growth and Organizational Change in the Multinational Firm" (unpublished doctoral dissertation, Harvard Graduate School of Business Administration, 1968), p. 19.

Chas. Pfizer & Co., Inc.: Pfizer International

In 1965 Chas. Pfizer & Co., Inc., was one of the world's leading pharmaceutical companies. Sales had grown from only $60 million in 1950 to over $540 million in 1965. Profits of $53.4 million in 1965 represented an increase in earnings of 19.5% over 1964 and almost 200% over 1955. For a 10-year financial history of the company, see Exhibit 1.

The rapid growth of Chas. Pfizer during the 1950s and early 1960s was attributed to a number of factors. Several important product developments, of which Terramycin was perhaps the most notable, had a significant effect on company sales and earnings, as did acquisitions which were believed to be responsible for about 20% of Pfizer's 1964 sales. During this period the company also accelerated the process of diversification, with pharmaceuticals (human antibiotics and other ethical prescription drugs) accounting for only 47% of sales in 1964. Pfizer's other major product lines and their shares of 1964 sales were: chemicals (25%), agricultural products (13%), and consumer products (15%).

A large amount of Chas. Pfizer's business was conducted outside the United States. In 1964 Pfizer International[1] sales reached $233 million, almost 50% of the Pfizer total. Manufacturing plants for pharmaceutical, chemical, agricultural, and consumer products were operated in 27 countries, and 17,000 employees worked for the International company as compared with 11,000 for the domestic company.

Pfizer International was responsible for marketing all Pfizer products outside the United States, and it conducted extensive development and manufacturing operations abroad. Pfizer International had its own board of directors and officers and, for the most part, operated independently of the parent company. Although Pfizer International purchased part of its raw materials from Chas. Pfizer, and generally marketed products that were part of the Chas. Pfizer product line, its executives were free to run the international business as they saw fit, with only general policy guidance from the parent company.

This case will present background information on Pfizer International's product lines and major activities. It will then describe the organization and activities of Pfizer International in early 1965 in both the New York headquarters and the field, and the means through which headquarters worked with the field organizations in the areas of reporting, control, and pricing. The final section describes changes in the organization in late 1965 and proposals for further change.

Product Lines

Like the parent company, Pfizer International was engaged in the development, manufacture, and sale of pharmaceutical, agricultural, chemical, and consumer products. There was some overlap among product lines, but in general they differed markedly in development, manufacturing, and marketing characteristics.

Pharmaceutical Products

The pharmaceutical product line consisted of antibiotics and other ethical drugs (sold only by prescription) and proprietary drugs (sold without a prescription). In 1964 pharmaceutical sales represented 59.5% of Pfizer International's sales volume and an even larger percentage of its profits.

Pharmaceutical Research and Development: A great deal of laboratory research and development work was needed in the pharmaceutical field in order to insure a continuing flow of new products. In 1965 Chas. Pfizer had a number of basic new drugs in various stages of clinical evaluation in the United States and overseas.

The bulk of Pfizer International's development work was carried out in its research and development labora-

---

[1] In this case Chas. Pfizer's various foreign subsidiaries will be treated as a single company, "Pfizer International."

tories in Sandwich, England. In addition, each pharmaceutical manufacturing plant had laboratory facilities which were necessary for quality control and also were used to develop new dosage forms and adapt products to local market conditions.

Pharmaceutical Manufacturing: There were two major phases in the pharmaceutical manufacturing process. In the initial basic manufacturing phase, the active ingredients in a given pharmaceutical product were produced in bulk form. In some cases this was done through fermentation; in others the basic process was one of chemical synthesis, or a combination of fermentation and synthesis. Whichever process was used, carefully controlled conditions and exceptional safeguards against impurities were required. The basic manufacturing process produced a basic ingredient, which was then packaged in bulk form for bulk sale or was further processed into finished goods.

The second phase of the pharmaceutical manufacturing process was carried out in what were known as pharmaceutical manufacturing plants. In these plants the bulk pharmaceuticals were transformed into final dosage forms such as tablets, capsules, ointments, syrups, liquids, and injectables. Prescribed dosages were often as small as one milligram, and in final dosage form the drug was mixed with a base so that it could be administered safely and conveniently in a form acceptable to the patient. As in the case of bulk manufacture, exceptionally sanitary conditions were essential.

Pharmaceutical Marketing: In general, pharmaceutical products were sold at the retail level by pharmacies. While there was wide variation in channels of distribution among the many countries in which Pfizer International sold its products, the company generally sold them either to drug wholesalers or directly to pharmacies. As national health plans proliferated, increasing sales were made directly or indirectly to governmental agencies. In some areas, moreover, pharmaceuticals were sold to practicing physicians who then supplied them to their patients.

Pfizer's pharmaceutical marketing effort was directed toward physicians. Detail men, who were often professionally trained, called on doctors to familiarize them with Pfizer drugs, so that they would prescribe or recommend Pfizer products to their patients. On detailing calls, the detail man generally pointed out the advantages of Pfizer products and left product samples and informative literature with the doctor.

Expenditures on advertising, other than the cost of samples and materials used by the detail men, represented a relatively small marketing expense. While advertisements were placed in medical and pharmaceutical professional journals, consumer advertising was rarely used by the pharmaceutical industry. In almost all countries, it was believed that doctors would not prescribe pharmaceuticals that had been advertised directly to the consumer.

Agricultural and Veterinary Products

Pfizer International's agricultural and veterinary products line consisted essentially of: (1) *animal feed supplements,* which primarily consisted of various vitamins and antibiotics in crude form and were added to proteins and minerals and then to a basic grain, such as corn or wheat, to provide a balanced animal ration, (2) a range of *veterinary products* such as antibiotic injectables, soluble powders, boluses, and animal vaccines, and (3) *pesticides,* formulations of standard compounds, which were marketed in France, Canada, Rhodesia, South Africa, and Brazil. In 1964 agricultural and veterinary products accounted for 13.5% of Pfizer International's total sales. Western Europe accounted for one-third of this total.

Development: Development of animal feed supplements and veterinary antibiotic formulations was generally carried out in Pfizer pharmaceutical laboratories. Although procedures for product testing and obtaining government approvals differed somewhat from those for human pharmaceuticals, the actual development processes were essentially similar. In many cases, Pfizer human pharmaceuticals were adapted to agricultural needs. Terramycin, for example, was the basic ingredient in a large number of Pfizer antibiotic animal health products.

Animal vaccines were generally developed in the area where they were marketed. Since strains of disease-producing organisms were usually confined to particular geographic areas, each area generally had to develop its own vaccines.

Manufacturing: The active ingredients, when manufactured by Pfizer, came from the same basic manufacturing plants as the pharmaceutical products. Animal feed supplements were then manufactured for the most part at local blending plants, through processes involving the blending of the active ingredient(s) with diluents to facilitate addition to feed formulation. Veterinary products were produced in Pfizer's basic pharmaceutical plants also. Purity dosage and packaging might differ from those for human pharmaceuticals, but the manufacturing processes were basically similar. Animal vaccines were usually manufactured locally, since these products frequently had applications restricted to limited geographic areas corresponding to locally specific disease-causative organisms.

Marketing: Feed supplements were generally sold to feed millers, who mixed them with other ingredients and basic animal feed stuffs and then sold the resulting balanced "mix" to farmers through retail feed stores. Pfizer salesmen usually placed major emphasis on convincing millers of the benefits of Pfizer feed supplements, including antibiotics, vitamins, and custom mixes and, when needed, helping them to determine the proper formulas for their markets. In recent years stress had also been laid on visiting the larger farmers and urging them to specify feed containing Pfizer supplements. Product excellence, technical service support, and competitive pricing enabled Pfizer to maintain a favorable position against constant competitive pressure.

Pfizer also sold direct to the farmer in some markets. In Nigeria Pfizer operated as a feed miller and marketed a variety of animal feeds. In Italy and certain other markets Pfizer sold "custom premixes" which allowed the farmer to mix his own feed. Custom premix was particularly successful in markets where large modern farms could achieve significant economies by mixing their own feeds and in less developed areas where feed manufacturers were not a significant factor (e.g., Brazil).

Animal health products salesmen generally called on veterinarians and tried to convince them to prescribe Pfizer products to the farmers in their area, or, in some cases, to sell Pfizer products themselves. In some countries, where regulatory and marketing practices permitted, Pfizer promoted its products directly to the farmer. This practice was particularly prevalent in marketing areas where the company had a strong position in proprietary medicines but veterinary medicine was still relatively underdeveloped.

Chemical Products

Pfizer International's chemical product line consisted of three categories of products: (1) fine chemicals, (2) petrochemicals and plastics, and (3) bulk pharmaceuticals. The chemical product line had experienced rapid growth in recent years and represented 14% of Pfizer International's sales in 1964. About 27% of Pfizer International's chemical sales were in the United Kingdom and about 28% in the rest of Europe.

Fine Chemicals: Fine chemicals were distinguished from other industrial chemicals in that they were usually of higher purity and price and required relatively complex manufacturing processes involving organic chemistry.

Pfizer's line of fine chemicals was extremely diverse with regard to manufacturing processes, end uses, and channels of distribution. Citric acid, oxalic acid, and gluconic acid were produced by a fermentation process. Pfizer International's fine chemicals were sold directly to food processors and other industries as well as other pharmaceutical companies.

Fine chemicals were sold with little product differentiation among suppliers, and at published, well-established prices. Pfizer International's competitors in the chemical field were mostly large chemical companies, many of which produced fine chemicals as well as basic chemicals. Competition, in Europe in particular, was becoming quite severe.

Petrochemicals and Plastics: Pfizer International's activity in the petrochemical field was limited to the manufacture of polyethers in the United Kingdom and of polyurethane foams in the European Economic Community.

The polyether produced by the U.K. plant was one of the basic ingredients in the manufacture of polyurethane foams. These foams were used as insulation in a variety of construction applications and as cushioning in furniture and automobile seats.

Polyurethane foams were manufactured by "foamers." Foamers were generally small companies, since distribution of their product was economic only within a radius of 200 to 300 miles. Foamers sometimes purchased polyethers on long-term contracts, with price and consistent quality the key elements in their buying decisions. Most of the polyether production of Pfizer's U.K. plant was sold to British foamers.

Pfizer owned two foamers in Europe, one in Belgium and one in France. While these foamers received some of their polyether from the Pfizer plant in the United Kingdom, tariff considerations forced them to buy most of their polyether locally. Pfizer sold its polyurethane foam to a large number of furniture manufacturers located near its plants. Furniture manufacturers generally purchased polyurethane on a month-to-month basis, largely on the basis of price. When a furniture manufacturer was ready to add to his polyurethane foam inventory, he generally asked several foamers for price quotations.

Bulk Pharmaceuticals: Bulk pharmaceuticals were considered part of the chemical rather than the pharmaceutical business. Pfizer International sold several pharmaceutical products in bulk form to other pharmaceutical manufacturers. These manufacturers then packaged the pharmaceuticals in final dosage form and sold them under their own labels. Most of the bulk pharmaceuticals which Pfizer sold to other pharmaceutical manufacturers were the so-called "narrow spectrum" antibiotics,[2] which were no longer patentable and were thus sold in much the same way as fine chemicals, with low margins, commodity pricing, and little product differentiation among suppliers. Also included in the chemical product line were a few Pfizer patented ethical drugs, which were sold in bulk form to a limited number of manufacturers who manufactured them into final dosage form and sold them under their own labels.

The marketing of bulk pharmaceuticals was the responsibility of country chemical managers. This assignment was intended to provide maximum incentive for bulk pharmaceutical sales. It was believed that pharmaceutical managers would lack enthusiasm for bulk pharmaceutical sales to their competitors.

Consumer Products

Pfizer International's consumer product line included three categories of products: (1) selectively distributed cosmetics and toiletries, (2) mass marketed toiletries and other consumer products, and (3) door-to-door cosmetics. In the cosmetics and toiletries field, Pfizer's major entries were the Coty line of cosmetics (Coty had been acquired by Pfizer in late 1963) and the Pacquin line of women's hand creams and lotions. Pfizer International's consumer products included vitamins, cough and cold remedies, analgesics, antacids, dietary products, baby formulas, and a line of health "tonics" sold only in Germany and Austria. Cosmetic and consumer products together accounted for 13% of Pfizer International's 1964 sales.

Pfizer did not make the basic raw materials for its consumer products, and supplies were often obtained from local supplies in the countries where the products were produced. The manufacturing process required mixing and filling operations, but was complicated by frequent changes in package design and product features. It was customary, for example, to introduce new lipstick shades each season.

The cosmetic and general health products were sold through separate sales forces to drug wholesalers and direct to pharmacies and other retail outlets. They were rarely sold by the same salesman who sold Pfizer's pharmaceutical products. Relatively heavy consumer advertising and promotional expenditures differentiated the marketing of these products from the marketing of pharmaceuticals. Moreover, Pfizer was beginning to experiment with door-to-door sales of cosmetic products, particularly in England.

Geographical Location of Pfizer International Activities

In early 1965 Pfizer products were sold in more than 100 countries and manufactured in 27 countries. In addition, Pfizer operated bonded warehouses (used as supply points) in Belgium, Hong Kong, and Panama, and had extensive research and development laboratories in the United Kingdom.

Pfizer's foreign operations took a variety of legal forms. In 13 countries, Pfizer operated through branches, which were legally considered local offices of a foreign company. In most cases, however, Pfizer operated through subsidiaries, which were locally domiciled corporations in the countries in which they operated. In early 1965 Pfizer had 84 foreign subsidiaries, a few of which were partially owned locally. In several countries Pfizer operated through several different subsidiaries, some of which were subsidiaries of still other subsidiaries.

In general, the legal form of a given operation was dictated by financial and fiscal considerations and had little relevance to the way in which it functioned. Some countries, for example, had different tax rates for branches of foreign companies and locally incorporated subsidiaries. Moreover, there might be different policies concerning remission of profits and reporting of financial data. In the case of partially owned subsidiaries, however, the local owners sometimes took part in the management of the company.

Manufacturing Plant Locations

Manufacturing operations differed markedly among countries and product lines. Bulk pharmaceutical fermentation plants were located in Argentina, Brazil, Japan, India, Spain, France, and the United Kingdom. The plants in France and Japan were only 50% owned by Pfizer. In general, the foreign bulk pharmaceutical plants produced only for their own national markets, with other countries receiving bulk pharmaceuticals, through the three bonded warehouses, from

---

[2] Narrow spectrum antibiotics were effective against a narrow range of disease-producing organisms while broad spectrum antibiotics were effective against a wider range of organisms. Terramycin, Pfizer's most important patented pharmaceutical, was one of the first broad spectrum antibiotics.

Chas. Pfizer bulk pharmaceutical plants in the United States. In some cases, however, bulk pharmaceuticals were shipped from the foreign plants to the supply points, for eventual shipment to other countries.

Pharmaceutical manufacturing plants, where bulk pharmaceuticals were manufactured in dosage form and packaged, were located in 24 countries. In addition, operations limited to pharmaceutical packaging were carried out in Puerto Rico and South Africa. The pharmaceutical manufacturing plants generally received bulk pharmaceuticals from one of the supply points, or directly from a bulk pharmaceutical plant if one was located in the same country. The output of these plants was transferred to warehouses which supplied the local market. Occasionally, finished goods were sent to one of the supply points for subsequent shipment to other countries.

Pfizer executives gave several reasons for the relatively large number of pharmaceutical manufacturing plants as compared with the number of bulk pharmaceutical plants. The reasons fell into three categories: economic, political, and marketing. On the economic side, the capital investment required for a pharmaceutical manufacturing or packaging plant was far less than for a basic fermentation plant; transportation costs for dosage forms were greater than those for bulk pharmaceuticals (the former included inert materials, which were often purchased locally, and packaging materials); economies of scale were far more significant in bulk production than in dosage production; and tariffs were usually higher on dosage forms than on bulk pharmaceuticals. On the political side, there was considerable pressure for at least some manufacture to take place in the country where a drug was marketed. Moreover, differences in national regulations concerning dosages and labeling often made local dosage manufacture almost a necessity. From a marketing point of view, Pfizer International found that medical and patient practices and tastes varied widely from country to country, and the ability to satisfy them under local management was a big advantage.

Agricultural and/or veterinary products were manufactured in Canada, Mexico, Brazil, Colombia, Argentina, Chile, Great Britain, France, Sweden, Germany, Italy, Spain, Belgium, Greece, Turkey, Egypt, Nigeria, Venezuela, Japan, India, Pakistan, the Philippines, and Australia. In addition, they were manufactured in plants owned by third parties in Denmark and Yugoslavia. In general, the bulk pharmaceuticals used in these products were produced at the basic manufacturing plants, and shipped to the agricultural and/or veterinary product manufacturing facilities through the three supply points. As in the case of the pharmaceutical manufacturing plants, the finished agricultural and veterinary products produced abroad were almost always sold in the same country in which they were manufactured.

Pfizer International chemical manufacturing plants were located in Australia, Canada, Argentina, Belgium, France, and the United Kingdom. These plants generally represented a large capital investment, and were limited by high tariffs and transportation costs to sale in their national markets. Some chemicals and bulk pharmaceuticals were exported from the United States and the United Kingdom, however.

Cosmetics and/or other consumer products were manufactured in Argentina, Mexico, Canada, Brazil, Chile,[3] South Africa, France, Germany, Italy, Sweden, Venezuela, Uruguay,[3] and the United Kingdom. These factories produced consumer products primarily for their local markets; but there was a considerable temporary movement of these products across national boundaries as this was still a relatively new business and volumes were not yet high enough to justify all desirable plants. This was particularly true of the Coty cosmetics line, a large part of which, for Europe, was manufactured in France.

Decisions as to which manufacturing facilities or supply points were to supply which markets were made by the Operations Services Department in New York under policies set by the President of Pfizer International. In making these decisions, the department took into account differences in manufacturing costs, tariffs, transportation expenses, and utilization of capacity. In general, a given logistics pattern, once established, was not changed unless a major development occurred. A new plant or above-capacity demands on an existing facility were typical reasons for making such changes.

In early 1965, as a considerable number of Pfizer's U.S. manufacturing facilities were reaching capacity levels, the Operations Services Department requested foreign manufacturing facilities with excess capacity to estimate unit costs at higher production levels. On the basis of these estimates, future logistics patterns were to be established. A typical problem was whether to increase the size of a plant then operating at capacity or increase the production level of a plant operating below capacity. According to the manager of the Operations Services Department, decisions of this sort required not only complex economic analysis, but

---

[3] Under license.

also consideration of the economic policies and trading patterns of the countries in which Pfizer International did business.

Geographic Distribution of Sales

Pfizer International sales varied considerably from country to country and among product lines. The accompanying table presents sales data for each business in a number of representative countries.

Net Sales by Country and Business (1964)*
(in thousands)

Country	Pharma-ceuticals	Agricultural and Veterinary	Chemicals	Consumer
France	$ 5,000	$ 400	$3,400	$2,400
Germany	9,200	1,800	400	9,000
Italy	10,000	5,000	800	900
UK	23,000	4,000	5,200	1,500
Benelux	11,000	1,600	1,800	280
Sweden	2,800	400	440	140
Norway	520	100	60	280
Finland	480	350	240	140
Greece	2,000	300	30	—
Iran	900	300	35	—
Spain	4,800	900	400	35
Egypt	920	200	200	—
Mexico	9,600	1,600	500	360
Brazil	6,800	3,200	170	1,600
Argentina	11,000	2,400	900	700
Guatemala	550	70	70	8
Colombia	3,200	700	600	140
Chile	2,400	1,200	100	2
Australia	3,000	800	3,200	2,000
Japan	2,400	30	2,200	200
Philippines	2,400	600	250	—
India	28,000	1,400	1,850	65

* Financial data not publicly available have been disguised.

Historical Development of Pfizer International Organization

The Pfizer International Organization, as it existed in early 1965, was the outgrowth of a series of organizational changes. In the early 1950s Chas. Pfizer had had an export department which sold fine chemicals (Pfizer's original product line) to distributors in a number of foreign countries. When Pfizer entered the pharmaceutical field in 1950, the export department sold some pharmaceutical products to the same distributors who handled the fine chemical line.

Then in 1951 Pfizer decided to export Terramycin, the broad spectrum antibiotic that was to play such a significant part in the company's future growth. At this time the company concluded that fine chemical distributors would not be an effective channel for marketing Terramycin, and decided to set up branches in the key foreign markets. As the result of a consultant's study, Pfizer decided to establish international subsidiaries to operate these foreign branches.

These subsidiaries soon became known as "Pfizer International." They had their own boards of directors, drawn from Chas. Pfizer and Pfizer International executives. Mr. John J. Powers, who had previously been a member of the Chas. Pfizer Board of Directors and Corporate Secretary, became President and Chairman of the Board of Pfizer International.

In the early 1950s Pfizer International operated as a highly centralized organization. At New York headquarters four Regional Directors, responsible respectively for Europe, Latin America, the Middle East, and the Far East, reported to the President of Pfizer International. Territorial Managers, who were also located in New York, were each responsible for several countries, whether branches or independent distributors. These Territorial Managers reported to the Regional Directors.

During this period Pfizer International attempted to manage its growing foreign operations from New York. Advertising and promotional brochures were prepared at headquarters and sent out to the branches. Territorial Managers made many operating decisions, particularly in the area of marketing. New York headquarters attempted to plan foreign activities in detail, and the Regional Directors spent most of their time traveling.

By 1956, as the business grew, it became clear that extreme centralization was an inefficient way to run Pfizer's international business. After considerable analysis, Mr. Powers decided to send the Regional Directors abroad and eliminate the Territorial Managers altogether. The Regional Directors were designated Area Managers and area headquarters were established in the United Kingdom (Europe, Middle East, Africa), Hong Kong (the Far East), and Buenos Aires (Latin America).[4] The managers in the various countries, who were now more likely to be managing subsidiaries than branches or distributors, were given increased responsibility, particularly in the marketing area, and were called Country Managers. These men reported to the appropriate Area Managers.

In 1956–1957 reorganization resulted in a highly

---

[4] Later divided into Northern and Southern Latin America.

decentralized organization. Mr. Powers' staff was limited to technical specialists, and there was no way for him to follow the operations of the regions and countries closely. The Area Managers developed their own headquarters organizations. The Country Managers had considerable autonomy in running the country businesses and complete responsibility for local marketing activities.

Although an organizational philosophy based on decentralization was firmly established in the late 1950s, Pfizer International's rapid growth soon suggested some changes. In particular, Mr. Powers felt that he needed some assistance in New York and that more areas should be established. As a result, he decided to divide the old areas into eight new areas, each under an Area Manager. The former Area Managers returned to New York. Mr. Richard Fenton, who had been in charge of the European Area, became an Operational Vice President responsible for the Area Managers located in Europe, Africa, the Middle East, and Canada. The former Southern Latin American Area Manager became an Operational Vice President and supervised Area Managers in Latin America and the Far East. The Far East Area Manager became Vice President in Charge of the New York Administrative Staff.

In late 1963 Mr. Powers was promoted to Vice Chairman of Chas. Pfizer & Co., and Mr. Fenton became President of Pfizer International. Under Mr. Fenton, the organization remained much as it had under Mr. Powers except that the positions of the Operational Vice Presidents were eliminated. As a result, the Area Managers reported directly to the President.

Organization in Early 1965

The basic organizational concept under which Pfizer International operated was that the key operating entity was the country business. In early 1965 there was a direct line relationship between ten geographic Area Managers and Pfizer International President Fenton. The Area Managers and the countries under their jurisdiction are shown in Exhibit 2. Each Area Manager was responsible for the Pfizer business in the countries in his area and exercised direct line authority over these Country Managers.

A number of staff departments, consisting of about 250 persons in early 1965, also reported to Mr. Fenton (Exhibit 3). In addition to providing various staff services, the headquarters staff by disseminating information coordinated world-wide Pfizer activities in the fields of product development, long-range planning, and production; and it advised Mr. Fenton (for line implementation) regarding transfer prices, logistics, and capital budgeting.

Members of the Pfizer International organization believed that decentralization of line authority to as great an extent as possible to the country business level was a major factor in the company's success. Executives on the headquarters staff traveled frequently, and had close working relationships with members of the line organization located in the field, but their role was limited to making suggestions to line managers or policy recommendations to Mr. Fenton.

The Line Organization

According to a Pfizer International position description, it was "the responsibility of each Area Manager to plan, develop, and carry out Pfizer International's business in the assigned foreign area in keeping with company policies and goals. This involves, for the area assigned, the managerial planning and integration of products imported from established plants located elsewhere; location and recommendation of potentialities of local manufacture; acquisition or establishment of plants or businesses; and direction of manufacture (where applicable) and marketing of products."

The memorandum went on to list a number of specific responsibilities charged to the Area Managers. The Area Manager:

1. Participates in top-level consideration of overall Pfizer International policies. Establishes area policies within limits of company general policies.
2. Initiates, evaluates, and determines long-range planning and annual and interim product plans for the area. Administers area's operations through delegation of responsibility to staff members and Country Managers (if applicable) for timely accomplishment of objectives. Guides and directs specific action, as required by emergency or change of conditions. Continually reviews and evaluates area's status and trends with the president, and recommends solutions to major problems.
3. Determines and establishes organization structure for the area's needs and objectives. Develops key personnel through example, counsel, job assignment, and establishment of standards of leadership at managerial levels. Assures conduct of development and training programs at lower levels.
4. Represents the company through participation in major negotiations in such matters as acquisitions of businesses or plants, securing necessary clearances

from foreign governments or international operators.
5. As applicable, assures that Country Managers—
   a. Maintain balanced product lines, determining product additions or deletions.
   b. Look after foreign-language labeling and packaging requirements.
   c. Establish selling prices and agency discounts and terms—requesting the N.Y. office approval when required by existing policies.
   d. Analyze sales volume and profit contribution of each product variety.
   e. Direct sales promotional plans, adapting domestic or other overseas promotions when feasible.
   f. Develop and maintain a field sales organization.

An Area Manager was generally located in the area for which he was responsible. Exceptions to this rule in early 1965 were the CIP (Canada, India, and Pakistan) Area Manager, who temporarily located in New York, and the SEE (Scandinavia and Eastern Europe), SEME (Southern Europe and the Middle East), and EEC (European Economic Community) Area Managers, all of whom were located in Brussels, where they shared a common staff.

The size and functions of the area staffs varied widely among the various areas. While all areas had staffs operating in the fields of control, personnel, and finance, some areas also had staffs concerned with production coordination and legal matters. Differences among areas in this regard were generally accounted for by differences in the complexity of their activities in these fields.

By early 1965 some areas with extensive nonpharmaceutical businesses were also beginning to set up product-oriented staff departments at the area level. No such staffs had yet been set up in Brussels, but chemical product specialists were operating in the SOLA (Southern Latin America) and JAN (Japan, Australia, and New Zealand) areas. In Europe the UKI (United Kingdom and Ireland) Area Manager also had line responsibility for chemical sales and manufacture in the EEC area. A member of his staff was located in Brussels, with responsibility for chemical activities in the EEC.

At the country level, one or more managers had profit responsibility for Pfizer activities in each country. In most cases, a single Country Manager had responsibility for all Pfizer activities in his country. In the EEC, however, the Country Manager was responsible only for the pharmaceutical and agricultural products businesses. Separate general managers, who reported to area management, were responsible for the chemicals and consumer products businesses. In countries where the businesses were divided, the Country Manager generally retained administrative responsibility for staff services, which were shared, and represented Pfizer International on occasions requiring a representative of the company as a whole. Organizationally, however, Country Managers and general managers in the EEC area were at the same level and reported directly to the Area Managers.[5]

Pfizer Organization in Europe: In early 1965 the chief exception to this organizational pattern was Pfizer's line organization in Europe, where three Area Managers (EEC, SEE, SEME) shared a common staff and a fourth Area Manager (UKI) was responsible for chemical operations in the EEC area (see Exhibit 4).

Pfizer's European organization took this form for a variety of reasons. The decision to bring the three Area Managers together in Brussels had been made in 1963, as part of a wider realignment of areas intended to reflect the growing importance of the European Economic Community. Once the three areas had been brought together, it had seemed logical to have them share a common staff, which was put under the administrative direction of the SEE Area Manager.

The decision to have the UKI Area Manager direct the EEC chemical operations, as well as his UKI area, from the United Kingdom was also due to a number of factors. The UKI Area Manager had not been moved to Brussels because of the magnitude of the UK operations and the location of Pfizer International's research laboratories in England. This manager had also taken the lead in establishing Pfizer International's chemical business, most of which was located in the United Kingdom. Since he had had far more experience with chemicals than the EEC Area Manager, he had been given responsibility for chemical operations in the EEC. Chemical business managers in the six EEC countries reported to an EEC chemical manager, who reported to the UKI Area Manager.

This arrangement caused some problems in the field of bulk pharmaceutical sales and licensing. As previously noted, bulk pharmaceutical sales were considered part of the chemicals business, so that pharmaceutical managers would not have to face conflicts between marketing Pfizer pharmaceutical products to the trade and selling or licensing Pfizer patented products to competitors. If a chemicals manager wished

---

[5] In the EEC area, the Area Manager had written a memorandum setting forth the relationship between country and business managers. See Appendix A for excerpts from this memorandum.

to make such a sale or licensing arrangement, the pharmaceuticals manager could present opposing arguments to his Area Manager, who would make the final decision. This procedure was followed in the SEE and SEME areas, where chemical and pharmaceutical managers reported to the same Area Manager. In the EEC area, however, such conflicts had to be resolved by Mr. Fenton, since chemical and pharmaceutical managers reported to different Area Managers.

The Headquarters Staff

In early 1965 Pfizer International maintained a headquarters staff of about 250 persons in New York City. Most of these personnel (193 persons) were located in eight staff departments, the managers of which reported to the Vice President-Administration. The Vice President-Administration reported to Mr. Fenton (see Exhibit 3, Headquarters Organization).

The administrative departments which reported to the Vice President-Administration were responsible for such functions as employee relations, long-range planning, production, control, legal matters, purchasing, pricing, shipping, and finance. The managers of these departments had no line authority, but influenced field activities through policy recommendations submitted to Mr. Fenton. In addition, these departments reviewed plans, budgets, and operating results of the field organizations, and submitted their analyses to Mr. Fenton, who met with the Area Managers several times a year. Moreover, the administrative department managers visited most of the larger countries on a regular basis in order to meet with the Area and Country Managers and their functional counterparts. On these occasions, they explained new policies and guidelines established by Mr. Fenton and made certain that existing policies were being implemented effectively.

The staff departments that reported directly to Mr. Fenton were government relations, public relations, product development, and projects. The government and public relations departments were responsible for Pfizer International's efforts in these areas in the United States, and they also had advisory relationships with their functional counterparts in the field organization. The product development department was responsible for coordinating the development activities of the areas and countries with those of the Pfizer International research laboratories in England and the Chas. Pfizer & Co. Laboratories in the United States. In addition, it made policy recommendations to Mr. Fenton concerning long-range development projects, and was responsible for making certain that Pfizer International made adequate use of product developments originating in the United States. Finally, a projects committee appraised the merits of capital investment proposals of more than $20,000 (US).

Profit Centers and Budgets

The cornerstone of Pfizer International's reporting and control system was a large number of decentralized profit centers (about 200 in early 1965). Each geographic area was a profit center and prepared annual area budgets. Within each area, the countries were also profit centers, preparing annual budgets for review and consolidation at the area level. In the larger countries, each business (i.e., pharmaceutical, agricultural, consumer, and chemical) was treated as a separate profit center.

Area budgets were reviewed, modified, and approved by Mr. Fenton at annual budgetary meetings held in New York each fall. In preparing their budgets, the Area Managers were guided by "guideposts" established by Mr. Fenton. For an example of such guideposts, see Appendix B.

Differences in customs regulations and fiscal policies among the countries in which Pfizer did business often required that external transfer prices be calculated individually for each country. If these external transfer prices were used in measuring the performance of each profit center, meaningful evaluation of operating results would have been virtually impossible.

For this reason, results for each profit center were measured by reference to an "internal" transfer price. A primary source of supply was established for each product, and the cost of manufacturing at the source of supply was used as the "internal" transfer price. Although secondary sources of supply were sometimes used, the internal transfer price could not be higher than that used for shipments from the primary source of supply, so as not to penalize those profit centers supplied by relatively high cost manufacturing facilities. This latter modification was particularly important since decisions as to which manufacturing facility or supply point would supply a particular country were made in the Operations Services Department in New York.

New York headquarters received interim financial reports from the profit centers each month. In addition, a number of standard operating reports were submitted to New York on a regular basis. Among these were reports dealing with production efficiency and inventory levels. The New York headquarters staff used these reports to discover significant trends before they began to show up in the profit centers' financial statements.

Pfizer International's growing diversification had significant implications for the company's reporting and control procedures. By early 1965 separate financial statements were being prepared for each of the four businesses, so that management could appraise the performance of each product line as well as each geographic area. Nevertheless, there were increasing complaints from consumer products managers, who contended that Pfizer's account structure at the market level was oriented to the pharmaceutical business and did not provide them with sufficiently detailed data. For example, the Pfizer accounting manual contained the category, "advertising expenses." This category was not broken down into types of media since consumer advertising was a relatively insignificant expense in the pharmaceutical business.

Pricing

New York headquarters exercised differing degrees of control over the to-the-market price of each of the four categories of products. Disregarding slight variations within each of the four businesses, the following generalizations give an indication of the differences.

In general, New York headquarters exercised the most control over pharmaceutical prices. When a pharmaceutical product was first introduced, basic price levels were determined by the Operations Services Department, with approval by Mr. Fenton. This procedure was necessary because of the broad international nature of most of the basic products.

For agricultural and chemical products, the Area Managers generally had final responsibility for pricing. Strong competition in most markets, considerable product variety by country, and the commodity nature of many of these products made this policy necessary. In some cases, however, floor prices were established by New York headquarters. Area Managers could not go below these floor price levels without headquarters approval.

In the consumer products field, Country Managers had considerably more autonomy, because of the distinctly national character of the consumer goods business. With the exception that Area Managers had to approve all major price changes, Country Managers and Consumer Products General Managers were relatively free to respond to local marketing conditions.

1965 Organization Changes

Pfizer Europe

In June 1965 Mr. Fenton announced that the EEC, SEE, and SEME areas were to be combined in a new regional grouping, Pfizer Europe. The former manager of the EEC area, Mr. James Green, was appointed Senior Vice President of Pfizer Europe and a Vice President of Pfizer International. He would continue to report directly to Mr. Fenton, but the SEE and SEME Area Managers would now report to him, as shown in Exhibit 5.

According to Mr. Fenton, the establishment of Pfizer Europe as a "management center" represented a step in the direction of further decentralization. At some time in the future he expected to set up similar management centers for Asia and Latin America. Eventually, three management center heads would report to him, each responsible for several of the old areas. Since each of the new management centers would be able to support relatively extensive administrative and field support staffs, it would be possible for Mr. Fenton to delegate more responsibility to the management center heads than he had to the Area Managers. Moreover, Country Managers would now be able to look to the management centers rather than New York for assistance in such matters as finance, product development, and plant construction. According to Mr. Fenton, the management center organization would alleviate many of the communications problems that had existed when the countries and areas had worked directly with the New York staff.

Mr. Fenton had decided to begin with Pfizer Europe for several reasons. Europe was the largest and most sophisticated market for Pfizer International products, and thus had become able to support an extensive headquarters staff sooner than other parts of the world. The growth of the EEC, the diversification of the product line, and the tendency for competition to view Europe as a single market had all contributed to the decision. Finally, Mr. Fenton believed that Mr. Green, who had done an outstanding job as EEC Area Manager, was ready for increased line responsibility, and that the SEE Area Manager, who had assumed various administration responsibilities for the Pfizer Europe headquarters, was well qualified to manage an expanded administrative staff.

Pfizer Europe Organization

When Mr. Green became Senior Vice President of Pfizer Europe, responsibilities for the combined Brussels staff and the SEE and SEME areas were added to his previous responsibilities as manager of the EEC area. Initially, he would retain responsibility for managing the EEC area, whose five Pharmaceutical/Agricultural Country Business Managers and four Consumer Products Country Business Managers would continue to report to him. Temporarily, the SEE and SEME areas would remain intact, and Country Managers in these areas would continue to report to their respective Area Managers, who would report to Mr. Green. The manager of the SEE area would continue to supervise the headquarters staff, and the manager of the separate UKI area would continue to have line responsibility for chemicals and basic research.

During 1966 and 1967, however, Mr. Green expected to begin making changes in the organization of Pfizer Europe. While he was not yet certain what form these changes would take, he outlined certain possibilities in the late fall of 1965.

As a first step, the UKI area might be brought into Pfizer Europe. This move would add a major market to Mr. Green's responsibility and bring UK/EEC chemicals and European basic research, which were presently under the UKI Area Manager, into Pfizer Europe.

If the United Kingdom were added, Pfizer Europe would then have seven countries large enough to have separate managers for the various businesses conducted in each (i.e., UK, France, Italy, Benelux, Germany, Sweden, and Spain). In each of these countries, for example, separate Country Business Managers might be appointed for: (1) the pharmaceutical-agricultural/veterinary business; (2) the chemicals business; (3) the consumer products business; (4) a door-to-door cosmetics business. Although these separate managers would probably share some staff services, each would have profit responsibility for his business, and would report directly to Pfizer Europe headquarters.

With this in mind, Mr. Green was considering a top organization that would ultimately consist of six vice presidents at Pfizer Europe headquarters. Three of these vice presidents would be responsible for products: (1) Vice President-Pharmaceuticals (including Agricultural); (2) Vice President-Consumer Products; and (3) Vice President-Chemicals. Each product vice president would have line authority over the Country Business Managers responsible for that particular product group in each of the seven large countries indicated above. The other three vice presidents would be: (1) Vice President-Administration, with responsibility for staff activities at the Pfizer Europe headquarters; (2) Vice President-Country Organizations, with responsibility for those smaller markets essentially involved in the pharmaceutical business with small agricultural and chemical operations; and (3) Vice President-Scientific Affairs, with responsibility for basic research in the British and Belgian research centers. The Vice President-Country Organizations would function in much the same way as the old Area Managers had, except that he would report to Mr. Green and work closely with the product line vice presidents (see Exhibit 6, Possible Organization of Pfizer Europe).

Pfizer International Staff Vice Presidents-New York

In early September 1965 Mr. Fenton announced the establishment in New York of four new vice presidential positions in a memorandum to Pfizer International Area Managers and New York division heads:

With the continued rapid growth and diversification of our International business, and our determination that this growth shall continue and that each of our separate businesses shall have full opportunity to develop in its own way, it has become necessary to provide for more and better strategic planning at New York Headquarters.

We are, therefore, creating four positions of Vice President for Development, each concerned with one of our separate businesses on an international basis and each reporting directly to me. These positions will be International staff positions, not line. That is to say, they will not intervene in the direct line of authority between me and Senior Vice President Green of Pfizer Europe or the Area Managers in other parts of the world, nor will they take responsibility away from these men. They will be responsible, in consultation with operating managements abroad, for formulating and recommending to me strategic policies for the International business with which they are concerned, and for ensuring that such policies, when agreed, are implemented through operating managements abroad. They will also be responsible for maintaining liaison with the Managers of the corresponding businesses in the United States with a view to ensuring that there is a free flow of technological and other information in both directions between the U.S. businesses and the business abroad, and also between our organizations in different parts of the world.

According to Mr. Fenton, the four staff vice presidents would complement the further decentralization of the geographic field organization. Since the management center heads would have almost complete control over Pfizer International activities abroad, Mr. Fenton believed he needed competent staff assistance in planning and guiding the world-wide development of the four broad Pfizer businesses.[6] The four new vice presidents were to perform this function and to assure that each business, with its unique characteristics, received adequate top management assistance and support.

In describing the duties of the new vice presidents, Mr. Fenton pointed out that each would have a somewhat different role to play. Since each of the four Pfizer businesses was at a different stage in development, the line organization would require differing degrees of assistance in policy formulation and implementation.

At one extreme, the Pfizer pharmaceutical business was highly developed, and the field organization had adequate experience and resources to deal with most of its problems. For this reason, the Vice President for Pharmaceutical Development would be primarily responsible for coordinating the flow of information between Chas. Pfizer research and development and the Country Pharmaceutical Business Managers, and for insuring that information concerning successful marketing approaches in one country was disseminated to the other countries. According to Mr. Fenton, the Vice President for Pharmaceutical Development would largely confine his planning activities to the fields of logistics and new plant construction.

The Vice President for Agricultural Development would also be involved with dissemination of information and logistics planning. In contrast to pharmaceuticals, however, there were still several major strategic issues for Pfizer to resolve in the agricultural field. In Nigeria, Pfizer had integrated forward into the manufacture of finished feeds, rather than concentrating on the sale of feed supplements to independent millers as it had done in most other countries. Mr. Fenton expected the new Vice President for Agricultural Development to study these and other strategic alternatives and to make recommendations as to what Pfizer's long-range strategy should be for the development of this business.

The Vice President for Consumer Products Development, who had been head of international marketing for Avon Cosmetics, would devote a large part of his time to the establishment of a Pfizer International door-to-door sales organization. By early December he had reviewed the experimental British direct sales operation. He had also assisted in the hiring of a direct sales specialist who was to build a direct sales organization in Italy. Although this specialist reported to Mr. Green, he would work closely with the Vice President for Consumer Products Development. After establishing an organization in Italy and training an Italian Direct Sales General Manager, the specialist was to move on to other European countries, setting up direct sales organizations on a country-by-country basis. Eventually he would move to Brussels, where he would be Mr. Green's Vice President in Charge of Direct Sales.

The new Vice President for Chemical Development had previously been an executive with a major international chemical company. Because Pfizer International was still relatively inexperienced in the chemical business,[7] the Vice President for Chemical Development would have a somewhat broader assignment than the other new vice presidents. According to an internal memorandum:

The Vice President of Chemical Development will be responsible, in consultation with operating managements abroad, for formulating and recommending to the President strategic policy for the company's world-wide chemical business outside the United States and for insuring that such policies when agreed by the President are implemented through operating managements abroad. He will also be responsible for maintaining liaison with the managers of the chemical businesses in the United States with a view to insuring that a really global point of view is taken to the extent that it is necessary. Specific responsibilities will include:

(1) Analyze and appraise the chemical business in those markets where it now represents an important part of the company's total business. In consultation with operating managements devise ways in which further profitable growth and development can be achieved.
(2) Evaluate opportunities for the profitable growth of the company's present line of chemical products in major markets where the chemical business has not yet been significantly developed. In consultation with operating managements, formulate plans and policies which will accomplish this development.
(3) Develop with operating managements opportunities for the establishment of new businesses in the chemical field in all major markets including the expansion of the company's present managerial, research, technical, and physical resources necessary to con-

---

[6] Pharmaceutical, Agricultural, Chemical, and Consumer Products.

[7] Pfizer International chemical sales were only $28 million in 1964 (excluding bulk pharmaceuticals). Chemicals and consumer products were the only businesses in which international sales volume were less than Chas. Pfizer's domestic sales volume.

duct such new businesses as well as the acquisition of or joint ventures with other companies, licensing arrangements, etc.

(4) Review and evaluate plans for the development and expansion of the company's chemical business which originate with operating managements. Analyze projects and recommend action to be taken.

(5) Review and appraise Chemical Division budgets and long-range plans submitted by operating managements to headquarters for approval.

(6) Insure coordination and liaison between operating managements abroad and in the United States to make certain that chemical products marketed in any market are evaluated for introduction in other markets. Assist operating managements in making such evaluations.

(7) Acquire and supervise a staff at headquarters necessary to carry out these responsibilities.

In defining the assignment of the Vice President for Chemical Development, Mr. Fenton pointed out that he would not be responsible for bulk pharmaceuticals. While Chemical Business Managers would continue to sell bulk pharmaceuticals, the Vice President for Pharmaceutical Development would have staff responsibility for bulk pharmaceuticals.

The Future

In late December 1965 Mr. Fenton made the following comments on the future of Pfizer International's organization:

As far as I can tell, our new organization will probably be adequate for the next five years or so. The management center heads and new staff vice presidents will make it possible for me to concentrate on the broader dimensions of our business, and, at the same time, give increased support to our philosophy of decentralized management at the country level.

It is difficult to predict what type of organization will be appropriate to our needs in the 1970s. We might want to go to line product divisions, as so many companies have done. Conversely, we might find that modern management techniques make it possible for geographic managers to operate a number of different businesses. After all, this is what I try to do for the company as a whole.

Exhibit 1. Chas. Pfizer & Co., Inc., and Subsidiary Companies, Ten-Year Financial Summary, 1956–1965

	1965	1964	1963	1962	1961	1960	1959	1958	1957	1956
Net sales	$542,620	$480,144	$414,290	$383,573	$312,433	$269,376	$253,673	$222,726	$207,152	$178,362
Other income	8,989	8,425	8,500	8,710	7,534	5,715	7,189	6,484	7,121	5,820
	$551,609	$488,569	$422,790	$392,283	$319,967	$275,091	$260,862	$229,210	$214,273	$184,182
Cost of goods sold and research expenses	$272,920	$242,816	$203,923	$188,150	$150,836	$140,283	$138,802	$116,966	$101,142	$ 91,440
Selling, general and administrative expenses	171,067	156,051	136,186	131,455	109,279	89,684	81,820	71,359	65,083	57,308
Other deductions	11,508	11,706	13,074	8,984	6,209	6,271	5,027	4,020	5,095	3,006
	$455,495	$410,573	$353,183	$328,589	$266,324	$236,238	$225,649	$192,345	$171,320	$151,754
Earnings before taxes	$ 96,114	$ 77,996	$ 69,607	$ 63,694	$ 53,643	$ 38,853	$ 35,213	$ 36,865	$ 42,953	$ 32,428
Taxes on income	42,700	33,300	29,300	27,200	22,200	12,670	10,350	12,900	20,044	14,174
Net earnings	$ 53,414	$ 44,696	$ 40,307	$ 36,494	$ 31,443	$ 26,183	$ 24,863	$ 23,965	$ 22,909	$ 18,254
Preferred stock dividends	—	—	—	—	24	128	150	165	192	497
Common stock earnings	$ 53,414	$ 44,696	$ 40,307	$ 36,494	$ 31,419	$ 26,055	$ 24,713	$ 23,800	$ 22,717	$ 17,757
Fixed assets net of depreciation	$192,185	$175,261	$154,988	$148,103	$121,348	$111,503	$ 97,768	$ 75,056	$ 44,438	$ 36,413
Working capital	126,399	110,882	101,046	98,467	86,502	78,464	79,405	69,366	74,896	72,590
Share owners' equity	338,165	301,448	275,120	244,137	199,647	170,462	154,849	138,434	127,081	115,051
Average number of common shares outstanding*	19,771	19,666	19,362	18,881	17,979	16,456	16,232	16,116	16,079	15,385
Earnings per share of common stock*	$2.70	$2.27	$2.08	$1.93	$1.74	$1.58	$1.52	$1.47	$1.41	$1.15
Dividends per share of common stock*	1.30	1.15	1.05	.95	.85	.80	.80	.75	.70	.58

(All amounts in thousands except per share data)

* Earnings and dividends per common share are based on the average number of shares of common stock outstanding during each year (excluding shares reacquired and held in the treasury) and restated for comparative purposes on the basis of the 3-for-1 stock split, April 20, 1959.

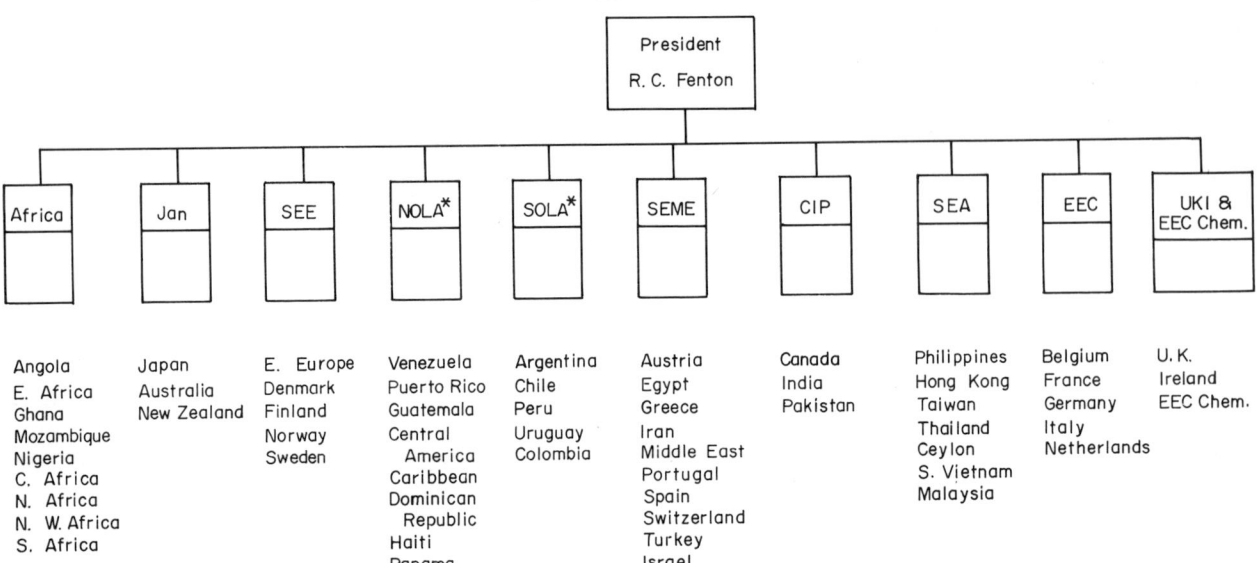

Exhibit 2. Line Organization in Early 1965

*In early 1965, Mexico reported directly to Mr. Fenton.
**In early 1965, Brazil reported directly to Mr. Fenton.

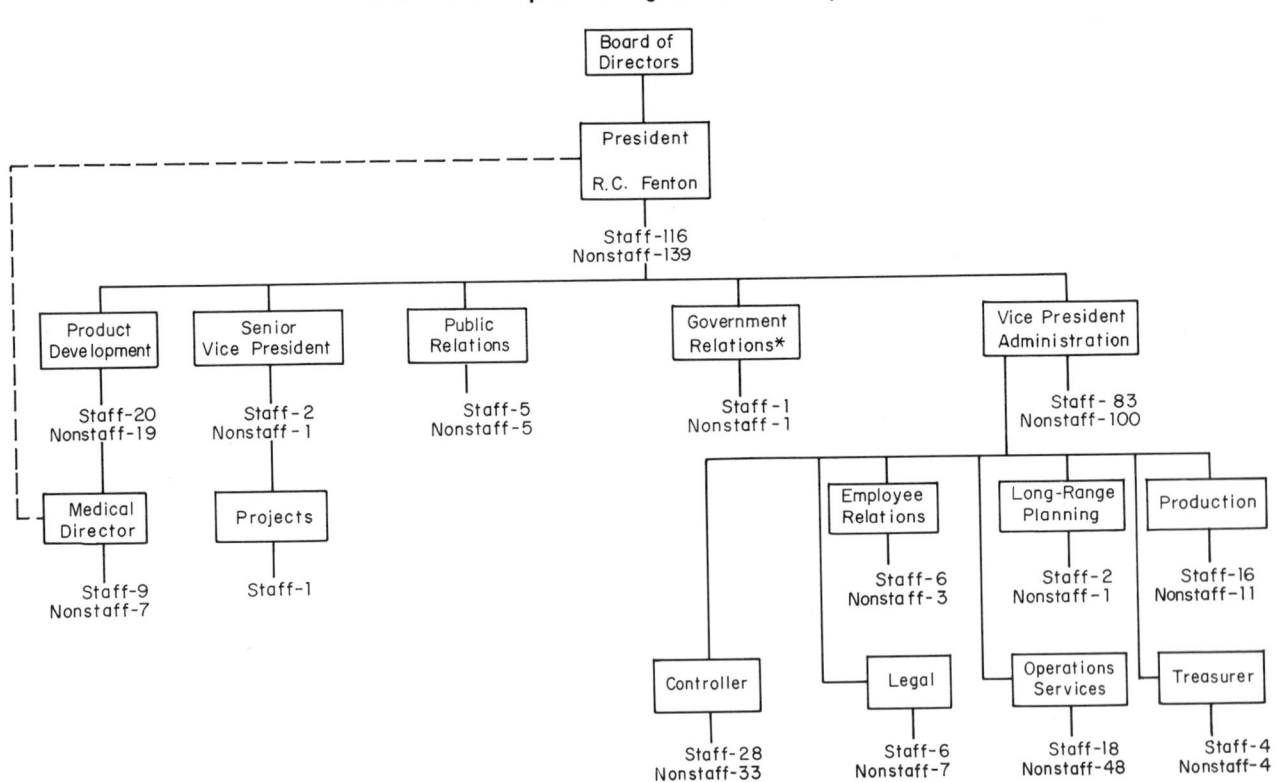

Exhibit 3. Headquarters Organization in Early 1965

*Also reports to J. J. Powers, Jr., President Chas. Pfizer

Exhibit 4. Organization of Areas in Europe in Early 1965

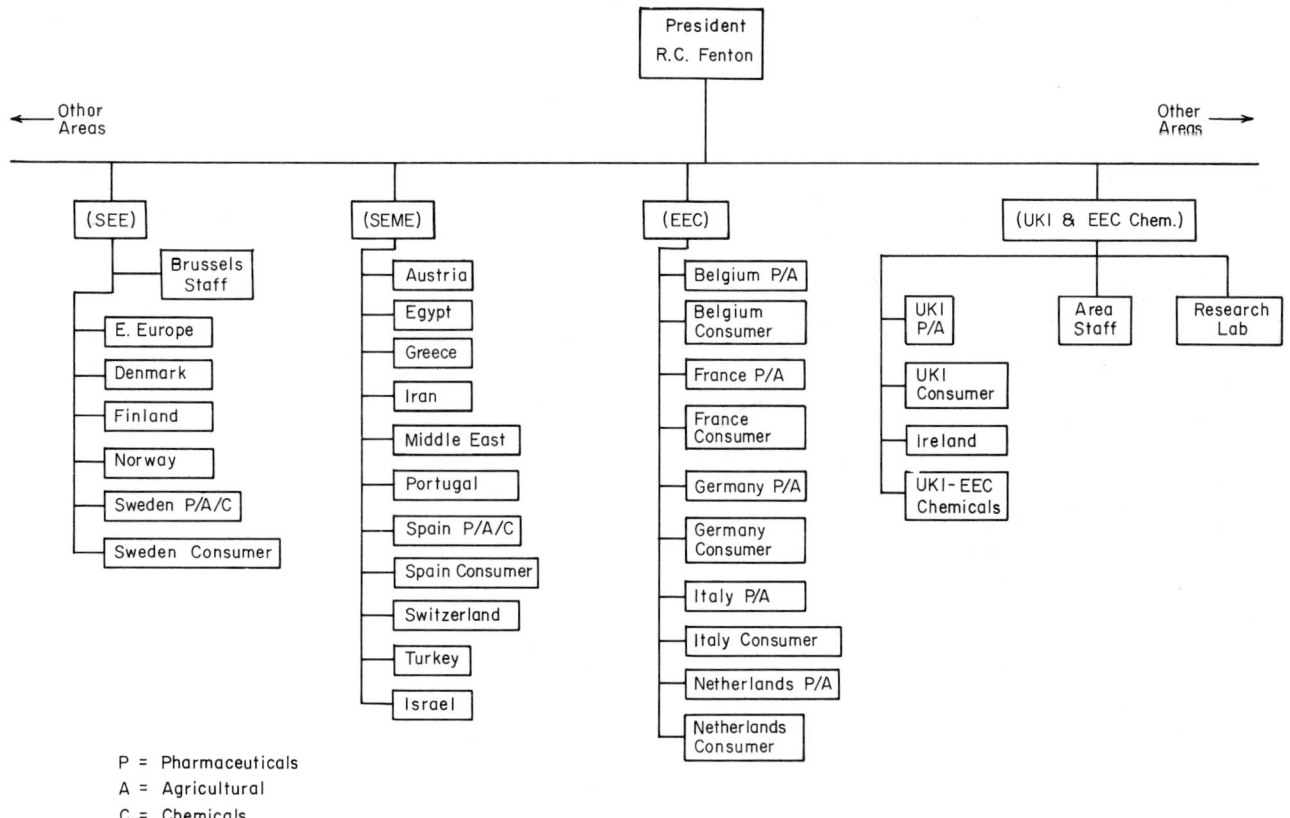

Exhibit 5. Organization of Pfizer Europe in Late 1965

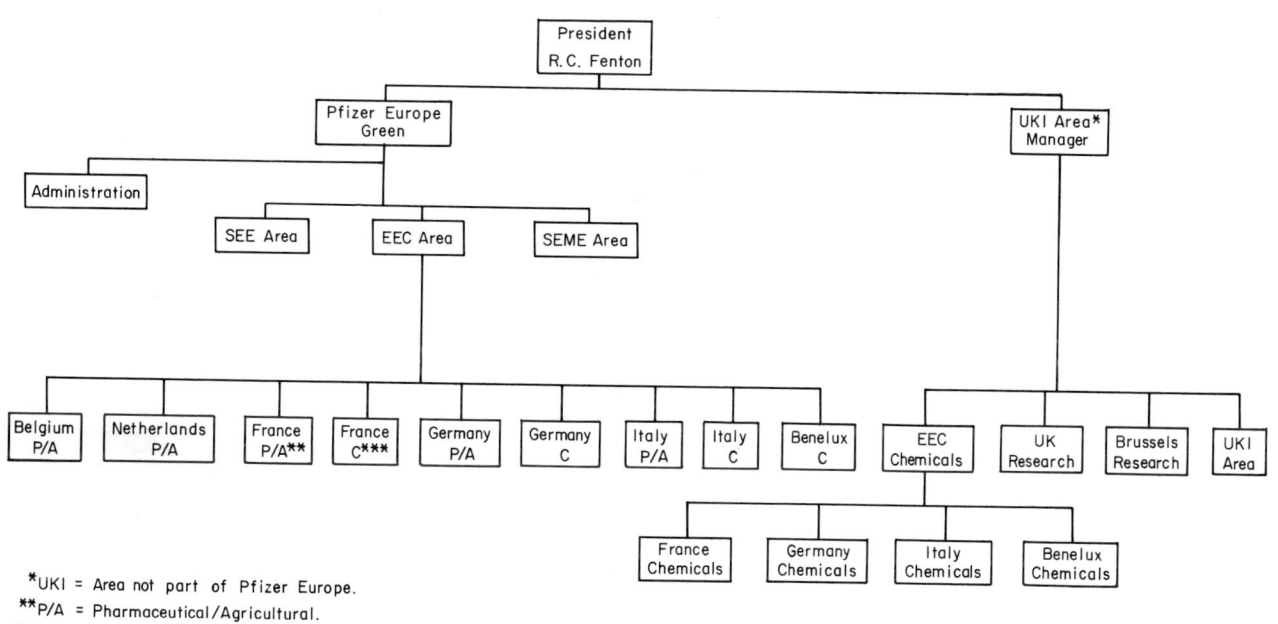

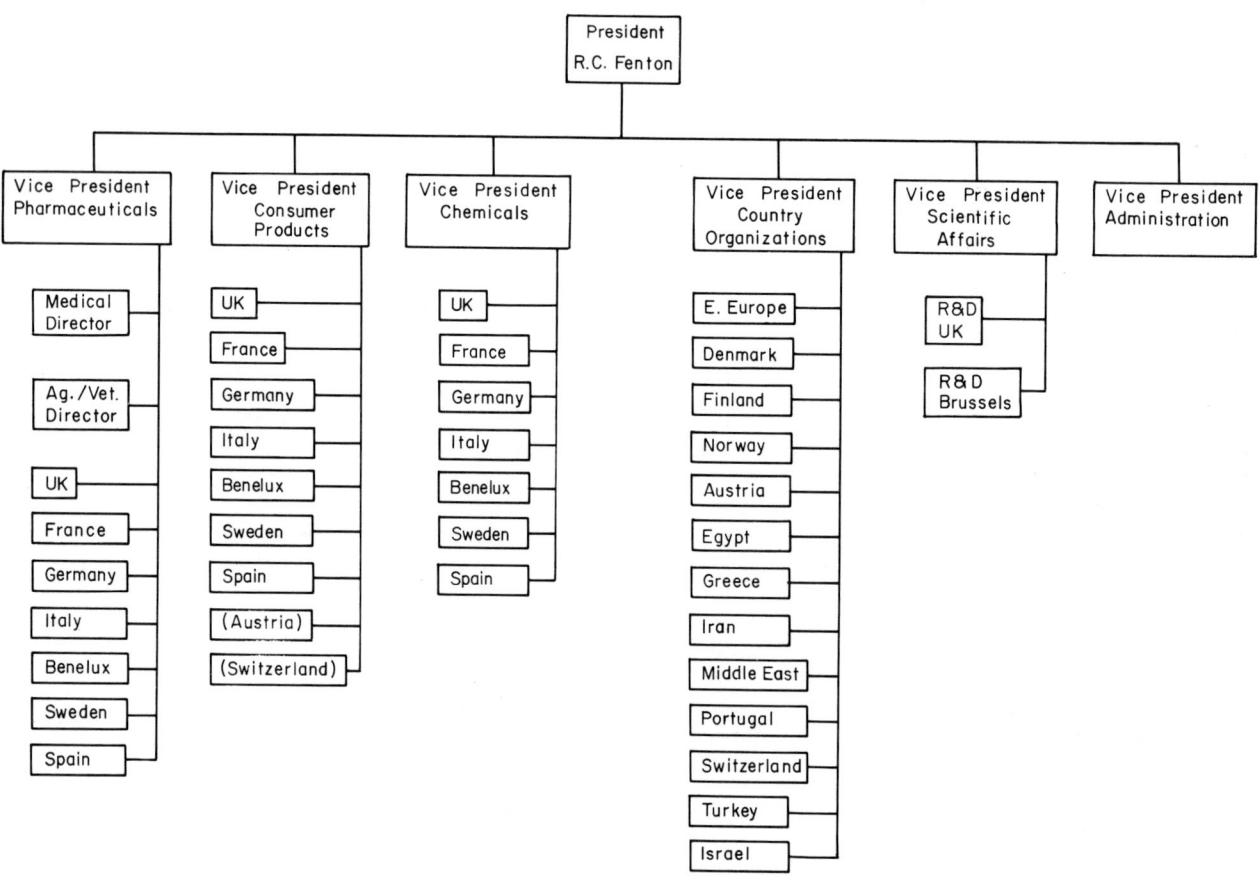

Exhibit 6. Possible Organization of Pfizer Europe

Appendix A

Extracts from: Interoffice Memorandum, Brussels Headquarters

TO: EEC Country Managers and Consumer Products General Managers
FROM: EEC Area Manager — Brussels
SUBJECT: Relationship between Country Manager and Consumer Products General Manager — EEC Area
DATE: November 9, 1964

. . . in the EEC Area, both the Country Managers and the Consumer Products General Managers are at the same level of operational authority and responsibility, which is the country manager level. The authority and responsibilities of a country manager level operational position are defined in more detail in the Pfizer International Accounting Manual as well as the Pfizer Europe Procedures Manual. Thus, in the EEC Area the Country Manager and the Consumer Products General Manager have complete profit and loss responsibility for their respective operations, complete budget responsibility, capital appropriations responsibility, pricing and new product development responsibility, to mention only a few of the most obvious criteria. There are, however, certain differences in the administrative and organizational responsibilities of the Country Manager versus the Consumer Products General Manager as outlined in the following paragraphs.

Country Manager

The Country Manager has complete responsibility for our Pharmaceutical and Agricultural operations in his country reporting directly to the EEC Area Manager. The Pharmaceutical and Ag/Vet Division Managers report to him. In addition, the managers of the service divisions, Technical, Finance, and Medical, report to him administratively. In addition to providing appropriate services for the pharmaceutical and agricultural operations the service division managers, under the Country Manager, have responsibility, likewise, for providing services to the consumer products operating divisions in their country. In addition to this operational responsibility for our pharmaceutical and agricultural activities and his administrative responsibility for the service functions, the Country Manager is also expected to exercise overall cognizance concerning governmental, community, legal, and social problems affecting Pfizer interests in the country as a whole.

Consumer Products General Manager

The Consumer Products General Manager has complete responsibility for all consumer products operations in his country reporting directly to the EEC Area Manager. The consumer products operating divisions report to him. He obtains services as a requirement from the Finance, Technical, and Medical Divisions in order to ensure the proper functioning of these operating divisions. In matters related to the consumer products operating divisions he is the final authority on finance, technical, medical, and personnel issues at the local country level. If consumer products operations affect our ethical pharmaceutical activities, he would consult the Country Manager, and if local agreement cannot be reached, the matter would be referred to the Area Manager.

Use of Service Divisions

If the organization as defined above is to function smoothly, managers must ensure that there is direct liaison between the service divisions and the operating divisions at all levels. The Country Manager and Consumer Products General Manager must not act as bottlenecks to the normal routine functioning of staff and service activities. Most routine activity must be accomplished by horizontal contact between division managers, department heads, and section heads down through the entire organization consistent with proper operating procedure. Any important problems of policy and priorities would be resolved as necessary between the Country Manager and the Consumer Products General Manager.

Decentralization of Authority to Division Managers

The proper functioning of the above organization is certainly dependent upon one aspect of good management practice which we assume is carried out in all our countries. This is the policy of decentralizing authority to the managers for both operating and service divisions. Essentially, this means that the country should run properly without the interference of the Country Manager or Consumer Products General Manager. This is particularly important in the operating divisions where the division manager must have complete profit and loss responsibility for his operations. This may involve only giving him responsibility for the *local* profit and loss situation: however, the basic principle is essentially the same. We would also hope that eventually all division managers could have the consolidated profit and loss responsibility.

In any event, it means that the operating division manager must be cognizant not only of sales and promotional expenses, but the financial, technical, and all other business aspects affecting his division as well. This does not give the Operating Division Manager direct authority over the Service Division Manager. For example, the Pharmaceutical Division Manager obtains services and has essentially the same relationship with the Finance and Technical Divisions

Appendix A (continued)

as the Consumer Products General Manager, and under him, the Coty or other consumer products division managers.

Charges for Services

The operating divisions, whether they be pharmaceutical, agricultural, or consumer products, are charged their proportion of the expenses of the service divisions in accordance with the general policy in Pfizer International of direct and indirect charges. Direct charges are those which can be positively and exclusively identified with the activity of a particular operating division. After these direct charges have been allocated, the remainder of the expenses of the service divisions are allocated to the operating divisions in direct proportion to the sales volume of each division. In a particular country the system of effecting direct charges to the operating divisions is the responsibility of the Finance Division Manager under the control of the Area Controller. The Country Manager and the Consumer Products General Manager must be cognizant of and approve the system of allocating direct expenses which is in use. The most important point is that this system must be defined in detail at the time of preparation of the budget and thereafter can only be changed with the approval of the Area Controller and the Area Manager.

Chemical Divisions

The service division managers under the administration of the Country Manager are responsible for providing service to the Chemical Division in each country in a manner similar to that provided for the consumer products activities as outlined above.

Dissemination of Above Procedure

Country Managers and Consumer Products General Managers should ensure that their Division Managers as well as other appropriate staff personnel are informed of the above procedures as they apply to their particular country.

Appendix B

Guideposts for 1966 Budget

The following is a memorandum from Mr. R. C. Fenton in New York to PI Area Managers:

With some of you, I have been able to discuss this subject during my recent trips, but this has not been the case with all of you. So, I am setting down in writing the main points that I can think of. These are not intended to be rigid rules, and if you have good reasons for breaking them and doing something different, you should, by all means, follow your own view in preparing the budget, but you should know that I will have to be convinced by you during your visit to New York. Therefore, it would be wise for you to give your reasons for departing from these principles in writing when you submit the budgets.

Pharmaceutical and Agricultural Business:

If the total expenses of promotion and S. & G.A. exceed 20% of sales, there should be some reduction in the percentage. There should not be any increase in the percentage whatever the present percentage may be.

Consumer Products Business:

I will not be prepared to approve any budget showing a significant loss unless a 5-year plan is presented at the same time which indicates when we will get into profit. There should be no significant expenditure in any country where a consumer products general manager has not been appointed. The emphasis should be on Coty unless we already have another major activity. Our long-range aim should be to achieve, at least, as good a percentage of the cosmetics market as we have of the pharmaceutical market, and in any country where we are concentrating on consumer products, the budget for 1965 should be framed as part of a program in this direction.

Personnel:

Adequate provision should be made for the management training programs discussed at the last Area Managers' meeting.

Public Relations:

Adequate provision should be made for serious industry programs in all major countries.

Net Income:

Generally, I will expect the net income after taxes of each country to grow by at least 10% unless there are good explanations as to why this cannot be done. The countries where we are making substantial effort with investment and people should, of course, be growing at a greater rate than this. We will always have problems in one part of the world or another which have to be absorbed by greater than average growth where it is within our power. Our over-all aim is for our net income after all taxes to grow by substantially more than 10%, so many countries must do better than this — after absorbing the losses which we will certainly have in opening up new markets for consumer products.

COMMENTARY

Like IBM and Lockheed-Georgia, Pfizer International went through great organizational changes in a relatively short time under the forced draft of a rapid growth in sales. In all three cases one may observe the emergence of a program structure. But at Pfizer International the outline of the program structure is not so clear and, in fact, seems still to be developing. A geographic dimension considerably more complex than at IBM and Lockheed-Georgia has been a dominant influence shaping organizational structure. But while major aspects of strategy are formulated at the area level, other key elements are decided at headquarters.

It may be well to look at how the organization has developed and then to appraise the factors currently influencing organizational development. Some of these seem to push in the direction of a centralization of program management responsibilities at New York headquarters. Others seem to lean in the direction of a decentralization of the program management by geographic area.

As the structure developed, the country organizational unit emerged as the basic unit for program planning and implementation. From the beginning, the Country Manager was given considerable autonomy in running his country. He devised programs for marketing Pfizer International products, arranged for product supply, and managed company resources — sales and manufacturing — located within the borders of his country. This degree of autonomy and the fact that Country Managers were profit responsible would confirm the idea that the locus of program management was at the country level.

A major reason for the geographic decentralization of strategic planning and operating was that each country provided a unique market and regulatory environment. In the case of pharmaceuticals and agricultural and veterinary products (Pfizer International's most important lines), national laws affected formulations, dosages, labeling, distribution, and often price. Trade restrictions affected the flow of materials, bulk pharmaceuticals and chemicals, and packaged products. And in many countries legislation might have the effect of requiring that Pfizer International establish manufacturing facilities within the country to supply local markets. Probably no other type of consumer goods is as subject to local government regulations as pharmaceuticals.

As sales volume grew it became possible to support a degree of specialization by product groups within countries and in areas where markets for Pfizer International products were relatively homogeneous. There were separate organizations for the pharmaceutical/agricultural/veterinary businesses and the consumer products business in France, Italy, Germany, Belgium, the Netherlands, and the United Kingdom. The chemicals business for UKI and EEC was centralized in the UK with chemical business managers in six EEC countries reporting to the UKI area managers. Then, in the new Pfizer Europe management center, the Senior Vice President for Pfizer Europe proposed the establishment of three vice presidents for products. Each vice president would be responsible for one of the three product lines — pharmaceuticals (including agricultural chemicals), consumer products, and chemicals.

It is important to note, however, that certain key program decisions were taken out of the hands of Country Managers and were made at New York headquarters. Plant location, capital investment decisions, and sourcing patterns for local markets were determined at New York headquarters. That was because bulk plants, to be cost efficient, had to be built and operated on a scale much greater than needed to supply one country. Economies of scale, then, required the centralization of manufacturing and sourcing decisions.

Depending on the product, pricing decisions ran the gamut from complete centralization at New

York headquarters to decentralization at the country level. Pharmaceutical pricing tended to be centrally controlled because prices in one country would have an impact on prices in other countries. It was likely that New York headquarters exercised particularly close control over to-the-market prices of proprietary products such as Terramycin. The prices of agricultural and chemical products were largely determined at the area level, with minimum prices being set on some products in New York. For these products the relevant market environment was the area, and Pfizer International's pricing had to respond to competitive conditions in the area.

In the case of consumer products pricing, decision making resided primarily at the country level. Some consumer products were made and sold in only one or two countries. As for the others, apparently, competition was local in character and manufacturing costs were locally controlled.

This suggests the idea that while program management was largely on a country by country basis, there was an "upward" coordination of programs on matters that went beyond the borders of each country — sourcing on bulk products and pricing on products that, in effect, had world markets.

In spite of the centralization of decision making on certain critical strategy elements, program responsibility at Pfizer International was essentially decentralized geographically. Would it continue to be so or were there strong pressures toward centralized program management responsibility by product line?

The establishment at New York headquarters of four new vice presidential posts (for Pharmaceutical Development, Agricultural Development, Consumer Products Development, and Chemical Development, respectively) would suggest the possibility of a centralized program management function. The description of the responsibilities to be assumed by the new managers, however, suggests that their roles would be limited. They did not have the broad range of concerns that would indicate that they would be, in fact, program managers responsible for planning world-wide programs and working to integrate Pfizer International resource effort in carrying them out. The Vice President for Pharmaceutical Development would confine his planning activities to logistics (sourcing) and new plant construction, matters that were already handled at headquarters. In addition, he would serve as a vehicle for disseminating information to Country Pharmaceutical Business Managers on research and development and marketing. The Vice President for Agricultural Development played a similar role. In addition, he would make recommendations on strategy alternatives for the long-run growth of this business.

The Vice President for Consumer Products Development would devote his attention simply to the establishment of a Pfizer International door-to-door sales organization. The Vice President of Chemical Development had broader responsibilities for "formulating and recommending to the President strategic policy for the company's world-wide chemical business outside the United States and for insuring that such policies when agreed by the President are implemented through operating managements abroad."

Only this last position would seem to fill a program management role. Moreover, all four posts were described as "staff positions, not line." At least at this point, then, the primary responsibility for devising and implementing product programs still resided at the area and country levels, except perhaps for chemicals. This exception is explained possibly by the fact that chemicals were a relatively undeveloped business for Pfizer International. In the case of the more developed businesses — pharmaceuticals and agricultural chemicals — strong country and area operations existed. The centralization, therefore, of program management responsibility at headquarters for these products would be perceived as contravening the authority and responsibility of strong, established country and area managements. In the brief history of Pfizer International, program management strength had developed at the country and area levels, making it difficult, possibly, to centralize the program management function at the headquarters level.

Moreover the same pressures for having world-wide product strategies do not exist here as at Monsanto. At Monsanto, competition among foreign subsidiaries, lack of coordination, conflict in dealing with multinational customers, and problems of product supply abroad were pressures leading toward centralization of program management. With a single sourcing system at Pfizer International and centralized control over key prices, the kinds of conflicts that Monsanto experienced in marketing abroad are not likely to develop at Pfizer. In addition, Pfizer International's markets are essentially local and its customers are not big multinational companies.

By Way of Prediction

Probably over the longer run market forces and manufacturing considerations would tend to result in somewhat different structures for the pharmaceutical, agricultural, veterinary, and chemical products, on the one hand, and consumer products, on the other.

In the case of the former the need for a single (ex-United States) supply system, the interrelationship of prices in different countries, and the desirability of disseminating new product developments quickly would point to the need for centralized program managements. At the same time, the impact of local market and regulatory environments on product formulations, packaging, labeling, and marketing practices indicates the need to allow for program modification at local levels. The nature and extent of modification would vary among these several product lines and also by area. For example, area managers might have more flexibility in pricing agricultural and chemical products than pharmaceuticals. Managers in countries with very different social, political, and economic climates (such as India) might have greater responsibility for adapting advertising, promotional, and selling programs to meet local market needs.

The essential facts, however, which characterize the consumer products lines of Pfizer International suggest that the locus of program management responsibility be at the area and/or country level. Manufacture was to a large extent local in character, depending on local supplies of raw materials. The economies of scale were such that manufacturing plants having the capacity for supplying the needs of one country were practical and efficient. Moreover, some consumer products were made and sold in only one or two countries. In particular, product, packaging, price, and promotional competition was primarily local in character. Under these circumstances, consumer product program management units might easily be decentralized by area in some parts of the world and by country in others. At headquarters in New York, the most useful function to be performed might be the dissemination of ideas on product line developments, packaging, and promotional campaigns among the several consumer products program management units.

Ford Motor Company: Tractor Division

The Ford Motor Company's Tractor Division was established in 1961, with full responsibility for coordinating Ford's tractor, industrial equipment,[1] and farm implement[2] businesses in all parts of the world. Prior to this time, the tractor, implement, and equipment business had been split between two organizations: the Ford U.S. Tractor and Implement Division in the United States and the Ford of Britain Tractor Group in the United Kingdom. Each organization had developed, manufactured, and marketed its own product line. Although the two product lines were based on completely different designs, both lines covered a similar range of sizes, horsepower ratings, and applications.

The Ford U.S. Tractor and Implement Division had been fully integrated, having its own development, manufacturing, and marketing resources. The Ford U.K. Tractor Group had been essentially a marketing activity, obtaining its products from the Ford of Britain engineering and manufacturing organization.

In other countries, Ford tractors had historically been marketed by automobile-oriented sales components. The Ford Motor Company had operating subsidiaries in 28 countries. Where such subsidiaries existed, they generally had had responsibility for tractors as well as cars and trucks. In countries where Ford did not have operating subsidiaries, tractors had been marketed by importer-distributors — generally the same importer-distributors who handled Ford's car and truck lines.

The Ford U.K. Tractor Group had been active in both domestic and export markets, exporting quite successfully to Latin America and the United States. The Ford U.S. Tractor and Implement Division had exported few tractors, but had been somewhat more active in exporting farm implements.

In 1960 Mr. Henry Ford II had requested a study of Ford's world-wide tractor business. Two major conclusions had emerged from this study:

(1) Ford's major competitors were organized as world-wide, full-line tractor and implement companies, whereas Ford operated through two independent tractor organizations. Only the U.S. organization offered a Ford-produced implement line.
(2) The high costs of designing and manufacturing two separate lines of tractors prevented Ford from realizing the economies of scale warranted by its total unit volume.

In accord with these conclusions, it was decided that the Ford U.S. and Ford U.K. tractor activities should be coordinated, and as far as was legally possible, the tractor activities of the two companies should operate as complementary parts of a single organization. Certain engineering was done by Ford of Britain, some by Ford U.S. Certain of the manufacturing facilities were owned by Ford U.S., some by Ford of Britain and its subsidiary.

The primary objectives of the new Ford Tractor Division were to standardize Ford's tractor and equipment product lines world-wide; consolidate manufacturing facilities to obtain production scale economies; provide specialized tractor sales and marketing attention to areas formerly supervised by automobile sales departments; and expand equipment product lines and sales in all markets.

Organization

The new Division[3] passed through several organizational stages between 1961 and 1968. In the first stage,

---

[1] Industrial equipment included products such as tractors equipped with back hoes and loaders and other attachments used for landscaping, trenching, etc. These products were generally based on standard Ford tractors.

[2] Farm implements included products such as plows, spreaders, harrows, combines, etc., generally (although not always) to be attached to a tractor.

[3] In 1967 the name of the Ford Tractor Division was changed to Ford Tractor Operations. For clarity the text of this case uses the name "Ford Tractor Division" throughout.

all purchasing, product engineering, and manufacturing operations were consolidated. At the same time, a Product Planning Group was established at Division headquarters in Birmingham, Michigan, with responsibility for planning the new world-wide product line. The new Division's key objectives, product line standardization and manufacturing consolidation, were thus placed under centralized world-wide control almost immediately.

During the next several years, various functions were removed from the U.K. operation and established on a world-wide basis at Division headquarters. These functions included programming and distribution, market planning and analysis, industrial relations, financial control, and administration. As a result of these moves, the U.K. and U.S. operations became essentially marketing activities, rather than fully integrated business units.

Shortly after the establishment of the new Division, a Tractor Manager had been appointed in each country where Ford operated through a subsidiary company. While these Tractor Managers were generally on the payrolls of the subsidiary companies, they coordinated their efforts with the Tractor Division. In other countries, tractor franchises of Ford importer-distributors had been transferred to the Tractor Division.

In 1967 three Assistant General Managers were appointed, responsible respectively for Product Development, Manufacturing, and Sales and Marketing. Each Assistant General Manager had world-wide responsibility for his function, and reported to the Division General Manager (see Exhibit 1). To the extent that one Ford company rendered service to another Ford company, it was paid a service fee by the receiving company.

Product Development

The Product Development Operation was divided into three offices: Tractor Product Planning, Tractor Product Engineering, and Equipment Product Development (product planning and product engineering).

Tractor Product Planning

When the new Division was established, its immediate objective was to establish a single, world-wide tractor product line. There were product planning units in both the U.K. Tractor Group and the U.S. Tractor and Implement Division, but primary responsibility for planning the new product line was assigned to the new headquarters Product Planning Group.

The new group began by assessing the strengths and weaknesses of the Division's 1961 product line. The major finding of this study was that neither the U.S. nor the U.K. product line was fully competitive with the product lines of the Division's stronger competitors.

In view of this analysis it was decided to start from scratch, rather than attempt to modify one of Ford's existing tractor product lines. The objective was to design a single line of tractors, consisting of five models. The basic components of each model would be the same, regardless of the country in which a particular tractor would be sold. Other components would be available in several versions, to permit "customization" of a model to meet local market requirements. All tractors of a given model would use the same engine, for example. Because several transmissions and rear axles would be available, however, it would be possible to modify the basic model to meet a wide range of agricultural and legal requirements.[4]

Provisions were also made to facilitate less substantial modifications of the basic models. German law required, for example, that fender tops be wide and flat (rather than curved) to allow passengers to ride on them. As a result, the new tractors would be designed in such a way that either a curved or a flat top fender could be used.

In developing the plan[5] for the new line, the headquarters Product Planning Group requested and utilized market information and product feature requests from the U.S. and U.K. product planning units. The U.K. product planning unit also collected and transmitted information from the various export markets in which it was active. While not attempting to fill all those requests, the Product Planning Group found them useful in determining the most commonly sought features for a new line of tractors, and for making provision for subsequent modifications and adaptations for local markets or applications.

By mid-1966 Ford's old tractor lines had been completely replaced by the new line of tractors. At this time the Product Planning Group described the new line of tractors as follows:

Ford has five agricultural all-purpose tractors to cover the entire market for 25 to 75 horsepower. The 1966 Ford

---
[4] Some countries had maximum speed requirements for agricultural tractors, for example. By removing the top gear of a transmission it was possible to meet these legal requirements without sacrificing efficiency or using a different transmission.

[5] The product plan was essentially a list of features, characteristics, and cost targets for the new line. This plan was transmitted to the Product Engineering Office, which translated it into detailed engineering specifications and drawings.

tractors incorporate a new family of rugged, efficient diesel engines. Four different types of transmissions are offered to meet varying market needs. . . .

Besides the five basic agricultural tractors, we now offer seven specialized agricultural derivative models and 11 nonfarm derivative models. The number of derivative models has increased from 10 in 1961 to 18 in 1966. And the number of all models in the Ford tractor line has increased from 15 in 1961 to 23 in 1966. . . .

Ford has three major world-wide tractor competitors: [Competitor X], which sells a slightly greater number of tractors than Ford, [Competitor Y] with sales of 75 per cent of Ford, and [Competitor Z] in fourth place selling one-half as many tractors as Ford. [Competitors X, Y, and Z] certainly do not constitute all of our competition around the world. These three major companies offer the principal world-wide tractor lines. Ford has severe competition from many local makes of tractors. One of the major advantages of our new tractor line is that it provides a product base from which we can secure derivative models to compete in local markets. Examples of this are the vineyard and narrow tractors primarily produced for France and the recently approved 3000 rice tractor for Japan and the Far East. Thus, our new tractor line has given us better coverage of the primary agricultural all-purpose market and also has improved our position in respect to derivative models required to meet local competition.

In early 1968 Ford was in the process of introducing an extra-large tractor. Although not the largest or most powerful tractor in the industry (Competitor Y was particularly strong in this segment of the market), the new 8000 tractor represented a major addition to Ford's tractor line. The market for the 8000 tractor was limited for the most part to the United States, but was expected to develop in other areas of the world in the near future.

U.S. marketing personnel were extremely pleased with the new series of extra-large tractors, since it would allow them to compete in market segments in which Ford had not previously been represented. Several U.S. executives pointed out that they would have had such a tractor sooner if top management had not decided to concentrate product development activities on products having the broadest world-wide market potential. While admitting that this decision had possibly limited Ford's short-run penetration of the U.S. market, these executives were emphatic in pointing out that this kind of trade-off, with the overall world-wide profitability of the business as a criterion, was the major benefit of having a world-wide organization.

Product Engineering

The Product Engineering Office was responsible for translating the product plans for the new line of tractors into detailed specifications and designs. The Office consisted of two operating components, one in the United Kingdom and one in the United States. Both components reported to the Chief Engineer, who was located in the United States.

The decision to maintain two engineering organizations had been based on several considerations. First, there was a shortage of qualified engineers, and it appeared to be more feasible to augment two existing organizations than to undertake a massive recruiting effort in either the United States or the United Kingdom. Second, some sort of engineering organization was needed in the United Kingdom in any event, since so much of the Division's basic manufacturing was to take place in that country.

While the decision to retain two engineering offices facilitated the personnel build-up required for the new line of tractors, it also placed a heavy communications burden on the management of the Product Engineering Office. As the Chief Engineer explained:

With the creation of an international organization came a tremendous problem of communication, not only within engineering, but also with other activities of the division. Starting early in 1962, we held regularly scheduled management meetings alternately on each side of the Atlantic. We also learned that by installing a taped telephone answering service in each office, we could leave messages for each other that would get immediate attention the next morning. By this means we reduced our telephone rates by taking advantage of after-hour reduced charges.

Recognizing the need for early problem resolution and control of problems, engineering has established problem control rooms in the U.S. and U.K. All problems are reported into the control rooms and from here they are controlled and followed up for earliest resolution. Information on problems and progress is exchanged daily between both rooms in U.S. and U.K. to permit visibility on both sides of the Atlantic for all members of engineering management.

In February 1966 the Engineering Office at Birmingham, Michigan, installed a teletype console. This console is linked into an elaborate computer complex at Dearborn, Michigan. A computer console is also being installed in the U.K. and will be linked into our central computer at Dearborn by trans-Atlantic telephone lines.

Naturally, we have had some problems in coordinating two engineering offices in the use of common procedures and common methods of disseminating engineering data to a complex international organization. This was accomplished by the development of a computerized system for handling parts lists and engineering information. Traditional manual systems became obsolete with the new organization, and the use of a computer method became necessary. Without this, the job of transmitting information would not have been done.

Nevertheless, I am still reviewing the possibility of realigning certain engineering responsibilities on both sides of the Atlantic to help improve communications. The trend has been to assign all Advanced and Forward Model Engineering to the U.S. Office and permit the U.K. Office to concentrate on Current and Past Model Engineering and provide assistance on Forward Model work as workload permits. It is also necessary to consider the requirements for specific talents as may be required for future Product Programs and new products, as these can have a strong influence on any organization plans.

Manufacturing

In 1961 Ford tractors had been manufactured at the large Ford automotive plant in Dagenham, England, and at the Ford tractor plant in Highland Park, Michigan. The two plants had operated independently of each other, each producing a full line of tractors.

Because of increased demand for the British automotive line, it had been necessary to move tractor production out of Dagenham by October 1964. A new plant was built in Basildon, U.K.; and an automotive assembly plant in Antwerp, Belgium, was converted to tractor production. By late 1964, therefore, the Tractor Division coordinated tractor manufacturing at three major manufacturing plants: Highland Park, Basildon, and Antwerp.

A major objective of the new organization was to rationalize tractor production, to have a single source for each major component. Basildon was to manufacture all engines, front axles, and hydraulic units; Antwerp all six-speed and eight-speed transmissions and rear axles; and Highland Park all ten-speed and four-speed transmissions. Other components were to be purchased from outside vendors, either in the country of final assembly or from a single source for subsequent shipment to the assembly points.

Each of the three manufacturing plants was to assemble tractors and components for its own use and use by other assembly plants. In general, Basildon was to assemble tractors for the U.K. and overseas export markets; Antwerp for the European Economic Community; and Highland Park for the U.S. market. There were, however, a number of exceptions to this pattern. Temporarily, for example, the new extra-large 8000 tractor was to be assembled only at Highland Park. If export demand materialized, Highland Park would export this model, in either finished or "knocked-down" form. Similarly, the Antwerp plant had responsibility for assembling vineyard tractors for export to wine producing areas throughout the world.

The new manufacturing system was intended to give Ford the advantages of high volume specialized production of components and, at the same time, the advantages of assembling completed tractors near their markets. To a large degree the new system would be dependent on the ability of Manufacturing to procure, produce, and transport components from one part of the world to another.

The Assistant General Manager-Manufacturing described these processes as follows:

Purchased Parts: A total of 5,532 different production parts are procured for the new tractor line alone. This excludes those parts which are associated with old model tractors, implements, service parts, and components. Each of the plants has the responsibility for procuring approximately 3,100 individual items or assemblies, of which some 600 to 800 are unique parts—unique to its own manufacture of engines, axles, transmissions, etc., in addition to some 2,000 common final line parts. Each tractor plant also has some several hundred final line or assembly end items which are used only at that plant to accommodate special marketing needs, legal requirements, and so on. The rest, however, are truly common parts; that is, they are identical, and in many cases a single source, most often located in the U.K., will furnish the requirements for all three plants.

Sourcing: The major portion of the tractor procurement is concentrated in the United Kingdom even though a tractor built at any one of our three assembly locations could have component parts or assemblies originally produced in any one of 12 countries.

The purchase of the unique parts by the purchasing activity in each plant is a relatively simple sourcing job. Virtually all of the Basildon requirements are sourced in the U.K.; Antwerp requirements come primarily from the U.K., with some parts coming from Continental sources and the U.S.; and the Highland Park requirements for unique parts are almost entirely sourced in the U.S. The latter are mainly 10-speed transmission parts, plus some four-speed components.

The common or final line parts, however, present an entirely different problem. Naturally, we are interested in minimizing tooling costs while at the same time assuring supply protection and the most economical prices for the division as a whole, even though in some isolated cases it could mean a slightly higher price for an individual plant. To make the proper analysis, each major item falling in this category and sourced before June 1964 was reviewed on the basis of soliciting quotations (insofar as possible) in the U.S., the U.K., and the Continent. Then these quotations were evaluated at division staff and a complete analysis made of the piece price, freight, duty, and other applicable costs for each plant from each source. . . .

Logistics: While sourcing the parts was one important phase of our activity in preparing for new tractor production, getting the materials to the plants was another problem. As you will also appreciate, moving the manufactured components, such as the engines, axles, and transmissions, from one plant to another is also a substantial task.

Insofar as possible, we try to take advantage of regular shipping schedules to minimize transport cost, but many conditions — often beyond our control — require emergency actions, including transoceanic air freight. As far as we have been able to determine, our division regularly ships more materials across the ocean than any other company in the world today. Our Traffic Department, which is an integral part of the purchasing activity, becomes involved with each of the following:

1. The movement of incoming parts from approximately 1,000 suppliers in 12 countries.
2. The movement of transmissions, axles, engines, hydraulics, and front axles between the three tractor plants.
3. The export of tractors and implements to approximately 60 countries.
4. The analysis, audit, and reporting of freight and duty payments in connection with the component movements outlined above.

In early 1968 there was general agreement in the Division that world-wide sourcing and shipment of components was working well. As one executive explained:

It is really amazing how few problems we have — considering the number of parts, countries, and assembly points involved. Occasionally we have a real snafu — like having to ship rear axles across the ocean by air frieght, for example, but such situations are extremely rare. Although it may be instructive to calculate the final cost of a completed tractor following such a snafu, there is no question that our world-wide system reduces our costs considerably.

An internal memorandum described the situation in late 1964 as follows:

During [recent] years, our efforts to build a full line of farm implements and industrial equipment have largely consisted of the time and effort left over after we handled the tractor responsibility. . . . We are second . . . in tractor unit sales. . . . In contrast to tractors we are weak in the implement and equipment business. . . . We are less of a factor than even the leading independents. . . .

Simply stated, we need the market — it does not need us. Our objectives are to become the principal supplier of implements and equipment to our dealers so that we may reap greater distribution profits, and to manufacture as many of our dealer requirements as possible to also obtain a manufacturing profit.

It is our belief that our dealers will need us as a source of implement and equipment supply although many of them do not presently recognize this. In many areas of the world they are pretty well able to obtain their present implement and equipment requirements. How long they will be able to do this we do not know but cases are regularly coming to our attention of mergers or acquisitions which limit the supply of good implements from independents. We want to be able to protect our dealers from any void in a quality implement and equipment supply — and we want the distribution and manufacturing profit.

In an effort to give "concentrated management attention" to the implement and equipment businesses, Equipment Operations was established in December 1964. Equipment Operations consisted of product planning, product engineering, manufacturing, and marketing planning units. According to an internal memorandum, Equipment Operations had "complete world-wide responsibility for the engineering, manufacturing, and market planning for Ford implements and industrial equipment." The Division's tractor marketing organizations were, however, to continue to be responsible for the actual sales of equipment and implements.

Equipment Operations

In late 1964 the General Manager of the Tractor Division concluded that the Division's "equipment business" was suffering from a lack of management attention. The "equipment business" consisted of two categories of products: industrial products (e.g., industrial tractors, back hoes, loaders); and farm implements (e.g., plows, cultivators, harrows, combines).

Sales and Marketing

In early 1968 Ford Tractor Sales and Marketing Operations was divided into three operating components: Tractor and Implement Operations-U.S. (T&I); Ford Tractor Operations-Europe (FTO-E); and Overseas Tractor Operations (OTO), which was responsible for marketing in other areas of the world. Each Sales and Marketing operating component was headed by a General Operations Manager, who reported to the Assistant General Manager-Sales and Marketing Operations. In addition, the Managers of the General Marketing Office and the Programming and Distribution Office also reported to the Assistant General Manager-Sales and Marketing (see Exhibit 1).

Each Sales and Marketing Operation was a profit center. According to the Assistant General Manager, the three General Operations Managers were given considerable autonomy. Each Operation submitted an annual profit plan, including volume and penetration objectives. When this plan was approved (generally after some discussion and modification), the General Operations Manager was relatively free to take any action he considered appropriate in attaining the objectives set forth in his plan. While certain decisions (e.g., pricing, number of personnel) required headquarters approval, the General Operations Managers were permitted to shift certain funds from one budgetary account to another without headquarters concurrence.

Each profit center's plan included an approved profit target. Profit center performance was appraised on the basis of percentage realization of this target.

Pricing

The Assistant General Manager-Sales and Marketing Operations commented on pricing as follows:

> Our overall strategy is to produce the highest quality agricultural products in the world. Our "pricing philosophy" is intended to insure that our prices in all markets are consistent with our overall strategy. For this reason, prices are established on the basis of the recommendations of the Sales and Marketing Operations.

Quarterly Marketing Reviews

Beginning in 1968 headquarters operating reviews were held quarterly. At these reviews the General Operations Managers and their staffs made brief presentations concerning their performance and problems and were given general direction and guidance by headquarters personnel. The Assistant General Manager used these meetings to obtain information concerning market share, dealer representation, sales volumes, and management development.

The General Marketing Office

The General Marketing Office consisted of four components: (1) Market Planning and Analysis; (2) several "Marketing Associates;" (3) Parts and Service; and (4) Equipment Marketing[6] (see Exhibit 2).

---

[6] Equipment Marketing consisted of a small group that conducted special studies for Equipment Operations.

Market Planning and Analysis: The Market Planning and Analysis Department was divided into two groups: (1) Marketing Planning and (2) Market Research and Analysis. The latter group was essentially responsible for marketing and sales accounting. According to the General Marketing Manager, "these are the people who keep score in all markets."

The Marketing Planning Group was responsible for certain aspects of the Division's short- and long-range planning processes. In the short-range planning area, each Sales and Marketing Operation was required to submit an annual marketing plan (by market) each year. Upon receipt of these plans, which included targets *and* specific action steps, the Marketing Planning Group prepared a comment sheet on each plan.[7] The comment sheets, which were sent to the Sales and Marketing General Operations Managers and their staffs, raised questions on specific elements of the plans. After the questions raised in the comment sheets had been answered, the Marketing Planning Group prepared a summary of the action steps (including completion deadlines) called for in each plan.[8]

When the three marketing plans had been approved by Division Management, the Sales and Marketing Operations were responsible for ensuring that the approved action steps were completed on schedule. Prior to each Quarterly Marketing Review, each Sales and Marketing Operation submitted a report of what had taken place in its markets, and which action steps had (or had not) been completed. The Marketing Planning Group summarized these reports for Division management before each meeting.

The Marketing Planning Group in 1968 was just beginning to develop its approach to the long-range planning part of its responsibilities. As the General Marketing Manager explained:

> Our objective is to develop long-range planning procedures, and lead the Sales and Marketing Operations to participate in long-range planning with us. If we make the plans here, and send them out, they will be difficult to implement because of conflicts with local priorities and resources. On the other hand, if *they* [the Sales and Marketing Operations] plan, it tends to be a one-year plan.
>
> I am hoping for the best of both worlds. I want the local operations to participate in the planning process for three reasons:
>
> (1) To tie the plans to the priorities and resources of the operations.
> (2) To make annual planning easier and more consistent.

---

[7] Exhibit 3 contains sample comment sheets.
[8] Exhibit 4 contains sample summaries.

(3) To make annual and long-range planning more ambitious. In our long-range plans, we will ask the operations to tell us what they can do ten years from now *if everything goes right.*

Marketing Associates: The four Marketing Associates were all seasoned T&I District Managers, whose appointments as Marketing Associates were considered promotions. According to the General Marketing Manager, the primary reason for these positions was "to have men with line operating experience in what [was] essentially a staff organization."

The General Marketing Manager used the Marketing Associates for special projects. For example, Ford Tractor's penetration in a particular OTO subsidiary market had recently declined significantly. OTO management had decided that it would benefit from a "line-experienced look" at the dealers, products, and country organization in this particular market. At OTO's request, a Marketing Associate was sent to the country in question for six weeks. He returned with a set of recommendations which were presented to OTO management and the Assistant General Manager-Sales and Marketing Operations. These executives agreed with most of the recommendations and instructed the country Tractor Manager to implement them.

Parts and Service: The Parts and Service Department carried out special studies in its field. Recently, the Department had conducted a study of world-wide parts profitability. In comparison with competitors and with other units of the Ford Motor Company, this study concluded, Ford Tractor's return on investment in the parts business could be improved. In order to bring about such improvement a committee was formed with the mission of examining the Division's parts pricing practices.

In the Service area, the Parts and Service Department performed the day-to-day function of analyzing world-wide warranty claims in order to direct the attention of Product Planning personnel to weaknesses in the Division's product line. In addition, it had recently designed a "dealer service upgrading program" for FTO-E.

The Programming and Distribution Office

The Programming and Distribution Office was responsible for developing monthly production programs for the manufacturing plants. Each Sales and Marketing Operation had a Programming Department, which received product requirements from the countries or districts under its jurisdiction monthly. These product requirements covered the next eight months and were broken down by month, model, and basic options. They generally were a composite of firm orders (for the next month), tentative orders (for the next several months), and forecasts (based on expected share of expected industry demand). The Programming Departments exercised judgment in consolidating these country or district requirements, making changes on the basis of their own knowledge of plant and in-transit inventories, and their own forecasts of industry demand and Ford market share.

Each Sales and Marketing Operation was sourced out of several assembly plants (depending on the model and the country to which it would be shipped). The Programming Departments divided their product requirements among the appropriate assembly plants, and these requirements were transmitted (by telex) to the assembly plant concerned and the Programming and Distribution Office in Birmingham. When an assembly plant received all its product requirements for the next eight-month period, it analyzed them and determined their implications for plant loading, overtime, etc. These data were then transmitted (by telex) to the Programming and Distribution Office in Birmingham.

The Programming and Distribution Office evaluated all product requirements and plant capacity analyses on a world-wide basis. When appropriate, it modified the original programs by changing sourcing patterns, shifting inventories from one area to another, or "smoothing out" production requirements over a period of time. The completed program was then discussed with Manufacturing personnel. On the basis of these discussions, it might be further modified.

Finally (about 15 days after the Sales and Marketing Operations had received requirements from the field), the final program was submitted to the Division General Manager for approval. When approved by the General Manager, the Program became the basis for an assembly schedule for the next month, and for a "planning" schedule used to order and manufacture components, plan changes in facilities and in work force levels, etc.

The Programming and Distribution Office was also responsible for recommending modifications in the basic program as the need arose. It received ten-day sales reports[9] from each of the three Sales and Market-

---

[9] The ten-day sales reports were based on post cards attached to each tractor. The dealer was to mail the post card when a tractor was sold. In practice, some dealers forgot to mail the post cards, or held them until the end of the week or month. It was possible to adjust the data for this factor, however, on the basis of historical experience.

ing Operations, and used these data to determine whether retail demand and the assembly program was still in balance. When necessary, the Programming and Distribution Office (working with the Manufacturing Programming Office) recommended changes in assembly schedules, resequencing of shipments, and transfer of inventories.

In commenting on the Programming and Distribution function, the Tractor Programming Manager explained:

The world-wide nature of our job really adds only two complications to the programming function. First, component shipping schedules make it necessary for us to plan and schedule production a month or two further into the future than would otherwise be necessary. While a month or two doesn't sound like a long time, it means you have that much less current sales data to work with.

Second, it is always necessary for Programming to exercise judgment in consolidating field product requirements. Because of the diversity of our markets (even within a single Sales and Marketing Operation), it is difficult to have adequate knowledge upon which to base such judgment.

Tractor and Implement Operations U.S. (T&I)

T&I was responsible for the sale and service of Ford Tractor Division products in the United States. Prior to 1961, T&I had marketed its products through 24 independent distributors and four company-owned sales branches, which sold in turn to approximately 2,100 independent dealers. When the Ford Tractor Division was established, a study of the U.S. distribution network was made. The study concluded that "this system of distribution created a very long pipeline between Ford and our customers and had many other disadvantages mostly concerned with profit limitations, and difficulties in developing stronger dealers." As a result, T&I was "authorized to acquire the interests of distributors as necessary and establish a direct franchising arrangement with dealers on a nation-wide basis."

T&I purchased the assets of many of its distributors and had succeeded in establishing a direct distribution system by late 1964. In early 1968, therefore, T&I marketed its products directly to a network of 1,750 franchised dealers, serviced by nine District Sales Offices and ten Supply Depots.

As may be seen in Exhibit 5, T&I was organized on a functional basis, with departments responsible for Marketing (marketing research and sales planning, market representation and dealer development, advertising and sales promotion, and training), Parts and Service, Control, Public Relations, Programming (i.e., ordering and logistics), Personnel,[10] and Sales.

Sales Department: This department included nine Districts (under a General Field Manager), a Sales Administration Department, a Wholegoods Distribution Department,[11] an Agricultural Sales Department and an Industrial Sales Department. The following paragraphs describe the Agricultural and Industrial Sales Departments and the Field Sales Organization.

The Agricultural Sales Department consisted of a manager and four Product Sales Managers. The Product Sales Managers were responsible respectively for tractors, hay tools, harvesting equipment, and implements. Each Product Sales Manager was concerned with the "merchandising" of his assigned products and with providing Product Planning with requests for new product features.

In the merchandising area, the Product Sales Managers designed dealer incentive contests, developed exhibits for agricultural shows and fairs, and suggested formats for product demonstrations. These merchandising tools were then used by the Districts. For the most part, the Product Sales Managers did not get directly involved with the preparation or scheduling of advertising.

In each District there were several Agricultural-Industrial Sales Representatives. The District Agricultural-Industrial Sales Representatives were responsible for implementing the merchandising programs developed by the Product Sales Managers. In addition, they were responsible for performing an annual "product audit." In this audit they were required to submit a list of the ten products (with the highest sales potential) most needing improvement; and a list of the ten products which, if added to the FTD product line, would contribute most significantly to District profits.

The Product Sales Manager then collated these product audits as background for requesting new products or product modifications from Product Planning. The Product Planning Group received such requests (with volume estimates) from all three Sales and Marketing Operations, and used them as a major input to the Product Planning process.

The Industrial Sales Department had responsibilities

---

[10] The responsibilities of the personnel in this department were essentially the same as those of their counterparts in the Ford Division. As described below, they generally worked with similarly specialized personnel in the District Sales Organization.

[11] The Wholegoods Distribution Department was responsible for the physical distribution of assembled products (wholegoods) *within* the United States.

similar to those of the Agricultural Sales Department, but was not elaborated to the same degree. The Department consisted of a Manager and two assistants, one responsible for Government and Original Equipment Manufacturer sales; and the other for attending trade shows, visiting other manufacturers, and keeping track of competitive developments. The Manager of the Industrial Sales Department worked with the Agricultural-Industrial Sales Representatives in the Districts in much the same way as his counterparts in the Agricultural Sales Department did.

District Organization: Exhibit 6 is an organization chart of a typical District. Reporting to the District Manager were Managers of Parts and Service Merchandising, Marketing, Service, and Wholegoods Distribution. These Managers and their subordinates were responsible for implementing the plans in their specialties that had been developed by their counterparts at T&I headquarters. In some cases personnel from the T&I headquarters staff departments were sent out to the Districts to assist their District counterparts on special studies or projects.

The District sales organization functioned very much like the Ford Division field sales organization, except that the T&I District Sales Offices were also responsible for parts and accessories sales, whereas automotive parts and accessories were now the responsibility of the Autolite-Ford Parts Division. A District was divided into a number of zones, each assigned to a Zone Manager. Within each zone, the Zone Manager called on all Ford tractor dealers to take orders and provide assistance; in addition he had a continuing responsibility for his zone, to assure, for example, that there were enough dealers to cover his zone effectively.

The Zone Manager also had reporting to him several Agricultural-Industrial Sales Representatives. The primary responsibility of these Sales Representatives was to provide technical support to the Zone Managers. They were, for example, expected to provide the Zone Managers with information to be used in responding to technical questions raised by customers or dealers.

In addition, the Agricultural-Industrial Sales Representatives were responsible for coordinating the implementation of merchandising programs emanating from the Agricultural and Industrial Sales Departments and for performing District Product Audits.

In commenting on the limited role of the Agricultural-Industrial Sales Representatives, one T&I executive pointed out that the dealer organization was not specialized on a product or market basis. While most dealers emphasized either one line or the other (depending primarily on location), virtually all dealers made at least some sales in both fields. As he went on to explain:

> We would undoubtedly obtain some benefits from further specialization. A dealer who sold only industrial products, and was called on by an industrial specialist, would probably do a better job selling industrial products than a dealer selling both lines. But there is not enough business to justify separate specialized dealers in all locations. Some farmers do come into the city to buy tractors and farm implements; even small farming towns occasionally require equipment for construction or industrial purposes. Unless we have someone on the spot, going after this business, the business will go to a competitor.

Ford Tractor Operations — Europe (FTO-E)

FTO-E headquarters were located in Brussels. Management consisted essentially of a General Operations Manager, a General Sales Manager, a Marketing Manager, and a Financial Analysis Manager (see Exhibit 7).

FTO-E was responsible for the coordination of sales and marketing in France, Germany, Italy, Austria, Belgium, Holland, Portugal, Switzerland, Denmark, Finland, Sweden, Norway, Ireland, and the United Kingdom. Spain and Greece, though located in Europe, had been assigned to OTO rather than FTO-E because they were direct dealer (i.e., importer-distributor) markets, rather than markets in which Ford Tractor was represented by Ford Motor Company subsidiaries. In all countries except Norway,[12] FTO-E worked through Ford subsidiary organizations; OTO worked primarily with direct dealers.

Each FTO-E country (except Norway) thus had a resident tractor organization, which was part of the local Ford subsidiary in that country. While these organizations varied considerably in size, all had functions corresponding roughly to those in the T&I districts. Exhibit 8 is an organization chart of a typical large FTO-E organization (Germany); Exhibit 9 shows the organization in a smaller FTO-E country (Netherlands).

The FTO-E country organizations were headed by Tractor Operations Managers. These managers had historically been highly autonomous, developing their own dealer networks, marketing plans, sales promotion and advertising materials, etc. FTO-E (or its predecessor headquarters organizations) had reviewed these plans and materials, but the Tractor Operations Man-

---

[12] Norway was not assigned to OTO because it would have been inefficient for OTO to cover a single market in Northern Europe.

agers had been relatively free to use their assigned personnel and budgets as they saw fit.

In early 1968 the relationship between the FTO-E headquarters organization and the country organizations was undergoing a significant change. Intensive study and analysis had convinced the new management team that the FTO-E headquarters organization should take a more direct role in working with the country Tractor Organizations. For example, FTO-E now prepared virtually all sales promotion materials, advertising copy, product introduction programs, and sales forecasts. Most of this work was done by the FTO-E headquarters Marketing Office and transmitted directly to counterpart offices in the country organizations. The FTO-E General Sales Office, consisting of a General Sales Manager and three regional sales managers,[13] worked with the country organizations to insure that the centrally prepared marketing plans were implemented effectively.

The FTO-E General Operations Manager commented on this changing role of his headquarters staff as follows:

The countries in FTO-E differ much more considerably from each other than do typical districts in T&I. We have major differences in language, culture, agricultural methods, government policies and regulations, and competitors[14] in our various markets. It is necessary, therefore, that our Tractor Operations Managers be the kind of people who thoroughly understand their markets and are able to develop plans (or modify our plans) to meet the needs of their markets. By the end of this year, all of our Tractor Operations Managers will be local nationals.

Nevertheless, it is certainly true that we can do a better job in many areas centrally than each country can do individually. In some cases it is a matter of cost; it is much cheaper to print several language-versions of the same product brochure, for example, than to prepare a separate brochure for each country. Similarly, we can afford to maintain a higher level of expertise in various specialties (e.g., advertising, market representation) here than any individual country could.

We must, of course, be careful not to lose sight of the significant differences which do exist among countries. Our headquarters personnel visit the countries frequently, and the Tractor Managers are encouraged to object to programs which do not meet the needs of their markets. Many of these objections are valid; others are not. We have to do a considerable job of education — through persuasion rather than directive.

Take two examples. We are presently introducing a new line of tractors in all our markets. Traditionally, each country would have developed its own introductory program. Our Marketing Office came up with a program to fly models of the new line into each country and hold dealer meetings at airports, using a common script and approach for all markets. Several Tractor Managers objected, saying, in effect, "It just won't work here." Our General Sales Manager and General Marketing Managers reasoned with the Tractor Managers, explaining how much more we could afford to do in each country this way than they could do individually. Finally, all agreed to try the program, and it has been working well.

Dealer contests are another example. Our Marketing Office came up with a program whereby the leading dealers in each country (by size category) would win a free trip to Beirut. Several Tractor Managers objected, claiming that the approach was "too American" for their markets. But we convinced them to try it, and it seems to have been quite successful.

This contest also had a provision for Ford sales representatives to win prizes, such as color television sets and other appliances. One Tractor Manager argued that he would rather use the money for free trips to Paris as prizes, and we agreed. The important thing is that we held a dialogue and worked out a modification of the program which was satisfactory to all parties concerned.

It is clearly a question of balance. And I am convinced that we are approaching the proper balance.

Overseas Tractor Operations (OTO)

OTO was responsible for marketing in 134 countries. The vast majority of these countries (125) were direct dealer markets, served by one or more importer-distributors. These importer-distributors generally had their own dealer networks. Many of the direct dealer markets were small (e.g., Jamaica), but others (e.g., Japan) represented a considerable amount of volume or potential volume.

OTO was also responsible for nine countries (South Africa, Australia, New Zealand, Canada, Brazil, Chile, Mexico, Uruguay, and Venezuela) where Ford had subsidiary companies. In these countries there was a separate tractor organization (headed by a Tractor

---

[13] The three regional managers were responsible respectively for coordinating the U.K. and Ireland; Denmark, Finland, Sweden, and Norway; and Austria, Belgium, Netherlands, Portugal and Switzerland. There were no regional managers for the three largest markets on the European continent: France, Germany, and Italy.

[14] The following table indicates the range of differences among selected FTO-E countries with regard to Ford's market share and major competitors.

Country	Major Competitors	Ford Market Share
A	a,b,c,d	8.5%
B	c,e,f	4.0
C	a,c,j	25.7
D	a,j,n	28.4
E	a,c,e	17.9
F	a,c,l	24.4

Manager), similar in most respects to the FTO-E subsidiary organizations.

The OTO headquarters staff (see Exhibit 10) was located in Detroit, Michigan. Although it was structurally similar to T&I and FTO-E, its function was quite different. The Marketing Office, for example, included managers of Dealer Planning and Business Management, Advertising and Sales Promotion, Sales Planning and Analysis, and Product Training. These departments prepared programs and materials (including advertising mats and sales promotion literature) for dissemination to the field. In general, however, the marketing organizations in OTO countries were considerably more autonomous than those in the FTO-E countries.

As the OTO General Marketing Manager explained:

We have a great many more countries than FTO-E, and they are spread over (virtually) the entire world. As a result, we are faced with much greater differences in languages, crops, income levels, distribution systems, and government regulations. For example, many of our countries have either partially or completely closed their borders to tractor imports, which is not a problem in FTO-E.

Moreover, most of our countries are direct dealer markets. Our Zone Managers call on these direct dealers on a regular basis, of course, but it is simply not economic to work as closely with them as a resident tractor organization could.

The OTO Sales Office was divided into three regions: South Eastern, Western, and Central. Each region was headed by a Regional Manager, reporting to the General Sales Manager. Within each region, the Tractor Managers of subsidiary companies reported directly to the Regional Managers. A Manager of Direct Dealer Markets also reported to each Regional Manager. He supervised several Zone Managers, each of whom was responsible for a number of countries. The Zone Managers called on their importer-distributors on a regularly scheduled basis, soliciting orders, disseminating marketing programs prepared at headquarters, and providing general counsel and advice. A Zone Manager might, for example, examine a direct dealer's dealer network in light of OTO market representation policies and make recommendations for modification as appropriate.

In recent months there had been a tendency toward centralization in OTO, although to a lesser degree than in FTO-E. Centrally prepared product literature (which the countries were free to use or not use) was a recent innovation, for example, as was the establishment of specific objectives for the Zone Managers. Nevertheless, several OTO Managers commented that the wide disparity of OTO markets, predominance of direct dealers, and lack of staff at the regional level would prevent OTO from going as far in the direction of centralization as FTO-E had.

Ford: Tractor Division   423

Exhibit 1. Organization Chart, February 1968

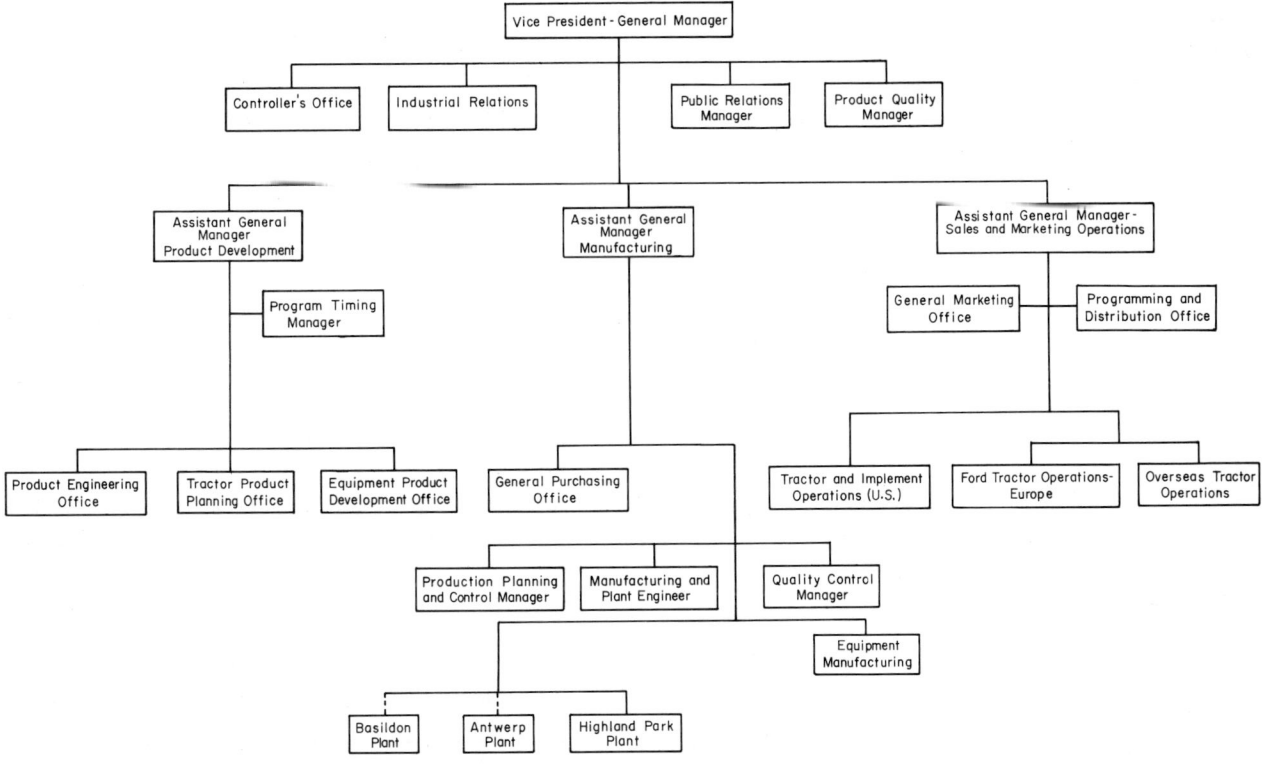

Exhibit 2. Organization Chart of General Marketing Office, February 1968

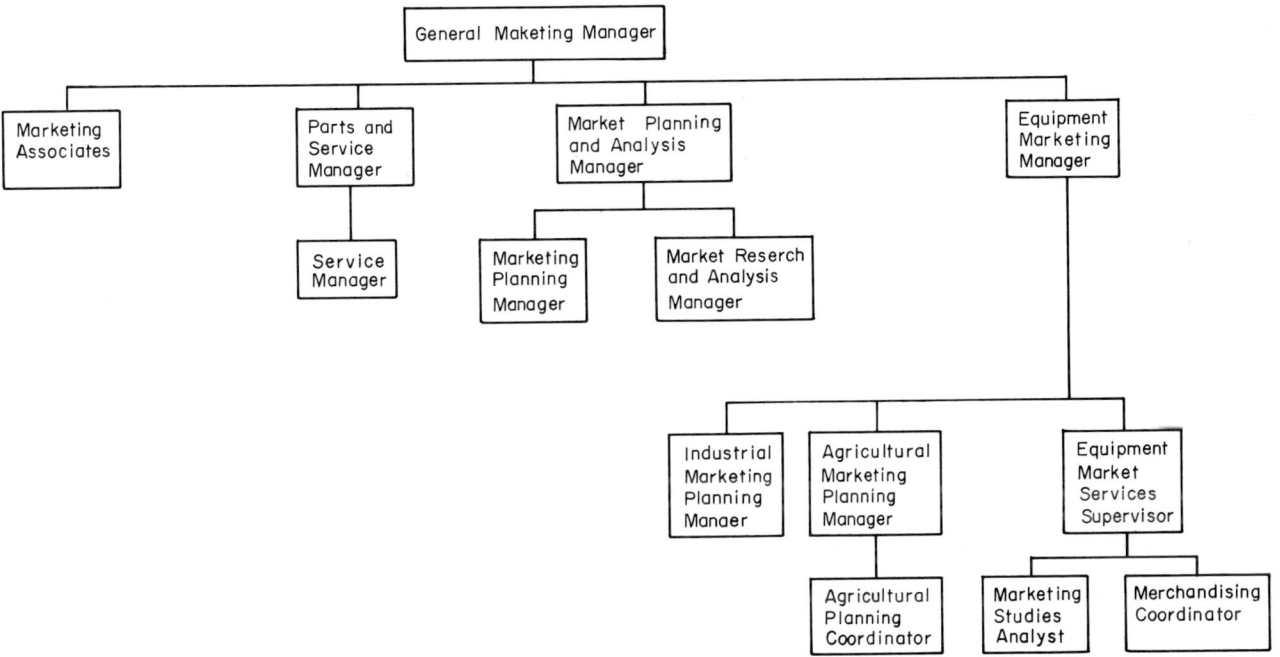

Exhibit 3. 1968 Marketing Plan Comment Sheets

Country A

Page 3   Is 7.4% penetration for 1967 a reasonable basis for projecting 1968 penetration? An unusual gain in penetration will be required the last five months of this year:

	July Cum.	Full Year
1967	6.5%	7.4%
1966	6.8	6.7
1965	8.0	7.9
1964	8.2	8.0

Page 3   Assuming 7.4% for 1967, is a 0.8% point penetration increase in 1968 reasonable to expect? Penetration growth stabilized starting in 1962.

1962	1963	1964	1965	1966	1967	1968
8.4	8.0	8.4	7.9	6.7	7.4 Forecast 6.7 Possible	8.0

Page 3   It should be noted that all support actions listed, except the 8000 series introduction, are rather general.

Page 8   1968 *industry* volume of 51,000 is reasonable in view of maturity of market. Heavy first quarter and light second quarter are based somewhat on competitive introductions.

Page 26   (a) Can additional salesmen be located and hired that fast?
(b) What likelihood is there that the new sub-dealer discount structure will be accepted, and *adhered to* subsequently?
(c) What kind of margin revisions are planned to encourage greater emphasis on Ford sales by dual franchise dealers?

Page 27   As of November 25, how is the review of dealer standards for Country A progressing? What form does it take?
As background for your dealer recruitment objectives, how many new dealers have been recruited so far in 1967?

Page 30   Are there more specific examples of "less attentive to farmer's needs"?

Page 33   Why would spontaneous knowledge of Ford tractors be lowest when Ford penetration is exceeded only by Companies W, X, Y, and Z?

Page 37   How will you assure full benefit from each 30-5 call?

Page 38   What incentive will there be for participation in the follow-up on Cheque Farmers?
Where will the demonstration personnel come from? Hired and trained by February 1st?

Page 40   What will be the basis of the Jan.–Feb.–Mar. Tractor Sales Contest?

Page 44   Can the one *additional* salesman be hired in every case?

Page 46   Where does the implement review study stand?

Country B

Page 1   Proposed 1969 industry volume assumes year similar to 1966–1967 and significantly below the 1962–1965 average of 25,000.
Forecast of 1967 industry volume has been adjusted slightly since #264, from 20,000 to 21,000.
Resulting increase for next year is 3.0%.

Page 2   Forecast penetration for 1967 has shown considerable fluctuation:

#262	#263	#264	#265	1969 P.B.
13.0	14.0	14.0	12.4	14.0

The last four months of 1969 seem to have been forecast optimistically compared to 1965–1966:

Exhibit 3 (continued).

	Jan.–Aug.			Sept.–Dec.		
	Ind.	Ford	Pen.	Ind.	Ford	Pen.
1965	14,000	2,100	15.0	11,051	1,300	11.9
1966	11,564	1,220	10.6	9,120	1,120	12.3
1967–#262	11,400	1,320	11.5	8,605	1,290	15.0
#265	11,400	1,320	11.5	9,075	1,325	13.7

Ten months actual was 12.6% which means the 1968 P.B. may involve a jump of 1.4% points.
Forecast 1967 Ford volume is currently 2,500 compared to 2,610 in #262. This will involve an increase of 550 units next year.
This objective attempts to regain the 14.0%+ historical share level in one year.

Page 3	Give some illustrations of success of fall marketing programs.
Page 4	When is the 8000 tractor to be introduced?
Page 9	When will the price and profit study on the Ford 8000 be completed, and field trials held?
Page 14	What are the pro's and con's of Company Y's interest in Ford?
Page 16	Why was dealer development help excluded from the 1969 budget?
Page 18	Does Ford need a two-year warranty for competitive reasons?
Page 19	Are Ford insertions intermittent in several different publications?
Page 24	Is not the 3000 A.P. underpriced versus Product L?
Page 25	Are all of these priority tasks?
Page 27	How successful have past dealer salesman recruitment campaigns been? What assurance is there that 16 contract workshops will be signed up? Laying down dealer requirements for the 8000 does not necessarily ensure selling capacities.
Page 28	When will "Model" dealer standards be completed? Are enough prospects available to accomplish dealer actions planned?
Page 29	So some of the dealer recruitment plans are merely goals! On what basis will the [Country B's language] speaking Representation Area Manager from FTO-E Brussels be available? Who will provide the business management assistance?
Page 30	Where will parts catalogs in [Country B's language] be obtained?
Page 31	Approximately how many dealers will be included in the service upgrading program?
Page 32	Why would Company X leave the tractor business when they currently have 34% of the Country B market? Unprofitable level of operations?
Page 33	What are the cab production plans? Is the localized unit a specific Ford model? How uncompetitive is our retail credit?
Page 36	Basically where will the mailing list come from? What percentage of dealers participated in co-op advertising in 1968?
Page 39	Decision to stay out of National Show probably feasible in view of [Company T's] nonparticipation. Are there enough other agricultural shows to justify trailer unit? When will used tractor merchandising package be ready?
Page 40	Concerning the Tractor Owners' Club, is the appeal sophisticated enough? Who will produce the customer magazine on a competent long-term basis? Challenge demonstrations sound specific and positive.
Page 42	What is the significance of closed wholesale territories?
Page 43	What locally sourced implements will be available for the 8000?
Page 47	Are media insertions full page, or less?
Page 48	Give more details of the company operated industrial demonstration program.

Exhibit 4. 1968 Marketing Plan Summaries

Country A

Priority Plans	Mktg. Plan Page	Completion Objective			
		1Q	2Q	3Q	4Q
1. Dealer Plans	27 Ex. III				
Territory Realignments (5)				2	3
Dealer Replacements (12)		3	3	4	2
Dealer Appointments (9)		2	2	2	3
Branch Openings (2)		1			1
Terminations (13)		4	4	3	2

	Mktg. Plan Page	Follow-up Date	Completion Deadline
2. Expansion of Dealers' Selling Capacity	26		
Salesmen's recruitment program		Feb. 1	Mar. 31
Sub-dealer meetings to promote standard sub-dealer discounts.		Feb. 1	Feb. 28
Primary Plans			
1. Service Upgrading Program	42		
Selection of Dealers		Jan. 1	Jan. 1
Publication of Service Manager Guide		Jan. 1	Jan. 31
2. "Cheque" Farmer Follow-up	38	Feb. 1	Feb. 28
3. 30-5 Program to encourage prospecting	37	Feb. 1	Mar. 31
4. Tractor Sales Contest	40	Jan. 1	Mar. 31
5. 8000 Tractor Introduction	44	Jan. 1	Mar. 31
6. Demonstration Support Program — involving four temporary personnel	38	Feb. 1	Mar. 31
7. Demonstration Tractor Assistance Program — providing 6 months interest-free credit on demos.	38	Mar. 1	Mar. 31
8. P&A Contest	41	Jan. 1	Dec. 31
Planning in Process			
1. Revision of margin programs to encourage greater emphasis on Ford	26	Jan. 1	Dec. 31, 1967
2. Used Tractor Merchandising Package for dealers	40	Feb. 1	Feb. 28
3. 2000 and 3000 Tractor Cheque Program	40	Mar. 1	Mar. 31
4. Proposal on 4000 Tractor Pricing	29	Jan. 1	Jan. 31
5. Resolution of P&A Depot Supply Problems	41	Feb. 1	Undetermined
Special Studies			
1. Review of Dealer Standards to establish models for varying sales potential	27	Jan. 1	Dec. 31, 1967
2. Detailed Parts Pricing Study	41	Jan. 1	Dec. 31, 1967
3. Major Review of Implement Future in key European markets	46	Jan. 1	Jan. 31

Country B

Priority Plans	Mktg. Plan Page	Completion Objective			
		1Q	2Q	3Q	4Q
1. Agricultural Market Representation	28				
Dealer Appointments (4)		2	1	1	
Dealer Replacements (2)				1	1

Exhibit 4 (continued).

2. Industrial Market Representation	47		
Dealer Appointments (2)		1	1
Upgrading Programs (2)	2		

	Mktg. Plan Page	Follow-up Date	Completion Deadline
3. Increase Dealer Sales and Service Capacity	27		
Salesmen's Recruitment Program		Mar. 1	Mar. 31
Contract Workshop Plan — to extend service where full-scale dealers unavailable (16)		Apr. 1	Dec. 31

Primary Plans

1. Demonstration Tractor Assistance — providing 6 months interest-free credit on demos.	38	Jan. 1	Jan. 31, 1968
2. Ford Premium Trade-In Promotion	39	Feb. 1	Undetermined
3. Used Tractor Merchandising Plan	39	Feb. 1	Feb. 28
4. "Cheque" Farmer Follow-up	40	Feb. 1	Feb. 28
5. Trailer Unit for Agricultural Shows	39	Feb. 1	Feb. 28
6. Ford Tractor Owners' Club	40	Feb. 1	Feb. 28
7. Tractor Sales Contest	40	Jan. 1	Mar. 31
8. Industrial Emphasis in Spring Contest	48	Jan. 1	Mar. 31
9. 30-5 Program	38	Feb. 1	Mar. 31
10. Development of Localized Unit	33	Feb. 1	Mar. 31
11. Company Operated Industrial Demonstration Program	48	Mar. 1	Continuous
12. Demonstration Support Program — involving four temporary personnel	38	Mar. 1	Apr. 30
13. 8000 Tractor Introduction	42	Mar. 1	May 31
14. Challenge Demonstrations	40	Sept. 1	Oct. 31
15. P&A Contest	30	Jan. 1	Dec. 31
16. Service Upgrading Programs	30	Apr. 1	Dec. 31
17. Supply Ford Engines to Company X	32	May 1	Undetermined

Special Studies

1. Study of Ford Retail Credit vs. Co-op	33	Jan. 1	Jan. 31
2. Long Range Implement Study	44	Feb. 1	Feb. 28
3. Detailed Parts Pricing Study	30	Mar. 1	Mar. 31

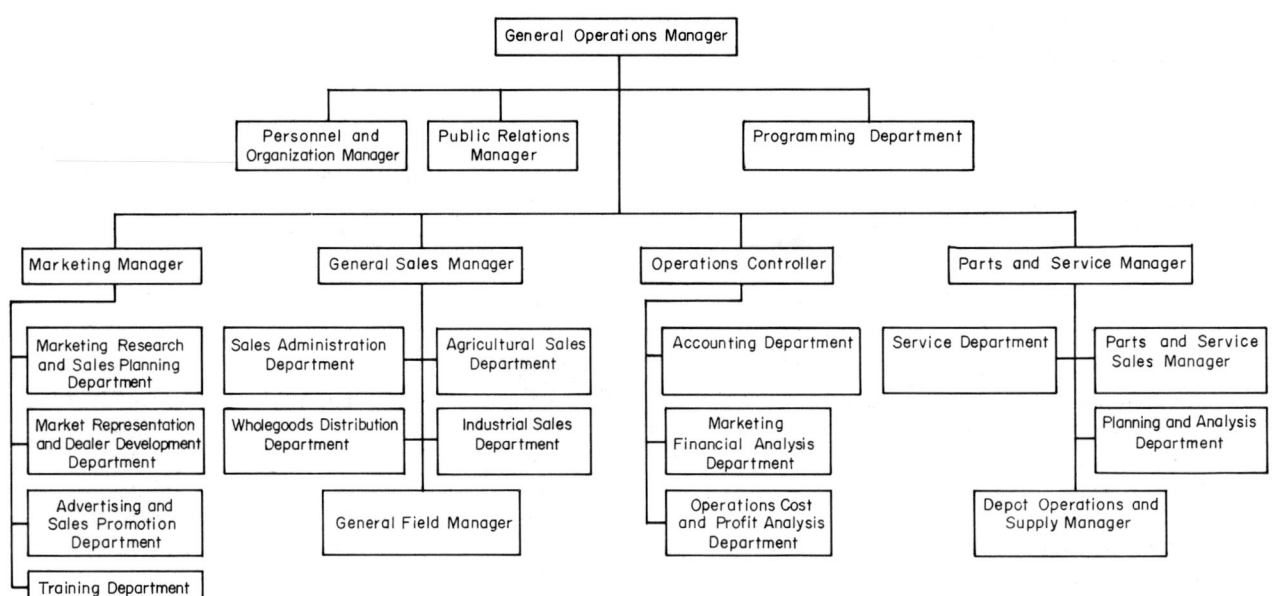

Exhibit 5. Organization of Tractor and Implement Operations (U.S.), 1967

Exhibit 6. Organization Chart of Typical District in Tractor and Implement Operations (U.S.), 1967

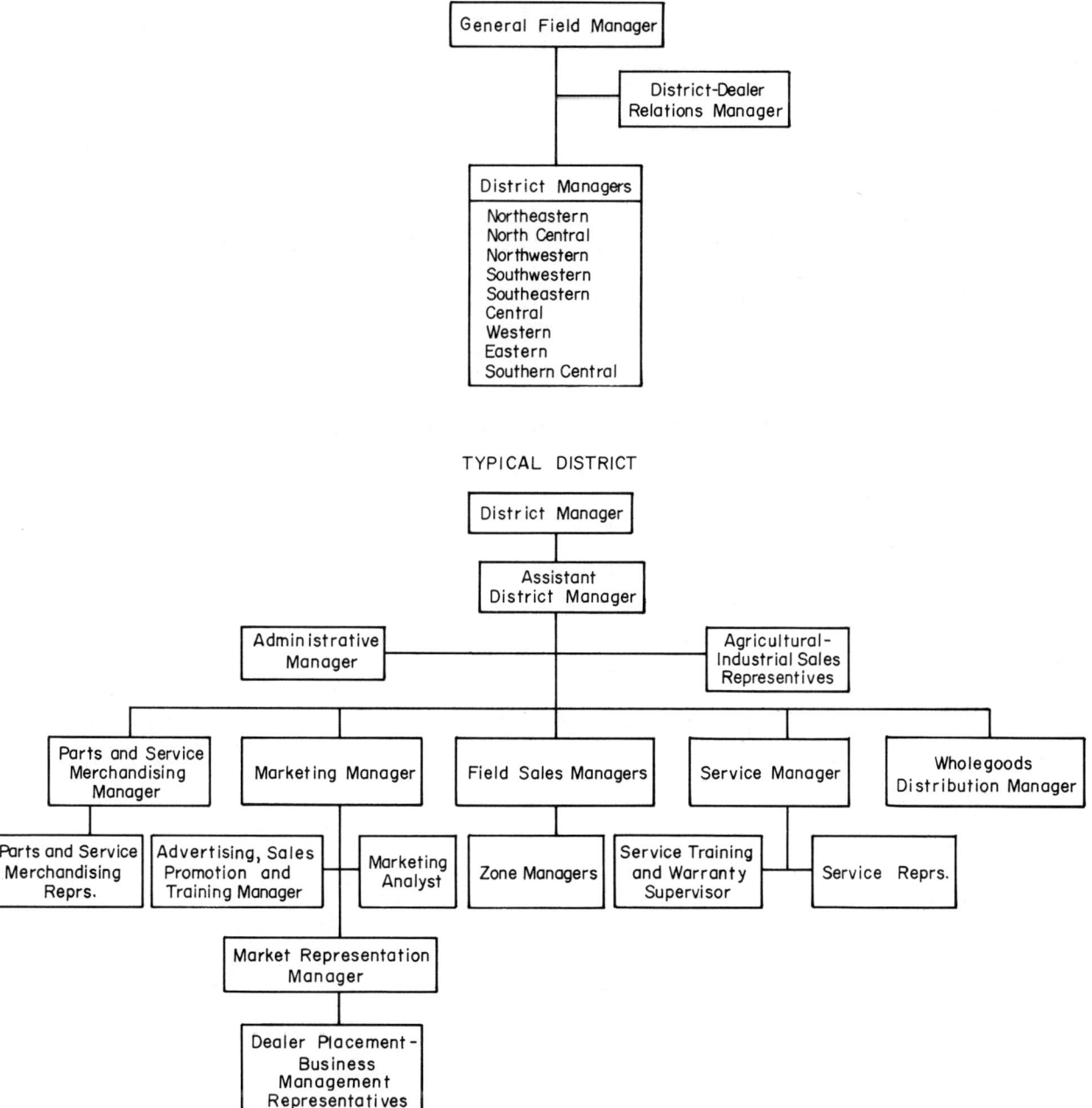

430 Cases and Commentaries

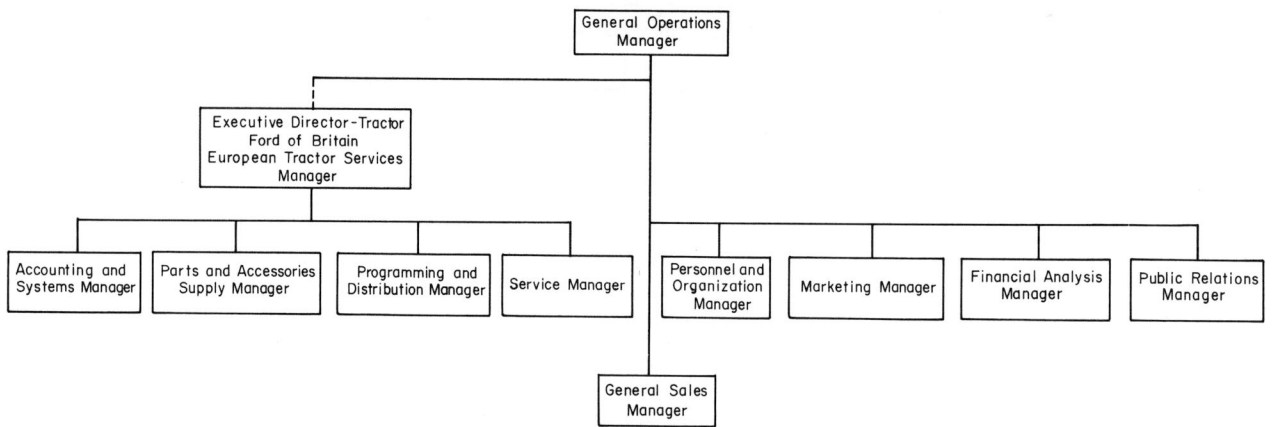

Exhibit 7. Organization Chart of Ford Tractor Operations — Europe, February 1968

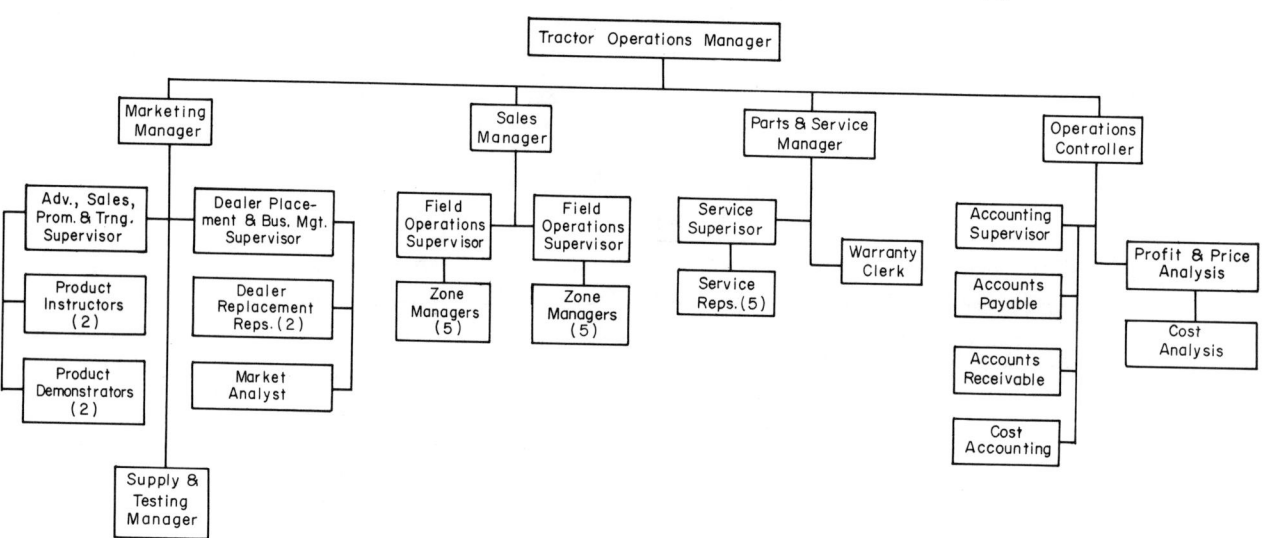

Exhibit 8. Organization Chart of Typical Large FTO-E Organization (Germany), March 1968

Exhibit 9. Organization Chart of Typical Smaller FTO-E Organization (Netherlands), March 1968

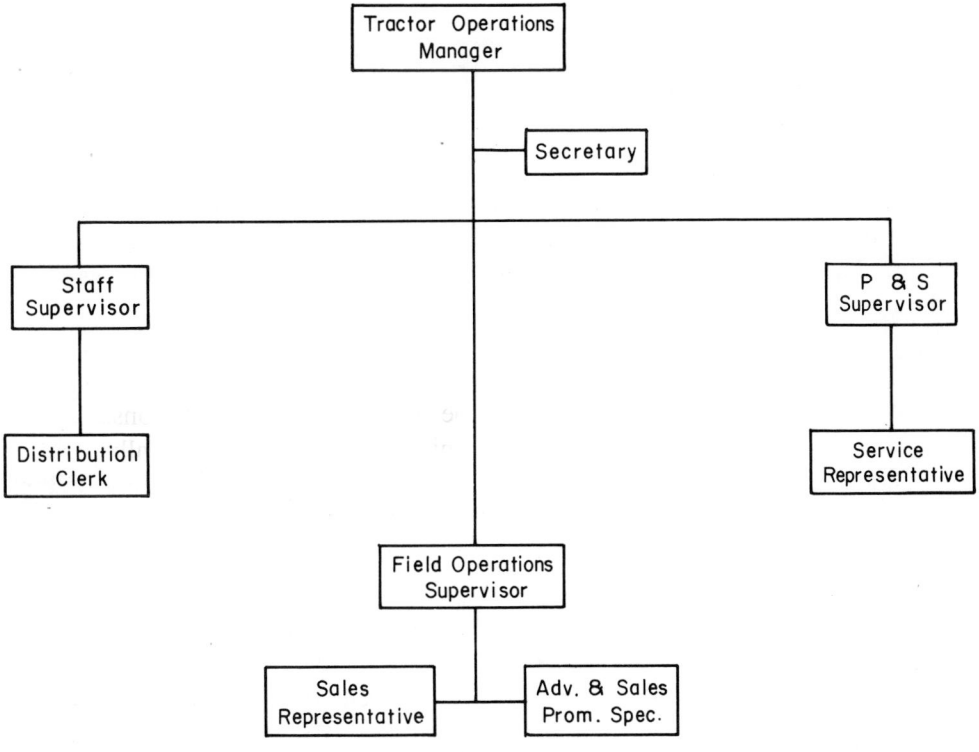

Exhibit 10. Organization Chart of Overseas Tractor Operations, February 1968

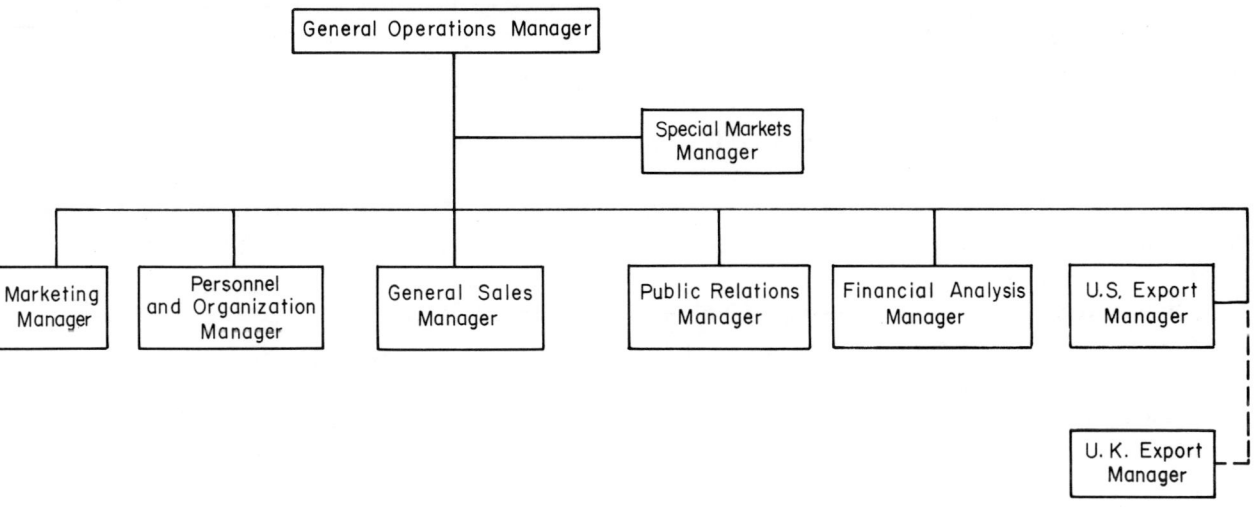

COMMENTARY

The Ford management's decision to establish a world-wide business for tractors stands in contrast to its organizational approach for trucks and automobiles. In the case of its automotive lines, Ford established separate integrated business units in North America (North American Automotive Operations) and in Europe (Ford of Europe), while Ford affiliated companies operated in seven Latin American countries, Australia, New Zealand, Malaysia, and South Africa.

There are several reasons for differentiating between automotive lines and tractors in this respect. The Ford management believed that world markets for tractors could be served with a single product line in which the basic models could be modified in accordance with local use conditions. By contrast European and United States mass markets for cars, to take Ford's two largest markets, called for fundamentally different designs — different in overall size, engine design, and styling. This is not to say, of course, that markets for European cars did not exist in the United States and vice versa. But the large markets in each case exhibited distinctively different needs.

A second reason had to do with the nature of competition; in the tractor business the major competitors were organized as world enterprises. Although major U.S. automotive manufacturers operated multinationally, they were organized, like Ford, as a series of integrated businesses serving particular countries or geographic regions.

Finally, it is useful to recognize that the consolidation of two tractor businesses, one in the United States and the other in England, was practical to contemplate. By comparison Ford's automotive operations in different parts of the world were so complex and involved so many diverse organizational structures that their consolidation into a single business unit would have been a gigantic undertaking offering, perhaps, little competitive or economic advantage.

Given the fact that world tractor market needs are relatively homogeneous, Ford anticipated achieving major economies in tractor design, tooling, and manufacturing expenses. Tractor and equipment product lines could be standardized world-wide and manufacturing facilities could be consolidated. Given the need to redesign substantially the whole Ford tractor line, it was practical to carry out the rebuilding of the line as a single effort. The tractor line could be designed to reflect market needs throughout the world and the new line could then be introduced through world-wide marketing operations.

In addition, the tractor sales operations could be brought into sharp focus and given strong direction under the new organization. (Ford tractors had generally been sold through subsidiary companies and importer-distributors who handled Ford car and truck lines as well.) The move to establish tractor managers in countries where Ford operated through subsidiary companies suggests that the tractor line may have suffered previously for lack of strong local attention on the part of the managements of the predecessor businesses, the U.K. Tractor Group and the Tractor and Implement Division in the United States.

Basic Organization

The basic organization of Ford Tractor Division (FTD) parallels that of Ford's North American Automotive Operations and Ford of Europe. The "troika" pattern is clearly seen with the Product Development, Manufacturing, and Sales and Marketing units forming the basic structure.

Product Development could be organized with little regard for geographic considerations. Hence, the product development functions were centralized in Birmingham, Michigan.

Manufacturing established a rationalized system in which there was a single source for each major component but three assembly operations serving the three broad market areas, EEC, the United States, and the U.K. and overseas export markets. The development of a single world-wide sourcing and manufacturing system was indeed a remarkable feat.

Organization of the Marketing Function

The fact that Ford Tractor could serve worldwide markets with essentially a single, integrated line of products made possible the establishment of monolithic manufacturing and product development functions. In addition, marketing and manufacturing could be coordinated through one Programming and Distribution office.

By contrast, the Sales and Marketing function was tailored to meet market conditions in different geographic markets. Hence, world markets were divided among Tractor and Implement Operations (T&I) in the United States, Ford Tractor Operations-Europe (FTO-E), and Overseas Tractor Operations (OTO) covering 134 different countries, in most of which Ford was represented by importer-dealers.

The T&I organization was the most fully developed. Market program management responsibility was located at headquarters and product program strategies were developed for different categories of agricultural and industrial tractor and equipment lines. Agricultural-Industrial Sales Representatives in nine districts coordinated the implementation of merchandising programs developed at T&I headquarters by the Product Sales Managers. They also fed back ideas to Product Sales Managers for product development and product line additions.

In FTO-E, Tractor Operations Managers in the several countries headed organizations which were similar to a District Manager's organization in the United States. Historically, these managers had been highly autonomous, which meant, in effect, that they had developed and implemented their own local marketing strategies. FTO-E headquarter's task was to centralize program management for the area, allowing for program modifications by country Tractor Operations Managers to suit local market conditions.

OTO's territory included the vast majority of countries in which Ford Tractor products were sold. Except in nine of these, the Division was represented by direct dealers. OTO might be regarded as one vast District in which the "zones" were widespread and greatly different as to market characteristics. The major task of OTO management was to maintain this organization, build its strength, and assure that it was supplied with products to sell.

T&I, FTO-E, and OTO differed fundamentally as to market concentration and in the degree of control headquarters groups could exercise over local market representatives. In the most concentrated markets (in the United States) program management was centralized and specialized by product line (agricultural tractors, tools, harvesting equipment, and implements; and industrial tractors and equipment). In the least concentrated markets, the OTO countries, major elements of the marketing program were apparently largely decentralized to region and zone managers and to the dealers themselves. There is no indication that program strategies were centrally developed by product categories as in the United States.

The Future

The Ford Tractor Division organization is one of the newest that we have considered. In analyzing the organization of its sales and marketing activities, it is useful to recognize that for organizational purposes there are four different ways of segmenting the world markets the Division serves. First, they can be segmented by the type of representation (direct dealer or subsidiary) that FTD has in each country. Second, markets can be divided geographically regardless of type of representation. (FTD's three existing Sales and Marketing Operations were delineated in terms of a combination of these two.) Third, markets can be segmented by products (e.g., agricultural tractors, implements, industrial tractors, and equipment). Finally, a logical segmentation scheme might be developed by type of application (e.g., vineyards, rice fields, road construction).

In the short run, FTD could possibly move in the direction of organizing its Sales and Marketing Operations by the type of representation that FTD has in each country. One Sales and Marketing Operation might, for example, be responsible for all countries in which FTD operates through Ford subsidiaries, while a second Sales and Marketing Operation might be responsible for all countries in which FTD markets through direct dealers.

Such an organizational scheme would recognize the fact that a Sales and Marketing Operation headquarters organization can exercise much less control over strategy formulation and implementation in countries where it is necessary to market through independent importer-distributors (direct dealers). In these countries Ford Tractor may not have the strong local sales units to assure that Ford strategies are carried out. In subsidiary countries, by contrast, strong specialized organizations have been built up at the country level. These organizations are well suited, in both structure and orientation, for the implementation of centrally prepared marketing strategies.

It would seem that the distinction between direct dealer countries and subsidiary companies is useful for organizational purposes. It might be more effective, therefore, to have two Sales and Marketing Operations — one for direct dealer countries and one for "company" countries — at least in the short run.

In time, however, one would expect FTD to develop more elaborate (and specialized) regional sales offices to work with importer-distributors and their dealer networks in those countries now identified as "OTO territory." At that point, the distinction between "direct dealer" and "company" countries would become less meaningful for organizational purposes.

It might then be possible to have a single Sales and Marketing Operation, which would serve world markets through homogeneous product offerings. Such an organizational unit might be structured something like the present Tractor and Implement Operations in the United States. FTD might then be able to establish a more finely articulated Product/Sales management structure for purposes of formulating and implementing marketing strategy by broad product categories. The fact that the product line is relatively diverse (from agricultural tractors to industrial equipment) would argue for a unilateral (market/product) type of program management structure.

Market/product programs could be tailored in different parts of the world to fit local market environments by managers in field offices functioning much like the Agricultural-Industrial Sales Representatives now located in U.S. District Sales Offices.

All of this suggests that even for businesses serving world markets, the initial segmentation for purposes of organizing the marketing function should not be geographic if the business serves its markets through a common line of products. In the case of the Ford Tractor Division, type of market representation ("direct dealer" and "company" countries) may provide a realistic basis for organizing the marketing function in the short run. It recognizes the hard facts of organizational history and the relative independence of Ford's importer-distributors in direct dealer countries. It also recognizes the fact that Ford has much stronger field sales organizations in some areas of the world than in others.

As time goes on, these distinctions among country markets may become much less meaningful. At that point, FTD might be able to realize important advantages in setting up a single organizational unit for Sales and Marketing, as it has for Manufacturing and Product Development.

Index to Companies and Commentaries

du Pont, E. I., de Nemours & Company: Textile Fibers Department, 5, 6–7, 10, 13–14, 15, 16, 18, 19, 20, 24–25, 29, 32, 41–42, 47, 146, 152, *197–200*, 225, 228, 254, 257, 332

Ford Motor Company: North American Automobile Operations, 5, 10, 11, 15–16, 23, 32, 36, 39, 47, 48, 146, 147, 254, *289–295*, 334, 432

Ford Motor Company: Tractor Division, 5, 56, *432–434*

General Electric Company, 2, 14

General Electric Company: Housewares Division, 5, 11, 16, 34–35, 47, 228, 229, *254–260*, 334

General Foods Corporation: Post Division, 5, 17, 18, 20, 23, 38–39, 42–43, 56, 152, *225–230*, 254, 256, 257, 259

International Business Machines Corporation: Data Processing Division, 1, 5, 18–19, 21–23, 25, 26, 28–29, 31–32, 33, 40, 47, 48–49, 56, *146–154*, 180, 183, 226, 229, 230, 332, 356, 388, 409

Lockheed Aircraft Corporation: Lockheed-Georgia Company, 5, 29, 30–31, 40, 43, 46, *102–107*, 146, 152, 154, 226, 409

Mobil Oil Corporation: North American Division, 5, 10, 12, 16, 21, 32, 36, 43–44, 146, *179–186*, 226, 254, 368–369

Monsanto Company: Agricultural Division, 5, 44–46, *367–369*

Monsanto Company: International Division, 5, 13, 16, 24, 28, 56, *385–389*, 410

Monsanto Company: Organic Chemicals Division, 5, 9, 13, 14–15, 16, 20, 42, 43, 47, 48, 49–50, 56, 146, *354–357*, 367–368, 388

Pfizer, Chas., & Co., Inc.: Pfizer International, 5, 23–24, 26, 56, *409–411*

Sears, Roebuck and Co., 5, 20–21, 23, 32, 36, 39, 56, *326–335*, 388